# ROME'S EMPIRE

# ROME'S EMPIRE

## HOW THE ROMANS ACQUIRED AND LOST THEIR PROVINCES

PATRICIA SOUTHERN

AMBERLEY

First published 2023

Amberley Publishing
The Hill, Stroud
Gloucestershire, GL5 4EP

www.amberley-books.com

British Library Cataloguing in Publication Data.
A catalogue record for this book is available from the British Library.

ISBN 978 1 4456 9432 0 (hardback)
ISBN 978 1 4456 9433 7 (ebook)

1 2 3 4 5 6 7 8 9 10

Typesetting by SJmagic DESIGN SERVICES, India.
Printed in the UK.

# Contents

# List of Illustrations

20. Arch of Severus in Forum Romanum recording the Parthian campaign.
21. Triumphal arch at Rheims.
22. Triumphal Arch of Constantine in Rome viewed from the upper level of the Colosseum.
23. Remains of the Horrea Epagathiana warehouses at Ostia.
24. The Pont du Gard.
25. The aqueduct at Segovia.
26. Landscape of the gold mining area of Las Medunas, north-west Spain.
27. Inscription dedicated to the Emperor Claudius at Leptis Magna, Libya.
28. The theatre at Merida (Emerita Augusta) in Spain.
29. Bust of the Emperor Trajan.
30. Scene from Trajan's Column recording the Dacian wars.
31. Site of the Dacian capital of Sarmizegethusa.
32. Inscription from Germany mentioning Brittones in the Roman army.
33. Modern copy of a statue of Hadrian near Castell Sant'Angelo.
34. Reconstruction of the Hadrianic palisade in Germany.
35. Scene from Trajan's Column showing a timber tower.
36. Reconstruction of a timber tower on the German frontier.
37. Hadrian's Wall at Walltown Crags, Northumberland.
38. Remains of Hadrian's Wall and the milecastle at Cawfields, Northumberland.
39. Arch of Hadrian at Gerasa (modern Jerash in Jordan).
40. Busts of the Emperors Marcus Aurelius and Commodus.
41. Bust of the Emperor Philip the Arab.
42. Persian rock carving at Naqs-I Rustam: the Emperor Valerian captured by Shapur.
43. The Porta Nigra at Trier.
44. The Roman amphitheatre at Trier.
45. The Kaiserthermen or Imperial baths at Trier.
46. The colonnade flanking the road at Apamea, Syria.
47. The town walls at Caerwent, Wales.
48. Coin portrait of the Emperor Aurelian.
49. The Aurelian walls of Rome.
50. The Porta Appia, one of the gates in the Aurelian wall of Rome.
51. The walls of Senlis in France, probably built by Aurelian's successor Probus.
52. Coin portrait of Diocletian.
53. Diocletian's Palace at Split.

# Acknowledgements

I owe thanks to several people who have helped me, Sue Howie, Isla Jones and Graeme Stobbs for drawing the maps, Carole McGivern for posting things when we couldn't meet, and Sue Howie again for listening to facts about Rome without yawning, ever since we both worked at the University of Newcastle upon Tyne, some years back now.

# Introduction

The original plan for this book was to give an account of Rome's history with particular reference to the acquisition of provinces and the reasons for doing so, recounting the development of provincial administration and government, and the involvement of provinces in various wars within the chronological framework. Then Covid 19 intervened, and libraries closed, something which I was probably not alone in failing to anticipate. In writing the long history of Rome, access to a university library is essential. No-one can own all the required literature and reference books, so thrown back on my own resources, I was thankful for never having undergone therapy for the inability to pass any kind of bookshop without buying something on entering. Nonetheless, the lack of library resources curtailed the intention to take the history of the Empire and its provinces into the late fifth century, and the traditional date of 476 when the western Empire fell. There are conventional choices for end dates before 476: the death of Constantine the Great in 337, or 395 when Theodosius I died and his two sons Honorius and Arcadius ruled the western and eastern halves of the Empire, not yet split into two separate Empires. Most terminal dates are artificial, since life went on after all of them. I have chosen to end the main narrative in 408 when Arcadius died and Honorius killed the capable general Stilicho, by which time the western Empire was starting to unravel. The final chapter describes what happened in the provinces after that date.

For modern historians, the Roman Empire generally denotes the period from the supremacy of Augustus in the first century BC, but if the term Empire means control of territory, then Rome possessed an empire long before then. Most of the provinces had been acquired by the end of the Republic, and the apparatus for governing them developed empirically from the administrative systems designed for a single city state.

Rome's acquisition of provinces has been labelled a search for safe boundaries, and in acquiring new territories the Romans constantly met new neighbours. Occasionally, the new neighbours objected. Sometimes wars were fought on behalf of other people, especially after Rome had emerged as a strong power which could be called upon for assistance. Rome fought Greeks on behalf of other Greeks, without annexing their lands until much later. Some territories were gifted to Rome, for example Attalus III of Pergamum and Nicomedes of Bithynia bequeathed their kingdoms to the Roman people.

The annexation of territory, bringing it under direct Roman administration, was a slow process. After the traditional foundation of the city in 753 BC it took the Romans five centuries to gain control over the different peoples of Italy, and just after this was accomplished, they also acquired their first provinces, Sicily, Sardinia and Corsica.

To a modern audience, province signifies a territorial unit, but to the Romans *provincia* originally indicated a specific task, assigned to an official such as a consul or praetor. The term covered anything from supervising roads, maintenance of woods and forests, building a fleet, or conducting a war. When Rome began to acquire territories, the same word *provincia* was applied to the task of governing them.

Administration of a territorial province called for manpower in the form of governors and clerical staff, and troops to keep the peace internally or to fight wars to police and protect the province. Roman militarism and imperialism are much discussed, unfavourably or otherwise, but it cannot be denied that expansion of territory eventually became embedded in the concept of *imperium sine fine*, power without end, either territorially or chronologically. The Romans showered praise on the men who extended territory, even after the process had slowed. The Emperor Septimius Severus earned his honorary label *propagator imperii* when he extended the frontiers in the North African provinces.

Before Rome gained provinces, alliances served the purpose of keeping the peace with the neighbours, instead of annexation. The terms of an alliance could be tailored to circumstances, but usually involved contribution of troops for the army to fight against mutual enemies, so that Rome could raise larger armies than most other individual states. Allied troops were supported by their own states, so no extra costs devolved upon the Romans, who did not pay their own soldiers until probably the fourth century BC.

Government of the provinces developed with practice. Rome was certainly in sole charge, but provincial administration was not on a rigidly applied, one-size-fits-all pattern. In the more developed states of the eastern provinces Rome often utilised the administrative and taxation systems that were already in place, but in less developed or less cohesive communities, Rome had to create the government machinery, conforming to whatever the province could yield, for example the Frisians of the modern Netherlands, whose resources were meagre, paid tax not in cash, but in ox-hides – the army alone required a vast quantity of leather.

Provincial communities, like the early allied states, governed themselves within the parameters set by Rome. When government and administration tipped over into outright exploitation, the Romans somewhat lethargically adapted their legal systems to try to curb and punish rapacious governors, not altogether successfully. Theoretically, the people who had been exploited could state their case at Rome, but it required determination to travel there and find an advocate to plead for them. Too many provincial governors exploited the provincials, but there were exceptions, such as Lucius Licinius Lucullus, governor of the province of Asia, approximating to western Turkey. He was honoured by the provincials for his fair and non-rapacious treatment of them during his conduct of the war against Mithradates of Pontus in the 70s and 60s BC.

The tribes or states beyond Rome's boundaries represented real and perceived threats. Warfare against raiders was an option for Rome, but that was expensive and success was not always guaranteed, as several military leaders discovered to their cost. The Emperors sometimes chose another option. Across the Rhine and Danube borders especially, the Romans ruled indirectly through the local elite, subsidizing the native chiefs, sending food, money and gifts, and in return the chief promised to keep the peace within his own tribe, and sometimes to defend Roman interests against other chiefs. It was resented at Rome, but on the whole it pre-empted wars and raids. When Hadrian drew the lines to delimit the Empire and enclose much of it within solid barriers, he still sanctioned the subsidies to peoples beyond the frontiers. Some Emperors chose to cancel the subsidies and paid the price in military defeat. A treaty was made with the Goths in AD 238 that included the payment of subsidies, but when the Romans under the Emperor Philip the Arab felt more secure in the 240s, the subsidies were stopped, and the Goths united under their leader Cniva. After the Romans won the war, subsidies were resumed.

Migration into the Empire was always an attractive proposition for the outlying tribes. Tribesmen sometimes arrived on Rome's borders because their lands were exhausted or spoiled, for example the incursions of the North Sea in the third century AD ruined the north-western coastal areas. Other migrants wanted to escape annihilation by other tribes. This is a relevant scenario in our modern world. During the Empire, migrants and refugees were settled on lands within the Empire and most often contributed soldiers for the army. The sources tell of 50,000 Getae settled in Moesia by Augustus; 40,000 Germans brought across the Rhine under Tiberius; Nero brought tribesmen across the Danube. The list goes on. In the later period, when Rome was hard pressed on the frontiers, the Empire would probably not have survived without the military contribution of the Germanic tribes, Sarmatians, Franks, Alamanni, and latterly the Huns. These people retained their customs and religious beliefs, dressed differently and spoke different languages, but they were absorbed into the Empire and fought in Roman armies for Rome, despite the fact that most of them had never even seen the city.

The Roman Empire survived as long as it did because although the Romans could be cruel and murderous, throughout their history they also assimilated and integrated other people. Romanization was not generally enforced but came about on a voluntary basis and was then encouraged. The provincials retained their own languages, customs, and religions. Native gods were equated as far as possible with Roman versions. The only exceptions were the orgiastic followers of Bacchus, suppressed during the Republic, and religions with widespread influence – the Druids, suppressed in the early Empire, and the Christians, who could form a separate state within the state.

In the provinces, non-Romans could get along quite nicely, running businesses, owning property or working for wealthier people, but there were considerable advantages at law and in civil and military life in gaining the privileges inherent in Roman citizenship. This was not impossible even for slaves, most of whom gained Roman citizenship when they were freed. Freeborn non-Roman provincials could acquire Roman citizenship by entering into the patronage of important Romans who could enfranchise them, and then they adopted the family names of their benefactors. During the Empire non-Roman auxiliary soldiers automatically become Roman citizens after serving for twenty-five years with an unblemished record. Civilians who served as magistrates on their town councils became Roman citizens, and some could rise in status to share in government of the Empire, and in command of the armies. In the early third century, the Emperor Caracalla granted citizenship to all freeborn inhabitants of the Empire. The name Roman never was a narrow ethnic description. It denoted a member of a vast commonwealth of mixed racial types enjoying or enduring varied social status.

Throughout this book the conventional dates that usefully divide Roman history into manageable segments are utilized. The traditional date for the foundation of the city of Rome is 753 BC, which was accepted by the Romans themselves. Similarly, 509 BC is the traditional date when the kings were expelled and the Republic was established, but the beginning of the Empire is not so sharply defined, one reason being the reluctance of Octavian-Augustus, the successor of Julius Caesar, to acknowledge that the Republic had died, so the Empire's beginning can be placed somewhere between the battle of Actium in 31 BC and 27 BC when Octavian theoretically gave back the government to the Senate. In the end, the Republic became the Empire so gradually that you couldn't really see the join.

# 1

# Seven Kings and One Republic

Cicero is the first known ancient author to note the geographical advantages of the site of Rome, praising Romulus, the traditional founder, for avoiding the dangerous coastal sites by settling near the river Tiber, where imports and exports were facilitated, the hills provided natural defences and springs provided fresh water. Cicero does not mention that the Tiber was prone to flooding. Livy adds that Rome was close enough to the sea to utilise the Tiber, but safe from sea-borne raids.[1]

There were several convenient landing places on the west coast of Italy, and the west was more fertile than the eastern zones. Rome controlled two main land routes, the north-south road linking Etruria with Campania across the ford downstream from the Tiber Island, and the east-west route, the Via Salaria, or salt road, led to the salt pans at the Tiber mouth. The geographer Strabo, writing under Augustus, says that later Romans were prisoners of these existing conditions.[2] Prisoners or not, the Romans made the best of those conditions for over a thousand years.

## The foundation of Rome: archaeology and legend
Rome was traditionally founded by Romulus, whose name is pronounced with a long O, as Rome-ulus. Consigned to myth by modern historians, he was vastly important to ancient Romans, though there were over thirty legends of the foundation of Rome.[3] Before the first century BC the Romans were not certain of the foundation date of their city. Extrapolating backwards through their history, late Republican scholars worked out dates ranging from the ninth to the

eighth century. It was the first-century polymath Marcus Terentius Varro who established the accepted foundation date, 21 April 753, as translated into modern calendrical terms. The Romans accepted Varro's conclusions and dated events by the number of years from the foundation of the city, *ab urbe condita*, abbreviated to *a.u.c.*

The hills of Rome were occupied long before 753. Primitive pottery from the Capitol indicates settlement from at least 1600, and post holes reveal that huts were continually rebuilt. On the south peak of the Capitol a terrace wall was built between 1350 and 1250 and an area of the Capitoline was long associated with metallurgy, the techniques becoming more sophisticated as time went on.[4] From about 1025 to 875 the inhabitants disposed of their dead at the foot of the hill, and a different necropolis was used by the Palatine settlements, probably two independent communities, but not necessarily separate races.[5] The Palatine Hill features in the Romulus legend, particularly the Cermalus, the higher ground to the south-west. Prehistoric nomads left flint tools there, and permanent habitation began *c.*1050, attested by post-holes. The hut walls were of pressed clay between timber uprights, and the roofs were probably thatched. Dating from the tenth century, a necropolis was laid out nearby, but in the ninth century a new settlement was established, partly overlying the necropolis.[6] On the Velia north-east of the Palatine, a defended settlement may be even earlier. By the second half of the eighth century, Greek imports were reaching the Velia, linking with the finds of eighth-century Greek pottery near the church of Saint Omobono, close to the Tiber. It is suggested that Greek traders settled in Rome, or Greek pottery could have arrived by way of Etruria.[7] Mussolini removed most of the Velia to build the modern Via dei Fori Imperiali.

The Romans claimed descent from Aeneas, who fled from Troy as it fell, but since there is a gap of centuries between Aeneas and Romulus, the Romans concocted a family tree to link them. Numitor, King of Alba Longa (Castel Gandolfo) was allegedly descended from Aeneas. Once Numitor was out of the way, his brother Amulius seized power, killing Numitor's sons and forcing Numitor's daughter Rhea Silvia to become a Vestal Virgin, forbidden to have sexual relations with any man so she could not produce an heir. Instead, she had sexual relations with the god Mars and gave birth to the twins Romulus and Remus, who were set adrift in a basket on the Tiber, coming to rest at the base of the Palatine, near the *Ficus Ruminalis*, the fig-tree of Romulus. The Tiber does not flow anywhere near Alba, but let's not quibble. A she-wolf, presumably with cubs, was able to suckle the twins, until the shepherd Faustulus and his wife Accia Larentia took them in.[8]

Archaeological evidence shows that huts on the northern slopes of the Palatine hill were destroyed to accommodate an early wall. Ritual deposits in the foundations provide the date-range 775 to 750. No-one would assert that these foundations were dug out just after breakfast on 21 April 753, or that Romulus wielded the spade. The construction techniques of the wall resembled that of the early huts. Chunks of tufa deposited in the trench steadied the timber posts inserted into it, and the posts supported the pressed clay wall. There was no internal bank of earth behind the wall, but its top was protected from rain by pieces of broken pottery. Three sections of the earliest wall have been found, sufficient to work out its course, enclosing the Palatine on its lower slopes, forming a near-rectangle, which Tacitus called *Roma Quadrata*.[9] The wall was rebuilt three times between c.700 and 550, in clay and finally in stone.[10]

Rome developed from several small hill-settlements, and the first signs of unification pre-date 753. The settlements of the *montes* or hills joined as the *Septimontium*, the early name for Rome according to Varro, seemingly referring to the famous seven hills, but the name may derive from *saepti montes* meaning fortified hills.[11] A unified proto-urban settlement of about 200 hectares was evolving, with more huts built on the summits and slopes of the hills. The older cemeteries at the bases of the Palatine and Capitol were abandoned and new cemeteries developed on the Quirinal and Esquiline.[12] The primitive villages shared religious rites, one being the ceremony of the Argei, a procession around all the settlements on 16-17 March.[13]

Some of the earliest buildings can be related to the traditional dates for the kings from Romulus onwards. Recent discoveries have shown that the earliest sanctuary of Vesta, built on virgin land and oriented to the cardinal points, dates from 750-725. Its construction techniques match the first Palatine wall. The earliest sanctuary of Vulcan, called the Volcanal, dates to 750-675.[14] The first cobblestone paving of the Forum was laid c.750.[15] The first firmly dated level of the *Comitium*, an open area meeting place in the Forum, is assigned to the end of the seventh century, and according to Cicero, King Tullus Hostilius built an enclosure around it.[16]

Rome's humble beginnings required communal effort, supervised by a Roman version of a project manager. A king, perhaps?

## The seven kings

During the 244 years between 753 and the establishment of the Republic
in 509, only seven kings ruled Rome, an improbably low number of
rulers in such a long time-span which prompts scholars to date the
foundation of Rome in the seventh century, shunting the seven kings into
the truncated time slot.[17] It is worth noting that in British history, George
III became king in 1760, and discounting Edward VIII, who abdicated
and was never crowned, only eight monarchs reigned in 260 years up to
the time of writing this book. In 2022 of course the number of monarchs
increased to nine as Queen Elizabeth was succeeded by King Charles III.
Greater security and better food and healthcare to sustain the rulers of
Britain were not readily available until the late nineteenth century.

Evidence for early kings derives from the area of the *Comitium*,
where a broken pillar or *cippus* was unearthed. Associated deposits
date from the first quarter of the sixth century. The *cippus* bore an
incomplete inscription with the word *recei* in the second line, 'to
the king' in archaic Latin.[18] On the site of the earliest version of
the Regia, the home of the kings, later the residence of the Pontifex
Maximus, a potsherd was found bearing the word *rex*, or king. The
two inscriptions attest to kings in Rome, but without names or dates.

The following sections tell the tale as the Romans told it. Voluntary
suspension of disbelief is mandatory.

## Romulus 753 to 716

The Romulus legend may not have been current until the fourth or third
century, possibly derived from Greek legends in which heroes and kings
were frequently rescued by animals, often a wolf.[19] The famous bronze
statue of the she-wolf in the Capitoline Museum in Rome, with the
twins added in the Renaissance, was considered to be a sixth-century
Etruscan work, suggesting that the legend was current at that time, but
on stylistic grounds and methods of manufacture it is now dated to the
early medieval era.[20] Other attested depictions of the she-wolf in Rome
date from periods much later than the eighth century BC.

Like other cities with a deficiency of people, Romulus invited
foreigners and refugees to settle in Rome. A sanctuary called the
Asylum was sited between the two peaks of the Capitol, where
incomers were granted Roman citizenship, no questions asked.[21]
The Romans assimilated migrants without obliterating their cultural
backgrounds and customs.[22] Romulus proposed rights of intermarriage
with nearby settlements but was rebuffed, so he invited neighbouring

peoples to a religious festival and seized the women.[23] The hills of Rome, settled for centuries, are unlikely to have had a complete dearth of female residents, but the legend tells how outraged fathers appealed for help to Titus Tatius, King of the Sabines. There was a battle, but the abducted ladies, now wives of Romans, stopped the fighting. Romulus and Titus Tatius agreed to share the kingship, and some Sabines moved to Rome.[24]

Romulus organised the Romans into thirty *curiae*, which eventually formed the people's assembly, the *comitia curiata*.[25] The *curiae* provided the basis for political functions and for the organisation of the infantry army, the cavalry being levied from three centuries of *equites*, or knights, called Ramnes/Ramnenses (Romans), Tities (Sabines), and Luceres (Etruscans), associated respectively with the Palatine, the Quirinal and the Caelian hills. Archaeology reveals no signs of cultural differences.[26] From among the aristocrats, Romulus chose 100 men as senators, designated as *patres*, or fathers, their descendants being patricians, but this is probably anachronistic.[27] Romulus also recruited 300 men as armed guards, known as the *Celeres*, meaning swift, possibly implying horsemen.[28]

Rome's neighbouring Etruscan communities of Veii (Veio) fought with the Romans for control of the salt pans near the Tiber, and at the river mouth, the Veientines established the rocky citadel of Fidenae (Castel Giubileo). Romulus ambushed and defeated the Fidenates and converted the town into a colony for the original inhabitants and Roman settlers.[29] A truce for 100 years was made with Veii, but Romulus demanded the territory of the *Septem Pagi*, or seven districts, near the Tiber, and the salt works at the river mouth. He freed his prisoners, granting Roman citizenship to those who asked, registering them in the *curiae* and providing allotments near the Tiber.[30]

There are different versions of how and where Romulus died.[31] He was deified, eventually equated with the god Quirinus, the origin of Quirites, an alternative name for Romans. Livy says that Romulus was more popular with the people than with the senators, and the soldiers loved him.[32] This epitomizes the later problems of the Republic.

### Numa Pompilius 716-673

Without a king, Romulus' 100 'senators' divided themselves into ten groups, each with a chosen leader or *interrex* holding power for five days, succeeded by another *interrex*. The *interreges* summoned the people to choose the next king, to be confirmed by the Senate, according to Livy, while Dionysius usually says that the Senate chose the king and the people ratified the choice.[33]

Numa Pompilius, a Sabine, became the second king. Plutarch attributes the dearth of information about Numa to invading Gauls, who destroyed records *c*.390.[34] The auspices were taken in the *auguraculum* on the summit or Arx of the Capitol to ensure that Numa's election pleased the gods. Remains identified as the *auguraculum* are visible in the small garden on the Capitol, overlooking the later Forum of Caesar.[35] Numa attended to religion, administration and law. He established a twelve-month lunar year, with intercalary months to correlate it to the solar year. He built the temple of Janus, the god with two faces, the guardian of gateways. The doors of this temple were closed only when there was total peace.

Numa presided over religious ceremonies in person, but eventually created a permanent priest of Jupiter to take over when the kings were absent from Rome. The new priest was granted special clothing and the use of the curule chair, or *sella curulis*, of Etruscan origin, and a symbol of office. When Numa died there was another *interregnum* and Tullus Hostilius was chosen as king.[36]

### Tullus Hostilius 673 to 641

In contrast to Numa, Tullus was devoted to war. Cross-border cattle raids by the Albans and the Romans were settled when Tullus and Mettius Fufetius of Alba arranged a treaty, the most ancient known to Livy. Tullus brought in the *fetiales*, priests whose role included making demands for restitution, formal declaration of war, and the sanction of treaties. An oath was sworn, so verbose that Livy, perhaps mercifully, declined to reproduce it. The matter was to be settled by combat between the three Horatii brothers from Rome and three Curiatii from Alba.[37] During the fight, two of the Horatii were killed, but the remaining Horatius killed all three of the Curiatii. The victory was Rome's, and peace was made. Tullus summoned his ally Mettius to help him in a war against Veii and Fidenae, but Mettius only feigned loyalty to Rome, planning treachery. Tullus foiled him.[38] Mettius was punished, Alba was destroyed and the people were settled in Rome as citizens. Houses were built with Roman help on the Caelian hill. Several distinguished Roman families descended from leading men of Alba.[39]

Ancient authors assume that senators existed from Romulus onwards, and that Tullus Hostilius built the first Senate House, the *Curia Hostilia*, in the Forum. Archaeological traces of it are sparse, and the existence of a permanent Senate with a defined number of senators is doubted, though different groups of aristocrats may have been summoned by the kings as advisors.

Tullus was said to have tried to subdue the Latins, who resisted, but then a treaty was made 'that left no rancour'.[40] When Tullus died an *interregnum* followed and Ancus Marcius became the next king.[41]

### Ancus Marcius 641-616

Ancus was traditionally the founder of the port at Ostia at the mouth of the Tiber, but nothing is attested there before the fourth-century Castrum, or fort. Even so, the Romans of the second century AD erected an inscription in the town, honouring Ancus as the founder.[42]

Ancus defeated the Veiientines when they tried to regain the Tiber salt pans. The people displaced in the fighting were settled in Rome.[43] The Latins raided Roman territory, declaring that the death of Tullus Hostilius invalidated their treaty.[44] Ancus is said to have formalised the procedure of declaring war, employing *fetiales* according to the laws of the Aequicoli, but Numa and Tullus Hostilius had probably preceded him.[45] In connection with Ancus, Dionysius enlightens his Greek audience about the role of *fetiales*.[46] Complaints against another community had to be reported to the *fetiales*, who despatched three of their number to ask for the return of stolen goods (*rerum repetitio*). If no response was received by the agreed deadline, one of the *fetiales* was nominated to declare war. Standing at the territorial borders of the people concerned, the *fetialis* threw a spear into their land. When Rome became involved with communities some distance away, the *fetialis* threw a spear into a patch of Roman land representing enemy territory, traditionally near the temple of Bellona, goddess of war.[47]

Ancus declared war on the Latins, destroyed some settlements, captured Politorium and brought the population to Rome.[48] The new settlers were given citizenship and housed between the Aventine and the Palatine.[49] None of this is attested archaeologically. The Janiculum Hill across the Tiber was fortified and connected to the city by the first bridge, the timber-built Pons Sublicius.[50] Ancus also constructed the *fossa Quiritium*, or the Quirites trench, to defend the most vulnerable eastern side of the city.[51] Such a trench has been identified in this area on the Esquiline near the so-called Servian wall, built by the later King Servius Tullius, and the geographer Strabo attributes the trench to this king.[52] In order to deal with the growing crime rate, which Livy attributes to the increase in the population of Rome, Ancus built a prison, or *carcer*, near the Forum.[53] It has not yet been identified. Ancus may have remodelled the sanctuary of Vesta since excavations show that it was rebuilt between 650 and 625, no longer oriented to the cardinal points. It was built in a much more monumental style, with a masonry base and a tiled roof.[54]

Taking advantage of Roman acceptance of strangers, the Etruscan Lucumo and his wife Tanaquil emigrated from Tarquinii. Lucumo's name derives from the Etruscan *lauchme* or *lauchume*, meaning king, but he is better known as Lucius Tarquinius Priscus.[55] Priscus gained supporters by distributing his wealth, and he made himself supremely useful to Ancus Marcius, almost financing his wars and serving in them. He commanded strongholds, keeping the Latins in order, and led the cavalry in the Sabine wars.[56] He was made a senator and named in the king's will as guardian of his children.[57] Ancus died of natural causes, but suspicion attached to Tarquinius, who sent Ancus' two sons out of Rome while he speeded up the election procedure, in effect seizing power.[58]

## *Tarquinius Priscus 616-579*

As the first Etruscan king, it was once thought that Priscus ushered in a period of Etruscan domination, but this is discredited. While the Etruscans influenced Rome, they did not take over politically or militarily, but from the accounts of Priscus' reign it seems that Rome became more aggressive.

Priscus' first war was with the Latins. The men of Apiolae raided Roman territory and Priscus took the town by storm. The population was sold into slavery and the town razed.[59] Other Latin towns succumbed one by one.[60] Priscus destroyed the lands of Corniculum, and then offered friendship, but the inhabitants refused the offer, expecting help from other Latins which never came. The town was burned and the men, women and children were enslaved.[61] The Etruscans and Sabines mobilized to help the Latins, Roman territory was invaded, but Priscus won a great battle and sold the prisoners as slaves. Happily, the end was better than the beginning. Remaining Latin towns surrendered and were treated leniently. They retained their forms of government, no-one was executed, exiled or enslaved, and no fines were levied. Dionysius concludes this episode with a triumph for Priscus.[62]

Priscus planned to build a wall around the city but was interrupted when the Sabines attacked. Fortunately, they quickly withdrew.[63]

Priscus concluded that he needed stronger cavalry, so he doubled the numbers of *equites* from the three Romulan tribes of Ramnes, Tities and Luceres.[64] Campaigns against the Sabines resumed, both armies camping near the river Anio. Priscus set fire to the bridge over the river and attacked while the Sabines were distracted by the conflagration.[65] The Roman cavalry posted on the flanks proved its worth. As the Roman infantry in the centre fell back, the horsemen turned inwards to attack the Sabines from two sides. Is this true, or is it based anachronistically on later practice? With no bridge, the Sabine retreat was cut off and many drowned. Prisoners were sent to Rome and Priscus arranged a six-year truce.[66]

Livy's description of the formal unconditional surrender of the Sabine town of Collatia (Lunghezza) may derive from an official document and is taken as the template for such procedures. Priscus questioned whether the envoys of Collatia were representatives of the people, whether the people were authorized to offer the surrender, and whether they were free to make this decision. Receiving affirmative answers, he demanded the surrender of the people, the town, the lands, water, boundary stones, shrines, utensils and all possessions for the service of the gods and the people. The envoys of Collatia agreed and Priscus received the surrender, installing his nephew Tarquinius Arruns Egerius as commander of a garrison in the town.[67] Dionysius adds that Egerius wielded absolute power over Collatia for life, and his descendants were all named Collatinus.[68] The people of Collatia were not absorbed as Roman citizens, no colony was established, and no alliance was made. Only total subjection sufficed for Tarquinius Priscus.

For nearly a decade Romans fought wars against the Etruscans, losing and regaining Fidenae, where new Roman colonists were installed. Fighting against the Sabines, he employed Etruscan auxiliaries and Latin allies. Peace was made and Priscus celebrated his third triumph.[69]

The contribution of Tarquinius Priscus to public works in Rome is difficult to detect archaeologically because it merges with that of Tarquinius Superbus, and the written sources also conflate the work of the two kings. Both Priscus and Tarquinius Superbus made the people work so hard on building the sewers that many of them committed suicide.[70] It is possible that Priscus began the building of the sewers on a modest scale. Livy and Dionysius describe how he built porticos and shops in the Forum, apportioning building lots around it, and since the Forum was prone to flooding it would make sense to attend to the drainage first.[71]

While at war with the Sabines, Priscus had made a vow that he would build a temple to Jupiter, levelling the site according to Dionysius, or laying foundations according to Livy.[72] The temple was not inaugurated until 509, the first year of the Republic, so why did it take so many decades to build it? The arguments for Tarquinius Superbus as the builder are described below. Priscus came to a bloody end, when assassins hired by the sons of Ancus Marcius felled him with an axe. Tanaquil concealed his death, announcing that while Priscus recovered, Servius Tullius, who lived with Priscus' family and was well-known in Rome, would deputise for him. Servius sustained the fiction, sometimes pretending as he gave judgements in court that he had to consult the king.[73]

## *Servius Tullius 579-535*

When it was announced that Priscus was dead, Servius was the first to become king without the formalities. There was no *interregnum* or election.[74] He expelled Ancus' sons and organised a magnificent funeral for Priscus. The reign of Servius generates more verbiage than any of the other kings, because of his overhaul of the political system and the army as described by the ancient authors, not entirely accurately. Servius reorganised Romulus' three tribes, dividing the increased population into four tribes, which were not ethnic groupings, but territorial divisions with clearly indicated boundaries, described by Varro.[75] Servius perhaps incorporated designated sectors of the rural areas (*pagi*) outside the city within each of the four tribes, or alternatively he created an unknown number of separate rural tribes, in addition to the four urban ones. The eventual total in the Republic, never exceeded, was thirty-five tribes, consisting of thirty-one rural tribes and four urban tribes.[76]

Servius' new tribal system required information about the people, where they lived, their status, wealth and property. The census was instituted, with penalties for not registering.[77] According to Fabius Pictor, quoted by Livy, 80,000 men capable of bearing arms were registered in the first census, far too many for a sixth-century city.[78] Using the census information the people were divided into *classes*, plural of *classis*, derived from *calare*, to call to arms. *Classis* was applied to any group of people. (The same word was used later for a fleet). The Servian *classes* were based on a sliding scale of wealth, capital not income, assessed from land, farms, agricultural produce, slaves and livestock, reckoned in *aes* or *as rude*, irregular lumps of bronze valued by weight, coinage not appearing until much later.

Divisions of the male population were based on property ratings and ability to provide arms and armour for army service. This would be a hoplite army, attested by finds of equipment dated from the late seventh and early sixth centuries. Opinion differs as to whether this army was introduced before, during, or after Servius' reign.[79] Hoplites were heavy infantry armed with a long spear and protected by a bronze breastplate, helmet, greaves and a large round shield, called *hoplon* in Greek, *clipeus* in Latin. The formation was called the phalanx, meaning roller, containing companies of about ninety-six men in a block twelve men wide and eight men deep, though these numbers could vary.[80] The army may have been called the legion from the beginning, since *legio* (plural *legiones*) means 'a choosing', or a chosen body, referring to the selection process called the *dilectus* from *diligo*, 'I choose'.

Using information from a later era, Livy and Dionysius describe the Servian system in detail, but differing about equipment.[81] The five infantry *classes* were supplemented by the wealthiest at the top of the scale and the very poor at the bottom. The wealthiest Romans provided eighteen centuries of cavalry, or *equites*. Horses are expensive to maintain, so the treasury granted 10,000 *asses* to each century of cavalrymen for the purchase of horses, and an annual grant of 2,000 *asses* per century for fodder and maintenance, levied from a tax on rich widows or unmarried women. The cavalrymen with horses paid for by the treasury were *equites equo publico*.

All able-bodied male citizens, except those with the lowest census rating, were obliged to serve in the army without pay, providing their own arms and armour. For the men of the first Servian *classis* the minimum property rating was 100,000 *asses*. There were forty centuries of *juniores*, aged seventeen to forty-five, for action in battle, plus forty centuries of *seniores* aged forty-six to sixty, for civil defence. This first *classis* was labelled the *classis clipeata* after the round shield. The second class was assessed at a minimum of 75,000 *asses* and comprised ten centuries of *juniores* and ten of *seniores*, using oblong shields and excused from providing armour. The third and fourth *classes*, respectively rated at 50,000 and 25,000 *asses*, also had twenty centuries, less well armed. There were thirty centuries in the fifth class, with a minimum rating of 11,000 *asses*, each man armed only with slings and stones. There were two centuries of engineers, probably attached to the first class, and two centuries of trumpeters probably attached to the fifth class. At the bottom of the scale the men with the lowest property rating were all assigned to just one century, counted by heads not wealth, and known as the *capite censi*, from *caput* (plural *capites*) meaning head. With no political power and little or no property, they were exempted from army service.

Some authors accept that Servius divided the people into multiple *classes* utilising to best effect all the available manpower, according to their ability to equip themselves.[82] Other authors suggest that Servius needed only one *classis* comprising men who could afford the hoplite equipment, and Cornell points out that the first *classis* was the only one possessing the arms and armour suitable for a hoplite army.[83] All the rest would be grouped *infra classem* as light armed troops. Another suggestion is that *classes* belonged to a later period.

The *classes* and centuries formed both the army and the *comitia centuriata* or voting assembly, and indeed the whole system as described by Livy and Dionysius is more suited to political purposes than to military formations. In the elections, the preponderant voting power lay with the wealthiest men. There were 193 centuries in total, the first eighteen centuries being cavalry, each century containing only a small number of men compared to other centuries. The first and second infantry *classes* totalled 118 centuries. It was the majority vote of each century that counted, not the vote of individuals. The cavalry and the first two *classes* cast their votes first, and these votes usually decided the issue, so the lower *classes* did not need to vote.[84] Cicero accepted that the system originated with Servius, thoroughly approving it because it gave the greatest number of votes to the rich.[85]

Servius is also credited with extending the boundary (*pomerium*) of Rome, in effect re-founding the city.[86] Generals had to relinquish their military powers before crossing the *pomerium*, so that they entered the city as civilians. After the extension of the *pomerium* in Servius' reign, the *Comitium* was inside it, so it remained in use for civil assemblies, while military assemblies were held in the Campus Martius, outside the new boundary.

The so-called Servian wall around the city is much disputed. Priscus planned a wall but never built it. A wall was built in the fourth century, and it is argued that this was the first wall. Servius' modern devotees insist that the earliest wall was built of *cappellaccio*, a friable grey tufa from Rome, used in nearly all archaic buildings from the seventh to the fifth century, and the fourth century wall was a rebuild using the yellow Grotta Oscura stone from the quarries of Veii.[87] The *pomerium* and the wall were not necessarily contiguous, so some parts of the city could be within the *pomerium* but not the defences, and vice versa.

Servius attended to the needs of the poor, allowing freedmen to become citizens enrolled in the four urban tribes, with the same rights as everyone else. The custom persisted through the Republic.[88] Servius investigated debt problems, passing a law forbidding anyone to lend money on the security of a free person, since the forfeit of property ought to suffice. He called for lists of debtors and paid off creditors from his own funds. He asked for names of men without land allotments and decreed that possessors of public lands should relinquish them, so that allotments could be given to landless men.[89] Not surprisingly, wealthy Romans were opposed to Servius, demanding an *interregnum* and an election, because Servius succeeded Priscus without these formalities. The people unanimously elected Servius, but the Senate refused to ratify the election.[90] Servius' household included Lucius Tarquinius, named Superbus, supposedly the son of Tarquinius Priscus, which Livy accepted, but Dionysius concluded, probably correctly, that Tarquinius and his brother Arruns were grandsons of Priscus.[91] Servius had two daughters, both called Tullia after the family name, one married to Tarquinius Superbus and the other to Superbus' brother Arruns. Tarquinius eliminated his wife and Arruns so that he could marry his ambitious erstwhile sister-in-law. Summoning the senators, Tarquinius had himself declared king. Servius was ejected as he arrived at the meeting, and it was said that Tullia ordered his death.[92] Livy says that never again would a king rule with justice and humanity, and Cicero considered that Servius ruled with profound understanding of constitutional matters.[93]

## Tarquinius Superbus 535-509

The second Tarquinius seized and held power like the Greek tyrants, which should not always imply a reign of terror, but Tarquinius Superbus comes close to it. He was permanently surrounded by guards, never stating times for his public appearances, granting no-one access to him unless he had personally summoned the visitor, prosecuting prominent men, killing some, banishing others, and taking their property.[94]

Superbus' daughter Tarquinia married Octavus/Octavius Mamilius of Tusculum, and by cultivating the leaders of other Latin communities, Superbus strengthened his power in Rome.[95] He persuaded the Latins that Tullus Hostilius' treaty needed updating to give them a greater share in the prosperity of the Romans. In reality, he restricted Latin freedom.[96]

By treachery and guile, Gabii (Osteria dell Osa) fell into Superbus' hands, followed by executions and banishment according to Livy, but with the grant of Roman citizenship and retention of all possessions according to Dionysius.[97] Superbus also made treaties with the Aequi, renewed a treaty with the Etruscans, and founded colonies at Signia (Segni) and Circei (San Felice Circeo), guarding routes around the mountain ranges of the Volsci.[98]

Archaeological investigation shows that under Superbus the city amenities advanced further and faster than ever before, and suggests that he built the Capitoline temple of Jupiter.[99] Foundations for the temple were laid out in a former residential area where continuous occupation dating from the Bronze Age ceased around the second half of the sixth century.[100] If this project was initiated solely by Superbus, awkward questions concerning Priscus as the builder, Servius' neglect of the work, and the alleged decades that it took to complete the temple, become redundant. Livy says that Tarquinius Superbus summoned workmen from every part of Etruria, and some work was done by Roman plebs (*fabris undique ex Etruria accitis...operis etiam ex plebi*).[101] Unless Livy did not want to use *faber* (plural *fabri*) twice in one sentence, there may be a distinction between Etruscan and Roman workers, the first having connotations of skilled craftsmen, and the second merely labourers.

The temple foundations were built in *cappellaccio* tufa blocks, and Coarelli argues that the materials and the building techniques date the work as sixth century, not the hypothetical fourth century reconstruction.[102] In Superbus' day this temple was larger than anything in Etruria. The central core of these vast foundations is housed in situ in the Capitoline Museum. It says a lot for the mind-set of Tarquinius Superbus. In Superbus' reign roads were laid out, and the Forum was paved with cobblestones for the fourth time.[103] The Cloaca Maxima, the famous sewer, is attributed to both Tarquinii. Some sources refer to it as *canalis*, or *canalicolae*, hinting that the sewer was only canalized at first. The Elder Pliny describes the sewer in detail.[104]

Needing wealth to continue his building work, Superbus launched an unprovoked attack on Ardea near the west coast, belonging to the wealthy Latin Rutuli.[105] His son Sextus lusted after Lucretia, the wife of Tarquinius Collatinus, first trying to seduce her and then raping her.[106] Lucretia killed herself, triggering political upheaval which had probably been brewing for a long time. Lucretia's husband Collatinus, and Superbus' nephew Lucius Junius Brutus addressed the people. Tarquinius Superbus was banished. He dashed to Rome but found the gates closed. Junius Brutus secured the allegiance of Titus Herminius and Marcus Horatius, commanding at Ardea. These officers abandoned the siege, arranged a fifteen-year truce with Ardea, and led the army to Rome.[107]

### The birth of the Republic and the regal inheritance

Traditionally, the Republic was established in 509. Dionysius and Polybius calculate the date using Greek chronology, and both come up with 508-507.[108] The same kind of political changes were happening in Italy and Greece.[109] Traces of destruction in Rome, dated *c*.500, suggest that the end of the monarchy was not peaceful.[110] Buildings strongly associated with the kings, the Regia, and the temples of Fortuna and Mater Matuta near the church of Saint Omobono, were destroyed.[111]

By listing Lucius Junius Brutus and Lucius Tarquinius Collatinus as the first consuls in 509, ancient authors imply that the Republican government arose from the wreckage of the monarchy like Athena from the head of Zeus. If the non-violent beginning of the Republic is unlikely, its instantaneous emergence is more so. It is pertinent to ask how much of the Republic grew out of the monarchy.

The achievements of the Romans during the Regal period, which laid the foundations of the Republic are succinctly summarized by Lintott.[112] By 509 the Romans had developed religious rituals and installed the major priesthoods. They had acquired experience of government and administration and dealing with other people, not always by making war but by arranging treaties and by integrating immigrants and foreigners. The Romans believed that the kings established the first colonies, according to religious and practical procedures of considerable antiquity.

The right of appeal against legal judgements began under King Tullus Hostilius. The Roman champion Horatius killed all three Curiatii of Alba, and on arrival in Rome, Horatius was enraged to find his sister, who was betrothed to one of the Curiatii, lamenting her lover's death. Horatius killed her. He was tried and condemned, but he appealed against the judgement, supported by King Tullus. The matter was put before the people, who acquitted Horatius.[113] The right of appeal was embodied in the Twelve Table of laws drawn up in 449.

Dionysius credits Romulus with the institution of client and patron.[114] This became one of the important features of Roman civil and political life, where free men placed themselves under the patronage of more influential men. The patron protected the client, and the client supported his patron in public life. Clients were not always poor, and a patron's status was enhanced if his clients were well-off. It is suggested that in the Republic, clients were neither patrician nor plebeian, but formed a group separate from both, but Livy says that when Marcus Furius Camillus called together his clients in 391, they were largely drawn from the plebeians.[115]

In warfare, the formalities had been laid down under the kings, who were supreme commanders, personally appointing subordinate officers. The use of *fetiales* to demand restitution first and only afterwards to declare war, justified the proceedings in the eyes of the gods.[116] The kings established the formula for the acceptance of surrender, which placed the defeated people and everything they owned into the hands of the Romans.[117] Religious rites applied when treaties and alliances were made, again involving the *fetiales*. Livy says that the same methods applied to all treaties, though the terms differed.[118] The term for a treaty was *foedus* (plural *foedera*), meaning a covenant or agreement, and the people thus allied with Rome were *foederati*, though allies were more usually referred to as *socii* (singular *socius*), which has connotations of partnership.

### After the kings: threats and dangers

When Tarquinius was outlawed, there was potential danger from adventurous leaders with soldiers in tow looking for the main chance, not uncommon at this period in Italy. Fortunately, one such leader, the Sabine Attus/Attius Clausus, was not hostile. Opposing his compatriots who wanted war with Rome, in 504 he brought 5,000 followers to settle in the city. All were given Roman citizenship, together with lands across the river Anio, and a new tribe, the Claudia, was created to accommodate them.[119] Attius became Appius Claudius, the ancestor of the most consistently troublesome politicians in the Republic. In 495, Appius was elected consul. Not bad for a landless Sabine immigrant who had been a Roman citizen for less than ten years, proof of Roman integration of people, conditioned by a preference for dealing with the elites of other communities.

Tarquinius Superbus posed a clear and present danger. He and his two surviving sons Arruns and Titus were at Caere (Cerveteri) in Etruria, where they raised an army, and fought the Romans at the battle of Silvia Arsia in 509. Arruns and the Roman consul Junius Brutus were killed.[120] Tarquinius and Titus found refuge with the King of Clusium (Chiusi), Lars Porsenna, who attacked Rome and occupied the Janiculum hill.[121] This era produced several Roman heroes, for instance Horatius Cocles. Single-handed, he stopped the Etruscans from crossing the bridge from the Janiculum into the city until it was cut down.[122] Patriotic bluster in the sources reflects all the Roman virtues, but there is a darker alternative. Tacitus believed that Rome surrendered to Porsenna.[123] In 506 Porsenna negotiated with the Romans on behalf of Tarquinius Superbus, but the Romans were not listening. Tarquinius complained that the Romans had seized his power collectively, because no-one among them was worthy to be king.[124] He failed to grasp that the Romans did not want a king, worthy or otherwise. Tarquinius and Titus went to Tusculum (Frascati) ruled by Tarquinius' son-in-law Octavus Mamilius, and all three joined with the Latins against the Romans at the battle of Lake Regillus, in 499/496.[125] The Romans won. Titus was killed. King Aristodemus of Cumae (Cuma) sheltered Tarquinius, who died in 495.[126] In Rome, the antipathy to kings in general and the Tarquinii in particular resulted in the exile to Lavinium of the consul Tarquinius Collatinus. Publius Valerius replaced him as consul, but he failed to arrange the election of a colleague to replace Junius Brutus, and his house on the Velia seemed more like a fortified palace. Public antipathy for his regal tendencies forced him to demolish the house, and to hold an election. Marcus Horatius, one of the commanders at Ardea, became consul.

## The government and magistrates of the Republic
In his narrative Dionysius of Halicarnassus invents a speech for Junius Brutus as spokesman, urging the Romans to abolish the monarchy, and recommending that the Senate should be supreme, government should never again be entrusted to a single man, and no magistrate should hold office permanently. Brutus put his proposals before the people's assembly.[127] This is retro-speak, based on the late Republican government that Dionysius knew.

Republican Rome was governed by the Senate and the People of Rome, denoted by the initials SPQR, still seen in Rome on mundane things like lamp posts and drain covers. The initials stand for *Senatus Populusque Romanus* (*que* at the end of a word means 'and'). The Senate, perhaps initially an advisory body, was made permanent, effectively controlling all affairs of state, internal matters, foreign relations, the army, the finances, and law and order, but the Senate's proposals had to be presented to the people's assemblies for ratification. Senators were not permitted to gather to discuss matters unless the Senate was summoned officially by a magistrate, but there is debate about which magistrates had the power to do this.

The people retained their assemblies, which were convened by a magistrate. The people were limited to voting for or against proposals. The oldest assembly, the *comitia curiata* formed from the thirty Romulan *curiae*, confirmed the appointment of magistrates by a law, the *lex curiata*. The *comitia centuriata* traditionally originated under Servius Tullius, but probably dates from a later period. This assembly voted by centuries to elect senior magistrates, the consuls and praetors, enacted laws which had been passed, and voted for or against going to war. The *comitia tributa* was a tribal assembly where the people voted by tribes to elect the junior magistrates.[128]

The magistrates, in descending order of seniority, were the Dictator and his Master of Horse, two censors, two consuls, and a praetor, increased to two praetors *c.*244. Junior magistrates were two plebeian aediles from 494, with two further patrician aediles added later, and two quaestors from 447. The most important magistrates were in place within fifty years after the expulsion of Tarquinius Superbus. Republican magistrates served out of duty to the state and were not paid. There was no sharp division between religious duties, civil magistracies and army commands, and Romans fulfilled all these functions without any formal training.

The Dictators, consuls, and praetors held *imperium*, authorising them to command armies. The *lex curiata de imperio*, passed by the *comitia curiata*, either conferred *imperium* on magistrates or merely confirmed it, so it is not clear whether elected magistrates held *imperium* only when the assembly bestowed it, or possessed it automatically, merely approved by the people.[129] Dictators held power for six months, consuls and praetors for one year. Later, when the Romans governed territories outside Italy, *imperium* was restricted to a specified geographical area.

### The Dictator

The Dictator had no colleague with equal powers, as the consuls did. He usually dealt with military emergencies, but he could also be appointed to subdue popular unrest, or to oversee the elections if both consuls were absent.[130] The Dictator held power over all the magistrates, including the consuls, who remained in office as his subordinates. His six-month term of office set him apart from the permanent Dictators in Aricia (Ariccia), Lanuvium (Lanuvio), Nomentum, and Tusculum (Frascati).[131] Instead of wasting valuable time with cumbersome electoral procedures, the Roman Dictator was nominated, usually at night. It is not known whether any magistrate holding *imperium* could nominate the Dictator.[132] An exception is Quintus Fabius Maximus, elected in 217 as Dictator by the *comitia centuriata*.[133] The Dictator chose his own *magister equitum*, or Master of Horse, and he provided a unified military command, once exercised by the kings.[134]

Twenty-four lictors were allotted to the Dictator, lictors being men who carried the *fasces*, the root word for Fascism and important symbols of power in ancient Rome. The *fasces* were bundles of rods, signifying the power to flog miscreants, and an axe within each bundle signified the power to execute people. Axes were not usually carried in Rome but were inserted for external expeditions. The *magister equitum* was allocated only twelve *fasces*, like the consuls, who each held the twelve *fasces* in alternate months. After six months, or when his task was concluded, the Dictator resigned.

### Consuls and praetors

Consul has a strange word-ending for a Latin form, and even the Roman scholar Varro was unsure of its ancestry. Traditionally the first consular elections were held in 509, supervised by Spurius Lucretius, appointed as *interrex* by Junius Brutus.[135] The consuls were eponymous magistrates, giving their name to the year. Although Dionysius says that consuls inherited the powers and insignia of the kings, they were definitely not regarded as kings.[136] They were always elected annually in pairs by the *comitia centuriata*, and the *comitia curiata* confirmed, or conferred, equal *imperium* on them. They took office on 15 March, but from 153, consulships began on 1 January. The institution of a dual magistracy as early as 509 is doubted, but Cornell wonders why it is so unimaginable.[137]

Though consuls are listed from the beginning of the Republic, the supreme magistrates may initially have been two praetors. Dealing with the events of the mid-fifth century, Livy says that consuls were originally called praetors (*now* he tells us!).[138] The chief magistrates of other early communities were praetors.[139] The title probably derives from *praeire*, meaning to go before, and Varro suggested that praetors were leaders in military and legal matters.[140]

The spanner in the works is the *praetor maximus*, mentioned in an ancient law on a tablet fixed to the Capitoline temple of Jupiter, concerning an annual ceremony on the Ides of September (13 September). It involved driving a nail into something, presumably the temple wall. Livy mentions the law when describing the flooding of the Circus Maximus in 363, when the Senate hoped that the ceremony would appease the gods and stem the floods.[141] Mommsen suggested that the term *praetor maximus* referred to whichever magistrate was most senior, not to a permanent post, but on grammatical grounds, *praetor maximus*, meaning greatest praetor, implies that there were three of them (great, greater, greatest).[142]

It is not known if the new title consul was substituted for praetor, or whether consuls were newly established with greater powers than those of the praetor. Consuls are not attested on inscriptions until the early third century, the first known being Lucius Cornelius Scipio Barbatus, consul in 298, by which time consuls were well established.[143] The inception of the consulship has been variously dated, to 449 after the Twelve Tables of laws had been drawn up, or when government by military tribunes came to an end in 367 (both episodes are described below). It is thought that in 367 a third praetor was elected and the two original praetors became consuls, or alternatively in 367 the consuls were merely restored to office, and the praetorship of that year was a new, additional, magistracy.[144]

The consulship is a purely Roman innovation. No consuls are attested in any other state. The Romans did not usually invent new posts with new titles when circumstances necessitated a change in government procedures. Instead, they used what they already had in stock, so to speak, adapting existing posts to accommodate new requirements. Such an adaptation occurred in 327/326 when the consul Quintus Publilius Philo, besieging Neapolis (Naples), was nearing the end of his term of office. There could not be two new consuls and a third still in office, so the Senate's decision, confirmed by the people, was that Philo must step down, but he could retain the *imperium* of a consul, with the title *pro-consule*, indicating that he was acting on behalf of a consul.[145]

The praetor was responsible for legal matters, and as a holder of *imperium* he could command armies. In the absence of the consuls the praetor became acting chief magistrate. In 244 an additional praetor was elected because legal and other business had increased in Rome, so the original praetor became the *praetor urbanus* responsible for home affairs, and the new *praetor inter peregrinos*, or 'over foreigners', but the title was probably not used at first, the extra praetor perhaps having military duties. Late, the *praetor peregrinus* most likely supervised legal cases involving *peregrini*, non-Romans, but he had many other duties besides this.

### Censors

The census was conducted by the consuls until 443, when the censorship was established. Censors, senior magistrates with no military responsibilities, always came in pairs, like consuls, who supervised the election of censors by the *comitia centuriata*. The duties and responsibilities were probably instituted by Servius Tullius.[146] All the people were listed, along with their tribes, ages, families, slaves, property and capital wealth. Between 339 and 318 the *lex Ovinia* was passed, empowering the censors to enrol and demote senators.[147] If a censor resigned, or died, the remaining censor was also expected to resign.

The censors enrolled recruits for the cavalry and the infantry, and supervised morals and conduct of the citizens.[148] They supervised the cultivation of land, the performance of civic duties, and dealt with cases of corruption or debt. Citizens could be expelled from their tribes, which would entail loss of citizenship privileges but perhaps not the loss of voting rights. Later, the censors were responsible for letting out contracts for building work, road construction, operation of mines, and for tax collection in the provinces and at harbours and ports.[149]

Censors were elected at irregular intervals, then every four years, and finally every five years, in theory. According to tradition, the censors retained their powers for the five-year term.[150] This does not sit well with Republican antipathy for long-term posts, even if no military powers were included. A law proposed in 434 by the Dictator Aemilius Mamercus limited the office to eighteen months. When Mamercus laid down his office, the censors retaliated, using their legitimate powers to disenfranchise him, remove him from his tribe, and levy a fine, eight times his property assessment.[151] On the completion of the census, one of the censors, chosen by lot, conducted a *lustrum*, a ceremonial for the religious purification of the city and the people, involving a procession with sacrificial animals. The ceremony averted evil, equivalent to a re-foundation of the city.

### Tribunes of the plebs

The first tribunes of the plebs were instituted in 494 after the grievances of the plebeians resulted in their temporary desertion of the city, an episode known as the First Secession, which was only a part of an ongoing struggle labelled by modern historians the Conflict of the Orders between plebeians and patricians. The origin of plebeians and patricians before the early fifth century is not fully elucidated. The ancient authors thought the distinction dated back to Romulus. It has been suggested – and refuted – that there was a racial split, or the plebs were the original inhabitants of Rome and the patricians were nobles arriving later to dominate them, or vice versa the patricians arrived first and the plebs muscled in.

Only plebeians could stand for election as tribunes, whose duties included protection of the plebs against arbitrary actions by the patricians. The plebeians elected the first two *tribuni plebis*, and the elected tribunes chose another three.[152] Not all historians agree that there were five tribunes in 493, but there were five by 471 and ten by 457.[153] Tribunes began their term of office on 10 December. In the later Republic, this gave them time to set their agendas before the consuls entered office on 1 January.

By the enactment of a sacred law, tribunes were sacrosanct. Anyone who injured one of them also injured the gods and was subject to legal and religious penalties. The culprit was declared *sacer*, which could mean sacred, or cursed, and a man cursed could be legally killed.[154] The tribunes could raise fines, imprison or execute people, and they had the right of *intercessio*, commonly labelled the veto, whereby they could stop proceedings which were likely to damage the plebeians.

Alongside the creation of tribunes, the *concilium plebis* or plebeian assembly was established, eventually incorporated into the government. Tribunes put proposals to the *concilium plebis* and the decisions (plebiscites) had to be obeyed by the plebeians. It took many years and several laws before the decisions of the *concilium plebis* achieved the same validity as laws passed in the other assemblies.[155]

### Aediles

The aediles were two new plebeian officials created to assist the tribunes. In 367-366, two additional aediles were created, known as curule aediles, at first drawn from the patricians, but eventually the post was open to plebeians as well. The title aedile derives from one of the duties of the post, the care of the *aedes* or temple of Ceres, the plebeian cult centre on the Aventine where an archive of senatorial proceedings was kept, informing the plebs of what had been discussed or decided.[156] The aediles may have shared the sacrosanctity of the tribunes to whom they were subordinate, but Livy decided against this because aediles could be imprisoned by more senior magistrates.[157] As time went on, aediles acquired more responsibilities, including care and maintenance of the streets and buildings of the city, the water supply, the food supply, and regulation of the markets. There was an allowance for the maintenance and repair of streets, public buildings, sewers and drains, attested by the fact that Marcus Vipsanius Agrippa, aedile in 33, repaired all these things without drawing his entitlement from public funds.[158] There would have been assistants for clerical work and slaves to carry out menial tasks. The aediles organised games and festivals, and organising lavish entertainment became a method of gaining popularity and votes in elections. There may have been an allowance from the public treasury for the games, but increasingly the aediles spent their own money or borrowed heavily. The aedileship was not a requirement for a senatorial career, but Cicero says it was the first step to higher office, primly asserting that as aedile he kept within his means, because remembrance of spectacles is transitory.[159]

## Quaestors

Quaestors were the most junior magistrates. The consuls appointed quaestors unofficially, perhaps as clerks dealing with judicial and financial matters. After 447, two quaestors were elected by the *comitia tributa*. From 421 there were four quaestors, and the post was opened to plebeians. From 267 there were eight, and in the first century under Cornelius Sulla there were twenty.[160] During the Republic the quaestors administered the *aerarium Saturni*, the treasury in the temple of Saturn, where state-owned bronze, silver and gold was lodged, along with official documents concerning financial and legal matters. After the acquisition of provinces, one or more quaestors accompanied the provincial governor. In the later Republic, Cornelius Sulla enlarged the Senate and from then onwards entry to the Senate for ex-quaestors was guaranteed.

## *The Twelve Tables of laws*

The political system was interrupted in 451 when the plebeians demanded codification of the laws, because in not knowing what the laws stated, the plebeians could inadvertently break them. Ten men or *decemviri* were appointed, with *imperium*, and all other magistracies, including the tribunate, were suspended. After producing ten tables of laws the task was not complete, so a second set of *decemviri* took over, producing only two laws, one of which reveals aristocratic disdain for the common people by forbidding marriages between plebs and patricians. Gaius Canuleius abolished this in 445 via the *lex Canuleia*, named as usual after its originator. The Twelve Tables of laws were displayed in the Forum inscribed on bronze tablets, which had disappeared by Livy's day, but the text was known and schoolboys had to learn it by heart.[161]

The villain of the piece is Appius Claudius Crassus Inregillensis Sabinus, who refused to lay down his powers at the end of the second decemvirate and discredited himself by lusting after, and raping, the beautiful Verginia, claiming that she was his slave. These events allegedly triggered the Second Secession of the plebeians, who were worried that tribunician powers would never be restored. Two rebellious Roman armies entered the city from the north-east at the Colline Gate, marching to the Aventine. Lucius Valerius and Marcus Horatius were sent to talk to the plebeians and order was restored. After an *interregnum*, Valerius and Horatius were elected consuls, and passed the Valerio-Horatian laws, which restored all that the plebeians had gained after the First Secession. *Tribuni plebis* were elected, their sacrosanctity was restored, and the right of appeal against a judgement was revived. Appius Claudius appealed after his condemnation, but he had gone too far to elicit sympathy and committed suicide.[162] The tyrannical Decemvirate, ending after the rape of Verginia, is suspiciously similar to the end of the tyrannical monarchy after the rape of Lucretia.

### Consular tribunes

From 445 to 367 another form of government was instituted, neither well documented nor consistently reported in the ancient sources, inviting copious modern speculation.[163] Traditionally, in 445 it was decided to suspend the consulship and substitute military tribunes of which there were usually six per legion. Their titles were *tribuni militum consulare potestate*, military tribunes with consular power, not to be confused with *tribuni plebis*.[164] The maximum number of consular tribunes was six, holding office for one year. The reasons behind this governmental change are not known, but the prolonged episode has been related to debts, land ownership, and plebeian demands for access to high office. Sometimes consuls were elected instead of military tribunes, usually in blocks of successive years.

At the beginning of 445 the tribunes of the plebs proposed a law that one of the consuls should be chosen from the plebeians, then nine *tribuni plebis* proposed a bill to allow the people to choose the consuls indiscriminately from plebeians or patricians. This was thwarted by the outbreak of war with Veii (Veio) and raids on the borders by the Volsci and Aequi peoples. Later, while the consulship was still restricted to patricians, consular tribunes could be elected from patricians or plebeians, so plebeians stood for election, but few were elected.[165] From 367 the Roman government was run on more familiar lines, via the Senate and the people's assemblies, with two annually elected consuls as the chief magistrates.

## Plebeians and the magistracies

The efforts of the plebeians to gain access to magistracies were rewarded in 409 when four quaestors were elected and only one of them was patrician. Livy says the plebs considered 'the way to consulships and triumphs were open to new men.'[166] The first plebeian consular tribune was Publius Licinius Calvus in 400.[167]

From 376 to 367, two tribunes of the plebs, Gaius Licinius Stolo and Lucius Sextius Lateranus, were re-elected every year, consistently proposing laws to tackle land distribution, debt problems, and plebeian access to the consulship. Despite patrician opposition, the tribunes finally passed the Licinio-Sextian laws in 367. One of these restricted land holdings of the *ager publicus*, or public land, to 500 *iugera*, roughly 330 acres. Appian provides information which may derive from later additions to the law: no-one should pasture more than 100 cattle or 500 sheep on their allotted 500 *iugera*, and there should be a number of free men employed on the farms to report what was going on – Rome as a police state?[168] The main drawback was that no viable method was suggested to facilitate the restriction to 500 *iugera*, because it involved reducing the large holdings of men who were wealthy and politically well connected.[169]

It is debated whether the Licinio-Sextian law concerning the consulship made it compulsory to elect one plebeian consul each year, or if the law simply allowed for one plebeian consul. If the former, the law failed. Elected in 367 for 366, Lucius Sextius was the first plebeian consul.[170] In 365 the plebeian Lucius Genucius was consul, and again in 362, but in most years both consuls were patricians. In 352 the tribunes of the plebs obstructed the consular elections to ensure that the Licinio-Sextian laws were observed. There was an *interregnum*, with power held by successive *interreges*, until the *interrex* Lucius Cornelius Scipio ordered the Senate to observe the law. This still does not elucidate what the law actually stated.

Lucius Genucius, son of the consul of 365 and 362, was tribune of the plebs in 342 and passed a law supposedly allowing for plebeians to hold both consulships.[171] Cornell suggests that the Licinio-Sextian laws allowed for one plebeian consul, and the Genucian plebiscite made it compulsory, because after 342 one consul was always plebeian.[172] Plebeians now had achievable goals, but attainment was slow. The praetorship had been in existence for three decades before the first plebeian was elected, Quintus Publilius Philo.[173] In his second consulship in 362, Lucius Genucius senior was the first plebeian to conduct a war under his own auspices, chosen by lot to command the army against the rebellious Hernici, but he was defeated and killed. Appius Claudius, opposed to plebeians and the Licinio-Sextian laws from the start, more or less said 'I told you so.'[174] A Dictator was nominated to continue the war.

The plebeian Gaius Marcius Rutulus demonstrated what plebeians could achieve. He was consul in 357 and the first plebeian Dictator in 355 when the Etruscans and the Romans were at war. Rutulus chose Gaius Plautius as the first plebeian *magister equitum*. Their military campaign was enormously successful. Rutulus was elected to his second consulship in 352, and shocked the patricians by his election as censor in 351. He held his third consulship in 344, and his fourth in 342.[175] The plebeian Marcus Popilius Laenas was consul in 350 and fought a successful campaign against the Gauls. Despite a javelin wound in his shoulder he carried on directing the battle and was awarded a triumph.[176] It was not until 173 that two plebeians reached the consulship together.

By 284, twenty-eight plebeian families had gained consular status. Plebeian society changed, and patrician and plebeian consuls sometimes colluded to promote mutual aims. After 342, nobility no longer depended solely on birth and bloodlines, but on consular ancestry. A new man or *novus homo* in later Roman politics was one who had no consuls in his family. Snobbery remained in good health, but its focus shifted.

## The fifth century: plagues, famines, debts, and land

A widespread economic decline in the second half of the fifth century has been detected in the archaeological record in Italy and other countries. Trade died off in the Greek colonies of coastal Italy, and even at Carthage. In Rome in the 480s, building work almost ceased.[177] Plagues of one sort or another, *pestilentia* in Livy's accounts, are recorded in Rome and among the surrounding tribes. In 492-491 the Oscan speaking Volsci were decimated by plague.[178] In 463 the Hernici east of Rome, around modern Monti Ernici, appealed to Rome for help. They were sandwiched between the Volsci and Aequi, who raided their farms. The Romans, afflicted by pestilence, were powerless to help, and the Hernici were encouraged to seek assistance from the Latins. Livy says that the contagion (*contagio* in Latin) was spread by mere contact (despairingly familiar in 2020), made worse by the influx of people fleeing from the countryside with their animals, fearing raids.[179] The plague subsided in the following year.

Between 508 and 384 fourteen famines affecting Rome were recorded.[180] In 491 grain (*frumentum*) was purchased from Sicily, and in 476-475 food was imported from Campania. Private stores of grain were brought out.[181] The frequent food shortages resulted from harvest failures, bad weather, lack of cultivation, or devastation of crops by Rome's enemies. The plebeians were blamed for neglecting the fields during the First Secession, when the price of grain rose, famine ensued, and agents (*frumentatores*) were sent by sea to buy food, probably hiring private merchants (*negotiatores*) with their own ships to sail northwards from Ostia along the coast of Etruria and southwards, bypassing Volscian settlements of the west coast.[182]

Rome was primarily an agricultural community, and in normal circumstances should have been able to feed the populace, until territorial expansion and increased population necessitated state control of home production and imports.[183] When the aediles were eventually put in charge of the food supply, the whole system had to be integrated, from procuring food, transporting it, building warehouses to store it, and then overseeing the distribution of it in Rome. After 384, famines seem to have ceased, perhaps because the continual wars and devastation of farms and fields had diminished, and Rome was better organised to import food on a regular basis.[184]

The so-called First Secession of the plebs, which resulted in the establishment of the tribunes of the plebs, was supposed to have been related to debts. The plebeians had been trying to elicit assistance from the Senate for men who had been bound over for debt. With no coinage at this period, the only way in which debts could be repaid was in bronze by weight, in goods, or by *nexum*, meaning the process whereby the debtor bound himself to work for the creditor if he could not repay a loan. *Nexus* refers to the person working in this way.[185] Modern authors have denied that this procedure even existed. The main grievances of the plebs concerned imprisonment and beatings by creditors and loss of property while serving in the army, when the creditors seized their farms.

In 495 Publius Servilius was levying troops to oppose the approaching Volsci, but no one agreed to serve in the army until Servilius issued a proclamation that no man should hold a Roman citizen in chains, preventing him from enlistment, and no man should seize or sell a serving soldier's property, nor interfere with his children or grandchildren. This was published, the people were reassured, and the army was levied.[186] Three separate wars were fought against the Volsci, Aequi, and Sabines in 494. Manius Valerius was appointed Dictator and issued an edict confirming Servilius' promises, so the people willingly enlisted in ten legions, four for the Dictator against the Sabines and three for each consul, who dealt with the Volsci and Aequi. When peace was restored, the Dictator honoured his promise that he would explain the soldiers' concerns to the senators. Achieving nothing, Valerius said he preferred to be a private citizen when the mutiny broke out.[187] Livy blamed money lenders (*faeneratores*, best translated as loan sharks), for causing the problems by their influence (*gratia*), and artfulness (*ars*).[188] The Senate did not disband the army, ordering the soldiers to march against the Aequi. *Maturata est seditio*, says Livy: the sedition matured.[189]

The First Secession had begun. The plebeians camped on the Sacred Mount three miles from Rome across the river Anio, or according to another source on the Aventine. They sat quietly for a few days. There were no demands for the cancellation of debts and no fighting. Harmony was restored, and tribunes of the plebs and the *concilium plebis* were instituted. So what about the debt problems? Penalties for money lenders had to wait until 344, when the aediles brought some lenders to trial.[190] Interest rates were dealt with in 342, when Lucius Genucius, tribune of the plebs, proposed a law to make it illegal to charge interest.[191]

Perhaps the plebeians had not objected to loans, debts, or even debt-bondage, but only to abuse by creditors.

Another perennial problem was the distribution of land. The *ager publicus* or public land around the city was open to all, but wealthy men were better able to cultivate the land via their dependants and clients and later, with slaves. The solution was *assignatio viritana*, individual allotments for each small farmer as his own property, but this meant that the wealthy farmers would have to reduce their holdings, which went down like the proverbial lead balloon. The first recorded land law was put forward by Spurius Cassius, consul in 486. Lands had been confiscated from the defeated Hernici, who allied with Rome afterwards. Spurius proposed to share the land between the Latins and the plebeians, together with some of the *ager publicus* appropriated by wealthy individuals, though rightly it belonged to the state.[192]

The *tribuni plebis* made twenty-five attempts between 486 and 367 to have laws passed for redistribution of land.[193] They resorted to preventing the levy of soldiers, hoping that the need for troops would force the Senate to put the land legislation to the vote of the people. When the plebs withdrew from Rome during the First Secession, there was concern about what would happen if the people refused to enrol in the army when a foreign war broke out (*externum bellum*).[194] At this stage, 'foreign wars' were almost on Rome's doorstep. Appius Claudius was blithely unconcerned, insisting the military contribution of the plebs was slight, and armies could be raised from among the clients of the patricians, but this speech is an invention of Dionysius, not an official record.[195] Could wars be fought without the plebs? If armies could be raised without the plebs, why did the *tribuni plebis* keep on trying to prevent the levy as an accelerant to getting the land laws passed? When the Aequi attacked the Latin city of Ortona in 481, and at the same time the men of Veii threatened Rome, the tribune Spurius Licinius persisted in obstructing the levy to force through a land bill. The consuls opposed him and the other tribunes stopped him, but the plebeians resorted to other methods.

Two armies were raised to take on the Aequi and the Veientines, under the consuls Caeso Fabius and Spurius Furius (Monty Python fans please desist).The army was assembled, but the plebeians would not fight.[196] This shows that plebs fought in the army in sufficient numbers to influence proceedings. In 480 the tribune Tiberius Pontificius obstructed the levy hoping to have the land laws passed, but he was defeated by Appius Claudius, who advocated assiduous subversion of the other tribunes to exercise their right of *intercessio*.[197]

The subversion of the tribunes may be an anachronism interposed from the later Republic, when it was quite usual for senators to keep tame tribunes in their pockets to veto potentially disruptive proposals. Caeso Fabius was elected consul again in 479. He proposed that the senators should pre-empt the tribunes by dividing up the land gained by conquest and bestowing it impartially on the plebeians, because they had fought in the battles that had won it. Needless to say, Caeso did not get far.[198] Distribution of land was as far away as ever.

### Roman control of other communities

The Romans were reluctant to govern lands or peoples directly. They thought in terms of controlling people, not territories, but they lacked the necessary personnel and administrative machinery to impose direct government on communities outside Rome, so they controlled other communities without annexing them and governing them directly. Influence sometimes sufficed to establish Roman control without employing troops, but it must be admitted that without *potential* use of the army, political methods alone would not have afforded the Romans long-term control even of a village. The Romans were not averse to using brute force, but they also found more peaceful methods. They established colonies, autonomous communities of Romans and/or other peoples with their own lands, linked to Rome and usually guarding outlying territory. Secondly, the development of *municipia* as self-governing communities helped to spread the Roman way of life and law, and thirdly the establishment of alliances bound communities to Rome, with mutual rights of protection in return for some obligations, without obliterating the autonomy of each ally.

During the third century the Romans established fifty-three colonies, protecting vulnerable areas or routes.[199] The Latin colonies, *coloniae Latinae*, began as settlements of mixed groups of Romans, Latins, and other allies, who renounced their former citizenship and achieved equal status as citizens of their colonies. Some were placed on lands confiscated after a war. They formed independent autonomous communities with the same obligations, rights and privileges as the Latin states, under the heading *ius Latii*, or Latin rights. This legal status could be granted to other communities, so that Latin colonies could be established anywhere, and they spread rapidly. Aulus Gellius labels colonies as images of the Romans.[200]

The first was established in 334, at Cales (Calvi Vecchia), originally a town of the Aurunci/Ausones. Alba Fucens in the Apennines was founded on land confiscated from the Aequi in 303, with 6,000 colonists. Cosa (Ansedonia) on the west coast was founded in 273 for 2,500 men, on land taken from Caere (Cerveteri). These last two sites have been excavated and their plans are known. Each was built on a hill, with a sturdy surrounding wall, and in each a forum, basilica, markets, temples and theatres have been identified.[201] During the third century the numbers of Latin colonies began to exceed the numbers of original settlements of Latium.

Roman citizen colonies were developed along the same lines as their Latin counterparts, but the citizens were registered in Rome. The early citizen colonies were usually smaller than Latin colonies and were sited near the coasts to guard harbours, river mouths and potential landing places. These were *coloniae maritimae*, more like forts than the colonies in towns, usually manned by 300 Romans, as at Castrum at Ostia. Another 300 settlers were sent to the *colonia maritima* established in 329 at Tarracina/Anxur (Terracina). Eight more colonies were established in 194, at least five of them settled by 300 Romans.[202] The settlers of the maritime colonies were excused service in the legions, except in dire circumstances. In times of war, the colonists were forbidden to be absent overnight, emphasizing their role as protectors of the coastal zones, probably against pirates and raiders, requiring an armed police force rather than an army.

Later in the second century, Roman citizen colonies became more widespread, generally larger than the *coloniae maritimae*. In parallel, the foundation of Latin colonies declined. As Roman power expanded, strategic needs altered, and the colonial system was adapted accordingly. During the Empire, the title *colonia* was applied to different kinds of settlements. Some *coloniae* were established for retired legionaries, such as the colony founded by the Emperor Claudius at Camulodunum (Colchester) for veterans of XX Valeria legion. One of the most famous veteran colonies is Timgad (Thamugadi), founded by the Emperor Trajan in the province of Numidia in North Africa. Eventually, *coloniae* became the highest status civilian settlements, overtaking the *municipia* which once outranked them.

The term *municipium* is said to derive from *munus* (plural *munera*), meaning a duty or service, and *capere*, meaning to take up, implying that a citizen of a *municipium* accepted duties and obligations.[203] *Municipia* were independent self-governing communities, retaining their own government, laws, languages, local customs, religious beliefs and ceremonials. They were not squeezed into a standard form of government approved by Rome. Tusculum became the earliest Roman citizen *municipium*, according to Cicero.[204] The citizens of any *municipium* could acquire full voting rights at Rome (*ius suffragii*), as in the case of Arpinum (Arpino), Fundi (Fondi) and Formiae (Formia) in 188, but this occurred only after complaints to Rome.[205] After the war with the Italian allies, called the Social War from *socii* or allies, Roman citizenship was finally awarded to all Latin cities and Italian allies. Most Italian cities then became *municipia*, except for the colonies, where there was no change. When the *municipia* spread to the provinces, some of them were given Latin rights (*ius Latii*), which came to be regarded as a step towards full citizenship. Under Augustus, a template municipal charter was issued for the provincial *municipia*, but the clauses could be adapted to the specific needs of each community.

By 264, Rome had made over 150 alliances with independent Italian states.[206] The Italians were referred to as allies and *amici*, or friends, but there is only limited evidence for formal treaties among the numerous alliances.[207] If a community had surrendered voluntarily, or after a defeat, the people became *dediticii*, subjects of Rome without rights, and it was probably the act of *deditio*, unconditional surrender, rather than a formal treaty that bound them to Rome. It was not happy ever after, since some allies rebelled and the Romans had to re-establish relationships, especially during the wars with the Samnites and later with Hannibal, when some allies were prised away from the Romans, or went over voluntarily. The main advantage to Rome was that allied communities were obliged to furnish troops for the Roman army, and the advantage for the allies was protection by Rome if they were attacked. By allying with so many communities, the Romans were able to increase their military manpower, enabling them to fight simultaneously on several fronts and to absorb losses that would have crippled any other state.

2

# The Assimilation of Italy and the First Provinces

*Rome, the Latins and the treaty with Carthage*
The first treaty between Rome and Carthage, traditionally dated to 509, was inscribed in archaic Latin on bronze tablets rediscovered in Rome around the middle of the second century BC, stop-press news for the historian Polybius.[1] The Carthaginians had made arrangements with Etruscan cities, as demonstrated by the three gold tablets inscribed in Phoenician-Punic and Etruscan, discovered in 1964 at Pyrgi (Santa Severa), the port for Caere (Cerveteri).[2] There may have been a treaty with Tarquinius Priscus or Superbus, so when the regime changed it was advisable to make some arrangement with the new Republic.

The treaty of 509 establishes friendship between the Romans and the Carthaginians and the allies of both. Neither the Romans nor their allies were to sail beyond the Fair Promontory (Cap Bon or Cap Farina). If a Roman or allied ship was driven onto the Carthaginian shore by storms or enemies, the crew would be allowed take away whatever was needed for repairs and for the worship of the gods, but they must leave after five days. Traders entering Libya or Sardinia were to conclude their business in the presence of a herald or town official, but since Carthage controlled only a part of Sicily, Romans entering the island would have the same rights as others.

The Carthaginians were forbidden to harm the peoples of Ardea (Ardea), Antium (Anzio), Laurentium, meaning Lavinium (Pratica di Mare), Circeii (San Felice Circeo), Tarracina (Terracina). These towns are near the west coast of Italy, accessible to Carthaginian ships, but the terms probably concerned privately owned merchant ships, not necessarily naval fleets.[3] The Carthaginians were not to harm cities of the Latins subject to the Romans. As for Latin cities not subject to the Romans, if the Carthaginians captured one, they had to relinquish it undamaged. They were not to build any fort in Latin territory, and if they entered the area carrying arms, they could not spend a night there.

The treaty reveals that some but not all Latin towns were subject to the Romans. Polybius provides no date for the second treaty with Carthage, but a likely context for it is 348. Diodorus says it was the first treaty, and Livy's extant text ignores the 509 treaty.[4] Four of the five named towns of the 509 treaty appear in the second treaty, except for Lavinium, captured by the Volsci in 488. Antium had also been taken by the Volsci, but in 467 it was made a colony for Romans, Volsci, Latins and Hernici.

## The Latins and the treaty of Spurius Cassius in 493

The Latins shared mutual rights but there was no political federation, as implied by the modern title Latin League, never used by Romans or Latins.[5] By 501 it was known that the Latins were conspiring against Rome, but in 499/496 the Romans defeated them at the battle of Lake Regillus. In 495 the Volsci allied with their neighbours the Hernici and tried to rouse the Latins to join them, but the Latins delivered the Volscian envoys to Rome. In gratitude, the Senate released 6,000 Latin prisoners, and referred to the incoming magistrates 'the treaty that they had deferred almost in perpetuity', suggesting that the Latins had unsuccessfully asked for a treaty more than once.[6] It seems that the Latins had been disarmed and forbidden to make war without Rome's consent. When the Aequi invaded Latium in 494, the Latins asked for assistance, or permission to take up arms, and the Romans preferred defending them to arming them.[7] In the later fourth century the Latin leader Lucius Annius Setinus said that the Romans forbade the Latins to defend their own frontiers by themselves.[8]

In 493 a treaty of alliance between Romans and Latins, recorded on a bronze column in Rome, was arranged by the consul Spurius Cassius. Romans and Latins were not to make war on each other, nor ask a foreign power to help them, nor allow hostile enemies to march safely through their territory. If Romans and Latins assisted each other in war, the spoils were to be shared equally.[9]

The Romans defeated the Hernici in 487 and made an alliance in the consulship of Spurius Cassius and Proculus Verginius.[10] Cassius arranged similar terms with the Hernici as with the Latins.[11] He confiscated two-thirds of Hernican land, dividing it between Latins and Roman plebeians. Suspected of seeking power, Cassius was executed when his consulship ended.[12] Latins and Hernici contributed soldiers to the Romans to fight the Volsci and Aequi on several occasions.[13] Their contingents would be commanded by Romans, but military expertise was not a Roman prerogative. In 476/475, the Latins and Hernici, with their own commanders, drove off Volsci and Aequi raiders and recovered their property. Feathers were ruffled at Rome.[14]

## Enemy at the gates

During the fifth century there were occasions when the enemy really was at the gates of Rome. The Volsci came within five miles of the city in 488, led by the renegade Roman aristocrat Gnaeus Marcius Coriolanus who defected in 491. He drew off when the women of his family came to plead with him, and never returned.[15] In 460 the Sabine leader Appius Herdonius seized the Capitol with 2,500 men, including slaves and Roman exiles. He intended to reclaim the lands of the exiles, free the slaves, and call in the Volsci and Aequi. Even in this dire emergency the tribunes tried to push through the land law, bringing the soldiers away from guard duty. The consul Publius Valerius sent them back.[16] As soon as the people of Tusculum (Frascati) heard of the situation in Rome, they decided to march to the rescue, helping the Romans to defeat Herdonius, who was killed, but so was the consul Valerius. The Capitol was ceremonially purified, and the Tusculans were appropriately thanked.[17]

The Sabines were at the gates once more in 458, and again the tribunes tried to prevent the levy, but Romans eagerly enlisted, forming two Roman armies, because the Aequi had also mobilised. The consul Gaius Nautius repelled the Sabines, while the other consul Lucius Minucius remained in camp long enough for the Aequi to fence him in.[18] Lucius Quinctius Cincinnatus was made Dictator. According to legend, he was ploughing his fields as the senatorial delegation arrived, but he assembled troops, asking the men to bring stakes to make a palisade to encase the Aequi. Attacked from two sides, the tribesmen surrendered. After only fifteen days, Cincinnatus relinquished his office, held a triumph, and went back to his ploughing.[19] The story may be largely fiction, but it inspired later Romans.

Fighting on more than one front was becoming normal for the Romans. The Sabines were on the warpath again in 449, while the Aequi and Volsci were also making strenuous preparations for war (*summa vi bellum apparare*).[20] This time, the tribunes did not obstruct the raising of two consular armies. The consul Marcus Horatius defeated the Sabines and Lucius Valerius defeated the Aequi and Volsci, capturing their camp and masses of loot.[21] In 446 the Volsci and Aequi approached the Esquiline gate, and again the tribunes did not obstruct the levy. Titus Quinctius Capitolinus and Agrippa Furius were elected consuls, agreeing that Quinctius should be the senior commander, a sensible practice not always followed by Roman generals. A battle was fought about ten miles from the city. Livy supplies great detail, suggesting the existence of official records.[22]

When the Volsci and Aequi went to war in 431, they entrenched their camp on Mount Algidus and drilled their men. Tribesmen were recruited under a *lex sacrata*, obliging every man to join the army or face penalties. The consuls were Titus Quinctius Cincinnatus and Gnaeus Julius Mento. Aulus Postumius Tubertus was nominated Dictator and chose Lucius Julius as *magister equitum*. The Romans and their Latin and Hernici allies fought the fiercest battle of the late fifth century. The Dictator received a shoulder wound, the consul Quinctius lost his arm, and Marcus Fabius the cavalry commander was nearly pinned to his horse by a spear though his thigh. The Volsci surrendered, and the tribesmen were enslaved. Their nobles were spared.[23] The citizens of Labici joined the Volsci and Aequi 419-418, defeating the Romans because the two consular tribunes would not co-operate. The Dictator Quintus Servilius Priscus with his son as *magister equitum* restored the situation. Labici was captured and was made a colony, with 1,500 colonists from Rome.[24]

As the raids of the Volsci and Aequi diminished, the Samnites arrived on the scene, from the hill country around the rivers Sangro, Trigno and Biferno. Modern place names recall them, such as Civitanova del Sannio north-east of Isernia, and Monti del Sannio, south-east of Campobasso. There were four main tribes, Hirpini, Caudini, Carricini and the wealthiest, the Pentri. The Samnites were expert fighters with capable commanders, as the Romans would soon learn.

## The tribes

The struggle between the Romans and the various tribes was a prolonged stalemate, with few decisive victories. The Romans could call on troops from their allies, but similarly Livy pondered the inexhaustible tribal manpower, suggesting that new generations replaced losses.[25] This cannot be the only explanation. The tribes comprised different independent segments, often incorporating other tribesmen who had been absorbed, so while one group might be disastrously defeated, other tribesmen were still at large. When Lucretius Tricipitinus routed the Volsci in 462, Livy says that the Volscian name was blotted out (*deletum est*).[26] Yet there they were again, large as life, in 459, when the Hernici reported that the Volsci and Aequi were arming. However, after their next defeat the Volsci temporarily abandoned their annual attacks.[27] Lack of unity made the tribesmen seem fickle. In 467 the Aequi asked for a treaty of friendship with Rome.[28] The consul Quintus Fabius arranged the terms. Like all allies, the Aequi were obliged to provide troops, supported at their own expense, and Fabius also demanded provisions for the army, two pieces of clothing per man, and money for the soldiers.[29] The Aequi took to raiding, breaking the alliance in 466. They obtained another treaty in 459 and broke it within a year.[30] This apparent perfidy suggests that different factions were operating independently. The Volsci quarrelled among themselves from 430 onwards because some wanted peace and others wanted war with Rome.[31]

In tribal organisation there was not always a single leader responsible for the behaviour of the entire tribe. Tribesmen made treaties with an individual, not with a state, so the death of a Roman who organised a treaty automatically invalidated it. There was not always a central place of 'government'. When the Volsci captured Antium it was regarded by the Romans as the Volscian capital, but it was just one of the Volscian dwellings, not the administrative centre of a united Volscian realm.

## Rome and Veii

The wars between Rome and Veii were quite different from tribal wars. Veii was a centralised, wealthy, sophisticated Etruscan city, way ahead of Rome. A road network had been established around the city long before Appius Claudius established the first properly made-up Roman road in 312. The water supply and drainage preceded Rome's. Various *cuniculi* or artificial water channels drained the city and the fields, while separate *cuniculi* brought water to fill the cisterns. The city lay on an elevated plateau above cliffs providing natural defences, but sometime before 450 the Veiientines enclosed the plateau within a wall, built in uniform style, suggesting that it was not a piecemeal development over several years.[32] According to Livy, in 480 all Etruria sent auxiliary forces to support Veii, but later he whittles down 'all Etruria' to 'some Etruscans'. The Romans won the battle but the consuls were killed.[33] The Fabii clan fought the Veiientines, disastrously, in 478-477. They were ambushed and the only survivor was the young Quintus Fabius Vibulanus, who became consul ten years later.[34]

The Veientines captured the Janiculum hill in 476. They were driven out, asking for a truce in 474, which the Romans granted for forty years in return for money and grain.[35] Before it expired, the Roman colony of Fidenae defected to Lars Tolumnius, King of Veii, who killed Roman envoys sent to protest. Mamercus Aemilius was made Dictator, with *magister equitum* Lucius Quinctius Cincinnatus, son of the famous Dictator. They cleared the enemy from Roman territory and defeated a combination of Veiientines and Faliscans, men of Falerii (Civita Castellana). Aulus Cornelius Cossus killed Lars Tolumnius, claiming the right of *spolia opima*, reserved for those who had personally killed an enemy leader, whose arms and armour were dedicated to Jupiter Feretrius.[36]

The Veientines and Fidenates marched on Rome in 435, but were chased into Fidenae, where the Dictator Quintus Servilius captured the town by mining into it. Disregarding their ten-year truce, in 434 the Veientines asked for Etruscan help, but were told that since they started the war on their own initiative, they should finish it the same way.[37] The men of Fidenae slaughtered the Roman colonists but were defeated, and a twenty-year truce was made.[38] It ended in 406, and the Romans sent *fetiales* to the Veiientines, who threatened to kill them. The Roman people rejected war against Veii because the Volscian war had not ended, but they eventually agreed and the siege of Veii began.[39]

According to Livy this was when the Senate decreed that soldiers should be paid from the public treasury. The people rejoiced, but the tribunes dampened their enthusiasm because tax (*tributum*) would have to be levied to pay for this apparent largesse. The senators set the example, ostentatiously bringing cart-loads of bronze to the treasury, followed by leading plebeians.[40] Volunteers flocked to enlist in the army. The introduction of pay for the soldiers, kept away from their farms at the siege of Veii, was a sensible move on the part of the senators, but it also imbues them with clairvoyance, because in 406 the Romans could not know that the war would last for the alleged ten years. It is suggested that the introduction of army pay may belong to the Samnite wars of the fourth century.[41]

Livy resumes the story of Veii in 403. The Romans built a double ring of fortifications around the city to defend their army from other Etruscans, but no Etruscans came because the Veientines had abandoned democracy and chosen a king, who had gravely offended all the Etruscans.[42] The men of Capena and Falerii assisted the Veientines in 402, defeating the Romans, but the Romans retaliated by devastating the lands of both these enemies.[43] In 396 the Capenates and Faliscans defeated the Romans again, and the soldiers besieging Veii ran away. The Dictator Marcus Furius Camillus levied troops and assisted by Latins and Hernici he dealt first with the Capenates and Faliscans, then returned to Veii and ordered the troops to dig a mine into the city, working in shifts night and day.[44] When the mine was ready, Camillus ordered an assault, while picked soldiers burst out of the tunnel inside the city, defeating the Veientines. Camillus ordered heralds to announce that all those who were unarmed would be spared, and the war ended.[45] The ten-year siege of Veii is suspiciously similar to that of Troy, especially the emergence of the Romans from the tunnel, like the Greeks bursting from the belly of the Trojan horse. Livy did not wholly believe the story of Veii.[46]

The Veiientine lands were annexed and allocated to Roman settlers, increasing Roman territory by more than half. The Romans also gained the quarries yielding the yellow Grotta Oscura tufa. Capena submitted to Rome in 395, and Falerii was captured by Camillus in 394.[47] Belatedly, in 388, the people of Veii, Capena and Falerii were incorporated as Roman citizens in four new Roman tribes.[48] After his successes, Camillus was indicted by a *tribunus plebis*, and went into exile at Ardea.

## Gauls in the city

The Gallic tribe which attacked Rome, traditionally in 390, were principally Senones, one of the last tribes to cross the Alps into northern Italy. They asked for lands around Clusium (Chiusi). The Romans agreed to help Clusium, sending ambassadors to the Gauls, but the Fabii among them turned violent. The Senate refused the request from the Gauls to surrender them.[49]

Six consular tribunes were appointed, including three Fabii, 'whose rashness had brought on the war'.[50] Their rashness persisted when the Gauls appeared. Without fortifying their camp, and without taking the auspices, they fought at the river Allia. The Gallic chief, Brennus, with considerable strategic ability, reasoned that Roman reserves on a nearby hill would attack the rear of the Gauls so he concentrated on the hill, eventually scattering all the Romans who fled to Veii, or to Rome, heading straight for the Capitol. The Gauls entered the city, killing the senators sitting outside their houses to await their fate.[51] The Romans assembled men of military age with their families, and weapons, grain and other provisions on the Capitol. The plebeians moved to the Janiculum and then to other cities, and the Vestal priestesses found shelter in Etruria at Caere (Cerveteri), taking some of their religious artefacts and burying everything else.

Furius Camillus raised troops at Ardea to fight off the Gauls approaching the town.[52] He was made Dictator, with Lucius Valerius as *magister equitum*, but before they arrived in Rome the Gauls attacked the Capitol. The story goes that the geese housed on the hill, sacred to Juno and resolutely not eaten by starving Romans, gave a noisy warning, arousing the garrison, and the Gauls were driven off.[53] The Romans agreed to pay Brennus one thousand pounds of gold, but discovered that the Gauls used false weights. Brennus swept aside protests with the famous phrase *vae victis*, 'woe to the conquered.' Propitiously, Camillus arrived, retrieved the gold, and told his soldiers to win back the city with iron. After a short battle the Gauls fled.[54]

Recovery was fairly rapid, convincing modern historians that the so-called sack of Rome was not so serious, which may be true, but it instilled in future generations of Romans a fear of the Gauls. A fund was started in case they attacked again. Houses were rebuilt, roofed with tiles (*tegulae*) supplied by the Senate, and everyone was permitted to quarry stone and cut timber wherever he liked, provided that building work was completed within a year. Livy complains that the Romans built wherever they wished, with no straight streets, so the sewers which followed the original streets from then on ran under houses.[55]

Roman attitudes changed after the Gallic invasion. In 388 two armies were levied, one to attack the Aequi, purely out of hatred according to Livy, and the other attacked Etruscan towns without sending *fetiales*.[56] The attitudes of Rome's allies also changed. Alliances had metamorphosed into domination. For the next thirty years or so the Romans and their allies and colonies warred against each other.

The people of Tusculum (Frascati), friendly to Rome from the time of the kings, joined the Volsci in 383. Fortunately, it did not end in tears. The Romans assembled an army under Furius Camillus but arriving at Tusculum he found the gates open. Peace was made. From 381 the Tusculans were full Roman citizens with voting rights, and their town became the most ancient *municipium*.[57] The Tusculans were enrolled in the Papirian tribe, and by sheer numbers could influence the vote of this tribe.[58]

The Tusculans were not governed directly by Romans, retaining their autonomy, their magistrates and laws, but had to travel to Rome to vote in elections. They possessed the legal right to intermarry with Romans (*ius conubii*) and to engage in business with them (*ius commercii*). They paid taxes and were obliged to furnish troops, but they had no right to assemble an army, or formulate their own foreign policy.

## Roman citizenship: boon or burden?

The ancient authors interpreted the grant of Roman citizenship as a generous award, but modern authors have proclaimed it positively detrimental, interpreting citizenship for the Tusculans as an act of domination. Cornell points out that Roman soldiers occupied Tusculum, but according to Livy troops were withdrawn when citizenship was granted.[59]

One small point is worth considering about the Tusculans. In other cases where Roman citizenship was granted, Livy's terminology is *civitas data*, or *in civitatem accepti/recepti*, or in older contexts, *Romani facti*, 'made Romans'. Describing how the Tusculans acquired Roman citizenship, Livy uses the verb *impetraverunt*, the plural form referring to the Tusculans doing whatever *impetraverunt* implies.[60] *Impetrare* means to achieve or obtain, but can mean to obtain something by asking for it. Was Roman citizenship imposed on the Tusculans, or did they seek it?

There are instances of various people refusing Roman citizenship. In 307-306 the Hernici fought against Rome, except for their communities of Aletrium, Ferentinum and Verulae. After the Roman victory, the Hernici were given *civitas sine suffragio*, citizenship without the vote,

devised thirty years earlier. The three communities which had not
fought the Romans rejected citizenship.[61] A few years later the Aequi
broke the terms of their treaty by joining the Samnites, complaining
that the Romans were trying to make them Roman citizens, just as the
Hernici had been 'punished'.[62] Much later, when Hannibal besieged
Casilinum in 216 the town was defended by several allied contingents,
including men of Praeneste (Palestrina). Before the soldiers starved,
Hannibal ransomed them and occupied Casilinum. The Roman
Senate rewarded the Praenestini, giving the soldiers double pay and
exemption from service for five years. Roman citizenship was offered,
but refused.[63]

## War with the Etruscans

The absorption of Veii extended Roman borders up the Tiber towards
Sutrium (Sutri) and Nepete (Nepi), founded as Latin colonies in 382,
'gateways and barriers' into Etruria, according to Livy.[64] Sutrium was
besieged by 'nearly all Etruria' in 389, and asked Rome to help. As
Sutrium surrendered, Furius Camillus arrived, meeting the ejected
population. Leaving soldiers to protect them, Camillus approached
Sutrium where the Etruscans were busy looting, neglecting to guard
the gates, but who would stand guard when everyone else was getting
rich? Camillus regained Sutrium on the same day that it was lost, and
the inhabitants were reinstalled.[65]

The Etruscans attacked Sutrium again three years later and were
defeated by Camillus and Publius Valerius, two of the consular tribunes
for 386, but another Etruscan army captured Nepete, betrayed by
its inhabitants. The Romans recaptured it, installing a garrison.
The people of Tarquinii (Tarquinia) raided Roman territory in 358,
offering no reparation when Roman envoys arrived. War was declared.
The consul Gaius Fabius was disastrously defeated, and 307 Roman
prisoners, an unusually precise figure, were killed at Tarquinii.[66]
In 356 the defeat of Tarquinii and Falerii (Civita Castellana) by the
consul Marcus Fabius Ambustus prompted other Etruscans to join
Tarquinii. The plebeian Dictator Gaius Marcius Rutulus and his
*magister equitum* Plautius drove the Etruscans out of Roman territory.
The people awarded Rutulus a triumph, but the Senate refused to
authorize it.[67] In another war, 358 men of Tarquinii, once again a very
precise figure, were scourged and beheaded in the Forum in Rome,
in retribution for Romans sacrificed at Tarquinii. No peace treaty is
mentioned.[68]

## The Samnites: first contact

In 354/353 the Samnites requested an alliance of friendship with Rome. The terms of the treaty are unknown, but there were Samnite contingents in the war with the Latins in 340.[69] The First Samnite War began when the Samnites attacked their long-standing enemies, the Sidicini, who appealed to the Campanians, prompting the Samnites to besiege Capua, the chief Campanian city.[70] When Capuan envoys arrived at Rome, the Romans refused to make war on their Samnite allies. Then the envoys made an offer that the Romans could hardly refuse. Capua surrendered unconditionally, with its people, lands, temples and shrines, making the Capuans *dediticii*, subject to Rome without rights.[71] This was a common feature of ancient diplomacy.[72] Roman ambassadors explained to the Samnites that the Campanians were now Roman subjects, but the Samnites nevertheless attacked the Campanians, and when Roman *fetiales* received no favourable reply Rome declared war on their erstwhile Samnite allies.[73]

Two armies were raised, the consul Marcus Valerius Corvus/Corvinus marching to Campania and his colleague Aulus Cornelius marching to Samnium.[74] Valerius attacked the Samnites, who fought fiercely. The Romans faltered. Then they got angry. The Samnites broke. Samnite prisoners explained that the furious expressions and blazing eyes of the Romans panicked them.[75] In Samnite territory the other consul Cornelius marched into a forested valley, neglecting to reconnoitre. The Samnites were arranged on the heights above him. His officer Publius Decius Mus asked permission to occupy a hill above the Samnite camp, holding the position until the Romans escaped, and in the night Decius and his men fought their way to Cornelius' camp, urging the consul to attack instantly, since the Samnites were split up. The Romans won the battle.[76] The Samnites were defeated again at Suessula (Cancello ed Arnone on the river Volturno). Peace was made in 341, renewing the alliance of 354. The Carthaginians congratulated the Romans and sent a golden crown for the temple of Jupiter.[77]

## Discord in Rome

In 342 Capua asked for Roman protection, receiving a Roman garrison, but the soldiers began to think of taking over the wealthy city. The consul Gaius Marcius Rutulus, appointed to Campania detected the soldiers' intentions, steadily dismissing the troublemakers by granting leave and discharging older men.[78] A mutiny began, in which the soldiers kidnapped the retired general Titus Quinctius (or

Gaius Manlius), forcing him to lead them to Rome. The situation was defused when the soldiers approached the city and met the Romans sent against them. They came to their senses, avoiding civil war.[79]

An indication of the seriousness of this affair can be deduced from a law passed by the people and authorized by the Senate, a *lex sacrata*, entailing dire punishment for anyone who disobeyed it.[80] The real problem was probably debt. One of the clauses of this new law made it illegal to remove the name of a serving soldier from the army list without his consent. Deletion of names converted serving soldiers into private citizens, so their farms and lands could be seized by creditors. In 495 the people had refused to enlist until it was made illegal to seize the property of a serving soldier.[81] The *faeneratores*, money-lenders, had most to gain from striking out soldiers' names, possibly by bribing or terrifying some clerks. In 342 the tribune Lucius Genucius proposed a law against lending at interest.[82] In 326/321 it was made illegal to imprison anyone for debt, limiting creditors to seizure of property. The men currently in prison for debt were released, and only those found guilty and awaiting sentence could be kept in shackles.[83]

## The Latin revolt 340-338

Signs of discontent emerged among the Latins in 348 when they refused to levy troops, preferring to fight for their liberty rather than for the Romans.[84] Eight years later, the Latin revolt was precipitated by a third party. By the terms of their alliance with the Samnites, the Romans agreed not to interfere in Samnite attacks on their enemies, the Sidicini, who tried unsuccessfully to surrender to Rome, then approached the Latins, who agreed to help, along with the Campanians who had no cause to love Samnites. The Romans received Samnite protests but explained that there was nothing in their treaties with the Latins to prevent them from attacking another state. The Romans could not admit that they had lost control of the Latins.[85]

Ten chief men of the Latins were summoned to Rome. Livy makes the Latin praetor Lucius Annius Setinus complain about the lack of equality and liberty, and the pretence of equal rights. There had never been a Latin consul or even a Latin senator in Rome. The meeting in Rome was acrimonious, revealing Roman prejudice, not entirely racial, but against insubordinate subordinates.[86] Latins, Campanians and Tusculans gathered near Capua.[87] Two Roman armies, including Samnite levies marched there under the consuls

Manlius Torquatus and Decius Mus, fighting a battle at the foot of Mount Vesuvius. When the Romans began to fall back, Decius Mus decided that he must sacrifice himself and the enemy army to the gods, according to a vision seen the night before. The religious ritual was performed, and with his head veiled Decius threw himself into battle and was killed. The Romans won.[88] After another battle the Latins surrendered, then rose again in 339 to be defeated by the consul Quintus Publilius Philo. It remained to subdue Pedum (location unknown), the centre of rebellion, supported by Tibur, Praeneste, Velitrae, Lanuvium and Antium. In 338 the consuls Lucius Furius Camillus and Gaius Maenius subdued all the Latins, installing garrisons in their towns.[89]

## The new organisation of 338

To their credit, the senators decided that not all the Latins and other peoples were equally guilty, so the consuls were asked to draw up proposals for each individual community.[90] Outlining the results, Livy carefully arranges his material in status groups. Lanuvium, Aricia, Nomentum and Pedum were given full Roman citizenship (*civitas optimo iure*). These Roman citizen communities formed an arc around Rome, from Nomentum in the north-east, to Aricia in the south-east. The Tusculans retained their citizenship, while a few ringleaders were blamed for the revolt.[91] Next on Livy's list are Velitrae (Vellitri) and Antium (Anzio). The people of Velitrae had long been Roman citizens, but because they had rebelled, their town walls were demolished. The Romans usually preferred to deal with and promote the elite classes, but in this case the elite of Velitrae were permanently banished, and colonists were settled on their lands, while the people were made citizens.[92] New colonists were sent to Antium, where everyone, including the Volsci, became Roman citizens. The Antiates, renowned pirates, surrendered their ships. Some were burnt, the rest were taken to the dockyards (*navalia*) of Rome, opposite the Tiber Island on the left bank of the river.[93] Some of the ships' metal rams or *rostra* (singular *rostrum*), were placed in the Roman Forum on the speakers' platform, which Livy says was built now and called, appropriately, the Rostra.[94] The new Roman citizens with voting rights were registered in 332 by the censors Quintus Publilius Philo and Spurius Postumius. Two new tribes were created, the Maecia for the people of Lanuvium, and the Scaptia for the people of Velitrae, bringing the total of tribes to twenty-nine.[95]

The Latin states were each allied separately to Rome and no other state. They remained as self-governing communities, but they lacked *ius commercium* or mutual trading rights, allowed to do business only with Romans, and *ius conubium*, the right to marry men or women from other Latin states, so they could marry only citizens of their own state or Rome. They had no foreign policy of their own and were forbidden to hold common councils (*concilia*), removing any possibility of reviving the so-called Latin League.[96] It was 'divide and rule' made manifest.

The *equites* or nobles of Capua were given *civitas Romana*, full citizenship, because they had not joined the Latin revolt.[97] The remaining Capuans had withdrawn from the final stage of the revolt, and received *civitas sine suffragio*, citizenship without voting rights. The Campanian lands were declared *ager Romanus*, providing for Roman settlers, theoretically keeping out the Samnites. Rome's territory was increased to an estimated 5,525 square kilometres (2,130 square miles).[98] According to Pliny, Latium was relabelled Latium Vetus, or Old Latium, and the new territories were called Latium Adiectum, Additional Latium. [99]

Fundi (Fondi) and Formiae (Formia) were given *civitas sine suffragio* because they had always allowed free passage for Roman armies. Cumae (Cuma), Suessula (Cancello) and later Acerrae (Acera) also became *civitates sine suffragio*.[100]

Privernum (Priverno) made war on Rome in 330, assisted by men from Formiae and Fundi. The consul Plautius Venox defeated Privernum, claiming that the people were not uniformly guilty. This town bordered on Samnite territory, and Samnite-Roman relationships had deteriorated, so *civitas sine suffragio* was granted to Privernum in 329.[101]

*Civitas sine suffragio* was an important innovation. The states with this type of Roman citizenship retained their own laws and elected their own magistrates, paid tax like other Romans and provided soldiers, but they were not directly governed by Rome. The Romans were good at doing new things with old tools, in this case separating the privileges, rights and obligations of citizenship from the franchise that tied it firmly to the city of Rome. *Civitas sine suffragio* could therefore be granted to distant communities, which would retain their internal government and administration, but pay tax and contribute soldiers to Rome.

Twenty years after the settlement of 338, Capua asked the Romans to quell internal strife. The praetor Lucius Furius established laws for Capua. Prefects, elected by Romans, began to be sent to the city, probably when necessary, not annually. Livy says that the praetor drew up the laws and the prefects administered the changes.[102] Later the people of Antium complained that they had no fixed laws and magistrates. As a Volscian state, with Roman colonists sent out more than once, they did not know whose laws they should be following. This time the Senate did not appoint a prefect, but they asked the Roman patrons of Antium to draw up laws. Communities often chose patrons from among influential Romans, who protected them and represented them at Rome. The practice continued into the Empire. Livy adds that Roman law was beginning to spread to other communities.[103]

## *Livy, Polybius and the change from the phalanx to the legion*

Livy says that after the soldiers began to serve for pay, traditionally in 406, the phalanx-legion was replaced by an open-order formation composed of maniples, 'handfuls' of soldiers derived from *manus*, meaning hand.[104] As mentioned above, military pay may have been introduced during the Samnite wars, a context which also fits the change from phalanx to maniples, because Samnite terrain was not conducive to the operation of the compact phalanx.[105]

Unfortunately, Livy's description of the reorganised army of the mid-fourth century is unreliable.[106] He had to rely on sources to describe an army which neither he nor his contemporaries had ever seen, whereas Polybius had observed the second-century Republican army in action. Some of Livy's description agrees with that of Polybius, especially with regard to Polybius' three main battle lines composed of *hastati*, *principes* and *triarii*, the *hastati* being the youngest and the *triarii* the eldest. These three groups were each subdivided into ten smaller units, variously called *ordines*, *manipuli*, or *vexilla*, the last two titles referring to maniples and the standard, or *vexillum*. There were two centurions for each maniple. Polybius and Livy disagree about the size of a legion. Livy opts for 5,000 infantrymen and 300 horsemen, whereas Polybius' legion comprised 3,000 men, plus *velites* or light armed troops, distributed equally among the maniples, and if the levy exceeded 4,000, the extra men were divided up between the *hastati* and *principes*.[107]

The date when the manipular formation was introduced is disputed. A case can be made for 311, when a law was passed allowing the

Roman people to elect sixteen of the twenty-four military tribunes, all of them hitherto appointed by Roman commanders.[108] Twenty-four military tribunes at six per legion indicate that by 311, when the Romans were fighting the second Samnite war, four legions were usually raised.[109] Is it too simplistic to suggest that it all came together in 311, with paid soldiers, a new style army, four legions instead of the usual two, and elected military tribunes?

### The allied troops

The process for raising allied troops may have been overhauled in the late fourth or early third century, when more allies had been gained, and more troops were required for frequent wars. It has been suggested that alliances were not always established by a formal treaty, because there is so little evidence.[110] If there were only a few formal, detailed treaties documenting the terms arranged with the allies of Rome, then the specifics of raising troops must derive from some other record, probably the *formula togatorum*, a document listing each state and its obligations.[111] It is not known when the *formula togatorum* was instituted. The greatest need for it would be when many Italian states were brought into alliance with Rome in the late fourth and early third centuries, and with so many communities involved, it would be much easier to preserve, consult, and amend the records if they were in one list. Polybius says that when it seemed that the Gauls were about to invade in 225, the allies were ordered to compile lists of men of military age.[112] This may be the start-date for the *formula togatorum*, but if so, it remains unexplained how the allies and the Romans levied their troops before this time. It was once thought that the *formula togatorum* specified the maximum number of soldiers to be contributed by each state, but this would require revision to take account of an increase or a decline in population. It is suggested that there never was a stated limit, and soldiers would be demanded according to circumstances.[113]

### The Second Samnite War 326-304

In 327 Romans living in Campania were attacked by the people of the Greek city of Palaepolis, meaning Old City, as opposed to Neapolis or New City (Naples). The Romans despatched *fetiales*, received no satisfaction, so war was declared. The consul Quintus Publilius Philo began to besiege Palaepolis, while the other consul Lucius Cornelius Lentulus guarded Campania.[114] The Samnites came to the rescue of Palaepolis, managing to install there 4,000 soldiers, and 2,000 men from Nola.[115] Publilius Philo's consular command was prorogued in 326, by the process known as *prorogatio imperii*, described above. Cornelius Lentulus and his troops remained in Samnite territory, though no declaration of war is recorded until 326 when Gaius Poetelius and Lucius Papirius Cursor (or Mugillanus) became consuls.[116] The citizens of Palaepolis decided to surrender to the Romans, and Publilius Philo assisted them to eject the Samnites and Nolans. The Greeks transferred their government to Neapolis, and a treaty was arranged with Rome.[117]

The long war between 326 and 304 was punctuated by truces, which according to the sources always resulted from Samnite requests for peace. It would never be admitted that Romans asked for peace, but perhaps they never did, displaying from earliest times their total intransigence in war, and their ability to raise army after army. The Samnites wanted peace after a defeat 325/324 but received a one-year truce.[118] In 318 Samnite ambassadors sought to renew the treaties of 354 and 341 but obtained only a two-year truce. Hostilities resumed in 316. The Romans had still not learned to reconnoitre, and the consuls Titus Veturius Calvinus and Spurius Postumius were famously trapped by the capable Samnite leader Gaius Pontius as they marched through the Caudine ravines, near modern San Martino Valle Caudina. Pontius decided to let the Romans go, on condition that they evacuated Samnite territory and withdrew their colonies. A Roman officer, Lucius Lentulus, advised that being wiped out was equivalent to betraying Rome, so the terms were accepted. The Samnites took 600 Campanian cavalrymen as hostages, and the Roman army, unarmed and dressed only in tunics, passed under the yoke, two vertical spears supporting a horizontal one, forcing them to bow down. The Capuans provided arms, horses, clothing and provisions for the march back to Rome.[119]

The war from 316 until 304 involved attacks on the allies of both sides, some of which were taken and retaken, and suffered accordingly. Roman colonies were established in 314-312 at Suessa Aurunca (Sessa Aurunca), the island of Pontiae (Isola Ponziana) and at Interamna Sucasina (Pignataro Interamna), between the Casinus and Liris rivers.[120] The consuls Gaius Sulpicius Longus and Marcus Poetelius won an indecisive victory near Capua in 314. Livy gives details of the dispositions of the troops, possibly from an official report.[121]

Alarmingly, in 312 the Etruscans were arming, but they were not allied with the Samnites. Hostilities did not begin until 311, and the Etruscans of Arretium (Arezzo) did not join in. The consul Quintus Aemilius Barbula was assigned by lot to the war and marched to Sutrium (Sutri), a Roman colony since 382, and now invested by the Etruscans. Sutrium was relieved by Quintus Fabius, consul for 310, taking over from Aemilius.[122] The Etruscans fled into the vast, uncharted Ciminian forest, which lay around the modern Monti Cimini. It was not visited even by traders. Quintus Fabius' brother explored it, met the Umbrians, and reported to the consul. The Romans then pillaged their way into Umbria and Etruria, and in response the largest Etruscan and Umbrian armies ever raised arrived at Sutrium. The Romans defeated the coalition, and envoys from the Etruscan cities of Perusia (Perugia), Cortona (modern Cortona) and Arretium (Arezzo) asked for peace and alliance with Rome. They received a truce for thirty years, but in 308 hostilities began again, the victory going to the Romans, who garrisoned Perusia.[123]

The Roman offensive in Samnium resumed in 310 under the consul Gaius Marcius Rutulus, son of the Dictator. The consul Quintus Fabius defeated the Samnites in 308 and again in 307 when his command was prorogued. The Samnites had been assisted by the Hernici, now prisoners of the Romans, prompting the rest of the Hernici to declare war except for three of their cities. The Hernici surrendered unconditionally to the consul Quintus Marcius Tremulus, and were awarded *civitas sine suffragio*, rejected by the towns which had not joined the fighting.[124] Facing two Roman armies, the Samnites unsuccessfully asked for peace. They raided Campania in 305 but were defeated and peace was made by treaty in 304. The Romans explained that the Samnites could have had peace much sooner if they had not continually sought it while at the same time preparing for war.[125]

### Between the wars

During a calm interval in 300, the brothers Gaius and Quintus Ogulnius, tribunes of the plebs, campaigned for plebeian access to the priesthoods, until now the preserve of aristocrats. It was proposed to increase the number of priests and augurs, and in 299 four plebeian priests and five plebeian augurs were created.[126]

The consuls for 299, Marcus Valerius and Quintus Apuleius, fought respectively against the Aequi and the town of Nequinum, where the Romans wanted to establish a colony to watch Umbria. The town, on a precipitous site, held out until 300, falling when two inhabitants tunnelled their way out and betrayed the place. A colony was duly established, and since the river Nar flowed nearby it was renamed Narnia (Narni).[127] No evidence has been found of lions, witches, or wardrobes. A rumour spread that the Gauls were joining the Etruscans in return for lands. The consul Marcus Valerius was given the command, and he devastated Etruscan lands without precipitating a pitched battle. Envoys from the Lucanians arrived to ask for assistance against Samnite raids into their territory, and *fetiales* were sent but were threatened by the Samnites and turned back. The people of Rome voted for a third Samnite war.[128]

### The Third Samnite War and the battle of Sentinum

The consuls for 298, Lucius Cornelius Scipio Barbatus and Gnaeus Fulvius were respectively allocated to Etruria and Samnium.[129] Scipio met the Etruscans at Volaterrae (Volterra), fought an inconclusive battle, and during the rest of the campaign the Romans devastated Etruscan territory, without attacking fortified settlements. The Roman people determined to elect Quintus Fabius Maximus Rullianus to the consulship, whether he was a candidate or not, so in 297 he became consul with Decius Mus as colleague. Envoys arrived from Sutrium, Nepete and Falerii, reporting that the Etruscans wanted peace, so the consuls concentrated on the Samnites.[130] Fabius' scouts, on one of the rare occasions when Romans reconnoitred properly, enabled him to avoid a Samnite ambush near Tifernum. Decius was based at Malventum (later renamed more propitiously as Beneventum). After defeating the Apulians he joined Fabius, devastating Samnite lands, leaving 930 Samnite dead and taking 2,900 prisoners.[131]

Four commanders took the field, Appius Claudius and Lucius Volumnius as consuls for 296, and Fabius and Decius with commands prorogued for six months.[132] Lucius Volumnius marched to Samnium with two legions and 15,000 allies, while Appius Claudius marched into Etruria with two legions and 12,000 allies, allegedly writing to Volumnius to ask for help, but denying this when Volumnius arrived. After a controlled spat, the consuls routed the Etruscans, took their camp and gave the booty to the soldiers. Volumnius then returned to Samnium, where the extended commands of Decius and Fabius were about to expire. The people of Cales (Calvi) informed Volumnius that the enemy were slowed down by carts laden with booty, so he attacked. During the battle 7,400 Roman prisoners freed themselves to join in the attack. It was a complete Roman victory.[133]

The Senate decided to secure Campanian territory by founding two colonies on the west coast, at Minturnae (Minturno) and Sinuessa (Mondragone). The prime purpose was not farming the land but guarding hostile areas, so volunteers were in short supply.[134] Appius Claudius reported that the suspected gathering of Etruscans, Umbrians, Samnites and Gauls was actually happening. The elections for 295 were due, with an instant clamour for Quintus Fabius as consul. He asked for Decius as colleague, and both were elected. Appius was elected praetor *in absentia*, returning to Rome when Fabius relieved him.[135] The Romans were about to experience the most serious threat and the largest battle that they had ever fought.

Raising new armies, Fabius placed troops near Clusium (Chiusi), under Cornelius Scipio Barbatus with the rank of propraetor. Appius Claudius, certain that two commanders were needed in Etruria, recommended that Decius should join Fabius, while Lucius Volumnius, with his consulship prorogued, took over in Samnium. Then the Senones attacked Scipio at Clusium.[136] Fabius stationed an army at Falerii under Gnaeus Fulvius and another in the Vatican fields under Lucius Postumius Megellus, both of whom were made propraetors. Meanwhile, enemy forces were gathering on the east side of the Apennines at Sentinum in Umbria. Fabius and Decius marched with four legions, Roman cavalry, the Campanian horsemen and other allies. Letters were sent to Fulvius and Postumius ordering them to attack Clusium to draw away the Etruscans to defend their lands.

The Romans harassed the enemy for two days, committing to battle on the third. Decius commanded the Roman left facing the Gauls, who pushed the Romans back, so he decided to emulate his father, offering himself and the enemy army to the gods. Marcus Livius Denter, serving as a priest with the army, presided over the ceremony and was made propraetor to command the army. Decius went into battle. Fabius sent troops to assist the Roman left, ordering the Campanian horsemen to circle round to attack the rear of the Gauls. On his own wing Fabius sent his cavalry round the Samnite lines to attack the enemy in flank. The Romans eventually won. The body of Decius was found next day and given a funeral on the battlefield.[137] The battle of Sentinum in 295 was a significant victory for Rome, but raids and skirmishes by the Samnites dragged on for another five years.[138]

The consuls for 293, Lucius Papirius Cursor and Spurius Carvilius, were assigned to Samnium. Thousands of Samnites gathered at Aquilonia. In an enclosure marked out with stakes and roofed with linen, they invoked their gods and made sacrifices, according to an old rite written on the same cloth. One at a time, the soldiers swore an oath, invoking a curse on himself and his family if he did not obey the generals, if he ran away, or refused to kill others who ran away. In this way the Linen Legion was raised, numbering about 16,000 men, with another 20,000 men in a different unit.[139]

Papirius had prepared well for the battle. He had ordered some men, probably soldiers' servants, to ride the baggage mules to a hill close by, with instructions to come down when battle was raging, raising dust as though an army was approaching. They were not cavalry, but mules at full tilt are not to be despised. The Samnites, routed, ran for their camp, where Volumnius captured them. Others fled into Aquilonia, and Cornelius Scipio attacked the city on his own initiative. Postumius joined him and Aquilonia was taken.[140]

During the next campaigns, the Romans fought on two fronts against Etruscans and Samnites. The final battle with the Samnites was won by Quintus Fabius Gurges, consul in 292, who did not do well until his father Quintus Fabius Maximus assisted him. The Samnite leader Gaius Pontius was displayed in Fabius' triumph and later beheaded. In 290 the Samnites sued for peace, and the treaty with the Romans was renewed, ending the third and last war.[141]

In 290 the Sabines and Praetutti were defeated by Manius Curius Dentatus and were awarded *civitas sine suffragio*. Some of their lands were distributed to Romans. Ten years later, Titus Coruncanius celebrated a triumph over the Etruscan cities of Volsinii and Vulci.[142]

The Gauls remained troublesome, though some of them made a treaty with the Romans in 334 and remained peaceful for thirty years.[143] The Gallic Senones defeated the Romans at Arretium (Arezzo), c.283. Manius Curius Dentatus sent envoys to the Senones to ask for the return of the prisoners. Appian provides the lurid detail – the envoys were literally cut to pieces.[144] The Romans mobilized, met the

Senones, defeated them and occupied their lands, later founding a Roman citizen colony at Sena Gallia (Senigallia). Polybius says that the planting of this colony alarmed the Gallic Boii, who joined the Etruscans, and together they fought the Romans at Lake Vadimon in the Tiber valley. The Gauls were defeated but raised another army of their youngest men. After another defeat, they sued for peace, remaining quiet for forty-five years.[145]

## Professional standing armies

The wars of the late fourth and early third century were quite different from earlier struggles, when a 'foreign war' was fought a few miles from the city. Fighting covered wide areas, and two consuls each commanding two armies were no longer sufficient. The Romans never increased the number of consuls but prorogued the commands of existing consuls or praetors. In 296 there were two consuls and two proconsuls, all commanding armies in different theatres. In 295, Quintus Fabius Maximus and Publius Decius Mus were consuls, Lucius Volumnius' command was prorogued, and there were four propraetors, Lucius Cornelius Scipio, commanding at Clusium, Gnaeus Fulvius Maximus Centumalus and Lucius Postumius Megellus commanding troops at Falerii and the Vatican fields, and at Sentinum, Decius used his consular powers to appoint Marcus Livius Denter as propraetor.[146] These four men had been consuls between 305 and 298, but when they were made propraetors two were serving in the armies, and two were private citizens. All four had *imperium* conferred on them to allow them to command armies.[147] From 295, *prorogatio imperii* required only a decree of the Senate.[148]

The days of campaigning in the summer and going home for the winter were long gone. Armies remained on active service for much longer, sometimes under arms when no wars were fought, as in 332, when the army remained in the territory of the Sidicini in case the Samnites attacked.[149] During protracted campaigns, the armies often passed intact from the outgoing to the incoming commander. Continuous long service contributed to the development of greater professionalism.

Large quantities of food, clothing, and pay were obviously required for sustained campaigning. The Romans began to make wars pay for wars. On arranging peace or a truce, they frequently extracted from the vanquished people quantities of grain (*frumentum*), pay (*stipendium*), and tunics (*tunicae*). The Etruscans obtained a truce in 308 in return for one year's pay for the soldiers and two tunics for each man. Three months' food, one tunic for each soldier, and one year's pay were extracted from the Samnites in 306. The Hernici provided pay and grain for two months and one tunic for each soldier. The two-year truce for the Etruscans involved payment of grain for two months and pay for one year. When the rebels of Falerii were defeated in 293, they were fined a vast quantity of bronze and one year's pay for the soldiers.[150] In each case the pay was presumably for the Romans, since the allied troops were supported by their own communities, but allies receive hardly any attention in the ancient sources.

Installing garrisons became more common. During the Latin war the consuls Furius Camillus and Gaius Maenius garrisoned all the captured towns.[151] Privernum was garrisoned in 338 and Sora and Calatia in 314, when they were recovered from the Samnites.[152] A colony was established at Cales (Calvi) in 334 after it had been garrisoned.[153] The Latin for garrison is *praesidium*, which literally means 'sitting before' with connotations of protection, but when expressed in Livy's terminology as *praesidium impositum*, from *imponere*, to impose upon, it throws a clearer light on what happened.

## Pyrrhus, King of the Molossians of Epirus

Pyrrhus was not the first foreign king to arrive in Italy, but he was the first foreign enemy whom the Romans encountered up close and personal. Archidamus of Sparta was summoned in 342 to help the city of Tarentum (Taranto) against the Lucanians and Bruttians. Alexander of Epirus followed two years later.[154] Agathocles of Syracuse assisted Tarentum *c.*297 but fostered ambitions to control all southern Italy and was assassinated in 289.

The Roman treaty with Tarentum dated from *c.*303, prohibiting the Romans from sailing round the promontory of Lacinium, near Croton in the Gulf of Taranto. The Romans upset the Tarentines on two counts. In 285 they agreed to assist the people of Thurii (Thurio) against the Lucanians. The Thurians consented to the installation of a Roman garrison. Soon afterwards, Locri (Locri Epizefiri, near modern Locri), Rhegium (Reggio di Calabria) and Croton (Crotone) also asked for and received Roman protection. The Tarentines did not like this, and when ten Roman ships sailed round the promontory of Lacinium in 282 the Tarentines sank four and captured one with the crew. The Roman garrison was ejected from Thurii. Roman envoys led by Lucius Postumius Megellus gained admittance to the Tarentine council only with difficulty, gaining nothing but mockery and insults, and war was declared.[155]

The Tarentines sent for Pyrrhus.[156] Plutarch questioned why the Tarentines failed to realise that Pyrrhus' ambitions were as grandiose as those of Agathocles.[157] Settling in at Tarentum, Pyrrhus' behaviour caused an exodus of the citizens, so he locked them out, not the best way to answer an appeal for help.

The Romans under Lucius Aemilius Barbula met Pyrrhus at Heraclea (Eraclea near Policoro) and lost the battle. Pyrrhus thought the Romans were beaten and sent the Thessalian Cineas to propose a treaty, offering return of prisoners without ransom on condition that the Romans left the Greek cities of Italy free, and restored to the Samnites, Lucanians and Bruttians all that they had taken. The aged and blind Appius Claudius warned that while Pyrrhus remained in Italy, he could be neither friend nor ally, so Cineas left without a treaty, but he witnessed how eagerly large numbers of Romans volunteered for the army. He reported to Pyrrhus, 'We are fighting a hydra.'[158]

Pyrrhus marched towards Rome, joined by Samnites, Lucanians and Bruttians, but Titus Coruncanius was marching back to Rome after defeating the Etruscans of Volsinii and Vulci. At Anagnia (Anagni) Pyrrhus turned back. In 279 at Ausculum (Ascolo Satriano) Pyrrhus won the battle, but said, in modern idiom, 'another victory like that and we're done for.'[159] The term Pyrrhic victory is now well known, but it was not used in Pyrrhus' time. It first appeared in the *Daily Telegraph* in 1885.[160]

Pyrrhus, married to Lanassa, daughter of the late Agathocles, was offered command of the Syracusan army and went off to fight the Carthaginians in Sicily, capturing four cities, but then he thought of invading Africa, forcing the Sicilians to raise money and provide ships. This threw the Sicilians into the arms of the Carthaginians, who were defeated by Pyrrhus. He tired of Sicily and sailing to Italy seventy of his 110 ships were sunk by the Carthaginians.[161] During Pyrrhus' absence the Romans subdued the Samnites, Lucanians and Bruttians, and were now able to turn their experienced troops on Pyrrhus. In 275 at Malventum (Benevento) Manius Curius Dentatus defeated Pyrrhus, and the king returned to Greece. He was killed in 272. It was not a noble death. A roof tile fell on his head.

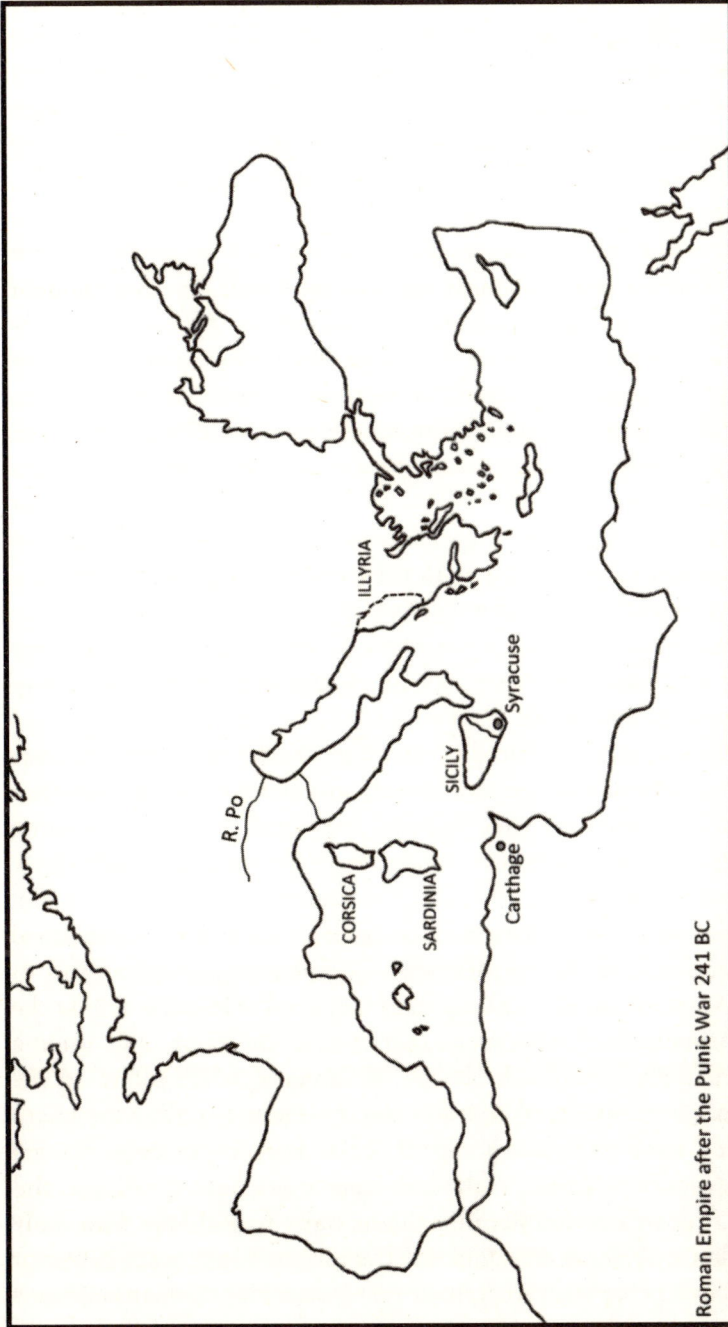

Roman Empire after the Punic War 241 BC

1. Rome's first provinces of Sicily, Sardinia and Corsica, taken over after the end of the First Punic War when the Romans defeated the Carthaginians in 241 BC. Illyria was not a province but Rome had protectorates there and some influence over the region. Redrawn by Sue Howie after Richardson 1976.

## The First Punic War 264-241

During the years between the battle of Sentinum in 295 and the outbreak of the war with Carthage, the Romans achieved control of the whole of Italy, except for the Gauls and Ligurians of the north. Even Polybius could not give the details, limiting himself to a single statement that the Romans attacked the rest of Italy, not as a foreign country but as if it rightfully belonged to them.[162] By 264, it did.

Complete unity was not achieved in Italy, but the Romans could draw on more military and naval resources than ever before to fight the Carthaginians in a war that they did not begin directly and could have avoided. Carthage was founded probably in the eighth century by the Phoenicians, known to the Romans as Poeni. They also used the term Carthaginienses, but the wars were labelled Punic wars. Carthage was the most important of the Phoenician colonies of Africa, possessing commercial and naval fleets with experienced crews that gave them a great advantage over the Romans, who obtained ships with crews from their allies or *socii navales* in coastal cities of southern Italy.[163] Rome's advantage lay with their tried, tested and experienced armies, whereas the Carthaginians had to rely on hired mercenaries, commanded by Carthaginian generals who held their posts until they succeeded or failed. The Carthaginians had an alarming tendency to crucify generals who failed.

The Carthaginians controlled much of Sicily but not Syracuse, the most powerful city on the island, originally a colony founded by Corinthian Greeks. After Pyrrhus left, in 275 a military coup enabled the general Hiero to become ruler of Syracuse. He had trouble with Messana (Messina) which had been captured by Campanian mercenaries originally hired by Agathocles. These were abandoned after his death, and calling themselves Mamertines, meaning sons of Mamers/Mars in the Oscan language, they took Messana, killing the men, appropriating the women, taking over the lands and raiding the surrounding countryside. Hiero of Syracuse finally defeated the Mamertines in the plain of Mylae (Milazzo). He was made King Hiero II, but the Mamertines still occupied Messana and – perhaps divided into two factions – they requested help from both Carthage and Rome.[164] Roman interference in Sicilian affairs would offend not only Hiero II but also the Carthaginians, friendly to Rome since 509, but hyper-inflated perceived threat made Rome fear that the Carthaginians would take over Messana, then Sicily, then the straits of Messina and southern Italy, then Rome. The propaganda helped the consuls for 264 to encourage the levy for intervention in Sicily. Booty was appended to the agenda. The people voted for war, justified by the appeal from the Mamertines for help.[165] Polybius allows his audience to construe the enemy of Rome as Carthage, but in 264 the Mamertines probably wanted help against Syracuse.[166] The consul Appius Claudius Caudex was ordered to Messana. The scrambled chronology and lack of detail makes it difficult to reconstruct what happened. King Hiero II allied with the Carthaginians, who installed a garrison in Messana which the Mamertines are said to have ejected.[167] The Romans perhaps hoped to avoid war, settling affairs by negotiation.[168] Diodorus Siculus records attempts by Appius to negotiate with Hiero and with the Carthaginians before he crossed to Sicily, but Polybius says this belongs to Appius' arrival at Messana.[169]

The Carthaginians attacked the Roman ships at sea but lost one of their quinqueremes to the Romans. Three years later, when the Romans built a fleet, their shipwrights copied it.[170] Appius entered Messana at night and then attacked Hiero, who returned to Syracuse. Next day, Appius scattered the Carthaginians and besieged Syracuse.[171] The Mamertines fade from history. Appius was replaced by Valerius Corvus and Manius Otacilius, consuls for 263, with four legions, each with 300 cavalry, and presumably allied forces. Hiero realised which way the wind was blowing and allied with Rome, releasing his prisoners without ransom and agreeing to pay an indemnity of 100 talents.[172]

Hiero was extremely helpful to the Romans. He established connections with other communities who could assist them, thereby keeping them out of Carthaginian hands. Sixty-seven states went over to Rome voluntarily, probably contributing troops for the Roman army.[173] The Carthaginians recruited foreign mercenaries, choosing Agrigentum (Agrigento) as their base, commanded by Hannibal – not the famous one; it was a common Carthaginian name. The new consuls for 262, Lucius Postumius and Quintus Mamilius, besieged Agrigentum.[174] Hanno arrived from Carthage and cut the Roman supply lines, but Hiero stepped in to supply food. The Carthaginians won one battle and lost another, abandoning Agrigentum to the Romans, who sacked the city, killing many people and enslaving the survivors, neglecting to inquire whether they supported the Carthaginians.[175]

Polybius says that at this juncture the Romans began to think of driving the Carthaginians out of Sicily.[176] More Sicilian communities joined the Romans, except for coastal towns fearing Carthaginian raids from the sea. The Romans needed to convert themselves from landlubbers to seafarers, building a fleet in 261. Polybius indulges in superlatives to describe the determination of the Romans, not mentioning the skills of Rome's *socii navales*.[177] One hundred quinqueremes were produced. They were not built for speed but for sturdiness to survive ramming, with decks high above the waterline serving as missile platforms. They carried soldiers in addition to their crews.[178] Twenty new triremes were built. Crews were recruited and taught to row on land, seated on benches arranged like those inside the ships, until all the oarsmen could operate in synchrony before training at sea.[179] The Romans also needed to control the coastal strong points in Sicily, so Panormus (Palermo) and Lilybaeum (Marsala) featured in later battles.

After Gnaeus Cornelius Scipio and seventeen ships surrendered to the Carthaginians at Lipara (Lipari), Gaius Duilius, commanding the army in Sicily, rushed to take command of the fleet. An unnamed crew member suggested building on each ship a platform that could be swivelled round, with an attached hinged extension kept in a raised position to be dropped onto the deck of an enemy ship. A metal spike on the underside would be embedded into the planking to hold it in place while the Romans boarded. It was labelled the Crow, or Raven, and equipping his ships with it, Duilius engaged the Carthaginians off Mylae, capturing thirty ships with their crews. The commander Hannibal escaped. Duilius' victory is recorded on an inscription in Rome.[180]

The Carthaginians attacked Roman allied troops, killing 4,000 men, one of the few mentions of allies in wars.[181] In 258 the Romans captured some of the towns claimed by the Carthaginians, and in 257 the consul Gaius Atilius Regulus won a victory at sea off Tyndaris (Tyndari). Operations were scaled up in 256 to take the war into Africa. Another fleet was built, commanded by the consuls Marcus Atilius Regulus and Lucius Manlius Vulso Longus. Somewhere off Ecnomus (Licata) on the sea route to Africa, the Romans won a naval victory.[182] Arriving on the African coast, Manlius Vulso was ordered to return to Rome with the prisoners while Regulus remained with 15,000 infantry and 500 cavalry.[183] Regulus wanted a quick victory in case a new commander arrived to take the credit, but when the Spartan Xanthippus arrived at Carthage with Greek mercenaries, the Romans were trounced. Regulus and 500 soldiers were captured.[184] Regulus was probably killed in battle, but this undeniable disaster became a tale of Roman courage and integrity, with Regulus promising to persuade the Roman Senate to make favourable terms, or if he failed, to return to Carthage to face execution. Polybius does not mention this, but Livy and Appian include the story.[185]

In 255 and 254, two Roman fleets were lost in storms.[186] Losses in storms are thought to disguise Roman defeats, but the Mediterranean is hardly a placid little lake. The losses halted Roman naval activity. Using Panormus as their land base the Romans captured Thermae and Lipara in 251, but the Carthaginian Hasdrubal installed troops and 140 elephants at Lilybaeum, which the Romans besieged in 250 using their new fleet. Lilybaeum was enclosed by a wall and deep ditch to landward, and by difficult shoals to seaward. The Romans camped on either side of the city, destroying the towers of the city walls, while the Carthaginians built counter-works inside and attacked the siege works, but the Romans maintained their position.[187]

A daring individual called Hannibal the Rhodian promised the Carthaginian government to bring news from Lilybaeum. In broad daylight he penetrated the line of Roman vessels guarding the harbour. The Romans tried to seize him as he left, but the Rhodian's oarsmen were too fast. Just out at sea, he slowed the ship as if challenging the Romans, then sped off. The scenario lends itself to Technicolor, stirring music by Erich Korngold, and a young Errol Flynn. The Rhodian ran the blockade frequently, until the Romans constructed an artificial bank in the shallows where another blockade runner was grounded. The Romans refitted this ship, using it to chase the Rhodian, and after capturing him the Romans refitted his ship as well.[188] Shortly afterwards, the Carthaginians burnt the Roman siege works, so the Romans blockaded the city from land and sea, waiting for the Carthaginians to starve.[189]

Publius Claudius Pulcher, consul for 249, hastily gathered crews and mounted a naval expedition to the Carthaginian naval base at Drepana (Trapani). Adherbal, the Carthaginian fleet commander, attacked him, and Claudius forgot that he was not commanding infantry, trying to make the fleet turn round. His ships got fouled up, and Adherbal put out to sea, turning to face the Romans. Claudius fled with thirty ships, leaving the rest to their fate. He was put on trial in Rome, and fined.[190] The Carthaginians would have crucified him.

The Romans had again lost control of the sea but still commanded on land, and Hiero II renewed his treaty in 248, assuring Roman supplies.

In 247 the Carthaginians chose Hamilcar Barca as naval commander. After raiding the Italian coastal towns, he returned to Sicily to base his army at Hercte (Monte Pellegrino) north of Panormus, still held by the Romans. For the next three years Hamilcar caused a lot of trouble. Polybius gives no details, moving swiftly on to 244, when Hamilcar seized the town of Eryx (Erice), trapping the Romans inside.[191]

The Romans had no funds to build a new fleet, but the senators provided loans to be repaid if the Romans won the war. Ships were copied from the Rhodian's vessel and the fleet was ready by summer 242, with Gaius Lutatius Catulus commanding it. He aimed for Drepana, gained control of the harbour and besieged the city. Catulus put all his energies into training the oarsmen and sailors. In 241 Hanno, commanding the Carthaginian fleet, brought supplies to the troops at Eryx and picked up Hamilcar Barca and some soldiers to serve as marines. Hearing of this, Catulus took the fleet to the Aegates islands off Lilybaeum, intending to fight next day. In the morning the wind favoured the enemy, but Catulus could not afford to wait for fair weather. His new ships were better designed, and his trained oarsmen coped well with adverse winds and heavy seas, capturing seventy Carthaginian ships with their crews and sinking fifty, ruining the Carthaginian fleet. Catulus moved off to Lilybaeum with 10,000 prisoners. Hamilcar Barca was authorized to treat with the Romans, and he and Catulus agreed terms. The Carthaginians were to evacuate Sicily and were forbidden to make war on Hiero or his allies. Prisoners were returned without ransom, and an indemnity of 2,200 talents was imposed on Carthage, payable over twenty years. The approval of the Roman people was required. Disinclined to mercy, they raised the indemnity to 3,200 talents, to be paid in ten years.[192] The Carthaginians could not afford to argue.

When hostilities ceased, the Carthaginian mercenaries were shipped from Sicily to Africa. Gisgo, replacing Hamilcar Barca, sent them off in batches, allowing time for the Carthaginians to pay them and send them home. Instead, the Carthaginians confined all of them, Libyans, Iberians, Celts or Gauls, Greeks, Ligurians and men from the Balearics, packing them off to Sicca with their baggage. No pay was forthcoming, so the aggrieved mercenaries marched to Carthage. Gisgo paid them, withholding the expenses they claimed for loss of horses. Rebellion broke out led by Spendius, an escaped Campanian slave, and Matho, a Libyan. Gisgo and his men were imprisoned, and the rebels roused the Libyan natives, diverting all the revenues intended for Carthage, and captured Tunis and Utica. Hamilcar Barca relieved Utica but the rebels scaled up the hostilities, brutally killing Gisgo and his men. They besieged Carthage.[193] Hiero II helped the Carthaginians, as did the Romans after remedying the problem of the Italian merchants, carrying supplies for the mercenaries. Polybius demolishes the tale that Italians were killed.[194] The Romans authorized the merchants to supply Carthage, but not the mercenaries. The terms of the treaty of 241 forbade Romans or Carthaginians to recruit soldiers in the territory of the other, but the Romans now permitted the Carthaginians to recruit mercenaries in Italy.[195]

In 238, Hamilcar cut the supply lines of the rebels besieging Carthage. They surrendered when no help arrived from Tunis, held by Matho, who risked battle and was defeated and imprisoned. Utica and Hippacritae capitulated after a siege. Carthage was back in control of Libya.[196]

## Sicily: the first Roman province

It took the Romans about five centuries to acquire their first territory outside the Italian mainland. They could have withdrawn from Sicily in 241, relying on their alliance with Hiero II to protect their main interests there, especially the supply of grain, but they were concerned to prevent the Carthaginians from regaining it – and the only way to do that was to keep hold of it. They decided to take over the island, leaving the kingdom of Syracuse, its lands and dependencies intact and autonomous.

Technically, as soon as the Romans decided to hold Sicily it became the first *provincia* in the territorial sense, but *provincia* was not used to indicate a governed territory until the first century, and it never lost its original meaning, denoting an allotted task. It is not certain if the Roman Senate labelled Sicily a *provincia* from 241 or used some other term.[197] Control of Sicily required a new approach. The Romans controlled most of Italy via their self-governing colonies and allied states, but this was not sufficient for supervising islands remote from the city, vulnerable to attack from other Mediterranean states. Another point is that control of Italy had not so far required a permanent fleet. If the Romans were to secure Sicily, they had to develop sea transport and control other shipping, especially pirates.

Officials were required to govern the island, but the Romans had nothing in their administrative repertoire to facilitate this, lacking a handy manual on how to create provinces and how to govern them.

There was never any question of creating extra consuls to govern their new acquisition. The officials next in rank to the consuls, holding *imperium*, were the *praetor urbanus*, and the *praetor peregrinus*, a post created in 244. This praetor may have governed the island by remote control in its first years as a province. The alternative was to create extra praetors, which is what the Romans chose to do, but not until 227, fourteen years after gaining Sicily, and eleven years after they gained Sardinia and Corsica, described below. The appointment of two extra praetors meant that the Romans were committed to governing these three islands. Gaius Flaminius was the first praetor to govern Sicily, and Marcus Valerius was praetor in Sardinia-Corsica, both serving while in their year of office. Later, when there were more provinces, praetors served in Rome for one year, and then governed a province as propraetor.

Once the first provinces were created, provincial government developed slowly and empirically. Although the Romans have been construed as rabid Imperialists, they had not envisaged that they would require a system for governing territory overseas. However, there was a procedure for establishing a colony. Usually, three commissioners were sent out to supervise the necessary religious ceremonial, and to survey the land and divide it into allotments for the colonists. Ten commissioners were often sent to organise new territorial provinces and a law was passed, called the *lex provinciae*, but Andrew Lintott has warned against the assumption that this always happened when a province was created.[198] Commissioners could be sent to areas which required arbitration or reorganisation after a Roman victory, without necessarily making those areas into provinces. In 167 when the wars in Macedonia and Illyricum ended, ten commissioners were sent out to Macedonia and five to Illyricum, and although organised by Romans, it was decided that the people in both states were to be free.[199]

Many years after 241, there is some evidence of a law being made for the establishment of Roman control of a province. Letters of the younger Pliny, governor of Bithynia in the reign of the Emperor Trajan (AD 98-117), make it clear that a law of Pompey the Great, who made the country into a province, was still relevant.[200] Probably in 57, Lentulus Spinther made a law concerning Cyprus, and a *lex Cornelia* regulated elections in Asia. The best example of a provincial settlement derives from a law concerning the organisation of territory in Africa in 111, by ten commissioners under the *lex Livia*. Commissioners were sometimes sent out long after the Romans had occupied a country. Two Spanish provinces, Hispania Citerior in the north and Inferior in the south, had been created in 197, requiring a governor for each, but the two areas were occupied military zones rather than provinces. Commissioners were not sent to Spain until 133-132, after Scipio Aemilianus had received the surrender of Numantia.[201]

For Sicily, a commission of ten men under Publius Rupilius, consul in 132, drafted a law, the *lex Rupilia*, which approximates to a so-called *lex provincia*, but it was more of a restructuring rather than an initial organisation. The date is disputed, since Rupilius had quelled the slave revolt which broke out in Sicily 136/135 in protest against the harsh conditions imposed by wealthy landowners, so his law could have been made then, or after the second revolt from 104-100, but since Rupilius was consul in 132 and governed Sicily in 131, this date of 132 for the law is more likely.[202]

Cicero referred to the *lex Rupilia* during his prosecution of Gaius Verres, the governor who exploited and robbed Sicily on an industrial scale.[203] The law seems to have been tailored to the circumstances of the lands and people of the province, distinguishing between four different classes of settlements. It is thought that Rupilius and the commissioners incorporated previous Sicilian treaties and regulations, especially those covering taxation and tithes. Rupilius' law also dealt with agriculture in general, trade, ports and harbours, and taxes levied on goods. Messana (Messina), Tauromenium (Taormina) and Neetum (unknown) were allied to Rome, retaining their own governments and laws, with jurisdiction over all their citizens including Romans. They were allowed to produce coins but denied foreign policies, and by the terms of their treaties they were obliged to furnish troops in time of war. External boundaries were in all cases the sea, except for the land boundary with Syracuse. In other provinces, external boundaries were neither rigid nor permanent.

There will have been administrators, probably quaestors, based in Sicily from 241 onwards, perhaps answerable to the *praetor peregrinus* in Rome. The base was probably Lilybaeum, the capital city where troops were probably stationed, but before 227 no Roman with *imperium*, the right of command, is known in Sicily.[204] The Romans usually relied on self-governing communities, cultivating local elites, in cities as well as in tribal societies, and a record was presumably made of the status and tax responsibilities or exemptions of each community. The sixty-seven Sicilian communities that went over to the Romans in 263 would originally be regarded as *dediticii*, people who had surrendered unconditionally, and these would be converted into *amici* of the Roman people, obliged to furnish troops. Some cities were free. Cicero refers to five *civitates sine foedera liberae ac immunes*, cities without a treaty, free and immune.[205] This implies self-government and immunity from taxes and obligations, but the date when these cities were declared free is unknown. Some communities became *socii navales*, obliged to provide ships and crews at their own expense, like the coastal allies of Italy. Messana was obliged to furnish one ship, but little is known of other naval allies. When Sicily was attacked in 218, the *socii navales* were asked to provide ships, with oarsmen and marines, and food for ten days. An inscription attests that two inland cities provided sailors, so perhaps contribution of crews was not limited to coastal cities.[206]

Probably from the first moment, the Romans adopted the form of taxation already in existence. In Syracuse, Hiero II drew up regulations for the tithe system in his dependent communities. It was called the *decuma*, one tenth of the grain harvest, and a percentage of fruit and vegetables, which may have already been in operation in much of Sicily. The Romans called these regulations the *lex Hieronica*, but it was not a *lex* passed by the Senate and people of Rome. Some of its details are known from Cicero's speeches in the trial of Verres.

During the war with Carthage much of the Sicilian farmland would have been destroyed as both Carthaginians and Romans ate their way through the harvests and devastated crops to deny produce to the enemy, or to bring a besieged city to terms. Archaeological evidence shows that in contrast to the kingdom of Syracuse, the rest of Sicily was greatly impoverished. The harvests in 241 and 240 would not have yielded a great deal, and the Romans may have levied a money tax in the early days, while aiding the necessary reconstruction.[207] A fixed tax in money bore no relation to the actual yield, whereas in the tithe system, the tax remained at one tenth of the harvest, no matter how large or small.

To operate the tithe system, officials of each city conducted an annual census of all the surrounding producers, from large landowners to people with rented holdings. Each farmer had to declare how many *iugera* he was cultivating that year, one *iugerum* being just over half an acre. The types of crop and the quantity of seed were recorded. The *decumanus*, responsible for the collection of the tithes, would bid for the contract at auction in the city, or alternatively the city officials could appoint their own *decumanus* or an equivalent.

The *decumanus* was ideally a local man who knew the area, the farms, and the characteristics of the diligent or lax farmers. He would need to understand soil types, weather patterns, and customary produce. He inspected the details provided by the cultivators and then made a written agreement, or *pactio*, with each farmer, estimating the likely yields. This was drawn up in triplicate, signed by the farmer and the *decumanus*, each of whom held one copy, and the third version was lodged with the relevant city officials. The tithes would be calculated after the harvests when the yield was known. Local men administered all this, not requiring Roman officials at grass roots level. The *decumanus* was allowed to take a small percentage of the tithe to cover his costs. He probably bid for the contract in wheat, not cash, although it was possible to convert amounts of wheat to cash values. When the Romans governed several provinces, the contracts for collection of most taxes were let out by the censors in Rome, but in Sicily it seems that contracts were organised in the island, though individual Romans could bid for them.[208]

## Sardinia with Corsica: the second Roman province

Polybius remarks that the Romans had designs on Sardinia; the context is 258, before the end of the First Punic War.[209] Two decades elapsed before the Romans acted on these designs. During the rebellion of the Carthaginian mercenaries, the discontent spread to the mercenaries in Sardinia, who killed their commander. The Carthaginians sent a new commander, Hanno, to recover Sardinia, but his men joined the rebels and crucified him. The mercenaries took over part of the island until the Sardinian natives drove them out. They took refuge in Italy.[210]

Just after the Romans agreed to help Carthage against the rebels in 240/239, the Sardinian mercenaries, presumably not yet refugees in Italy, asked the Romans to occupy the island, but the Romans refused.[211] Yet in 238, they accepted a second invitation from mercenaries who had deserted to them from Sardinia.[212] It is debated why the Romans did not take over Sardinia when it was first offered but then did so in 238. It is possible that the mercenaries mistimed their first invitation to Rome. Italian merchants may still have been supplying Carthage, and Carthaginians may have been recruiting mercenaries in Italy.[213] If this was the case, the Romans probably decided against assisting Carthage with one hand and taking over Sardinia with the other. The second invitation to Rome occurred after Carthage had regained control of Libya. The Romans accepted.

The Carthaginians assembled troops and ships to regain Sardinia. The Romans chose to interpret this as a declaration of war, and since the Carthaginians were too weakened to fight Rome again, they relinquished Sardinia, agreeing to an extra indemnity of 1,200 talents, which was to be paid immediately. Polybius called this a robbery, daylight robbery in fact, and a cause of the Second Punic War.[214] Lazenby accepts that Roman control of Sardinia and the sea lanes protected Italy, but says that the Romans thought only of their own interests.[215] Harris cannot find any defensive strategy in the takeover of Sardinia, and Rosenstein labels it a calculated act of cynical opportunism, especially as the indemnity of 1,200 talents weakened the Carthaginians even further.[216] The reality or otherwise of defensive needs was probably not so important to the Romans as the threat of Carthaginians in Africa and Sardinia, with Sicily between the two.

From 238, Sardinia, combined with Corsica, was technically the second Roman province, but as in Sicily, the Romans did not immediately develop administrative apparatus because it was a zone of military occupation which had to be pacified, initially by the consul Tiberius Sempronius Gracchus in 238, fighting hostile communities and supporting and defending friendly ones.[217] The terrain of both islands was ideal for guerrilla warfare. Strabo describes the land as rugged and never at peace.[218] The fighting continued for years, requiring consuls to lead the armies, and brigandage was not suppressed even in the early Empire.[219] Fortunately for the Romans they gained Sardinian allies, who provided food and other supplies for the soldiers during the Hannibalic war.[220]

It is not known if the tithe system like that of Sicily was applied by the Romans, but Sardinia possessed fertile areas, despite its mountainous terrain. Polybius says the island could support a large population, and Strabo says that Sardinia was blessed with all products, especially wheat.[221] By the middle of the second century Rome was importing enough wheat from Sicily and Sardinia to overshadow the Italian producers.[222]

# 3

# Hannibal, and the Provinces of Spain and Macedonia

After the first war with Carthage the Romans fought in Italy, Sicily, Sardinia, Corsica and Illyria. Pyrrhus of Epirus had ruled part of Illyria, but after his death King Agron of the powerful tribe of the Ardiaei expanded the Illyrian kingdom, seizing Corcyra (Corfu), Epidamnus (later Dyrrachium, now Durres in Albania) and the island of Pharus (Hvar).[1] When Agron died in 231 his second wife Teuta ruled the kingdom, enlarging the fleet and the army, and authorizing privateers, some of whom attacked Italian trading vessels.[2] Gaius and Lucius Coruncanius arrived to protest. Teuta explained that Illyrian kings did not restrain their subjects from piracy. In 229, the Romans prepared an army and a fleet, and declared war.[3]

When the Roman fleet arrived under the consul Gnaeus Fulvius Centumalus, the Corcyrans ejected the Illyrian garrison commanded by Demetrius of Pharus (Hvar) and became friends of the Roman people. Demetrius quickly reasoned that opposing the Romans would be bad for his health, and he joined them. The fleet moved on to Apollonia, in modern Albania, to meet the other consul, Lucius Postumius Albinus. Epidamnus was taken into Roman protection. The Illyrian tribes surrendered, two of them becoming friends of the Roman people. The island of Issa became a Roman protectorate. The Romans captured some coastal cities, but at Nutria (not identified) they lost men, their quaestor, and some military tribunes. Queen Teuta fled to a fortified town. Fulvius, nearing the end of his consulship, took most of the navy and troops back to Rome, but Postumius, presumably as proconsul, remained in Illyria with forty ships, establishing headquarters at Epidamnus. He enrolled a legion from local natives under Roman protection.[4] This was a double first: the first occasion when a general's command was prorogued while operating outside Italy, and the first time that non-Italian troops were raised by a general on the spot. Queen Teuta surrendered in 228. She agreed to an indemnity, to give up parts of Illyria, and not to sail beyond Lissus (Lezhe, Albania) with more than two unarmed ships.[5] Pinnes, Agron's young son by his first wife, inherited a reduced Illyrian kingdom as a friend of the Roman people, forbidden to harm Corcyra, Issa, Pharus, Epidamnus, and the Illyrian tribe of the Atintani, all protected subjects of Rome. Apollonia was declared a free city, and Demetrius of Pharus was given control over some fortified locations.[6]

Six years later, Demetrius joined forces with the vigorous new King of Macedon, Antigonus Doson, and his adopted son Philip, natural son of the previous king. Demetrius attacked the Illyrian cities under Rome's protection, triggering the Second Illyrian war. By 219 the Romans had liberated the threatened cities, defeated Demetrius, and destroyed his home city. He fled, joining Antigonus' adopted son, now Philip V of Macedon. The Romans did not annex Illyrian territory and did not disturb Macedon, but they would encounter Philip V again.

## Ligurians and Gauls

In 238 the Romans fought against the Cisalpine Gauls and the Italic Ligurians, whose territory stretched from Arretium (Arezzo) to Pisae (Pisa), and into south-eastern France.[7] The Ligurians, both men and women, were extremely tough.[8] Two of the several generals earned triumphs, Publius Cornelius Lentulus Caudinus and Quintus Fabius Maximus. A separate war broke out with the Gallic Boii, possibly in protest about the Latin colony of Ariminum (Rimini) established on their land in 268. The Boii surrendered, but after another colony was established at Sena Gallica (Senigallia) and Gaius Flaminius, tribune of the plebs for 232, distributed lands in Picenum to the Roman people, the Boii perceived a threat, calling in other Gauls, and in 225 they marched into Etruria. The Romans raised troops from the Umbrian and Apennine tribes, sent the consul Lucius Aemilius to Ariminum (Rimini), and recalled the consul Gaius Atilius from Sardinia. An unnamed praetor guarded the frontier of Etruria.[9]

Polybius explains that the Italians readily co-operated with Rome because the Gauls endangered them all. He breaks off his narrative to produce an oft-quoted estimate of the potential numbers of men that could be raised by Rome and her allies: 80,000 infantry and

5,000 cavalry from the Latins, 70,000 infantry and 7,000 cavalry from the Samnites, 50,000 infantry and 16,000 cavalry from the Iapygians of Apulia and the Messapians around Brundisium, 20,000 infantry and 4,000 cavalry from the Frentani and Marrucini of the Adriatic coast, the Marsi around the Fucine Lake, and Vestini of the Apennines. Four legions were raised, each 5,200 strong with 300 cavalry. Two reserve legions were placed in Sicily and at Tarentum, each with 4,200 infantry and 200 cavalry. Romans and Campanians together could furnish 250,000 infantry and 23,000 cavalry. The totals are 700,000 infantry and 70,000 cavalry.[10] Scholars reduce these figures to 580,000 infantry and 54,000 cavalry.[11]

The Romans, ambushed by the Gauls, lost 6,000 men, but near the coast at Telamon (Talamone), the Gauls were trapped and defeated.[12] The Gallic Insubres were subdued after some fighting, finally submitting when Cornelius Scipio captured Mediolanum (Milan). In 219 colonies were planned at the towns of Placentia (Piacenza) and Cremona. The fortifications were strengthened in a hurry. Hannibal was heading to Italy.

## Hannibal and the Second Punic war

Deprived of Sicily and Sardinia, the Carthaginians turned to Spain, much of which they had once controlled, but now possessed only trading post at Gades (Cadiz). Hamilcar Barca determined to restore the losses. His eldest son Hannibal told how, as a boy, he was asked by his father to swear on an altar that he would never be a friend to Romans.[13]

Hamilcar extracted wealth from Spain, especially from the silver mines. Alerted to the growth of Carthaginian power, the Romans investigated, and Hamilcar reminded their envoys that he needed wealth to pay the indemnities they had imposed.[14] Hamilcar was killed in 229. Hannibal was only eighteen, so Hamilcar's son-in-law Hasdrubal took over, founding Carthago Nova (Cartagena) as a supply base and winter quarters for his troops.[15] The Romans sent an embassy to Hasdrubal in 226/225, proposing that Spain should be divided by the river Ebro, which the Carthaginians were not to cross in arms. Modern authors suggest alternatives, but only the Ebro is an effective boundary line, running almost all the way from western Spain to the Mediterranean.[16] Livy and Appian erroneously assumed that the Romans were forbidden to extend south of the Ebro.[17] Complications arise over Saguntum (Sagunto). Appian says that Saguntum, originally a Greek colony, asked for Roman protection. He places Saguntum north of the Ebro, but it lies to the south, well within the Carthaginian domain. The Romans agreed to help Saguntum, and a formal treaty has been postulated and doubted.[18]

Hasdrubal was assassinated in 221. Hannibal took command, first subduing the Spanish tribes, then accusing the Saguntines of sheltering under Roman protection while raiding settlements.[19] The Saguntines appealed to Rome, and envoys met Hannibal to warn him off. He besieged the town. It has been debated why the Romans allowed Saguntum to fall to Hannibal, while ambassadors went to Carthage, but before describing this embassy, Livy describes preparations for war, implying that the Senate's decision was already made.[20] At Carthage, the senior Roman ambassador held out the folds of his toga. They held both war and peace, he said. Which should he drop? The Carthaginians left the choice to him. He dropped war. The Carthaginians replied, 'We accept.'[21]

## Hannibal enters Italy

Not for one moment did the Romans imagine that the war would be fought in Italy. They designated Spain and Africa as the consular *provinciae*, assembled ships, raised six legions and as many allied contingents as the consuls thought fit.[22] Publius Cornelius Scipio set off for Spain by sea, and Tiberius Sempronius Longus embarked for Lilybaeum in Sicily, a staging post to Carthage.

Hannibal marched directly for Italy, leaving his brothers Hasdrubal and Mago to command in Spain. Publius Scipio's fleet arrived at the mouth of the Rhone to learn that Hannibal had already crossed it, heading for the Alps.[23] A less far-sighted general would have abandoned the Spanish campaign, but Scipio sent his brother Gnaeus into Spain with command of the greater part of the troops, probably making him propraetor. Publius returned to Italy and Sempronius Longus was recalled.[24] Hannibal spread the message that he came to fight Romans, not their allies, and he freed allied captives, detaining only Romans. Livy produces a list of the allies which defected, combining them for maximum effect, regardless of when they changed sides.[25] It was usually last in, first out, such as the Gauls of the north, and the Bruttians and Lucanians, only recently absorbed by Rome. Latin communities and colonies are conspicuously absent from Livy's list. They would never desert Rome.

The first battles were disastrous for the Romans. At the river Ticinus (Ticino), west of Ticinum (Pavia), Hannibal's Numidian cavalry wounded Publius Scipio and almost trapped his soldiers. Publius Scipio junior rescued his father, and they and survivors reached the colony at Placentia (Piacenza).[26] At the Trebia the consul Sempronius Longus and Publius Scipio were separately defeated.[27] The consuls for 217 were Gnaeus Servilius and Gaius Flaminius. The next disaster was at Lake Trasimene. Flaminius would not wait for Servilius, and without reconnoitring, and in thick fog, he entered a defile between the lake and the mountains. Hannibal sprung his ambush. The Romans had no time to form up. Flaminius and many soldiers were killed. Some drowned trying to swim across the lake in their armour. The Carthaginian Maharbal offered to spare the prisoners. Hannibal overruled him, detaining Romans but freeing allies.[28]

After Trasimene, Servilius left troops to guard the north and took the rest to protect Rome. He was appointed fleet commander.[29] In the absence of consuls to nominate a Dictator, Quintus Fabius Maximus was elected to the post, with Publius Minucius Rufus as *magister equitum*. Avoiding pitched battles, Fabius earned the name Cunctator, the Delayer, perhaps waiting for a favourable opportunity to attack.[30] The Romans agitated for quick results, culminating in a plebiscite bestowing Dictatorial powers on Minucius, without making him a second Dictator, as some ancient sources claim. The command was divided. Before long, Minucius was ambushed by Hannibal and rescued by Fabius. He apologised to Fabius and the armies were reunited.[31]

## The battle of Cannae and the aftermath

The consuls for 216, Gaius Terentius Varro and Lucius Aemilius Paullus, commanded on alternate days. Varro was commander on the day of the battle of Cannae (Canne, south-west of Barletta). Varro was blamed for ignoring Paullus' advice not to fight, but Polybius says that the Senate, not Varro, decided on battle.[32]

The Romans had eight legions, 5,000 strong, with 300 cavalry, with 5,000 allied infantry and 600 cavalry. In August 216 Romans faced the Carthaginians at Cannae.[33] On the day of battle, with cavalry on the flanks, the depth of the infantry in the centre exceeded the length of the front, the theory being that with close formation and greater depth the Romans could break the Carthaginian centre, then turn and demolish the remaining soldiers.[34] Hannibal put his Celtic and Spanish troops in the centre, with his African troops armed with salvaged Roman weapons on both flanks, and cavalry on both wings. The Carthaginian centre advanced beyond the Africans on either side, forming a projecting crescent.[35] The Romans pushed back the Carthaginian centre, drawing level with the Africans, who turned inwards. Encircled, the Romans were annihilated. Scars on the Carthaginian dead revealed that the Romans had literally fought tooth and nail. In a separate cavalry engagement, Aemilius Paullus was killed. The young Publius Cornelius Scipio, son of the consul, and Fabius Maximus, son of the Dictator, rallied the survivors, leading them to Canusium (Canosa di Puglia), where Varro formed them into two legions.[36] Maharbal encouraged Hannibal to take Rome.[37] Hannibal knew better. If he captured Rome, he would have to obliterate it or hold it, tying down his troops. Besides, Rome was a federation, so even if the city fell, he would not be master of the Romans.

Late in 216, the Boii of northern Italy killed Lucius Postumius, consul elect, wiping out his army. The Romans decided that the priority must be Hannibal, so left northern Italy undefended.[38] Launching a desperate recruitment drive, the Romans stubbornly refused to ransom the prisoners from Cannae, or to re-enlist the survivors, who were disgraced and sent to Sicily to live in tents.[39] Four legions were recruited from debtors, criminals and 8,000 slaves, under the Dictator Marcus Junius Pera. Tiberius Sempronius Gracchus trained the slaves, instructing officers that they were to be regarded as equals of the soldiers.[40] In 214, Gracchus consulted the Senate, and freed many of the slaves. In Rome, the owners of the freed slaves demanded payment, but had to wait until the war ended. Gracchus was killed in 212, and the slaves deserted, their loyalty being to him, not the state. Officers were sent to find them.[41]

## Capua 216-211

For a while after Cannae, Hannibal found it easier to win over Rome's allies. He gained three south-coast towns, Tarentum (Taranto) by betrayal, Metapontum went over voluntarily, and so did Thurii when the Roman garrison was defeated.[42] At Nola, the populace favoured Hannibal, but the nobility favoured Rome and appealed to the praetor Marcus Claudius Marcellus, who installed soldiers. The people of Nuceria refused to join Hannibal, escaping to Campanian towns loyal to Rome. Nuceria was burned. The same fate befell Acerrae in Campania.[43] The most serious loss to Rome was Capua. The people were Roman citizens *sine suffragio*, tied to the Romans by marriage alliances and business relations. A powerful faction in

Capua submitted to Hannibal, provided that they retained their own laws and magistrates, and only willing Campanians were recruited. They demanded 300 Roman prisoners to be exchanged for their cavalrymen, sent to Sicily after Cannae.[44] Fulvius Flaccus and Appius Claudius, consuls for 212, encircled Capua with two earthen ramparts and two ditches, one set facing inwards and one outwards.[45] If the Romans could not take Capua, it was also clear that Hannibal could not relieve it. His allies now knew that if Hannibal was absent, the Romans took back their cities and towns, and were not merciful.[46]

Hannibal marched to Rome, camping eight miles from the city to draw the consuls from Capua, but the siege was not lifted. Fulvius Flaccus marched to protect the vulnerable north-eastern parts of Rome. According to Livy, Hannibal moved off when he learned that lands around the city were being sold to raise funds and those around his camp sold for the normal price.[47] In 211, Capuans surrendered because Hannibal had moved to Rhegium. The Romans sent the instigators of the rebellion to Cales (Calvi) and Teanum (Teano). Fulvius appointed himself judge and executioner. At Teanum he executed all the Capuans. At Cales, a decree from the Senate arrived with instructions not to kill the prisoners, but Fulvius did not read it until he had done exactly that.[48]

The city of Capua survived, but most of the people were killed and the rest sold. The lands around it, fertile and productive, were declared public property of the Romans. The farmers, tradesmen, foreigners and freedmen were allowed to remain, without government, magistrates, or an army. A Roman *praefectus iure dicundo* was elected each year in Rome, to administer justice.[49]

### Illyria and the First Macedonian War 215-205

In 215, the praetor Marcus Valerius Laevinus was in Apulia with twenty-five ships patrolling the coast between Tarentum (Taranto) and Brundisium (Brindisi).[50] He captured five vessels, one with passengers carrying a treaty between Philip V of Macedon and Hannibal, revealing that Philip and Hannibal promised to aid each other. One of the clauses stated that when the Romans were defeated, they would be forced to relinquish their protectorates of Corcyra, Apollonia, Epidamnus/Dyrrachium and Pharus. The news greatly disturbed the Senate.[51] Laevinus' command was extended in 214. He embarked for Oricum in modern Albania, which had asked for help when captured by Philip. The First Macedonian War began without a formal declaration of war.[52] Laevinus drove Philip from Apollonia and the Roman troops and fleet wintered at Oricum. Laevinus' command was prorogued again for 213, now covering Greece and Macedonia.[53] He initiated talks with the Aetolians, making an alliance in 211, the first known example of a formal written treaty with a Greek state.[54] Laevinus was elected consul for 210 *in absentia*, and Publius Sulpicius Galba, consul in 211, replaced him.[55]

Sulpicius captured the island of Aegina, a member of the Achaean League, to provide anchorage for the Roman fleet. He sold the people as slaves and gave the island to the Aetolians, who promptly sold it cheap to Attalus of Pergamum, a bribe to secure the assistance of his fleet.[56] A Carthaginian fleet arrived in 208 and again in 207, but little was achieved.[57]

Discussions began between the Aetolians and Romans about how to end the war. In 205 Sulpicius was replaced by the proconsul Publius Sempronius Tuditanus, bringing 10,000 infantry and 1,000 cavalry, by which time Philip had made peace with the Aetolians on his terms. Peace with Rome was arranged at Phoenice in Epirus.[58] The Romans had shown themselves intransigent in dealing with their opponents, but they did not annex territory after the war ended.

### Sicily and Syracuse 215-205

King Hiero II of Syracuse died in 215. His son Gelo having predeceased him, he was succeeded by his grandson Hieronymus, aged fifteen, easily manipulated by the pro-Carthaginian party. The praetor Appius Claudius Pulcher, governor of Sicily outside Syracuse, tried and failed to negotiate, then garrisoned the border between Roman and Syracusan territory, and the Roman fleet patrolled the seas.[59] In 214, Hieronymus held a council to declare war on Rome and then, having outlived his usefulness, he was assassinated, leaving the pro-Carthaginian party in control. Marcus Claudius Marcellus, consul in 214, began the siege of Syracuse from land and sea. Dates are disputed, the fall of the city traditionally dated to 211, but some authors prefer 213. Marcellus captured Sicilian communities favouring the Carthaginians but returned to Syracuse when the Carthaginian Himilco landed in Sicily west of Agrigentum (Agrigento) with troops. Appius Claudius was reinforced by one legion from Rome.[60]

One of the Romans noticed that at the Trogili harbour the city walls were low, counting the courses of stone to estimate the height.

He reported to Marcellus, who had learned that the festival of the goddess Diana was due; and because food supplies were low, the main sustenance would be wine. Marcellus produced ladders matching the height of the wall at the harbour and launched an assault late at night, when the revellers would hopefully be comatose. His soldiers climbed over the wall, opened a postern gate and Marcellus led in his whole force.[61] Syracuse was taken street by street, over several days. Marcellus tried to prevent a massacre, but during the proceedings the scholar Archimedes was killed, allegedly while studying designs on the floor, which he asked the soldiers not to disturb.[62] Envoys arrived at Marcellus' headquarters to make terms. It was agreed that all the possessions of the Syracusan kings should now belong to the Romans, and it was well known that Marcellus appropriated many art works for the embellishment of Rome and his estates. The Sicilians were to be free, subject to their own laws. The pro-Carthaginian leaders were executed.[63] Then the Carthaginian fleet arrived at Agrigentum under Hanno.

The consuls for 210 were Claudius Marcellus and Valerius Laevinus, assigned respectively by lot to Sicily and the war with Hannibal, but Sicilians had arrived in Rome, complaining about Marcellus' ruthlessness, so he received the Italian command, and Sicily and the fleet were assigned to Laevinus and the praetor Lucius Cincius Alimentus, who was authorized to create two legions from the remaining soldiers of Cannae.[64] Agrigentum was recaptured, and Hanno escaped by sea. Some towns surrendered voluntarily to Laevinus, twenty were betrayed, and the Romans took another six by storm. Laevinus gathered 4,000 troublemakers, sending them to Regium, where the people were looking for a band of brigands to devastate lands of the Bruttii. In 209 Fabius Maximus employed them for this purpose.[65] When Sicily was pacified, Laevinus encouraged the Sicilians to reinvigorate agricultural production. The grain harvest fed the people and soldiers of Sicily, the city of Rome and the soldiers at Tarentum.[66]

Laevinus was summoned to Rome in 210, leaving Cincius commanding Sicily. Marcus Valerius Messalla was sent on reconnaissance to Africa and reported that soldiers were being assembled for Hasdrubal in Spain, and a large fleet was being prepared to regain Sicily. Laevinus informed the Senate and was ordered to nominate a Dictator, but his choice of the absent Valerius Messalla was rejected because no Dictator should be appointed outside Italy. Laevinus' command was prorogued for 209, and he abandoned the Dictator debate, leaving secretly for Sicily.[67] Laevinus was authorized to attack Africa, probably in 208. He attacked the Carthaginian fleet, capturing eighteen vessels and sinking four. In 206 he was recalled to Rome, succeeded by the praetor Gaius Servilius.[68]

### Hannibal in Italy 211-203

From about 211, Hannibal's fortunes decline. The Senate decided in 210 to discharge the legion in Illyria and to replace the army of Sicily by the two legions recruited from the Cannae soldiers. One consul was sufficient to fight Hannibal, and the recovery of Italy began. The men who had served in the most campaigns were to be discharged and the remaining soldiers formed one legion. Allied forces were to be reduced to 7,000 infantry and 300 cavalry. Twenty-one legions remained, some facing Hannibal, the rest in Cisalpine Gaul, Etruria, Apulia, Campania, Spain, Sicily, Sardinia and Macedonia.[69]

In 209, twelve of the thirty Latin colonies declared that they could supply no more soldiers. The remaining eighteen Latin colonies reassured the Romans that their men were ready for service, and they could provide more. That year, Quintus Fabius Maximus Verrucosus, in his fifth consulship, recaptured Tarentum, where the spoils were of great value in gold, silver, and works of art. Livy observes snidely that Fabius was not as rapacious as Marcellus.[70] While Fabius was preparing for the Tarentum campaign, he had asked his consular colleague Fulvius Flaccus and the proconsul Marcus Claudius Marcellus to keep Hannibal busy. After being defeated near Canusium (Canosa di Puglia), Marcellus treated his soldiers to an explosive pep talk, exceeding the wrath of any football manager, and drove Hannibal into Bruttium.[71]

Marcellus was consul again in 208, with Titus Quinctius Crispinus. They joined forces near Venusia (Venosa), and both consuls, on a reconnaissance mission, were killed in an ambush.[72] Hannibal had not lost his touch. News arrived that Hannibal's brother Hasdrubal, defeated in Spain 208, was marching for Italy. One of the consuls for 207, Marcus Livius Salinator, marched northwards to await Hasdrubal, and the other consul Claudius Nero blocked Hannibal in Bruttium, where the Romans intercepted a messenger carrying a letter from Hasdrubal informing Hannibal where to meet him. Their two armies must not be allowed to join. Nero set off with most of his army on the long journey to join Salinator at Sena Gallica (Senigallia). Hasdrubal's army was wiped out at the river Metaurus (Metauro). Hasdrubal was killed and Nero returned south immediately, carrying Hasdrubal's severed head to be thrown in front of Hannibal's outposts. Hannibal now recognized what fate had in store for Carthage, says Livy.[73]

There was plenty of fighting in Italy in 206, but not with Hannibal. The Romans began to punish communities aiding the Carthaginians. Livius Salinator, with his command prorogued, operated in Etruria. The *praetor peregrinus* Quintus Mamilius devastated the lands of the Gauls who joined Hannibal. Other Gauls were raiding in the north, around the colonies of Placentia and Cremona, so Mamilius was sent against the tribes.[74]

Livy portrays Hannibal raging and gnashing his teeth when he received the recall to Carthage, but Lazenby suggests that Hannibal was not so devastated.[75] If Hasdrubal had reached him, it would have been a different story. Hannibal left Italy probably in autumn 203. The final chapter was played out in Africa, but first attention must be turned to Spain.

### The war in Spain 218-206

In 218 Gnaeus Scipio continued to Spain while his brother Lucius returned to Italy. He secured much of the coastal areas and advancing inland, he defeated the commander Hanno. Gnaeus' achievements in Spain have been labelled as largely fictitious, but it is accepted that he established a base at Tarraco (Tarragona).[76] Early in 217, Gnaeus learned that Hasdrubal's army and the Carthaginian fleet were approaching the Ebro. He decided on a naval battle, and won a victory, which persuaded the Senate to send Publius Scipio to Spain. The brothers led their forces south of the Ebro, subduing some of the tribes, camping at Saguntum.[77]

In 216 the Carthaginian Senate sent Himilco to Spain with reinforcements and a fleet, to allow Hasdrubal Barca to go to Italy. The Scipios combined forces to defeat Hasdrubal, but he escaped. Some Spanish communities joined the Romans. The Scipios asked the Senate to send food, clothing and pay for soldiers and naval crews. The tasks were put out to contract, three companies bidding for them.[78]

Prevented from going to Italy, Hasdrubal Barca blockaded the Roman garrison and the people of Iliturgi near the Mediterranean coast. Gnaeus relieved the town, but during a battle at Munda he had to withdraw with a javelin wound in the thigh. He won the next battle, directing it from a litter. The Scipios then expelled the Carthaginian garrison from Saguntum and brought back the inhabitants. The Romans could now extend beyond the confines of eastern Spain.[79]

In 212-211, Hasdrubal Gisgo, Mago and Hasdrubal Barca commanded in Spain. With two-thirds of the army, Publius faced Gisgo and Mago, and Gnaeus faced Hasdrubal Barca with the rest of the Romans, supplemented by 20,000 Celtiberian mercenaries. Tiberius Fonteius commanded the camp while Publius marched to prevent Indibilis, chief of the Suessetani, from joining the enemy, but he was trapped and killed. Gisgo and Mago joined Hasdrubal Barca against Gnaeus, having bribed the Celtiberians to desert. Gnaeus was also killed. Roman survivors from both disasters reached Fonteius' camp. A soldier, Lucius Marcius, formed them into an army, and was elected as leader. He fortified the camp, collected supplies, drove off a Carthaginian attack and captured two of the enemy's camps.[80]

Lucius Marcius called himself propraetor in his report to the Senate. It was a dangerous precedent for soldiers to elect their commanders, and Marcius was not officially a propraetor. The Senate hastily appointed an authentic propraetor, Gaius Claudius Nero, who blockaded Hasdrubal Barca and his troops in a pass in the eastern Pyrenees. Hasdrubal proposed a withdrawal from Spain if his army was released. Did Nero really believe this? Naturally, Hasdrubal prolonged negotiations while successive batches of soldiers escaped.[81]

In Rome an election was held for a proconsul to command in Spain. Publius Cornelius Scipio, son of Publius and nephew of Gnaeus, was chosen unanimously by the *comitia centuriata*, though he had held no magistracy. He arrived in Spain late in 210 with 10,000 infantry and 1,000 cavalry, accompanied by the propraetor Marcus Junius Silanus and Gaius Laelius, Scipio's friend, in command of the fleet of thirty quinqueremes. Scipio settled into winter quarters at Tarraco.[82]

In 209, Scipio left Silanus to command the camp and marched to Carthago Nova (Cartegena) which possessed a harbour large enough to accommodate the Roman fleet. The arrival of the fleet under Laelius was synchronized with the appearance of Scipio's army. The harbour protected the southern defences of the city and on the northern side there was a lagoon in which the level of the water sometimes dropped, caused by wind action, not by tides as ancient authors said. Scipio's troops crossed the lagoon, and when the army attacked the main gate and the fleet attacked from the harbour, these men climbed over the wall into the city, which was captured. The Carthaginians holding the citadel eventually surrendered. Scipio released the citizens, restoring their property. He declared all factory workers to be public slaves of the Romans, promising them freedom in return for manufacturing equipment for the army. Some slaves and non-citizens were assigned as oarsmen, and eight captured ships were added to the fleet. Sixty-three merchant ships were captured with their cargoes, and in the city there were vast stores of grain, gold, silver, siege engines and military equipment.[83]

The capture of Carthago Nova induced Spanish communities to come over to the Romans. Hasdrubal needed to stop this, and Scipio was keen to fight in the absence of the other Carthaginian generals. [84] Battle was joined near Hasdrubal's camp at Baecula, near the head of the river Baetis (Guadalquivir). Hasdrubal occupied an elevated plain above the valley. Scipio ordered his troops to climb the hill. It wasn't as high as the walls of Carthago Nova, he said. Hasdrubal escaped, collecting as many soldiers as he could, heading for the Pyrenees and Italy, to meet the fate described above.[85]

The captured Spaniards were freed but the Africans were sold, except for a striking young Numidian horseman called Massiva. His uncle was Masinissa, ruling eastern Numidia. The boy was sent home with a gold ring, a fine cloak, and a horse with his own trappings and equipment, and Masinissa became one of Rome's most loyal allies, after he could stop pretending loyalty to Carthage.[86]

Hasdrubal Gisgo prepared for battle at Silpia/Ilipa, location unknown, and Scipio won an undoubted victory. A thunderstorm prevented any follow-up. Gisgo's Spanish troops deserted, so he embarked at Gades for Carthage, sending ships back for Mago. Scipio returned to Tarraco, leaving Silanus to besiege the Carthaginians who fled to a hill. Many Carthaginian soldiers deserted, including Masinissa.[87]

In Rome, Lucius Scipio reported that Spain had been recaptured, as though it had been in Rome's possession all along. Pacification was necessary, but news that Scipio was ill precipitated revolt among the Spanish allies. Two brothers, Mandonius and Indibilis, from the lands around Barcino (Barcelona), occupied the territory of the Sedetani, threatening Roman communications, but Scipio defeated the brothers and made terms, extracting pay for the soldiers from Mandonius.[88]

According to Livy, while Publius Scipio fought battles in Spain, he already had his eye on Africa.[89] There was no longer any Carthaginian presence in Spain, but Roman armies were still necessary to protect the Spanish allies and to discourage other communities from aggressive action. In 206 Scipio established Italica (Santiponce, near Seville) to house his wounded soldiers.[90] A *praefectus* had been installed at

Gades, indicating that there was a Roman garrison there. Scipio left Spain to stand for the consulship for 205. The Senate's decision about what to do with Spain is given below.

### *Africa and the battle of Zama*

As consul for 205, Scipio continually urged the invasion of Africa. Fabius Maximus opposed him, because Hannibal was still in Italy. The Senate assigned Africa as Scipio's *provincia* in strict secrecy.[91] No troops were allocated to him, but he was authorized to recruit volunteers. Ships and troops were assembled at Lilybaeum, but it took time, so it was as proconsul in 204 that Scipio embarked for Africa.[92]

On landing in Africa, Scipio camped near Utica, destroying crops and farm lands, and then besieging the city.[93] He brought supplies from Sicily, Sardinia and Spain, and the Senate prorogued his command until the war in Africa ended.[94] Peace talks were initiated, prolonged by Scipio to allow experienced centurions disguised as slaves accompanying the envoys to observe the numbers of different troops, the camp entrances and exits, and locations of the sentries and outposts.[95] When he broke off the talks, he positioned troops above Utica and sent out ships as if to attack from the sea, disguising his plan to attack the Carthaginian camp at night. It was a Roman victory.[96]

Another Carthaginian army was raised by Hasdrubal Gisgo and Syphax, ruler of western Numidia, but they were both defeated at the battle of the Great Plains. Syphax ran for home but was captured and sent to Italy. His kingdom was given to Masinissa, who provided cavalry for the Romans. The Carthaginians made overtures for peace and Scipio arranged a truce and dictated terms, but what he really wanted was the recall of Hannibal.[97]

Hannibal arrived in Africa probably at the end of 203, basing his men at Hadrumetum (Sousse). After skirmishing, Hannibal requested a meeting with Scipio. They talked in an open space to avoid ambush, but peace was not achieved. The generals returned to their armies and met next day in battle at Zama. The name is famous, but there are several places called Zama, so there is debate about which is the correct one.[98] Hannibal employed elephants, and Scipio ordered the Romans to leave gaps between their ranks to allow the animals to charge through them. What was it like to stand still while several elephants, taller than men, weighing tons, carrying armed men and probably trumpeting their heads off, came by at speed? During the battle the Roman cavalry drove the enemy horsemen off the field but did not pursue, turning back to charge the rear of Hannibal's army. It was all over. Hannibal addressed the Carthaginian Senate, explaining that there was no choice now except to make peace.[99]

Carthage was disarmed. All the elephants were given up, and no more were to be trained. All the warships, except ten triremes, were surrendered. Carthaginians could not make war without Rome's permission. A large indemnity was imposed, grain was demanded for Roman troops, hostages were taken, and all prisoners and deserters were to be returned. The Carthaginians retained the territory held before the war, and were to make a treaty with Masinissa, confirming him as ruler of Mauretania, bordering Carthage. The city and its buildings were not destroyed, and the people were to be free, ruled by their own laws. The Romans did not take over, and Polybius says that Scipio did not take anything for himself from Carthage.[100]

In the following years Hannibal tried to reform Carthaginian government and finance, but gained little support, so when the Romans demanded his arrest because of his correspondence with Antiochus III, king of Syria, the Carthaginians were glad to let him go. He arrived later at Antiochus' court.

Hannibal was the cleverest, wiliest commander the Romans had ever faced, never side-tracked in his long struggle against them. No-one could have kept together an army for as long as Hannibal did, in a foreign country, not knowing the languages, or the terrain, which he nonetheless exploited brilliantly, setting successful ambush after successful ambush for the Romans. Hannibal welded together so many people with different languages, laws and gods, yet they never turned against him, which Livy, quite rightly, finds remarkable.[101]

## The Spanish provinces
After the Carthaginians evacuated Spain in 206 and the battle of Zama, the Romans could have withdrawn from Spain, as they had done from Illyria and Macedonia. The difference between Spain, and Macedonia and Illyria, is Carthage. While the Carthaginians had little interest in Macedonia, they had great interest in Spain, and they had to be prevented from regaining it to build up another trading empire, accumulating wealth to hire mercenaries. Perceived threat gave the Romans every reason to hold onto the country, which was in any case still a war zone, and would remain so for years.

In 197, Spain was divided into two sections, Hispania Citerior and Hispania Ulterior, or Nearer and Further Spain. The ancient authors used Ulterior and Citerior for commands in Spain predating the formal establishment of the two provinces. Livy used the singular *Hispania* for the command of the senior Publius Scipio in 218 and 217, but for 212, Livy uses *Hispaniae* in the plural, indicating the commands of Publius and Gnaeus Scipio. When the proconsul Publius Scipio junior and the propraetor Junius Silanus commanded in Spain, Livy says that they controlled 'their own Spains and their own armies' (*sui Hispaniae suique exercitus*).[102] Strictly, this denotes two occupied war zones, not two provinces.

Lucius Lentulus and Lucius Manlius Acidinus took over from Scipio in 206. Livy calls them propraetors, but they were private individuals with *imperium* bestowed on them, operating as proconsuls, which remained the official title of all later commanders, whether or not they had been consuls. From 206 to 197, it is not known if the commanders were assigned to a specific area. Lentulus and Acidinus were not so restricted, since they united their armies in 205 to fight an amalgamation of Spanish tribes, stirred up by the chiefs Indibilis and Mandonius of the Ilergetes of the lower Ebro valley. The Romans won a great battle, received the surrender of Mandonius and took him prisoner. Hostages were taken from over thirty tribes, tribute was extracted, and pay and clothing for the soldiers.[103]

The commands of Lentulus and Acidinus were extended for 204 by a unanimous vote of the tribes (the *comitia tributa*), and again for 203 by decree of the Senate.[104] Lentulus returned to Rome in 200, demanding a triumph. The Senate agreed that he deserved one, but having been only a private citizen upon whom *imperium* was bestowed, he did not qualify. He was awarded an *ovatio*, or lesser triumph. Fantastic amounts of silver and gold were brought to Rome, 43,000 pounds of silver, 2,450 pounds of gold, and 120 *asses* for each soldier from Lentulus; 6,000 pounds of silver and thirty pounds of gold by Acidinus; from Hispania Citerior Gaius Cornelius Blasio brought 1,515 pounds of gold, 20,000 pounds of silver, and 34,500 *denarii* in coin, indicating that coins were minted in Spain; Blasio's colleague Lucius Stertinius deposited 50,000 pounds of silver in the Roman treasury from Hispania Ulterior.[105]

Private individuals with *imperium* in Spain caused problems in Rome. Before the battle of Sentinum in 295, *imperium* was bestowed on non-magistrates temporarily, and the recipients were subordinate to the senior commanders, but individuals given *imperium* in Spain were not subordinate to senior commanders. This was unconstitutional, providing grounds for a *tribunus plebis* to block Acidinus' *ovatio* granted by the Senate. It was decided in 198/197 to elect two new praetors for the two Spains, to hold *imperium pro consule* like their predecessors.[106] Hispania Citerior and Hispania Ulterior were not formally established as provinces until 133.[107] Some document was probably produced recording the agreements, concessions, and treaties which had been made by commanders on the spot and ratified in Rome, but this goes beyond the evidence. Fighting did not cease after 133, and the pacification of Spain took a very long time.

## Gauls and Ligurians

The Romans began to stabilize Italy before the victory in Africa. Remnants of Mago's troops remained in northern Italy, joining the Gauls and Ligurians in 203 to attack the Roman colonies of Placentia, which was sacked, and Cremona, which closed its gates and sent word to the praetor Lucius Furius Purpureo at Ariminum.[108] Furius had only 5,000 allies and Latins, and but was ordered to swap these for two legions of the consul Aurelius Cotta in Etruria. He defeated the Gauls and relieved Cremona, and his campaign was finished off by Cotta.[109] In 197 the consuls Gaius Cornelius Cethegus and Quintus Minucius defeated the Gauls, and the Ligurians surrendered.[110] An extensive program of colonization was begun to secure Cisalpine Gaul, annexed in the late 220s, but the arrival of Hannibal temporarily stopped the colonization. In the 180s, Bononia (Bologna), Parma and Mutina (Modena) became colonies.

## The Second Macedonian War

The second war with Philip V began as a result of appeals from communities on the receiving end of his expansionist activities. The Athenians appealed to Rome for help when Philip devastated their lands, and the Romans declared war.[111] Marcus Valerius Laevinus, experienced in Illyrian and Macedonian affairs, was given propraetorian authority and command of the Roman fleet, and on arrival in Macedonia he was warned that Philip was gathering troops and ships, possibly to invade Italy.[112] The Romans were further alarmed on hearing that Philip had allied with Antiochus III of Syria, agreeing to conquer various territories around the Mediterranean, especially Egypt.[113] Most modern authors deny that Philip V and Antiochus III harboured any designs on Italy or Rome.

The consuls for 200 were Publius Sulpicius Galba and Gaius Aurelius Cotta. War was firmly on the Senate's agenda, but it was not on the agenda of the voting centuries. The people rejected the proposal, but next day Sulpicius repackaged it, warning that Philip might invade and the Lucanians and Samnites would join him; it was better for Macedon to have this war, not Italy.[114] War was declared. The consul Aurelius Cotta commanded in Italy, and Sulpicius was to oppose Philip. The consuls were authorized to raise two new legions and demobilize all the veterans.[115]

At Abydus, under siege by Philip, the king reminded the Roman ambassador Marcus Aemilius Lepidus of the treaty of 205. Nonetheless, the Romans notified Greek communities of their intentions against Philip. Abydus fell, and all the inhabitants committed suicide. A Macedonian garrison was installed.[116] Philip heard that Sulpicius was wintering in Apollonia and the Roman fleet was at Corcyra (Corfu). The legate Gaius Claudius Centho was sent with twenty ships and 1,000 men to Athens, to deter raids on the city lands.[117] Centho received exiles from Chalcis, one of the so-called Fetters of Greece, strategic strongholds controlled by Philip, the others being Demetrias in Thessaly and Corinth in Achaea. Centho captured Chalcis, burning it along with Philip's food stores, siege engines and equipment, and returned to Athens.[118]

Sulpicius camped between Dyrrachium and Apollonia, receiving support from communities bordering on Macedon. Attalus of Pergamum brought his fleet and was sent to Aegina, and the Rhodians were asked to join the Romans.[119] The Aetolians refused to ally with either side. Philip was drawn off when tribesmen attacked Macedonia. Sulpicius returned to Apollonia.[120]

The Aetolians returned to their friendship with the Romans. In the autumn Sulpicius was replaced by the consul for 199, Publius Villius Tappulus, whose first task was to pacify mutinous soldiers. It is not certain whether Villius' victories belong to him or to his successor Titus Quinctius Flamininus, consul for 198, bringing reinforcements.[121] Attalus returned home because Antiochus III had almost surrounded Pergamene territory.

When Flamininus attacked Macedonia, Philip offered peace, but refused to relinquish the captured Greek states. The Romans defeated him, and he fled into Thessaly, leaving the Romans free to attack his garrisons in towns and cities, taking up time and manpower. Flamininus tried another tack. The Achaeans had driven out the pro-Macedonian faction, so now Flamininus offered them Corinth, once part of the earlier Achaean League. Romans and Achaeans besieged Corinth, and an alliance was made between Rome, the Achaeans, Pergamum, and Rhodes, ratified in Rome.[122]

In 197 Flamininus' command was prorogued until a successor was appointed by senatorial decree, which left Flamininus uncertain about how long he would retain his post. A truce for two months was arranged.[123] In Rome envoys from Philip were met with the blunt question: was the king prepared to give up the Fetters of Greece? The answer was inevitably no. Flamininus realized that the Senate wanted a victory, and Philip realized that he would have to fight. He gave the city of Argos to Nabis of Sparta, causing trouble for the Romans later on.[124] The last battle was fought in Thessaly at Cynoscephalae, or Dog's Heads, named after the shape of the nearby hills. Philip had not expected to fight there.[125] In thick fog Flamininus' reconnaissance party of cavalry and 1,000 infantry stumbled into Philip's troops sent to occupy the hills. The skirmish developed into a battle. The Aetolian cavalry held off the Macedonians, allowing the Roman infantry to reorganize themselves until Flamininus brought out his whole army, as did Philip. Two legions and two phalanxes became separated and fought two separate battles.[126] Philip left the battlefield when one phalanx crumbled, and the Macedonians in the other phalanx raised their spears to indicate surrender. When Flamininus learned what it meant, it was too late to stop the carnage.[127]

Philip headed back to Macedonia. Peace talks began and Flamininus called together the Greek allies to discuss terms. Much was owed to the Aetolians, but they pillaged as though their lives depended on it, not the sort of message that Flamininus wanted to broadcast. He knew that if Macedonia and Philip were removed from the scene, the Aetolians would become masters of Greece. He explained that without a strong Macedonia, Greece would be left open to Thracians, Illyrians and Gauls, not mentioning that no-one wanted the supremacy of Aetolia either.[128]

At the meeting at Tempe, Philip agreed to whatever terms were offered, which were referred to the Senate. The Roman people voted for peace.[129] Ten commissioners were sent to Greece with the terms. All Greek states were to be free. Philip was to return prisoners and deserters, his army was limited to 5,000 men, all elephants were to be given up, and only five ships and Philip's royal galley could be retained. He required Rome's consent to make war outside Macedon and was to pay 500 talents immediately and another 500 over ten years. Flamininus argued that if Rome retained the Fetters of Greece, Roman dominance would simply replace Philip's, but he conceded that until the intentions of Antiochus III were known, it was advisable to place Roman garrisons at Corinth, Demetrias, Chalcis, Oreus and Eretria.[130] At the games in 196 at Isthmia, east of Corinth, it was announced that the Greek cities, including those taken by Philip, were to be free and independent under their own laws. Flamininus was nearly killed by the joyous mob.[131]

There was some clearing up to do. Flamininus' command was extended for a year. Reinforcements were sent. There was still the question of Argos controlled by Nabis of Sparta. The Senate decided on war. When the decree arrived, Romans and Greeks attacked Argos, until Aristaenus of the Achaeans announced that they wanted to liberate Argos, not destroy it, and he was going to attack Sparta. Flamininus agreed.[132] Nabis asked for peace. The Greeks deferred to Flamininus, who drew up terms. Nabis was to withdraw all garrisons, return prisoners and deserters, return ships taken from the coastal communities, and limit the number of his own ships. He was not to hold forts in Crete or anywhere else. He was to pay 100 talents immediately and fifty every year for eight years. After a slight glitch, the peace terms were finally put into effect.[133]

In Rome it was decided that all Roman forces and garrisons could be withdrawn from Macedonia. During the winter, Flamininus dispensed justice and sorted out problems, establishing a senate and judges for the Thessalians, from wealthy men with vested interests in keeping the peace among the unruly tribes. At Corinth he explained that he could not crush the ancient city of Sparta, but Nabis was powerless. He asked for a search for enslaved Roman citizens, sold by Hannibal when the Senate refused to ransom them. The Greeks agreed and compensated the owners of the slaves. The garrisons of Chalcis, Demetrias, Oreus and Eretria marched out. Flamininus' triumph in Rome occupied three days, displaying weapons and works of art – taken from Philip, Livy hastens to add.[134]

No-one can say that the Romans had not profited from the war, but they had not annexed any territory, installed permanent garrisons, or established colonies. Holding onto Greece would have involved maintaining the balance of power between proud, independent, intelligent, warlike people. The Romans were proud of having fought for the freedom of the Greeks, but the Greeks would soon realize that Roman supremacy was a reality not to be challenged.

## War with Antiochus III, 192-189

Antiochus was heir to the kingdom of one of the companions of Alexander the Great, Seleucus, who gained control of Babylonia in 321, and extended his empire to the Mediterranean. Antiochus III was determined to reconstitute the Seleucid Empire. When he moved towards Thrace in 197, he sent an embassy to Rome, but the Romans feared that he would assist Philip V.[135]

After the announcement of the freedom of the Greeks, ten Roman commissioners met envoys from Antiochus, and dictated terms. Antiochus was not to make war on the free cities of Asia (western Turkey). He was forbidden to take an army to Europe, claiming to liberate people, since the Greek states were not subjects of anyone. A short time later, three commissioners, Publius Cornelius Lentulus, Lucius Terentius Massiliota and Publius Villius Tappulus, met Antiochus at Lysimachia. They repeated the terms, accusing Antiochus of intending to attack the Romans, meaning Roman achievements in Greece.[136] Antiochus withdrew into Syria, receiving Hannibal with whom he communicated after Zama.[137]

Polybius says that the Aetolians set alight the war between the Romans and Antiochus.[138] In 192, Roman commissioners toured Greece, discovering that the Aetolians were turning communities towards Antiochus, who was persuaded that all Greece eagerly awaited him as liberator.[139]

The Romans prepared for war in 192, declaring the consular *provinciae* as northern Italy against the Gauls, and wherever the Senate decided. Troops were enlisted and ships were built.[140] The war did not begin until 191when Antiochus arrived at Demetrias with a relatively small force of 10,000 infantry, plus cavalry and elephants. He expected Chalcis to surrender, but the pro-Roman party declared that they did not reject friendship with Antiochus, but they did not require liberation, thanks all the same. They explained that no city had a Roman garrison, paid tribute to Rome, or had undesirable laws imposed upon them. Antiochus returned to Demetrias.[141] For the Romans, war was justified when Antiochus captured Chalcis and attacked Romans at Delium. The consul for 191, Manius Acilius Glabrio, obtained Greece as his *provincia* by lot.[142]

The Romans rejected offers of grain, gold and troops from Philip V and Ptolemy, food supplies from Carthage, and the Carthaginian offer to pay the outstanding amount of their indemnity.[143] The Romans preferred regular instalments, keeping Carthage in debt.

The Boeotians joined Antiochus, but the Epirotes, reluctant to join or fight Antiochus, offered to receive him in their cities and harbours.[144] At a meeting at Demetrias, Hannibal advised the assembled leaders to make an alliance with Philip V, if only to prevent him from aiding the Romans. He was ignored. Philip joined the Romans.[145]

Antiochus forcibly liberated cities that did not want to be liberated, but he proved unable to stick to any plan.[146] He marched to the pass of Thermopylae, garrisoning the entrance, but the Romans made short work of his troops. The Aetolians sued for peace, surrendering themselves and possessions to the good faith of the Romans, *in fidem se permittere*. Acilius Glabrio asked did they really know what this meant? To the Romans, the Aetolians were offering permanent unconditional surrender. [147] On learning the truth, the Aetolians decided to continue the war, assembling at Naupactus (Nafpactus), which Glabrio besieged. Philip V asked and received from the consul permission to recover communities which had joined Antiochus. Titus Quinctius Flamininus arrived, with no official position but enormous prestige, pointing out that Philip was busily gaining cities and becoming too powerful.[148]

The consuls for 190 were Lucius Cornelius Scipio and Gaius Laelius, respectively brother and friend of Scipio Africanus. Lucius was appointed by senatorial decree to command in Greece, and Africanus accompanied him as *legatus*. Lucius took over Acilius' army, raised reinforcements, and was authorized to cross into Asia.[149] Antiochus never expected the Romans to march into Asia. Hannibal said he was only surprised the Romans were not already there.[150] Antiochus tried to make peace with Rome, Pergamum and Rhodes at the same time, but failed.[151] He suggested an alliance with Prusias, King of Bithynia, but Lucius Scipio convinced Prusias that Rome was a better bet, because the Romans left kings greater than they found them.[152] The praetor Aemilius Regillus commanding the Roman fleet won a naval battle off Myonnesus, between the island of Samos and Teos (Sigacik, Turkey). Antiochus' offer of peace was refused.[153] Lucius Scipio, eager to fight before winter set in, defeated Antiochus at Magnesia (Manisa, Turkey). Peace was made, and the treaty was confirmed in 188 at Apamea (Dinar, Turkey). Antiochus agreed to stay out of Europe, to withdraw beyond the Taurus mountains, to pay Rome 15,000 Euboean talents, to pay Eumenes of Pergamum 400 talents, and allow the Romans to choose twenty hostages. Above all, he was to surrender Hannibal, and other named individuals.[154]

Hannibal found refuge with Prusias of Bithynia, but in 183/182, Flamininus persuaded the king to give him up. Hannibal preferred poison.

## The Third Macedonian War

Antiochus was not deposed, and the Romans did not withdraw. Of the consuls for 189, Marcus Fulvius Nobilior drew the command against the Aetolians by lot, and quickly brought them to terms. Gnaeus Manlius Vulso drew Asia.[155] At Rome, Eumenes of Pergamum, successor of Attalus who died in 197, explained the problems caused by the freedom of the Greeks. Some cities were tributary to Pergamum, and Eumenes worried that the Rhodians would seek to free them. Eumenes urged the Romans to avoid trouble by taking over the territory on the near side of the Taurus mountains.[156] The Romans saw that they would have to forsake Flamininus' policies of freedom, or alienate Pergamum and Rhodes. In the final settlement, Asia Minor was divided roughly at the river Meander, flowing westwards from the mountains of central Turkey. The lands north of it were to be controlled by Pergamum, those to the south by Rhodes. Philip V was to control central Greece, and the Peloponnese was to belong to the Achaeans.[157] The Romans hoped that by placing strong states over smaller autonomous communities, the whole of Greece and parts of Asia Minor would be peaceful and self-sufficient, without the need for a constant Roman presence. It nearly worked.

Philip died in 179, succeeded by his elder son Perseus. Polybius and Livy insist that Perseus inherited Philip's intentions against Rome along with the kingdom.[158] Perseus was recognized as King of Macedon, and the treaty of friendship was renewed.[159] Probably in 174 it was rumoured that Perseus was in touch with the Carthaginians. The Romans sent three ambassadors to Macedonia, and four to Aetolia, where civil war was starting.[160] When all the ambassadors returned at the beginning of 173, they reported that they had witnessed Perseus' preparations for war, and the Aetolian situation was worsening.[161]

The Romans denounced the treaty of friendship with Perseus.[162] Ships and crews were assembled, allied troops were called in, grain was purchased in Apulia and Calabria, and later a double tithe was imposed on Sicily and Sardinia.[163] Elections were held early. Publius Licinius Crassus and Gaius Cassius Longinus became consuls for 171. The proposal was put to the people for war against Perseus, with a let-out clause 'unless he offered satisfaction'.[164] Licinius Crassus received

Macedonia by lot. Eager volunteers and veterans almost begged to enlist. Envoys were sent to various states, most especially Rhodes. If the Rhodians would not join the Romans, it was vital that they at least remained neutral.[165] Perseus' overtures for peace were rejected.

The Romans arrived at Larisa, making camp on the river Peneus, while the Pergamene and Roman fleets came to Chalcis.[166] It was a demoralizing surprise when the Romans lost the first battle, which would have been a rout but for the Thessalian cavalry joining with Eumenes' troops to shield the fleeing Romans, and then advancing on Perseus' army.[167] Perseus offered peace, again. The Romans, stubborn even after defeat, demanded unconditional rights to decide the general policy of Macedonia.[168] Perseus could hardly agree to that.

In 170 the consul Aulus Hostilius Mancinus was assigned to Macedonia, and the praetor Lucius Hortensius commanded the fleet. Livy's coverage of the period is lost. There was no war in Macedonia, but in 170 Appius Claudius was sent to deal with Gentius, King of the Illyrians, who favoured Perseus. Appius tried to take a town belonging to Perseus and was defeated.[169] In 168 the praetor Lucius Anicius Gallus relieved Appius Claudius, defeated Gentius, and locked him up, to be paraded in his triumph in Rome.[170] Anicius took Gentius' main city of Scodra in modern Albania, and other cities surrendered. The conclusion of the Illyrian campaign was reported at Rome before it was known that Anicius had begun it.[171]

The Romans needed reinforcements, but contrary to previous Roman zeal, men refused to give in their names. The censors of 169 ordered all men liable for service to report to them, and they examined reasons for discharge of soldiers. In Greece several states complained of over-zealous requisitioning of all kinds of supplies. The Senate decreed that no states should supply anything unless it was voted by the senators. It was timely, because some Greeks were wavering.[172]

Marcius Philippus, consul for the second time in 169, received the Macedonian command. He sailed to Ambracia and marched into Thessaly, while the fleet commander Gaius Marcius Figulus, Philippus' cousin, harassed the coasts of Thessaly, joining up with the army later. Philippus finally penetrated Macedonia by negotiating a difficult mountain pass which emerged on the heights overlooking Perseus' camp in the northern Thessalian plain. Perseus did not believe that an army could approach from the pass because the route down was almost vertical, but the Romans of necessity had to get down it, with their horses and baggage animals. For the elephants, they built a series of platforms that could be lowered at one end to make each animal slide down onto the platform below, and so on until they reached the bottom. Perseus fled, taken by surprise. The Romans camped at Dium, whose inhabitants had left for Pydna.[173] Before going into winter quarters in Thessaly, Philippus reported to the Senate, explaining that he had gathered supplies and the Epirotes had contributed wheat and barley which should be paid for when their envoys reached Rome. He asked for clothing for the troops and 200 horses, which the Senate arranged.

The consuls-elect for 168 were Lucius Aemilius Paullus and Gaius Licinius Crassus. Aemilius Paullus, who was to command in Macedonia and received permission to send envoys to the war zone to gather information.[174] In early spring he arrived in Macedonia, and the praetor Gnaeus Octavius, commanding the fleet, sailed to Oreus on the northern coast of Euboea.[175]

Perseus stationed guards on the pass north of Mount Olympus.[176] Paullus thought a night attack would overpower the guards, sending Scipio Nasica to clear the route.[177] Perseus made his stand at Pydna.[178] The battle began accidentally. One of the Roman baggage animals bolted across the river, captured by two Thracians on the opposite bank. The Romans killed one Thracian and took the animal back. A few Thracians chased them, then more and more of them turned out and finally the armies were drawn up. Paullus scattered the Macedonian left. The legion under Lucius Albinus in the centre broke up the Macedonian phalanx. Paullus admitted that when he saw the solid mass of spears, he maintained a cheerful expression, but he was more afraid than he had ever been in his life.[179]

The Roman victory ended the war. Almost all Macedonian cities surrendered. When Perseus arrived at Amphipolis he was chased out and Paullus arrived shortly afterwards. Gnaeus Octavius, commanding the fleet, chased Perseus to Samothrace, and received the king's surrender, conveying him to Amphipolis.[180]

## The four Republics of Macedonia

The Senate prorogued the commands of Paullus and Lucius Anicius in Macedonia and Illyria, debating how to settle these states without a monarchical government. Ten commissioners were sent to Macedonia, and five to Illyria. Macedonia was to be divided into four independent republics, each with its own laws, and likewise Illyria was divided into three, the fine details to be worked out on the spot by the commissioners and the commanders.[181]

Ten leading men from all the cities were summoned to meet the commissioners at Amphipolis, where the terms were read in Latin and Greek. The Macedonian republics were to be free, would keep their cities and lands, and the assemblies were to elect annual magistrates to administer the state. Tax was to be paid to the Roman people at half the rate levied by the kings. The capital of the first republic was to be Amphipolis; of the second, Thessalonica; of the third, Pella; and of the fourth Pelagonia. All trading and marriages were to be conducted within the boundaries of each republic. Leasing of mines and farming estates was to cease, avoiding aggressive competition among contractors. Gold and silver mining was stopped, while copper and iron mining could continue, with a tax at half the rate imposed by the kings. Salt was not to be imported from outside each zone and no-one was allowed to cut timber for shipbuilding.[182]

## Aftermath

The Roman commanders did not emerge from the campaigns with much credit. There had already been repercussions in Rome concerning the appalling behaviour of Roman officers. The consul Publius Licinius Crassus and the praetor Gaius Lucretius Gallus commanding the fleet had conducted their campaigns with excessive cruelty and greed.[183] Gaius Lucretius and his brother Marcus besieged Haliartus, which was destroyed and the citizens were sold, though they had surrendered.[184] Haliartus, friendly to Perseus, was at least a legitimate target, whereas Chalcis, an ally of Rome, was also treated roughly by Gaius Lucretius and his successor, the praetor Hortensius. Lucretius was tried in Rome and fined one million *asses*.[185] Lucius Hortensius had demanded 100,000 *denarii* and 50,000 measures of wheat from Abdera.[186] The citizens could not meet the demands and asked to send envoys to the consul Aulus Hostilius Mancinus, assigned to Macedonia in 170. On reaching him, they heard that their city had been stormed, the leading citizens beheaded and the people sold as slaves. Two envoys were sent to free the enslaved population and restore them to their city.[187]

Roman discipline had evaporated. The only avenue for maltreated people was to appeal to the Senate, involving a long journey with no guaranteed redress. Roman commanders could not be prosecuted until they returned to Rome, and a trial depended on envoys claiming reparation or Romans, usually young men beginning their political careers, bringing a charge against an individual. A special court, the *quaestio de repetundis* was created in 149 to judge cases of extortion.

The states which had helped the Romans, such as Pergamum and Rhodes, were not treated with gratitude. Eumenes of Pergamum had come under suspicion while the war was still in progress.[188] Discerning that Perseus did not want war with Rome, Eumenes spied a chance to arrange peace, for a price.[189] He had a kingdom to run near the war zone, and he had expended resources on helping the Romans. In 167 the Romans had begun to foster his brother Attalus, reluctant to see Pergamum gaining strength.[190]

The Rhodians had assisted Rome, and they too had attempted to make peace between Rome and Perseus.[191] War destroyed commerce, their life-blood. They were suspected of disloyalty and were consequently nervous about Roman reactions. When Gaius Popilius was sailing to Egypt to broker a peace settlement between Antiochus and Ptolemy, the Rhodians invited him to come to their city so that they might hear the opinion of the Senate. Popilius enumerated all the faults and transgressions of the Rhodians, while his colleague Gaius Decimus blamed only a few dissidents. The Rhodians promptly executed citizens favouring Perseus.[192] Even worse, the *praetor peregrinus* Marcius Juventius Thalna urged war against Rhodes, for which he had no authority. The Rhodians were allowed to present their case, supported by Cato the Censor, whose speech was still extant in Livy's day.[193] By their own choice, Rhodes had never been an ally of Rome, but now they sought an alliance, granted in 164.[194] The treaty made the Rhodians subordinate to Rome, containing a clause binding them to 'uphold the greatness of Rome in friendly fashion', which according to Cicero did not appear in all treaties.[195] Roman protection entailed giving up independence.

After peace was established, witch-hunts began in Greece. The war had split many communities and Greeks, Macedonians, Epirotes and Illyrians were just as brutal to each other as the Romans had been in Greece. From 168, in various states, supporters of Perseus were punished, sometimes bloodily, in fear of retribution from the victorious Romans. Occasionally, Romans assisted, or at least did not interfere. On his way back to Demetrias after his tour of inspection around the main cities of Greece, Aemilius Paullus met a group of Aetolians obviously in mourning, and discovered that the pro-Roman leader Lyciscus had executed 550 Aetolians who supported Perseus. Roman soldiers under Aulus Baebius, the garrison commander, had surrounded their Senate house while the deed was done. Paullus summoned the leaders to meet him at Amphipolis. Lyciscus and his henchmen were acquitted, Aulus Baebius was punished.[196]

Denouncing those who had sided with Perseus served the purpose of getting rid of opponents, and in most states pro-Romans secured all the magistracies. Polybius says that Paullus did not necessarily believe all the accusations.[197] All the same, he had to be seen to act on the information, and he summoned named individuals from Aetolia, Acarnania, Epirus and Boeotia to follow him to Rome to stand trial. The case of the Achaeans was examined more closely by two of the ten commissioners, because although letters had been found among Perseus' archives from the other states, none were found from the Achaeans. It was also thought that the Achaean Callicrates, a fanatical supporter of Rome, might need protection.[198] He had submitted the names of 1,000 Achaeans suspected of not being sufficiently pro-Roman, and they were held without trial in Rome. Fortunately for students of ancient history, one of them was Polybius.

Paullus was quite prepared to carry out punishments on his own account, identifying all the communities and individuals which had helped Perseus in the smallest way.[199] His most appalling act was his treatment of Epirus. Only a minority of Epirotes had supported Perseus, but Paullus sent for ten men from each city, ordering them to display all their gold and silver for Roman cohorts to collect. The departures of the troops were timed so they would all arrive at their destinations on the same day, when looting and worse began. 150,000 people were enslaved and the booty was sold, raising enough to pay hefty sums to the cavalrymen and infantry. Polybius lays all the blame on the Senate for this, not Paullus, and Waterfield points out the pressing need for slaves to farm the large estates in Italy.[200]

Paullus could have refused to treat Epirus so brutally, but the lack of booty would have disappointed his soldiers. In fact they were discontented when they arrived back in Rome, feeling that they had been cheated of profit. Marcus Servilius claimed that Paullus did not usually cater to the greed and ill-discipline of the soldiers.[201] Paullus' triumph took three days from 27 to 29 November 167. Perseus and his children were paraded through the streets.[202] Under guard at Alba Fucens, Perseus died within about two years. Gentius of the Illyrians was similarly detained at Iguvium (Gubbio). Tragedy struck for Paullus. His two sons by his second marriage, aged about twelve and fourteen, died within days of each other.[203]

The year 167 was notable for the abolition of *tributum*, the tax based on property, for all Roman citizens living in Italy. This resulted from the tangible profit of the acquisition of provinces. Romans living outside Italy still paid the property tax.

## Andriscus, or Philip VI of Macedon

Greece and Macedonia were still unsettled after 167. There was no war, but troublesome outbreaks. In 156-155, the unrest in Illyria required two successive commanders to quell it. Illyria remained split into three areas, the southern part being friends of Rome. The central area never recovered its former prosperity.

In Macedonia unexpected trouble broke out with the arrival of Andriscus in 149. He looked very much like Perseus, and claimed to be his son, gaining enough supporters to form an army. Andriscus, as Philip VI, took control at Pella without opposition. In trying to gain Thessaly he was foiled by soldiers of the Achaean League commanded by Scipio Nasica, sent to negotiate with the 'False Philip'. On receiving Nasica's report, the Senate sent Publius Iuventius with one legion, thinking that Andriscus would be quickly eliminated. Instead, it was the Romans who were quickly eliminated, necessitating the assembly of another army. The praetor Quintus Caecilius Metellus defeated Andriscus in Macedonia, and again in Thrace. Metellus took the victory title Macedonicus, and he displayed Andriscus in his triumph.[204]

## The province of Macedonia

In Macedonia the choices were to leave well alone, try to make the four Republics work, or to reunite the country. The northern and eastern border areas were vulnerable to attacks from tribesmen. The Macedonians were not allowed to raise large numbers of troops, so effective protection required Roman troops. It was not exactly formal annexation, but from 148 Macedonia was an occupied zone, permanently garrisoned by Roman troops, with successive commanders sent out to attend to administration. The province of Macedonia was formally established in 146, when a large part of Greece was added to it. The four Macedonian republics were converted into administrative divisions, each supervised by local officials, most probably local dignitaries, who would deal with day-to-day government, while more serious problems would be referred to the commanders on the spot rather than reporting to Rome and waiting for a reply. Gradually, this practice would require secretarial staff, rudimentary administration, record-keeping, accumulation of local knowledge, relationships with local leaders, all of which was a good foundation for provincial government.[205]

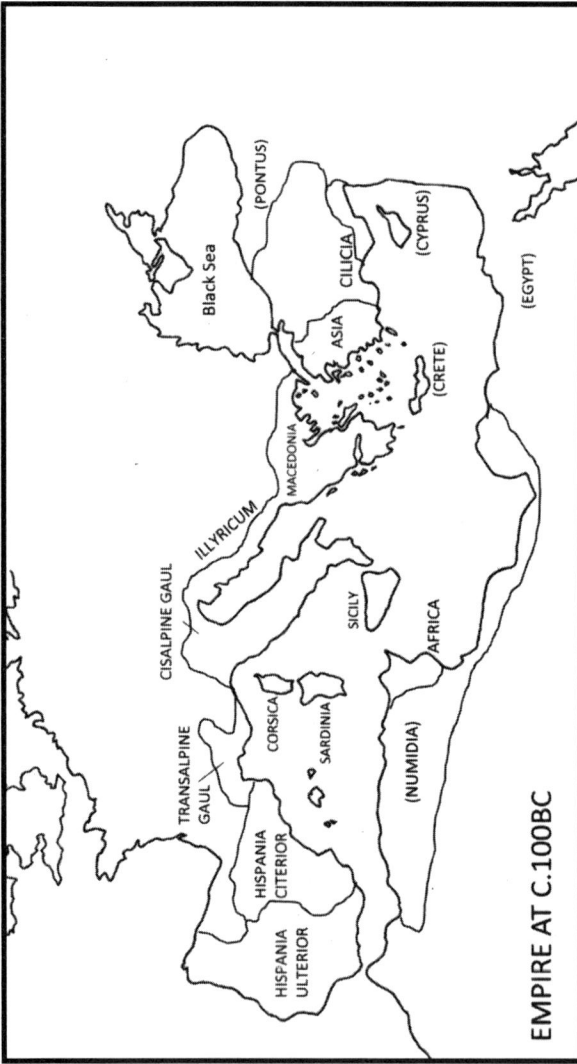

EMPIRE AT C.100BC

2. Provinces and territory under the influence of Rome by 100BC. Names in brackets indicate areas where Rome had influence, but had not annexed territory. Numidia, Crete, Cyprus, Egypt, Syria and Pontus remained outside Roman control until the first century BC. Cisalpine Gaul was annexed by 222 and colonies were planted, but progress was interrupted when Hannibal arrived in Italy in 218 and the area was not re-annexed until the first century BC. After the defeat of Hannibal and the end of the Second Punic War in 201, the Romans gained a foothold in Spain, dividing it into two occupied zones of Hispania Citerior or Nearer Spain, and Hispania Ulterior or Further Spain. In Macedonia, Rome fought wars and withdrew more than once, but maintained influence over the country until its annexation in 146 BC, and in the same year the territory of Carthage was annexed and became the province of Africa. When King Attalus III of Pergamum died in 133 he bequeathed his kingdom to the Roman people, but it was not annexed until 129 as the provinces of Asia. Roman armies marching into Spain used a route through Transalpine Gaul, which was traditionally annexed c.121 BC, but the date is disputed. Cilicia was occupied from 102 BC because it was a base for Mediterranean pirates, but it was not annexed at that time. Redrawn by Sue Howie after Richardson 1976.

# 4

# The Two Spains and the Provinces of Africa, Asia and Transalpine Gaul

Although the two Spains were *provinciae* in the sense of an allotted task, they were far from settled territories. They were not urbanised, except for the towns developed by Greek colonists and the Carthaginians, and there was as yet no permanent administrative centre in either *provincia*. The Romans did not even control the whole of the peninsula. The north-western areas remained unconquered until Augustus' reign.

The first two praetors, Gaius Sempronius Tuditanus in Hispania Citerior, and Marcus Helvius in Hispania Ulterior, were magistrates in their year of office, like the praetors commanding in Sicily and Sardinia-Corsica. They were asked to define the boundary between the two Spains, but it is not known if they did.[1] Even if the boundary was established, Roman troops occasionally crossed from one province to the other, as in 194 when Sextus Digitius in Citerior was assisted by Scipio Nasica from Ulterior.[2]

The Senate had to be involved in all provinces to ratify treaties and agreements with various communities or tribes. Appian says that in 151 Licinius Lucullus in Hispania Citerior attacked settlements of the Vaccaei without senatorial authorisation, and Appian mentions this twice more, in different contexts.[3] Given the unavoidable time lag communicating with Rome and receiving replies, it is likely that within a broad general brief, governors were allowed to make their own decisions on the ground, including attacks on communities suspected of scheming against Rome. The Senate only occasionally took direct action in a province, but in Spain such interventions increased in the later second century.[4] Extortion of the natives was too frequent, and since governors could not be prosecuted until they returned to Rome, they were not always condemned even when there was incontrovertible evidence of guilt. In the 170s, envoys from both Spains brought complaints to Rome and from 149 courts were established to try cases of extortion, but even then, blatantly guilty men escaped punishment.

There was almost continual fighting in Spain from 197 onwards, mostly against Lusitanians of the west and Celtiberians in the north, but these tribes contained different factions, like the tribes of fifth-century Italy. Livy says that when not provoked the Lusitanians were peaceful, which conveys a lot more than he perhaps intended about Roman dealings with Spanish tribes.[5] In 197 tribes joined together against the Romans.[6] Warfare intensified in Citerior, prompting the Senate to appoint the consul Marcus Porcius Cato, accompanied by the praetor Publius Manlius, in 195-194. Livy used Cato's own account of his achievements.[7] Cato imposed taxes (*vectigalia*) on production of the iron and silver mines, probably north of the Ebro, and revenue was also drawn from public land, salt works, and other mines.[8] Cato proclaimed Citerior pacified, and in 194 the Senate withdrew most of the troops and reinstated praetors as proconsular governors.[9]

Reinforcements were authorized for Spain in 188, since troops were available after the defeat of Antiochus III in Asia. The praetors for 186, Gaius Calpurnius Piso and Lucius Quinctius Crispinus, decided to work together according to a coordinated plan. They lost a battle near Toletum (Toledo), but with help from Spanish allies they won the next one in 185, ensuring peace for a while.[10]

In 180-178, Tiberius Sempronius Gracchus in Citerior and Lucius Postumius Albinus in Ulterior also cooperated with each other. Postumius moved north through Lusitania and then east into Celtiberia, where Gracchus was operating, ultimately receiving the surrender of the Celtiberians.[11] Livy says that Gracchus captured 103 cities, Polybius says 300. Strabo quotes Posidonius, who sneers that Polybius classed a fortified tower as a city.[12] Gracchus and Albinus celebrated triumphs in 178.

More pertinent for provincial development, Gracchus converted some tribes into friends of Rome. He drew up clearly defined and carefully worded treaties, confirmed by oaths of the Romans and Spanish leaders. Gracchus allocated lands to the poorer classes and arranged the usual tribute payments and contribution of troops from the tribes.[13]

These treaties probably formed the basis of later agreements between Rome and the tribes.[14] Up to this time, in the absence of regulated tax assessments, military commanders extracted whatever they could in money and grain.[15] Gracchus reorganised the supply of grain for the army and regulated the financial administration. The Spanish tribes never forgot Gracchus or his laws, which were probably incorporated in the organisation of the two provinces in 133.

After 179, military actions declined, and from 171 until 167 one commander administered both provinces, the first being the praetor Lucius Canuleius. He delayed his departure to receive envoys of the Spanish communities of both provinces, as mentioned above, complaining of the rapacity of some commanders. Canuleius assigned five senators to act as judges in the case of the accused Romans and authorized the Spanish envoys to choose their own Roman advocates. The cases were heard, but not all the accused were punished. At least the Senate decreed that the price for grain should not be set by Roman officials, and no Romans should collect money from Spanish towns, indicating what Romans had been doing.[16]

More Spanish envoys arrived in Rome in 171, explaining that about 4,000 men, sons of Roman soldiers and Spanish women, wanted somewhere to settle. Marriage of Romans with native women was illegal, so the men were Spanish *peregrini*. They were settled at Carteia, already occupied, on the coast of the Bay of Algeciras. The inhabitants remained, but all lands were re-apportioned. Carteia was a Latin colony, the first outside Italy, and it included any freedmen (*liberti* or *libertini*) of the *peregrini*, reflected in its title *colonia Latina libertinorumque*.[17]

Sources for the 160s in Spain are almost non-existent. The Lusitanians and Celtiberians defeated the praetor Lucius Mummius in Ulterior in 153, but Mummius rallied and chased them through southern Spain, across the Straits of Gibraltar and into Africa, earning a triumph. His successor in 153-152 was the praetor Marcus Atilius, to whom some tribes surrendered.[18] The consul Quintus Fulvius Nobilior was assigned to Citerior for 153, and consuls commanded in this province until at least150. Nobilior demanded tribute from Segeda, which was exempt according to the treaty arranged by Sempronius Gracchus. Nobilior attacked it anyway but was defeated, losing his supply base at Ocilis. Tribesmen moved into the stronghold of Numantia, which Nobilior failed to capture.[19] In 152 the consul Marcus Claudius Marcellus replaced Nobilior, recovering Ocilis and inducing three tribes, the Arevaci, the Belli and the Titthi, to send envoys to Rome. The Senate rejected peace until tribes at Numantia surrendered unconditionally.[20] Marcellus achieved a negotiated peace before the consul Lucius Licinius Lucullus replaced him in 151. Lucullus wanted money and fame, so without official sanction he attacked settlements of the Vaccaei, accusing the people of harming a pro-Roman tribe.[21] Lucullus killed all adult males at Cauca, installing a Roman garrison. People fled from him, burning everything to deprive Lucullus of supplies. He besieged Intercatia but had to arrange a treaty in return for hostages, clothing, and cattle. His next failure was against Pallantia, the chief city of the Vaccaei and allegedly wealthy. Lucullus soon had to withdraw, without the wealth. The history of Citerior is patchy for some years after 150.

In Ulterior, the praetor Servius Sulpicius Galba, proconsul from 151, was notorious for an unprecedented atrocity. He and the consul Lucullus fought the Lusitanians in Ulterior and Citerior, inducing the tribesmen to ask for peace in 150. Galba promised to resettle the Lusitanians on fertile lands to replace their unproductive farms. They turned up at the assembly points and were divided into three widely separated groups, to be shown their allocated lands. Galba then killed all the tribesmen, moving from group to group, the fate of the others being unknown to each one.[22] Only a few escaped, including one man, Viriathus, who was to make life miserable for the Romans for a decade.

Galba's conduct was deplored in Rome. He had sold Lusitanian survivors as slaves, who were taken to Gaul. He was prosecuted for this, not the massacre. Lucius Scribonius Libo, tribune of the plebs, proposed that the enslaved Lusitanians should be freed. Libo's proposal was a *rogatio*, a bill that would have become law if it was passed, and Galba might have been condemned. But he went free.[23] From 149 other wars loomed, first with Carthage and later with the Achaeans.

## The Third Punic War

Masinissa of Numidia encroached on Carthaginian territory, and as his ally, Rome was asked to settle the dispute in 157. The Roman envoys noted the wealth of Carthage. Marcus Porcius Cato, possibly one of the ambassadors, pronounced that Rome would never be secure while Carthage flourished and at the end of every speech, regardless of the subject, Cato allegedly added *Carthago delenda est*,

Carthage must be destroyed, or more accurately Carthage should cease to exist, and Scipio Nasica always replied that Carthage should continue to exist. It was reported in 153 that ship timbers were being collected at Carthage.[24] It was decided that war could be avoided if the Carthaginians burnt the fleet and disbanded their army, but then the Carthaginians attacked Masinissa. Livy says they deserved war. Polybius says that the Romans had simply been waiting for a suitable opportunity for war.[25]

The slow move towards war as reported by Livy is dismissed as fabrication by Harris, who points out that the Roman treaty with Carthage did not forbid possession of ships, or soldiers to protect their borders. He accuses the Romans of encouraging Masinissa's attacks.[26] The Carthaginians attempted to appease the Romans by condemning to death their general Hasdrubal, who had conducted the war against Masinissa. Hasdrubal rebelled, camping outside Carthage with 20,000 men.

War against Carthage was formally declared. The consul Marcus Manilius was assigned to the army and his colleague Lucius Marcius Censorinus to the fleet. Appian says they were secretly instructed not to end the war until Carthage was obliterated. Carthaginian ambassadors in Rome were asked for 300 children as hostages, then they could retain their city and lands.[27] The Romans landed at Utica, which surrendered. Another Carthaginian embassy arrived there, to be told to surrender all arms and war engines. They agreed, on condition that the Romans dealt with the renegade Hasdrubal. Then impossible demands were made. Carthage was to be destroyed, replaced by a new site ten miles from the sea, a death sentence, since Carthage depended on overseas trading. The Carthaginians protested that they had agreed to all Roman demands and had scrupulously paid the massive indemnity imposed in 201.[28] The Carthaginians had not realised that it was their ability to pay these enormous sums, yet still prosper and grow rich, which attracted Roman hostility. The Carthaginians resolved to fight, and hastily manufactured new weapons. Hasdrubal's death sentence was revoked and he was asked to defend the city from outside, while another Hasdrubal commanded inside.

Livy and Appian make much of the exploits of Scipio Aemilianus, serving as military tribune in the army.[29] Masinissa, a friend of Scipio Africanus, Scipio's grandfather by adoption, asked the young man to discuss legacies to his sons, and the government of his kingdom after his death. He was ninety and died before Scipio arrived.[30] Scipio rewarded Masinissa's illegitimate sons and then apportioned the lands and governmental roles between the three legitimate sons, Micipsa, Mastanabal and Gulussa, who was persuaded to contribute troops. Shortly afterwards, Scipio also persuaded a Carthaginian commander, Phameas Himilco, to change sides.[31]

The new consul Calpurnius Piso arrived in spring 147 with Lucius Mancinus in command of the fleet. The campaign seemed to be stalling. Scipio returned to Rome to stand for election as aedile, but the people wanted him as consul. He had held no magistracies and was too young for the consulship, but the Romans excelled at circumventing their own laws, and authorized the tribunes of the plebs to repeal the relevant law and then reinstate it. Scipio, consul for 147, was appointed commander in Africa, obtaining volunteers from allied kings.[32] Arriving at Carthage, he dug a ditch across the peninsula accompanied by a wall with towers, blocking the land approach to the city. From the sea, supply ships could reach Carthage only with favourable winds.[33] Carthage began to starve, and the Romans captured it section by section. The people crowded into the stronghold of Byrsa, the hill where Carthage was founded. The city, now burning, fell after six days. Scipio agreed to let numbers of people under guard to pass through one of the gates, except for 900 Roman deserters, who took refuge in a temple, set fire to it, and died. Carthage was obliterated in 146. Scipio shed tears over it, contemplating the fate of empires, including that of Rome.[34]

## The province of Africa

The new province was clearly not the entire African continent, but the territory previously controlled by Carthage, *c.*5,000 square miles. Ten senatorial commissioners assisted Scipio in the formation of the province in 146. Information about the establishment derives from a *lex agraria* passed in 111, preserved on an incomplete inscription.[35] The surviving text also covers Italy and Corinth, Africa being dealt with in paragraphs 45 to 95. One clause mentions 'the land or ground where the city of Carthage formerly stood' and another mentions 'the land or ground left or assigned to the people of Utica by the ten-man commission appointed or created under the Livian law'. This *lex Livia*, otherwise unknown, may have formally established the province of Africa in 146, recording who held titles to which lands. Seven cities were declared free, *civitates liberae et immunes*, listed as Utica, Hadrumetum, Tampsus or Thapsus, Leptis, Aquileia/Acholla, Teudalis, and Uzalis. The cities kept their original lands and by 111 were friends of the Roman people. The lands given to the 2,200 Carthaginians who deserted to Rome under Phameas Himilco were confirmed as their private possession. All other land was *ager publicus*, belonging to the Roman people. On the less valuable lands, Broughton suggested that the natives may have rented their farms from new owners. The law of 111 also contains information about the various categories of land and the methods of cultivating it. Initially, farmers may have continued to grow the varied crops of the Carthaginians, but later they probably turned to cereals for the Roman markets.[36]

Africa was to be governed by a praetor, not a newly created magistrate as for Sicily, Sardinia with Corsica, and the two Spains. The Senate decided to keep the total at six praetors, only two of whom could hope to become consuls after their year of office, while the other four provided provincial governors. This meant that from now on, prorogation of commands was obligatory to provide enough governors. The praetor of Africa was based at Utica, which was granted extra territory from Carthaginian lands, but this territory did not possess the same legal status as the free city of Utica.

Settlement on the site of Carthage was cursed. The ground was not cursed, but was infertile, having been sown with salt. The cities of Tunis, Neferis, Neapolis and Clupea/Aspis were destroyed for assisting the Carthaginians. A land tax was imposed and a personal or head tax was levied on men and women. Public and private lands around Carthage were declared *ager publicus*, and could be sold to individuals, probably wealthy Italians who became absentee landlords. Occasionally, land was purchased complete with the men who worked it, mostly Libyans. The lands beyond the western borders of the province belonged to Numidia.[37] Autonomous self-government was the preferred method of Roman control, while the praetors and their staff kept law and order and ensured that taxes were paid.

### War in Achaea

Concurrent with the African war, the Achaeans went to war with the Romans in 147. Sparta had gained near-independence within the Achaean League, bolstered by its relationship with Rome. The Achaeans asked for Roman advice, received an imprecise reply, and began to quarrel. Lucius Aurelius Orestes arrived with the Roman verdict, which was to declare Sparta, Corinth, Argos, Orchomenus and Heraclea near Thermopylae independent.[38] Fisticuffs ensued between

Romans and Greeks. The Achaean general Critolaus declared war on Sparta with help from other Greeks. The Senate authorized Quintus Caecilius Metellus, commanding in Macedonia, to march to Greece. He defeated the Achaeans at Thermopylae, and then at Chaeronea. Critolaus disappeared, replaced by the Achaean Diaeus.[39] The consul Lucius Mummius arrived in Greece, defeating the Achaeans at the Isthmus of Corinth. The Senate ordered him to destroy Corinth. Obeying the order, Mummius killed or enslaved the Corinthians, razed their city, and sent ship-loads of art treasures to Rome. The walls of Thebes and Chalcis were pulled down, though Livy denies it.[40]

Ten commissioners were sent to Greece. The main source for the settlement is Pausanias, and it is clear that though the Romans controlled Greece by 146, they did not formally make it a province.[41] Cities and towns governed themselves and their areas, as the Romans preferred. Polybius, living in Rome as a hostage since 168, was sent to settle disputes.[42] There were no treaties, but tribute was levied and some indemnities were imposed. Thebes had to pay fines for the benefit of Heraclea and Euboea.[43] Lands were confiscated, declared *ager publicus* and were rented out, primarily to the city of Sicyon.[44] The policy was to split up the various leagues and isolate the cities. This was reversed a decade later, though the leagues were not fully reconstituted.[45]

Macedonia is usually said to have been made a province in 148/147, and from 146 it had a permanent garrison and a governor, usually a praetor, but it may not have been made into a formal province until the later Republic. At an unknown date, possibly in the 130s, the Via Egnatia was built, the major road eventually connecting the Adriatic coast with Byzantium, facilitating movement of armies and traders.[46] The governors of Macedonia probably supervised the affairs of Greece after 146, with the right to intervene if necessary. In later times it was not unusual for provincial governors to take responsibility for areas outside but close to his province.

After the destruction of the major ancient cities of Carthage and Corinth in 146, no-one could deny the power, determination, and ruthlessness of Rome.

### Spain: the rebellion of Viriathus

After his infamous massacre of the Lusitanians in 150, Sulpicius Galba's legacy was Viriathus, still a national hero in Portugal. The Lusitanians who escaped overran the southern part of Hispania Ulterior and were defeated by the praetor Gaius Vetilius, probably in 146. Vetilius called the tribesmen to an assembly, promising to provide lands, but it was too soon after Galba's ruse. Viriathus extricated the Lusitanians from the assembly, drawing up as if to give battle, but then at his signal, everyone scattered in all directions. Vetilius could not chase all of them, so he went for Viriathus and 1,000 men holding off the Romans then fleeing on swift horses. Vetilius was killed. His quaestor rounded up survivors, probably west of the river Baetis (Guadalquivir).[47] Nothing succeeds like success, so other Spanish tribes joined Viriathus. They defeated the next praetor Gaius Plautius in 145, forcing the Senate to take Viriathus more seriously. Quintus Fabius Maximus Aemilianus, consul in 145, began to restore the balance.[48]

There is no information for the years between 144 and 142, when the consul Quintus Fabius Maximus Servilianus arrived in Ulterior. He was the natural brother of Fabius Aemilianus, but both were adopted by different families. Viriathus defeated Servilianus and peace was made, ratified by the people of Rome. Viriathus was declared a friend of the Romans and his followers were confirmed as holders of the lands they had taken.[49] The next commander was the consul of 140, Quintus Servilius Caepio. Perfidiously, the Senate authorized him to harass Viriathus clandestinely. Then it was decided to break the peace overtly and declare war. Viriathus was defeated but escaped. Caepio resorted to dirty tricks. When envoys arrived to negotiate peace, Caepio bribed them to kill Viriathus, which they did, probably at the end of 140.[50] Fighting continued under a leader called Tantalus, defeated by Caepio. Decimus Junius Brutus, consul in 138, took over in Ulterior, remaining there until 133.[51]

## The siege of Numantia

The Numantine war began in Citerior, during the struggle with Viriathus. From 150-146 it is not known who commanded the province. Praetors governed 145-144, succeeded by two consuls, and senatorial Roman counsellors arrived with reinforcements for the army, implying serious problems.[52] The problems probably derived from Roman commanders, whose performances in ensuing years were abysmal.

The senators arrived just after the consul Quintus Pompeius, governing Citerior from 141-140, secretly approached the Numantines about making peace. The tribesmen agreed, tiring of the war. Pompeius persuaded them to surrender unconditionally because the Senate and people of Rome would accept nothing less. But then the consul for 139, Marcus Popillius Laenas, arrived, and Pompeius denied that he had made any agreements with the Numantines. His own officers backed up the Numantines. Pompeius and Numantine representatives were sent to argue the case in Rome. Hostilius Mancinus replaced Popilius in 137, got himself trapped in his camp, and surrendered. Mancinus' quaestor was Tiberius Sempronius Gracchus whose father had arranged treaties with the Spanish tribes in 180-178, and because of his family connection, the young Tiberius negotiated a way out of the dilemma. Mancinus was recalled and put on trial, while his consular colleague Aemilius Lepidus replaced him. Lepidus ignored Numantia and attacked the nearby Vaccaei. Appian denies, then confirms, that the Vaccaei assisted the Numantines.[53] Lepidus invited his relative Decimus Junius Brutus governing Ulterior to join him in attacking Pallantia. Messengers from Rome brought a senatorial decree ordering him to stop, because he had begun an unauthorized war. Lepidus ignored the Senate, but Pallantia held out and Lepidus and Brutus withdrew in disorder. Lepidus was deprived of his command as proconsul, recalled to Rome, and fined.[54]

The Senate decided to deliver Hostilius Mancinus to the Numantines, who declined the offer. Two more consuls were sent to Spain, Lucius Furius Philus in 136 and Quintus Calpurnius Piso in 135, but their achievements, whatever they were, pale into insignificance besides those of the next consul for 134, Publius Cornelius Scipio Africanus Aemilianus, who had been Lucullus' quaestor in Spain. As consul for the second time, Scipio recruited 4,000 volunteers, 500 of them from his own clients and friends, and many more were sent to him on grounds of personal friendship by certain cities and kings.[55]

Rome's miserable track record in Spain demanded tough measures. Scipio restored discipline and morale at Numantia, trained soldiers, dismissed hangers-on, reduced superfluous pack animals and wagons, declaring that the remaining mules were not to carry loads that were too heavy for them, not entirely from a sense of animal welfare but to toughen up his men who carried the excess baggage themselves. Scipio reconnoitred the territory all around and on the march he made the soldiers of the vanguard and some horsemen watch the surrounding terrain while camps were made, even specifying how long construction should take.[56]

He made war on the Vaccaei to stop them supplying Numantia. While he was in winter quarters near Numantia, extra troops including archers, slingers, and twelve elephants arrived from Numidia with Jugurtha, the grandson of Masinissa. In 133, the siege of Numantia began in earnest. The town was encircled by a stone wall, regularly spaced towers, and seven camps for the soldiers. The camps have not been obliterated, and the layout of the soldiers' living accommodation confirms that the troops were organised in manipular formation.

The Numantines offered battle but Scipio did not fight, choosing to starve them out. When the Numantines were allegedly reduced to cannibalism, the city surrendered, asking for one day to arrange their suicides. Survivors were sold as slaves, except for fifty of them for Scipio's triumph. Numantia was razed. Appian discusses the motives: vindictiveness, glory for Scipio in destroying a city that resisted for so long, or was it all for the advantage of Rome?[57]

### The formal establishment of the Spanish provinces

In 133, the first steps were taken towards creating a system for provincial administration. Spain was a large territory, populated by many disunited tribes, and neither all the people nor the entire country were controlled by the Romans until much later. There was no urbanisation, and no ready-made administrative system as there had been in Sicily, and the formal establishment of the province was tardy. Spain had been in Roman hands since 206, divided into two areas controlled by praetors in 197, and yet Appian says that in 133 ten senators arrived in the 'newly acquired provinces' to settle them on a basis of peace.[58] The names of the ten senators are not known, and their activities are not elucidated. Appian says they covered both provinces. Lands would be surveyed and assigned to officially recognised communities, their varying statuses would be acknowledged, the internal boundaries between the towns and cities would be set, and all this and the regulations would be recorded, probably in the name of the individual who saw it through to confirmation; in this case, the younger Cornelius Scipio Africanus. No *lex Cornelia* is known, however.

After 133 the organisation of Hispania Citerior and Hispania Ulterior is not documented. The Spanish provinces were under military occupation and fighting continued. It requires peace and security to establish new cities and a network of roads, and it was not until the later second century that military bases were eventually converted to civilian use, probably settled by natives, Italians and Romans, possibly living in their own specified areas within the town or city. In the valley of the river Baetis, Roman and Italian farmers established agricultural communities. There would be different types of cities, towns and other communities, with different relationships with Rome and different status categories. One of the oldest settlements was Emporion, or Emporiae (Empuries) between Barcelona and Girona, probably originally a Greek colony, eventually controlled by Massilia (Marseilles). When Gnaeus Scipio headed for Spain in 218, there were few choices of landing places where he would not have to fight the Carthaginians, and since the Romans had established friendly relations with the Massilians in the past, Emporiae was where Gnaeus Scipio landed his troops. It was used for the same purpose in 211 and 195. A Roman town was established there *c*.100 and it became a *municipium* under Augustus, but began to decline by the end of the first century AD.

Carthago Nova or New Carthage (Cartagena) was a Carthaginian colony founded by Hasdrubal, son-in-law of Hamilcar Barca, probably in 228. The harbour is probably the best on the east coast of Spain, with access to the silver mines in the vicinity, which made it highly important to the Carthaginians and then to the Romans after they captured it in 209. Polybius visited the city in the mid-second century, reporting that the mines produced 25,000 *drachmae* for Rome every day. Assuming that Polybius equated the *drachma* with the Roman *denarius*, Richardson calculates that if the mines were worked every day, they would yield 10,800 pounds of silver per annum.[59] Worth hanging onto, then. And these were not the only mines.

Cicero mentions a treaty between Rome and Gades (Cadiz), first established by Phoenicians, the main attraction being the minerals of the area, especially the Rio Tinto silver mines.[60] The original Roman arrangements with Gades were made by Scipio in 206, when the city surrendered, but until 78 there seems to have been no formalised treaty or *foedus*.[61] Tarraco (Tarragona) on the east coast was founded sometime after 218 by Gnaeus Scipio, as a landing place and a base for the Roman army. Traders soon followed. Tarraco gave its name to Tarraconensis, the largest of the three Spanish provinces created by Augustus, the other two being Lusitania and Baetica. Italica (Santiponce) was founded by Cornelius Scipio in 206 for his wounded soldiers.[62] The site was already occupied, and it is not known what happened to the original inhabitants. Its status is uncertain, because the Roman Senate did not have any part in its foundation. It was not until the later first century, under Julius Caesar or Augustus, that it became a *municipium*. Italian families settled there, among them the Ulpii and the Aelii, respectively the ancestors of the Emperors Trajan and Hadrian.

In 123, Quintus Caecilius Metellus Balearicus settled 3000 Romans from Spain in the Balearics, as his name suggests. They may have been retired soldiers and ordinary civilians, settled in two Latin colonies at Palma and Pollentia, possibly with people of mixed descent from soldiers and unofficial Spanish wives.

Some foundations were intended for native settlers. The Latin colony of Carteia has been mentioned above, established after 171 for the children of Roman soldiers and Spanish women. Marcus Marcellus founded Corduba in the valley of the Baetis (Guadalquivir), but the date is uncertain.[63] Strabo says that specially selected Romans and native Iberians were chosen as the inhabitants, which is attested by archaeology. It was the first Roman citizen colony in that area, founded by either by Julius Caesar or Augustus. The native settlement of Gracchuris, established by Tiberius Gracchus in the upper Ebro valley, had gained Latin rights by the time of Augustus. Valentia (probably Valencia) was founded in 138, likely on vacant land, by Decimus Junius Brutus. Livy calls Valentia an *oppidum*, usually the name for a native town in Spain and Gaul, and the followers of Viriathus were settled there, far from their homelands in the west.[64]

After 133 only a few names of praetors are known in the two Spains, and virtually nothing of what they did, probably because of the ongoing internal and external troubles that began in the same year.[65]

## Internal strife

For part of the first half of the second century, the political and military history of Rome becomes the history of outstanding politicians and generals. The Gracchus brothers dominated politics for more than a decade, starting with Tiberius Sempronius Gracchus, *tribunus plebis* in 133. Tiberius supposedly realised the need for reforms when he travelled through Italy on his way to Spain to serve as quaestor under Hostilius Mancinus. He noted how the large estates of wealthy men, worked by slaves, were obliterating the small farms, forcing out farmers who would have provided allied soldiers.[66] Slaves created more slaves, and their labour was not interrupted by their removal to fight wars. Only in dire emergencies did the Senate authorize recruitment of slaves.

As tribune, Tiberius drew up a land law, assisted by his father-in-law Appius Claudius Pulcher, and by Publius Licinius Crassus Dives Mucianus, and Publius Mucius Scaevola, consul for 133. In his first bill Tiberius arranged compensation for those who would lose land.[67] The Senate asked the tribune Marcus Octavius to interpose his *intercessio*, or veto. Tiberius redrafted his proposals, making them harsher. It was to be illegal for any individual farmer to hold more than 500 *iugera* of public land, as once proposed in 367 by the Licinio-Sextian laws. Occupying farmers could keep 500 *iugera* rent-free, with an extra 250 *iugera* for each child, up to a maximum of four children, which would provide a farm of 1,500 *iugera*, approximately 900 acres, enough to maintain a comfortable villa.[68] The remaining public land was to be allocated to landless men in small parcels of thirty *iugera* each, which they were not allowed to sell.[69] A commission of three men was to be set up, called *tresviri agris iudicandis adsignandisque*, three men to judge and assign lands. These were to be Tiberius, his brother Gaius, and Appius Claudius.

The tribune Octavius vetoed the re-drafted bill. Tiberius asked him nicely to desist, Octavius refused, and Tiberius drew up a bill to depose him. Before everyone had voted it was clear that Octavius would be removed. He was mauled and one of his slaves was blinded trying to protect him.[70] Tiberius, urged to prove that he had not violated the sacrosanctity of a fellow tribune, replied that the tribune Octavius was supposed to act in the interests of the plebs, but was acting against them by opposing the bill. Sources differ as to who replaced Octavius.[71] The land law was passed, but at the instigation of Publius Cornelius Scipio Nasica the Senate refused to vote the usual expenses for transport and accommodation for the commissioners.[72]

In rearranging landholdings, the commissioners found that landownership was not straightforward. Some farmers had bought extra lands and would lose not only the land but the money paid out. Others had borrowed money on the security of their estates, and sometimes lands were designated as dowries for farmers' daughters.[73] Titles to allotments were lost or never recorded, nor were subsequent sales. Not all the lands acquired by conquest had been properly surveyed, and boundaries between private and public land were blurred.[74]

At this moment, a potential source of funds presented itself. King Attalus III of Pergamum died, bequeathing his kingdom to the Roman people. Tiberius drafted a bill to allow Attalus' legacy to provide money to help new farmers to purchase tools and seed. As for the Pergamene towns and cities that came with the bequest, the people would decide on their status and government.[75] The claim to the legacy was contested by Andronicus, illegitimate son of King Eumenes II, and the Romans had to fight to gain their inherited kingdom.

Tiberius had more reforms in mind, but his office would expire in early December 133, so he stood for a second term for 132. The Senate blocked him, according to a law passed in the 180s making it illegal for anyone to seek re-election to the same office until ten years had elapsed. Tiberius adjourned the voting session.[76] Next day, Tiberius gathered his supporters for the assembly. He seemed to be aiming for kingship, and Publius Cornelius Scipio Nasica, senator and Pontifex Maximus, urged Tiberius' death. The consul Publius Mucius Scaevola, who had helped Tiberius to draft his land law, refused to authorize such a momentous action without a trial.[77] Undeterred, Nasica led out the senators to confront Tiberius, who was killed along with many followers and thrown into the Tiber.

An enquiry was set up. As Pontifex Maximus Scipio Nasica was not supposed to leave Rome, but he was put at the head of a commission of five senators and quietly removed to Pergamum to take over the kingdom of Attalus III. Nasica never returned to Rome.

Appian's verdict was that Gracchus had an excellent design, too violently pursued.[78] The violence did not stem from Gracchus alone. Senators had over-reacted. Three land commissioners, Fulvius Flaccus, Gaius Papirius Carbo and Gaius Gracchus, went ahead with the redistribution of land.[79] The tribune Papirius Carbo proposed a law to allow repeated re-election of tribunes, but Scipio Africanus opposed it, declaring that Tiberius had been justly killed.[80]

Gaius Sempronius Gracchus, nine years younger than his brother, initially showed no ambition for a political career.[81] He served in the army at Numantia, and on Tiberius' land commission. He was quaestor in Sardinia, under Lucius Aurelius Orestes, consul for 126. The command of Orestes, and Gaius' quaestorship, were prorogued for 125 and 124, but before his term ended Gaius returned to for Rome for election as tribune for 123. He was questioned for leaving early, and he explained that he had served in the army for two years beyond the mandatory ten, stayed in post as quaestor for longer than the usual year, and he had returned from Sardinia no wealthier than he was when he got there.[82] Livy judged Gaius a better orator than Tiberius.[83]

Gaius had senatorial supporters, among them his friend Fulvius Flaccus, consul in 125. Plutarch claims that Gaius' first proposal of 123 concerned magistrates who had been legally deposed, banning them from subsequent magistracies. It was aimed at the tribune Marcus Octavius, but Gaius' mother Cornelia persuaded him to withdraw the bill. Gaius then advocated the prosecution of any official who banished a Roman citizen without trial, targeting Popillius Laenas, consul in 132, instructed by the Senate to act against the surviving supporters of Tiberius, without trial. Popillius went into voluntary exile.[84]

Plutarch considered Gaius' laws benefitting the people were intended to damage the power and prestige of the Senate, and Appian says that Gracchus claimed to have broken the power of the Senate. Livy, staunchly senatorial, labels Gracchus' laws as pernicious.[85] Gaius was elected tribune for a second term in 121, so it is not always possible to assign each law to a specific year. One of his laws made it mandatory to allocate the provinces before the elections, to avoid scrambles for posts which were usually allocated after the elections, and the new procedure was to be immune to tribunician veto.

Though the property qualification for army service had been lowered to embrace impoverished farmer-soldiers, there was a growing reluctance to enlist for wars fought mostly overseas for long periods. Gaius made it illegal to recruit men younger than seventeen, and soldiers were relieved of the burden of paying for their clothing and equipment.[86]

The work of the original land commission continued, each commissioner serving for one year. Gaius introduced a bill imposing rents on new allotments and he removed some of the public land from redistribution, possibly to rent it out to non-Romans.[87] A programme for founding new colonies in Italy was started at Tarentum, and less certainly at Capua. Gaius also organised more road building.[88] He tried to arrange fair treatment for provincials. In 123 Quintus Fabius Maximus Allobrogicus, praetor in Spain, sent requisitioned grain to Rome, but Gaius persuaded the Senate to sell it and send payment to the Spanish tribes. He tried to curb extortion by putting the courts in the hands of the equestrians, since senatorial judges were reluctant to condemn their colleagues.[89]

The food supply was one of the perennial problems at Rome, attracting the attention of several politicians. Gaius wished to pre-empt food shortage by providing grain at low cost, via the *lex frumentaria*, from *frumentum*, grain.[90] Grain was to be purchased by the state, supplementary to the grain collected from Sicily and Sardinia, stored in warehouses specially built in Rome and distributed each month, though there was no permanent distribution site in the city for another 150 years.[91] The people would pay six and one-third *asses* per *modius*, the standard measure for grain.[92]

Near the site of Carthage, Gaius proposed the foundation of a colony called Junonia, to accommodate 6,000 settlers from Rome and Italy, each with an allocation of 200 *iugera* of land (130 acres). In 122, Gaius was allowed to break the rule that tribunes should not leave Rome during their term of office and travelled to the colony with Fulvius Flaccus, but the site was beset by troubles. Wolves uprooted the foundation markers, attesting to the wasteland that once was Carthage. The colony failed. Julius Caesar tried to revive it, but it was Augustus who established it, and the renewed Carthage flourished, becoming the capital of the province of Africa, renamed Africa Proconsularis.

Marcus Livius Drusus, tribune for 122, very anti-Gracchus, proposed the founding of twelve colonies, each accommodating 3,000 people. Nothing came of it. Gaius' plan to give citizenship to Latins and Italians also came to nothing. Livius Drusus proposed an alternative to citizenship, recognizing that the main concern for Latins and Italians was to put an end to arbitrary treatment by magistrates, and to obtain the legal right of redress against such treatment. Drusus began by proposing that Latins should be immune from flogging, even while serving in the army under Roman officers. [93]

When Gaius decided to stand for a third term as tribune, an assembly was called in 121 to present a bill annulling one of his laws. Gaius attended and fighting broke out. A lictor of the consul Lucius Opimius was killed. The Senate summoned Gaius and Fulvius Flaccus, who stayed away. Opimius was empowered to secure the safety of the state. History repeated itself. Gaius, Flaccus and many followers were killed and thrown into the Tiber.[94]

A new division had been created in Roman public life. Instead of patricians and plebeians there were *populares*, politicians ostensibly working on behalf of the people, and self-styled *optimates*, 'the best men' working with the Senate. Conflict and violence eventually became civil wars.

## The province of Asia

The kingdom of Pergamum, bequeathed to the Roman people by Attalus III in 133, was to become the Roman province of Asia, not to be confused with modern Asia. As well as Pergamum and other cities, the Attalid realm also included Mysia, Lydia, Phrygia and parts of Caria, all in western Turkey. Aristonicus, son of Eumenes II by a concubine, claimed the kingdom, gathering a following of slaves and discontents, including many citizens of Pergamum. A Greek inscription records the hurried response of the Pergamene government in depriving the followers of Aristonicus of their rights, and hastily bestowing citizenship on several classes of people to provide more fighting men. The text also mentions that Attalus' will had still to be ratified in Rome.[95]

At first the Romans were content to allow rulers of neighbouring states to suppress Aristonicus. These included Mithradates V of Pontus, Nicomedes II of Bithynia, Ariarathes V of Cappadocia, and Pylaemenes of Paphlagonia. Some of them were rewarded after Asia was settled. Ariarathes V was killed in the fighting and his heir received Lycaonia and perhaps Pisidia and Pamphylia. Much of Phrygia was given to Mithradates V of Pontus, but when he died in 120, succeeded by his young son Mithradates VI, the Romans took it back, regretting it later.

In 131 the Roman commission of five men sent to settle the kingdom had to be quickly replaced by an army under the consul Publius Licinius Crassus Dives Mucianus, who was also Pontifex Maximus and ought not to have left Rome. Aristonicus defeated and killed Crassus in 130. The Romans called on their client states to provide troops. The consul Marcus Perperna defeated and captured Aristonicus, but died at Pergamum.[96] Manius Aquillius, consul of 129, subdued rebellious cities. A commission of ten men assisted Aquillius in organizing the kingdom.[97] An undated inscription refers to the collection of revenues in Pergamene territory, but although the text mentions Manius Aquillius, it does not prove when tax collection began because there was another Aquillius in Asia, consul in 101. A praetor and some troops governed the province of Asia. The eventual settlement may have been confirmed by the *lex Aufeia*, of which only a few details are known.[98] Pergamum was made friend and ally of the Roman people as reward for assistance against Andronicus, and the city along with Ephesus, Aphrodisias and Laodicea-on-Lycus were to be free allies of Rome. Some cities of Caria in the south-west of modern Turkey, and the Lycian League, in southern Turkey, became independent allies of Rome.[99]

The Romans were unwilling to make sweeping changes in the new province. Greek was the administrative language, but the province was multi-lingual. Aramaic and the native languages spoken before the Greeks arrived did not die out. Latin was a minority language, spoken in the veteran colonies, mostly founded by Augustus, and in the four Latin *municipia*.[100] Cities and towns of the new province were to govern themselves according to their own laws and customs, and as usual the Romans cultivated the wealthy elite, who were responsible for law and order, and those possessing lands paid for food and entertainments for the people. The city states possessed considerable freedom, as indicated by the number of communities issuing their own coins. Foreign policy was controlled by Rome and, at least in the later history of the province, administration of justice was also in Roman hands.[101]

The Romans would collect tribute, and revenues from port dues (*portoria*) and from the lands belonging to the Pergamene kings, declared public land and divided up to be rented out. Unfortunately, the tax farmers of Asia were notoriously extortionate, and when war broke out with Mithradates the inhabitants regarded him as their deliverer from Roman greed.[102]

## The province of Transalpine Gaul

The province of Gallia Transalpina was traditionally, but not certainly, established in 121, comprising Roussillon, Foix, Languedoc, the Dauphiné and Provence.[103] The Romans called it *Provincia* or The Province, hence the modern name Provence. The Romans were familiar with the territory because it was their route into Spain. The most important city was Massilia, founded at the end of the seventh century as an independent colony of Phocaean Greeks. Massilia founded further colonies, sometimes by military means, according to Strabo, three of them in Spain, at Hemeroscopeium, Emporium, and Rhodus, all situated between the river Sucro (Jucar) and Carthago Nova (Cartagena), protecting the area from Iberian tribes.[104] The furthest colony east of Massilia was at Nicaea (Nice), and the others were Tauroentium, Olbia, and Antipolis (Antibes), strongholds against the tribe of Sallyes, the Greek version of the Latin Salluvii, still called Salyens in French.[105] One of their chief places was the *oppidum* or town of Glanum (near St Rémy) which became a Roman city. Influenced by Massilians and Greek traders, the Gauls wrote their contracts in Greek and used Greek letters for their own language, and where Greek was firmly embedded Latin did not prevail even in Roman times.[106]

The Roman relationship with Massilia dated back probably to the early fourth century, when the Massilians sent help to Rome after the attack of the Gauls. There may have been a treaty between Rome and Massilia from that time. The Massilians did not join Hannibal, and in 218-217 they provided naval support for Gnaeus Scipio.[107] They assisted the Romans in 181 to eradicate pirates, mostly Ligurians in the Mediterranean, and Cilicians in the Adriatic. In 154 the consul Quintus Opimius fought the Ligurians west of the Alps because they had attacked the Massilian towns of Antipolis and Nicaea.[108]

Transalpine Gaul was probably an occupied military zone during the campaigns of 125 when the Massilians appealed to Rome for help against the Salluvii. It was suspected that Salluvian raids had been instigated by King Bituitus of the Arverni, a powerful tribe controlling a large area of Gaul and several smaller tribes. Marcus Fulvius Flaccus, friend of Gaius Gracchus and consul in 125, obtained the command late in the season, beginning the campaign in 124.[109] Flaccus fought successfully against Ligurians, Vocontii and Salluvii, and held a triumph over all three in 123. The next commander, Gaius Sextius Calvinus, established a fort close to hot springs. It became the town of Aquae Sextiae, the waters of Sextius (now Aix-en-Provence). It was close to the hilltop stronghold of Entremont, probably the tribal capital of the Salluvii, where archaeological investigations have revealed signs of siege and destruction, perhaps by Sextius, who drove the tribesmen back from the coast, giving the vacated lands to Massilia. He celebrated a triumph in 122.[110]

Salluvian survivors fled to the Allobroges, and around the same time, the Aedui, perhaps already friends of the Romans, complained that the Allobroges had devastated their lands. The Romans went to war against the Allobroges. Gnaeus Domitius Ahenobarbus, whom Livy calls proconsul, was commander.[111] King Bituitus of the Arverni asked pardon for the Salluvii, but Domitius refused to negotiate. In 121 he defeated the Allobroges, who were then joined by Arverni. Domitius asked for more troops. The consul Quintus Fabius Maximus arrived with about 30,000 men to face a horde of 180,000 Gauls. Ignoring the hyperbole, it was still a big battle, which Fabius won. Bituitus escaped, to be captured by Domitius. Both generals held triumphs, but the Allobroges surrendered to Fabius and it was the formal surrender rather than the victory that counted for the honour of a triumph. Fabius was the first of his family to become a patron of the Allobroges, who kept up their association with the Fabii for many years.[112] Domitius went on to establish the Via Domitia, west of the Rhone. The route had existed from prehistoric times, so it is assumed that Domitius gave it a better surface (not all Roman roads were paved). Domitius placed milestones along it, bearing his name. The road probably began at Ugernum (Beaucaire), running to Narbo Martius (Narbonne), and from there it continued into Spain, attested by the discovery of one of Domitius' milestones twenty miles south of Narbonne.[113]

The territory of Transalpine Gaul remained a military zone. There is no evidence that it was officially annexed and made a territorial province by Domitius in 121, the traditional foundation date. Gaius Marius may have organised the province when he was stationed east of the Rhone from 104 to 102. He dug a canal, the *Fossae Marianae* leading to the sea, probably at the modern Fos sur Mer.[114] Another candidate is Licinius Crassus who led colonists to Narbo in 118 and was proconsul in Gaul in 94. A third possibility is Gnaeus Pompeius Magnus, or Pompey the Great, commanding in Spain.[115] The date when Transalpine Gaul became a province is still not proven.[116]

## The War with Jugurtha

Of the three sons of Masinissa of Numidia, it was Micipsa who emerged as the most important, ruling alone after the death of his two brothers. He had two sons, Hiempsal and Adherbal, and eventually adopted his nephew Jugurtha, illegitimate son of Mastanabal.[117] Jugurtha was sent to Spain with the Numidian cavalry to assist Scipio Africanus at Numantia. After Micipsa's death in 118, Hiempsal, Adherbal and Jugurtha divided the kingdom. Jugurtha assassinated Hiempsal, and defeated Adherbal, who turned to Rome for help.[118] The Romans sent ten commissioners to Numidia, headed by Lucius Opimius, to oversee the division of the country into two, the eastern part for Adherbal, the western area for Jugurtha, bordering on the kingdom of Mauretania ruled by Bocchus, Jugurtha's father-in-law.

Jugurtha captured and killed Adherbal at Cirta (probably Constantine) by 112. The city was sacked, and Italian traders and businessmen living there were killed or injured.[119] The consul Lucius Calpurnius Bestia was assigned in 111 to Numidia.[120] Jugurtha already understood the power of money in dealing with Romans, and he pretended to surrender while in reality buying peace from Bestia.[121] Jugurtha was summoned to Rome, and Massiva, grandson of Masinissa, was encouraged to claim Numidia. Jugurtha arranged

Massiva's assassination by remote control from Rome. The consul Spurius Albinus renewed the war when Jugurtha went home.[122] Albinus returned to Rome for the elections, leaving his brother Aulus in command, but Jugurtha trapped Aulus and his army. From this position of strength, Jugurtha hoped for a treaty, but treaties were not arranged between Romans and victorious enemies.[123]

Quintus Caecilius Metellus was given the Numidian command in 109. Like a whirlwind he descended on Albinus' army, tightening up discipline, expelling camp followers, soldiers' slaves and excess baggage animals and carts, training the soldiers, setting them on route marches, and stopping looting and illegal requisitioning. Then he invaded Numidia, capturing Vaga, one of Jugurtha's main cities. Italian traders in residence were ordered to supply the army. After a battle with Jugurtha, who forced the Romans to take refuge on two hills, Metellus changed tactics, avoiding pitched battles and resorting to raiding farms and lands. Kings who failed to protect their people lost favour very quickly.[124] Jugurtha harassed the Romans rather than attacking, so Metellus decided to besiege Zama (not the one near Carthage). It was taken with difficulty. Metellus' command was prorogued.

One of Metellus' officers was Gaius Marius, a relatively unimportant cavalry commander.[125] He was a good soldier, but politically unremarkable. After serving as praetor in Rome in 115, he was proconsul in 114 governing Hispania Ulterior.[126] On his return from Spain he made a good marriage with Julia, sister of the elder Gaius Julius Caesar, thus becoming uncle of the younger and more famous Gaius Julius Caesar. Marius asked for leave to go to Rome for the consular elections, but Metellus advise him to wait, not what Marius wanted to hear. He set his friends in the army and trading communities to criticising Metellus' conduct of the war, and promoting himself as commander, boasting that he would have Jugurtha in chains within days.[127]

Marius arrived in Rome only a few days before the elections, but his friends had worked well on his behalf. Elected consul, Marius had to persuade the Senate to give him the command in Numidia.[128] Obtaining it, he called for volunteers, recruiting the *capite censi*, the poorest men counted by heads, not property, and Plutarch says that he recruited slaves.[129] Marius was blamed retrospectively for this, since men with no property looked to their commanders for assistance on discharge, making them loyal to the generals and not the state, and ultimately enabling these commanders to seize power.

Metellus had marched to Thala, home of Jugurtha's family and treasury. It took forty days to reduce the city, which was burned. Then he heard that Marius was to replace him.[130] Jugurtha had joined forces with his father-in-law Bocchus, but they split up as Marius arrived in 107. Marius gave his new troops experience by attacking scantily defended towns, and then attacked Capsa, loyal to Jugurtha. It was taken and burned, the adult males killed and the rest sold as slaves, the profit going to the soldiers.[131] Slave dealers were presumably close by, like vultures round a dying beast.

While Marius was attacking a hilltop fortress near the river Muluccha, the boundary between Numidia and Mauretania, his quaestor arrived, Lucius Cornelius Sulla, an aristocrat with hardly any money and even fewer scruples. He brought cavalry recruited in Italy. With no experience of war, he became one of the best soldiers in Marius' army.[132] The hill on which the fortress sat was too steep to climb, and the inhabitants destroyed siege engines by dropping rocks onto them. One of the Ligurian allies in Marius' army went to search for water around the side of the hill. Discovering a quantity of snails, he climbed up the cliff to gather them, eventually reaching the top overlooking the town, which was not guarded. He reported to Marius, and next day Marius launched a vigorous attack to distract the attention of the defenders, while the Ligurian led some soldiers to the top. The fortress was taken.[133] Jugurtha was now losing the faith of his people. He offered Bocchus part of his kingdom if he would join him. The two kings attacked Marius as he was heading for winter quarters on the coast, trapping the Romans on a hill. The night was spent in silence by the Romans and in rejoicing by the Numidians, who finally quieted down towards morning. Marius attacked them while they slept and routed them.[134]

Bocchus could tip the balance by joining Jugurtha or the Romans. He requested a meeting. Sulla attended it, and thereafter worked hard to persuade Bocchus to deliver up Jugurtha, so the war ended by treachery instead of battle.[135] Jugurtha was sent to Rome, imprisoned until he walked in Marius' triumph with his two sons. Then he was strangled, or possibly starved to death.

Numidia was not annexed. For some years after the Jugurthine war ended little is known about the country and its rulers, and the ancient historians lost interest in it, because other dangers threatened

Italy and Rome. Marius had persuaded Gauda, Jugurtha's brother or half-brother, that he would rule eastern Numidia once the Romans won, and in 105 the promise was fulfilled.[136] Three more names of rulers are known, Mastanabal II, Hiempsal II, and Hiempsal's son Juba I, who was king until 46, when the eastern part of Numidia was annexed and named Africa Nova, tacked onto the old province, now renamed Africa Vetus. Both were made into a single province, Africa Proconsularis, by Augustus.

Bocchus retained western Mauretania, succeeded by his two sons Bogud and Bocchus II, who split the kingdom between them. Bogud joined Mark Antony, on the losing side against Octavian-Augustus, so Bocchus II ruled a united Mauretania until 33, bequeathing it to Rome. In 25 Juba II was installed as king, married to Cleopatra Selene, daughter of Cleopatra VII and Mark Antony. Ptolemy, son of this marriage, succeeded them. Mauretania was not annexed until AD 44 by the Emperor Claudius, who divided it into Mauretania Caesariensis in the east and Mauretania Tingitana in the west, bordered by the Atlantic.

## Rome's other wars

While the major wars were going on the Romans also fought in wars serious enough to warrant consular commanders. These events take a back seat to the more important wars and the political upheavals at Rome. The sources provide hardly any information about the provinces, what was happening and who administered them, infinitely more boring than battles and heroic deeds.

There was ongoing trouble in Illyricum, where the Dalmatians raided Rome's subjects. In 156 the consul Marcius Figulus conducted the war, suffering a setback when the tribesmen attacked the troops laying out the camp. The Romans scattered, but later Figulus drove the tribesmen into Delminium, the origin of their tribal name. The town was too elevated for effective use of siege engines, so Figulus attacked other towns, then returned to Delminium and took it by catapulting burning brands into the town and setting it on fire. Appian says the war ended then, but Livy includes a campaign in 155 led by the consul Cornelius Nasica, who held a triumph. Much later in 119 Lucius Caecilius Metellus fought the Dalmatians, but while Livy says that Metellus subdued them, Appian says that Metellus wintered with the Dalmatians as a guest at Salona. Both authors agree that Metellus held a triumph in 117, and that he took the name Delmaticus.[137]

The Illyrians under Roman protection were raided by other Illyrian tribesmen, who refused to comply when Roman ambassadors arrived to stop their raids. In 135/134 the Romans collected 10,000 infantry and 600 cavalry to make war on the tribes, who sent ambassadors to say they were sorry but declined to make reparations to those they robbed. Appian describes the subsequent campaign under the consul Gaius Fulvius Flaccus as only a raid, though Livy credits Flaccus with a victory.[138]

According to Appian, Gaius Sempronius Tuditanus, consul for 129, and Tiberius Pandusa subdued the Iapydae living south of the Alps, but Livy says Tuditanus was unsuccessful at first, and Decimus Junius Brutus repaired the damage. All the same, Tuditanus triumphed over the 'Iapudae'.[139] Other tribes are listed fleetingly, such as the Sardi of Sardinia who had risen in arms and were defeated by the consul Lucius Aurelius Orestes, who held a triumph in 122.[140] The consul for 118, Quintus Marcius, routed the Styni of the Alps, triumphing over them as the 'Ligurian Stoeni'.[141]

In Thrace, the most troublesome people were the Scordisci, who defeated the consul Gaius Porcius in 114, possibly in Macedonia. The tribesmen ventured into Greece, reaching Delphi.[142] In 113 Gaius Caecilius Metellus held off the Scordisci, defeated in 112-111 by Livius Drusus, consul of 112. In 109/108 the proconsul Minucius Rufus, consul in 110, defeated the Thracians, but the majority were probably Scordisci.[143] Wars against this tribe were not ended until Augustus' reign.

5

# From Marius to Pompey and the New Eastern Provinces

Towards the end of the second century the Germanic Cimbri, Teutones and Ambrones, not yet acting in concert, began to move towards the Roman world from what is now Jutland, where the sea was gradually inundating the lands, forcing the people to find new homes. In 114/113 the tribes plundered Illyricum, then moved into Noricum, not yet a Roman province but uncomfortably close to northern Italy. The consul Papirius Carbo was defeated in 113, probably near Noreia (Neumark, Austria).[1] In 110/109 the Cimbri asked the Romans for lands on which to settle but were refused. Moving on, the tribesmen defeated the consul Marcus Junius Silanus in the Rhone valley.[2]

The greatest disaster came in 105 at Arausio (Orange) in Gaul, when the Cimbri defeated the consuls Gnaeus Mallius/Manlius and Quintus Servilius Caepio in a battle fought on both sides of the river Rhone. 80,000 Romans died, together with 40,000 servants and camp followers (*calones* and *lixae*).[3] Caepio was prosecuted for not helping Mallius and his property was confiscated.[4] The Cimbri marched into Spain. Gaius Marius was still in Africa. He was elected consul for 104 *in absentia*, and assigned to Gaul, but first he triumphed over Jugurtha. He wore his triumphal finery to attend a meeting of the Senate, upsetting the senators.

Marius marched to Transalpine Gaul to await the return of the Cimbri from Spain. It was the native Celtiberians who forced them out. While waiting, Marius tightened up discipline in the standard manner, banishing hangers-on, carts and pack animals, and making the soldiers carry their entrenching tools, rations for at least three days, and pots and pans for cooking. They called themselves Marius's

138

mules. He set his soldiers digging a canal to the sea to bring in supplies, and he built a fortified camp near the Rhone to protect his stores.[5] Publius Rutilius Rufus, consul for 105, had reassembled the survivors after Arausio and had trained them to fight like gladiators. Marius liked what he saw, adopted the same methods, and got the credit, but he acknowledged Rutilius' contribution in 104 by selecting his better trained and disciplined troops for his army.[6] Marius finalised the change from maniples to cohorts and introduced the single legionary standard, the eagle, or *aquila*, abandoning the five standards possibly associated with the five so-called Servian classes.

Back in Rome, Marius entered his fourth consulship for 102, then returned to the army in time for the reappearance of the Cimbri, one group moving around the Alps to meet the other consul, Lutatius Catulus, in Noricum, and another group entering Transalpine Gaul, where they joined the Teutones and Ambrones coming through Ligurian territory.[7] Marius kept his soldiers in camp until the Teutones and possibly the Ambrones moved off. He followed, fortifying camps at each halt. At Aquae Sextiae (Aix-en-Provence) the tribesmen were defeated in two battles. Plutarch comments that there were enough bones to make the fields fertile for years.[8] Marius was awarded a triumph and elected consul *in absentia* for 101. In the meantime, Catulus had been pushed back into Italy and Marius joined him, abandoning the triumph. The Cimbri waited for the Teutones, not knowing of their defeat at Aquae Sextiae.[9]

For the coming battle Marius is said to have adapted the *pilum*, removing one of the two metal pins which secured the iron head to the shaft, replacing it with a wooden pin which broke easily, so that when the *pilum* embedded itself in an enemy's shield it dropped down, making the shield too cumbersome to use. If this is so, he was not the innovator, since archaeological remains from Numantia reveal bent *pila* of Scipio Aemilianus' day. In summer 101 Marius and Catulus defeated the tribesmen at Vercellae (Vercelli) in Cisalpine Gaul.[10]

## Marius, Saturninus and Glaucia

Marius obtained his sixth consulship in 100, accused of bribery.[11] A better general than politician, he chose the wrong associates, Lucius Saturninus, tribune for the second time in 100, and Gaius Servilius Glaucia, praetor in the same year. These two were already blacklisted, and the censors of 102 argued over removing these men from the list of senators but refrained because trouble would have followed.[12]

The ancient sources roundly condemn Saturninus and Glaucia as black-hearted villains passing their legislation by violence and eliminating rivals. It cannot be denied that it could be fatal to get in their way. There are different versions of what happened in 101 when Aulus Nunnius (or Ninnius or Nonius) took the tenth and last place in the elections for the tribunes for 100, leaving Saturninus out in the cold, but we know Nonius was dead by next day.[13]

Some of Saturninus' and Glaucia's laws were designed to assist provincials, not to damage the state. The *lex Servilia de pecuniis repetundis* was probably introduced by Glaucia as tribune in 101, to help provincials to recover stolen money.[14] The law made it illegal for jurors to vote repeatedly that they were unsure of the judgement, thus necessitating retrials until the prosecution gave up. The new law limited retrials to two, and then jurors must vote for acquittal or condemnation. Another clause amended the *lex de repetundis* which allowed prosecution only of magistrates, not non-magistrates, so the guilty men could put stolen money into the hands of a non-magistrate who was promised his cut. Glaucia's law facilitated prosecution of whoever ended up with the cash (*quo ea pecunia pervenerit*) and the provincials could be reimbursed. All the jurors were to be *equites*, not senators.[15]

## Laws concerning provincial government

Another law dating from 101-100 is known from a Greek inscription found at Delphi in the nineteenth century in which the surviving text was devoted to combatting Mediterranean pirates, so it was labelled the pirate law. A similar inscription concerning the same law was discovered in 1970 at Cnidus on the Aegean coast of Asia Minor. It revealed that the law was more extensive than previously thought, so it is renamed the *lex de provinciis praetoriis*, about praetorian provinces, not necessarily confined to annexed territorial provinces and concerning praetors' responsibilities for organising provincial affairs and/or commanding troops. The surviving sections concern only Asia, Macedonia and Cilicia. It is possible that the missing text covered all the praetorian provinces.

Extant ancient literature ignores the *lex de provinciis praetoriis*, which was rooted in the context of 101-100. It stated that new levies were not to be sent to Macedonia and that praetors governing this province were obliged to oversee the collection of tribute, and to spend sixty days visiting the Caenic Chersonese, recently added to

Macedonia on its south-eastern side. The governor of Asia was to secure Lycaeonia situated to the south-east of the province, perhaps already acquired and requiring pacification, but it is suggested that the governor of Asia was to operate there in conjunction with Marcus Antonius (grandfather of Mark Antony) who was campaigning against pirates in Cilicia.[16] Cilicia was not annexed until *c*.80, but the law designated it a praetorian task because the country was needed as a base for the pirate campaign. The law instructed the consuls to foster good relations with Rhodes and the kings and rulers around the Mediterranean who could assist against pirates.

The law repeats or augments parts of the *lex Porcia*, predating 100, outlining the duties of provincial governors, who were not to move outside their provinces except for reasons of state or for travelling to fulfil certain tasks. The regulation presupposes the establishment of borders clarifying where a province ended and another province or a non-Roman territory began. If an appointed governor was absent from his province, the man taking his place was to take on his full powers of jurisdiction.

The *lex Porcia* and the *lex de provinciis praetoriis* are the first known attempts to provide a general framework for provincial government.[17] Now at last, after about 130 years of ruling territories outside Italy, some Romans were trying to bring regulation and order to the whole.

### Land allotments and the fall of Saturninus and Glauca

Saturninus tried, probably unsuccessfully, to revive Gaius Gracchus' law to distribute grain at low prices. He proposed, in the teeth of opposition, to provide lands for Marius' veterans and those who had fought in northern Italy, Greece and Sicily. Allotments were proposed for Roman citizens in Cisalpine Gaul and colonies were to be established, probably for the Italian allies. Marius was authorized to bestow citizenship on a limited number of new colonists. He had spontaneously bestowed citizenship on 1,000 allied soldiers from Camerinum (Camerino in Umbria), who had showed exceptional bravery. When told this was illegal, he said that he could not hear the law in the noise of battle.[18] He was the first to bestow citizenship in this way, and other commanders would emulate him. When the law was put to the vote, Saturninus posted Marius' veterans to guard the assembly area, and there was some fighting.[19] Saturninus forced the senators to swear an oath to uphold the laws. This was neither unusual nor illegal. Caecilius Metellus Numidicus, inimical to Marius for filching the command against Jugurtha, refused to swear the oath. Saturninus proposed a law to banish Metellus, who went voluntarily to Rhodes. Penalties were prescribed for anyone attempting to recall Metellus.[20]

When Saturninus stood for re-election as tribune for 99, he also tried to obtain the consulship for Glaucia, but as a serving praetor Glaucia could not legally stand for election, and Marius, as consul presiding over the elections, disallowed his candidacy. Saturninus proposed a law to overturn Marius' objection, and in the ensuing riot Memmius, another consular candidate, was killed. It was a step too far, and Saturninus, Glaucia and their followers took refuge on the Capitol. Somebody cut the water supply. The Senate passed the decree authorising the consuls to secure the state, and Marius persuaded Saturninus and Glaucia to surrender to him, promising that there would be no executions. He locked them into the Senate House. There are different versions of how they were killed.[21] Marius left Rome when his consulship ended, to visit Cappadocia and Galatia to honour the Mother Goddess to whom he had prayed during the battles against the Cimbri. Plutarch suspects Marius of stirring up the Asian cities against Mithradates VI of Pontus to cause a war, for which he wanted the command.[22]

### Marcus Livius Drusus

Drusus was tribune of the plebs in 91. His father, also Marcus Livius Drusus, had proposed settlements on the land and citizenship for the allies, in opposition to Gaius Gracchus. The younger Livius Drusus resurrected the proposal to provide cheap grain and proposed a restructure of the juries for the courts. The *equites* had been put in charge of the *de pecuniis repetundis* courts by Glaucia's law, but showed a malevolent bias against senators on trial, so Drusus suggested that 300 *equites* should be added to the Senate, possibly imagining that this would reduce biased judgements, but it turned senators and *equites* against him.[23]

Drusus advocated the establishment of colonies in Italy and Sicily, pleasing the Roman people, but worrying the Italians because the establishment of colonies might encroach on their cultivated lands.[24] Almost as an afterthought, Drusus proposed Roman citizenship for the Latins and the Italian allies.[25] After 125, Latins who had served as magistrates on their town councils automatically became Roman citizens, but other people found illegal methods of obtaining Roman

142

citizenship. The consuls of 95, Lucius Licinius Crassus and Quintus Mucius Scaevola, passed the *lex Licinia Mucia* establishing a *quaestio* to investigate false claimants. This was simply to prove or disprove legal status, not to remove people from Rome, or to exclude them from citizenship in the future.[26]

One evening an unknown assailant stabbed Drusus to death.[27] Afterwards the *equites* persuaded the tribune Quintus Varius to pass a law to prosecute anyone who helped Italians to gain citizenship. The real target was not Italians, but senators who favoured them. Other tribunes vetoed the bill, but the *equites* wielded daggers, so it was passed. Prosecutions of senators began immediately, and some went into exile. Mummius, destroyer of Corinth, went to Delos, forever. Italians noted Roman attitudes.

## The Social War

The title Social War derives from *socii*, allies, specifically Italians. It is suggested that the war involved more than a demand for citizenship. Perhaps the Italians wanted complete independence from Rome, possibly a new state with Rome obliterated. These and further suggestions are lucidly discussed by Christopher Dart.[28]

The Italians formed a league and exchanged hostages for good faith.[29] They chose Corfinium as their capital, renaming it Italica, with a Senate and magistrates. Coins were issued with legends in Oscan, the most common language among the allies. States which did not want war were coerced.[30] The Greek states of the south kept clear of trouble. Of the Latin colonies, only Venusia joined the Italians. In some communities the aristocrats favoured Rome, and the people favoured the Italians. Livy and Appian list the principal rebels, who could muster 100,000 soldiers.[31] One of the commanders mentioned most frequently was Quintus Poppaedius/Pompaedius Silo, the leader (*dux*) of the Marsi, and the originator (*auctor*) of the war. Poppaedius features in Plutarch's life of Marius, who remained in camp even when encircled by a ditch. Poppaedius challenged him: 'If you are a great commander, come out and fight.' Marius replied, 'If you are a great commander, make me fight.'[32]

The Romans, deprived of allied troops, had to recruit from elsewhere. Troops were raised from Cisalpine Gaul, Spain, Sicily and Numidia. Gauls and Spaniards served in the army of Gnaeus Pompeius Strabo, who awarded Roman citizenship in November 89 to some Spanish cavalry.[33] Appian says that Numidian and Mauretanian infantry and cavalry and 10,000 Gallic infantry served in the Roman army, but he confuses the activities of the consul of 91, Sextus Caesar, with those of the consul of 90, Lucius Caesar.[34] Eventually, the Romans had to enrol freedmen in 89, and freedmen also garrisoned the west coast, and the coastal cities of Greece and Asia Minor provided ships.[35]

The war began probably at the end of 91, and Plutarch says dramatically that it nearly obliterated the hegemony of Rome.[36] Requiring several commanders all over Italy the Senate appointed *legati*, deputies of the consuls. In 90 the consuls, Publius Rutilius Lupus and Lucius Julius Caesar, were each assisted by five legates.[37]

Appian explains that in those days proconsular praetors governed parts of Italy. The proconsular praetor nearest to Asculum was Quintus Servilius, who was informed of suspicious activity in this town. He went to investigate.[38] The Italians thought that the rebellion had been discovered. Servilius was killed along with his legate Fonteius, and all other Romans living in the town. Subsequently, there was a string of defeats for the Romans. The consul Rutilius and many of his men were ambushed and killed, and after the funerals in Rome the Senate decreed that the dead should be buried where they lay, to avoid such depressing sights in the city.[39]

The first Roman victories were over the Marsi at Firmum.[40] Asculum provided refuge for Italians, so Pompeius Strabo besieged the place. He was succeeded by the proconsul Sextus Caesar, who died there.[41] The Etruscans and Umbrians joined the rebellion late in 90, separately defeated by Lucius Porcius Cato and the legate Aulus Plotius. Via the *lex Julia* of Lucius Julius Caesar the Romans finally offered citizenship to those who had kept to their alliance.[42] The offer of citizenship was accepted by some, but it did not stop the fighting. Lucius Cornelius Sulla's reports, as relayed by Appian, tell how Sulla unsuccessfully attacked the Italian Lucius Cluentius, then won a victory, besieged Nola, defeated the Hirpini, killed many Samnites and took Bovianum, where the rebel council was now held because Corfinium was in Roman hands.[43] Sulla returned to Rome for the consular elections for 88, and during that winter Marius subdued the Marsi, Marrucini and Vestini.[44]

The *lex Plautia Papiria* of 89 was passed by the tribunes Marcus Plautius Silvanus and Gaius Papirius Carbo, offering Roman citizenship to all the allies enrolled in Italian towns and currently living in Italy, provided that they applied to the urban praetor within sixty days. The Transpadane Gauls north of the Po were awarded Latin rights by the consul Gnaeus Pompeius Strabo, and Marius may have bestowed Latin rights on some of the Ligurian tribes living south of the Po.[45] Strabo was able to bring the war to an end in the north by a combination of diplomacy and fighting.

Fighting continued into 88, but this year marks the end of the Social War as far as Appian, Livy and other ancient authors were concerned. The Samnites and Lucanians held out for much longer, and the fighting against them segued into the civil wars of Marius and Sulla. In 87 the Samnites were exhausted, but still refused Roman citizenship, and the Lucanians tried to seize Sicily rather than surrender.[46]

The conversion of Italians into Roman citizens was still going on in 49, when Julius Caesar reorganised Italy. There was no census between 86 and 70, so newly enfranchised people were not assessed for their property class qualifying them for the centuriate assembly. In 86 the census recorded 463,000 citizens. In 70 there were 900,000 adult male citizens, according to Livy. Other sources differ.[47] Unless there had been a massively increased birth rate and decreased death rate, the figures must represent the addition of the Italians. The enfranchised Latins were distributed in sixteen tribes, but the Italians were placed in only a few of the thirty-one rural tribes, which restricted their voting power, and agitation for their distribution among all the tribes became a sensitive issue for future generations of politicians.[48]

The Italian states would become self-governing *municipia*, subject to Roman law but without making sweeping changes to their political organisation.[49] Roman officials probably organised the establishment of *municipia* and the installation of their first magistrates. Some fragments of different municipal charters have survived, and sufficient details have been gleaned from them to indicate that there was probably a uniform template or set of guidelines, perhaps outlined in the *lex Plautia Papiria*, but it seems that in usual Roman fashion it was not a case of one-size-fits-all. Local magistrates could alter their charters according to local circumstances.[50] The territory of the *municipia* would have to be properly defined, and in the case of tribal peoples, their chief town or *oppidum* would become their administrative centre.

## Lucius Cornelius Sulla

Sulla was born in 138 to a thoroughly patrician family without wealth or prestige. Between his service under Marius in Africa and his self-advertised heroics in the Social War, Sulla served in the war against the Cimbri, and was at the final battle at Vercellae. He served as aedile in Rome, excelling his predecessors in putting on games and shows, reducing the lion population of Africa when his friend King Bocchus sent him quantities of animals to be slaughtered for the entertainment of the people. Dates are not certain for his term as urban praetor or as propraetor in Cilicia. Between 96 and 92 he conducted a diplomatic mission to re-install Ariobarzanes, dislodged as king of Cappadocia by Mithradates VI of Pontus. Plutarch says that Sulla's real mission was to watch Mithradates.[51]

From the end of the second century, Mithradates steadily extended his control of territories and peoples around the Black Sea, the Euxine Sea in Greek, perhaps a propitiatory title, meaning 'hospitable sea', exactly what it isn't. Paphlagonia, south of the Black Sea was divided *c.*107, one part added to Mithradates' kingdom of Pontus to the east and the other to Nicomedes' kingdom of Bithynia to the west. Rome protested but was not in any position to intervene while fighting Jugurtha and then the Cimbri.[52] During the Social War in Italy, Mithradates annexed Bithynia and Cappadocia, dislodging Ariobarzanes yet again.

The Romans said they would help Nicomedes and Ariobarzanes if they warred against Mithradates, and war began. Lucius Cassius assembled his army, split into three divisions, commanded by himself, Manius Aquillius and Quintus Oppius. Nicomedes of Bithynia provided infantry and cavalry. Mithradates had an enormous army and 500 ships, but the Roman fleet guarded the mouth of the Black Sea, closing it to ships from Pontus. Nicomedes was the first to engage and the first to be defeated, and Manius Aquillius was next, finally killed at Pergamum.[53] The son of Mithradates, Ariarathes, was now threatening Macedonia and Thrace, and the Athenians, unhappy with the government installed by the Romans, went over to Mithradates. Many Romans and Italians were killed, including those on the island of Delos when it was captured by Mithradates' naval commander Archelaus.[54] Later, in 88 Mithradates failed in his attempt to gain control of Rhodes.[55]

The command against Mithradates was assigned by lot to Sulla, consul in 88. Marius teamed up with the tribune Publius Sulpicius, labelled by Plutarch as a perfect tool for destroying the state.[56] Sulpicius' agenda included recall of exiles, distribution of the Italians among all the thirty-five tribes, and the removal of Sulla from his command in favour of Marius.[57] Sulla and Pompeius Rufus suspended all public business. During the ensuing riot Sulla had to run for his life, famously ending up in Marius' house, and was forced to rescind the suspension of public business.[58] Removed from their commands, both consuls headed for the army at Nola, and Marius obtained the Mithradatic command, but his military tribunes attempting to take over the army were killed.[59] Sulla's response was to lead his army to Rome. Of his officers, only his quaestor Lucius Licinius Lucullus agreed to accompany him across the *pomerium* of the city in arms. Pompeius Rufus guarded the Colline gate while Sulla commanded at the Esquiline gate. Marius and Sulpicius gathered troops and met Sulla's forces, lost the battle, and left Rome.[60] Sulla restored order. One measure was to declare the Marians enemies of the state. All Sulpicius' legislation was annulled.[61]

Marius narrowly escaped death more than once, ending up in Africa, where his landing was prevented by the praetor Sextilius commanding the province and unwilling to be embroiled in the political turmoil. Marius moved on to Numidia, joined by some supporters.[62]

### Sulla and Mithradates VI Eupator

As Sulla prepared for war, he sent Pompeius Rufus to take over the army of Gnaeus Pompeius Strabo in Italy but he was killed, and Strabo was blamed for his death.[63] Sulla feared for his safety, joined the army at Capua, and continued to Asia in 87 with his quaestor Licinius Lucullus.[64] The new consuls for 87, Lucius Cornelius Cinna and Gnaeus Octavius, had sworn under oath that they would not alter Sulla's legislation.[65] Cinna had no intention of keeping the oath. With luck, Sulla might get killed.

Achaea, Sparta, Boeotia and Athens had gone over to Mithradates, whose naval commander Archelaus held Piraeus, the port for Athens.[66] From autumn 87 to spring 86, Sulla besieged Piraeus, eventually resorting to blockade and starvation. Then he turned his attention to Athens, sending Lucullus to Alexandria and Syria to find ships.[67] On 1 March 86, Athens, but not the Acropolis, surrendered, amid tremendous slaughter.[68] Ordering Gaius Scribonius Curio to besiege the Acropolis, Sulla burnt Piraeus, drove off Archelaus and followed him into Thessaly, defeating him at Chaeronea.[69] It was Plutarch's birthplace and he provides great detail about this battle.

Thanks to Cinna, Sulla was now *hostis*, but his family escaped and joined him in Greece, along with several Romans. Plutarch says that Sulla was surrounded by a veritable Senate.[70] A Roman army under the consul Lucius Valerius Flaccus was despatched to Greece, which Sulla naturally interpreted as an effort to replace him. Before encountering Flaccus, Sulla won a second battle against Archelaus at Orchomenus.[71] After this defeat, Mithradates ordered Archelaus to make peace but then rejected some of the terms. He still controlled the Aegean and Sulla had no ships.[72] Archelaus tired of Mithradates and turned to Sulla, becoming an official friend and ally of the Roman people.

Appian portrays Flaccus as greedy for gain and Livy reports that the soldiers hated him.[73] Gaius Flavius Fimbria, of unknown rank, may have instigated the mutiny in which Flaccus was killed.[74] Fimbria easily took over the army, defeating the commanders of Mithradates one by one, and then four of them all at once at the river Rhyndacus. By the middle of 85 Mithradates sued for peace, with Sulla, not with Fimbria, who was still pursuing the war. Sulla and Mithradates met at Dardanus in north-west Asia, south of the Hellespont. Mithradates was to be a friend of the Roman people and was to keep his kingdom of Pontus, minus the lands he had overrun. Bithynia and Cappadocia were to be restored to their kings. The Romans demanded 2,000 talents according to Plutarch, 3,000 talents in another source.[75] Eighty ships were surrendered to the Romans. Urgently needing to return to Rome to avoid political annihilation, Sulla was vividly aware that the war had not reached the optimum conclusion. Mithradates also thought the war unfinished, and when the Romans refused to ratify the treaty of Dardanus, he was certain.

Fimbria, who had done much to end the war, committed suicide when his soldiers deserted to Sulla.[76] These men formed the garrison of Asia under Lucius Licinius Murena, commander of the left wing of Sulla's army at Chaeronea.[77] Spending the winter of 84 in Greece, Sulla began the settlement of the disrupted areas, declaring freedom for the people who had co-operated with the Romans, or had suffered damage because of supporting them. These were made friends of the Roman people. Appian names Ilium, Chios, Lycia, Rhodes, Magnesia 'and others'.[78] Elsewhere, cities and communities of Cappadocia were punished for siding with Mithradates.

Sulla convened a meeting with leading citizens of Asia at Ephesus, where he reminded them that the Romans had freed them from Antiochus and left them free. He enumerated their crimes, emphasizing the massacre of Romans and Italians in Asia. He demanded a total of 20,000 talents and billeted his troops on their cities to keep order, and the soldiers reduced their hosts to penury.[79] Five years' tax was to be paid immediately, plus his expenses in waging the war and settling the province of Asia. The cities had already suffered the depredations of the Roman tax collectors and then Mithradates, so the citizens had to borrow from Roman bankers to pay the Roman general. It did not win hearts and minds in Asia.

## Factional strife in Rome

Gnaeus Octavius and Lucius Cornelius Cinna, consuls of 87, opposed each other from the start. Cinna tried to push through legislation to distribute the Italians among all the voting tribes. He was blocked by tribunes who were probably purchased by Octavius. The citizens rioted. Plutarch calls it open warfare.[80] Octavius organised a senatorial decree to deprive Cinna of his consulship. Cinna left the city and began to recruit soldiers. Octavius arranged the election of Lucius Cornelius Merula, *flamen dialis*, a priest, but so set about with rules and regulations that he could hardly operate as consul.[81]

Subsequent events are confused. This is Appian's version: the consuls sent for Gnaeus Pompeius Strabo, commanding in the north. He camped with his troops outside the Colline Gate. Marius left Africa with fellow exiles and 500 slaves, joining Cinna with 6,000 Etruscans. Marius, Cinna, Carbo and Quintus Sertorius besieged Rome. The consuls sent for Metellus Pius, commanding an army against Samnites still fighting the Social War. Marius and Cinna muscled in, agreeing to grant whatever the Samnites wanted and making them allies, but both men were sent packing by Octavius and Strabo.[82] Soon afterwards Strabo died, from plague or a lightning strike, or as a result of a plot.[83]

Plutarch's version tells how Marius arrived in Italy with Moorish cavalry, Italians from Africa, and forty ships with crews, which blocked food supplies to Rome. They captured coastal towns, sacked Ostia and occupied the Janiculum in Rome. Metellus Pius arrived, but when Octavius' soldiers tried to go over to him, he left Rome in despair.[84] Merula committed suicide and Octavius was killed. His head was displayed in front of the Rostra, together with heads of other senators. Without benefit of election by the people, or by elections held with only two candidates, in 86 Cinna and Marius became consuls.[85] Carnage followed as Marius and Cinna eliminated their enemies, but Marius died after a consulship of seventeen days.[86] Livy wondered whether his services in war outweighed the damage he caused in peace.[87]

Cinna was consul for the third time in 85, with Gnaeus Papirius Carbo as colleague. They raised an army and made certain of their re-election for 84. Sulla had written to the Senate recounting all his achievements and hinting about vengeance. The Senate, momentarily resuming control, sent an embassy to Sulla and halted the recruiting until his reply was received.[88] Cinna and Carbo intended to fight Sulla in Greece, but Cinna was killed at Ancona in a mutiny, leaving Carbo as sole consul. There was no choice now except to fight Sulla in Italy. He arrived in spring 83 with five legions, 6000 cavalry, and 1,600 ships (1,200 according to Plutarch). The people of Brundisium were too wise to try to stop him and were later exempted from customs dues.[89]

## Civil war in Italy

Sulla's troops were experienced and loyal. Opposing him were the troops recruited by the consuls Lucius Cornelius Scipio Asiaticus and Gaius Norbanus, and ex-consul Papirius Carbo. Supporting Sulla, Marcus Licinius Crassus had escaped the Marians by going to Spain and then had joined Metellus Pius in Africa, but they quarrelled. Crassus set off in 84 to join Sulla before he sailed for Italy.[90] Metellus Pius returned from Africa and Gnaeus Pompeius, twenty-three-year-old son of Pompeius Strabo, recruited a legion from his estates in Picenum. He later raised two more. Before Sulla arrived, Pompey had defeated three armies sent against him by Carbo.[91] Meeting Sulla, Pompey hailed him as Imperator and Sulla returned the compliment, endorsing Pompey as independent commander.[92]

Sulla defeated the consul Norbanus and negotiated with the other consul, Lucius Scipio, whose men came over to Sulla. Scipio and his son went free.[93] One of Scipio's officers, Quintus Sertorius, set off for Spain, where he soon established himself with an army.[94]

Papirius Carbo entered his third consulship in 82, with the under-age Gaius Marius, nephew of the elder Marius. At Signia (Segni) most of young Marius' troops deserted him when facing Sulla. The remaining soldiers and Marius ran to Praeneste, where the gates were closed before everyone had entered. Marius was hauled up by ropes, but everyone left outside was killed or captured. The Samnites among them were all killed on Sulla's orders. Sulla ordered Lucretius Ofella/Afella) to blockade Praeneste. Carbo sent eight legions to relieve the city, but Pompey ambushed them. Lucanians and Samnites coming to aid Praeneste were driven off and Marius' attempts to break out were foiled.[95]

Sulla ordered affairs in Rome, installed a garrison, and pursued Carbo, fighting indecisively at Clusium. The governors of Spain sent Celtiberian cavalry for the Marians, but 270 of them joined Sulla.[96] Discouraged, the consul Norbanus sailed to Rhodes, while Carbo sailed to Africa leaving his soldiers near Clusium to be overwhelmed by Pompey. Lucius Philippus took over Sardinia, killing the praetor Quintus Antonius Balbus, and Quintus Sertorius controlled parts of Spain for some years.[97] Thus the war spread into the provinces.

With Pompey commanding in the north, Sulla and Licinius Crassus headed for Rome, racing against Carbo's abandoned officers and Samnites. Near the Colline gate Sulla faced the Samnites and all was very nearly lost.[98] Sulla thought that Crassus was dead, but that evening, some of Crassus' soldiers arrived, requesting the men's dinner. Crassus had driven the enemy off and chased them into Antemnae. He had saved the day.

Marius committed suicide when Praeneste surrendered, and his head was sent to Rome. The Romans at Praeneste were told they deserved death, but they were freed. Everyone else was killed. Representatives of the soldiers driven into Antemnae asked for peace. Sulla promised them their lives if they attacked the people of the town, which they did, but soldiers and civilian survivors were taken to Rome and herded into the Circus Maximus. Nearby at the temple of Bellona, Sulla met the senators, calmly reporting on the war against Mithradates to the accompaniment of screams from hundreds of prisoners being killed by his soldiers. A few criminals being executed, said Sulla, not batting an eyelid. The Romans realised that they had exchanged one monstrous tyranny for another.[99]

### Sulla's regime

Sulla eliminated opponents without opposition, until some senators asked him either to list those to be spared or those who were to be removed, so proscription lists were posted up, the proceedings to end on 1 June 81. Cash rewards were given to the murderers, unless they were slaves, who received freedom. The property of the proscribed was sold at auction, to the tune of 350,000,000 sesterces for the state.[100]

Italians who had held commands under the Marians were searched out and Sulla destroyed pro-Marian communities through crippling fines, or by demolition of walls and buildings. Elsewhere, he installed garrisons. His opponents were hunted down in the provinces. Metellus Pius fought Sertorius in Spain, and the Senate obligingly bestowed propraetorian powers on Pompey to command troops against Carbo, who had moved from Africa to Sicily, governed by the confirmed Marian, Marcus Peperna, or Perpenna. As Pompey took possession of Sicily, Perperna fled and Carbo was captured and executed.[101] From this episode Pompey earned his reputation as *adulescentulus carnifex*, or the boy butcher, but this label was only applied much later, in a speech by Helvius of Formiae.[102] Plutarch says that Pompey had no choice except to punish well-known enemies of Sulla but adds that Pompey also let several people escape, citing the case of the people of Himera, on the north coast of Sicily. Pompey arrived to punish them, but their spokesman Sthenius said that it was unfair to punish innocent people while letting the guilty person go free. 'Who is the guilty person?' asked Pompey, and Sthenius said it was himself, because he had persuaded the inhabitants to act as they did. Pompey pardoned Sthenius and everyone else.[103]

Pompey's brother-in-law Memmius was put in charge in Sicily, and on Sulla's orders Pompey went to Africa where Domitius Ahenobarbus commanded the refugee Marians. The legitimate governor Gaius Fabius Hadrianus had been burned to death in a riot at Utica.[104] Domitius allied with Hiarbas, currently but not legally king of Numidia. Pompey split his forces into two groups, landing at Utica and Carthage, and instead of meeting an army he found 7,000 deserters wanting to join him. For a while there was no fighting because one of Pompey's soldiers found a pile of coins in the sand, so the troops spent all their time and energy in digging holes. Pompey let them exhaust themselves until they were ready to fight.[105]

Domitius was entrenched behind difficult ground, with no intention of moving, but eventually both sides drew up their forces for battle. A rainstorm began and Domitius gave the order to return to camp, not expecting Pompey to attack, but he did, and Domitius was killed. The soldiers hailed Pompey as Imperator, but he refused the victory title because the war was not finished. He obeyed orders to remove Hiarbas and reinstate Hiempsal, the legitimate king of Numidia.[106] Pompey now had useful friends, Sthenius in Sicily and Hiempsal in Numidia. The soldiers called him Magnus, the Great, perhaps after a hint from Pompey, exploiting his resemblance to Alexander the Great.[107] When Pompey returned home with his army, Sulla also addressed him as Magnus.

Pompey demanded a triumph. Sulla reminded him of his youth, and lack of senatorial status. Pompey replied that more people worshipped the rising than the setting sun. While onlookers clamped their lower jaws back into position, Sulla asked him to repeat what he had said. He did. After a silence, Sulla shouted 'Let him triumph!'[108] Sulla had judged Pompey correctly. He wanted glory and recognition, but not supreme power. Not yet, anyway. Pompey was the youngest ever *triumphator* and the only equestrian.[109] Since Romans did not triumph over Romans, Pompey triumphed over Hiarbas, a suitably foreign enemy. He was thwarted in one respect. He wanted elephants to draw his chariot but the city gates had not been built to cater for them, so he had to make do with horses like ordinary men.[110]

## Sulla the Dictator

Sulla's long-term project for the overhaul of the state could not be achieved as consul for one puny year. He required supreme power, immune from challenges, but he needed to attain it within the legal framework. Both consuls were dead, and in accordance with ancient Roman practice Sulla ordered the Senate to choose an *interrex* while he withdrew from Rome. The appointee was Valerius Flaccus. Sulla instructed him to revive the Dictatorship, dormant since 202. There was no need to mention candidates. The powers suited Sulla's purpose, but a six-month term did not, so Sulla proposed that the Dictatorship should be in force until the state had been restored.[111] Towards the end of 82, Flaccus presented the bill to make Sulla *Dictator rei publicae constituendae*, to reconstitute the Republic. Valerius Flaccus was *magister equitum*. Sulla took the precaution of obtaining ratification of his laws up to that date, and also had all his future actions authorized. A new law gave him the power to inflict the death penalty without trial.[112]

The Senate was enlarged to 600 members.[113] A trickle of new senators would be available every year after Sulla passed a law to give quaestors automatic entry to the Senate when their term ended. He increased their numbers to twenty, and they would all owe their advancement to Sulla. So would the 10,000 slaves of the proscribed men, given their freedom and Roman citizenship, and the name Cornelius. Lands throughout Italy were distributed to the soldiers of twenty-three legions, some of them receiving allotments from public land, others settled in devastated areas so that they could revive the towns and villages, and some of them on lands of various cities and towns allowed to commute fines imposed on them to land grants.[114] There was massive disruption when some veterans were allocated plots of land all around the city of Rome.

The jury courts were returned to senatorial control and the permanent courts were reorganised. One of Sulla's measures concerned embezzlement of public money. He may have reconstituted a court already in existence, or instituted a *quaestio peculatus* for such cases.[115] Sulla was consistent in bolstering the powers of the Senate, reviving the laws regulating the senatorial career path or *cursus honorum*. A minimum age was imposed for holders of magistracies, ensuring that that no-one reached the consulship before he was forty-two. There was a strict order of magistracies, and election to any of them was forbidden to men who had not held the previous ones. The ten-year gap between consulships was reinforced. Lucretius Ofella (Afella) flouted the law by his intention to stand for the consulship without having held any magistracy. As one of Sulla's officers, he perhaps thought himself immune from Sulla's retribution. He found out his mistake when Sulla had him killed.[116]

Tribunes of the plebs were banned from holding any further magistracy, precluding a political career. All proposals from tribunes had to be approved by the Senate. Some of the laws of previous tribunes were annulled, especially those for distribution of subsidized grain. Sulla would hardly be expected to mollycoddle the people.

Sulla held onto the Dictatorship until the end of 81 and then resigned, holding only the consulship for 80, with Metellus Pius. It was Sulla's second consulship, only eight years after his previous consulship, but no-one was likely to remind him of the ten-year rule, if it was in force at the time. He refused a third consulship and retired without losing his political influence. In 79 Marcus Aemilius Lepidus stood for the consulship of 78, having fulfilled all the criteria, but Sulla disliked him, and Pompey became *persona non grata* by supporting Lepidus. Soon afterwards Sulla died, possibly from syphilis. The consul Lepidus opposed a state funeral for him, but Pompey assisted the other consul Quintus Lutatius Catulus to organise it.[117]

### Pompey and Metellus in Spain

Pompey may have deliberately backed the wrong horse in supporting Lepidus, in anticipation of trouble, so he could suppress it.[118] Lepidus opposed the tribunes of the plebs agitating for repeal of the law forbidding them to hold further office, and then inexplicably changed his mind. His policies, if he had any, were contradictory. He planned to stop veteran settlement and restore confiscated lands to the original owners. Displaced landowners of Etruria attacked the veterans and when Lepidus and Catulus were sent to restore order, Lepidus joined the discontents, demanding a second consulship. Marcus Perperna, who had precipitately left Sicily, reappeared and joined Lepidus.[119] The affair was becoming dangerous and widespread. For 77, Lepidus had been assigned to Transalpine Gaul, and his deputy Junius Brutus raised troops there.[120] Catulus' consulship was prorogued to enable him to oppose Lepidus, and Pompey, with no official post but with an excellent track record for suppressing rebels, was chosen, possibly as propraetor, to oppose Junius Brutus, besieging him at Mutina (Modena). Brutus' surrender was negotiated. Pompey informed the Senate, imprisoning Brutus while awaiting the verdict. Then Brutus was killed trying to escape, sullying Pompey's reputation.[121] Catulus defeated Lepidus, and Pompey defeated him again near Cosa. Lepidus fled to Sardinia and died there. Perperna joined Sertorius in Spain.[122]

Pompey ought to have disbanded his army but wanted the Spanish command. In 79 Quintus Caecilius Metellus Pius and Domitius Calvinus had been assigned respectively to Hispania Ulterior and Citerior. Calvinus was quickly killed by one of Sertorius' officers, and in 78 Lucius Manlius, governor of Transalpine Gaul, was also killed.[123] Metellus may have asked for Pompey to be sent out, since they had worked well together on behalf of Sulla. Sertorius was now well-established in Spain, with an army of Roman settlers and native Spaniards. He had instituted a Roman-style government with a Senate and magistrates and had set up a school for sons of the tribal chiefs. Sympathetic to the Lusitanians, he avoided the oppressive methods of Roman governors. He stopped the exploitation of resources and the vicious taxation and came to a successful understanding with the ruling elite, winning over most of the tribes and cities of northern Spain, but he was implacable against opponents.[124]

The consuls of 77 showed no inclination to go to war anywhere, so Lucius Marcius Philippus suggested that Pompey should be sent to Spain. When Philippus was challenged for bestowing proconsular power on Pompey, he replied that he was sending him *non proconsule sed pro consulibus*, not as proconsul, but on behalf of the consuls.[125]

On arrival in Spain in spring 76, Pompey secured the coastal towns to facilitate supply by sea, but at a later stage in the war he would be severely hindered by pirates allied with Sertorius.[126] The inhabitants of Spain were brought into a war that was neither of their making, nor fought for their benefit. It centred on winning over tribes and cities and capturing those that resisted. Sertorius besieged Lauro because the inhabitants would not co-operate with him, drawing Pompey to the rescue.[127]

In 75 Pompey defeated Sertorius' generals Perperna and Herennius and captured and destroyed Valencia, but when he attacked Sertorius near the river Sucro without waiting for Metellus, he was defeated. When Metellus Pius arrived, Sertorius withdrew, saying that he would have thrashed the boy if the old woman had not turned up.[128] By joining forces Pompey and Metellus were better protected, but there were more mouths to feed and supplies were scarce. At the river Turia near Saguntum, Pompey's scouts reported that Sertorius and Perperna were approaching with their whole army. Battle was joined. Pompey's brother-in-law Memmius was killed and Metellus had to be rescued by his soldiers using their shields to form the *testudo* over their general and themselves. Sertorius installed his troops in the city of Clunia, where the Spanish people supported him.[129] Pompey and Metellus besieged the city, but then went into winter quarters at the end of 75.

Sallust reproduces the letter sent by Pompey to the Senate, asking for supplies and reinforcements.[130] Pompey reminded the Senate that he had supported his army from his own resources for three years, exhausting his credit. He warned that the war could be brought into Italy.[131] The consuls Lucius Licinius Lucullus and Marcus Aurelius Cotta, about to start a new war against Mithradates, ensured that supplies and two legions were sent to Spain, because disaster in Spain would mean fewer troops for the east.[132]

In 74, Pompey and Metellus concentrated on Spanish cities loyal to Sertorius. At Pallantia and Callagurris, Pompey was driven off by Sertorius, but the tide was beginning to turn as some of Sertorius' men deserted to Metellus, and Sertorius lost support by punishing the rest.[133] Sertorius favoured his Spanish troops over the Romans, so when Metellus announced pardons for anyone who joined him, Romans deserted Sertorius, and the Spanish troops realised that even if Sertorius won this war, another army would arrive, and Spanish communities would continue to suffer.[134]

In 73, Metellus and Pompey redoubled their efforts against Sertorius' loyal Spanish communities.[135] Sertorius allegedly lost his grip, resorting to wine, women and song. Perperna invited him to dinner and killed him. Then he fought Pompey, while Metellus was operating elsewhere. Pompey won, capturing and executing Perperna, and burning the correspondence between Sertorius and people in Rome.[136] Pompey did not want a witch-hunt for closet Sertorians.

At last Spain could be pacified and reorganised. Unfortunately, administration probably bored ancient historians, so there is little evidence for Pompey's settlement of Spain. Seager says that Pompey utilized the same shrewd blend of humanity and self-interest as he had shown in Sicily.[137] Pompey cultivated Spanish communities or individuals as his clients. The most famous is Lucius Cornelius Balbus of Gades, given citizenship by Pompey *c.*72. Balbus became Caesar's secretary and after Caesar's death he became the first provincial to achieve the consulship, in 40. Metellus also recruited friends and clients, and bestowed citizenship on individuals. The consuls of 72 ratified these grants of citizenship.[138] On his way home, Pompey set up a monument at Col de la Perche in the Pyrenees. His statue was placed on top, and an inscription proclaimed his conquest of 876 cities (any fortified settlement) between the Alps and the borders of Further Spain.[139]

## Other wars

There was no lack of wars to fight while Metellus and Pompey were in Spain. Publius Servilius, consul in 79, gained successes as proconsul fighting in Cilicia in 78-77, and in 75-74 he defeated the Isaurians of Cilicia, storming the strongholds of the pirates, taking the name Isauricus.[140] In 77-76 the proconsul Appius Claudius Pulcher defeated the Thracians in several battles.[141] The proconsul Curio fought the Dardanians in Thrace, scoring some successes in 75 and winning a victory in 73, but in 72-71 Marcus Terentius Varro Lucullus, consul in 73, fought the Thracians again.[142] There were ongoing attempts to defeat the Mediterranean pirates. More important, the war began against Mithradates of Pontus in 74/73.

In Italy, the gladiators under Spartacus and Crixus escaped in 73, defeating the legate Appius Claudius Pulcher and the praetor Publius Varenus, but in the following year Crixus was defeated by the propraetor Quintus Arrius, who was then defeated himself, along with two consuls, Gnaeus Lentulus and Lucius Gellius. Spartacus was on a winning streak, defeating Gaius Cassius, proconsul of Cisalpine Gaul, who tried to prevent the gladiators and slaves from moving north. After the defeat of the praetor Gnaeus Manlius, the praetor Marcus Licinius Crassus was put in command, winning the final battle in 71, when most of Spartacus' soldiers died, the remainder being crucified.[143] Some 5,000 survivors fled north, defeated by Pompey as he entered Italy. Plutarch says that Pompey met the gladiators and slaves entirely by chance, but in his biography of Crassus he says that Crassus had asked for the recall of Pompey from Spain.[144] Pompey informed the Senate that he had eradicated the war.[145]

## The consulship of Pompey and Crassus in 70

Pompey wanted the consulship. He was too young, had not been quaestor or praetor, and had so little knowledge of senatorial proceedings that he had to ask his friend Terentius Varro to write a handbook for him.[146] He asked to stand *in absentia* for the consulship, since he could not cross the *pomerium* into Rome until after his triumph. He promised to disband the troops after the celebrations. The Senate waived the regulations to enable Pompey to stand for election.[147] On the last day of 71, Pompey held a splendid triumph, and became consul for 70 along with Marcus Licinius Crassus, also elected consul *in absentia*, having been awarded an *ovatio*. There may have been no other candidates.

As consul designate in 71, Pompey promised to restore tribunician power, reform the courts, and improve provincial government.[148] Pompey actually did very little to improve the government of the provinces, and it was the praetor Lucius Aurelius Cotta who dealt with the reform of the jury courts. His *lex Aurelia* changed the composition of the juries, now drawn equally from senators, *equites*, and *tribuni aerarii*, relieving the burden on senators. The *tribuni aerarii* were originally treasury officials responsible for military pay and collecting tribute, but the office had lapsed. It is not known why the *tribuni aerarii* should have been selected as a discreet group, and if they were *equites* as is supposed, it would seem that two-thirds of the juries were equestrians, outnumbering the senators. Livy says simply that Cotta transferred the juries to the *equites*, and Velleius Paterculus says that service on the juries was divided equally between senators and equestrians. The modern jury is still out on this question.[149] The *tribuni aerarii* were removed by Julius Caesar and disappeared from view.

As for the muzzled *tribuni plebis*, several politicians had tackled the problem. From 76 to 73, various proposals to restore full powers to the tribunes were squashed, but at least in 75 the consul Gaius Aurelius Cotta made it possible for tribunes to hold further offices.[150] Pompey and Crassus co-operated for the first and only time in their year of office to restore the legislative powers of the tribunes.[151]

As mentioned above, in 70 the census was held. The censors were Gellius Poplicola and Cornelius Lentulus Clodianus, consuls in 72.

The membership of the Senate was revised and sixty-four senators lost their senatorial status.[152] Two bills were presented by the tribune Plautius /Plotius, one to extend an amnesty to the followers of Lepidus and Sertorius, which was passed, and another to provide allotments for Pompey's veterans, also passed. But no veterans were settled.

After his consulship Crassus returned to city life. Pompey lay low.[153] He could not expect to have the rules waived for a second consulship, and he failed to install his adherents in any of the magistracies.

## Pompey and the pirates

During his three-year retirement, it cannot be doubted that Pompey had devoted thought to the pirate problem. His extensive planning was behind Aulus Gabinius' bill for the pirate command in 66.[154] The campaign would have to cover the whole of the Mediterranean and the lands around it, requiring vast resources and personnel. The first attempt to co-ordinate Roman and provincial resources to combat piracy was made 101-100 with the *lex de provinciis praetoriis*. Publius Servilius successfully attacked the pirate strongholds of Cilicia in 77 but deprived the defeated individuals of any means of making a living, so they resorted to piracy again. Mark Antony's father, Marcus Antonius, praetor for 75, was given a special command in 74, with an extended term of three years and powers over a broad territory, possibly up to fifty miles inland in the provinces around the Mediterranean, though not necessarily with authorization to override the powers of the appointed governors.[155] Antonius was defeated, dying in office in 71. Quintus Metellus took over in Crete in 68 and flushed out pirates, but in 67 a pirate fleet appeared at the mouth of the Tiber, defeated a consular commander and attacked the harbour at Ostia.[156]

In 67, the tribune Aulus Gabinius introduced his bill. No commander was named, but no-one was fooled as to who it would be.[157] Gabinius specified a three-year command and 200 ships, divided into squadrons under fifteen legates of at least praetorian rank, subordinate to the supreme commander, who would be a consular, with the right to levy troops when necessary, access to the funds of the main treasury in Rome, and the tax resources of the provinces. His authority should extend up to fifty miles inland in all the provinces bordering the Mediterranean. Modern scholars debate the extent of the powers of the commander. Velleius Paterculus labels it *imperium aequum*, powers equal to other commanders, but Tacitus compares the *imperium maius* or alleged greater powers of Domitius Corbulo under the Emperor

Nero with that of Pompey during the Mediterranean command.[158] It has been argued that there was no such thing as *imperium maius*.

The senators were dubious about putting such enormous power into the hands of one man. The Senate recruited two tribunes to veto the bill, Lucius Trebellius and Lucius Roscius Otho, but they were silenced.[159] Quintus Lutatius Catulus, consul of 78, was asked for his opinion in the assembly. He suggested that the proposed legates should have independent commands. This would have negated co-ordination in planning and action. The contentious issue was that the legates were responsible to the commander, not the Senate. Catulus ended his speech by questioning who would take over if the commander was killed. The people shouted 'You, Catulus'.[160] Gabinius' law was passed.

A second law was necessary to put Pompey in command. When he was named, the price of grain fell.[161] The provisions of the first law were amended. There were to be 500 ships, and there were to be twenty-four legates (twenty-five in some sources).[162] Pompey divided the entire Mediterranean and the coasts into thirteen regions, each under a legate. Appian and Florus preserve a list of thirteen names of high-ranking men, but they are not identical.[163] The legates with inland commands are unknown.

The pirates were first driven from the seaways of Sardinia, Sicily and Africa, sources of Rome's grain. Some of the pirates surrendered, others took refuge in Cilicia. Pompey had to return to Rome because Gaius Calpurnius Piso, governor of Transalpine Gaul, peevishly obstructed recruitment within his province for Pompey's command, and had discharged troops already in arms. Gabinius prepared to depose Piso, but Pompey stopped him, relying on the anger of the people against anyone who disrupted the pirate campaign. Maybe Piso forgot that he and Pompey worked for the same firm.

Part of the fleet was at Brundisium, while other ships patrolled the eastern Mediterranean coasts, except those of Cilicia, to encourage the pirates to gather there. The pirates who surrendered told Pompey of the Cilician hiding places, which were captured one by one. The last of the fighting was at Coracesium (Alanya). The pirates were converted into farmers, given lands in settlements destroyed in wars. The Cilician city of Soli was re-founded and called Pompeiopolis, and pirates were settled on destroyed sites at Dyme in Achaea, and Mallus, Epiphaneia and Adana in Asia Minor.[164] The pirate menace was eradicated, for the time being, anyway.

Pompey had a spat with Quintus Metellus, consul in 69, assigned to Crete in 68 to deal with the pirates there. Word had spread that Pompey was lenient, so the pirates decided to surrender to him, not Metellus, who escalated attacks on the cities favouring Pompey. The quarrel became less important when Pompey heard that he had been awarded the command against Mithradates.

## Pompey and Mithradates

When King Nicomedes died in 75/74, he bequeathed his kingdom of Bithynia to the people of Rome, but Mithradates seized it. The consuls of 74, Marcus Aurelius Cotta and Lucius Licinius Lucullus, scenting war with Mithradates, wanted the command. By various political intrigues they exchanged their allotted commands, gaining Bithynia and Cilicia with Asia as their *provinciae*. When war commenced, Cotta was rapidly bottled up in Chalcedon, and was relieved by Lucullus.[165] On learning that Mithradates had begun to besiege the port of Cyzicus (in modern Turkey), Lucullus followed, camping on a virtually impregnable hill where he could be easily supplied, while he concentrated on cutting Mithradates' supply lines. The inhabitants of Cyzicus vigorously defended their city, and eventually lack of food forced Mithradates to move off.[166] Lucullus had been successful without risking a battle, and now he aimed at Mithradates' kingdom of Pontus with his five legions, drawing Mithradates after him. There was no decisive battle, but Mithradates' troops were decimated by Lucullus.

Mithradates approached his son-in-law Tigranes, ruler of Armenia, who housed him on one of his estates in a sort of gilded cage, entertained but not helped to win back Pontus, which Lucullus took over.[167] Asked to surrender Mithradates or face war, Tigranes chose the latter, so Lucullus marched to Armenia in 69 to besiege and capture Tigranocerta.[168] In 68, Tigranes and Mithradates gathered a new army, but with the onset of winter Tigranes retreated into Armenia, and Mithradates marched to Pontus and defeated Lucullus' officers.[169] Worse still, in Armenia, Lucullus' soldiers refused to march. They had been fighting for years, and the Armenian winters were extremely harsh.

Lucullus abandoned his march. This was his turning point. From 69 onwards there had been political movements to replace him, doubtless at Pompey's instigation.[170] Roman and Italian businessmen claimed that Lucullus had damaged their interests in Asia, by which they meant that they could not get away with extortion and various means of enriching themselves because Lucullus' administration was fair and even-handed, so unusually benevolent that the provincials erected statues of him and celebrated festivals called Lucullea. He had temporarily stopped the many Roman abuses and had revived the prosperity of communities struggling to pay off the money borrowed from Roman lenders to pay the indemnities imposed after the previous Mithradatic war. The province of Asia was detached from Lucullus in 68 and given a praetorian commander.[171] Cilicia was given to the consul Marcius Rex, who refused Lucullus' requests for assistance when Mithradates and Tigranes descended on Asia and Cappadocia. In 67, the tribune Aulus Gabinius detached Bithynia and Pontus from Lucullus, assigning both to Manius Acilius Glabrio, but by the time Glabrio arrived, Mithradates had regained control.

In 66 the tribune Gaius Manilius proposed installing Pompey as commander. There was opposition, but several senators supported the bill, notably the praetor Marcus Tullius Cicero. The bill became law. Cicero published his speech afterwards, called *de Imperio Gnaei Pompei*. Pompey was to take over the troops of Lucullus, Acilius Glabrio and Marcius Rex. He was authorized to make war or peace according to his needs, to judge nations as friends or enemies, and to conclude treaties with whoever he wished, effectively controlling Rome's foreign policy in the east.[172] He chose legates, Lucius Afranius who had served in Spain, Quintus Metellus Celer, half-brother of Pompey's wife Mucia, Aulus Gabinius, and Lucius Valerius Flaccus who had served under Quintus Metellus in Crete. Probably the legates of the pirate war were included.[173] Before he moved, Pompey arranged diplomatic settlements with states surrounding the eastern territories, sending a mission to Phraates, King of Parthia, with whom Lucullus had established good relations. Phraates, enemy of Tigranes, was encouraged to attack Armenia, tying down Tigranes while Pompey concentrated on Mithradates.[174]

Alarmed by Pompey's approach to the Parthians, Mithradates tried to make peace, but Pompey wanted a decisive surrender. Mithradates withdrew into the mountains. Before following him, Pompey met Lucullus at Danala in Galatia. There was a furious row.[175] Lucullus retained 1,600 men for his triumph; Pompey took the rest.

Pompey drew Mithradates into Lesser Armenia, but the king refused battle and withdrew, narrowly escaping Pompey's ambush in a pass.[176] Mithradates approached Tigranes again, but was repulsed, because

Tigranes thought that Mithradates had encouraged his son to rebel against him, and when Tigranes junior was defeated, he submitted to the Romans. Using the younger Tigranes as a guide, Pompey invaded Armenia, receiving the submission of Tigranes senior. Pompey imposed an indemnity of 6000 talents on him, also demanding the surrender of Cappadocia, Syria, Cilicia, Phoenicia and Sophene, which was given to Tigranes junior, until he proved troublesome. He was then arrested and eventually sent to Rome. Tigranes senior assisted Pompey in the next campaigns and became a friend and ally of the Romans.[177] It was from this moment in 66 that Pompey dated the possession of the province of Syria.[178]

In 66/65 the Romans wintered in three groups. King Oroeses of the Armenians engaged separately with Pompey, Metellus Celer, and Valerius Flaccus, failing in all cases.[179] The campaign of 65 was against Oroeses, and the Iberians (not the Spanish tribe) under King Artoces. The two kings laid an ambush for Pompey near the river Cyrtus and were defeated.[180] Artoces, defeated again, eventually made peace, sending his children as hostages. Oreoses was defeated, and Pompey made peace with him, also arranging a truce with tribes of the Caucasus.[181] These tribes extended to the Caspian Sea, which Pompey tried to reach, but turned back because of the poisonous snakes, and tarantulas whose bite made people literally die laughing. Some of the geographical and scientific information that was gathered survives in the works of Strabo and Pliny. Seager dismisses the suggestion that Pompey was simply looking for glory, since control of the Iberians and Albanians protected the east and north-east of Pontus, which Pompey took over late in 65.[182]

In the meantime, Phraates invaded Gordyene, belonging to Tigranes. Pompey sent Afranius to restore it to Tigranes.[183] Phraates' envoys asked Pompey if the frontier was to be the Euphrates. Pompey replied that it would be wherever he thought best. Phraates later reasserted himself, warning Pompey not to cross the Euphrates.[184]

Needing representation in Rome, Pompey sent Metellus Celer and Valerius Flaccus home as candidates for the praetorship of 63; both were elected but achieved little for Pompey. With Mithradates out of the way and relatively harmless, Pompey set up headquarters at Amisus (Samsun, Turkey), and at Antioch he ousted Antiochus XIII, Seleucid king of Syria, recognised as such by Lucullus. Antiochus asked for recognition from Pompey, but was refused, and then he asked for help from Sampsigeramus, ruler of Emesa, who killed him.[185] Pompey annexed Syria, though technically, since Tigranes had conquered Syria, and had then surrendered himself and all his conquests to Pompey, Syria automatically belonged to Pompey, or rather, Rome. Pompey travelled there in autumn 64 to claim the province. This meant eradicating the remaining heirs to the Seleucid kings, and suppressing bandits. His legates had dealt with them in the northern areas, but in the south the bandits were still active. Once they were subdued, organisation of the province could begin. According to Dio, Coele Syria and Phoenicia were combined into one province and received laws so that they were governed in Roman fashion.[186]

Ptolemy XII Auletes, ruler of Egypt, sent gifts, money, soldiers, and clothing for Pompey's army.[187] There were strings attached. Ptolemy needed help to quell riots among his own subjects in Alexandria, but Pompey's remit did not extend as far as Egypt. Licinius Crassus urged the Senate to annex Egypt, proposing that the young Julius Caesar should be sent out to supervise the process. Catulus crushed the proposal.

On his way to Damascus early in 63, Pompey flushed out bandits and punished hostile local leaders, executing some and fining others. Friendly communities were rewarded. Others were left alone and their authority recognised.[188] At Damascus, Pompey summoned Hyrcanus and Aristobulus, at loggerheads over the rule of Judaea. Their quarrel went back three or four years, when Hyrcanus had appealed to Aretas of Nabataea and together they besieged Aristobulus in Jerusalem. Pompey's legate Aemilius Scaurus had forced Aretas to withdraw, but Pompey refused to pronounce judgement until Aretas was neutralised. Aemilius Scaurus marched to Nabatea, and peace was established at the instigation of Hyrcanus' envoy Antipater.[189] After the meeting Aristobulus went to Jerusalem and fortified the city, ready to fight the Romans. At Jericho, Pompey heard that Pharnaces, son of Mithradates, had rebelled, since the old king had begun to eliminate people purely on suspicion. Josephus says Pharnaces killed his father.[190]

Pompey besieged Jerusalem. Aristobulus came out to negotiate and was imprisoned, but his supporters held out for three months until Pompey's troops forced a way in. Pompey respected most Jewish customs but insisted upon entering the inner sanctuary of the temple, a sacrilegious act. He reported that there was nothing inside, but Josephus says that the sanctuary contained the golden table with its lampstand and libation vessels, and money, which Pompey did not touch.[191] Hyrcanus was made High Priest, not king, and some of his territory was added to Syria. It suited Pompey to create a relatively weak Judaea on the frontiers of his new Syrian province. He returned to Amisus, where Pharnaces had left gifts, and his father's body. Pompey arranged for Mithradates' funeral at Sinope.[192] Good relations with the new ruler of Pontus were forged. Pharnaces asked Pompey's permission to retain the old kingdom within its original boundaries, which was refused, but Pompey agreed to Pharnaces' control of the Bosporus, except for the city of Phanagoria, which was to be independent, governed by a pro-Roman. Pharnaces became a friend and ally of the Roman people.[193]

## Pompey's organisation of the east

In the eastern territories Pompey judged the leaders of various communities on their merits, executing some whom he considered unsuitable, and extracting hefty fines from those who could be useful. He rewarded leaders who had helped him, such as Antiochus I of Commagene, who received Seleucia and the conquered areas of Macedonia, and he made other prominent men kings of various territories. Some of the conquered communities were freed, and became allies, according to Appian, who follows up with a list of cities that Pompey founded.[194]

Pompey spent the winter of 63-62 in organising the east. In general, without bleeding the east dry, Pompey took over what was governable, defensible and profitable, and in these provinces the long-established city-states with their own autonomous governments provided the infrastructure of Roman provincial administration, adapted to local circumstances as far as possible without imposing completely new systems. Other territories were placed under friendly pro-Roman rulers.

Cilicia was reorganised, some parts of it bestowed on King Ariobarzanes of Cappadocia, but elsewhere Cilicia was extended into parts of the surrounding territory, with two legions for protection against potential threat from Armenia or Parthia. Parts of Paphlagonia were to be ruled by Attalus.[195] Part of Pontus was amalgamated with Bithynia, and some sections of Pompey's law establishing the new province of Bithynia-Pontus are known from quotations in Pliny's correspondence with Trajan. Dio notes that in his day, the third century AD, Pompey's laws were still current.[196] Pompey rejected the former centralised government of Bithynia and Pontus, deciding in favour of self-governed communities, creating such communities where none existed, or if that was impracticable, he installed other rulers to keep the peace. Some lands formerly in Pontus were given to Deiotarus of Galatia, along with the kingdom of Lesser Armenia, and the remaining part of Pontus was divided into eleven districts with an administrative centre in each.[197] Around Bithynia-Pontus, Pompey created client kings, or confirmed them in their existing possessions.[198] Not all their names are known, but the principle holds good for all of them, in that the territories that Rome was not prepared to administer directly were governed by rulers who would keep the peace and protect their own and Roman territory against attacks.

In Syria, the cities freed by the Seleucids retained their freedom, while rulers of other cities became clients of Rome. With two legions Aemilius Scaurus commanded in Syria, without official rank, except as a legate of Pompey. The first propraetor arrived in 59, Lucius Marcius Philippus.[199] The next governor of Syria was Gnaeus Cornelius Lentulus Marcellinus in 58, and after him the governors were proconsuls, reflecting the importance of Syria. The first was Aulus Gabinius, from 57 to 55. Then Marcus Licinius Crassus took over, preparing for his Parthian campaign.

Pompey exacted tribute from some of the territories.[200] Some of the territorial rulers were possibly exempt, but those established by Pompey on lands taken from Syria or Pontus probably paid tribute. Pompey's arrangements protected taxpayers to a certain extent. While censors in Rome continued to lease contracts for the taxes of Asia and probably Bithynia, the Cilician and Syrian arrangements differed, in that contracts for individual communities were auctioned by proconsular governors. No single group of *publicani* could gain an overall monopoly. Local officials made a *pactio* with their relevant *publicani* for a fixed sum, and collected it themselves, obviating direct contact between *publicani* and provincials.[201]

On his way home Pompey visited Mytilene on the island of Lesbos, the home of his friend Theophanes. He restored the city to freedom, lost because the people supported Mithradates. In the theatre, poets recited works honouring Pompey, who commissioned several drawings of the building, using them to build the first stone theatre in Rome, with a temple and a portico attached.

Pompey landed at Brundisium at the end of 62, expecting to hold a triumph, to settle his veteran soldiers on the land, and to secure from the Senate ratification for his organisation of the eastern provinces and friendly states. Pompey's administration was sensible, sound, and better still, mostly long-lasting. Three decades later, Octavian-Augustus owed a lot to Pompey's special extensive commands and his administration.

6

# Caesar, the Conquest of Gaul, and the Civil War

There had been political fun and games in Rome while Pompey was absent. His enemies prosecuted men who had assisted him, one being Gaius Manilius, the tribune of 66 who had passed the law giving Pompey the Mithradatic command. Cicero spoke in his defence, but there was violence at the trial, and when the court reconvened, Manilius did not appear and was condemned.[1]

*Rullus' land bill*
Early in 63, several tribunes drafted a bill for redistribution of land and the tribune Publius Servilius Rullus presented it. Two of the tribunes were Titus Labienus and Titus Ampius Balbus, Pompey's men, and while the aim of the bill was to resettle the poor, reduce their numbers in Rome and ease the strain on food supplies, Pompey's veterans were to be catered for, but Pompey himself was excluded from the proposed ten-man, five-year commission. Public funds were to be used to purchase land, but only from people who wanted to sell, avoiding compulsory purchase and evictions. Gruen says that Rullus' law was intelligent in design and farsighted in conception.[2]

Marcus Tullius Cicero, consul for 63, declared that Rullus' bill damaged Pompey's interests. Seager says this view will not bear examination.[3] Cicero quashed the bill. His speech against it, *de Lege Agraria*, is the only source for the episode, and Wiseman labels it 'a speech of brilliant chicanery'.[4]

168

## Cicero and Lucius Sergius Catilina

Cicero was responsible for the detection and eradication of the so-called conspiracy of Lucius Sergius Catilina, more familiarly Catiline, praetor in 68, and governor of Africa for two years, after which he was prosecuted for extortion. He was acquitted, but he could not stand for election as consul while the trial proceeded.[5] He was a candidate for the consulship of 63, but voters preferred Antonius Hybrida and Marcus Tullius Cicero. As consul Cicero began to collect information, writing an account of the episode, called *de Consiliis Suis*, forbidding publication until after his death. Without Catiline's own version, his motives are obscure.[6] Catiline had used borrowed money to bribe voters. Marcus Porcius Cato threatened prosecution, but Catiline issued a bigger threat of creating havoc. Tighter laws were demanded against electoral bribery. Cicero passed a new law adding banishment for ten years to the usual penalties.[7] In November Catiline joined the army of poor men assembled by a centurion, Gaius Manlius, in Etruria. Debt and debt-bondage were still the main problems, and a deputation from Manlius to Marcius Rex, sent against him with an army, gained nothing except advice to address their problems to the Senate.[8] The poor had lost faith in that process: there no hope of relief, except maybe with Catiline.

In December, a group of Allobroges came to Rome to see their patron, Quintus Fabius Sanga, complaining of extortionate governors. They also informed him that a certain Publius Umbrenus had approached them, explaining that that there was a plan that would end their grievances. When Catiline arrived at Faesulae (Fiesole) with his army, the consuls were to be killed.[9] Fabius Sanga informed Cicero. Gaius Cornelius Cethegus was arrested because he had a collection of weapons disguised as his museum. More suspects were arrested, including Mark Antony's stepfather Lentulus Sura, also involved with the Allobroges.[10]

In the Senate on 5 December, Cicero advocated the death penalty. Senators agreed. Gaius Julius Caesar disagreed. He was praetor elect for 62, and also Pontifex Maximus, having been elected to the office in spite of stiff competition. Religion and politics were compatible in Rome. Caesar argued that each suspect should be placed under guard in a different Italian town.[11] The Senate voted for the death penalty, and the suspects were strangled in prison.[12] There had been no trial.

Catiline headed for Transalpine Gaul with his army, pursued by the consul Gaius Antonius Hybrida. Quintus Metellus Celer with three legions in Picenum managed to turn Catiline back. In the final battle, Antonius put his subordinate Marcus Petreius in command, a much better soldier. Catiline and many of his associates were killed. His head was sent to Rome.[13] Before Catiline's death was announced, the tribune Metellus Nepos, one of Pompey's officers, supported by Gaius Julius Caesar, proposed the recall of Pompey to restore order. The tribunes Porcius Cato and Quintus Minucius Thermus tore the proposal out of Nepos' hands, but he continued speaking from memory. A riot began. Cato and Thermus were attacked, but their supporters fought back. Nepos returned to Pompey. Caesar was removed from office, but crowds of protestors clamoured for his return. He was soon reinstated and allotted the province of Hispania Ulterior. Governors of the Spanish provinces held the title of proconsul, though they were usually ex-praetors.

Before Caesar's departure, the festival of the Bona Dea, celebrated only by women, was held in his house, since he was Pontifex Maximus. Publius Clodius Pulcher gate-crashed the proceedings dressed as a woman and was thrown out by Caesar's mother, Aurelia. Caesar did not initiate a prosecution because no law had been broken, but he divorced his wife Pompeia, no relation to Pompey, explaining 'Caesar's wife should be above suspicion.'

On arrival in Spain, Caesar raised ten cohorts to supplement his troops already in the province and then marched against the Lusitanians, who were raiding the Baetis valley.[14] Having defeated them and another tribe, Caesar turned to civil matters, principally debt, ruling that creditors should take two-thirds of the debtors' income each year, allowing debtors to keep their property and one third of their incomes until debts were paid. Since Caesar was also vastly in debt, probably to Crassus, he copied his predecessors and grew wealthy in Spain.[15]

Caesar had been awarded a triumph, so on returning to Rome in 60 he could not legally cross the *pomerium* while still commanding troops. He asked permission to stand *in absentia* for the consular elections for 59 but was refused, so he abandoned the triumph and was elected consul, with Marcus Calpurnius Bibulus as colleague. The tasks already set for retiring consuls of 59 were maintenance of woodlands and pathways and combatting bandits in Italy. The Senate wanted to keep Caesar down.

## Caesar's consulship

As consul for 59, Caesar joined forces with Pompey, whose arrangements for the eastern provinces and client kingdoms had not been ratified and his veterans still lacked allotments of land because of the Senate's delaying tactics. At some disputed date the two men were joined by Marcus Licinius Crassus, their association dubbed by the people the *Tricaranus*, or Three Headed Monster (easily confused with the tricorynus, or deathwatch beetle).[16] The modern title First Triumvirate for the three partners is based on the later official Triumvirate of Octavian, Mark Antony and Aemilius Lepidus. The Latin term is *Tresviri*.

Caesar's large voting majority over Bibulus entitled him to be the first to hold the *fasces* and introduce his legislation in January. His first law authorized the publication of the *Acta Senatus* recording the discussions of the Senate, supplementing the *Acta Diurnia*, already in existence, recording events, ceremonials, speeches and lawsuits.[17]

It was certain that Caesar would introduce a land bill. Cicero wrote to Atticus in December 60, uncertain whether to oppose or support it.[18] Land bills were usually presented by *tribuni plebis*, but Caesar presented the bill himself. Allotments were to be provided for the urban poor and land was to be bought only from willing vendors, with the current census ratings as the price-guide. The Campanian lands, settled by Romans for a long time, were not to be touched, and there was to be no disruption to Sulla's veterans. Only Dio mentions that Pompey's veterans were to be settled.[19] Caesar was excluded from the commission of twenty men who would oversee the proceedings.

The bill was so well drafted that it was difficult to fault it. Speakers in the Senate were called upon in ranking order, so it was late in the day when Cato, not yet praetor, was asked his opinion. Unable to shred the bill clause by clause, he argued that it was not the right time for the bill. If he continued speaking until darkness fell, the Senate would be adjourned. Caesar called his lictors to take Cato to prison. Marcus Petreius left too, preferring prison with Cato than the Senate with Caesar.[20] Cato was released.

On the following day, Caesar addressed a public meeting from the Rostra. Bibulus, asked for his opinion of the land bill, told the people 'You shall not have it this year, even if you all want it.'[21] Crassus and Pompey declared support for the bill.[22] Emulating the Gracchi, Caesar bypassed the Senate, taking his bill to the popular assembly.[23]

The land bill was passed amid turbulence. Cato was physically ejected twice. Bibulus had a chamber pot emptied over him. Caesar administered an oath to uphold the law. Die-hards Cato and Metellus Celer refused until Cicero persuaded them that they were more useful in Rome than in exile.[24] Bibulus retired to his house to watch the skies for bad omens, which could potentially halt all public business, invalidating anything enacted on those inauspicious days.[25] With Bibulus inactive, the year 59 was dubbed the consulship of Julius and Caesar.

Pompey and Crassus were members of the committee of twenty to put the agrarian law into effect. In order to provide enough land, Caesar had to renege on the promise not to divide up Campanian lands. Men with three or more children qualified for allotments, probably of twenty *iugera*, not to be sold for twenty years. 20,000 men applied.[26] It remained to ratify Pompey's organisation of the eastern provinces. Caesar neutralised Lucullus, the main opponent, by threatening to prosecute him for his conduct during the Mithridatic War. At last Pompey's administrative and diplomatic work was legalized.[27]

Caesar passed a law to relieve the equestrian *publicani* of one third of their self-imposed burden, because they had bid too high for the tax farm of Asia.[28] He passed the *lex Julia de repetundis* in an attempt to curb exploitation of provincials. He incorporated previous legislation but spread the net wider, over governors, lesser officials, and assistants. Each type of offence was defined and measures were outlined for dealing with them. Claims for expenses were capped. Provincial accounts were to be sealed to prevent tampering and were to be published in two major cities of each province, as well as in Rome. There were penalties for governors or officials who left their provinces, crossed territorial boundaries, or made war, without senatorial permission. There were also measures to improve procedures of the extortion courts, which surfaced in later law codes.[29]

Around May or June, Bibulus warned Pompey of a plot to kill him. This was the mysterious Vettius affair, which will probably never be solved. After revealing plots to murder Caesar and Pompey, Vettius died in prison, by strangulation, poison, or suicide. Dio calls it murder, and Suetonius assumed that Caesar was behind it all.[30]

In summer 59, Pompey married Caesar's daughter Julia, whose previous betrothal was broken off. Pompey had divorced his wife Mucia on returning from the east and his attempt to make a marriage alliance with Cato's family was rebuffed, but his new marriage was a happy one. Caesar married Calpurnia, daughter of Lucius Calpurnius Piso, consul in 58. Pompey and Piso would look after Caesar's interests while he was absent, not caring for woods or combatting Italian bandits, but as governor of Gaul.

## Caesar and Gaul

In 62-61 there had been an uprising of the Allobroges in The Province, later Gallia Narbonensis. The governor Gaius Pomptinus put down the revolt, with difficulty.[31] The consul for 60, Metellus Celer, had been assigned to The Province for 59, but died before taking office. Around the same time the Helvetii of what is now Switzerland were under threat from Germanic tribes, and they were about to migrate through Gaul.[32]

The tribune Publius Vatinius proposed a law in the people's assembly to give Caesar command of Cisalpine Gaul and Illyricum with three legions for a fixed term of five years, with no discussion until 1 March 54. Pompey urged the Senate to transfer Metellus Celer's command to Caesar, with one legion, from January 58 for one year.

Consuls for 58 were Caesar's father-in-law Calpurnius Piso and Pompey's adherent Aulus Gabinius. Cicero lamented that there was no hope of ever having free magistrates again.[33] Caesar as consul and Pontifex Maximus, and Pompey as augur, supervised the adoption of the aristocratic Publius Clodius into the plebeian family of Publius Fonteius, so he could become tribune.[34] Taking office on 10 December 59, Clodius' legislation outlawed anyone who had executed Roman citizens without trial. Cicero now realised that he should have accepted Caesar's offer of a post on his staff, or the deceased Cosconius' place on the land commission.[35] He went into exile. Clodius removed Cato, sent to govern Crete, and forbade anyone to obstruct public business by watching the heavens. He also introduced free distribution of grain for the poor. Caesar's hand in all this is tangible.

Caesar arrived in Gaul in March 58. He was authorized to appoint legates, Titus Labienus and Publius Vatinius being two of them. The first seven books of Caesar's *Gallic War* were written by Caesar himself, while the eighth book, linking the end of the Gallic war with the account of the civil war, was written by Caesar's officer Aulus Hirtius, who probably completed the *Alexandrian War*. Caesar provides the only extant detailed description of a late Republican Roman army on campaign, and once the self-glorification is noted, there is much detail about practicalities, food supply, troop dispositions, deployment of cavalry, ruses to mislead the enemy, use of scouts (*exploratores*), and interpreters (*interpretes*) who spoke the various tribal languages. Caesar describes the nature, habitats and customs of the tribes.

Caesar first campaigned against the Helvetii, whose migration threatened the Aedui and Allobroges. He destroyed the bridge constructed by the Helvetii across the Rhône and constructed a fortified line along the river valley. Leaving Labienus in command, Caesar enrolled two new legions in Cisalpine Gaul. The Helvetii were sent home to guard against Germanic activity.[36]

The Romans had not been entirely absent from the unconquered part of Gaul, called Gallia Comata or Long-Haired Gaul. Gallic tribesmen served in the Roman army.[37] Rome had made the Aedui allies of Rome, as a counterweight to the power of the Arverni. Diviciacus, chief of the Aedui, had appealed to Rome for help against the Sequani, who called in Ariovistus, king of the Suebi, the largest and most powerful tribe beyond the Rhine.[38] During Caesar's consulship Ariovistus had been confirmed as friend of the Roman people but he now claimed that having defeated the Aedui they were tributary to him.[39] Caesar asked him to relinquish lands that he had taken, and to prevent movement of Germans across the Rhine. Ariovistus refused. Dio accuses Caesar of making impossible demands to justify war against a friend of Rome.[40] Caesar marched to Vesontio (Besançon), capital of the Sequani, whose fierce reputation panicked the Romans, but Caesar threatened to take the trustworthy Tenth legion alone. The Germans were defeated and Ariovistus escaped.[41] Titus Labienus commanded at Vesontio while Caesar wintered in Cisalpine Gaul attending to civil government.

Rome was currently under Clodius' thumb. He turned against Pompey and tried to annul all Caesar's legislation. Eventually, Pompey assembled a private army under Titus Annius Milo to counter Clodius' street gangs. In 57 Pompey arranged the recall of Cicero from exile, and after food riots he was put in charge of the grain supplies with five legates and proconsular powers for five years.[42]

In spring 57, with the two legions raised in Cisalpine Gaul, Caesar began the campaign in north-western Gaul against the Belgae, a federation of tribes whose territory covered a third of all Gaul, according to Plutarch. Some of them raided other tribes.[43] The Belgic Remi, of modern Rheims and Châlons, submitted to Caesar and were placed under Roman protection, so when the Belgic Bellovaci attacked them, the Romans drove them off. The Belgae were defeated at the river Axona (Aisne), and lacking food, they retreated.[44] Caesar put garrisons into settlements of the Bellovaci and Suessiones (around Soissons). At the river Sabis (Sambre), Caesar fought the Nervii, Viromandui and Atrebates, arranging terms with the surviving Nervii. They kept their lands and other tribes were warned not to attack them.[45] The Senate voted Caesar an unprecedented fifteen days of thanksgiving.[46]

In winter 57/56 Caesar went to Illyricum, while his soldiers remained in Gaul among the Carnutes, Andes and Turones. In Rome, Caesar's agrarian law came under threat, and in 56 Lucius Domitius Ahenobarbus, brother-in-law of Cato, agitated for Caesar's recall, desiring the Gallic command himself.[47] Caesar revived the Three Headed Monster. Unable to leave his province, in 56 Caesar summoned Crassus to Ravenna, at the southern boundary of Cisalpine Gaul. In April, he met Pompey at Lucca (Luca). It is uncertain whether Crassus joined them. It was agreed that Pompey and Crassus were to be consuls for 55 and would extend Caesar's Gallic command for another five years.[48] Money and the power of the three and their associates would accomplish this. Cicero had been right to say there would be no more free magistrates.

In Gaul in 56, Publius Licinius Crassus, son of Marcus Crassus, was sent to win over the Veneti of modern Normandy and Brittany. The tribesmen were made friends of the Roman people, but on demanding the return of their hostages they imprisoned Caesar's envoys, who were sacrosanct. War followed. Veneti strongholds were subdued, but at sea Caesar's oared warships were no match for the Veneti sailing ships, until the Romans under Decimus Brutus crippled the ships by pulling down the yardarms using hooks on long poles. The Veneti leaders were executed and the people enslaved. Neighbours of the Veneti were subdued. Only the Morini and Menapii remained free.[49]

Caesar planned a British expedition in 55, but was delayed when the Usipetes, Tencteri and other tribes, displaced by the Suebi, crossed the Rhine, demanding lands in Gaul, but were ordered to return home. A truce was made, but after the tribes attacked Caesar's Gallic cavalry, Caesar chased them back across the Rhine, which he then crossed himself on a timber bridge built by his soldiers in ten days. The bridge is described in Caesar's *Gallic War* and much has been learned in modern attempts to build it. Caesar spent eighteen or twenty days in

German territory. Returning to Gaul, Caesar destroyed the bridge to prevent the tribes from using it.[50]

Late in the year, Caesar invaded Britain, a reconnaissance rather than a campaign. His officer Gaius Volusenus was despatched to find landing places, and Commius, king of the Atrebates in Gaul, was sent to the British Atrebates to persuade them and other tribes to submit to Caesar. There was a flourishing trade between Britain and Gaul conveying Roman goods, so traders were questioned about the coastal areas.[51] Vital information that Caesar did not gain, or ignored, was the behaviour of the tides. In his account of the British campaign, he admits ignorance that at full moon tides are higher.[52]

The expedition sailed probably from Boulogne and Ambleteuse. Caesar took the Seventh and the Tenth legions and some cavalry. Famously, the legionaries were reluctant to disembark, until the eagle bearer of the Tenth legion leapt into the water, risking the capture of the standard, so the legionaries quickly followed.[53] Storms prevented the horse transports from landing and wrecked ships at anchor. Caesar remarked that the Britons still used chariots in war, long since abandoned in Gaul.[54] The Britons submitted and Caesar returned to Gaul, the only Roman general to set foot in Britain, marked by twenty days thanksgiving. After returning to Gaul, about 300 soldiers were marching for the Roman camp and were surrounded by the Morini. The Romans formed square, and then their cavalry arrived from the camp. The Morini fled, surrendering later to Labienus. The Menapii were attacked by Quintus Titurius Sabinus and Lucius Aurunculeius Cotta, and their lands were destroyed.[55]

Pompey and Crassus, consuls for 55, extended Caesar's command for another five years, and via the tribune Gaius Trebonius they each secured provincial commands to be taken up in 54, the two Spains for Pompey, and a Parthian command for Crassus.

The second British expedition in 54 was delayed while Caesar dealt with an alliance of Gallic chieftains under the hostile Aeduan, Dumnorix. The Gallic chiefs were summoned to meet Caesar at Portus Itius (Boulogne) and he kidnapped the untrustworthy ones, conveying them all to Britain where he could watch them. Conveniently, Dumnorix was killed trying to escape.[56] In July 54 while Labienus maintained order and secured food supplies in Gaul, Caesar reached Britain, but had to search for the natives, finding them assembled on high ground. He drove them into the nearby wood, but all the entrances were blocked by felled trees. Meanwhile, the ships had collided at anchor in the high winds and some were wrecked. Little had been learned from the last disaster. Caesar returned, hauled ashore the repairable ships, and constructed a fortified line all around them, attached to the guards' camp. He instructed Labienus by letter to build more ships. [57]

Against custom, the Britons united under a leader, Cassivellaunus, chief of the Catuvellauni. Caesar met the Britons at the Thames, where they had fortified the river bank with stakes, but the Romans prevailed. Cassivellaunus unsuccessfully attacked the naval base. Caesar approached the Trinovantes, enemies of Cassivellaunus. He had killed their king, whose son Mandubracius had fled to Caesar in Gaul. The Trinovantes willingly submitted. Cassivellaunus asked for terms, realising that Caesar could not stay in Britain without endangering his achievements in Gaul. Caesar made peace, demanding hostages and tribute. The Romans embarked for Gaul.[58]

In autumn 54, Caesar's daughter Julia died in childbirth. The people of Rome conducted her funeral in the Campus Martius, a considerable honour since funerals were supposed to take place outside the city.[59] New marriage alliances were proposed but came to nothing. Pompey married Cornelia, daughter of Quintus Cornelius Metellus Scipio, an anti-Caesarian, but there are no signs that the partnership was starting to break up. The two men continued to co-operate for another four years.[60]

Caesar's troops wintered in separate quarters in Gaul in 54/53. Earlier, Caesar had passed over Indutiomarus in favour of Cingetorix, not to be confused with Vercingetorix, as leader of the Treveri. Indutiomarus held a grudge, and persuaded Ambiorix, chief of the Eburones, to attack the Romans encamped at Aduatuca/Atuatuca (Tongeren) commanded by Quintus Titurius Sabinus and Lucius Aurunculeius Cotta. Ambiorix told the Romans that Gauls and Germans were about to attack all their camps simultaneously, advising Sabinus and Cotta to join Quintus Tullius Cicero, brother of Marcus, in Nervian territory. Despite Cotta's reluctance, the Roman army marched into annihilation, only a few survivors reaching Labienus' camp. The rebellion spread. The Nervii could not tempt Quintus Cicero to move out, so they enclosed his camp, torturing his captured messengers within view of his soldiers. A slave finally got a message to Caesar, who persuaded a Gallic horseman to carry the reply to tell Cicero that he was coming. The Gaul blended with the attackers, attached the message to a spear and threw it, embedding it in a tower. It was found two days later.[61]

Indutiomarus pinned down Labienus, so Caesar gathered troops from his other legates, arriving near Cicero's fort before the Nervii knew he had marched. They were defeated.[62] Indutiomarus left Labienus' camp, then returned with Senones and Carnutes, but was killed. Hostilities ceased, until the Treveri allied with the Eburones. Caesar raised two more legions in Cisalpine Gaul, and borrowed another from Pompey, who was in Rome while technically governor of Spain. In spring 53, Caesar summoned the Gallic chiefs to a conference, but the Treveri, Senones, and Carnutes stayed away. Caesar, based at Lutetia (Paris), marched on the Senones and Carnutes, receiving their surrender.[63]

Supported by the loyal Aedui and the Remi, Caesar focused on Ambiorix and the Eburones and their allies, Menapii and Treveri. He successfully attacked the Menapii at the mouth of the Rhine, isolating Ambiorix and destroying the lands, crops and homes of the Eburones, encouraging rival tribes to attack them: let the Gauls risk their lives, rather than his soldiers.[64] Ambiorix was never captured. The German Sugambri crossed the Rhine to attack the Roman camp at Aduatuca, where Quintus Cicero commanded the Fourteenth legion and 200 cavalry. He held out and the Germans retreated. Finally, Caesar arrived, executing the leader of the Senones and stationing six legions in their lands, to be supplied by the tribe.[65]

### Pompey as sole consul

In Rome the elections for 53 were delayed by riots, until finally Domitius Calvinus and Valerius Messalla were elected consuls.[66] News arrived in summer 53 of the disastrous defeat and death of Licinius Crassus and his son in Parthia. Even without Crassus, there is no indication of a rift between Caesar and Pompey. In 52, the government of Rome was virtually non-existent. *Interreges* were appointed. Eventually Pompey was made sole consul, an anomaly, avoiding the title Dictator. When the state was settled, Quintus Caecilius Metellus Scipio, Pompey's father-in-law, became consul. Dio detected a change in Pompey, who now started to work with the Senate.[67]

Pompey extended his Spanish command for a further five years (Plutarch says ten years) and he was voted money to maintain his troops. His first concern was to end the violence caused principally by Clodius, who had been killed outside Rome by Titus Annius Milo and his gang. Milo had to be prosecuted, on several counts, but Clodius' two nephews brought a charge of violence, enough to condemn him. Cicero, defending Milo, was put off his stride by soldiers all around the tribunal. Milo was exiled to Marseilles.[68]

Pompey's legislation as sole consul in 52 embraced the most serious problems of the state. He set a limit of four days on court hearings, three to examine witnesses, and on the fourth day allowing two hours for speeches of the prosecution and three hours for the defence. He chose 360 jurors, comprising 120 men from senators, *equites* and *tribuni aerarii*. All the jurors were to hear the examination of witnesses. Eighty-one jurors were to be selected for the final day. No-one could bribe 360 jurors. Another law facilitated retrospective prosecutions, from 70 onwards, of any office holder.[69]

When his term in Gaul ended, Caesar had been allowed to stand for election *in absentia* by the law of ten tribunes, passed in 52 with Pompey's support, or at least without opposition.[70] Pompey's *lex de iure magistratuum* apparently overturned this by stipulating that candidates for election to any magistracy must present their names in person. Pompey added an addendum to the law, exempting Caesar from personal attendance. In legal terms this was useless, and in any case the law of ten tribunes was still in force.[71]

Pompey's *lex de provinciis* interposed a five-year gap between a magistracy in Rome and a promagistracy in a province, which in turn imposed a five-year gap between bribing one's way into higher magistracies and recouping expenses as provincial governor. It obviated the need to select tasks for outgoing consuls before the elections, and the five-year gap initially meant that provincial governors had to be appointed from a pool of ex-consuls and ex-praetors. Marcus Tullius Cicero had to govern Cilicia from the summer of 51 to the summer of 50. Caesar could now be replaced at any time from this pool of ex-consuls.

## Caesar and Vercingetorix

Early in 52, Gallic tribes began to unite. Roman traders at Cenabum (Orleans), chief town of the Carnutes, were killed. Vercingetorix of the Arverni was chosen as leader. He knew that pitched battles were not the answer. Caesar had placed the Boii, dependents of the Aedui, at Gorgobina, which Vercingetorix besieged, obliging Caesar to defend the town or lose the faith of the Aedui.[72]

Vercingetorix adopted a scorched earth policy and ordered the destruction of undefended towns, but the Bituriges refused to destroy

Avaricum (Bourges). Caesar brutally did it for them, killing everyone, regardless of age or gender, in revenge for Roman traders killed at Cenabum, which he also burnt. As a result, Vercingetorix gained more allies. The Aedui, who provided most of the food for the Roman army, had to be coaxed back into friendship with the Romans.[73]

The Gauls assembled at Gergovia (Gergovie), an Arvernian settlement on a high plateau, which could not be taken by storm. Caesar attacked and captured Le Roche Blanche, where the tribesmen guarded the water supply and pasture. The Arverni bribed Aeduan nobles to start a rebellion against the Romans, but Caesar appeared and they surrendered.[74] Caesar returned to Gergovia without punishing the Aedui. He needed their services and food. Attacking Gergovia directly, Caesar lost 700 soldiers and forty-six centurions, explaining in the *Gallic War* that the soldiers did not hear the recall – a flimsy cover up for a blunder.[75] Caesar moved into Aeduan territory.

Roman headquarters were established at Noviodunum in Aeduan territory on the Loire. Some of the Aedui changed sides, but the Remi, Lingones, and the Allobroges of southern Gaul remained loyal to Rome. Caesar met up with Labienus, who had marched south with his four legions, thinking himself cut off when the siege of Gergovia was abandoned. Some of the Aedui defected from the Romans to try for leadership of the Gauls, but the vote was for Vercingetorix, and he continued cutting off supplies to the Romans, adopting guerrilla tactics.[76] He established headquarters at Alesia (Alise Sainte-Reine), in Mandubian territory, on a plateau surrounded on three sides by rivers, the Ose and Oserain to the north and south, both flowing into the river Brenne on the west. The only option was a blockade, so Caesar built two encircling sets of defences, facing both ways, distributing the troops in camps along the fortifications. After losing a battle with the Romans, the Gauls fled to the town, but Vercingetorix shut the gates. That night, since he could not feed the horses, he sent away his cavalry to rally all the Gauls. From then on Vercingetorix stayed within the defences, rationing food.[77]

The relief forces were on their way with a large Aeduan contingent, and Commius, chief of the Atrebates joined them. They occupied high ground south-west of Alesia and attacked next day, at the same time as attacks were launched from the town. Caesar's German horsemen scattered the relieving force. The Gauls attacked Caesar's inner and outer lines by night, without success. Then there was prolonged fighting at a gap in the defences where rivers joined, guarded by two legions. The relief force attacked both legions and simultaneously Vercingetorix attacked in different places. Caesar sent in Labienus and six cohorts to help the two legions, finally taking command himself when the Gauls began to tear down the inner defences. He sent troops round the outside to come up behind the relief force, and allegedly the Gauls gave way as they recognised Caesar's red cloak, leading to their defeat.[78]

Vercingetorix surrendered. His true genius was that he united the tribes for so long. He rode into Caesar's camp, dismounted, and laid down his arms. After six years in prison in Rome, he marched in Caesar's triumph and was then strangled. He is honoured by his huge modern statue at Alise Sainte-Reine.

The Aedui resumed their former status as friends of the Romans, retaining their own government. For the winter, the Romans were distributed among various tribes while Caesar remained at Bibracte (Beuvray) in Aeduan territory.[79] At the beginning of 51 the Bituriges rebelled, and Caesar marched against them, leaving Mark Antony in command of the winter camps.[80] This is the first mention of Antony by name in the *Gallic War*, though he had joined Caesar probably in 54.

After the defeat of the Bituriges, Caesar restricted himself to taking hostages.[81] Instead of attacking the Romans, the tribes attacked each other. The Carnutes made war on the Bituriges, who appealed to Caesar for help, and Commius of the Atrebates encouraged the Bellovaci to attack the Suessiones. It required an energetic Roman campaign to bring order, but after the final battle other tribes submitted to Caesar voluntarily. Mopping up the last resistance was bloody. Labienus fought the Treveri. The remnants of the Eburones were massacred but Ambiorix escaped.[82] Uxellodunum (Puy d'Issolu) surrendered when Caesar cut off the water supply. He assembled all the warriors and chopped off their hands. It was a just punishment in Roman eyes, but horrific to modern eyes.[83]

The last of the Gauls to surrender was Commius, who sent deputies to Mark Antony promising to go anywhere, provided that he never had to see another Roman. No large-scale campaigns were conducted in 50. Caesar lightened the burdens imposed upon the Gauls and distributed prestigious gifts.[84] He visited the enfranchised peoples of Cisalpine Gaul soliciting support for himself as consular candidate. Placing Labienus in command in the Cisalpine province, Caesar chose to ignore rumours of his disloyalty.[85] He stationed three legions in Belgae territory under Gaius Trebonius, and three under Gaius Fabius among the Aedui.[86]

## The Gallic provinces

There was no question of giving up Gaul after Caesar's conquests, so the country remained as an occupied zone, providing a base for operations to repel raids incursions from across the Rhine, or mount expeditions into Germany. Provincial organisation was slow to develop, even accounting for the interruptions of the civil wars. When development did begin, much of it depended on Caesar's assessment of the various communities. Each tribe, or group of smaller tribes, was assigned to their own self-governing *civitas* capital. The friendly *civitates* could be attached to Rome, which at first meant attached to Caesar, encouraged by gifts and privileges. Caesar promoted the Arverni and the Aedui, obliterating their support for Vercingetorix. The Romans adopted their usual policy of cultivating elite groups, whether of large tribes or small independent communities. Romanization was not enforced, but infiltrated gradually from The Province/Gallia Narbonensis, or by Gauls who served in Roman armies, returning with experience of Roman customs, and of course via trade in both directions.

Eventually, a Gallo-Roman culture grew up. Three colonies were established in Gallia Comata, at Raurica, later Augusta Raurica (Augst), Noviodunum (Nyon), and Lugdunum (Lyon). The programme was Caesar's, but it lapsed during the civil wars. These colonies were for time-served soldiers, forming quasi-military settlements intended to protect the routes from the Rhine into Italy.[87] Caesar did not have enough time to organise Gaul, but he provided a framework for Octavian-Augustus, who consolidated his power in 27, after which he could devote time to Gaul, dividing it into the three separate provinces of Aquitania, Lugdunensis and Belgica.

## Prelude to civil war

From 54, Pompey had remained in Rome while commanding Spain via his legates, Marcus Petreius and Lucius Afranius. The anomaly had not been challenged, and it served as a useful precedent for the provincial organisation of Octavian-Augustus. The consuls for 51 were Servius Sulpicius Rufus and Marcus Claudius Marcellus, who was virulently anti-Caesar. Blatantly ignoring the law making it illegal to flog Roman citizens, Marcellus did exactly that to one of the ex-magistrates of Comum (Como), which Caesar had made a Latin colony where magistrates automatically gained Roman citizenship. Marcellus, targeting Caesar, had merely thrown the Transpadane Gauls into Caesar's arms. Cicero called Marcellus' action disgraceful.[88]

Marcellus argued for Caesar's recall. The other consul Sulpicius objected to the removal of a magistrate in mid-term, indicating that Caesar's post was still current.[89] Probably no terminal date for Caesar's command had been set. The ban on discussion about it until 1 March 54 was not a terminal date. Since Caesar's command was renewed for five years in 55, then 50 should be the terminal date, and Marcellus chose 1 March of that year.[90] Pompey managed to convert that into the earliest date for discussion.

The consuls for 50 were Lucius Aemilius Paullus and Gaius Claudius Marcellus, cousin of Marcus Marcellus. Gaius Scribonius Curio was tribune.[91] Curio was anti-Caesar, but in February 50 Caelius informed Cicero that Curio had turned into a Caesarian.[92] Caesar may have settled all Curio's debts. When the consul Gaius Marcellus proposed to recall Caesar, Curio suggested that Pompey should also give up his provinces, and consistently pursued this argument as tribune.[93]

In the summer, Pompey was seriously ill, and the public prayers for him and the rejoicing at his recovery convinced him that the whole population supported him.[94] Curio labelled him a tyrant, proposing that if Pompey and Caesar did not give up their commands simultaneously, they should both be declared public enemies.[95] The Senate quashed the idea.

In November 51, news came that the Parthians were advancing through Commagene towards Syria.[96] Troops were assembled. Caesar and Pompey were asked to contribute one legion. Pompey offered the legion that he had lent to Caesar. Without protest, Caesar returned this legion and sent one of his own. No Parthian campaign was begun, and Pompey stationed the two legions near Capua. Hirtius, finishing off the eighth book of the *Gallic War*, refers to 'the armed tyranny' of Pompey.[97]

Curio's suggestion that Caesar and Pompey should lay down their commands simultaneously was carried by 370 to twenty-two votes.[98] Acting independently, Marcellus appeared at Pompey's Alban villa offering him a sword and command of troops in Italy. Pompey agreed that if no better solution was found, he would take command.[99] Curio's term of office ended on 9 December, but Caesar secured the election of Mark Antony and Cassius Longinus as tribunes. Antony had also been elected as augur, replacing the orator Hortensius, who had died. In this post Antony would be able to supplement his tribunician right of veto by declaring the omens unfavourable if anyone proposed actions damaging to Caesar.

Caesar offered to retain Cisalpine Gaul and Illyricum with only two legions until he became consul. Pompey agreed. The Senate refused.[100] Cicero arrived in Italy from Cilicia in November 50, to find that the choice was between Caesar as consul, or fighting him.[101] Mark Antony spoke against Pompey in the Senate on 20 December. Five days later, Cicero and Pompey conversed all afternoon at Formiae. Cicero concluded that Pompey did not want peace.[102]

Consuls for 49 were Lucius Cornelius Lentulus Crus and Gaius Claudius Marcellus, the third Marcellus to hold the consulship. In January 49, Caesar sent a proposal to the Senate that he and Pompey should lay down their commands simultaneously.[103] This was rejected. A terminal date was nominated for Caesar to give up his command or be deemed an enemy of state. Antony and Cassius vetoed it. War was inevitable. The senatorial decree was passed on 7 January, authorising the consuls, praetors, tribunes and all the men of proconsular rank near the city to take steps to secure the safety of the state.[104] Pompey was not named as commander until later.

Violence was threatened if Antony and Cassius vetoed the declaration of war. They may have been thrown out of the Senate. Violence against tribunes was sacrilegious, and it gave Caesar his excuse for war.[105] Antony and Cassius fled to Caesar dressed as slaves, joined by Curio and Caelius.[106] Suetonius and Dio make it clear that before the four young men reached him, Caesar had already illegally left his province by crossing the Rubicon, the boundary between Cisalpine Gaul and Italy, but only Suetonius and Plutarch name it.[107] The Rubicon is so famous that it is surprising that nobody really knows where it was.[108] Caesar allegedly hesitated at the boundary on the night of 11 January, debating the enormity of what he was about to do. He led the army across, saying some kind of variation on 'the die is cast.'[109] Whatever he said, Caesar ended the gestation period of the civil war by presiding over its birth on 10 January 49.

## The Civil Wars

Pompey and the senators were not ready for war. The consular provinces were hastily assigned by lot, Syria to Pompey's father-in-law Metellus Scipio, The Province to Lucius Domitius Ahenobarbus. Sicily, Sardinia with Corsica, and Africa were designated praetorian provinces, assigned respectively to Marcus Porcius Cato, Marcus Aurelius Cotta, and Lucius Aelius Tubero.[110] Pompey began recruiting in Campania on 17 January.[111] On 22 January, Titus Labienus joined Pompey. Caesar sent all his baggage after him.[112] Negotiations were attempted and failed.[113] Likewise, negotiations failed after Caesar had reached Corfinium, and again at Brundisium when Pompey was about to leave Italy.[114]

Caesar's rapid march into Italy was halted at Corfinium by Domitius Ahenobarbus, to whom Pompey patiently explained by letter that splitting forces into small packets would not win victories, but not having been named as supreme commander, he could suggest but not command. When Domitius had to eat humble pie and ask for help, Pompey refused to stake everything on a pitched battle in the north.[115] Domitius went free and his troops became Caesar's.[116]

Pompey marched for Brundisium.[117] Caesar followed, too late. The consuls and much of Pompey's army had sailed for Dyrrachium, and Pompey got away when the ships returned. Entering Brundisium, Caesar found the streets barricaded. Across most of them there were trenches concealing pits containing sharpened stakes, a masterpiece of defensive planning, delaying Caesar until after Pompey sailed.[118]

Caesar had a choice, follow Pompey, or neutralize Spain. He chose the latter. Italians were ordered to round up ships to be sent to Brundisium, and to build two new fleets. Caesar sent Curio to Sicily, where Marcus Porcius Cato had delayed his arrival, and now fled to Pompey.[119] Curio moved on to Africa, locking up Attius Varus in Utica. Then Juba and his Numidians attacked and Curio was killed.[120] In Rome, Caesar appropriated the money stored since 390 BC in case the Gauls attacked. He said he had conquered the Gauls, so the money was not needed.[121] He ensured the loyalty of Italy and the provinces to which he had access. Marcus Crassus governed Cisalpine Gaul and gave the inhabitants Roman citizenship. Marcus Aemilius Lepidus commanded in Rome. Then Caesar marched to Spain, saying that he was going to fight the army without a leader, and would return to fight the leader without an army, meaning Pompey in Greece.[122] Massilia closed its gates because the citizens were friends of Caesar and Pompey and would not favour one above the other. Gaius Trebonius was put in charge of besieging the city, receiving its surrender while Caesar fought in Spain.[123] The Pompeian commanders in Spain were Terentius Varro in Hispania Ulterior and Marcus Petreius and Lucius Afranius in Citerior. Caesar's legate Gaius Fabius met these two at Ilerda (Lerida), and Caesar arrived and dispersed them. They marched to the Ebro, but turned back to Ilerda, making camp on a hilltop with no water supply, and surrendered. Varro did the same.[124] Returning to Italy, Caesar quelled a mutiny, principally of the Ninth legion, executing twelve of 120 agitators.[125] He was elected Dictator to hold the elections, relinquishing the office when he became consul for the second time in 48, with Publius Servilius Isauricus as colleague. The other magistrates were elected and the vacant priesthoods were filled.[126] Caesar tried to help debtors by passing a law to have the value of land assessed and to oblige creditors to accept land in lieu of payment.[127] He distributed grain to the people and used his warships to guard the sea-lanes, protecting the food supply from Sicily and Sardinia, sending Aulus Albinus and Sextus Peducaeus to govern the two islands. Decimus Brutus took over the new province of Gaul, and Marcus Aemilius Lepidus was sent to Spain.[128]

In naval engagements the Pompeians defeated Caesar's admiral Cornelius Dolabella. Pompey requisitioned ships and crews from Egypt, Phoenicia, Cilicia, Syria, Bithynia, Pontus, Athens, Corcyra, and Asia, and was having more ships built. He had five legions and raised two more from veterans settled in Cilicia, Greece and Macedonia. The consul Lentulus raised another two from veterans in Asia. Troops were raised in Thessaly, Boeotia, Achaea and Epirus.[129] Senators who accompanied Pompey finally made him commander of all the forces.

At Brundisium, Caesar had only enough ships to ferry 15,000 legionaries and 500 cavalry to Greece. Antony was to bring the rest when the ships returned, but Calpurnius Bibulus captured thirty of the returning transports, burning them with the crews on board. Pompey intended to put his troops in winter quarters at Dyrrachium, Apollonia, and towns on the Adriatic coast, but Caesar arrived, captured Apollonia and was admitted to Oricum, Pompey's supply base.[130] Both armies camped near Dyrrachium. Pompey's fleet ensured supplies by sea, whereas Caesar was short of food. Soon both armies moved to the river Apsis near Apollonia.[131]

Antony was blockaded at Brundisium by Scribonius Libo. Caesar went to find a boat and crew to sail to Italy to investigate why Antony had not sailed, but he was not master of the weather or the seas and had to turn back.[132] Antony refused a truce with Libo and Bibulus, but soon afterwards Bibulus died and Antony broke out from Brundisium. He landed at Nymphaeum and marched south to join Caesar, evading Pompey's ambush.[133] The race began for Dyrrachium. Pompey camped near the city gathering his supply ships in the large bay. All that Caesar could achieve was to prevent Pompey from foraging, and to this end he built small forts on the hills east of Pompey's camp, linking them by trenches. Pompey built an inner ring of defensive lines enclosing as much territory as possible, forcing Caesar to extend his own lines, eventually building a double circuit.[134]

Caesar's problem was in finding food. Pompey's problem was with his officers, who urged battle, while Pompey knew that it was best to conserve energy while Caesar starved. Cicero had joined Pompey in June, and he lamented that most officers thought only of getting rich.[135] Caesar cut Pompey's water supply, forcing him to remove all animals to Dyrrachium, but he had to bring them back when Caesar cut off the foraging areas.[136] Informed of a gap in Caesar's defences, Pompey investigated, discovering that Caesar's two parallel circuits were open where they met the sea. He very nearly succeeded in overwhelming Caesar's troops, but Antony arrived, followed by Caesar. Pompey built a small camp to protect his foraging grounds and his ships coming to shore. Caesar tried and failed to take it, losing many men. It was time to go in search of food.[137]

Pompey joined Metellus Scipio's army. Caesar made camp near Pharsalus. By the calendar it was August, by the seasons it was midsummer. The crops were still ripening.[138] Caesar drew up in battle order each day, but Pompey's troops were stationed behind rough ground not risking battle. Caesar decided to find food elsewhere, but as he broke camp, Pompey drew up further out than usual. Some days earlier he had outlined his battle plan. The cavalry was to attack the flank of Caesar's right wing, then move round the rear to encircle Caesar.[139] Observing the movements of the horsemen on Pompey's left, Caesar guessed what was planned, and detached some cohorts from the third battle line to make a fourth line, hidden opposite Pompey's cavalry.[140] At the first onslaught Pompey's infantry stood firm. Complying with Pompey's plan, Labienus led the cavalry attack on Caesar's right wing, and Caesar brought out his fourth line. The

Pompeians fled and Caesar's troops began to encircle the Pompeian left, making his victory a certainty.[141] Pompey rode back to camp, moving on when Caesar's men broke in. Some Pompeian troops made a last stand, surrendering when Caesar cut their water supply.[142] The historian Asinius Pollio was probably with Caesar when he saw the enemy dead and said that he had been forced to rely on his army to avoid condemnation by his enemies, reported variously by Suetonius, and by Plutarch:[143] 'They would have it so; they brought me to such a pass that if I, Caius Caesar, after waging successfully the greatest wars, had dismissed my forces, I should have been condemned in their courts.'

Needing to follow Pompey, Caesar sent Antony to command in Rome. In autumn 48, Caesar was appointed Dictator for one year, and Antony was made *magister equitum*, also for a year, after some argument.[144] In the absence of consuls and praetors Antony controlled military and political matters, upsetting the senators by wearing his sword at meetings.[145] Cornelius Dolabella tried to arrange cancellation of all debts and a riot broke out in the Forum. The Senate authorized Antony to restore order. He brought up his troops, but the crowd did not disperse, so Antony sent in his soldiers, resulting in several deaths. Disturbances continued until Caesar returned to Rome. Antony's actions could not be condoned, so Caesar dropped him.[146]

### Caesar in Egypt

Pompey was heading for Egypt, where in the past he had assisted the late Ptolemy XII Auletes (the Flute Player) to retain power, for a price. It was Pompey's associate Aulus Gabinius, proconsul of Syria, who had employed his troops to restore Auletes to his kingdom in 55. Some of Gabinius' soldiers were still in Egypt and might join Pompey, and there was the chance of more troops and money from the young Ptolemy XIII. Pompey landed at Pelusium (Tell el-Farama) east of the Nile delta. Ptolemy's advisers, Achillas, commander of the Royal army, Pothinus, the finance minister, and Theodotus, Ptolemy's tutor, all decided that they should rid themselves of Pompey before the inevitable arrival of Caesar. Pompey was killed, and his head and signet ring were presented to Caesar.[147]

Ptolemy XIII and his sister Cleopatra VII had been designated joint heirs of Ptolemy Auletes, but were currently at war with each other. Cleopatra was with her army outside Alexandria, and traditionally she arrived at Caesar's feet rolled up in a carpet, or according to

Plutarch, in a bag for storing bedding.[148] The Royal palace sheltered all surviving children of Auletes, Ptolemy XIII and his sibling Ptolemy, and the sisters Arsinoe and Cleopatra. Caesar began to fortify the palace, gathering food, fodder, and weapons, and summoning ships from around the eastern Mediterranean. He sent a message to his ally Mithradates of Pergamum asking him to recruit soldiers in Syria and Cilicia and bring them by sea.[149] He executed Pothinus, and Arsinoe escaped to join Achillas, arranged his death, and replaced him with Ganymede, who let in the sea to spoil Caesar's fresh water supplies. The Romans survived by digging wells.[150] Supply ships arrived from Domitius Calvinus commanding the eastern provinces, but contrary winds and then a naval battle delayed their entry.[151] Caesar needed to gain control of Pharos Island, which gave its name to the lighthouse, and of the causeway and its two bridges connecting the island to the mainland. While fortifying the island, Caesar was attacked and many of the soldiers drowned. Caesar had to swim for his life.[152]

Mithradates of Pergamum had by now captured Pelusium. In the meantime, Ptolemy XIII had been allowed to join his army, housed in a strong camp, with a branch of the Nile between it and Caesar's line of march. It was a hard-fought battle to overwhelm Ptolemy's fortifications, but finally the Egyptians were routed, and Ptolemy drowned in the Nile.[153] This conferred divinity according to Egyptian tradition, so Caesar had the body retrieved and displayed, to deprive dissidents of the chance to rebel in his name.

Cleopatra was made Queen of Egypt with her young brother Ptolemy XIV as consort.[154] Caesar accompanied her on a trip down the Nile.[155] Allegedly he married Cleopatra, scandalous if true, because marriage of Romans to foreigners was illegal. Ptolemy Caesar, or Caesarion, born of this union, was accepted by Caesar as his son.

Probably in June 47, Caesar left Egypt to prevent Pharnaces, the son of Mithradates of Pontus, from taking over Lesser Armenia, Cappadocia and Galatia. Deiotarus, king of Galatia, had sought help from Domitius Calvinus, governor of Asia.[156] Pharnaces defeated Domitius near Nicopolis, and went on to kill many Romans in Pontus, while Domitius returned to Asia.[157] Caesar caught up with Pharnaces at Zela in Pontus. Negotiations failed, so Caesar fortified the high ground close to Pharnaces' camp but separated from it by a deep gully with steep slopes. Pharnaces nearly succeeded in a frontal attack on the Roman camp, but the Sixth legion managed to force the enemy back down the hill, up the opposite slope, and into their camp.

Pharnaces escaped.[158] Caesar left two legions in Pontus, describing the campaign in a letter to his friend Gaius Matius, using the famous phrase *veni, vidi, vici,* I came, I saw, I conquered.[159] Domitius Calvinus was left in command in the east, and Caesar returned to Italy. On the way he collected money pledged to Pompey by various kings, and he fined communities which had helped the Pompeians. Caesar said that two things created and protected sovereignty: money and soldiers.[160]

## The African War

Caesar presided over the elections in Rome as Dictator for the second time. His officers Fufius Calenus and Publius Vatinius became consuls from September 47, and several senators and equestrians were promoted. Caesar's great-nephew Gaius Octavius, now aged about sixteen, was made *praefectus urbi* or city prefect, during the festival of the *Feriae Latinae.* This post, nothing to do with later city prefects, was bestowed on young members of upper-class families when all the magistrates left Rome for the Alban Mount to conduct religious ceremonies commemorating the conquest of Alba Longa. Gaius Octavius was technically head of state for a few days but attracted little notice.

Surviving Pompeians had gathered in Africa, where another war was to be fought. Some of Caesar's soldiers chose this moment to mutiny, chasing away Caesar's representative Gaius Sallustius Crispus (Sallust), and killing the praetors Cosconius and Galba.[161] Caesar met the soldiers outside Rome. They asked for discharge. What they really wanted was money to dissuade them, but Caesar accepted their request at face value, addressing them as *Quirites,* citizens, instead of *comilitones,* fellow soldiers. He said he could fight the war in Africa with other troops. The mutiny collapsed.[162]

The Pompeians in Africa were commanded by Metellus Scipio, with fourteen legions, cavalry and light armed troops, some elephants, and many ships. King Juba of Numidia brought infantry, cavalry and archers. When Scipio ordered the massacre of the pro-Caesarian citizens of Utica, they were saved by Cato, who had occupied the city after expelling the governor.[163]

The Pompeians outnumbered Caesar, and he could not land his whole force because his transports from Lilybaeum (Marsala) were scattered in a storm. With only 3,000 men and 150 cavalry, he landed near Hadrumetum (Susa), held by the Pompeian Considius Longus. Caesar stumbled on the beach, but rose again with handfuls of sand, saying 'I hold you, Africa.'[164] Juba's cavalry attacked Caesar, who beat them off and then marched south-east down the coast, camping near Ruspina, which became his naval base. On 1 January Caesar was welcomed at Leptis Minor (Lemta), where some of the missing ships arrived, disembarked their soldiers and sailed back to Sicily for the rest of the troops. Publius Vatinius searched for missing vessels.[165]

Leaving six cohorts at Leptis, Caesar returned to Ruspina. He led out a forage party, narrowly escaping encirclement by Labienus. Caesar ordered every other cohort to turn round so that his men faced in two directions, and moving in battle formation they fought their way to a hill to evade the Numidians, waiting until dark to regain their camp.[166] Everything had to be imported, not only food, but timber, iron and lead from Sicily, to make weapons in the arms factories that he established, so Caesar built fortifications from Ruspina to the sea to bring in cargoes safely.[167]

As in all wars, hostilities involved civilians. Caesar received food supplies and assistance from various towns, where the people risked retribution by the Pompeians. Settlements were besieged by both sides, lands were devastated, food was seized for soldiers and animals, or stores were destroyed to deny supplies to the opposing side. Either way, civilians suffered. The natives near Caesar's camp asked for protection; if Caesar failed to provide it, the inhabitants could easily turn to the Pompeians.

King Juba and his Numidians had to leave Scipio when King Bocchus of Mauretania and his Roman general Publius Sittius took Cirta (Constantine), the wealthiest Numidian city.[168] At the end of January 46 Caesar collected the newly arrived Thirteenth and Fourteenth legions, with cavalry, archers and slingers, and returned to Ruspina, where he fortified the ridge around the nearby plain.[169] As work started, Caesar drove off Scipio and Labienus when they attacked. It was not a spectacular victory, but Scipio marched off to Uzitta about a mile away, his main source of water and supplies, and reinforcements from King Juba joined him.[170] Caesar reached the town with no baggage, and a rainstorm spoiled all the food. Deserters from Scipio began to join Caesar, among them two Gaetulians originally sent as spies. Caesar persuaded them to foment a rebellion in Numidia to draw off Juba once again.[171] The Pompeian commander Varus burnt the transports at anchor and captured two quinqueremes. Caesar rode for Leptis, put to sea in a small boat and leaped on board one of the ships of a detached squadron. He pursued Varus, re-captured a trireme and a quinquereme with the enemy crew, and fired the enemy transports at anchor.[172]

Needing a victory more than ever, Caesar found a battlefield near Thapsus where he could place his troops in a seemingly disadvantageous position. The terrain was not advantageous for the Numidian cavalry. In the hinterland of the town, there was a narrow strip of land between the sea and an inland lake. Caesar built a camp near the town, and another camp south of it between the coast and the lake, ordering his fleet to guard the approaches from the sea. Then he began the siege of Thapsus, forcing Scipio to come to the rescue.[173]

Scipio stationed Juba and Afranius near Caesar's southern camp and built another camp at the northern end of the lake. Caesar was ready. The fleet blockading Thapsus was ordered to sail round the promontory to the rear of Scipio's army, and at a pre-arranged signal to make a lot of noise as if fresh troops were disembarking – but the battle seems to have been won without the fleet. As Scipio drew up in battle formation, his troops began to dash about as if panicked. Caesar resisted those who urged an attack, but without orders one of the trumpeters sounded the charge, and Caesar had to let the battle take its course. When the Numidian horsemen left the field, the Pompeian army collapsed. Thapsus held out under Gaius Vergilius, besieged by the Caesarian proconsul Caninius Rebilus. Scipio's surviving soldiers fled to Utica, where they killed many of the inhabitants, until Cato bribed them to leave. His name Uticensis was well earned. He made provision for his family, then killed himself, preferring death to Caesar's mercy.[174]

Pompeian resistance was confined to Thapsus and Thysdra, both of which eventually surrendered. Afranius was captured and executed. Scipio was drowned trying to escape by sea. Juba and Petreius fought each other to the death, arranging for the winner to be killed by a slave.[175] Utica, Hadrumetum and Uzitta were occupied by Caesarians. Juba's kingdom was divided, one part given to Bocchus of Mauretania, and the other incorporated into the new province of Africa Nova, where the first governor was the proconsul Gaius Sallustius Crispus (Sallust). Dio says he plundered the natives.[176]

Fines were levied from communities which had supported the Pompeians. The property of Roman officers serving with Juba was confiscated. Thirteen million sesterces were raised from Hadrumetum and Thapsus, and the people of Utica, already mauled by Pompeians, ransomed themselves by paying two hundred million sesterces over three years. Caesar settled some of his veterans in colonies in towns along the coast, to guard the area against the Pompeian fleet.[177]

## Caesar returns to Rome

In April 46 Caesar entered his third Dictatorship, which was to be a ten-year term. He and his *magister equitum* Aemilius Lepidus were also consuls. The Senate decreed an unprecedented forty days' thanksgiving. Caesar did not accept all the honours voted to him. He was permitted to sit between the consuls and speak first in debates, and was made *praefectus moribus*, prefect of morals, for three years, with censorial powers to promote or demote senators, and Dio says that he created senators from soldiers and sons of freedmen.[178] At the end of September 46 Caesar held four triumphs, over Gaul, Egypt, Pharnaces, and Juba, avoiding the unhappy theme of victory over Romans.[179] After six years in prison Vercingetorix was paraded through the streets and then executed, and Arsinoe, sister of Cleopatra walked in the Egyptian triumph before being released. She was killed some years later by Cleopatra and Mark Antony.[180]

Attending to the food supply, Caesar distributed more than the normal amounts of grain and olive oil. The vast booty from the wars enabled him to pay 400 sesterces to each claimant of the corn dole, but he reduced the numbers of people eligible for it from 320,000 to 150,000. [181] Legates were appointed to purchase lands for veteran settlement, and rewards were introduced for families with several children, prompted by the reduced population figures revealed by the census.[182] Caesar passed laws to assist debtors. The jury courts were reorganized, the *tribuni aerarii* being removed and juries were henceforth drawn in equal numbers from senators and equestrians. Provincial government was reformed and regulated, propraetors governing for one year and proconsuls for two.[183]

In carrying out his legislation Caesar avoided senatorial debate. Cicero wrote to Lucius Papirius Paetus in October 46, explaining how all government emanated from Caesar's house. Whether or not Cicero attended the Senate, his name was included among the signatories of decrees, and he received letters from grateful kings he had never heard of, thanking him for approving their new-found kingly status bestowed by Caesar.[184]

The reform of the calendar was long overdue, the seasons being out of synchronization with it. The new calendar was probably based on the calculations of Egyptian astronomers and implemented by Sosigenes, one of Cleopatra's courtiers. Two months were added between November and December, and from 1 January 45, there were 365 days to the year with one extra day to be inserted every four years.[185]

Cleopatra was invited to Rome and housed in Caesar's villa across the Tiber. She brought her young brother/consort Ptolemy XIV. Her father Ptolemy Auletes had been a friend and ally of the Roman people, a status now officially granted to her. She hoped that if Caesarion succeeded her, Egypt would remain free, allied to but not subject to Rome. Caesar erected a statue of Cleopatra in his temple of Venus Genetrix, which he had vowed at the battle of Pharsalus. He had already purchased land to build his Forum, in which the temple was the showpiece. Temple and Forum were dedicated in September 46 in an unfinished state, and Augustus completed the work. The tribune Helvius Cinna said that Caesar had asked him to present a bill to the people, allowing Caesar to marry any woman in order to beget children.[186] The woman was probably Cleopatra, and it was said that Caesar would make Alexandria the capital of the Roman world.[187]

## The Spanish War

The war against the Pompeians in Spain was originally to be conducted by Caesar's legates, his nephew Quintus Pedius, and Quintus Fabius Maximus, but the Pompeians had enlarged their armies by recruiting Spanish natives. Pedius and Fabius required reinforcements, and most of all they needed Caesar.[188]

Gnaeus Pompeius, Pompey's elder son, was the first to arrive in Spain after recovering from illness. His brother Sextus and Titus Labienus brought the fleet and the troops from Africa.[189] The only source for the war in Spain, probably written by an anonymous centurion, is *The Spanish War*, not in the same league as *The Alexandrian War* or *The African War*. Chronology is murky and there is no attention to supplies and logistics, or topographical details and the construction of fortifications, usually well-documented by Caesar and Hirtius.

In November 46 Caesar left Rome, inviting his great-nephew Gaius Octavius to accompany him, but the boy was ill. In Spain, Sextus Pompeius held Corduba to the north, with two legions, and Gnaeus Pompeius was besieging Ulia, which held out for Caesar. Before

Caesar arrived, Pedius and Fabius had made camp east of Corduba, and Caesar besieged the city to draw Gnaeus away from Ulia.[190] The plan worked, but Gnaeus was too wise to offer battle. Caesar's food supplies were low, so he moved from Corduba to capture the Pompeian grain stores at Ategua. He cut off the town by a palisade and ditch, establishing outposts to guard against the approach of Gnaeus. Caesar arrived in thick fog, overwhelming the outposts. Ategua surrendered.[191]

At the river Salsum, where Caesar's soldiers held both sides of the river, the Pompeians attacked. On one side of the river Caesar's troops wavered until two centurions from the Alaudae legion dashed across the river and succeeded in stiffening resistance. Both were killed. Caesar's cavalry dispersed the Pompeians. There was another inconclusive skirmish next day near Soricaria.[192]

Eventually, the two armies arrived at Munda, unidentified, possibly west of Urso (Osuna). Not expecting battle, Caesar was breaking camp when Gnaeus Pompeius began to form up. Caesar put out the battle flag.[193] Gnaeus Pompeius had every chance of winning the battle. There was a marshy area between the two armies, which the Caesarians crossed with difficulty. The Pompeian right wing was pushed back by Caesar's Tenth legion and had to be reinforced.[194] At one point Caesar had to dash to the front to rally his troops, and then the Pompeian left wing began to crumble. Gnaeus ordered Labienus to move from the right to assist the left, but before he got into position Caesar ordered up his ally king Bogud of Mauretania with his horsemen and they drove Labienus away. Realizing that Bogud's forces were moving towards the Pompeian camp, Labienus followed, but other Pompeians could not see why he moved. If he was leaving the battlefield, then the battle must be lost. The Pompeians ran away. Caesar said afterwards that he had often struggled to achieve victory, but this time he fought for his life.[195] Labienus was killed and buried where he fell. Gnaeus Pompeius escaped but was captured and, like his father, he was decapitated, his death graphically described in *The Spanish War*.[196] Sextus Pompeius fled from Corduba, leaving his two legions, and took to the sea.[197] Caesar built fortifications enclosing Munda, placing Fabius Maximus in command, instructing him to continue attacking until it fell. Corduba was taken with tremendous slaughter. At Hispalis (Sevilla) near the river Baetis (Guadalquivir), Caninius was put in command of a garrison, but most of his soldiers were killed. Wanting to capture Hispalis intact, Caesar waited until the Pompeians made a sortie, sent his cavalry against them and captured the town. Shortly afterwards, Hasta (Nesa de Asta) surrendered to him and others followed suit, sometimes by coercion.

Caesar rewarded communities which had helped him.[198] Land was taken from defeated towns and given to loyal communities, and taxes were reduced. Caesar bestowed Latin rights on some towns, and founded several Roman citizen colonies, obliged to defend their lands. The best-known citizen colony is Urso (Osuna) sixty miles east of Seville, its charter granted by Caesar early in 44. It is the only known colonial charter, much of the text surviving on bronze tablets. There were more than 134 clauses, the first fifty-nine and some at the end being lost.[199] Settlers were drawn from the Roman plebs. The colony would be autonomous, governed by two duoviri and aediles with the same duties as those in Rome. Each magistrate was entitled to clerical and administrative staff, paid at rates laid down in the charter.

Only a few other colonies can be attributed to Caesar. It is not always possible to distinguish between Caesar's work and foundations by Augustus. Richardson suggests that Caesar's colonies were in the war-zone, including Tarraco (Tarragona) and possibly Cartago Nova (Cartagena) in Hispania Citerior. In the Baetis valley, besides Urso, there were colonies at Hasta (Nesa de Asta), Hispalis (Sevilla), and Ucubi (Espejo).[200]

After the battle of Munda, Caesar's great-nephew Gaius Octavius reached Spain with Marcus Vipsanius Agrippa and other friends. Octavius played an active role in the foundation of colonies and the settlement of legionary veterans and Spanish troops. He received envoys from Spanish towns and supported the people of Saguntum in their defence against certain charges. On the journey back to Rome Octavius travelled in Caesar's carriage.

Antony set off to meet Caesar, not sure whether he was still in disgrace over his brutal crowd dispersal. He was accompanied by Gaius Trebonius who, according to Cicero, tried to bring Antony into a plot to kill Caesar.[201] Antony was obviously not swayed and possibly did not reveal the plot to Caesar, but it is also possible that he did, and if so he and Caesar decided to wait and see.[202] The reunion with Caesar went well, and Antony travelled in Caesar's own carriage, with Octavius following behind.[203] Antony was to be consul with Caesar for 44. The future looked bright.

*End game*

The Roman government was already in Caesar's hands, and once in Rome he tightened his grip. He planned campaigns in Dacia and Parthia and put trusted men in key posts in Rome and the provinces. Antony's brother Gaius was praetor, and his other brother Lucius, as tribune, passed a law in December 45 empowering Caesar to nominate both consuls for the following years, and half of all the magistrates.[204] The elections were not quite dead, but it required more than the kiss of life to resuscitate them. Aulus Hirtius and Vibius Pansa were to be consuls for 43. Decimus Brutus was to govern Cisalpine Gaul, and Lucius Munatius Plancus was assigned to The Province, each for one year, after which they were to be consuls for 42. Aemilius Lepidus was to relinquish his post as *magister equitum* to govern Hispania Citerior with part of southern Gaul, and Asinius Pollio was to govern Hispania Ulterior. Gaius Cassius Longinus was to be praetor. He had expected more. After the disastrous outcome of Crassus' Parthian expedition in 53, Cassius as quaestor had gathered the remnants of the army, saved the province of Syria, and reconstituted the Roman position in the east. He quietly festered.

In 44 Caesar was in his fifth consulship, but on 15 February he became Dictator for life, so he resigned as consul in favour of Dolabella. For Antony, Dolabella was the worst choice of colleague. As augur, Antony did a Bibulus, declaring that the omens were unfavourable, preventing Dolabella from becoming consul. He got away with it. Caesar was not pleased but did nothing.[205] The Senate granted unprecedented honours and marks of distinction to Caesar. Cassius and a few others held back.[206] Fairly rapidly, Caesar became an autocrat, remarking that Sulla was an idiot to lay down his Dictatorship. He did not consult the Senate about his proposals or allow debate. In the end, it was not so much his measures that upset the senators, but the methods that he used to put them into effect.

After Caesar's return from Africa, a statue of him was placed in the Capitoline temple facing the statue of Jupiter, with an inscription allegedly proclaiming his divinity. It caused offence, so Caesar had the words removed, but even so he seemed to have developed a disturbing inclination to become a living god. He had a shrine set up to himself and his *Clementia*, and Antony was appointed as priest of his cult, though he did not take up the office until 39.[207] In the eastern territories, worship of a living ruler was normal, but the Romans did not deify rulers even if they were safely dead. Another habit from the east was coinage routinely bearing portraits of rulers, but up to now Roman coins never displayed a portrait of someone living. Early in 44, coins were issued bearing Caesar's portrait. After him the practice never ceased, providing archaeologists with valuable dating evidence.

Caesar was suspected of wanting to be king, or worse, to establish a hereditary monarchy. The Senate had granted him the title Imperator as a hereditary name, so that was a start. At the festival of the Lupercalia in February 44, Caesar, or Antony, or both in collusion, may have tried to eradicate the rumours that he aimed at kingship. The Lupercalia was an ancient fertility rite, the Lupercal being the cave where the she-wolf suckled Romulus and Remus. Antony joined the scantily dressed young men running through Rome with strings of goat skin, whose touch was supposed to make women fertile. He approached Caesar, presiding over the festival, to offer him a diadem or crown. Caesar refused it, to general rejoicing. Antony offered the crown again. Caesar rejected it again. The crowd roared approval again. Caesar had rejected monarchy. What exactly was going on here? Possibly Caesar and Antony wanted to demonstrate that Caesar did not want to be king. According to Dio, Antony hoped to convince the Dictator not to go too far.[208] Plutarch says that Caesar wanted the kingship, and the Lupercalia was staged to test the waters, but the people rejected the idea.[209] Caesar dedicated the crown to Jupiter on the Capitol, and he ordered the scribes to record in the *Fasti* that he had refused the kingship.[210]

The opposition to Caesar crystallized. Marcus Junius Brutus cannot have failed to notice that he shared his name with the man who had overthrown the tyrant Tarquinius Superbus. The Senate was to meet on 15 March, the Ides, in rooms in Pompey's theatre. The Senate House was not in use because during Clodius Pulcher's funeral in 52 the people had somehow contrived to burn it down. A soothsayer warned Caesar to beware the Ides of March, and on the night of 14 March Calpurnia had a bad dream and pleaded with Caesar not to attend. Decimus Brutus came to his house to make sure that he did attend, since Caesar intended to leave for the Parthian campaign on 18 March.

When Caesar arrived at Pompey's theatre, Gaius Trebonius temporarily distracted Antony because Marcus Brutus had argued against killing him.[211] Caesar was stabbed several times, and on seeing Brutus about to stab him, he famously questioned 'Et tu, Brute?', but he more likely said 'you too my son?' in Greek.[212] The senators and conspirators fled, leaving Caesar's body at the foot of Pompey's statue.

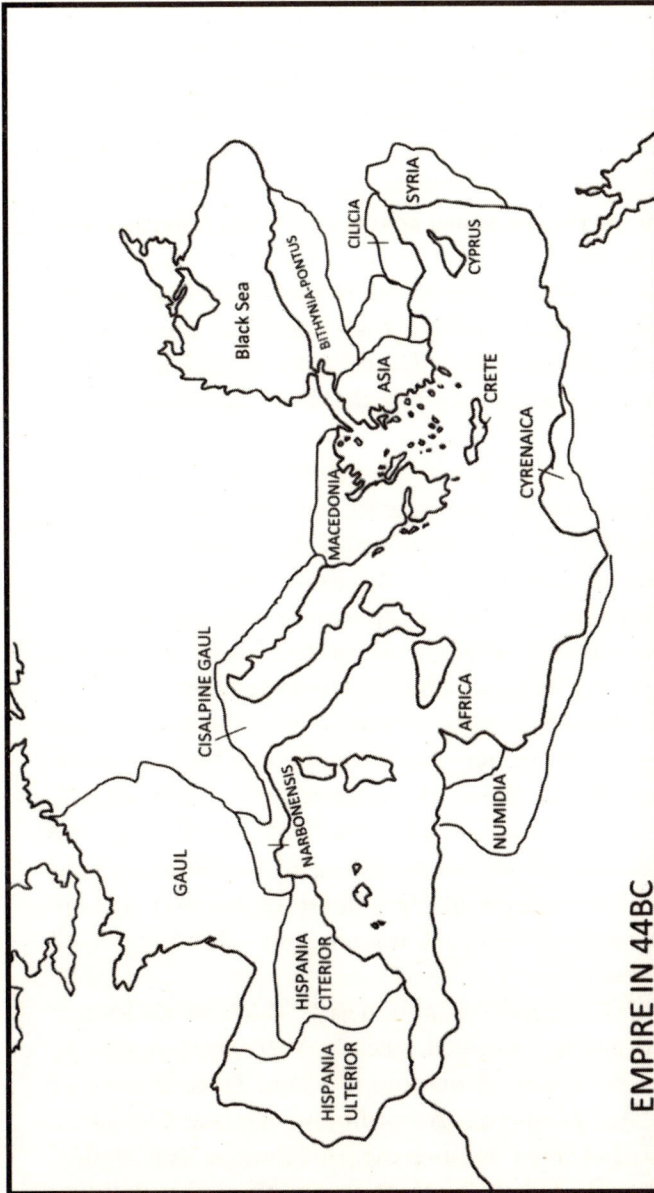

**EMPIRE IN 44BC**

3. By the year of the assassination of Julius Caesar in 44 BC the Empire had grown via Pompey the Great's conquest of Mithradates VI of Pontus, and his subsequent reorganisation of the territories and allied kingdoms. Pompey annexed Bithynia-Pontus and Syria, whose governor was placed in charge of Judaea. Illyria, occupying the relatively narrow coastal strip of the eastern shore of the Adriatic, was allotted to Julius Caesar in 59 BC as his province, renamed Illyricum. He governed it along with Cisalpine Gaul, while he was engaged in the ten-year conquest of Gaul, which annexed, distinct from Cisalpine and Transalpine Gaul, he renamed The Province, and later Gallia Narbonensis. The eastern part of Numidia was made a province called Africa Nova, neighbouring the original province of Africa, renamed Africa Vetus. Redrawn by Sue Howie after Richardson 1976.

### The Liberators

After Caesar's death, Brutus, Cassius, and their friends expected unmitigated gratitude, declaring to the people that liberty was restored. They were quickly disillusioned, and gathered on the Capitol, barricading the entrances. They imagined that the Republic would spring back to life after Caesar was removed, and they had not planned how to govern the state. Cicero said they had done the deed with the courage of men but acted like children.[213] As aristocrats whose liberty was oppressed by Caesar, the Liberators were out of touch with the people and the soldiers, who were accustomed to being oppressed, and had benefited from Caesar's rule.

Antony ran home and locked himself in, not knowing if he was on the hit-list.[214] Aemilius Lepidus collected his troops on Tiber Island, taking them to the Campus Martius, and informing Antony that he was prepared to use them as Antony directed. The two of them blockaded the Capitol.[215]

Antony averted potential civil war. Unwilling to play the tyrant, he tried to revert to normal government, arranging a meeting of the Senate on 17 March in the temple of Tellus, near his house. He had posted Lepidus' soldiers all over Rome to prevent armed gatherings. He may have visited Calpurnia to gather Caesar's papers. Calpurnia possibly thought it better to give them to Antony rather than risk their seizure by someone else.[216] Antony also gained the services of Caesar's secretary Faberius, with all his considerable knowledge. He may have sought out Gaius Oppius and Cornelius Balbus, Caesar's close associates. Most of all, Antony needed money. Soldiers could turn against him if they were not paid. Cicero accused Antony of removing 700 million sesterces from the treasury of the temple of Ops, pointing out that Antony owed forty million sesterces before Caesar was killed, but by April he had cleared the debt.[217]

On 17 March Cicero proposed an amnesty, which was adopted. Caesar's acts could not be annulled, because then there would be no magistrates, no provincial governors, no land laws, or any of Caesar's remedies for problems. Accordingly, Antony confirmed all Caesar's acts rather than teasing out those to be repealed.[218] He managed to include Caesar's intentions in this all-embracing confirmation. Cicero wrote to Atticus from Fundi on 12 April 44, complaining that Caesar's appointments of magistrates and tribunes were upheld, and that all the acts, notes, words, promises and projects of Caesar now had more validity than when he was alive. In another letter he wrote, 'We bow down to his notebooks,' referring to Caesar's papers in Antony's hands.[219] He also voiced the suspicions of others that Antony was forging documents.[220] Possibly Antony backed up his own ideas by fabricating plans and policies which he said he found among Caesar's jottings. In mid-April, Cicero summed it all up, telling Atticus: 'The tyrant is dead but the tyranny lives.'[221]

Antony amended his unconstitutional position as sole consul by making Cornelius Dolabella his colleague, Caesar's original choice. Antony sent his infant son to the Liberators on the Capitol, to vouch for his goodwill. Demonstrating their new understanding, Lepidus dined with Brutus and Antony dined with Cassius, asking him if he had a dagger, and Cassius replied that he had a large one, in case Antony turned tyrant.[222] Antony's bodyguard of 6,000 men no doubt confirmed Cassius' suspicions. As a political gesture Antony abolished the Dictatorship, but according to Dio, Cicero said that in itself the title did no harm, and even without it, Antony was acting the part.[223]

On 18 March the Senate agreed to ratify the terms of Caesar's will, which was read out by Calpurnius Piso in Antony's house.[224] Caesar left his gardens to the public, and money to each Roman citizen. There were legacies for some of his assassins. One quarter of his fortune was to be divided equally between his male relatives, Quintus Pedius and Lucius Pinarius. Antony was in the second rank of legatees. The main beneficiary was Gaius Octavius, Caesar's great-nephew, who was currently with five legions at Apollonia in Macedonia, where Caesar had sent him at the end of 45 to prepare for the projected campaign in Parthia, long overdue since Crassus' death in 53. Via a codicil attached to his will Caesar adopted Octavius as his son. Adoption of an heir was normal, but it was usually done while the adopter was alive. Testamentary adoption may not have been legal, as modern scholars have argued.[225]

Antony arranged Caesar's funeral for 20 March. He displayed Caesar's bloodstained toga, read the will, and said a few words of his own.[226] Cicero calls it a moving oration, and Dio and Appian use their versions of Antony's speech to express their own views. The Roman mob took Caesar's body to the Forum, ignoring the pyre already prepared in the Campus Martius, and using benches and anything flammable, they cremated him. [227]

As Cicero's friend Atticus had predicted, the public funeral for Caesar sounded the death knell for the Liberators.[228] Some of the conspirators went to the provinces assigned to them by Caesar, Decimus Brutus to Cisalpine Gaul, and Gaius Trebonius to Asia. Junius Brutus and Gaius Cassius, serving magistrates, were not supposed to leave Rome, but Antony put them in charge of the corn supply in Sicily and Asia before they entered their provincial commands for 43.

It is not known how long Cleopatra stayed in Rome after Caesar's death. She would need confirmation of the friendship of the Roman people, and of Caesarion as heir to Egypt. Antony promised to present Caesarion's case to the Senate, and at some unknown date, he did so.[229] With Antony in charge in Rome, Cleopatra's position was as secure as she could hope for. She could not know that the Romans would fight another civil war, ending at Alexandria with the obliteration of her kingdom in 30.

7

# Antony Falls, Octavian Rises

## Gaius Octavius

In March 44, Octavius was with the legions in Macedonia as Caesar's *magister equitum* when he heard of Caesar's death, probably by letter from his mother Atia.[1] With a few friends, including Marcus Vipsanius Agrippa, and Gaius Maecenas, Octavius set off for Italy. At Brundisium, Octavius found letters from his mother and stepfather Lucius Marcius Philippus explaining that he was heir to most of Caesar's fortune, and was now Caesar's son, entitled to call himself Gaius Julius Caesar Octavianus, indicating adoption from the Octavii into the Julii. History knows him as Octavian, but he never used this name. He was Gaius Julius Caesar, rejecting Philippus' advice to refuse the inheritance and the name.[2]

Octavian, only nineteen, was an unknown quantity. Cicero regretted that the young man was going to take up 'that inheritance' (*illum hereditatem*) but was relieved that Octavian had not brought the Macedonian legions to Italy with him.[3] Octavian was living in Philippus' villa, practically next door to Cicero's.[4] Octavian easily gained the allegiance of Caesar's supporters, the most important being Cornelius Balbus and Gaius Oppius. Balbus had acted as a filter for Caesar, scrutinizing correspondence before it got any further.[5] Balbus had no obligation to join Octavian, but the two met on 19 April at Naples, Cicero being the only source for this.[6] Balbus and Oppius presumably controlled a network of people in Rome and the provinces that was now at Octavian's disposal. They would be able to provide funds, and when Octavian began to recruit soldiers he did not lack money. According to Nicolaus of Damascus, Octavian had access to Caesar's treasury for the Parthian campaign and had also received a year's tribute from Asia.[7] Blink and you would miss it, but how on earth was this arranged? Was it earmarked for Caesar's campaigns? Nicolaus does not elaborate.

Octavian was in Rome in June or July 44, arranging games in honour of Venus Genetrix, instituted by Caesar in connection with his new temple.[8] Antony was reluctant to stir up the people in Caesar's name, so he refused Octavian's request to display Caesar's golden chair and wreath during the games.[9] He also refused to release the money bequeathed to Octavian, probably because he had used it to pay his soldiers.[10] Octavian had his adoption confirmed in writing and witnessed before the urban praetor Gaius Antonius, Antony's brother, but when he tried to legalize it via a *lex curiata*, Antony blocked him. No matter. Octavian was good at waiting. From his own resources Octavian paid to the people money left to them by Caesar. Then he declared his intention of avenging Caesar's death, as admitted in the *Res Gestae*, his account of his reign.[11] Octavian kept Caesar's memory fresh, utilizing the comet that appeared during the games celebrating Caesar's victories. It was declared the *sidus Iulium*, the star of Julius, a sign that Caesar had become a god. Octavian placed a star on Caesar's statues and on coins.

Antony was to have governed Macedonia during Caesar's campaigns, but in May 44, by means of the *lex de permutatione provinciarum*, he exchanged his province for Cisalpine Gaul, currently governed by Decimus Brutus, who did not go to Macedonia. Next, Antony transferred four of the five Macedonian legions to Italy.[12] When Antony met them at Brundisium, two of them went over to Octavian, as did Caesar's veterans, settled near Capua where Cornelius Balbus was patron.[13] Without legal sanction, Octavian raised an army of about 10,000 loyal and experienced men. He had no excuse – but Antony provided him with one, as he marched north with his legions – for claiming Cisalpine Gaul from Decimus Brutus. Would Antony march on Rome, like Sulla?

On 4 November, Cicero reported that Octavian offered to work through the Senate.[14] Cicero advised him to go to Rome, but it was too soon. Octavian gained no support and went off to raise more troops. Cicero returned to Rome, having been absent since September, when he had reviled Antony in the first of his *Philippics*, named after the orations of Demosthenes against Philip II of Macedon.

Antony summoned the Senate for 24 November, intending to declare Octavian *hostis*, but having lost favour he continued to Cisalpine Gaul, rapidly bottling up and besieging Decimus Brutus in Mutina (Modena).[15] The consuls designate Aulus Hirtius and Vibius Pansa were not yet in office, so Octavian's army was the only one available, and he was sent to oppose Antonius.[16] Cicero proposed on 1 January 43 that Octavian should be made a senator, and propraetor with *imperium*.[17] Octavian declared at the beginning of the *Res Gestae*: 'At the age of nineteen on my own initiative and at my own expense, I raised an army with which I successfully championed the liberty of the Republic when it was being oppressed by the tyranny of a faction.'[18]

Cicero persuaded the Senate to declare war on Antony. On 15 April, at Forum Gallorum near Mutina, Antony defeated the consul Vibius Pansa, who died of his wounds. Though Antony had been the victor, public thanksgiving for fifty days was voted in the names of the Imperators Pansa, Hirtius and Octavian, who counted this as his first in a series of acclamations as Imperator. On 21 April at the second battle of Mutina, Hirtius was killed and Antony was defeated, withdrawing across the Alps into Gaul.

The Senate ordered Octavian to co-operate with Decimus Brutus. Octavian had simply wanted a military command, but he never intended to assist a murderer of Caesar. Possibly at this time Octavian heard of Cicero's witty remark about him, *laudandum adulescentem, ornandum, tollendum*, meaning that he should be praised and honoured.[19] *Tollere* has a double meaning, the alternative being 'to eliminate'. If Octavian needed Cicero only to gain his military command, then Cicero needed Octavian only as long as he was useful.

In July, 400 soldiers arrived in Rome to demand the consulship for Octavian.[20] The Senate refused the request. When Octavian appeared on the doorstep with eight legions, the Senate promised the soldiers lots of money to desert, but this failed. Octavian was allowed to stand for the consulship *in absentia*, provided that the army remained 100 miles from Rome.[21] The Senate summoned two legions from Africa, and a third legion was to defend the city. All three joined Octavian.

As Octavian entered the Campus Martius, six vultures were seen, a splendid omen, harking back to Romulus.[22] Octavian's mother Atia and his sister Octavia were safe with the Vestals, but Atia died soon afterwards and Octavian gave her a splendid public funeral.[23] One month short of his twentieth birthday, he became consul on 19 August, originally called Sextilis, but named after him when he accepted the name Augustus. Quintus Pedius, nephew of Caesar, became Octavian's consular colleague.[24] Before the election, Octavian persuaded the Senate to pay the soldiers the money they would have spent on persuading them to desert. Reneging on promises to soldiers could be harmful. Octavian's consulship was short, but he used it well. He paid Caesar's remaining legacies, the sources of money being obscure.[25] He legalized his adoption via a *lex curiata*, legally inheriting willing members of Caesar's extensive *clientelae*, and his property. As Caesar's son, he was obliged to avenge his father's death, and as consul he outlawed the conspirators via a special court to try the absent assassins and anyone who had withheld information about the conspiracy.[26] All were condemned, and their property was confiscated.

For Octavian, since he could not defeat the conspirators alone, everything pointed towards an alliance with Antony. After Mutina, Octavian had returned Antony's captured officers with messages of friendship.[27] With the ground prepared, Octavian could ally with Antony, and as consul with an army he would not have to play second fiddle. Antony was gaining strength in Gaul. Publius Ventidius Bassus brought three legions for him, raised on his own initiative. He had marched them through Italy, avoiding battle.[28] Possibly Octavian let them through. By the end of May, the light had dawned on Lepidus, so he joined Antony. The Senate declared him *hostis*, like Antony, also *hostis* thanks to Cicero. Asinius Pollio with two legions from Hispania Ulterior joined Antony in the summer, as did Munatius Plancus, governor of Gallia Comata. Decimus, outnumbered, aimed for Ravenna, then north-west for the Rhine. His troops deserted him, and he was killed by a Gaul.[29]

While Octavian marched north, officially on behalf of the Senate, he had something to offer Antony. His fellow consul Pedius persuaded the Senate to revoke the laws declaring Antony and Lepidus *hostes*.[30] Antony, Octavian and Aemilius Lepidus met near Bononia (Bologna), where Antony had many clients. Appian places the meeting near Mutina.[31] The three men required all-embracing powers while avoiding the dread title Dictator, which Antony had abolished. Their association was formally constituted on 27 November 43 by the *lex Titia* passed by the tribune Publius Titius. Henceforth

Antony, Octavian and Lepidus were given powers under a new title for their association, *Tresviri Rei Publicae Constituendae,* three men for the reconstitution of the Republic, derived from the anomalous Dictatorships of Sulla and Caesar. One lesson learned from Caesar was that there should be no depressing hint of perpetuity, so a five-year limit was imposed on the *Tresviri,* 31 December 38 probably being the end date.[32] The legal basis for the powers of the *Tresviri* is uncertain and has been intensively studied.[33] In 36 Augustus drew a veil over this episode, ordering the destruction of all documents from 44 onwards.[34]

The *Tresviri* were empowered to make laws and to nominate magistrates and provincial governors. Since the Liberators had claimed most of the eastern provinces, the *Tresviri* took provincial commands in the west, not of single provinces, but groups of them. Antony was to govern all Gaul except The Province, which went to Lepidus along with Hispania Citerior. Octavian governed Italy, Africa, Sicily and Sardinia.[35] The agreements made by the *Tresviri* were written down, signed and sealed, and the main provisions were announced to the soldiers. For the settlement of veterans, eighteen cities in the most productive areas of Italy were chosen.[36] It would be Octavian's problem to apportion the allotments.

Lepidus was chosen as one of the *Tresviri* for his patrician status and his prestige as Pontifex Maximus, but he was overshadowed. He retained three of his legions to keep order in Rome and Italy, surrendering the rest to Antony and Octavian for the war against the Liberators. He did not play a significant part in the war and was quickly disempowered when he tried to assert himself.

Before Octavian and Antony could fight Brutus and Cassius, they first had to install their adherents in the government in Rome and the provinces. Ventidius Bassus became consul with Gaius Carrinas for the remaining term of 43. Existing praetors were made governors of provinces, and new praetors were appointed. Consuls for 42 were to be Lepidus and Munatius Plancus.[37] Consuls for 41 were to be Publius Servilius Isauricus and Antony's brother Lucius, followed by Asinius Pollio and Gnaeus Domitius Calvinus in 40.

The grislier goal was eradication of opponents. The *Tresviri* produced a list of seventeen men to be eliminated, including Cicero and his brother Quintus. These were sent to the consul Pedius, who put the executions into effect, dying soon afterwards.[38] Ancient and modern authors blame Antony for the carnage, especially for the murder of

Cicero. Antony had personal reasons for wanting Cicero's death, because during the Catiline episode, Cicero had executed without trial Lentulus Sura, Antony's stepfather, and had refused to release the body for a proper funeral.[39] Was Octavian as innocent as people like to believe? Cicero had said that he should be eliminated, and besides, he hated Octavian's association with Caesar. Cicero met the soldiers bravely on 7 December.[40] On Antony's orders, Cicero's hands and head, which had composed and spoken the *Philippics* vilifying Antony, were nailed to the Rostra in the Forum, and allegedly mutilated by Fulvia.

Another 130 names were added to the original seventeen proscribed men.[41] The *Tresviri* did nothing when more names were added, and the ultimate death toll according to Appian was 300 senators and 2,000 equestrians.[42] Entire power-blocs of senators were eliminated, their families, friends and associates, their equestrian business agents, and their financiers. Some of the city magistrates in Rome were proscribed, their posts bestowed on loyal supporters of the *Tresviri*, and soldiers took over the duties and property of proscribed magistrates in Italian cities and towns.[43]

The seizure and sale of the property of proscribed men yielded profit for the *Tresviri* but only the soldiers readily purchased the estates. The revenues of the eastern provinces were diverted to Brutus and Cassius, and the western provinces were never as wealthy as their eastern counterparts, so the *Tresviri* lacked funds. A percentage tax on wealth was levied by Lepidus and Plancus, consuls of 42. Women were taxed, until three of them protested. Hortensia, the daughter of Cicero's rival lawyer Hortensius, Octavian's sister, and Antonius' mother, offered voluntary contributions if Italy was endangered, but since women were not allowed to vote or to take part in government, they declared the tax unfair. The *Tresviri* removed the majority of women's names from the tax list and then seized the personal savings of individuals entrusted to the care of the Vestals.[44]

On 1 January 42, the *Tresviri* administered an oath to the senators and magistrates who swore to maintain the acts of Caesar the Dictator. Having secured Caesar's earthly acts, the *Tresviri* made every effort to confirm his divinity. Coins issued by Octavian in 40 bore the legend DIVI JULII F(ILIUS), the earliest evidence that he designated himself son of the divine Julius, but he was probably already using this title before 40. It was decreed that a temple to *Divus Julius* should be built in the Forum on the site of Caesar's funeral pyre.[45] It was dedicated in 29. The cult of *Divus Julius* was established in Italy by the *lex*

*Rufrena*, preserved on an inscription.[46] It was not unusual for Roman families to claim divine descent, but Octavian was the first to claim it from a recently deceased individual transformed into a new god.

## War against the Liberators

Before the *Tresviri* gained control in Rome, Brutus and Cassius took over Syria and Macedonia because of their strategic value and wealth.[47] Caesar had appointed Cornelius Dolabella as governor of Syria, but before going there Dolabella marched into Asia, where the Senate's appointee Gaius Trebonius was proconsul, collecting money and troops for Brutus and Cassius. The Senate, not yet under the collective thumbs of the *Tresviri*, declared war against Dolabella after he defeated and killed Trebonius.[48]

Brutus had raised three legions in Macedonia, and recruited troops in Thrace, where Antony had installed his brother Gaius as governor, but he was blockaded and captured in Apollonia. Acting on Cicero's advice, Brutus executed Gaius Antonius.[49] The Senate, also on Cicero's advice, gave Brutus command of Macedonia, Greece and Illyricum.[50] Cassius was popular in Syria for restoring order after the defeat of Licinius Crassus in 53, so he gained control of about twelve legions without lifting a finger. Eventually the Senate decreed that provincial commanders and all soldiers between the Adriatic and the Orient should obey the orders of Brutus and Cassius.[51]

Dolabella was besieged by Cassius at Laodicea. With no hope of relief, he committed suicide. His troops were absorbed by Cassius, who heard that Antony and Octavian were crossing the Adriatic. Octavian was ill and had to remain at Dyrrachium, joining Antony later at Philippi, where the two sides fought in 42. The Liberators had positioned their troops in two camps between mountains and a marsh.[52] In the first battle, Octavian's camp was captured by Brutus, while Antony took Cassius' camp without winning the victory, but Cassius thought all was lost and killed himself.[53] Supplied by sea, Brutus could have held out until Antony and Octavian had to move to find food, but his subordinates, like Pompey's at Pharsalus, nagged him into action. He gave in. His defeat was decisive. Suicide was his only option. His troops were captured or escaped to join Sextus Pompey, who left Spain after Munda, assembled a fleet, and remained at sea. All the captives associated with the Liberators were killed by Octavian, not always by swift execution. The soldiers saluted Octavian as Imperator but reviled him for his cruelty to prisoners.[54]

Appian and Dio portray the deaths of the Liberators as divine retribution for the murder of Caesar, identifying the battle of Philippi as the turning point between the Republic and the Empire. Appian says that 'the form of government was decided chiefly by that day's work, and they have not yet gone back to democracy,' while Dio says the war had 'exhausted the democratic element and strengthened the monarchical'.[55] All this is true in retrospect, but at the time it was perhaps not so certain. Antony was still the chief partner of the *Tresviri*. The victory at Philippi was his. He was to control the Gallic provinces via his legates Fufius Calenus, Munatius Plancus and Publius Ventidius, with about seventeen legions between them, and he controlled the eastern provinces in order to stabilize and reorganize them.

## Octavian in the west

Under Octavian, Cisalpine Gaul was incorporated into Italy as common recruiting ground for Octavian and Antony, but still required a governor, currently Asinius Pollio, Antony's legate.[56] Aemilius Lepidus, governing The Province and Hispania Citerior, had a previous record of co-operation with Sextus Pompeius, who had taken over much of Spain from him. The Province was now given to Antony, who already commanded Gallia Comata, and Lepidus was re-assigned to Africa.[57]

The promised settlement of veterans was a priority in Italy, but there was a shortage of land. Lawrence Keppie narrows down Appian's total of 170,000 veterans to 46,000.[58] This embraces veterans from the western provinces, Africa, and the legions from Philippi, whichever side they had fought for. Some veterans were settled in the provinces. In Italy, dispossessed farmers converged on Rome. Osgood pieces together the evidence of the upheaval.[59] There had to be a better way of providing for veterans than this continual merry-go-round of booting out existing farmers, re-assigning their lands to veterans, thereby increasing the landless poor in Rome, finding lands for them, repeat from beginning.

The consuls, Lucius Antonius and Servilius Isauricus, did not assist Octavian.[60] Lucius combined forces with his sister-in-law Fulvia, arguing that Antony's veterans should be settled by his own agents. Octavian took the wind out of Lucius' sails by agreeing with the proposals, thus winning round one, but round two began when Lucius took up the cause of dispossessed farmers.[61] Antony knew nothing about this, according to Plutarch and Appian, but he seemed to be sitting on the fence, awaiting the outcome.[62] The outcome was war.

Uncertain about Antony's intentions, Octavian put a legion in Brundisium in case troops arrived from the east, and Lepidus with two legions guarded Rome. Salvidienus Rufus, with six legions, was marching to Spain to drive out Sextus Pompeius, but was now recalled. Marcus Vipsanius Agrippa commanded whatever troops Octavian could assemble. Lucius Antonius clamoured for the dissolution of the union of the *Tresviri* and tried to stop Salvidienus and his six legions. Agrippa trapped him between his and Salvidienus' armies. Lucius and Fulvia took refuge in Perusia (Perugia), hoping that Asinius Pollio and Ventidius in Gaul were marching to the rescue, but these two commanders refused to fight Agrippa. Munatius Plancus and his veterans never budged from Spoletium. Octavian invested Perusia, firing lead sling bullets into the city, bearing the name *Divum Julium*. When the citizens of Perusia were starving, Lucius surrendered. His soldiers were not punished. Lucius was freed, continuously under observation. Fulvia and Munatius Plancus sailed for Greece.[63] Octavian's soldiers were allowed free-range pillage, and Perusia burned.[64]

## Antony in the east

After Philippi, Antony inspected the damage to the eastern provinces, acknowledging that not all communities had willingly supported Brutus and Cassius. Some had been coerced, and others had resisted at great cost. Antony dealt with each case on its own merits, imposing fines, levying tribute, or rendering assistance where necessary. There is little detail of his efforts. For the winter of 42-41, Antony went to Athens, where he could keep in touch with the eastern provinces.[65] In spring he began to organize the provinces and surrounding kingdoms, and he sought funds. Lucius Censorinus administered the Greek states with six legions, while Antony went to Ephesus with two legions to ask for ten years' tax to be paid in one year, reminding them that they had paid this much to Brutus and Cassius within two years. He settled for nine years' tax to be paid over two years. He toured the east, remitting taxes for some cities, declaring some of them free, and adjusting boundaries.[66] For economic and political reasons, Athens and Rhodes were given control of islands in their proximity. Antony released the Jewish prisoners taken by Cassius and found in favour of Herod, son of Antipater, when Judaean envoys complained of the latter's mistreatment.

Rome and Parthia were not at war, but the first line of protection for Roman territories comprised Parthia's neighbouring states, whose goodwill had to be maintained. Antony neutralised the kingdoms bordering Parthia, and then turned to the problem of finance. He sent Quintus Dellius with an invitation to Cleopatra VII of Egypt to visit him at Tarsus in Cilicia.[67] Cleopatra arrived in her spectacular ship, entertained Antony and friends to a spectacular feast, and allegedly Antony fell spectacularly head over heels for her.

Cleopatra needed to maintain diplomatic relations with the Romans to ensure that they kept their own and everyone else's hands off Egypt. She would be perfectly aware that Antony wanted money, and Antony would be aware that Cleopatra wanted security for Egypt. Augustan propaganda portrays the spineless bewitched Antony as Cleopatra's willing slave, so she could be blamed for Antony's subsequent behaviour and the civil war. For the time being, Antony and Cleopatra fulfilled their immediate needs. Antony was invited to visit Alexandria, which he did after an attack on Palmyra, for which his motives are obscure, somehow bound up with trouble caused by the collection of tribute in Syria. According to Appian, Antony imposed more tribute, placed his reliable officer Decidius Saxa in command of Syria, and dashed off to Alexandria before sorting everything out, which sounds unlikely.[68]

The Alexandrians said that in Rome Antony wore his tragic mask, but for them he wore his comic mask. The precise relationship between Antony and Cleopatra was explained beyond doubt when, after the appropriate interval, the Queen gave birth to twins, a boy and a girl, and Antony acknowledged them.

Antony received news that Decidius Saxa had been killed and the Parthians had invaded Syria, encouraged by Quintus Labienus, son of Titus, erstwhile legate of Caesar. Quintus had been sent to Parthia by Brutus and Cassius, but the battle of Philippi intervened and he decided to stay. The Parthians invaded Judaea, installing as ruler Antigonus, son of Aristobulus. Herod of Judaea fled to Egypt and was kindly received by Cleopatra, who lent him a ship to sail to Rome, where he was formally recognized as King of Judaea; but as yet he could not control his kingdom.[69]

Ventidius Bassus had gathered the Antonian troops after the fall of Perusia, and Antony sent him to restore order in the east, allowing Antony to respond to Octavian's request for a meeting at Brundisium. He briefly joined Fulvia in Athens. She was very ill, and Antony, not wanting to subject her to a sea voyage, left in haste to meet Octavian. Fulvia died before he returned.

## The Treaty of Brundisium in 40

Domitius Ahenobarbus now joined Antony. He had kept command of his fleet since Pharsalus and used it to attack Italian coastal towns without endangering Rome's food supply. Antony and Domitius approached Brundisium, once attacked by Domitius. Octavian's troops were already there, and the city gates were closed.[70] Antony besieged the town. War was imminent. Octavian ordered Publius Servilius Rullus to drive Antony away, but he failed and his soldiers joined Antony.

The only men with any common sense in this episode were the soldiers, who remembered that they were all Caesarians.[71] Talks were arranged in autumn 40, Maecenas speaking for Octavian and Asinius Pollio for Antony. Octavian was emerging as the stronger party, having taken over the legions of the deceased Fufius Calenus, Antony's legate in Gaul.

The Treaty of Brundisium of 40 rearranged the Roman world. Antony's command of the east and Octavian's command of the west were confirmed. Antony secured ratification of all his acts, past, present and future.[72] The treaty was celebrated in Rome. Antony married Octavian's sister Octavia, whose husband Marcellus had died. The mourning period of ten months had not expired but the Senate authorized the marriage.[73] Antony finally became *flamen divi Julii*, the priest of the cult of the divine Caesar.

Antony and Octavian made an agreement with Sextus Pompeius in 39, at Misenum.[74] Sextus had placed his fleet at the disposal of the Liberators, taken in their soldiers after Philippi and then penetrated Spain, where Salvidienus Rufus was heading when Octavian recalled him. In 39, Sextus disrupted the grain supply for Rome. In that year, Octavian hoped to make diplomatic peace with Sextus by marrying Scribonia, the sister of Scribonius Libo, whose daughter was Sextus' wife. At Misenum, in return for leaving the grain convoys alone, Sextus was offered control of Sicily, Sardinia, and Corsica, was made an augur, promised the consulship for 33 and control of the Peloponnese for five years, carved out of Antony's eastern territories. After the treaty was signed, Sextus entertained Antony and Octavian on board ship, scrupulously resisting the suggestion of his admiral Menodorus that they should set sail to arrange an aquatic accident for the guests.

Sextus soon resumed his interruption of Rome's food supply. It was clear that only war would stop him, and in 38, on the day that their daughter Julia was born, Octavian divorced Scribonia, having discovered Livia Drusilla. After Livia's divorce from Tiberius Claudius Nero, Octavian married her with indecent haste. Livia's elder son was the future Emperor Tiberius, and she was pregnant with her second son, Drusus. War was declared against Sextus. Menodorus deserted to Octavian, who now controlled Sardinia and Corsica, along with some ships, but was twice defeated by Sextus. Vipsanius Agrippa finally defeated Sextus, after first deepening a lake where he trained the crews for the new ships, and in the naval battle at Naulochus on 3 September 36, Sextus lost, fleeing to the east, seeking alliance with Antony, then with the Parthians, then with King Amyntas of Galatia, only to be delivered to Antony's general Titius. He executed Sextus, possibly on his own initiative.[75]

While the struggle with Sextus was going on, in 40 Ventidius Bassus had driven out the Parthians from Syria and Asia Minor and restored order. He levied tribute from various cities, especially those which had assisted the Parthians under Pacorus. During the winter of 40-39 Antony was in Athens with Octavia, preparing for the next Parthian campaign. He did not have exclusive control of the eastern provinces, since it seems that Octavian could send instructions directly to one of Antony's agents called Stephanos, as shown by inscriptions from the city of Aphrodisias, and the eastern states could send petitions to Octavian, bypassing Antony.[76] Possibly Antony enjoyed the same rights in the western provinces.

In spring 38, the Parthians pre-empted Antony by attacking Syria once more, and at the same time Octavian summoned Antony to the west. Ventidius took command against the Parthians while Antony sailed to Brundisium, but again Octavian was not there. Antony turned back to Syria where Ventidius had won a crushing victory over the Parthian Pacorus, who was killed.[77] Antiochus, King of Commagene, was sheltering Parthian refugees at Samosata on the right bank of the Euphrates, so Ventidius besieged it until Antony arrived, then returned to Rome to hold a well-deserved triumph in November 38. Antony negotiated a settlement at Samosata and wintered in Athens.

Octavian and Antony finally met at Tarentum in 37. It was agreed that Antony would give Octavian 120 ships in return for 20,000 soldiers. The ships were delivered, but the soldiers never materialised.[78]

There was another matter to settle. The powers of the *Tresviri* had expired in 38. Their *de facto* power derived from their command of troops, but it required legal sanction. A law of the Roman people renewed their powers for another five years.

Antony spent the winter of 37-36 at Antioch in Syria, while Octavia remained in Italy with their daughter Antonia and Antony's two sons by Fulvia, Antyllus and Iullus Antonius. Antony invited Cleopatra to Antioch, with their twins Alexander Helios named for the sun (Helios), and Cleopatra Selene, named for the moon (Selene). It was said that Antony married Cleopatra according to Egyptian rites. It was all grist for Octavian's mill.

As part of his settlement of the east, Antony granted to Cleopatra Crete, Cyrene and Cilicia, Phoenicia, Nabataean Arabia, and important coastal cities of Syria, except for Tyre and Sidon, all territories once ruled by Egypt.[79] For the preliminary stages of the Parthian campaign, Antony secured protection for the flanks and rear of his invading troops by installing trusted rulers in surrounding lands. Canidius Crassus was sent to secure Armenia, defeating King Artavasdes, who broke his alliance with Parthia to ally with Rome, but the King of Media, another Artavasdes, strengthened his Parthian alliance. The new King of Parthia, Phraates, ruled by dint of killing all his potential rivals.[80] Antony sent an embassy to Phraates to ask him to return Crassus' military standards lost in 53. The refusal was predictable. At Zeugma on the north-eastern border of Syria, opposite Carrhae, the site of Crassus' defeat, Antony assembled his army as if to invade Parthia from this point, but marched through Armenia to besiege Phraaspa (Phraapa or Phraata), the capital of Media. On the way there, the Parthians destroyed his siege train, but it looked like a blockade of Phraaspa would probably reduce the city.[81] It didn't. Antony retreated in the harsh winter. The army marched in square formation, with skirmishers on the flanks and scouts to reconnoitre the route. Plutarch's account reads like a military manual on how to retreat in rough terrain in winter.[82]

Domitius Ahenobarbus and Canidius led the army out of Armenia, while Antony headed for Leuke Come, between Berytus and Sidon on the Mediterranean coast. Cleopatra answered his summons to bring clothes and food. She had recently given birth to Antony's son, Ptolemy Philadelphus, but she still sailed. After settling the troops, Antony and Cleopatra returned to Alexandria.

In 36, when Sextus Pompey lost the battle of Naulochus, Aemilius Lepidus had seized Sicily, but he hardly resisted when Octavian took it back, along with Africa. Lepidus was sent to live in Italy, remaining Pontifex Maximus, but closely monitored until his death in 12. Then Octavian, by this time Augustus, become Pontifex Maximus himself.[83] Octavian settled some of his legionaries in the provinces and justified his command of the rest by launching a campaign in Illyricum. He needed a military reputation. He gained popularity in Rome by authorizing building works and road construction, provision of food, clean water, and an improved sewage system, repaired in 33 by Agrippa in the lowly role of aedile.[84]

### The road to civil war

Antony did not campaign in Parthia in 35. Octavia arrived at Athens with money, troops, ships and supplies from Octavian, but not all that had been promised. Was Octavian trying to provoke Antony to a showdown?[85] By callously sending Octavia back to Rome without even seeing her, Antony was making it clear that the relationship with Octavian was at an end.[86] It was what Octavian wanted anyway, and had been working towards, but it was essential that he himself was totally innocent of any blame.

On 1 January 34, Antony was consul *in absentia*, relinquishing the office on 2 January to Lucius Sempronius Atratinus.[87] The daughter of Artavasdes of Media was brought to Alexandria for betrothal to Alexander Helios. The Parthian campaign resumed. Antony opened diplomatic exchanges with Artavasdes of Armenia, to no avail. He marched for the Armenian capital Artaxata, accompanied as far as Nicopolis by Cleopatra and his son Antyllus. Antony invited Artavasdes to a conference and arrested him. Armenia was annexed, garrisoned, and made a Roman province. Roman settlers and traders followed. Antony issued coins in Alexandria bearing the legend ARMENIA DEVICTA, or Armenia conquered.

In Alexandria in the autumn of 34 Antony put on a display in honour of his favourite god Dionysus, very much like a Roman triumph, parading his Armenian captives through the streets. Antony must have known what use Octavian would make of his parade. Antony compounded the sacrilege of denying spoils to Jupiter by another ceremony now known as the Donations of Alexandria, in which he redistributed territories, some of which were not yet conquered, to the immediate benefit of Cleopatra and her children, who became nominal rulers of various kingdoms.[88]

Caesarion was proclaimed successor to the kingdom of Egypt, and the legitimate heir of Caesar, and coins declared Cleopatra, 'Queen of kings and of her sons who are kings'. King of Kings was a customary title in the east, but it sounded very dangerous to Romans.

Octavian was consul in 33, relinquishing it on the second day. After the victory at Naulochus in 36, he had been granted tribunician powers and sacrosanctity, and was strong enough to make his first verbal attack on Antony, probably as the second term of the *Tresviri* was coming to an end. He renounced his power as one of the *Tresviri* and severed relations with Antony.

Antony was beginning another campaign against Parthia. The conversion of Armenia into a Roman province meant that he could arrive in Parthian territory without having to fight *en route*, and he could over-winter there. The army was ready in summer 33. The last thing that Octavian wanted was a successful Antony. He focused on Cleopatra, a suitably foreign enemy. Egyptian wealth may have had something to do with Octavian's inclination for war.

Antony was in Armenia when he heard what had been happening in Rome. He finally realized that his alienation had progressed too far for him to reverse it. Abandoning the campaign, he concentrated on gaining support in Rome. He began by asking once again for formal ratification of his acts in the east, and offered to lay down his powers, if Octavian would do the same. In November 33, Canidius led the army from Armenia to winter quarters at Ephesus. There were protests when Cleopatra joined him there, but Canidius reminded the soldiers where their pay came from.

The consuls for 32 were Antony's friends Gaius Sosius and Domitius Ahenobarbus. Antony sent a letter to be read out in the Senate, but allegedly it was too inflammatory and Sosius and Domitius did not obey. Octavian broke the rules by sitting between the two consuls and threatening to produce documents condemning Antony.[89] This does not seem sufficient to warrant the panic that ensued, with the consuls and a couple of hundred senators immediately going east to join Antony.

## Bellum civile

Antony divorced Octavia in May or June 32, severing his connection with Octavian. Dio thought that this probably triggered the desertion of Antony's officers Publius Titius and Munatius Plancus to Octavian.[90] Octavian found the ideal tool to sway any remaining doubtful senators when Titius and Plancus told him that Antony's last will and testament was lodged, as normal, with the Vestals. Octavian obtained it, reading it in private. The main points in the will, or so Octavian said, were that Antony reaffirmed Caesarion as Caesar's son, and as heir to the Egyptian throne. Antyllus was to be Antony's own heir, and there were legacies to his children by Cleopatra, illegitimate in Roman law.[91] Antony asked to be buried alongside Cleopatra in Alexandria.[92] He had renounced Rome! Octavian used all this to good effect. Did he amend the will to serve his purpose, as modern authors suggest?[93]

Octavian took the precaution of having all of Italy swear an oath of allegiance to him, except for towns where Antony had clients, chiefly Bononia (Bologna). This was an oath to Octavian personally, not to Rome or the Senate. It is arguable whether or not this was the basis of later oaths sworn to each new Emperor. In the *Res Gestae*, Augustus stretches credibility by claiming that the oath was sworn spontaneously by all of Italy.[94] The war had to be justified, to defend Rome against Cleopatra and her scheme to dominate the world. The fetial ritual was observed by throwing a spear into a patch of earth designated as Egypt, enemy territory. Octavian and his army set off to the east from Brundisium.

Antony's forces comprised 500 ships, eleven legions (sixteen according to Plutarch) and native levies, especially cavalry.[95] He had established food depots and his naval communications were good, but he had to guard the long, craggy coast of Greece from Corcyra to Methone, while the bulk of the army camped near the Gulf of Ambracia. Octavian set up a base on Corfu, and on finding that Antony' ships had been withdrawn, he rapidly claimed the northern peninsula of the Gulf of Ambracia. Antony camped on the southern peninsula, sending troops to cut off Octavian's water supply. His native troops deserted to Octavian, followed by Amyntas, ruler of Galatia.

Marcus Vipsanius Agrippa, chief architect of the victory at Naulochus in 36, commanded Octavian's fleet. He captured Methone, won a naval victory at Leucas, captured Patrae and then Corinth, cutting Antony's connections with Alexandria. More important, Agrippa blocked the mouth of the Gulf of Ambracia, bottling up Antony's ships and defeating Sosius when he tried to break out.[96] Now encircled, Antony's supplies were endangered and his camp was in an unhealthy location. Dysentery and malaria were rife.[97] His trusted officers went over to Octavian, among them Domitius Ahenobarbus, who was ill, and Quintus Dellius, the born survivor.

Antony further alienated his allies and his senatorial colleagues by punishing officers and allies, instead of using his charm. The loyal Canidius remained, advocating a march into Macedonia to fight on land. Cleopatra suggested garrisoning strategic locations, then using the ships to break out from Actium with the rest of the troops.[98] Antony committed to this plan. Unable to crew all the ships, he burnt some, and on 2 September he ordered the break-out, telling the crews to take their sails with them. They might need to pursue the enemy, he said, rather than explaining that sails would help them to escape using the winds that usually blew up in the afternoons. When battle commenced, Antony tried to turn Agrippa's ships, but Agrippa would not close up, and the two fleets stretched out, thinning the centre, giving Cleopatra the chance to escape on the flagship *Antonia* carrying the treasure chests and probably documents, suggesting that this move was prearranged, though Dio accuses Cleopatra of fleeing.[99] Antony transferred to a small boat and followed her, getting away with probably fewer than 100 ships, leaving the rest to their fate.

## The fall of Alexandria

Antony could base himself in Egypt, regain his strength and regroup his army, which Canidius was leading overland from Greece to Egypt, but this required energy – and from the moment Antony transferred to Cleopatra's ship, his determination evaporated. He offered his friends money and the means of escape before reaching Egypt.[100] Octavian purchased all Canidius' soldiers, but Canidius would not be bought, and continued to Egypt.

Antony and Cleopatra landed at a small harbour far to the west of Alexandria, and Cleopatra decorated her ships for victory, betraying no hint of defeat as she approached the city. She executed Artavasdes of Armenia as a warning to his rival, Artavasdes of Media. With more courage than Antony, who was neither hopeful nor helpful, Cleopatra organized a united defence. Caesarion was made Ptolemy XV, and Antyllus assumed the *toga virilis* marking him as an adult. Antony finally emerged, creating the Society of the Inseparables at Death.[101]

Octavian and Antony communicated via envoys, but Dio says that Cleopatra negotiated secretly and separately with Octavian.[102] Both Antony and Cleopatra knew that what Octavian really wanted was Egypt, quickly, in case the Queen destroyed all her treasure before he could seize it. For the moment, all Egypt was united behind the Queen, who had attended to the needs of the people more extensively than previous Ptolemies. As Caesar's son Caesarion had no chance of survival, since Octavian intended that there should be only one son of Caesar, so in spring 30 Caesarion was sent into Upper Egypt, perhaps to cross the Red Sea or continue into Ethiopia.[103]

Antony was defeated when he opposed Octavian's officer, Cornelius Gallus, attacking Egypt from the west. In the east, Cleopatra's general Seleucus at Pelusium did not try to stop Octavian's troops. Taking some cavalry to meet Octavian's advance guard, Antony routed the soldiers, celebrating his victory in Alexandria. That night, haunting music accompanied a procession of unseen people leaving the city – the god Dionysus and his revellers deserting Antony. The real battle began next day. The crews of Antony's fleet approached Octavian's ships and put up their oars. There was no point in getting killed for a defeated Queen and Roman general. Antony's cavalry and legionaries ran away.

Suspecting that Cleopatra had betrayed him, Antony rode back to Alexandria, where he found that she had stayed loyal, locked in her tomb, already dead. Antony asked his slave Eros to kill him, and Eros promptly killed himself. Antony fell on his sword but did not die. Cleopatra's slaves explained that the Queen was alive, waiting for him. The romantic death in Cleopatra's arms is probably true, and even if it isn't, the legend wins hands down. The same can be said of Cleopatra's death by the bite of an asp, which according to Egyptian lore bestowed divinity on the victim. On being informed of what had happened, Octavian immediately sent for the *psylli*, trained to suck out poison from snake bites. Perhaps he wanted her alive for his triumph, but on the other hand her death at her own hands was preferable to executing her, risking uprisings of her faithful Egyptians.[104]

Antony's son Antyllus, aged fourteen, was discovered and killed, but Iullus Antonius, Antony's second son by Fulvia, and Alexander Helios, Cleopatra Selene, and Ptolemy Philadelphus were all spared and sent to Rome. The ultimate fates of the two boys are unknown, but Cleopatra Selene married king Juba of Mauretania and lived out the rest of her life in North Africa. Iullus Antonius married Marcella, Octavia's daughter by her first husband, becoming consul in 10, and governing the province of Asia from 7 to 6, but in 2 he was involved in a scandal with Octavian's daughter Julia and was executed.

Octavian buried Antony and Cleopatra in the same tomb, never found. The news of Antony's death was read out to the Roman Senate by Cicero's son Marcus, a pertinent choice. Antony's birthday, 14 January, was declared *nefastus*, when no public business could be conducted.[105] Antony was damned forever, all his statues and busts were destroyed, and his name was erased from all monuments. Only the coin portraits remain to show what he looked like.

## Egypt becomes a province

In the *Res Gestae* Augustus casually mentions: 'I added Egypt to the Empire of the Roman people,' without explaining that he kept it for himself.[106] Possession of Egypt secured the grain supply for Rome, and the Royal Treasury for Octavian. The equestrian Cornelius Gallus, who marched from the west towards Alexandria while Octavian approached from the east, became the first governor of Egypt. An inscription from Philae, with the text in Latin, Greek and hieroglyphics, attests his full title, *Praefectus Alexandriae et Aegypti*.[107] Alexandria was regarded as separate from Egypt, and people spoke of going from Alexandria to Egypt or vice versa. An equestrian governor and the title prefect departed from the norm. Octavian deliberately chose Gallus, banning senators from even setting foot in the province without his permission, a ban that his successors upheld.[108]

Egypt was unlike any other province in nearly all respects. The highly centralised government of the Pharaohs had been taken over more or less intact in 323 by Ptolemy Soter. He made Egypt one of the successor states after the death of Alexander, whose body Ptolemy brought to Alexandria. The ancient administrative districts were not autonomous, and were retained as such by the Ptolemies, but re-labelled *nomes* in Greek, and governed by *strategoi*, which strictly denotes military commanders, but in Egypt they were administrative officials. The *strategoi* were subordinate to three *epistrategoi* who governed the three major districts of Egypt, the Delta in the north, the Arsinoite district in Middle Egypt, and the Thebaid in Upper Egypt.[109] The native Egyptians retained only minor posts under the Ptolemies, who brought in Greeks to fill most governmental roles. Egyptians serving in the Greek army were replaced by Macedonians.

When Octavian took over Egypt, he did not bend the government to fit Roman systems. In other provinces the Romans relied on self-governing communities, but not in Egypt. The high degree of centralisation was retained and Egyptian communities were not given autonomy. The only change was the division of some of the *nomes*, and creation of new ones, all administered by *strategoi*. The local agricultural systems continued, much improved when Augustus repaired the irrigation systems. Native customs, religious practices, festivals, and languages were left alone, provided they did not contravene Roman law or threaten security. Pharaonic temples were repaired and further adorned.[110] The Egyptian calendar continued in use, so even under Roman rule the Egyptian administrative and religious year began on 1 Thoth, or 29 August by the Roman calendar. Every four years there was an intercalary day, and the year began on 30 August. Dates were assiduously attached to papyrus and other records and can be used to establish chronology elsewhere in the Empire. Greek was used for most records, though the use of hieroglyphics, the shorthand version called hieratic, and demotic script, survived until the late third century AD. Transliteration of Egyptian into Greek letters resulted in the emergence of Coptic, used in the Egyptian Christian communities.

The Prefect of Egypt was to all intents and purposes the new king, in charge of the army, justice, and finances, until a procurator took charge of the latter. The ban on senatorial access to the province meant that the two legions had to be commanded by equestrians, with the title *praefectus legionis*, subordinate to the *Praefectus Aegypti*. For the purpose of administering justice, there was a fixed circuit embracing Alexandria, Pelusium, and Memphis, where the Prefect would hear cases. The Roman army had its part to play in administration and law. Centurions dealt with local matters, appeals and minor legal cases, such as assault, theft, vandalism, disputes between people over inheritances, or land holdings, and problems with misbehaving soldiers and tax collectors. Although the *strategoi* were not primarily involved, cases were recorded in their documents.[111]

## After Alexandria

Octavian wintered on the island of Samos. On 1 January 29, the Senate confirmed all Octavian's acts to date.[112] Becoming consul for the fifth time in 29, Octavian was back in Rome by August to celebrate three triumphs for victories in Dalmatia/Illyricum, at Actium, and in Egypt. After this he never celebrated another triumph, promoting his image as the bringer of peace. During the Republic, the triumph had boosted the popularity of generals to dangerous levels. Augustus confined future triumphs to his own circle, but he could not abolish all rewards, so in place of the procession through Rome, he awarded visible adornments of a triumph (*ornamenta triumphalia*). The first challenge came when Marcus Licinius Crassus, son of Crassus killed in Parthia in 53, had personally killed a Moesian chieftain in his campaigns from 29-28, and claimed the honour of *spolia opima*, dedicating the spoils to Jupiter Feretrius. The precedent dated back to 437, when Aulus Cornelius Cossus had been granted the honour. Octavian thwarted Crassus by declaring that Cossus was acting under his own auspices as consul, whereas Crassus was operating under Octavian, not in an independent command. This tale underlines exactly who was in charge of the Roman world.

### January 27: the so-called first settlement

On 11 January 29, signifying peace in the Roman world, Octavian closed the doors of the temple of Janus, which were left open permanently while Rome was at war.[113] The propaganda value was enormous, and from then onwards Octavian nurtured his image as saviour of the state. The Senate made a dedication to him, proclaiming *re publica conservata*, the Republic saved.[114] In 28 Octavian reformed the treasury, revoked the illegal acts of the Triumvirate, and restored free elections.[115] When Octavian addressed the Senate on 13 January 27, he restored the government to the senators, who promptly handed it back. It was not a spontaneous gesture. Octavian had prepared well for the scenario; a spontaneous gesture risked a spontaneous acceptance from the senators saying thank you very much. Not what Octavian was aiming for.

Is the end of the Republic and the birth of the Empire to be dated to 31, after the battle of Actium? Or 30, when Antony and Cleopatra conveniently removed themselves? Or was it 27 when Octavian received the name Augustus and control of the provinces containing armies? Velleius favours this date, proclaiming validity restored to the laws, authority to the courts, dignity to the Senate, and the power of the magistrates reduced to former limits.[116] Suetonius says that Octavian thought of restoring the Republic at least twice, but reconsidered because it was not safe to entrust the state to the control of more than one person.[117] Dio lived in an age of monarchical rulers, and also perceives the beginning of the Empire as in 27, when Octavian's supremacy was ratified by the Senate and the people.[118]

## Augustus and the provinces

After describing Octavian's address to the Senate in 27, Dio launches straight into the reorganisation of provincial government. The provinces were grouped into two categories, senatorial or public provinces, and imperial provinces.[119] The senatorial provinces were Africa, Numidia, Asia, Greece with Epirus, Illyricum, Macedonia, Crete with Cyrenaica, Bithynia-Pontus, Sardinia with Corsica, and Baetica, part of Spain.[120] These were the most peaceful provinces, and governors would all be titled proconsuls, governing for one year, and only a few proconsuls commanded troops.

Augustus' provinces were Gaul, Spain, Syria, Cilicia, Cyprus, and Egypt. Some of these provinces were not fully pacified, others bordered on foreign powers, and all of them required armies.[121] Augustus limited command of his provinces to ten years, avoiding the concept of perpetual rule.[122] Following the precedent set by Pompey, who remained in Rome as consul while also governing Spain via *legati*, Augustus governed via *legati Augusti propraetore*, legates of Augustus with propraetorian powers, abbreviated on inscriptions to *leg. Aug. p.p.*, or sometimes *pr. pr.* The *legati*, personally chosen by Augustus, were usually ex-consuls for provinces with two or more legions, or ex-praetors for provinces requiring fewer troops. Augustus' innovation in establishing equestrians as governors provided more manpower for smaller provinces, some of them containing auxiliary troops.

These provincial arrangements were not immutable. Changes were made according to circumstances. Certain imperial provinces might be pacified and could be converted to senatorial provinces, or a peaceful senatorial province might face external threat, requiring a *legatus Augusti pro praetore*.

When Augustus relinquished the consulship after 23 he required proconsular *imperium* to continue to govern his own provinces, about which there is extensive debate, despite Dio's assertion that Augustus was granted *imperium proconsulare* for life.[123] It is suggested that Augustus held proconsular power from 27 onwards, possibly limited to five- or ten-year blocks, renewed without difficulty.[124] Augustus was allowed to cross the *pomerium* into the city of Rome without laying down his powers.[125]

It is debated whether Augustus was entitled to send instructions to proconsular governors of senatorial provinces, as suggested by an inscription from Cyme on the coast of Asia Minor.[126] It concerns a letter from the proconsul Vinicius to the magistrates of Cyme, in which he refers to an order of Augustus (*iussu Augusti Caesaris*). The inscription dates to 27, when Augustus was consul. Lacking the consulship after 23, it is less certain whether he had authority over the governors of the senatorial provinces. Dio was certain that he did.[127] The legal mechanism is much discussed. Two categories of proconsular power have been suggested, *imperium aequum*, or equal powers, and *imperium maius*, greater than anyone's powers, which would entitle Augustus to give orders to senatorial governors, but *imperium maius* has not been conclusively proven to exist.

Augustus tried to limit extortion of provincials. It was never entirely eradicated, but governors were not as free to exploit the provincials as they had been under the Republic. Senatorial proconsular governors and *legati Augusti pro praetore* were subject to scrutiny and could be prosecuted, and their future careers depended on their standing with Augustus and succeeding emperors. All governors now earned salaries and there was no excuse for lining their own pockets.

Direct government of provinces still depended on an infrastructure of local self-governing communities. During the later Republic, colonies became the highest status communities, with *municipia* in the second rank. Some inhabitants were already Roman citizens, while others were granted citizenship en bloc. In lower ranking but still autonomous self-governing states, the local magistrates automatically obtained citizenship. Smaller settlements could be tributary to larger communities. Settlements could be upgraded to higher status. In less urbanised areas the tribal capitals, or *civitas* capitals, were usually self-governing, often with two men or *duoviri* in charge of judicial matters, taking the census every five years, and overseeing the minutiae of administering a town, such as regulation of the markets and street cleaning, combining in one post the scaled-down versions of the quaestors, aediles and praetors in Rome. In the eastern provinces with long histories of local government, existing systems were usually retained.

The imposition and collection of taxes were often behind the troubles of the provinces in Republican times. The Romans usually adapted to the circumstances of the provinces with regard to what they could pay, but the unsupervised attentions of the *publicani* caused trouble. Augustus enumerated the resources of all the provinces by means of the census, the basis for assessing tax on land (*tributum soli*) paid by owners and renters, and the property tax (*tributum capitis*), which sounds more like a poll tax, and indeed was used as such in undeveloped areas. In general, the direct taxes were no longer put out to contract as they had been during the Republic, but there were still some *publicani* who assisted the quaestors in charge of finances and tax collection in senatorial provinces, and contractors bid for the collection of indirect taxes. The taxes of the imperial provinces were collected by equestrian procurators, and revenues from imperial estates in other provinces were also collected by equestrian procurators. There were plenty of opportunities for devious operators to cheat the natives. It was never going to be perfect.

The two provinces of Africa Nova and Africa Vetus were amalgamated under Augustus to form Africa Proconsularis, with more territory added, stretching from the border with Cyrenaica in the east to Numidia in the west. The capital was Carthage, where Caesar revived Gaius Gracchus' colony, and Augustus sent 3000 veterans to the city. In 28, Carthage became autonomous, governed by *suffetes* as the Punic city had been, and issuing its own coins.[128] Africa Proconsularis, as its name suggests, was governed by a senatorial proconsul, but unusually Africa contained a legion, IX Hispana, until AD 23, when Tiberius sent it back to Pannonia.[129]

Augustus went to Gaul in 27, when he may have divided the country into three new provinces, Aquitania, Lugdunensis, and Gallia Belgica, all governed by Augustus' legates. Strabo describes the divisions briefly, explaining how Aquitania as Caesar knew it was augmented by the addition of fourteen tribes, from the area between the rivers Garumna (Garonne) and the Liger (Loire).[130] It is not universally accepted that this occurred in 27, and a case has been made for the division into three in 16, during Augustus' next visit.[131] There is some evidence for administrative centres in the three Gauls, the least well attested at Burdigala (Bordeaux) for Aquitania, at Durocortorum Remorum (Rheims) for Belgica, and for Lugdunensis the capital was at Lugdunum (Lyon), where the Altar of the Three Gauls would be established in 12, unifying the Gauls in the worship of Rome and Augustus. Drinkwater identifies some of the smaller centres, based in the capitals of the various *civitates* of the provinces, with honorary names such as Augustodunum Aeduorum (Autun) and Augusta Treverorum (Trier), hence its French name Treves.[132]

Augustus intended to go to Britain, but remained in Gaul because the Britons seemed ready to come to terms, whereas the Gauls were restless.[133] An inscription recording a speech of the Emperor Claudius refers to a census taken by Augustus, which caused trouble because the Gauls were unaccustomed to it.[134] Livy and Dio also refer to the census, and Dio adds that Augustus 'regulated life and government' of Gaul.[135]

The Province was renamed Gallia Narbonensis after the capital at Narbo (Narbonne), having been pacified successively by Gaius Carrinas and Marcus Valerius between 31 and 27, their work completed by Augustus.[136] More peaceful than the other parts of Gaul, in 22 it became a senatorial proconsular province.[137]

Augustus' next visit to Gaul in 16 was triggered by an invasion of Germanic Usipetes, Tencteri and Sugambri. They raided Gaul and 'Germania' where some Celts, a.k.a Germans, had occupied the Belgic territory on the left bank of the Rhine, giving the territory its name.[138] Further incursions from Free Germany could be stopped only if the Romans controlled all the Germanic tribes. Augustus decided to convert 'Germania' into a province, or more correctly an occupied zone, in preparation for a campaign across the Rhine launched by Tiberius' brother Drusus in 12. He fortified bases at the junction of the rivers Lippe and Aliso.[139] In 9 he invaded the territory of the Chatti and Sugambri, subduing the tribes with difficulty and bloodshed. He contemplated crossing the Elbe but turned back, dying before reaching the Rhine, from disease as Dio says, or traditionally after a fall from his horse.[140] Tiberius rode in record time to see his brother just before he died, and took over the campaign. Most Germans sued for peace. Tiberius was made consul and awarded the title Imperator and a triumph. Only the Sugambri held out, and unless this tribe submitted Augustus refused to arrange a general peace. German campaigns continued up to the Elbe, and in AD 1 Domitius Ahenobarbus crossed it.[141] Modern scholars have suggested that the Elbe was Augustus' ultimate goal, but whatever he planned, the disaster in AD 9, when Quinctilius Varus and three legions were lost, put a stop to further advance. The Romans had miscalculated, thinking the Germans pacified. The Rhine remained the frontier, guarded initially by eight legions.

Not long after Augustus' death in AD 14, the eight Rhine legions were divided into two groups, four legions in each of the two sections of Germania on the left bank of the Rhine. The most westerly part with its capital at Cologne projected into Gallia Belgica and stretched from the Rhine mouth to Bonn and Remagen in the south.

The other section straddled the middle and lower Rhine, embracing Coblenz in the north-west, Wiesbaden and the capital Mainz in the north-east, Dijon, Besancon and Nyon in the south-west, and the Black Forest and Windisch in the south-east.

The two Germanies were zones under military occupation, controlled by army commanders of the Rhine, but administered from Gallia Belgica, one of the three Gallic provinces created by Augustus.[142] It was not until the reign of Domitian (AD 81 to 96) that the Germanies were converted into provinces in their own right, called Germania Superior or Upper Germany, and Germania Inferior or Lower Germany, Superior indicating the province nearer to Rome, Inferior being further away.

After the census in Gaul, Augustus travelled to Spain in 26 and remained there until 25, campaigning in the unpacified north-west, with two armies under Publius Carisius and Gaius Antistius Vetus, with whose help Augustus subdued the Astures and Cantabri, and the doors of the temple of Janus were closed once again, proclaiming peace in the Roman world. As usual, the tribes did not lie down. In 22 and 19 Carisius and then Vipsanius Agrippa fought the Cantabri all over again.[143]

The date when Spain was divided into three is uncertain, possibly after the subjugation of the Astures and Cantabri in 19, or in 16-13 when Augustus was again active in Gaul. Baetica in the south-west was the smallest, governed by proconsular senators, none of them attested until Tiberius' reign. The capital was Corduba (Cordoba). The capital of Lusitania, a much larger province, was the new colony of Emerita Augusta (Merida.) The largest province of all was Tarraconensis, named after its capital at Tarraco (Tarragona). Tarraconensis and Lusitania were governed by *legati Augusti pro praetore*.

In the east, Galatia was made a province in 25. It is to be distinguished from the similarly named and larger area to the west and east of Ancyra (Ankara). Galatia was taken over with relative ease when King Amyntas was killed in battle. He had sided with the Liberators, but deserted them in 42, and in 40 he had succeeded

Deiotarus as ruler of Galatia. Deiotarus had raised and trained two legions to fight on behalf of Caesar against Pharnaces, and one of them, XXII Deiotariana, is named after him. In 37-36 Antony confirmed Amyntas as king and gave him Lycaonia, Pamphylia, Pisidia and part of Phrygia. Amyntas and Archelaus of Cappadocia were the only kings who retained their extended territories when Octavian removed rulers who had helped Antony.[144] As a province, Galatia gave the Romans protection against marauding mountain tribes, and served as a buffer between Roman territory and Parthia.[145]

Augustus aimed to stabilize the Rhine, the Alps, the Danube zones, and the tribes beyond. The Danube was a natural frontier, protecting areas to its south, and the routes into Italy and Asia Minor.[146] The Romans fought three campaigns before they gained control over the territories up to the Danube, which were converted into occupied zones controlled by military commanders, only later becoming the provinces of Raetia, Noricum, Pannonia and Moesia, annexed at different dates.

The position of Raetia and Noricum, bordered by the Danube in the north and the Alps in the south made annexation imperative to guard routes into Italy, possibly in 15. Raetia was initially governed by legionary centurions as *praefecti* and later by equestrian procurators, who commanded troops as well as administering their provinces, based at Augusta Vindelicorum (Augsburg). Noricum was named after the Norici, who had contributed troops for Caesar's campaigns, but they are strangely anonymous in the sources, as Appian noted.[147] Noricum was known to the Romans long before it was annexed, mainly because of its iron deposits.

In 181 the Romans founded a Latin colony at Aquileia at the northern end of the Adriatic, primarily as a defence against the tribes beyond it, and the colonists, whom Livy splits into centurions, infantry and cavalry, received generous land allotments.[148] With its good harbour, Aquileia was in an excellent position for trade and rapidly grew into a port and emporium.[149] Iron from Noricum was shipped through Aquileia, and within Noricum another emporium developed at the Magdalensberg (Klagenfurt). Strabo says that the Norici, Vindelici and other tribes raided Italy and Gaul from the Alps. Publius Silius Nerva campaigned in Illyricum and the south-eastern Alps in 16, and in 15 Tiberius and Drusus stopped the raids during their Alpine campaign.[150]

Velleius Paterculus says that Noricum was made a province by Tiberius, by whose campaigns from 16-12 Vindelicia, Raetia, Pannonia and the territory of the Scordisci were pacified.[151] There is evidence for a *praefectus civitatium* in Noricum, and Gaius Baebius Atticus is attested as equestrian procurator, based at Virunum, south-west of the Magdalensberg.[152]

East of Noricum was Illyricum. In the *Res Gestae*, Augustus says that during his campaigns in 35-33 he advanced the boundary of Illyricum to the Danube.[153] This conquest was prolonged and bloody. Vipsanius Agrippa fought the Pannonians in 13 but died the following year. From then Tiberius fought a long war against the Delmatae and in 10 he received the submission of the tribes.[154] Possibly after Tiberius suppressed the Pannonian revolt, in AD 9 Illyricum was split into two provinces, Pannonia in the north and Dalmatia in the south.[155]

Pannonia was governed by a consular *legatus propraetore*, and Velleius names the consular Vibius Postumus as governor of Dalmatia, labelling him *praepositus*, normally indicating an officer standing in for someone else.[156] Pannonia was a source of auxiliary cavalry, *alae*, or wings, and infantry cohorts, sent to serve elsewhere. Like Raetia and Noricum, Pannonia protected Italy from the northern tribes, and it secured the route from northern Italy through Dalmatia to Macedonia and Greece. Its border to the north and the east was the Danube, as the river flows eastwards to a point just north of Aquincum (Budapest), then turns south and then east again, towards Singidunum (Belgrade) on the western border of Moesia.

Control of Moesia was necessary to guard the lower Danube zones, but the date when Moesia was annexed is uncertain. The earliest attested legate is Aulus Caecina Severus, who in AD 6 fought against the Pannonians who attacked the Roman base at Sirmium.[157] Gaius Baebius Atticus, who had served as *primus pilus* of V Macedonica, is attested as *praefectus civitatium Moesiae*, probably under Augustus, then as tribune of a Praetorian cohort, and then procurator in Noricum under Tiberius.[158] Only under Claudius (reigned AD 41-54) did Moesia became a province, bordered by the Danube from Belgrade to the Black Sea. Moesia was further protected when the Emperor Trajan created the province of Dacia north of the Danube.

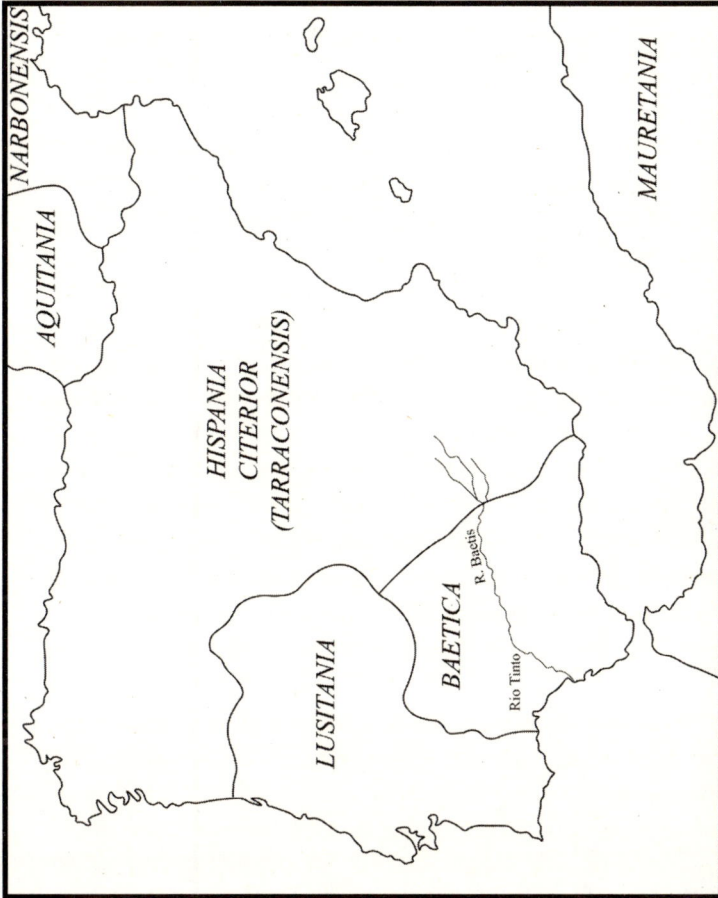

4. Spain after its division into three smaller provinces. Baetica was the smallest but the wealthiest, producing quantities of gold and exporting olive oil and fish sauce or *garum*. In the late period, the governor of Baetica also had authority over Mauretania Tingitana from where the tribesmen raided Spain. Tarraconensis was not urbanised, but the single legion, VII Gemina, was stationed in the province at Leon, and silver was mined at Carthago Nova (Cartagena). Lusitania also exported metals and fish products but was even less urbanised, so the Romans created the administrative infrastructure. Redrawn by Isla Jones after Richardson 1996 and various sources.

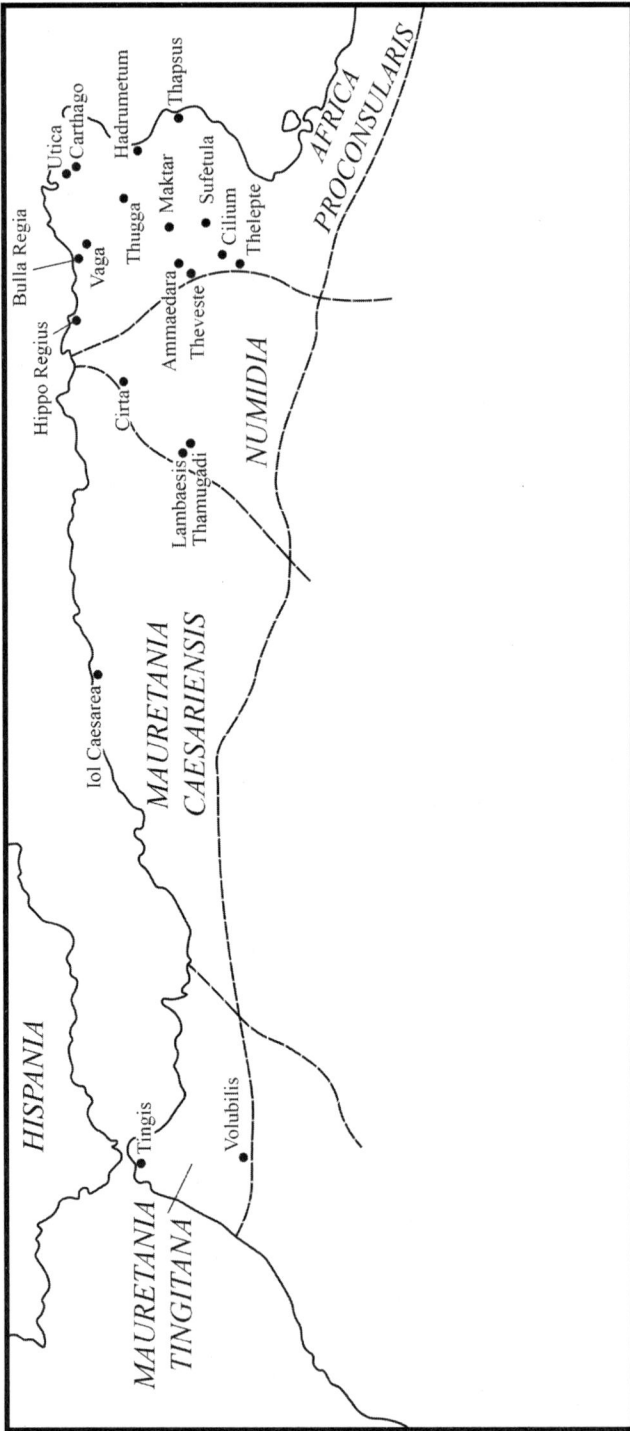

5. The provinces of North Africa. In the early AD 40s Suetonius Paullinus and Hosidius Geta subdued Mauretania, from which Claudius created Mauretania Tingitana and Mauretania Caesariensis. Numidia was once much larger, but under Augustus its eastern part was merged with Africa Proconsularis, until Severus created a new Numidian province in 197. Redrawn by Isla Jones after Goodman 1997.

## Military power: Augustus and the army

After 30, Octavian commanded about sixty legions and controlled the wealth of Egypt. Much needed to be done to repair the damage of the civil wars. Reducing the sixty or so legions to a manageable number was an urgent priority. There were Roman troops in Spain, Gaul, along the Rhine and Danube, in Syria, Asia Minor, Egypt and northern Africa. About twenty-eight legions were kept under arms, while the soldiers of the other legions would need to be disbanded and settled somewhere on the land. From 31 onwards, veteran settlers were to be exempt from taxation and requisitioning of supplies, according to Octavian's edict issued in that year.[159] In the *Res Gestae* Augustus says that in 31 and again in 14 he used his own funds to purchase lands for veteran settlement, totalling 600,000,000 sesterces for lands in Italy, and 260,000,000 for provincial lands.[160] It is estimated that 40,000 to 50,000 veterans were settled in Italy, from a total of twenty-five to thirty legions, but the number settled in the provinces is unknown. The Egyptian treasury probably funded much or all of this after 30, as well as the cash pensions that Octavian awarded to some soldiers, especially to those with homes to go to.[161] Keppie estimated that the price paid for lands in Italy would have purchased generous allotments of about fifty *iugera* for 24,000 veterans.[162]

According to Augustus, 120,000 veterans were settled in colonies, and he gave each man 1,000 sesterces (250 *denarii*).[163] Colonies were established in Africa, Sicily, Macedonia, the two Spains, Achaea, Asia, Syria, Pisidia, and in Gaul around Narbo.[164] Colonies founded by Caesar and Augustus all share the name Julia, so it is not possible to distinguish them from each other.

The standard term of service in the later Republic was sixteen years, and significantly in 14 there was another batch of veterans to be settled, sixteen years after the reorganisation of 30, when younger recruits replaced discharged veterans of the twenty-eight legions. During the massive settlement programmes after 30 and in 14, there does not seem to have been too much disruption involving evictions of existing farmers, but lands were not limitless and the system could not continue forever. With this in mind, Augustus introduced a pension scheme. In 13, cash payments were substituted for allotments of land. For the first two decades this was paid for from Augustus' own resources, including the further settlements listed in the *Res Gestae* in the years 7, 6, 4, 3, and 2.

Soldiers were to serve for sixteen years and then an additional four years as reservists, excused from fatigues. Probably in AD 5, not attested in any source but assumed to be the case, the term was extended to twenty years with five in reserve, which became standard practice. The cash payments for discharged veterans were fixed at 12,000 sesterces for each soldier in AD 5, and in AD 6, Augustus established the military treasury (*aerarium militare*). He boosted its resources by donating 170,000,000 sesterces, and it was topped up by a one per cent tax on sales at property auctions in Italy, and a five per cent tax on inheritances left to non-family members.

The provision of assured pensions obviated the struggles between the Senate and the returning generals for land allotments, and also made service in the army more attractive. There were many advantages in maintaining a permanent army establishment. There was already a cadre of men who had made a career for themselves serving in successive armies raised for the constant wars, but during the Republic, soldiers could not guarantee that they could re-enlist in a new army with the rank attained in a previous campaign. In a standing army there was a career structure where talents could earn rewards and promotion, as well as pay.

The soldiers of Republican armies each swore an oath of loyalty and obedience to the consuls, but in the standing army all the soldiers swore an oath of loyalty to Augustus, renewed every year, and transferred to succeeding emperors. Augustus was supreme commander, paymaster, and controller of all the higher appointments and promotions. Late in his reign, he appointed senatorial legates to command the legions, which until then had been commanded for one month at a time by two of the six military tribunes. The six tribunes were retained, the most senior being the *tribunus laticlavius*, literally the broad stripe tribune, of senatorial rank, and after about a year he could begin a career combining administrative posts and military appointments. The other five tribunes were non-senatorial *tribuni angusticlavii*, or narrow stripe tribunes, serving for a one or two years, moving on to command an auxiliary unit. All the tribunes were subordinate to the legionary legate, who was in turn subordinate to the provincial governor, but appointments of legionary legates were in Augustus' gift and controlled by him, as were further promotions, depending on performance and behaviour.

The *praefectus castrorum*, or the prefect of the camp, was next in seniority to the legate, and the *primus pilus*, literally 'the first spear' was next in line to the camp prefect. Both had usually been centurions, probably in more than one legion. Sixty centurions commanded the sixty legionary centuries, each containing eighty men. Six centuries formed one cohort, ten cohorts being the full complement of a legion. So far there is no evidence for a cohort commander. This was the organisation of Caesar's day and Augustus did not alter it, nor did he change legionary pay, set by Caesar at 225 *denarii* per annum. Provincial taxes provided the funds.

Although there were probably twenty-eight legions, they were not numbered in a straight sequence from I to XXVIII. The highest number assigned to the legions under Augustus was XXII. Legionary names and identities were important and symbolic, so Augustus retained them. During the Empire, some numbers were duplicated, such as III Augusta, III Cyrenaica, and III Gallica, IV Macedonica and IV Scythica, V Macedonica and V Alaudae, VI Ferrata and VI Victrix, X Fretensis and X Gemina. The name *Gemina* usually indicates that the remains of two legions had been formed into one.

The development from native levies to regular auxiliary units is not elucidated, and it was not complete even in the mid-first century AD. Tacitus says that there were as many auxiliary troops as there were legionaries, but their numbers fluctuated and they were frequently moved according to circumstances, so he did not list their bases. It is possible that tribesmen fighting under their native leaders were still being recruited, and there were probably no standard terms of service, or even size of units. In the evolved system, the auxiliary troops consisted of cavalry units, the *alae*, and infantry units called cohorts, and *cohortes equitatae* or mixed units combining some mounted men and some foot soldiers. Each unit's paper strength was either quingenary or 500-strong, or milliary, 1,000-strong. The equestrian commanders of these units would follow a prescribed career path, beginning with about three years commanding an infantry cohort of 500 men and then commanding a 500-strong cavalry unit. There were only a few 1,000-strong infantry units, and even fewer 1,000-strong cavalry units, of which no province had more than one. The commanders of the large cavalry units were important officers who could expect to go on to further military commands and prestigious civil posts.

The disposition of the armies in the provinces was authorized by Augustus, constantly changing according to developments in the Empire. The closest that historians can get to the locations of the legions under Augustus is Tacitus' list of naval and military forces dating to AD 23, nine years after Augustus' death.[165] The fleets at Misenum and Ravenna guarded the west and east coasts of Italy, and another fleet based at Forum Julium (Fréjus) protected Gaul, though this town is now about a mile from the coast. Eight legions on the Rhine could deal with problems in Gaul and Germany, three legions in Spain (finally subdued by Agrippa in 19), two in Africa (normally only one, but the revolt of Tacfarinas necessitated the presence of IX Hispana from Pannonia) and two in Egypt. In Syria and the lands bordering the Parthian Empire there were four legions, and two each in Dalmatia, Pannonia and Moesia. There are only twenty-five legions in Tacitus' list, because three legions had been wiped out in the Varian disaster in Germany in AD 9, probably XVII, XVIII and XIX, never heard of again, never reconstituted, and no other legions were given these numbers. Outside the provinces, Mauretania was controlled by King Juba II, who had been brought up in Rome, and allied kings kept order in Thrace.

As well as commanding the provincial armies, Augustus established permanent bodies of troops in Rome, for which there was no precedent. He created the Praetorian Guard with a full complement of nine cohorts, six of them stationed in various locations in Italy, and three housed in Rome. The Praetorian camp was not established until Tiberius' reign, when all the Praetorians were brought to the city. Whereas no cohort commanders are known for the legions, the Praetorian cohorts were commanded by tribunes, often high-ranking ex-legionaries. Overall command of the Praetorians was given to equestrians, usually but not always in pairs.[166]

Most of the Praetorians were Italians, and on discharge they usually received grants of land. Many had served in the legions, and their experience would be useful on the rare occasions when the Praetorians were called upon to fight in campaigns. They sometimes performed police work, but their duties in Rome were largely ceremonial. The three Praetorian cohorts in Rome under Augustus guarded his residence on a rotational basis, each serving for a month. The Praetorians were of higher status than legionaries, earning more pay. In 13, Augustus set their terms of service at twelve years, while the legionaries served for sixteen years, and when legionary service was extended to twenty years in AD 5 service in the Praetorian Guard was set at sixteen.[167]

Alongside the Praetorians, Augustus created a police force and a fire brigade, respectively the Urban Cohorts (*cohortes urbanae*) established in 13, and the *Vigiles* created in AD 6. The Urban Cohorts and the Praetorians were closely associated, and the cohort numbering system was shared, I to IX for the Praetorians, and X to XII for the three Urban Cohorts. The Emperor Domitian added an extra Praetorian cohort, making a total of ten, so the Urban Cohorts were renumbered from XI. The *praefectus urbi* or city prefect supervised the Urban Cohorts. Previously, the *praefectus urbi* was a temporary appointment, nothing to do with this more recent post, usually held by ex-consuls. Three tribunes commanded the three Urban Cohorts, with centurions commanding the centuries of each one. The soldiers served for twenty years but did not have to remain as reserves, as the legionaries did. It is not known how Augustus employed them, but under his successors they kept the peace and policed the city. The *praefectus urbi* had jurisdiction over petty crimes.[168]

Marcus Licinius Crassus assembled the first known fire-brigade in the first century BC. He was not officially appointed, but put out fires for his own ends, bringing his slave fire-fighters to burning buildings and offering to buy the property. If sales were agreed the slaves quenched the fire, and at least prevented it from spreading, while Crassus either repaired the buildings or put up new ones. In Augustus' day the aedile Egnatius Rufus assembled another slave fire-brigade, which put out fires and rescued people. Augustus put a stop to his enterprise, but Egnatius had gained popularity and lots of electoral support, becoming praetor. He aimed for the consulship. Gaius Sentius Saturninus was sole consul in 19 because Augustus would not admit Egnatius' candidacy, and refused the consulship for himself. Velleius says that Egnatius formed a conspiracy against Augustus, and the Senate condemned and executed him while Augustus was absent in the east.[169]

Three years before this, Augustus had assembled 600 public slaves of the board of *tresviri nocturni* responsible for the night watch, extending their duties to watching for fires. Better arrangements were put in place after a serious fire in 7. Augustus divided the city into fourteen regions, subdivided into a total of 265 *vici*, each one with a *vicomagister* in charge.[170] The slave fire-fighters were placed under the *vicomagistri*, but this proved too complicated and unwieldy for effective fire-fighting. After another fire in AD 6, Augustus created the *Vigiles* as a standing force, combining a city watch, a police force, and a fire service. The overall commander of the *Vigiles* was an equestrian, with the title of *Praefectus Vigilum*. The soldiers of the *Vigiles* were recruited from freedmen, divided into seven cohorts commanded by seven tribunes, who had usually served as *primus pilus* of a legion. The seven centuries in each cohort were commanded by centurions from the legions. One cohort controlled two of the fourteen Augustan regions. The *Vigiles* as fire watchers may have been able to put fires out if they were caught in time, but without special equipment all they could do was to demolish buildings in the path of a great conflagration. Fires were frequent and the *Vigiles* operated patrols, especially at night, watching for fires, but they probably also arrested people acting suspiciously, taking him, or her, to the office of the *Praefectus Vigilum* who was most likely on call during the night.

Christopher Fuhrmann estimates the number of military police and guardsmen of the Praetorians, the Urban Cohorts, and the *Vigiles* as 23,840 men, equivalent to four legions.[171] All the men swore an oath of allegiance to Augustus and succeeding emperors. Somehow Augustus managed to convince most Romans that all this potential force was for the benefit of Rome and its people, rather than support for his rule.

## Political power: little by little

Tacitus sums up Augustus' acquisition of powers, saying that step by step he united in his own person the functions of the Senate, the magistracy, and the legislature.[172] Octavian-Augustus held the consulship every year from 30 until 23, when he fell dangerously ill. He recovered but everything changed. He did not become consul in 22. His monopoly of the office until 23 was unusual and did little to persuade the Romans that he was not aiming at permanent supreme power. It also reduced by half anyone else's chances of holding the consulship. By 23, Octavian had become Augustus and his position was much stronger, so he relinquished his hold on the consulship, creating a vacancy for other candidates.

Without the consulship he required some other form of power, not necessarily of a military nature, but a legal and customary form with no hints of arbitrary sovereignty, or any whiff of permanence. *Tribunicia potestas*, or tribunician power, fitted the bill perfectly. This was conferred on him by law in 23. It enabled Augustus to step down as consul but retain legitimate control of the state.[173] It is suggested that from 36 onwards, Octavian-Augustus possessed tribunician sacrosanctity, obtaining the other attributes of the tribunes gradually, ultimately gaining all powers of the tribunes. He never used the title, and never held the actual office, but enumerated his tribunician years on inscriptions and coins, usually abbreviated to *trib.pot*, followed by a number.

The importance of tribunician power cannot be over-emphasized. Tacitus labelled it the title of supreme eminence (*summi fastigii vocabulum*).[174] It gave the holder the usual tribunician rights, to act on behalf of the plebs, to convene the Senate, to introduce legislation, and to veto any proposals, but while ordinary tribunes were subject to the veto of other tribunes, Augustus and his successors were not. Tribunician power alone did not enable Augustus to govern the state, but when combined with proconsular power and its inherent *imperium*, Augustus and his successors possessed the fundamental tools of government.[175]

Augustus employed literature, art and coins to promote his achievements and ideals. His portraits never showed any signs of ageing. His advantage over Caesar was youth, enabling him to introduce his proposals slowly and cautiously, if necessary backtracking and beginning all over again.

Octavian-Augustus had no intention of relinquishing control, but did not flaunt his powers, relying on influence, part of his *auctoritas*, but 'authority' in English does not convey its full meaning. It had no legal basis.[176] Augustus adopted the title *Princeps*, which embodied no political or military overtones, but outranked the honorary Republican status of *princeps senatus*, which Augustus also valued. It may have been awarded to him by the Senate in 29 or 28, and it gave him the right to speak first at meetings of the Senate.[177]

The eastern provinces had no problem with worship of Augustus as a living god, but Augustus merely allowed worship of his *Genius* or spirit, eventually combined with the goddess Roma, which became the basis of the Imperial cult.[178] In the western provinces the Imperial cult was celebrated in open-air sanctuaries, with an altar but no temple. The Altar of the Three Gauls was established at Lugdunum (Lyon), and an altar (*ara*) was established at Oppidum Ubiorum on the Rhine, renamed as the Altar of the Ubii, or Ara Ubiorum (Cologne). These altars were initiatives of the provincial assemblies, not forced on people by Augustus or the Senate. The priests who conducted ceremonials were provincials, called *sacerdotes*, as opposed to Roman *flamines*.

The numerous honours voted to Octavian-Augustus played their part in promoting his image. Dio enumerates the tributes from provincials and Romans.[179] The honours gave him privileges, such as the use of the name Imperator, and distinctions in dress. Statues, celebratory arches and monuments were erected in Rome, Italy and the provinces. The *lex Saenia* passed in 30 gave him the right to create new patricians.[180] Octavian did not accept all honours. He refused the cash payments that substituted for the *aureum coronarium*, customarily sent from Italian cities for triumphing generals.[181] The civil wars had impoverished the cities, so Octavian gained some credit, at little cost to himself.

Augustus' political powers gave him legal authority over the Roman world, and his command of finances and the army gave him a very secure edge, but he had to temper the potential use of force by a carefully groomed moral supremacy, part of his image as a benevolent and beneficial ruler, enabling him to retain the faith of the Roman people. Fortunately, after 27 until his death in AD 14, he had four decades to accomplish his aims.

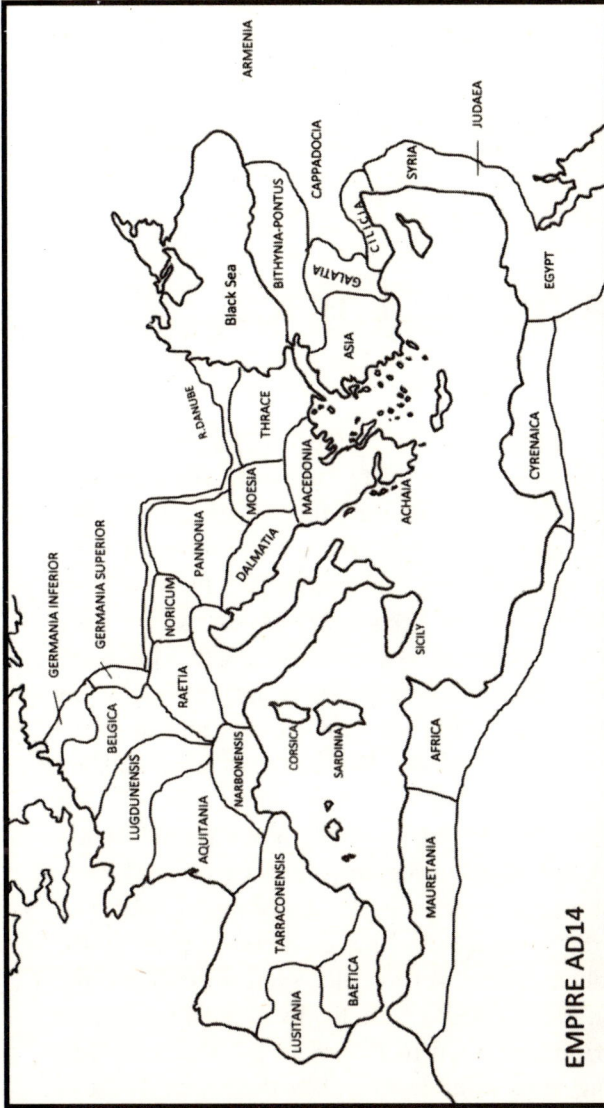

**EMPIRE AD14**

6. When Augustus died in AD 14 the Romans had extended control around the Mediterranean, which they called *Mare Nostrum*, Our Sea. Egypt was annexed after the defeat of Antony and Cleopatra in 30 BC. Augustus divided Spain and Gaul into smaller provinces, and combined Africa Nova and Africa Vetus to form a single province labelled Africa Proconsularis. Its name derives from the title of its senatorial proconsular governor, after Augustus reorganised the provinces, some of them Imperial provinces governed by the Emperor himself via legates, and the rest governed by senators. Germania Superior and Inferior were occupied zones of the left bank of the Rhine, not formally made provinces until c.AD 90 under the Emperor Domitian. Raetia, Noricum and Moesia were annexed, and the provinces of Pannonia and Dalmatia may have been created out of Illyricum by Augustus before AD 9, but they are not attested by these names until later. Thrace did not become a province until AD 46, but the Romans frequently had to intervene in the country as soon as they annexed Macedonia, sometimes leading armed expeditions to reinstate various rulers. Redrawn by Sue Howie after Goodman 1997.

# 8

# Augustus to Nero; the Provinces of Greece, the Danube, Britain and Thrace

The emperors from Augustus to Nero were labelled Julio-Claudians, claiming descent from Julius Caesar via Augustus, or from the Claudians via Augustus' wife Livia. Tiberius, the son of Livia by her first husband Tiberius Claudius Nero, had no trace of Julian ancestry.

The year 23 was an eventful one. Agrippa was sent to govern Syria, but remained on the island of Lesbos, governing the province via legates.[1] It was said that Agrippa had quarrelled with Marcellus, married to Augustus' daughter Julia, and generally considered as Augustus' heir and successor. It was an odd story, and Agrippa's task may have been surveillance of the Balkans, and also Parthia. Augustus intended to join Agrippa but was ill, and at the end of 23 his son-in-law Marcellus died. The alleged rivalry between Marcellus and Agrippa was now ended, but Agrippa remained in the east until 21.

There was a severe shortage of grain in 22. Once again, Augustus delayed his journey to the east and used his own resources to boost the food supply. Probably as a result of his success he was offered the consulship in perpetuity. He rejected it.[2] He finally arrived in the east and stayed on after Agrippa returned to Rome. In 20, the Armenian populace appealed to Augustus, wanting to replace their ruler Artaxias by Tigranes, a refugee in Rome. Tiberius was summoned, gathered troops, and installed Tigranes without bloodshed. The next event was the result of protracted diplomacy. King Phraates of Parthia asked for friendship with the Romans, and returned the military standards taken from Licinius Crassus in 53. It was a major political coup, treated as a military victory.[3] Augustus lodged the standards in the unfinished temple of Mars Ultor, the Avenger, which he had vowed at Philippi. On the breastplate of the statue of Augustus in the Vatican Museum, the main scene depicts the handing over of the standards, and coins were issued with legends proclaiming *signis receptis*, the standards returned.

Dio stands alone in mentioning that Augustus took the consulship for life on returning to Rome in 19, when the people begged him to set the state to rights and make whatever laws he liked, and it has been argued that from 19 onwards, without actually being consul, Augustus possessed full consular powers.[4] Tacitus describes Augustus' gradual assumption of all the Imperial powers; in Lacey's terms, a gradual encroachment on control.[5]

Before 19, many if not all the consuls reached their posts by dint of personal recommendation of Augustus. After 19 Augustus made fewer personal recommendations for office, and there was a tangible increase in numbers of nobles reaching the consulship from Italian communities as well as from Rome. Social mobility increased and regular career paths were established, but most appointments and promotions were in Augustus' gift. Experience in government and administration was necessary for senatorial careers, and provincial governors and commanders of the armies required praetorian or consular rank. In order to provide more personnel with consular experience, in 5, Augustus introduced the regular practice of allowing suffect consuls to take over from the *consules ordinarii* who gave their names to the year. From 5 onwards, the *consules ordinarii* entered office on 1 January but resigned at the end of June, and *suffecti* took over on 1 July. Later, numbers of *suffecti* in one year increased.[6]

In the years 19, 18 and 11, the Senate and people agreed that Augustus should be 'appointed alone as guardian of laws and customs with supreme power'.[7] In 19, Augustus was elected supervisor of morals (*praefectus moribus* or *curator morum*) for five years, passing legislation in 18 and 17 to improve moral conduct.[8] The legislation of 18 curbed bribery in elections, and sumptuary laws limited displays of wealth. The laws failed. Augustus promoted marriage via the *lex Julia de maritandis ordinibus*, encouraging men to marry. Men aged twenty-five to sixty and women aged twenty to fifty had a duty to marry and raise children. After divorce, or the death of a partner, remarriage was ordained within a specified period of three years, as stated in the *lex Papia Poppaea* passed in AD 9 by the consuls Marcus

Papius Mutilus and Quintus Poppaeus Secundus, ironic really, as neither of them was married.[9] Augustus penalised married men with no children, while married men with children were fast-tracked for promotions. Unmarried men and women could not inherit legacies, so there were probably some hasty marriage proposals around the death-beds of rich relatives. Senators were to marry women of their own class, not their freedwomen, which had become common. The Romans were forced into a moral straitjacket, and informers would spring out of the woodwork for all the various reasons that motivate such people.

After enforcing legitimate marriage, Augustus made adultery an offence by the *lex Julia de adulteriis coercendis*, hypocritical because he had adulterous affairs himself, but the law was aimed at women, to ensure that their children were legitimate. Wives having affairs were to be divorced, and husbands ignoring the adultery of their wives could be prosecuted as pimps. Women did not share these rights. In 2, the scandalous behaviour of Augustus' daughter Julia, wife of Agrippa, could no longer be ignored, and doubt was cast as to whether Agrippa was the real father of Gaius and Lucius, adopted by Augustus. Julia was exiled to the island of Pandateria, where she died.

The adultery laws prohibited unnatural vices, but provided that aberrant sexual practices were not performed on free citizens of Rome, free Romans could pay any sort of attention to anyone else.

## Social ranks

Caesar had increased the number of senators to an unwieldy 900 members, which Augustus reduced to 600, still double the 300 senators of the Republic. Augustus increased the financial threshold for senators to 1,000,000 sesterces. Dio invents a speech for Augustus' friend Maecenas, recommending that unworthy senators should be removed, and conversely if senators of good repute lacked resources, they should be assisted financially.[10]

The property qualification for equestrians was set at 400,000 sesterces. Equestrians were entitled to wear a gold ring, and sons of senators held equestrian status until they entered the Senate. Equestrians could be demoted, or promoted to senatorial status. They held army commands and administrative posts in Rome and the provinces, culminating eventually in the four great equestrian prefectures. The Prefect of Egypt was the earliest, the first being Cornelius Gallus. The Praetorian Prefects were established probably in 2, and the posts of *Praefectus Vigilum* commanding the *vigiles*, and the *Praefectus Annonae*, in charge of the food supply, were created respectively in AD 6 and somewhere between AD 8 and 14.

A problem had developed with the large numbers of freedmen in Rome. A five per cent tax was levied on manumissions by a magistrate when slaves were freed in the formal manner, with witnesses. These freedmen received Roman citizenship, and qualified for the corn dole. The alternative, avoiding the tax, was to announce that certain slaves were free and put them on the street, minus the grant of citizenship. Between 17 BC and AD 4 the *lex Junia*, the *lex Fufia Caninia*, and the *lex Aelia Sentia* reduced the number of informal manumissions and dealt with freedmen lacking citizenship. The *lex Junia* bestowed Latin status on freedmen who did not hold Roman citizenship. These became known as Junian Latins, whose property reverted to their former masters. The next two laws limited the number of slaves that could be freed at the same time, and made it illegal for anyone under twenty to free his slaves without good reason. Freed slaves had to be over thirty.[11]

## The succession

It was important for Augustus to declare his successor, but his problem was that his choice of successor was a kiss of death, allowing Tacitus, Dio and modern authors to blame Augustus' wife Livia for ensuring the succession of her son Tiberius by killing all other candidates.[12]

Augustus' nephew and son-in-law Marcellus was probably intended to be the heir, but he died in 23, and his widow Julia was quickly married to Marcus Vipsanius Agrippa. They had three sons, Gaius, Lucius, and Agrippa Postumus, born after his father's death. There were two daughters, Julia and Agrippina, the latter married to Tiberius' nephew Germanicus. This couple's offspring included their son Caligula and their grandson Nero. When Augustus was ill in 23, before Marcellus died, he gave his signet ring to Agrippa, as the only man capable of holding everything together.[13] After Agrippa's death in 12 his widow Julia was hastily married to Augustus' stepson Tiberius, who was devastated by having to divorce Vipsania, Agrippa's daughter by his previous marriage.[14] Tiberius sincerely loved Vipsania, and his new marriage was disastrous.

Augustus adopted Gaius and Lucius, sons of Agrippa and Julia, introducing both into public life.[15] Augustus was consul for the twelfth time in 5 to chaperone Gaius as his colleague. He held his thirteenth consulship in 2, with Lucius as colleague. Lucius, travelling to Spain, died in the same year at Massilia.[16] In AD 1 Gaius was sent to the east and came to an understanding with the new Parthian ruler Phraates V (Phrataces in Dio's narrative).[17]

There may be a connection here with Tiberius' seven-year stay on Rhodes, beginning in 6 BC. He was supposedly in disgrace, even though he had just held a triumph and received *tribunicia potestas* for five years. The year before Tiberius left Rome, King Tigranes III of Armenia had died, leaving his kingdom prey to Parthian kings, so Tiberius' destination was Armenia, but he never went there. Like Agrippa on Lesbos, Tiberius on Rhodes may have been watching and reporting to Augustus. Governors going out to their provinces detoured to visit him.[18] Were they being briefed about potential troubles? Gaius' mission had perhaps averted a potential crisis, enabling Tiberius to return to Rome. After making terms with Phraates V, Gaius was wounded in a skirmish when war broke out with Armenia. Relieved of command, he died on his way to Rome in AD 4.[19]

Tiberius now received tribunician power for ten years and was adopted as Augustus' son, along with Agrippa Postumus.[20] Drusus, son of Tiberius and Vipsania, was in the second rank of heirs, and Tiberius adopted his nephew Germanicus, the son of his brother Drusus. Augustus had provided himself with four potential successors, reduced to three in AD 7, when Agrippa Postumus was involved in a plot and banished.

In summer AD 14, Augustus fell ill on the way to Capri. He stopped at Nola, where he owned property. Making himself presentable to receive his friends, he asked if they had enjoyed the performance.[21] He died on 19 August, the anniversary of his first consulship. Tiberius inherited two-thirds of his estate, but refused the names Augustus and Imperator, which is presumably what Dio means by the Greek *Autokrator*.[22]

Augustus' long reign, from *c*.30 BC to AD 14, indicates that if plots were made against him, they were never successful, and in fact opposition to Augustus was perhaps never very serious.[23] Suetonius groups all the opponents together, prefacing the collection of names with the reassurance that plots were either detected or betrayed.[24]

Augustus left other documents besides his will. The *Res Gestae* recounted all his acts, and there was a summary of the armies and finances.[25] Dio mentions a letter for Tiberius, urging him to keep the Roman world within its present limits.[26]

## Accession of Tiberius

Tiberius was purely Claudian, with the inbred arrogance of the clan.[27] Dutifully administering the Empire, Tiberius was a reluctant ruler.[28] Velleius Paterculus, who idolized Tiberius, having served under him for eight years, says that Tiberius resisted government of the Empire longer than many others spent in gaining it, but gave in because whatever he did not protect would perish.[29] Tiberius used to repeat a Greek proverb that governing the state was like holding a wolf by the ears.[30]

Augustus' ashes were deposited in his Mausoleum, built in 28 BC.[31] Augustus was deified and Livia was made priestess of his cult. Tiberius was now son and heir of a god, but rejected attempts to worship him, writing to the people of Spain, who wanted to erect a shrine to him, that he was mortal and his work was the work of men. [32]

The Romans did not know what to make of Tiberius. He was well-educated but obscure in speech, never saying what he really wanted, and even if he did, he usually meant the opposite.[33] The oath of loyalty was sworn to the new emperor by senators, officials, and the Roman people, and Tiberius wrote to the armies, the real source of power. Tacitus says that he did so because he feared that Germanicus would seize power.[34] Backed by the military, Tiberius did not need honorific titles but retained proconsular *imperium* and his tribunician power, which he eventually accepted for life, without annual renewal, by now merely a legal device.

Dealing with the Senate, Tiberius presented proposals and encouraged debate. He took the momentous step of transferring election of the chief magistrates from the people to the Senate, recommending a few candidates.[35] The people still elected lesser magistrates. Trials for treason, *maiestas*, increased in number, informers multiplied, distrust and fear increased among the people. There was no clear definition of treason, and Tacitus says that in the old days only actions were punished, not words, but Augustus began to prosecute people for libel, as did Tiberius, supporting informers as guardians of the state.[36]

## Mutinies in Pannonia and Germany

Tiberius' familiarity with the troops may have led the soldiers to believe that he would be a soft touch for pay rises and privileges, and not long after his accession, some of the troops revolted. The Pannonian legions demanded the reduction of twenty years' service to the former sixteen years, and daily pay of one denarius (sixteen *asses*, six more than Caesar had paid them). Junius Blaesus, commanding three legions in one camp, managed to calm everything down and sent envoys to Tiberius, whose son Drusus was sent to deal with the mutiny, accompanied by some Praetorians, and the German bodyguard with their commander Aelius Sejanus. The soldiers were eventually pacified, and the ringleaders executed.[37]

The legions also rebelled in Germany. In Germania Inferior, commanded by Aulus Caecina, several centurions were killed, while Gaius Silius commanding in Germania Superior simply watched. Tiberius perceived a greater threat, from Germanicus, who was in Gallia Belgica, assessing payment of tribute when he heard of Augustus' death. With him were his wife Agrippina and their youngest son Gaius, called Caligula (Little Boots) by the soldiers, after the boots (*caligae*) specially made for him. When news arrived of the mutiny on the Rhine, Germanicus confronted the legions. The soldiers listed their grievances, one or more of them pulling his fingers into their mouths to prove that they had lost their teeth and grown old in army service. The soldiers were behind him if he wished to become emperor. Germanicus threatened to kill himself, and one of the soldiers offered his sword, saying that it was sharper. Germanicus escaped to his tent and wrote letters in Tiberius' name, promising to discharge men who had served for twenty years, and to excuse from fatigues all those with sixteen years' service. Augustus' bequest of 300 sesterces per legionary had not been paid, so double this sum was promised when the soldiers went into winter quarters. This was not good enough, so the discharges and payments were arranged immediately. Envoys arrived from Tiberius, and trouble broke out again. Germanicus was about to send away Agrippina and little Gaius, which shamed the soldiers and calmed them, except for two of Aulus Caecina's legions. Germanicus wrote to Caecina to say he was on his way to execute the ringleaders unless the soldiers did so themselves, which they did, bloodily, worse than any civil war.[38]

The best means of suppressing the mutiny was to mount a campaign against Arminius who had defeated Varus in AD 9. Germanicus built a bridge over the Rhine at Vetera (Xanten) and crossed into Free Germany, receiving the surrender of some of the tribesmen and the spoils from Varus' army. The site of Varus' disaster was discovered and the bones of the soldiers were buried. The war against Arminius continued, but a rumour spread that Germanicus had been defeated.

The Rhine bridge would have been destroyed, cutting off Germanicus' troops, if the indomitable Agrippina had not prevented it.[39]

In 16, Germanicus began to plan for another expedition into Germany, with a fleet to infiltrate from the rivers. Gaius Silius in Germania Superior was ordered to attack the Chatti, but the war soon involved other tribes, such as the Angrivarii who lived east of the river Weser. Germanicus crossed this river, winning a great victory, for which Tiberius was proclaimed Imperator. The next battle was also a victory, and most of the troops were sent by sea along the North Sea coast to winter quarters, but a storm wrecked some ships. The campaign resumed in the following spring, but Tiberius recalled Germanicus and put his son Drusus in command. Germanicus came home to a rapturous welcome and a triumph.[40] Tiberius gave 300 sesterces to the people in Germanicus' name, but he was probably also thinking of honourable ways to remove him from Rome.[41]

## Germanicus in the east

The ideal appointment for Germanicus arose when Parthian interest in Armenia intensified. The Senate voted Germanicus command over the provinces beyond the sea, with powers over provincial governors if necessary. At the same time Tiberius made his friend Gnaeus Calpurnius Piso governor of Syria in place of Creticus Silanus. Piso's real task was to suppress the ambitions of Germanicus, possibly on secret instructions from Tiberius and/or Livia.[42] This may have been invented retrospectively after the unfortunate outcome, but Tacitus says that his elders talked about Piso having a document containing Tiberius' instructions about Germanicus.[43]

Germanicus became consul for the second time in 18. He installed Artaxias as ruler of Armenia and received an embassy from King Artabanus of Parthia seeking renewed friendship with Rome.[44] After his successes, Germanicus visited Egypt in 19. He was Antony's grandson, and the Alexandrians loved him. Tiberius sent a letter admonishing Germanicus for disobeying Augustus' ban on senators entering Egypt.[45]

In Syria, having cancelled all Germanicus' orders, Piso left of his own accord, or was expelled by Germanicus, who was at Antioch, where he suddenly fell ill, accusing Piso of poisoning him. After Germanicus' death, all manner of spells and curses were found hidden in his house. Agrippina, widowed with several children, sailed to Rome bearing Germanicus' ashes. Tiberius could do nothing to help

Piso, who was acquitted on the charge of poisoning Germanicus, but then condemned for seeking to take power. He committed suicide.[46]

## The rise and fall of Sejanus

Lucius Aelius Sejanus had been made Praetorian Prefect in 14, as colleague of his father Lucius Seius Strabo, who became Prefect of Egypt in 17, leaving Sejanus as sole Praetorian Prefect. The Praetorians were distributed among cities in Italy, but Sejanus installed them all in a single camp on the north-eastern side of Rome, where he said that they would be better disciplined. Tiberius made him praetor, despite his equestrian rank.[47]

Velleius praises Sejanus' capacity for work, claiming no honours while assisting Tiberius in all the burdens of empire.[48] Tacitus, not mincing words, labels Tiberius a tyrant and the source of power for the tyrant Sejanus.[49] In the early days Velleius was probably correct, as Sejanus busily worked his way into Tiberius' favour, capable, efficient, trustworthy, indispensable, concentrating all business in his hands and filtering all approaches to Tiberius. Nothing was transacted that Sejanus did not know about, says Dio.[50]

Tiberius' own son Drusus died in 23, possibly poisoned by Sejanus, who was having an affair with Livilla, Drusus' wife.[51] After the death of Drusus, Tacitus detects the deterioration of Tiberius and his reign.[52] Sejanus presumed to marry Livilla, but Tiberius refused to connect him with the Imperial family.[53] Sejanus then began to remove potential opponents, often by persuading or coercing his clients to bring charges against his victims, men or women.[54] Dio provides a list, not complete, of people brought down by Sejanus.[55] Germanicus' widow Agrippina played into Sejanus' hands by persistently criticizing Tiberius. First, Sejanus prosecuted and removed Agrippina's friends, and then banished her in 29, with one of her sons. In 30 Sejanus imprisoned her other son, Drusus.[56] They all died, leaving Gaius Caligula as sole survivor.

In 26 Tiberius settled on the island of Capri, never returning to Rome.[57] His trust in Sejanus had been strengthened because in a cavern near modern Sperlonga, Sejanus had leaned over him to protect him from a rock fall.[58] On Capri, Tiberius perhaps dealt only with items that Sejanus allowed him to see.

For Sejanus the tide had turned by 31. He felt secure as consular colleague of Tiberius, with proconsular powers voted to him by the Senate.[59] Tiberius announced that he intended to bestow tribunician powers on Sejanus, but at the same time he appointed Naevius Sertorius Macro as Praetorian Prefect, giving him secret instructions. When the Senate convened in the temple of Apollo on the Palatine, Macro gave Sejanus a letter from the Emperor to be read out, then posted the *Vigiles* around the area and made rapidly for the Praetorian camp. Tiberius' letter very gradually conveyed that he was finished with Sejanus, who fell from power instantly. He was killed that day, as were his son and his young daughter, who was raped first, avoiding the charge of killing a virgin.[60] People searched for and killed Sejanus' adherents, and his remaining followers were picked off by legal means.[61] Later, Tiberius dispensed with courts and ordered the deaths of all Sejanus' associates already in prison.[62] After trusting Sejanus completely, when the scales fell from his eyes Tiberius began to be suspicious of everyone.

Two years before he died, Tiberius named his heirs, Tiberius Gemellus, his grandson, and Gaius Caligula, son of Germanicus. Gemellus was too young, and Caligula was not stable, hardly surprising after Sejanus, unchecked by Tiberius, killed his entire family. When he fell ill in 37, Tiberius decided to return to Rome, but died at Misenum. Legend has it that Caligula smothered him. Tiberius was not deified, and Caligula succeeded him.

## Provinces under Tiberius

The provinces receive little attention in the literary sources after 14, the emperors taking priority. As instructed by Augustus, Tiberius kept the Empire within the established limits, rarely interfering with provinces. Governors remained in post for long periods, the most extreme example being Poppaeus Sabinus, governing Macedonia and the two Moesias for twenty-two years.[63] Provided that governors were benign, continuity benefited the provincials, but Romans were denied experience of provincial administration.[64]

Tiberius helped provincials wherever possible, rebuking governors who were too eager to extract taxes. Dio and Suetonius tell different versions of how and when Tiberius said that a good shepherd sheared his sheep, but did not skin them.[65] In 17, earthquakes damaged several cities of Asia, and Tiberius remitted taxes for some years and sent large sums to help recovery. He took similar action in 23 when earthquakes struck Asia again, and Greece.[66]

There were two rebellions in the provinces, in Africa under Tacfarinas, and in Gaul under Florus and Sacrovir. Tacfarinas was a Numidian who had served in Roman auxiliary forces. In 17 he began to assemble natives, the Musulamii of the desert frontier and the Moors or Mauri of eastern Mauretania, under their leader Mazippa. Tacfarinas trained them to fight in Roman fashion and began raiding. The proconsul Furius Camillus was outnumbered with one legion, IX Hispana, and auxiliaries, but managed to rout the Africans. Tacfarinas escaped.[67] In 20 he resurfaced, raiding and rapidly withdrawing, and overwhelming a Roman unit. Lucius Apronius, taking over from Camillus, first decimated some of his troops to encourage them not to be overwhelmed, while Tacfarinas laid siege to Thala, a military post near Ammaedara, the future legionary base. Tacfarinas was driven off by 500 veterans and was defeated near the coast.[68] For some time he disappeared, then he sent an embassy to Tiberius, threatening war unless he received lands. Allegedly, Tiberius had an apoplectic fit. Junius Blaesus was appointed to deal with the rebels. He established strong points to deliver attacks on Tacfarinas all year round, achieving a stalemate which Tiberius interpreted as an end to the war, awarding triumphal insignia to Blaesus and sending IX Hispana back to Pannonia. This deprived the new proconsul Publius Cornelius Dolabella of troops, but nonetheless he managed to defeat Tacfarinas, who killed himself.[69]

The rebellion in Gaul was not so long-lived. In 21, Julius Florus of the Treveri and Julius Sacrovir of the Aedui, both Roman citizens, seized power among their own people. Their grievances probably concerned debts. The Gauls had probably borrowed from foreign moneylenders to pay taxes, or to recoup funds raised for Germanicus' campaigns.[70] Gaius Silius, commanding the legions of Germania Superior, defeated Florus, who killed himself.[71] Silius moved on to Augustodunum (Autun), defeating Sacrovir, who escaped but killed himself later.

On the Danube under Augustus, Macedonia and Achaia were senatorial provinces, but in 15 Tiberius amalgamated them with the two Moesias and made them Imperial provinces. Poppaeus Sabinus, already governing Moesia, remained as governor of this vast territory until 35. Beyond the Danube attempts had been made to keep the peace by allying with native chiefs, and Tiberius settled one expelled chief, Vannius, on the north bank of the Danube with some Suebi and Marcommani, to guard against attacks or attempts to cross into Roman territory.

Tiberius annexed Cappadocia in 17, and also Commagene, the latter for only a short time. Cappadocia had been ruled by Archelaus, confirmed by Mark Antony and retained by Octavian. In Archelaus' old age, Augustus sent a Roman equestrian procurator to govern on behalf of the King.[72] Cappadocia bordered on the Black Sea to the north, and the Euphrates in the east. Beyond Cappadocia was Armenia, sandwiched unhappily between Rome and Parthia. Cilicia, now amalgamated with Syria, formed Cappadocia's southern boundary and on the western side were Pontus and Galatia. In Roman hands Cappadocia protected provinces further west from Parthian attack, and it provided a base to gather intelligence about what was happening across the Euphrates. Archelaus had proved unaccommodating to Tiberius, and he was summoned to Rome, where he died.[73] Cappadocia was annexed and governed by an equestrian procurator until Vespasian enlarged its area and appointed a consular legate.[74]

## Gaius Caligula

After Tiberius' death Caligula adopted Gemellus as his heir, and bestowed the consulship on Claudius, his uncle, for July and August 37. Claudius had been kept out of public life because of his limping gait, his stammer, and a tendency to drool. He was far from unintelligent, however, and would reach greater heights.

Caligula had not held any magistracy except quaestor, but he was popular with the people because of the reputation of his father Germanicus. Suetonius says that Gaius Caligula fulfilled the highest hopes of the Roman people, foreign rulers were hopeful of him, and even Artabanus, King of Parthia, asked for his friendship. This was due to Lucius Vitellius, governor of Syria, who forestalled Artabanus' march on Armenia, and at a meeting with him near the Euphrates Vitellius arranged peace and friendship with Parthia.[75]

Dio produces a list of Caligula's good acts, and another, rather longer, of his not so good acts.[76] Caligula is said to have published accounts of public funds, and restored elections to the people, but the small turnout of voters indicated lack of interest, so elections were abolished again.[77] Among Caligula's bad acts, there were murders, executions and forced suicides, and copious sexual aberrations. He stole wives from their husbands, married them and cast them aside on a whim. In 39, he married Milonia Caesonia, who was already pregnant, so that he could be the father of a child within a month.[78]

Government of the Empire is obliterated among all the depravity, provincial governors being named only when Caligula killed them. Caligula restored to the Senate the capacity to make decisions and abolished the treason trials that had proliferated under Tiberius, but quite soon Caligula took total control of the government and restored the treason trials. The Praetorian Prefect Macro assisted him until Caligula compelled him and his wife to commit suicide.[79]

Not long after his accession, Caligula fell seriously ill. Romans spent the night around the palace, some offering their own lives if the new emperor were spared. They were punished if they were still alive after Caligula recovered.[80] Caligula exhausted the treasury and killed the client king Ptolemy of Mauretania for his money.[81] In 39 he went on an expedition to Gaul, allegedly interested only in appropriating wealth.[82] It was also said that Germans beyond the Rhine were hostile, and Suetonius says that Galba, briefly Emperor in 68, quickly put down an incursion of the barbarians into Gaul.[83] The alleged incursion may have been a cover for Galba's suppression of a plot hatched by Gnaeus Lentulus Gaetulicus, commanding in Germania Superior.[84] The plot involved Aemilius Lepidus, married to Caligula's sister Drusilla, who was made heir to Caligula's property in 37 when he was ill.[85] When Drusilla died, Lepidus began an affair with Caligula's other sister, the younger Agrippina, but he was soon executed.

Caligula planned an invasion of Britain in 40, reaching the coast of Gaul where he made his soldiers collect seashells, but the word for shells can mean siege engines, and Caligula lined up *ballistae* on the seashore.[86] The trip was not a complete waste of time, since Caligula ordered the building of a high tower from which lights were to shine at night to guide ships, the origin of a lighthouse at Boulogne.[87] Suetonius says that Caligula received the surrender of Adminius, the banished son of Cunobelinus, ruler of the Catuvellauni from his capital at Colchester. Caligula possibly intended to reinstate Adminius, but nothing happened. Possibly the soldiers refused to embark, which may be why Caligula butchered the legions, charging them with mutiny and causing trouble for his father Germanicus in AD 14.[88] Returning to Rome, Caligula acted as conqueror of Britain. He began to think himself a god on earth, and was angry that the Senate had not had the good sense to disobey his orders that he should be voted no honours.[89]

Not long afterwards Caligula was killed by two tribunes of the Praetorian Guard, Cassius Chaerea and Cornelius Sabinus. During a performance in the palace, Caligula went to meet boys from Greece who were to sing a hymn in his honour. In a narrow passageway, Chaerea and Sabinus stabbed him. Dio says that Caligula learned by experience that he was not a god.[90] Not surprisingly, Caligula was not deified.[91]

At this moment the government could have changed. The senators debated this, but being unable to agree they were not fast enough to resurrect the Republic.[92] When Caligula was killed, Claudius ran off to hide in fear for his life. A Praetorian found him and took him to the barracks, where Claudius was declared Emperor. He offered each Praetorian 15,000 sesterces.[93] As for the Praetorians, where would they be without an emperor to protect? Claudius belonged to the Imperial family, and it hardly mattered that he limped, stammered and drooled.

## Claudius

On his accession Claudius was fifty-one years old, the least likely candidate for Imperial rule. He had remained out of public view, studying history, languages and many other subjects. As Emperor, Claudius executed Chaerea and others, ensuring his own safety rather than avenging Caligula. He honoured all his family, including his grandfather Mark Antony.

Claudius held the consulship in 42 and 43, in 47 and 51, stepping down usually after two months to allow suffect consuls to take his place.[94] He provided entertainments for the people of Rome, and attended to the food supply, providing rewards for builders of merchant ships and improving the harbour at Ostia, also building a lighthouse there.[95] He built the Aqua Claudia which brought water from Subiaco, fifty miles east of Rome, built new roads to the coasts and to the Alps, repaired Pompey's theatre after a fire, and in the Circus Maximus he replaced the timber and tufa barriers with marble.[96] He put an end to the treason trials, and made courts permanent, abolishing summer and winter sessions. His judgements were based on circumstances, not the letter of the law, but he was inconsistent, and therefore unreliable.[97] Using censorial powers in 48, Claudius ejected some senators, without pursuing a vendetta against those who had reviled him during his earlier life, but if they were prosecuted by someone else he was vengeful. Senators were dismissed for non-attendance in the Senate, and those without the financial qualification were allowed to resign. He made a speech advocating full Roman citizenship for the Gauls, which would allow them to become magistrates at Rome. Most of the text survives on a bronze tablet found at Lugdunum (Lyon).[98] He reminded people that citizenship had been gradually extended through Italy and then to the Gauls north of the river Po. Men from Gallia Narbonensis were already senators, and thanks to Claudius, the loyal Aedui became the first senators from Gaul beyond Narbonensis.[99]

According to Suetonius, Claudius regularised equestrian careers.[100] Claudius is credited with centralizing and rationalising the administrative machinery in Rome, supported when Suetonius labels the two most influential freedmen, Narcissus and Pallas, respectively as secretary (*ab epistulis*) and treasurer (*a rationibus*). These titles may have originated in a later period, and separate administrative and financial departments were probably not fully evolved under Claudius.[101]

Claudius feared plots and rebellions, the unavoidable consequences of being an emperor. There was a failed rebellion in 42 when Annius Vinicianus contacted Furius Camillus Scribonianus, commanding the army in Dalmatia. They aimed to revive the Republic, but their soldiers had no grudges against Claudius. The two plotters and others in Rome committed suicide.[102] During his reign Claudius executed about thirty-five senators and 300 *equites*, some of whom were perhaps clients of senators.[103] Once convinced of danger, Claudius was as ruthless as his predecessors, and his associates played on these fears to achieve elimination of their rivals.

Claudius' marital history was not a success. He rejected his first betrothed, and his second betrothed died. He married and divorced Plautia Urgulanilla, and then Aelia Paetina. His next two wives were catastrophic. By Messalina he had a son later named Britannicus, and a daughter Octavia. Messalina's outrageous sexual behaviour was known to virtually everyone except Claudius, until Narcissus informed him. Messalina and several others were killed.[104] Claudius' niece Agrippina, daughter of his brother Germanicus, ensnared him. She had a son by her husband Gnaeus Domitius Ahenobarbus, and young Domitius was soon betrothed to Claudius' daughter Octavia.[105] Claudius adopted the boy in 50. Agrippina was not only determined that Domitius would be emperor, but also aimed at ruling through him. She began by removing

17. Ruins of the city of Carthage on the eastern side of Lake Tunis in modern Tunisia Originally founded as a colony of the Phoenicians, Carthage became a wealthy maritime trading city. Carthage and Rome made treaties in 509 and 348 BC to protect their mutual interests, but in the third century BC Rome and Carthage came into conflict in the first Punic War, which led to the creation of Rome's first provinces. Before the war the Carthaginians controlled most of Sicily, and after their defeat by Rome in 241, they created their first two provinces of Sicily, and Sardinia with Corsica. There will have been several motives for the take-over, but primarily Rome did not want Carthaginians in control of islands so close to Italy. More wars followed and in 146 BC the Romans obliterated Carthage. The tribune of the plebs Gaius Gracchus tried to revive the city in 123 BC as did Julius Caesar sometime later, but it was Augustus who succeeded in rebuilding the city, which became one of the prosperous cities of the Empire. The ruins shown here are those of this later city.

18. Modern reproduction of a statue of Augustus in Rome, placed in front of the ruins of his temple of Mars Ultor, vowed at the battle of Philippi against Brutus and Cassius in 42 BC. By Augustus' time Rome already controlled several provinces and had established a system of governing them, but after 27 BC when Octavian was renamed Augustus, he reorganised provincial government. The important provinces containing armies were governed by Augustus and then successive emperors via consular legates, each with the title *legatus Augusti pro praetore*; the other provinces were governed by senators with the title proconsul. The status of a province could change from senatorial to imperial and vice versa according to circumstances.

19. The inner panel of the Arch of Titus in the Forum Romanum in Rome. In the first century AD the Romans had long since begun to profit from governing the provinces, tipping over into exploitation. This photo shows the spoils of the Jewish war, in which Vespasian commanded on the orders of Nero. Titus finished off the war when Vespasian was declared Emperor in AD 69. The profits from this war financed the building of the Colosseum, and enslaved Jews provided labour.

20. The triumphal Arch of Septimius Severus, awarded to the Emperor by the Senate and erected next to the Senate House in the Forum Romanum in Rome. On both sides of the monument square panels above the two smaller arches depict scenes from Severus' Parthian war. On the top panel across the entire arch, the final word of the second line from the bottom on the centre panel is *propagatum*, the full phrase indicating that Severus had expanded the dominion of the Roman people, as expressed by his title *propagator imperii*. This Emperor also fought against the northern Britons, and extended Roman territory in Africa, pushing the frontiers further south.

21. Triumphal arches were not limited to Rome. The Porte de Mars at Rheims in France was built probably in the later second century at the peak of Empire-wide public building works, before the pressure on the Rhine, Danube, and eastern frontiers escalated. This is one of the largest triumphal arches but it was not known until the seventeenth century, because it had been buried five centuries earlier and used as the foundation for a castle. Its top storey is missing. The inner sides of the central arch depict monthly agricultural tasks, but only the panels representing June to December survive. Life in Roman Gaul was agriculturally prosperous and technologically advanced.

*Right:* 22. The Arch of Constantine viewed from the upper level of the Colosseum, now fenced off. It was voted by the Senate and People of Rome to celebrate the re-establishment of the state after civil wars, and dedicated in 315. The only decoration of Constantinian date is the narrow frieze depicting episodes in Constantine's struggle against Maxentius, running all the way round the four sides, just above the central arch. Most of the other decoration was looted from monuments of Trajan, Hadrian and Marcus Aurelius, but the heads of these Emperors were re-carved to represent Constantine.

23. Part of the Horrea Epagathiana, a range of large warehouses arranged round a square at the port at Ostia at the Tiber mouth. In the early Republic the Romans fought with the city of Veii for control of the salt pans of the Tiber, and the salt trade became important enough to Rome to warrant the building of a fort to protect it. Trade increased as Rome acquired provinces, providing a wide range of commodities from all over the Roman world and far beyond it. Ostia initially suffered from the lack of a good harbour, until the Emperor Claudius created a better harbour at Portus, two miles north of Ostia. A lighthouse was built and a canal constructed to join the Tiber in the fifth century.

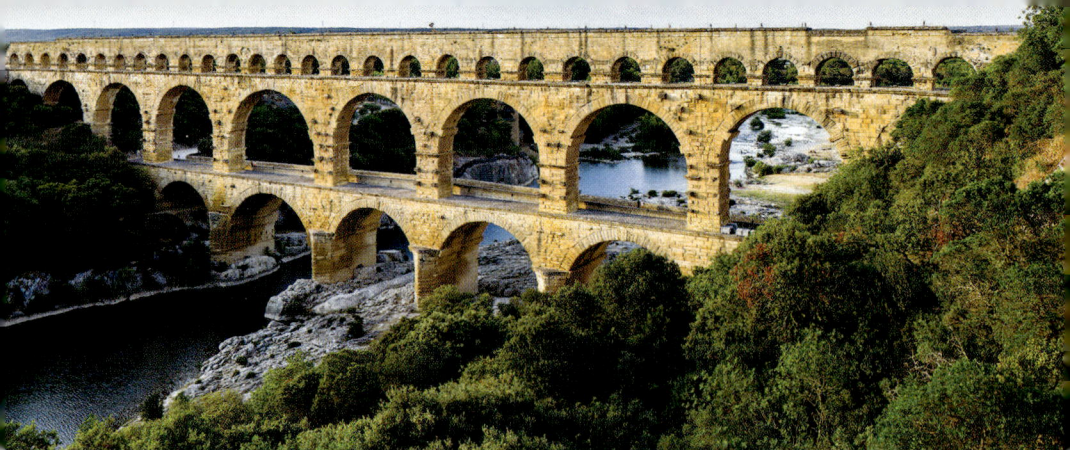

24. The Pont du Gard, France. Many of the provinces became Romanised, and benefitted from the excellent water engineering skills of the Romans, as shown by the Pont du Gard, an aqueduct built in the middle of the first century AD to carry water to Nemausus (modern Nimes). The rugged landscape precluded building the aqueduct in a straight line, so the necessary diversions ultimately increased the route to 35 miles, but the engineers managed to keep the flow of water steady over the various gradients. In this photo the aqueduct crosses the river Gardon, and three storeys were necessary to achieve sufficient elevation for the water to flow at the correct rate.

25. The Roman aqueduct at Segovia. Some provincial communities built their own amenities, sometimes successfully, and in other cases they required help from the Romans. Pliny's letters to Trajan reveal the difficulties which some communities got into. At Segovia the Spanish civic authorities had built an aqueduct prior to the reign of Trajan, but it was this Emperor who ordered its repair, and the local magistrates undertook the task, indicating that their town and they themselves were prosperous enough to do so.

26. The landscape of the gold mining area of Las Medunas of north-west Spain. During the Republic much of Rome's wealth came from the gold and silver mines in Spain, taken over after the defeat of Hannibal and Carthage in 201 BC. The mines were worked by slave labour, and in Spain were managed directly by the Roman state, but in other mines all over the Empire, management could be put out to contract.

27. An inscription from Leptis (or Lepcis) Magna near Tripoli in modern Libya. It was founded as a trading centre by the Phoenicians c.600 BC, and along with the cities of Oea and Sabratha, Leptis formed the area of Tripolitania in western Libya, Tripolis meaning three cities. It prospered under Augustus, its wealth derived from trade and agriculture. The Emperor Septimius Severus was born here, and he embellished the city. The inscription is a dedication to the Emperor Claudius by the consul Marcus Pompeius Silvanus. Note the local script under the Latin text.

*Above:* 28. Romanization began early in Spain through its long contact with Rome from the later third century BC. The hallmarks of Romanization are the building of a forum, a basilica, temples, and theatres. The theatre shown here is one of the earliest in Spain, donated by Marcus Vipsanius Agrippa to the *colonia* of Emerita Augusta (modern Merida) where Augustus settled many army veterans in 26 or 25 BC.

*Left:* 29. Bust of the Emperor Trajan, styled *Optimus Princeps*, the best ruler. Trajan inherited the Dacian war from Domitian, who was preparing for a campaign when he was assassinated. Trajan then campaigned in the east, but died at Selinus in modern Turkey. The Roman Empire reached its greatest extent under Trajan who annexed Dacia, Arabia, Armenia and Mesopotamia. From the Palazzo Bevilaqua, Verona.

30. Scene from Trajan's Column in Trajan's Forum in Rome. It was erected to celebrate Trajan's two Dacian wars in AD 101-102 and 105-106. The scenes spiral round the column from the bottom up, and while the depiction of soldiers, arms, armour and buildings are idealised, there is no better source for study of the Roman army. Depicted here are soldiers building a fort during the first war, with Trajan in the centre, gesturing to a legionary kneeling down.

31. The site of the Dacian capital of Sarmizegethusa in modern Romania, which Trajan captured in AD 106 at the end of the second Dacian war. He made Dacia a province north of the Danube, protecting the province of Moesia south of the Danube. Hadrian gave up territory to the east and west of Dacia, which was held until the Emperor Aurelian evacuated the inhabitants at the beginning of the AD 270s, settling them in parts of Moesia, and transferring the provincial name Dacia to the new areas.

*Above:* 32. Reproduction of an inscription attesting Brittones (second line from top) in the Roman army in Germany. It is known from inscriptions that the Britons were grouped into small units called *numeri*, which were formed from natives of several provinces to guard routes and patrol territory. The Brittones are well attested in Germany, housed in the fortlets on the Odenwald frontier running from the river Main to the river Neckar, where they guarded and patrolled the broken hilly country to the east of the line. It is not certain who first recruited them, possibly Trajan, after he abandoned Scotland and brought the troops in Britain to the line between the rivers Tyne and Solway. It is also possible that Hadrian brought them to Germany but this has not been conclusively proven. Under Antoninus Pius the Odenwald frontier was abandoned and the line was moved further east, occupied by the same *numeri* of Brittones.

*Left:* 33. Modern copy of a statue of Hadrian near Castell Sant'Angelo. Whereas Trajan enlarged the Empire and created new provinces, his successor Hadrian gave up territory, and enclosed much of the Empire within running barriers, especially on the northern frontiers and in Britain and Africa. Other frontiers lacked solid barriers but were protected by lines of forts and watchtowers accompanied by an outer ditch. The frontiers differed in design, probably according to perceived threat, and the purpose of all types of barrier was to protect the provinces behind the frontiers.

34. Hadrian's frontier in Germany consisted of a ditch fronting a timber palisade, as reconstructed in this photo. Much of the line followed the frontier area set out by Vespasian and Domitian, running from the Rhine to skirt the northern edge of the northwards projecting Taunus-Wetterau, then running south towards the Upper Danube, but for some time the frontier did not meet that of neighbouring Raetia. Hadrian fortified this new frontier by means of a palisade, with timber watchtowers and small forts close to the line, backed up by auxiliary forts and legionary fortresses some distance behind it. Without a convenient tourist to add scale, it looks smaller and flimsier than it is, but Roman frontiers were not intended to be impermeable.

35. This scene on Trajan's column depicts a timber watchtower used during the Dacian campaigns, not on a frontier but to guard the territory where the army operated. The torch protruding from the top level may have been used for signalling, or for illuminating what was happening in the dark, or both purposes. This tower is protected by a fence and has an upper gallery for better surveillance.

36. Modern reconstruction of a timber tower on the German frontier, based on archaeological remains and the depiction of the tower on Trajan's column. Sometimes evidence for wide gaps has been found in the palisade on the German frontier, with a timber tower set back from the line, facing the gap for surveillance of movement across the frontier. It is likely that soldiers used the gaps to go beyond the line on patrol.

37. Hadrian's Wall in Northumberland at Walltown Crags. The Wall was built on Hadrian's orders from 122 onwards, running from the Tyne to the Solway. It would be much higher than this remnant, and every Roman mile there were small forts, called milecastles in modern Hadrian's Wall parlance, and between each milecastle there were two towers, called turrets. In the central sector the Wall followed the heights of the Whin Sill, a northward facing cliff providing good views to the north, which runs west to east and then turns northwards to provide foundations for Bamburgh Castle on the east coast. This photo shows clear views to the north at Walltown Crags, east of Brampton. Despite good views northwards, a deep wide ditch, now called the Vallum, was dug all along the south side of Hadrian's Wall, indicating a need for defence of the hinterland, or at least a need to control movement from north or south.

38. Hadrian's Wall and milecastle at Cawfields, Northumberland, with clear views to the north and south. The milecastles had two gates, one on the north and one on the south, providing crossing points, but it is debatable whether civilians were allowed access through all of them. East of Housesteads fort there is a gap in the wall at Knag Burn guarded by a tower, probably an official crossing point. There were two gates here on the north and south sides, possibly to allow people and goods in, then with both gates closed their baggage could be checked and probably taxed, as they travelled across the frontier line. When Antoninus built a new frontier in Scotland the system would be redundant, but after the withdrawal of troops from Scotland *c*.158, Hadrian's Wall was recommissioned.

39. Hadrian was a great traveller, visiting most of the provinces of the Empire, and he showed an interested in virtually everything, reorganising things, putting right certain problems. This arch was erected in his honour in Gerasa (modern Jerash) in Jordan when he visited in 129.

*Above left:* 40a. A bust of Marcus Aurelius, Emperor 161 to 180. It was in Marcus' reign that the pressure of the northern tribes on the frontiers escalated, and some tribesmen reached Italy, unheard of since the Gauls took Rome in 390 BC. More inclined to philosophy than fighting, Marcus spent much of his life with the armies, though he did not neglect the provinces and their administration. He died in 180 on the northern frontier.

*Above right:* 40b. Marcus' son Commodus, who was made co-emperor with Marcus in 177. After his father's death Commodus made a lasting peace with the tribesmen threatening the northern frontiers, building watchtowers called *burgi* along the Danube frontier, intended to increase surveillance of raiding parties coming into the provinces. For the rest of his reign he was more interested in being a gladiator, but was killed on 31 December 192 by members of his household. Then a scramble for the Empire began, the winner being Septimius Severus.

41. A portrait of the Emperor Philip the Arab, born in Syria and reigning from 244 to 249. As Praetorian Prefect he accompanied the Emperor Gordian III on campaign against the Persian king Ardashir and his son Shapur, and after Gordian was killed he continued the campaign, and then he made a negotiated peace and successfully brought the Roman army out of the east.

*Above right*: 42. The year 260 was disastrous for the Romans. Every frontier was overrun, the Emperor Gallienus was struggling to regain control of the provinces of the breakaway Gallic Empire, and the Emperor Valerian was captured on campaign against the Persians. The Persian king Shapur ordered bas reliefs to be carved into rock faces at Naqs-i Rustam to celebrate his victories. This is one of the scenes, showing Valerian standing, his wrist and hand held firmly by Shapur, which to the Persians indicated that the enemy had submitted. The kneeling figure may be Philip the Arab who negotiated peace without having decisively won the war.

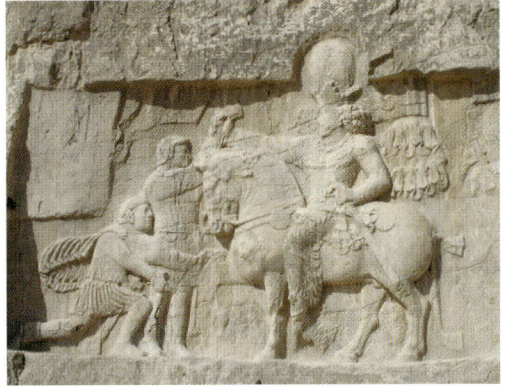

*Right*: 43. The Porta Nigra at Trier. The city defences of Trier were among the earliest in the western provinces, built in the mid-second century, before the pressure on the frontiers in the third century reached the point where the inhabitants of many cities began to think about building protective walls. Built before the so-called third century crisis, the Porta Nigra is more elaborate than defensive and was probably built to impress.

44. Remains of the amphitheatre at Trier. As well as possession of a forum and baths, a sign of Romanization was the building of an amphitheatre. This one was improved in the later 290s when Trier benefited from the presence of the Imperial court under the Tetrarchy founded by Diocletian, when each Tetrarch chose a headquarters in one of the provinces. Trier was chosen by Constantius, father of Constantine. When defensive walls were built the amphitheatre was incorporated into them, and it was probably due to the Imperial use of the city that the 6-km circuit remained intact, at a time when other cities were shrinking. When the court left for Amiens, Trier was attacked several times by the Franks.

45. The Kaiserthermen or Imperial baths at Trier, one of the two large bath complexes in the city, the largest in the Empire save for Rome. The Barbarathermen was the older, while the Kaiserthermen belonged to the Imperial palace complex, begun probably in 293, the year when Constantius became Caesar to Maximian Augustus and used Trier as one of his bases. What remains of these Imperial baths survived because the building was adapted to new uses.

46. The grand colonnade flanking the main street at Apamea, on the river Orontes in Syria. The city was originally established by King Seleucus of Syria as a stud farm for breeding war elephants, and then afterwards became a predominantly Greek city. From the Severan dynasty onwards Roman troops were stationed here when campaigns were being mounted into Persia. Inscriptions attest the presence of *Legio* II Parthica, or detachments of it, in the mid-third century, but Apamea was not a permanent legionary base.

47. The town walls and a polygonal tower at Caerwent, the capital of the Silures, in Wales. Romano-British cities and towns began to erect defences earlier than those of other provinces, even though there was not such an urgent need for them in Britain until later. Usually there was a rampart of earth with an external ditch, but during the later third century civic authorities began to replace the earth defences with stone, and in towns without defences they built new stone walls. At Caerwent the walls are not precisely dated, but they were probably built well before the fourth century, when the projecting polygonal towers were added, except on the west and east sides.

48. Coin portrait of the Emperor Aurelian wearing the radiate crown and cuirass. During his reign the northern tribes crossed the frontiers and entered Italy, in one instance penetrating as far as Milan. They moved fast, and though they were defeated in more than one battle they kept regrouping, and Aurelian learned two things: he needed mobile troops which could keep up with the tribes, and Rome would have to be walled. Drawn by Trish Boyle.

49. In 274 Aurelian discussed with the Senate the project of building new walls to defend Rome, which had not been walled since the fourth century BC. The walls were built fairly rapidly, mostly of brick, but the builders utilised whatever was to hand, including existing buildings, such as the aqueduct carried by what is now the Porta Maggiore, and the small Amphitheatrum Castrense on the south-west of the city. The circuit was over 18 kilometres, with eighteen gates of different designs, and closely spaced projecting square towers along the walls. The original walls were not so tall, but were increased in height in the early fifth century by the Emperor Honorius. The section of the walls shown here is on the south side of Rome, from the Porta Ardeatina looking towards the Porta Appia, also named the Porta San Sebastiano.

50. The Porta Appia, or Porta San Sebastiano, in the Aurelian Walls of Rome. The Via Appia, the first properly constructed road built in the fourth century BC, still runs out of Rome through this gate. The Porta Appia originally had two arches, reduced to one in later times, flanked by two projecting round towers, 28 metres high. The lower sections of these towers were eventually encased in square structures, the bottom halves faced with marble, not quarried, but hastily obtained from tombs and monuments. Alterations were made to the walls by the short-lived Emperor Maxentius (AD 306-312) and they were heightened by the Emperor Honorius (AD 393-423).

51. Many city councils all over the Empire began to think of erecting defences in the later third century. The photo shows part of the Roman walls of Senlis, France, with two of its projecting u-shaped towers, which display bands of tiles between the layers of stone work. There are similar towers with tile courses in the walls at Amiens, Soissons and Beauvais, which may indicate a corporate defensive programme to guard against tribes attacking the Gallic provinces from the north. Such a scheme may have been introduced by Aurelian's successor, the Emperor Probus (AD 276-282), who was said to have restored sixty Gallic cities.

52. Coin portrait of the Emperor Diocletian, with the fierce frown which characterised all artistic portraits of emperors in the troubled later third century. Diocletian undertook a major reorganisation of the Empire, its army and its provinces. He tried to reform the taxation system, to regulate the currency and the prices of commodities all over the Empire, and he introduced an extra layer into the hierarchy of provincial government, grouping the provinces into a number of larger units called dioceses, while at the same time splitting individual provinces into smaller provinces with new names. These changes required a vast number of administrative staff. Drawn by Trish Boyle.

53. Diocletian's palace at Salona (modern Split). This is the peristyle inside the vast complex, which was built like a square fortress, with one side facing the sea, towers at the corners and three gates with flanking towers, but though it looked like a fort it was not intended to be a military base. Diocletian was born in Dalmatia, which was once part of Illyria, and during his reign his focus was mainly on the eastern Empire. The architecture of the palace displays eastern influence. Court rituals became more rigid and emperors relied on magnificent display from Aurelian onwards, so Diocletian's peristyle was designed to allow him to proceed in grand style from his private areas into the public arcaded court.

her real or potential opponents, allegedly assisted by Pallas, with whom she was having an affair.[106] Claudius began to favour his son Britannicus, so Agrippina decided to act quickly, serving up Claudius' favourite dish of mushrooms, with deadly additives. Suetonius admits that it is not known precisely who poisoned Claudius.[107] Remaining undiscovered is the sign of an efficient poisoner. Claudius died on 13 October 54, aged sixty-four, bequeathing to the world his adopted son Domitius, better known as Nero.

## The provinces under Claudius

Provincial governors could still be prosecuted for extortion during the Empire, but Claudius attempted to control governors by refusing to give anyone a new appointment until some time had passed after holding a previous post. He appointed some governors himself, usually for two years in one province.[108] He also passed a law that all governors must leave Rome to take up their posts by 1 April, indicating that some of them had been dilatory.[109]

Caligula had summoned Ptolemy of Mauretania to Rome and killed him, and there was a rising of Ptolemy's people in 40-41, put down by Marcus Crassus Frugi. Claudius claimed the victory, while Frugi was awarded *ornamenta triumphalia*. The Mauri, or Moors, rebelled in 42, and Gaius Suetonius Paullinus campaigned as far as Mount Atlas. He was succeeded in 44 by Gnaeus Hosidius Geta, though Dio groups all their activities in 42. Probably when the rebellion was crushed, Claudius created two provinces, Mauretania Tingitana, with its capital at Tingi or Tingis (Tangiers), and Mauretania Caesariensis with the capital at Caesarea (Cherchel), both governed by equestrians.[110] The Mauri, not wholly pacified, began to raid Africa Proconsularis, where the governor Sulpicius Galba earned triumphal decorations for defeating them and restoring order in his province.[111] The Mauri were excellent horsemen, like the Numidians, and provided cavalry for the Roman army.

Lycia in south-west Asia was a self-governing area, occupying the coastal zone of south-west Turkey, between Caria to the west and north-west, and Pamphylia to the east stretching along the coast to the border with Cilicia. The Lycians were the only ancient people who were able to retain national unity while at the same time their cities were autonomous, a position which they had reached by the second century BC.[112] The Lycians came under the control of other states, one of them being Ptolemaic Egypt, and they were conquered by Antiochus the Great. After the Romans defeated Antiochus in 189, Lycia was given to the Rhodians, but they complained to Rome and were freed in 169. Mark Antony freed them all over again after they had suffered for not joining Brutus in the civil war. The federal assembly of the Lycian League continued in operation, but the autonomous cities began to quarrel with each other, continually appealing to Rome for assistance, so to put an end to this nuisance Claudius joined Lycia to Pamphylia in 43, forming a single province under a *legatus pro praetore*.[113] The freedom of the Lycians may have been restored by Nero, or possibly Galba, and then revoked once more by Vespasian.[114]

Two years after his accession Claudius authorized the invasion of Britain, the best way of earning a triumph, says Suetonius.[115] Augustus had contemplated the conquest of Britain, recording that he had received British rulers fleeing to him for refuge.[116] In Strabo's opinion, Britain was not worth the expense of conquest because soldiers would need their wages, and to impose tribute would reduce the revenues from import and export duties, which the Britons readily paid.[117] Archaeological evidence shows that the Catuvellauni in particular imported quantities of wine from the Roman world.

When Claudius received Verica or Berica, King of the Atrebates, expelled from his kingdom, it was decided to reinstall him. The aggressors were the Catuvellauni, who had been expanding their territory for some time. Their leaders were Caratacus and Togodumnus. Claudius' commander for the expedition, Aulus Plautius Silvanus, commanded four legions. Only II Augusta is definitely attested as part of the invasion force, while the other legions normally associated with Claudius' invasion, IX Hispana from Pannonia, XIV Gemina and XX Valeria from the upper and lower Rhine, are not firmly attested until the rebellion of Boudicca in 60/61. There were also auxiliary troops, probably detachments of other legions, and possibly some or all the men of VIII Augusta. The story goes that the troops were reluctant to embark at Gesoriacum (Boulogne) until Narcissus chivvied them along, but it is not known what he said.[118] When the foothold was secure enough, Plautius, as instructed, summoned Claudius, who brought elephants with him. Several tribes submitted to him, and the troops hailed him Imperator more than once. He left after about sixteen days, telling Plautius to subdue the rest.[119] Easier said than done, and the Romans never subdued all of Britain.

In Free Germany, Claudius aimed for the maintenance of good order and friendly relations with the tribes, which would help to protect the two Germanies and Gallia Belgica. Friendly relations could be upset by the Romans themselves. In 12 BC, Tiberius' brother Drusus arranged with the Frisii of modern Friesland that they could pay their taxes in ox-hides. This became problematical when the legionary *primus pilus* Olennius, commanding the area, demanded hides of the same dimensions as the aurochs, a massive undomesticated beast, now extinct. Catching one would be lethal, so several ox-hides would be required to approximate to one aurochs hide. The Frisii rebelled in 28 and killed 900 Romans. Lucius Apronius commanding in Germania Inferior gathered his troops plus some from Germania Superior and squashed the rebellion, without pacifying the Frisii.[120] Sanquinius Maximus, commanding Germania Inferior, was killed. Gnaeus Domitius Corbulo was appointed to succeed him in 47. He dealt first with seaborne raids on the coasts of Gaul by the Chauci. While doing so, he marked out an area for the Frisii, who were to be self-governing according to their own laws, with their own magistrates and a senate, confirmed by Claudius.[121] It was probably wise to pacify them and continue to collect the hides for the armies. Just as Corbulo had begun a new campaign against the Chauci in Germany, Claudius recalled him, bringing garrisons back to the left bank of the Rhine. Corbulo complained that Republican commanders had not been so restricted. Dio hints that Corbulo was becoming too powerful for Claudius' comfort.[122]

Late in Claudius' reign in 50, Agrippina persuaded her husband to create a colony for army veterans at her birthplace on the left bank of the Rhine at Ara Ubiorum, the settlement of the Ubii who had been brought across the river *c*.38 BC. Ara Ubiorum became Colonia Claudia Ara Agrippinensium (Cologne). The inhabitants possessed the rights of Roman colonists.[123]

The Danube provinces were protected without campaigning in the lands beyond the river. Probably in 46, Claudius annexed Noricum, converting it into a province as opposed to an occupied zone, enhancing control and protection of the Danube frontier.[124] The trading centre of Magdalensberg was not suitable as an administrative headquarters, and fell into disuse when the new headquarters was established at Virunum to the south-west. Further east, the Danube was potentially threatened when Vannius, ruler of the Suebi, was expelled. Claudius ordered Palpellius Hister, governor of Pannonia, to station one legion and auxiliary troops on the bank of the Danube as a deterrent to prospective invaders, obviating the need for a military expedition. Claudius offered refuge to Vannius and his followers, who were picked up by the Danube fleet and settled on lands in Pannonia, while his nephews Sido and Italicus succeeded to his kingdom.[125]

Tiberius had combined Achaia and Macedonia with Moesia, but Claudius split up this vast territory, probably in 44, when Aulus Didius Gallus became governor of Moesia alone, still very large. Achaia and Macedonia were assigned to two proconsular governors, both ex-praetors chosen by lot. In 46 Claudius annexed Thrace, where the in-fighting between members of the Royal House had been perpetually troublesome, requiring Roman intervention.[126] Control of Thrace protected Macedonia. Under the kings, Thrace had been divided into *strategiae*, roughly based on the tribal areas, much like the Roman *civitates* of the western provinces, but there the similarity ends because the Roman preferred to rely upon self-government of the *civitates* by their most prominent men, whereas the *strategiae* were governed by *strategoi* appointed by the central government, who had no connection with the tribal groupings. Claudius took over the Thracian arrangements more or less intact, except that the local community provided the *strategoi* so that the system of government approached that of the Roman western provinces. The governors of Thrace were equestrian procurators, commanding auxiliary troops. The *strategoi* were responsible to the procurator, creating a hierarchy of local government like that of Egypt.[127] Overall defence was the responsibility of the governor of Moesia.[128]

Claudius annexed Judaea probably in 44 after the death of Herod Agrippa I, who had grown up with Claudius in his mother Antonia's house. He had encouraged Claudius to become Emperor.[129] Agrippa had been rewarded with control of Judaea and Samaria, answerable to no Roman governor. All was well until he began to fortify Jerusalem.[130] Just before his death Agrippa arranged a conference of the kings of Lesser Armenia, Pontus, Chalcis, Emesa and Commagene.[131] It was not a secret conclave, but the governor of Syria, Vibius Marsus, broke up the meeting, and since Vibius made a meal of it all, Claudius suspected that Agrippa was relying on their long-standing friendship to gain more power. Soon afterwards, Agrippa died. Claudius sent Antonius Felix as procurator to Judaea, subordinate to the governor of Syria.[132] Felix was a freedman, brother of Pallas, Claudius' treasurer, both of them once slaves of Antonia, hence his name Antonius. Tacitus implies that Felix governed Samaria before Caligula was murdered, while Ventidius Cumanus governed Galilee.[133] Felix was still in office under Nero, when he continued to put down brigands, but he also had the High Priest Jonathan murdered.[134]

An extensive programme of establishing colonies was undertaken in Claudius' reign in many of the provinces. In Britain a colony was founded at Camulodunum (Colchester) for veterans of XX Valeria legion. Besides the colony already mentioned at Cologne, there were others in Mauretania, the Gauls, the two Germanies, the two Spains, Syria, Thrace and Cappadocia.

As an alternative to annexation and direct government, the Romans preferred control by influence, making rulers their friends and allies and supporting them if necessary, sometimes by armed intervention, or by subsidizing them with money and food. In return, the rulers usually kept order among their own dependents. The Bosporan kingdom on the northern shores of the Black Sea was important for the supplies of grain from what is now Russia, and therefore had to be kept friendly.[135] Mithradates was installed as king of the area in 41, and was at first compliant, but around 46 he turned against Rome. He sent his brother Cotys to Rome, but Cotys immediately spilled the beans and was made king in place of Mithradates.[136] Cotys was assisted by Didius Gallus, governor of Moesia, and then by soldiers under Julius Aquila when Mithradates, trying to reclaim his kingdom, was captured and brought to Rome.

In Parthia, a struggle began between two contestants for the throne, Vardanes and Gotarzes, and when Vardanes was murdered the Parthians split into two factions, one for Gotarzes and the other for Meherdates, descended from Phraates, and currently a hostage in Rome. Gotarzes proved to be excessively cruel, so Parthian envoys arrived at Rome in 47 to ask for the release of Meherdates. Gaius Cassius Longinus, *legatus Augusti pro praetore* of Syria, was ordered to escort Meherdates to the Euphrates. Gotarzes defeated Meherdates but died of disease, succeeded by Vonones for a short time, then Vonones' son Vologaeses took over, much more troublesome to Rome.[137]

Armenia was always a bone of contention between Parthia and Rome, ruled by kings favoured by one side or the other. Claudius installed yet another Mithradates as king in 41. The arrangement lasted for ten years, until Radamistus, nephew of Mithradates, killed his uncle. Ineffective moves on the part of the Romans allowed the Parthians under Vologaeses to install his own king of Armenia. Nero inherited the problem.[138]

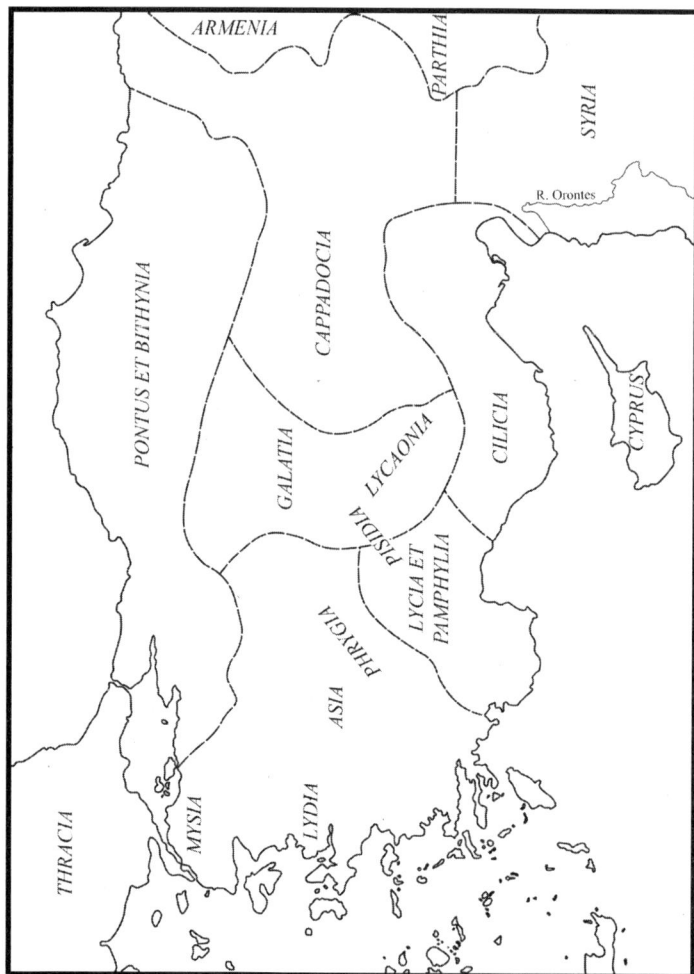

7. The provinces between the Mediterranean and the Black Sea. Asia, bequeathed to Rome in 133 BC and a province since 129, contained several regions including Mysia, Lydia and Phrygia. Pamphylia also belonged to Asia, but it was subject to several changes, first being attached to Cilicia, then to Asia, and then joined with Galatia. It was probably Claudius who put it with Lycia to make a separate province. Pisidia was made part of the province of Galatia, which was created in 25 BC, also containing Lycaonia, but changes continued. Under Vespasian, Galatia and Cappadocia were combined to form a massive province bordering Armenia and Parthia to its east, until in AD 112 Trajan split them into single provinces again. The province of Pontus and Bithynia south of the Black Sea was created by Pompey the Great after the defeat of Mithradates VI of Pontus in 63 BC, and he annexed Syria in 66. Redrawn by Isla Jones after Goodman 1997.

## Nero

After the death of Claudius was announced, the Praetorian cohort guarding the Imperial residence hailed Nero as emperor on the Palace steps. Nero did not bring Britannicus with him. He entered the Praetorian camp, where he promised the same amount of cash that Claudius had given the Praetorians, 15,000 sesterces per man, and was hailed as Imperator. Lastly, he appeared before the Senate, and the senators confirmed him as Emperor.[139] Aged seventeen, with the essential goodwill of the Praetorian Guard and the agreement of the Senate, Nero became ruler of the Roman world.

Claudius was deified after his funeral, modelled on that of Augustus.[140] Nero's reign began well and remained stable for about five years. He promised to rule according to the principles of Augustus. He held the consulship only four times, and never for the full year, in 55, 57, 58, and 60. It was not so much restraint as lack of interest in government. Tacitus says that the Senate was able to frame regulations freely, so some shadow of the Republic remained.[141] Under Claudius, quaestors administered the treasury, but Nero appointed praetors. The people of Rome were given 400 sesterces apiece, senators whose wealth had declined were assisted financially, the four per cent tax on sales of slaves, imposed by Augustus to fund the *Vigiles*, was amended so that the foreign vendors paid it, but as Tacitus says, the vendors simply added it to their prices and the purchaser still paid it in a different way.[142] Suetonius says that in judging court cases, Nero asked jurors to write down their opinions. He read these and delivered judgements in written form next day. Some abuses were suppressed, freedmen were barred from becoming senators, and those who had reached this status were ejected. Pantomime actors were banished, forgeries of wills were punished, and anyone writing a will on behalf of another person was forbidden to inherit. These early measures probably owed much to Nero's advisers, his tutor Lucius Annaeus Seneca, and the Praetorian Prefect Sextus Afranius Burrus.

Then there was Nero's mother, Agrippina, the greatest influence of all, who came as close as she dared to being emperor herself. She was quite content to take over all state business, and at first Nero was content to let her.[143] She dealt with all correspondence, and her head appeared on coinage, not unusual except that she was depicted on the obverse instead of the more usual reverse. Meetings of the Senate were held in the Palace where she could attend.[144] She overstepped the mark when an ambassador from Armenia came to Rome. Nero,

Seneca and Burrus received him on a tribunal, but Agrippina marched towards it to join them. She was forestalled when Seneca urged Nero to step down to meet her and introduce her to the Armenian. No-one remounted the tribunal, and everything passed off as normal. Dio says that after this episode, Seneca and Burrus took rule of the Empire into their own hands, and Nero was happy to oblige.[145]

Agrippina had removed her rivals under Claudius, and under Nero she continued as she had begun. Tacitus opens his thirteenth book with the first death of the new regime in 54, the proconsul of Asia, Marcus Junius Silanus, poisoned by Imperial agents in Asia. Agrippina had already killed Silanus' brother to prevent him from marrying Claudius' daughter Octavia.[146] Nero supposedly knew nothing of this, but he knew that Narcissus was forced to commit suicide. Sometime later, Pallas was deprived of his post and exiled.[147] The fate of Britannicus was never in doubt. Agrippina seemed to favour him, probably to make Nero jealous and do as he was told. [148] Britannicus was poisoned in 55, probably Nero's second attempt to kill him. Agrippina was taken by surprise. After a hasty funeral, Britannicus' ashes were placed in the Mausoleum of Augustus.[149]

Agrippina and Nero supposedly had an incestuous relationship, which may have been one of her methods of controlling him. She also threatened and criticized him, until Nero asserted his independence in 56, removing her from his residence.[150] Three years later Nero resolved to rid himself of her permanently, because while Agrippina was alive he would never be able to divorce Octavia and marry his new passion, Poppaea, who was already married to Nero's friend Marcus Salvius Otho. He first asked Burrus for advice about how to eliminate Agrippina, and Burrus promised to help if it could be proved that she was guilty of something.[151] She was difficult to kill. Poison was tried, but she habitually took antidotes, so nothing worked. Nero arranged for a ceiling to fall on her. She survived. Finally, he had a collapsible ship constructed, and at the festival of Minerva in late March 59 he invited her to Baiae for dinner and sent her home in the beautiful new ship. The collapse of the ship was too slow, and she swam ashore. Panicking, Nero had to order her death, unable to claim that it was an accident.[152]

Nero first rid himself of Octavia by divorcing and banishing her, and then he removed Poppaea's husband Otho by sending him to govern Lusitania in 58, where he remained for ten years. With all obstacles out of the way, Nero married Poppaea in 62. A daughter was born to them, Antonia, who lived only three months, and when Poppaea was pregnant again in 65, Nero kicked her to death.[153] Octavia was accused of adultery and executed. Nero married Statilia Messalina after killing her husband.[154]

Dio says after Britannicus was killed, Seneca and the Praetorian Prefect Burrus were content if they could manage affairs with moderate success and stay alive.[155] Burrus died in 62, replaced as Praetorian Prefect by Ofonius Tigellinus, of ill repute. Some remnant of good influence on Nero might have lingered if Seneca had not retired into private life. Nero had probably gone off the rails already, and was now free of all control. He leaned more and more towards acting, singing, dancing and poetry, which would have been acceptable within the walls of his residences, but he insisted on performing in public. He developed a passion for chariot racing, and did not keep that as a private hobby, either.[156] He established a five-yearly arts festival or *quinquennium*, called the Neronia to celebrate music and gymnastics, with ex-consuls presiding, which would have been an uplifting and entertaining competition if Nero had not somehow managed to win all the prizes.[157]

The ancient sources dwell on the scandals and sexual intrigues of Nero's court, incest with Agrippina, his passion for deflowering girls and boys, his so-called marriage to a boy called Sporus, whom he had castrated to convert him into a woman. Sporus was one of the few who remained with Nero to the bitter end.[158] Nero was given to roaming the streets at night with his gangs, looting shops and beating up and even killing anyone they encountered.[159] In one instance the gang met up with a senator, Julius Montanus, who defended his wife vigorously, and Nero was so badly bruised that he could not venture out for some days. The senator apologised, which was a mistake, because he had obviously known that he was beating up Nero, and worse still, Nero now knew who he was.[160] Silence would have been prudent as well as golden, and Montanus' only option was suicide. There were many other murders, and some people were killed or persuaded to commit suicide because they were seen as rivals for power, or because Nero wanted their wealth and property.[161]

Little is known of the plot attributed to Gaius Piso in 65. Tacitus names people but admits difficulty in identifying the instigator.[162] It was planned to murder Nero at his villa at Baiae, and then the location changed to the games celebrating the goddess Ceres in the Circus in Rome. A freedman betrayed the conspirators, and then all manner of people were hunted down. The Praetorians were involved, and Nero had to buy their loyalty afterwards.[163] Seneca was not linked to Piso but was forced to commit suicide. He cut his own veins and those of his wife Paulina, but she was rescued.[164] According to Suetonius, another conspiracy was unearthed later, organised by Vinicius, about whom even less is known. Punishments, perhaps for both sets of conspirators, extended to the children of the convicted men. These were banished, poisoned or starved, and after these conspiracies were crushed, Nero began to put to death anyone he pleased.[165]

## Rome burns

Nero was at Antium (Anzio) in 64 when the fire began in Rome. There are different versions of where and how it began, either accidentally, or purposely set at different locations on Nero's orders. 'Each version had its own sponsors,' says Tacitus, less sensationally than other authors. Nero hastened to the city. He allowed homeless people into his own gardens and opened up the Campus Martius and the buildings that Vipsanius Agrippa had erected there. He had temporary shelters constructed and arranged for supplies of food and other necessities to be brought from Ostia and the surrounding countryside.[166] His sensible measures did not prove sufficient to restore his damaged reputation. Rumours circulated that he had intended to destroy Rome, and that he sang of the sack of Ilium while watching the conflagration from the tower of Maecenas' house on the Esquiline.[167] The suspicion that he had wanted to clear away most of Rome was fuelled largely because of what he did next, building his *Domus Aurea*, or Golden House, occupying a huge area of the city, saying that he could at last be housed like a human being.

The fire burned for six days, and of Augustus' fourteen regions, three were levelled, remnants of buildings were left in seven of them, and four survived.[168] The cumulative archaeological evidence shows that destruction was not quite total. One of the results of the fire was the formulation of building regulations. Tacitus says that broad streets were laid out with open spaces, and water supplies were to be laid on for the public at more points than ever before. Fire-fighting equipment was to be kept on view outside houses. Nero offered rewards if new tenements and houses were completed within a certain time. A height restriction for buildings was imposed, and fireproof stone was to be used for building, each house was to be surrounded by its own stone walls, and timberwork was forbidden, especially in flimsy partitions between houses. Before building commenced the sites had to be cleared, and Nero ordered that the grain ships coming into port should carry the debris and ash back to Ostia to be dumped in the marshes there.[169] Suetonius notes, not connected to his description of the fire, that Nero ordered porticoes to be erected at his own expense on the fronts of houses and apartments blocks, and arranged for fire-fighting from the flat roofs.[170] These regulations were timely and sensible, and suggest that Nero had listened to advisers. The broad streets did not please everyone – they let in too much sunshine and heat.

Less salubriously, in appeasing the gods after the fire Nero found someone to blame: the Christians. He was not the first to persecute them, but he did it with unnecessary violence. Crucifixion was not enough, so he was said to have made human torches out of crucified Christians in his gardens.[171]

## Provinces under Nero

Nero formulated plans for great expeditions, sending a party of soldiers to march along the White Nile into Ethiopia in 62-63, probably exploration, since no territory was annexed. He planned to march to the Caspian Gates.[172] Miriam Griffin explains that this is not as fantastical as it sounds, since the Elder Pliny says that the intended destination was the Caucasus, not the Caspian Gates, so Nero may have intended to strengthen the Danube zone against attacks by the Sarmatian tribes.[173] Tacitus names the Albani as the foe, which Pliny corrects to the Alani, a group of tribes of northern Pontus who sometimes threatened Roman territories. When Polemon II retired as independent ruler of eastern Pontus, not altogether voluntarily, Nero annexed the lands, amalgamating them with Cappadocia-Galatia, probably as part of his strategy against the Alani. Nero may have aimed to control the Black Sea and surrounding areas, mainly to master supplies of wheat, and Miriam Griffin connects the wheat supply with Nero's scheme to cut a canal through the Isthmus of Corinth, originally suggested by Julius Caesar.[174]

Apart from annexing eastern Pontus, Nero was not noted for enlarging Roman territory, though a small province was created in the Cottian Alps, named after the ruler Marcus Cottius. An equestrian governor took over the province.[175] In 58, Nero bestowed Latin rights on the inhabitants of the Maritime Alps annexed by Augustus and governed by a procurator.[176]

After Claudius annexed Thrace, the acquisition of major provinces ceased altogether for sixty years. The Roman ideal was not forgotten, expressed as *imperium sine fine*, power without end, and emperors who did expand Roman territory were usually lauded, the honorary epithet *propagator imperii* being one of high praise, as applied to Septimius Severus at the turn of the second and third centuries AD. Tacitus, writing at the end of the first century, clearly expected that Roman rule would one day be extended across the Rhine into Free Germany, explaining that 210 years had passed since the Romans first met the Cimbri, and that was how long the conquest had been going on (*tam diu Germania vincitur*). He thought that conquest was still in the pipeline.[177]

## Armenia and Parthia

The Caucasus expedition was never carried out, possibly because the Romans had their hands full with the Parthians and Armenia. At the beginning of Nero's reign the Parthian Vologaeses overran Armenia, but had to withdraw because of the rebellion of his son Vardanes.[178] Gnaeus Domitius Corbulo was chosen to save Armenia, arriving in the east in 55 to take over half the army of Ummidius Quadratus, governor of Syria, and to take command of Cappadocia and Galatia, where more soldiers were raised.[179] An attempt was made to negotiate with the Parthians, which gave Corbulo some time to train his Syrian troops, not ready for battle until he toughened them up. Tacitus says that they did not know how to make a camp, and that they lacked equipment. The campaign probably began in 57 when the army spent its first winter in the snows of Armenia, quite a shock for soldiers accustomed to the Syrian climate.[180] Vologaeses had installed his brother Tiridates as ruler of Armenia, who raided the people to keep them down. King Antiochus of Commagene, and the Moschi, allies of the Romans, also raided the country on Corbulo's orders. A meeting was arranged with Tiridates but it did not take place, so Corbulo pressed on to Artaxata, an important city of Armenia, beating off attacks on the way. The city capitulated and was burnt, probably in 58. The troops hailed Nero as Imperator and the Senate ordered thanksgiving in Rome.[181] Corbulo marched 300 miles south to the other major city, Tigranocerta, which opened its gates and escaped destruction. The people who submitted were spared, but escapers were pursued.[182] By this time Nero had despatched Tigranes of Cappadocia, a hostage in Rome, as the new Armenian king. Most Armenians preferred him to the Parthians. Corbulo withdrew to Syria, where Quadratus had died, leaving the province without a governor.[183]

Vologaeses was naturally unhappy with the Roman candidate for Armenia, especially when Tigranes raided Adiabene beyond Armenian borders, and the people appealed to the Parthians for help. Corbulo sent two legions to assist Tigranes, but in order to dissuade Vologaeses from attacking Syria he installed garrisons at crossing points on the Euphrates, or to guard water supplies.[184] An agreement was reached with Vologaeses, who agreed to withdraw the Parthians from Tigranocerta and to send an embassy to Nero about the Parthian claim to Armenia. Corbulo advised Nero that a separate commander was required to protect Armenia, and in due course Caesennius Paetus arrived, taking over three legions and auxiliaries from Pontus, Cappadocia and Galatia. Corbulo kept three legions and put even more posts on the Euphrates, but then had to rescue Paetus, who had surrendered. When Corbulo was only about two days' march away, Vologaeses let Paetus go, removing his troops from Armenia, while Corbulo removed his from the Euphrates.[185]

Rome declared war, with Corbulo as commander. All Roman governors including Gaius Cestius in Syria, and all native rulers, were ordered to take orders from Corbulo. He marched towards Tigranocerta and met envoys from Vologaeses and Tiridates. Corbulo advised alliance with Rome rather than fighting. Tiridates agreed to go to Rome to receive the crown of Armenia from the Roman Caesar.[186] The war ended in 66 with a splendid ceremony put on by Nero in Rome to receive Tiridates.[187] Armenia was governed for the next six years by Tiridates until the kingdom was overrun by the Alani from northern Pontus.

### Britain

When Nero became Emperor in 54, the governor of Britain was Aulus Didius Gallus, who maintained the status quo among the Silures of south Wales, and assisted Queen Cartimandua of the Brigantes, allied to Rome, to prevent her estranged husband Venutius from ousting her. Didius was replaced by Quintus Veranius in 57 but he died in 58, claiming that given another two years he could have conquered the entire country.[188] The next governor was Gaius Suetonius Paullinus, who subdued some of the tribes, probably in north Wales, and attacked the island of Mona (Anglesey), where the Druids gathered, thought to be actively supporting rebellious Britons. Meanwhile, King

Prasutagus of the Iceni died, leaving half his kingdom to Nero, so the Imperial procurator Catus Decianus, or his soldiers, arrived at the Iceni settlement to collect. Tacitus does not mention Catus by name until the rebellion had begun, explaining that it was his centurions who flogged Prasutagus' wife Boudicca, and raped her two daughters.[189] More trouble was caused when Catus called in the loans that Claudius and perhaps Seneca had made to eminent Britons.[190]

Debts and oppression probably affected several tribes. Boudicca was able to unite the tribes to fight for a common cause. The date of the rebellion is given in the ancient sources as 61, now more commonly dated to 60. Boudicca took the new cities of southern Britain by surprise, aiming first for the colony established for veterans of XX legion at Camulodunum (Colchester). Catus Decianus responded to appeals for help by sending a paltry 200 soldiers, but Camulodunum was overwhelmed. The veterans died in the temple of Claudius. Petilius Cerialis, legate of IX Hispana, marched to the rescue. His troops were annihilated, and he was lucky to escape with the cavalry. Catus fled to Gaul.[191]

Verulamium (St Albans) was attacked and destroyed next. Suetonius Paullinus tidied up his Anglesey campaign without completing it, and marched for Londinium (London), but had too few troops to defend it. He marched away, joined by XIV Gemina and parts of XX Valeria to encounter Boudicca's attack somewhere in the midlands. The Romans won the battle. Boudicca was believed killed.[192] Dio exaggerates, saying Britain was lost, but it was bad enough for Nero to think of abandoning the island. He was dissuaded and 2,000 legionaries, eight auxiliary cohorts and 1,000 cavalry were sent from Germany.[193]

Tacitus's father-in-law Julius Agricola was in Britain with Suetonius, so he was presumably the source of Tacitus' criticism of Suetonius' draconian methods in dealing with the Britons.[194] The new procurator Julius Classicianus recommended the governor's recall, and Suetonius was replaced by Petronius Turpilianus, derided by Tacitus for inactivity.[195] In reality, inactivity and peace were exactly what was required. Two years later Turpilianus was replaced by Trebellius Maximus, governor from 63 to 69. He was greedy and mean, with no military background, but a mild governor, so the Britons indulged in pleasant vices, by which Tacitus means that they became Romanized.[196] Trebellius' mistake was to fail to keep the armies busy. Corbulo would have had soldiers digging canals, building harbours, surveying terrain and making roads, ensuring that they were tired every night. Just as

Nero's reign was ending, with four successive candidates claiming the Empire, soldiers in Britain rebelled. Roscius Coelius, legate of XX Valeria, took charge, Trebellius fled, and the military men ruled Britain.

## Judaea

The revolt in Judaea had been simmering for some time. The freedman Antonius Felix, mentioned above, was tolerated until Gessius Florus became procurator from 64-66, when war broke out.[197] Trying to suppress this rebellion, Cestius Gallus, governor of Syria, met more defeats than victories, and died suddenly. News reached Nero in Achaia, where he was giving musical performances. Having forced Corbulo to commit suicide, Nero sought for a commander of ability, and noticed among his entourage Titus Flavius Vespasianus, aged fifty-seven, undistinguished but reliable. He had fought in Germany and in the conquest of Britain.[198] Vespasian was to take command of the legions of Syria, where Nero appointed Licinius Mucianus governor. Vespasian's son Titus was sent to Alexandria to collect XV Apollinaris, then V Macedonica and X Fretensis, while the Syrian troops marched overland to Judaea. The war lasted for four years, and Vespasian and Titus were still in Judaea when Galba, Otho and Vitellius made their bids for the Empire.

## The last of the Julio-Claudians

Reluctant to cut short his performances in Achaia in 68, Nero ignored increasingly urgent messages from Rome advising his return. His freedman Helius, in charge of affairs in Rome, had to sail to Achaia to try to impress upon his master the urgency of returning to Italy.[199] People hoped that Nero would perish at sea.[200]

Events had begun in Gaul that would lead to Nero's downfall. Gaius Julius Vindex, a Roman citizen descended from the royal family of Aquitania, was governor of Gallia Lugdunensis. He began the rebellion in protest at the levies of money in Gaul. His purpose was probably limited to overthrowing Nero, but his actions were interpreted as a nationalist Gallic uprising. Dio says that Vindex rebelled on behalf of Sulpicius Galba, governor of Hispania Tarraconensis, and he wrote to Galba, asking him to make himself 'leader of the human race'.[201] The commander in Upper Germany, Lucius Verginius Rufus, marched against Vindex, and their armies met at Vesontio (Besancon), which Rufus besieged. Vindex eventually committed suicide.[202] The soldiers declared Verginius Rufus Emperor, but he refused the honour. Galba in the meantime declared his loyalty to the Senate, unequivocally rejecting the sovereignty of Nero, and now determined to succeed him. In Rome the Praetorian Prefect Nymphidius Sabinus offered 30,000 sesterces in Galba's name to each Praetorian guardsman.

Nero did not take the revolt of Vindex seriously, and probably did not realise that not only Galba but also Marcus Salvius Otho opposed him, hardly surprising since Otho had governed Lusitania since 58, when Nero stole his wife Poppaea. Nero's envoy to Galba joined the rebels.[203] Nero made wild plans. He would go to Parthia, or Alexandria to make himself Prefect of Egypt, or he would summon his guards and his friends. Too late; they had all fled. Nero rode to the villa of his friend Phaon, where he had to crawl into the house. Intercepting a letter addressed to Phaon, Nero learned that he was now an enemy of the state. He declared, before he committed suicide, 'What an artist the world is losing.'[204] His ashes were placed in the tomb of the Domitii. He died on 9 June 68, the day of Servius Sulpicius Galba's accession as Emperor of Rome.

## The year of four emperors

In autumn 68 Galba arrived in Rome, accompanied by Otho and Titus Vinius, legate of VI Victrix which was left in Spain. Elimination of potential rivals was Galba's first concern. Vespasian's brother Flavius Sabinus was not killed but lost his post as city prefect. Vespasian sent his son Titus from Judaea to Rome to declare allegiance to Galba.[205] Others were not so fortunate. The Praetorian Prefect Nymphidius Sabinus was murdered. Clodius Macer in Africa, and Fonteius Capito commanding in Germania Inferior, were raising troops to use against Galba.[206] The legionary commanders Cornelius Aquinus and Fabius Valens killed Fonteius.[207] Galba made Aulus Vitellius commander of Germania Inferior, saying there was nothing to fear from a man whose only concern was for eating.[208]

Failing to pay the Praetorians any donative, let alone the 30,000 sesterces promised by Nymphidius, was Galba's serious mistake. He compounded this by discharging the Praetorians in batches. The legions of Germania Superior refused to take the oath to Galba, swearing allegiance to the Senate instead.[209] Galba responded by adopting an heir, Lucius Calpurnius Piso Frugi Licinianus, whose brother Gaius had unsuccessfully plotted against Nero. Piso was presented to the Praetorians, whose officers accepted him, but still no donatives were offered.[210] The naming of an heir dashed Otho's hopes of succeeding Galba.[211]

On 2 January 69 the legions of Germania Inferior declared for Vitellius who began the march to Rome, joined by Fabius Valens and Aulus Caecina Alienus, legionary legates in Germania Superior.[212] Otho offered to share power with Vitellius, offering him his daughter in marriage.[213] On 15 January, Galba was murdered on Otho's orders, with the support of the Praetorians.[214] Vespasian's son Titus heard about the death of Galba while still on his way to Rome, and turned back.

Otho reigned for three months and two days. He reinstated Flavius Sabinus as city prefect at the request of the troops, who were already thinking of Vespasian.[215] Vitellius had divided his army into two parts, sending one force to Italy under Valens and Caecina, and leading the other through Gaul. Otho was outnumbered. The Danube legions declared for him, but were far away. Otho decided to fight Vitellius' advance troops before they reached Rome. Valens and Caecina had crossed the Alps, but Otho could perhaps stop them at the river Po. Otho's generals Suetonius Paulinus and Marius Celsus won victories, but after Otho was persuaded to withdraw to Brixellum (Brescello) these two experienced generals were ignored. The real power remained with the Praetorian Prefect Licinius Proculus, and Otho's brother Titianus.[216] Otho kept sending orders to hurry up the troops, but Suetonius and Celsus advised waiting because their soldiers were weary and weighed down with baggage, whereas the enemy was moving more freely. Otho was defeated on 14 April near Cremona, and committed suicide. His troops sent a delegation to Vitellius' commanders and received terms.[217] Flavius Sabinus as city prefect administered the oath of loyalty to Vitellius to the people and to the Praetorians, the Urban Cohorts, and the *Vigiles*, possibly also to the remaining troops of Galba and Otho. Vitellius arrived in mid-July and held a triumph.[218] Sabinus had kept everything calm, but now he was in danger, because on 1 July his brother Vespasian had been hailed as emperor in Alexandria, and the Prefect of Egypt, Tiberius Alexander, administered the oath of loyalty to the two legions based at Nicopolis. The same oath was sworn in Judaea two days later, and twelve days after that, the four legions and all the cities of Syria swore allegiance to Vespasian.

This cannot have been a spontaneous development in which soldiers in all three provinces suddenly thought 'wouldn't it be good if Vespasian was Emperor?' Persuasion, promises, and best of all, cash, would have featured. The legionaries and their legates in the eastern and Danube provinces could easily have upset or delayed Vespasian's elevation, so it is to be assumed that Vespasian had already been in contact with the relevant personnel. The organisation behind this required time, careful planning, and secrecy. Josephus takes the Flavian party line that it was only when Otho and then Vitellius caused turmoil in Italy and Rome that Vespasian began to think of making a bid for power, but Tacitus implies that Vespasian and Mucianus started planning much earlier.[219]

Licinius Mucianus, governor of Syria, was not a special friend of Vespasian, but the two men worked together, corresponding at least since 67 with Titus as intermediary. Tacitus says that Mucianus found it easier to bestow imperial power than to hold it himself. [220] An ideal supporter for Vespasian, Mucianus was capable, industrious, discreet but not afraid to tell the truth. Mucianus secured support for Vespasian in Syria and among the surrounding client kings and free allies. Vespasian took care of Syrian affairs and then went to Egypt to gather money and grain, sending Mucianus overland to Italy with some of the troops from Judaea, where Titus was left in command.[221] The legions of Moesia had decided to go over to Vespasian and their defection from Vitellius was the first to be made known. Vitellius sent to Germany, Britain and Spain for reinforcements, but Hordeonius Flaccus, Vitellius' commander on the Rhine, Vettius Bolanus in Britain, and the commanders in Spain, were also turning to Vespasian.[222] Galba had created a new legion, VII Galbiana (later VII Gemina), and sent it to Pannonia, and its legate Antonius Primus was eager to march against Vitellius before his reinforcements could reach him. Primus had little trouble in taking control of the Danube legions, and reached Italy before Mucianus, gaining Padua and Verona. Vespasian allegedly ordered Primus to wait at Aquileia until Mucianus arrived.[223] This is probably retrospective propaganda. Vitellius' general Caecina Alienus was sent against Primus but decided to join the Flavians. His soldiers agreed, then changed their minds, arrested Caecina and fought Primus, losing what is known as the second battle of Cremona. Dio says that Vitellians sacked the town.[224] Tacitus blames Vespasian's freedman Hormus, while Vespasian blamed Antonius Primus for the sack of Cremona.[225] When Primus captured Rome on 18 December, he could not prevent his troops from rioting. His fate was sealed.

Vitellius was willing to abdicate, but his followers continued fighting. Flavius Sabinus, who was certain that the Senate would remove power from Vitellius and confer it on Vespasian, was soon disillusioned, having to flee with the Flavian supporters and Vespasian's younger son Domitian to the Capitol, besieged by Vitellians. When they broke through, Sabinus was killed and Domitian escaped. In disguise he joined a procession of priests of Isis, or alternatively found refuge in a friend's house.[226] Vitellius was killed in December.

Mucianus reached Rome after the advent of Antonius Primus. Tacitus says the turmoil in the city lasted for some days, while Josephus opts for a shorter time, relating that Primus' soldiers were quickly brought to order. Flavian propaganda could not admit to anarchy.[227] Domitian, aged nineteen, was hailed as Caesar, and delivered a speech to the soldiers, who each received 100 sesterces.[228] Mucianus administered affairs alongside Domitian.[229] Antonius Primus was neutralized, vaguely promised a provincial command which he never received. Foiled of promotion, Primus retired for the rest of his life to his home town, Tolosa (Toulouse) in Gallia Narbonensis. Mucianus sent the legions back to their respective bases. At the end of 70, the Emperor Vespasian returned to Rome.

# 9

# From the Flavians to Trajan, and the Provinces of Dacia and Arabia

Vespasian's *dies imperii* was 1 July, the day of his acclamation in Alexandria in 69. Unrelated to the Julio-Claudian family, Vespasian had no rights of inheritance and therefore required legal backing. The *lex de Imperio Vespasiani* was passed by the Senate, confirming him as Emperor. The second part of the law is preserved on a broken bronze tablet found in Rome in the fourteenth century.[1] Vespasian was authorized by this law to take actions necessary for the good of the state, to deal with allies and enemies without consulting the Senate, and to select candidates for the elections, but historians are hampered by the loss of the first part, because the law could have limited or enhanced Vespasian's powers.[2]

Vespasian had no scruples about monopolizing the consulship. Between 70 and his death in 79 he was consul every year except for 73 and 78. His official nomenclature was Imperator Caesar Vespasianus Augustus, setting the pattern for other emperors. Imperator was part of his name, to be distinguished from the victory titles gained by acclamations by the troops.[3]

## The revolt of Julius Civilis

Before Vespasian took control in Rome, a revolt broke out in Gaul and Germany, led by Julius Civilis, a Batavian who had served in the Roman army and gained Roman citizenship. Originally part of the Germanic Chatti, the Batavi had crossed the Rhine to settle on the Gallic side near the coast, paying no tax but contributing soldiers for the Roman army.[4] Civilis declared for Vespasian, but it was said that he planned to shake off Roman rule in Gaul, motivated by the death of his brother and his own his imprisonment in Rome in summer 68 for supporting the uprising of Vindex. Galba released Civilis, but he was arrested again by the Rhine army, and released again by Vitellius, who rigorously recruited Batavi, but Civilis turned the recruits back to Gaul. He won over the Canninefates, neighbours of the Batavi, and the Frisii from the right bank of the Rhine. They defeated Vitellius' depleted garrisons, encouraging Germans from across the Rhine to join then.[5] Hordeonius Flaccus sent two legions and auxiliaries against Civilis, who defeated them. The survivors fled to the fortress at Vetera (near Xanten). Civilis had his army swear allegiance to Vespasian and besieged the fortress at Vetera because the garrison remained loyal to Vitellius.[6]

When the Gauls and Germans heard that the Capitol had been besieged and burnt during the civil war, they seized the chance to reclaim Gaul. Julius Classicus and Julius Tutor of the Treveri, Roman citizens who had served as Roman auxiliaries, joined Civilis, along with another Gallic leader, Julius Sabinus of the Lingones. Tutor was put in charge of the Rhine bank, as *praefectus ripae Rheni*, possibly not choosing Latin to describe his post. He besieged Cologne. The Rhine troops began to surrender, including those at Vetera. Classicus made all the soldiers swear allegiance to *Galliarum*, the Gauls, and the troops were allowed to march out, but they were massacred by the Germans.[7]

Not all Gallic states wanted war. The Sequani fought against Julius Sabinus, forcing him into hiding, and the Remi held aloof, encouraging other Gauls opposed to war to join them.[8] Licinius Mucianus selected Petilius Cerialis and Annius Gallus to put down the rebels. Cerialis, eventually commanding six legions, rounded up Vitellius' troops and concentrated on regaining Gaul. He was criticized for allowing the Gauls and Batavi to concentrate at Trier, but he managed to destroy their camp.[9]

The victory at Trier did not end the war. The people of Cologne killed their German garrison, the Canninefates attacked the Roman fleet on the Rhine and then roused the Nervii against Rome. Civilis gave up when Cerialis prised his adherents away. From here Tacitus' work is lost, so Civilis' fate is unknown.[10]

One lesson learned by the Romans was to send locally recruited troops away to distant locations, and to give them Roman commanders, not native leaders.

*Vespasian's tasks*

There were many problems requiring Vespasian's attention. Rome had suffered damage, the Capitol had been burned, the finances were at an all-time low, taxation needed to be overhauled, confidence and prosperity had to be revived over the whole Empire. Troops needed to be sent back to their bases or redistributed, and the borders of the Empire had to be guarded. Maintenance of the army required lots of money, the sinews of war, as Mucianus used to say.[11] Recruitment was necessary on a large scale to keep the armies up to strength, to protect and police the provinces.

Vespasian explained that forty thousand million sesterces were required to shore up the treasury.[12] The figure has been disputed, reduced, variously explained.[13] The main treasury was the *aerarium*, in the temple of Saturn, and there were other treasuries, but the relationship between them is not clear. The distinctions blurred as centralization developed. The Romans did not produce an annual budget, but the Imperial finance minister, *a rationibus*, probably documented revenues and expenditure. It is not known when the freedman Tiberius Julius became *a rationibus*. He held the post all through the reigns of Vespasian and Titus, but Domitian dismissed him.

Vespasian revived taxes which had been revoked and increased taxes generally. He allegedly sold official appointments and acquittals in court, and resorted to buying commodities and selling them for profit, gaining a reputation for being mean and grasping.[14] Some of his money-making schemes were novel, such as the oft-quoted tax on urinals, the urine being used by fullers of cloth for its ammonia content. When Titus objected, Vespasian handed him some coins, asking if they smelled.[15]

Expenditure was necessary to restore the damage in Rome. The repair of the Capitoline temple of Jupiter began as soon as possible, supervised by an equestrian, Lucius Vestinius, who cleared the site, observing the religious protocols. When building work began, Vespasian carried the first load of soil himself, to encourage citizens to share the labour.[16] Three thousand bronze tablets had been destroyed in the fire, recording treaties, alliances, and senatorial decrees, and Vespasian ordered their regeneration from remaining copies. Previous fire damage of 64 had not yet been repaired, so contractors were allowed to build on vacant lots if owners failed to do so.[17] Vespasian restored many buildings in Rome, but his most famous work is the construction of the Colosseum, paid for mostly by spoils from Judaea. It occupied part of the gardens of Nero's *Domus Aurea*. Vespasian dedicated it before it was finished, dying shortly afterwards. Titus and Domitian completed it, with the barracks for the gladiators nearby.

Empire-wide censuses were conducted. Domitian was sent to Gaul in 70 to oversee proceedings there. The census usually established provincial and city boundaries, important for tax purposes.[18] It would highlight the status, wealth and resources of the provincials, facilitating a realistic tax assessment, hopefully noting the decline in some areas due to wars, and therefore relating tax to the ability of the provincials to pay without ruining their economy. There was no point in taxing communities out of existence, especially if they produced food for Rome.

## The army and the frontiers

Vitellius had dismissed the Praetorian Guard and created a new one from his own legionaries, increasing the number of cohorts from nine to sixteen. It was an expensive move.[19] Vespasian reverted to nine or ten Praetorian cohorts. Since the Praetorian Prefect wielded great power, Vespasian gave the post to Titus in 70.

Eventually the constant movement of troops, characteristic of the Republic and early Empire, slowed down, as several provinces became more settled, even if they were still under military occupation. The Roman army fulfilled all the tasks of many modern uniformed officials, as police, guards of various officials, and sometimes assisting in construction of amenities, such as the water supply and drainage schemes.

The armed forces had begun to move to the edges of the Empire, and the nascent stages of fortified frontiers can be detected under the Flavian emperors, Vespasian, Titus and Domitian. There are dangers in mapping known sites for Roman legionary or auxiliary bases, because it cannot be assumed that they were all occupied at the same time. Bases were given up as units moved out, others may have been abandoned, then reoccupied later, elucidated only via archaeological excavation. At some sites there is evidence of a legionary or auxiliary presence without archaeological evidence for any fort.[20] Gradually legionary bases remained in occupation for longer periods, but units were still relocated according to circumstances. In Britain under the Flavians the legionary fortresses were moved to new sites where they remained until the later Empire, at Caerleon (derived from *Castra Legionis*), Deva (Chester) and Eboracum (York). Along the Rhine the legionary bases of Germania Inferior were at Noviomagus (Nijmegen, in the Netherlands), and in modern Germany the fortress of Vetera (Xanten) was rebuilt, and legions were placed at Bonna (Bonn) and Novaesium (Neuss). In Germania Superior two legions occupied Mogontiacum (Mainz) in Germany, one was based at Vindonissa (Windisch, Switzerland), and one at Mirebeau, near Dijon, France. In the Danube provinces, Pannonia was garrisoned by legions at Carnuntum (Petronell near Bad-Deutsch-Altenburg, Austria), Aquincum (Budapest, Hungary), Poetovio (Ptuj, Slovenia), and a fortress is suspected but not attested archaeologically at Sirmium (Sremska Metrovica, Serbia). In Moesia Superior, legionary bases were Singidunum (Belgrade) and Viminacium (Kostolac) both in Serbia. The legions of Moesia Inferior were at Oescus (Gigen) and Novae (Svistov), both in Bulgaria. There was a growing disquiet north of the Danube, which escalated during the next centuries.

The eastern provinces and their troops were reorganised by Vespasian. Suetonius lists the acquisition of provinces, and the following are connected with the protection of the eastern frontier.[21] Commagene, previously ruled by Antiochus IV, was taken over probably in 72 or 73 and combined with Syria. Lesser Armenia had been absorbed probably in 71 at the expense of its king Aristobulus.[22] Cappadocia was reunited with Galatia and two legions were installed near the eastern border of Cappadocia, at Satala (Sadak) and Melitene (Malatya), both in Turkey. There was a legionary base in north-eastern Syria at Samosata (Samsat, Turkey), and another is postulated from finds at Zeugma, at a crossing point of the Euphrates, but no fortress is known. There was a fortress at Raphanea (Rafniye) in modern Syria, and another in Jerusalem. In Egypt two legions shared the fortress at Nicopolis near Alexandria, and in Africa the single legion III Augusta left Ammaedara (Haidra, Tunisia) to move westwards to Theveste (Tebessa, Algeria). These dispositions in the east facilitated defence of the margins of Rome territory and provided bases for an invasion of Parthia.

The regular auxiliary units of the Imperial Roman army gradually became part of the standing army, evolving slowly from Augustus onwards. Under the Flavians these troops were settled in more permanent locations, their forts became more standardized, as did their terms of service, the size of units, their titles, and their pay, which may have equalled that of legionaries, though this is much debated because of lack of indisputable evidence. After completing twenty-five years' service without blemish, auxiliaries were given pensions and Roman citizenship. If they had seriously misbehaved, men could be dishonourably discharged, without pensions or citizenship. Auxiliary units usually served in provinces where they had no affiliation with the natives, especially after the disastrous example of Civilis, a Roman citizen with experience of the Roman army and detailed knowledge of the people and the territory. It used to be thought that once these auxiliaries were established in other provinces, new recruits would all be local men, but evidence has come to light for continued recruiting of batches of men from the homeland of the original soldiers, mixed with local recruits.

## The provinces

The civil war had damaged Italy and the provinces as battles were fought or armies simply marched through. Some communities were forced to supply the armies, suffering if they refused. At Divodurum (Metz) Vitellius' soldiers looted and murdered, and when Vitellius stayed at Lugdunum, Junius Blaesus, governor of Lugdunensis, received him lavishly, placing extra burdens on the city.[23] Mucianus' march overland from Syria to Italy also strained provincial resources. The Flavians assisted recovery and rebuilding in some provinces.

According to Pliny, Vespasian gave Latin rights to all Hispania, and Richardson says that Spain was from now on regarded as a core province of the Empire.[24] Baetica was the most urbanised of the three Spanish provinces, while Lusitania and Tarraconensis were less so, but in Tarraconensis a number of *municipia* started to appear with the additional name Flavium. The magistrates of the *municipia* would become Roman citizens, together with their families and descendants. They would then be subject to Roman law, while the non-citizens had lesser privileges and were subject to the municipal laws, especially in the private sphere. Municipal laws gradually became compatible with Roman practice.[25] It probably took time to finalise Vespasian's policies in Spain, which may explain why the extant municipal charters belong to Domitian's reign, as described below.

During the civil war, troops had been taken from Spain, which now had no legion. Vespasian installed VII Galbiana, renamed VII Gemina which title probably indicates that remains of another legion had been amalgamated with the original legion.[26] An inscription records that part of the legion and some native communities built a bridge at Aquae Flaviae.[27]

Suetonius, providing no firm dates, lists the provinces which Vespasian created or redeveloped, Achaea, Lycia, Rhodes, Byzantium, and Samos.[28] Vespasian also took over part of Cilicia, and Commagene, previously ruled by kings. These were not major conquests, but additional territory taken over mainly for financial gain. Probably early in his reign, Vespasian made Achaea a senatorial province, governed by a proconsul and Achaea's tax immunity was revoked. Lycia was probably combined with Pamphylia.[29]

Though Vespasian did not embark on conquest of new provinces, he extended Roman rule in existing ones. In Britain forward movement had ceased after the rebellion of Boudicca, and the civil war of 69 stopped the advance into Wales. In Brigantia in northern England Queen Cartimandua was loyal to the Romans, as she had demonstrated in 51 when she handed over the British chief Caratacus, who sought refuge with her after his defeat. Tacitus called her treacherous.[30] This takes no account of Cartimandua's responsibility for her kingdom and tribe of the Brigantes. Caratacus' war was not her war, and helping him would have turned the Romans against her, undoing all she had done to keep her tribe at peace with them. There was no nationalist unity among British tribes, so Boudicca's war was not Cartimandua's war either. During the civil war of 69 when Vettius Bolanus was governor, Cartimandua's estranged husband Venutius took over her kingdom. Cartimandua had to be rescued by Roman forces. Tacitus says 'the kingdom was left to Venutius and the war was left to us.'[31]

The war against Venutius began in earnest when Petillius Cerialis was sent to Britain in 71. He had been legate of IX Hispana during the Boudiccan revolt. He brought another legion with him, II Adiutrix, replacing the much travelled XIV Gemina, removed from Britain by Nero, returned by Vitellius, and finally removed in 70 to fight against Civilis. Lincoln was the base for II Adiutrix for a short time, then the legion moved to Chester while IX Hispana moved to the new fortress at York.

Cerialis may have inherited some forts bordering on Brigantian territory, and several marching camps are known, but lack of precise dating makes it impossible to distinguish Cerialis' movements from his predecessors or successors. Tacitus says that most of Brigantia was overrun, without explaining by which governor, or how far north the Romans went.[32] Archaeological evidence suggests that Cerialis built the first timber fort at Carlisle, and probably campaigned in southern Scotland.

Sextus Julius Frontinus replaced Cerialis in 74/75, and he is credited with completing the conquest of the Silures of south Wales.[33] Tacitus says vaguely that Frontinus shouldered the burden, implying continuation of Cerialis' work in northern England, but Tacitus reserved all the credit for the conquest of the north for his father-in-law Agricola, the next governor.[34]

Gnaeus Julius Agricola was the last governor of Britain appointed by Vespasian, probably in 77, or 78. Tacitus describes the campaigns by seasons, not consular dates, so there is great debate about the chronology. Agricola served in Britain three times, as military tribune during the rebellion of Boudicca, then as legate of XX Valeria.[35] His first season as governor was spent in completing the conquest of north Wales, and in his second season he subdued new peoples, taking hostages and establishing forts. No new part of Britain came over with so little damage, says Tacitus, indicating that Agricola was operating much further north than Brigantia, otherwise he would not have met 'new tribes'.[36] In the third season Agricola advanced as far as the river Tay (Taus), one of the few place-names in Tacitus' narrative. There was time to establish forts (*praesidia*) for the winter, from which the Romans harassed the natives, denying them any means of recouping their losses of the summer.[37] At Chester moulded lead pipes reveal that the water supply was being laid down for the fortress in the ninth consulship of Vespasian and the seventh of Titus, dating the work to 79, with Agricola as propraetorian legate.[38] When Vespasian died on 23 June 79, succeeded by his son Titus, the forward advance was perhaps halted. The fourth season in 80 was devoted to consolidation. Titus presumably authorized a further advance into what is now Scotland in 81. He died in September of that year.

During the winters, Agricola addressed problems in administration, identifying and curbing abuses in the first winter. Tacitus refers to schemes to cream off profit in levying grain and collecting taxes. One such device may be illustrated by the famous corn measure from Carvoran in Northumberland, dated to Domitian's reign, though the fort is later. It is a false measure, holding much more than it claims. Another scam was to make the Britons deliver their grain to places far distant, and though Tacitus does not specifically say so, soldiers no doubt extracted money from farmers wanting to avoid the journey.[39] Agricola assisted communities which wanted to build Roman-style towns, which was always left to civilian initiative. Tacitus sneers that the Britons thought of this as civilization, but it was actually enslavement.[40] In the second half of the second century more towns were created with all the latest amenities.

Under the Flavians there was an extension of territorial control between the Rhine and the Danube. These rivers provided natural frontiers, but though their headwaters are fairly close together, they diverge to the west and east to form a re-entrant angle extending southwards. Vespasian advanced into the most southerly part of this gap, and sent troops across the upper Rhine, probably to control the lands between it and the Neckar, and he made a road from Argentorate (Strasbourg) through the Black Forest to the upper Danube in Raetia. It was not built to subdue Germany but facilitated communications between the Rhine and Danube.[41] There was still a re-entrant angle, but not of such depth.

## Vespasian's reign

The decade of Vespasian's reign was mostly peaceful, apart from fighting in Judaea and Britain. Conspiracies were rumoured, but nothing came to fruition. It was mostly the philosophers, Stoics and Cynics, who objected to Vespasian, in particular the Stoic Helvidius Priscus. He and his family were at least consistent, having opposed Nero and suffered for it. Helvidius did not want power, nor did he want to topple Vespasian, but constantly nagged. His first speech in the Senate after Vespasian was made Emperor was well received, containing no false flattery.[42] Afterwards he treated Vespasian as an ordinary citizen, addressing him by his personal name, not his titles voted by the Senate.[43] As praetor in 70, Helvidius issued edicts without the Imperial titles. His purpose is obscure. He comes over as obstructive for the sake of it, with no constructive suggestions. In 71 Vespasian proposed to bestow tribunician power on his elder son Titus, causing increased obstreperousness in Helvidius, who was first exiled from Italy, and later executed.[44]

Vespasian promoted both Titus and Domitian in accordance with their age and experience. Titus was censor with his father, reviewing the Senate and bringing in new men from Italy and some of the provinces to fill vacancies after the civil wars of 69. The spread of

Roman citizenship, coupled with opportunities for social mobility, strengthened the Empire. One of the problems inherent in the rule of one man was the stultification and consequent apathy of the senators, until political and military careers were standardized from Augustus onwards, replacing the Republican scramble for honour and glory with something that was equally worthwhile, with achievable goals. With more provinces to be governed and more armies to command, there was scope for senators and equestrians to rise to important posts, gradually opened up to provincials as well. The Roman world was never going to be an egalitarian society. The elite with close ties to the ruler would flourish, the wealthy would always thrive, snobbery would never die, and there would always be a miserable oppressed substratum, but that could equally describe medieval or Victorian Britain.

Vespasian died in June 79, in his seventieth year, at his home town of Reate. He made his famous joke 'Dear me, I think I'm becoming a god.'[45] If his death did not instantaneously make him a god, Titus completed the process and deified him officially.

## Titus

Vespasian's designated heir, Titus, was not loved by people or senators. He had a ruthless streak, beginning his reign with an evil reputation. He executed Aulus Caecina in 79 for preparing a speech to the soldiers, interpreted as a bid for power.[46] As Emperor, Titus was said to have warned potential conspirators to think again, inviting them to dinner, and even sending a message to the mother of one of them, explaining that her son had not been killed.[47] Titus reigned from June 79 to September 81, so it is difficult to discern whether he would have been an oppressive tyrant or a benign ruler. At least there were no treason trials.[48] Perhaps Titus mellowed, or merely learned to play his part well.[49] He had grown up in Claudius' court as a companion of Britannicus, whose death he witnessed. His experience under Nero presumably taught him distrust and wariness.

The new Emperor ensured that entertainments were frequent. He put on games for one hundred days in the Colosseum, not yet built to its full height.[50] He opened his new baths on part of the site of Nero's Golden House, organising gladiatorial shows to inaugurate them. He proclaimed the day wasted if he had not been able to give presents or do favours for people.[51]

While Vespasian was alive, Titus was officially known as *Augusti filius*, son of the Augustus, by now a title. Later, the name Caesar was used for the designated successor. Titus had long military experience, in Britain, Germany and Judaea. He had shared all the major offices with Vespasian and had carried out much of the administrative work of the Empire. He had been given more powers than previous designated heirs. He became the first non-equestrian commander of the Praetorian Guard, he held tribunician powers, and the consulship six times in ten years. He had served as censor with his father in 73-74, and as Emperor he became Pontifex Maximus.

Titus received fourteen Imperial acclamations before he became Emperor, and his fifteenth acclamation celebrated Agricola's conquests in Britain. Tacitus prepares for Agricola's fifth campaigning season with the comment that a frontier could have been established between the Forth and Clyde (*Clota et Bodotria*) 'if only the ardour of the army and the glory of Rome had allowed it.'[52] The fifth season in 81 was authorized by Titus. The only action that Tacitus reports is the defeat of peoples hitherto unknown, and that Agricola sailed across something in the leading ship, presumably the river Clyde, since Tacitus' previous text concerns the rivers Clyde and Forth, and the Forth is ruled out because after the crossing Agricola arrived at a point facing Hibernia (Ireland).[53] An Irish chief had sought refuge with Agricola, so there was an excuse to invade Ireland to reinstall him. Agricola thought that he could conquer Ireland with one legion and some auxiliaries. English monarchs also underestimated Irish warriors. The sixth and seventh seasons belong to Domitian's reign, and are described in that context.

Titus was faced with three major disasters, the eruption of Vesuvius, not known as a volcano, that obliterated Pompeii and Herculaneum in August 79, then the fire in Rome in 80, and a serious plague. Titus sent commissioners to Campania to assess the damage after the eruption. Dio suggests that Titus was there when news came of the fire in the city, and he appointed two ex-consulars to continue the Campanian work.[54] In Rome he provided workers and money to help victims to rebuild their homes, selling much of his own property to contribute to the relief fund. He made sacrifices to the gods to avert the plague, and searched for medicines, but nothing human or divine provided a cure.[55]

Titus dealt with the problem of the *delatores*, or informers. In 70 it had been proposed that all the files on informers should be opened, presumably with the intention of hunting them all down. Mucianus was in charge of the city, and the young Domitian advised the senators that any decision should be deferred until Vespasian returned.[56] The files must have been opened and the names revealed, since Titus as Emperor finally drove the *delatores* out of the city, scourging some of them, selling some as slaves and banishing others to remote islands.[57] Probably no-one sympathised with them.

Titus died of an unknown illness in September 81. The Emperor may have succumbed to the plague. Domitian was suspected of killing Titus, but he was said to have used such a wide variety of methods that the charge becomes ridiculous. Domitian deified Titus about a month after he succeeded him.

## Domitian

Domitian's reign ended badly, and the ancient authors revile him. Tacitus in particular had an axe to grind, principally on behalf of his father-in-law Agricola, who never received any further posts after his long service as governor of Britain, and even his conquests were quickly abandoned. Tacitus had experienced Domitian's rule in the dark years of suspicion and fear, but he had escaped personal harm, and by his own admission his own career had progressed under Vespasian, Titus and Domitian.[58]

Like Titus, Domitian had been given honorary titles and posts providing him with experience of government during Vespasian's reign. While Mucianus pacified Rome in 69, the urban praetor, Julius Frontinus, stepped down to allow Domitian to take up the post. According to Suetonius, in a single day Domitian appointed twenty officials in the city and the provinces, but Tacitus says that Mucianus held the real power.[59] Domitian was consul six times in Vespasian's reign, always three consulships behind his father and one behind Titus, and he was usually suffect consul, except in 73, and in 80 under Titus when he was *consul ordinarius*.

The troops in Rome hailed Domitian as Imperator on the day of Titus's death, though Dio accuses Domitian of leaving Titus for dead and dashing for the Praetorians.[60] The Senate confirmed him as Emperor next day, with the title Augustus. Within a few days of his accession, Domitian awarded the title Augusta to his wife, Domitia, daughter of Domitius Corbulo, and previously the wife of Aelius Lamia, from whom Domitian stole her.[61] Only three Imperial ladies had been given the title, Augustus' wife Livia, Claudius' mother Antonia, and Agrippina, mother of Nero.

During his reign Domitian was *Imperator Caesar divi Vespasiani filius Domitianus Augustus*, indicating that he was the son of the divine Vespasian. He was also *pater patriae*, father of his country, and took Titus' place as Pontifex Maximus. During his fifteen-year reign he held ten consulships, serving for a few months, then allowing senators to gain experience as suffect consuls. *Tribunicia potestas* gave him real power over the Senate and people. He was also *censor perpetuus* from 84, the only man to be given this honour according to Dio.[62] As censor, Domitian could control who became and remained a senator, and after his reign all emperors held censorial powers.[63]

Probably in 86, Domitian decided that his title should be *dominus et deus*, lord and god.[64] Slaves or workers customarily addressed their owners or employers as *dominus* or *domina*. Pliny had no problem with addressing Trajan as *dominus* in his letters, and the people of Rome readily acclaimed Domitian and Domitia as *dominus et domina*, but senators baulked at addressing Domitian as *deus* while he still lived. The Imperial cult promoted worship of the genius or spirit of the reigning emperor, not a living god. With only Caligula as an unfortunate precedent, Domitian was said to have demanded obeisance as well, prefiguring the third-century Emperor Aurelian, also *dominus et deus*; and rather better at it.

## Senators, equestrians and administration

The relationship between Domitian and the senators has been studied in depth by B. W. Jones, who concludes that early in his reign Domitian tried to pre-empt potential opposition by friendly means.[65] Later, the relationship between Senate and Emperor soured. Suetonius groups together in a depressing list all the senators who were executed, the reported reasons for their deaths being flimsy, such as having written derogatory verses or made jokes about Domitian.[66] Was the death sentence so arbitrary all though Domitian's reign? Clearly it was never the entire Senate which opposed Domitian, and it seems that in 96 the Senate was not involved in his assassination.

Membership of the Senate was extended to provincials, notably from the more urbanised eastern provinces. The process began under Vespasian and the first suffect consuls of eastern origin were appointed under Titus. More senators from the eastern provincials appeared under Domitian.[67] Senatorial status was prestigious, but the executive power of the Senate diminished. New business was introduced by the emperors, who also made the final decisions on most matters. The Senate could be by-passed to avoid time-wasting discussion. Domitian wrote directly to the proconsular governor of Cyrene, a senatorial province, authorizing him to delineate land boundaries.[68]

Domitian continued Vespasian's policies of promoting equestrians, appointing more and more of them to administrative posts, replacing the freedmen who normally occupied them. At some point in 82 or 83 he dismissed the freedman Tiberius Julius, his financial secretary, or *a rationibus*, who had served under Vespasian and Titus. An equestrian probably succeeded him. The freedman *ab epistulis* Abascantus, known from the poet Statius, was replaced by the equestrian Titinius Capito. The existence of any sort of regular career structure for equestrians has been challenged, but the four prefectures, with command of the Praetorian Guard at the peak, remained as goals for equestrians, though advancement would depend on the goodwill of the emperor and the successful fulfilment of a string of previous posts. In Domitian's reign the Praetorian Prefect Lucius Julius Ursus was promoted to the Senate, and then the consulship. Another equestrian was temporarily appointed to take charge of a proconsular province when the governor was executed for reasons unknown.

Suetonius says that Domitian gave scrupulous attention to the administration of justice, and the administration of the Empire was reasonable and fair.[69] Domitian was not greedy, refusing to accept inheritances if there were surviving offspring.[70] When Nerva became Emperor in 96, he found no need for a wholesale cancellation of Domitian's edicts and legislation. Domitian took steps to prevent extortion in the provinces. The lack of trials for extortion probably means that governors were more careful to cover their tracks, but Suetonius says that at no time were the city officials and provincial governors more honest.[71]

When Domitian discovered that the food supply was deficient in cereals but there was at the same time an abundance of wine, he tried to promote the production of grain and reduce that of wine, forbidding the planting of new vines in Italy and removing half of the vines in the rest of the Empire. The law has attracted much speculation as to Domitian's motives, but it probably was a sincere attempt to increase vital cereal production. In the end, it was allowed to lapse. Suetonius says that Domitian was frightened by threatening verses, but he probably just listened when the communities of Asia, and possibly of other provinces, appealed against the vine edict.[72]

Some light is shed on local government of the *municipia* by three municipal charters from Spain, all dating to Domitian's reign. Charters from Malaca (Malaga) and Salpensa (Facialcazar), both incomplete, had been known for some time.[73] Another from Irni, a town not previously known, was discovered in 1981. Charters from one part of the Roman world cannot be taken as the standard form of municipal government in all the provinces, except in so far as these Spanish charters are very similar in composition and wording, suggesting that they were all drawn up according to the same format. The three towns belonged to the province of Baetica and were all denoted as *municipium Flavium* followed by the name of the people of the community, Malacitani, Salpensani and Irnitani. Charters may yet be discovered in Tarraconensis.

Some clauses of the charter of Irni suggest that intermarriage was allowed between Romans and native Spanish women.[74] This was normally illegal but not impossible, since the precedent was set by Claudius in Mauretania Tingitana, where he elevated Volubilis (Oubilis, Morocco) to a *municipium*, giving the Romans of the town the right of intermarriage with non-Romans.

The three Spanish charters show that *municipia* were self-governed by the *ordo*, the local Senate, comprising usually about 100 decurions, but numbers varied with the size of the community. Two magistrates, usually *duoviri*, were elected annually, responsible for administration. They chose some of the decurions as judges in the law courts where the less serious cases would be tried. More important cases involving violence or sums of money over 1,000 sesterces would be referred to the provincial governors. There were also two aediles responsible for the food supply, buildings and public works, with slaves owned by the *municipium* to assist them. There were sometimes two quaestors dealing with finances and tax collection. The municipal government was modelled on that of Rome, and the men who had served in the above posts earned Roman citizenship. The laws for the *municipia* were quite detailed, but noticeably less so than those of the charter for Urso under Julius Caesar.[75] The municipal authorities seem to have been allowed considerable freedom of action in governing their towns, and town councils, not forced into a straitjacket by a plethora of detail, could probably adapt general rules to fit local circumstances.

## Rome and the people

Domitian distributed cash gifts (*congiaria*) three times, paying 300 sesterces to each person.[76] The populace was kept entertained by the usual shows and games. On one occasion the Colosseum was flooded to stage a naval battle, and Domitian had a large pool constructed on the Tiber for other naval displays.[77] Although he attended all the shows, Domitian displeased the audience because he dealt with his correspondence while supposedly watching the action, possibly because, according to Suetonius, in his early years Domitian did not like bloodshed, and before he was Emperor he had contemplated a law forbidding the sacrifice of oxen.[78] This does not sit well with his later activities when he was perfectly content as an accomplished archer to kill animals, though the same tale is told of Commodus.[79]

Domitian finished the buildings begun by Vespasian and Titus. He completed the interior of the Colosseum and its fourth storey, and finished the baths of Titus, of which little remains, but the site is known. The buildings destroyed by fire in 80 were restored or rebuilt and on the Capitol Domitian built a new temple to Jupiter Custos. He searched for copies of books that had been destroyed so they could be reproduced.[80] According to Suetonius he put his own name on the renewed buildings as the restorer, without naming the original builders.[81] Suetonius probably wanted to please Hadrian, who rebuilt Vipsanius Agrippa's temple, putting only Agrippa's name on it. The temple is now known as the Pantheon, the best preserved complete ancient building in Rome. A list of buildings attributed to Domitian is preserved in a work of the fourth century AD, but not all the sites can be identified.[82] Remains of Domitian's Odeum devoted to the arts have been identified in the Campus Martius, and the Meta Sudans, the conical fountain attributed to him, is marked by its circular remains near the Colosseum, and it appeared on Domitian's coins with the Colosseum in the background. At the south-eastern end of the Imperial Fora in Rome the remains of Domitian's Forum and temple of Minerva can be seen, now known as the Forum Transitorium, or the Forum of Nerva, who inaugurated it. On the Palatine, Domitian built his own palace, the *Domus Augustana*, and a magnificent villa at Alba, now Castel Gandolfo, the summer residence of the Popes.

At the end of 82 Domitian started to overhaul the mint in Rome. As an obsessive perfectionist, he issued silver coinage of the highest standard, the most pure in silver content of any that had gone before or was issued afterwards, but he had to devalue the coinage later in his reign.

## The army

It may have been Domitian who introduced the Imperial mounted guards known as *equites singulares Augusti*.[83] Julius Caesar employed German horsemen as guards. The Emperor Galba disbanded them, and thereafter there is no evidence for such units until 98, after Domitian's death. *Equites singulares* already existed as guards of military commanders and of governors in the armed provinces. The horsemen were usually drawn from the mounted units serving in the province, and they remained attached to their original *alae*, to which they returned after serving in the guards. They were chosen for their skills, their service record, and for their personal appearance, since they took part in ceremonials and displays as well as fighting when necessary. Their title as *equites singulares Augusti* distinguished them from the provincial *singulares* and made it clear that they belonged to the reigning emperor.

In 83 Domitian raised soldiers' pay by about one third. There had been no increase for over a century after Julius Caesar awarded legionaries 225 denarii per annum, paid in three instalments of 75 denarii, equal to three gold aurei, probably on the first day of January, May and September. Domitian raised this to 300 denarii per year, possibly adding a fourth pay day or *stipendium*, but if this is correct, three pay days were restored later.[84] Praetorians were paid more than legionaries, and Praetorian and legionary officers were paid at an even higher rate. Pay scales for auxiliaries are debated.[85] Suetonius says that Domitian robbed people to fund this pay rise, and he reduced army numbers, exposing the empire to attacks by barbarians. Dio's version is that Domitian regretted the pay rise, but instead of retracting it (imagine what would have happened if he had tried!) he reduced the number of soldiers, leaving too few men to defend the empire, still at enormous cost.[86] The assertion that the armed forces were reduced in size may refer only to the reduction of troops on the Rhine in order to strengthen the more threatened Danube zone. The citizens of Rome and Italy expected their defence to come cheap, but they were no longer connected to the soldiers, who were once Romans who went away to fight wars and then the survivors came home. That familial relationship had been lost. The legions were full of Roman citizens not native to Rome, and the auxiliaries were not even Romans, yet all this money was flowing their way.

### Campaigns in Britain

Domitian authorized Agricola's advance further into Scotland in his sixth and seventh seasons, which were once dated 83 to 84 but now arguably belong to 82 to 83. In the sixth season Agricola may have left part of IX Hispana at York to guard the north of England, which would explain why this legion was understrength on campaign. Alternatively, it is suggested that Domitian took troops from Britain for his war against the Chatti of Free Germany in 83. As ever, dates are much disputed. Tacitus reports that IX Hispana was attacked by night and Agricola rescued it.[87]

In the seventh season the final battle at Mons Graupius was fought. The Grampians were named after Tacitus' account, and therefore do not prove that the battle was fought in the Highlands. It can only be said that Agricola fought near a mountain, and in Scotland. Searching for the battle site is like searching for the proverbial needle in a haystack. The battle was probably in the far north, if Tacitus is correct in making the British leader Calgacus 'The Swordsman' explain that there was no land beyond, and even the sea provided no refuge, patrolled by the Roman fleet. Agricola's speech to his assembled army also refers to 'the place where world and nature end'.[88]

Agricola's real talent was forcing the northern Britons to unite to fight him. They could have retreated into the mountains and waited for the invaders to run out of time and food, as happened later in Scotland's history. Agricola's fleet could have supplied the troops, but not indefinitely. The ships were used to make raids into the countryside near the coasts to induce the natives to fight.[89] Calgacus allegedly said of the Romans, 'they make a desert and call it peace,' probably Tacitus' own view.[90] Tacitus describes Agricola's troop dispositions, the legionaries in reserve, the auxiliary infantry cohorts in the centre flanked by the cavalry, with some horsemen in reserve for emergencies. This is likely to have come from Agricola himself, who extended the line because the Britons drawn up on the hillside outnumbered the Romans. Ignoring suggestions from his staff to call in the legionaries, he sent away his horse and stood in front of the auxiliaries, who won the battle on their own. The defeated Britons ran into the woods, and Agricola sent in cavalry, ordering them to fight on foot.

After the battle Agricola sent out scouts, who reported that the Britons were not regrouping, so the Romans progressed slowly southwards taking hostages from a tribe called the Boresti. While the army marched south, the fleet was ordered to sail round Britain.[91] Tacitus prepared his audience for this in an earlier passage where he says that for the first time, under Agricola's governorship, Britain was proved to be an island, as some of Agricola's auxiliaries, the Germanic Usipi, discovered. They mutinied, killing their Roman officers, and seized boats to go home. They are supposed to have sailed north, ending up on the other side of Britain.[92]

Evidence of Agricola's campaigns is provided by marching camps around the north-east of Scotland, a line of watchtowers on the Gask Ridge skirting the western edge of Fife, and camps and forts along the southern edge of the Highlands guarding the exits and entrances of the glens. The Tay valley was guarded by the legionary fortress of Inchtuthill near Dunkeld. It is not known for certain whether the glen forts belong to Agricola or his successor. The towers of the Gask Ridge are accompanied by two forts at Ardoch and Strageath, each of which has two Flavian phases, the second phase perhaps part of the post-Agricolan arrangements, which were very short-lived. The above brief description gives no inkling of the amount of scholarly debate on this topic.

Agricola returned to Rome probably in 84, and within a short time his conquests were given up, except for part of southern Scotland. Tacitus was bitter on Agricola's behalf, not just in his biography of his father-in-law. In his *Histories* he says *perdomita Britannia et statim missa*, Britain was subdued and immediately abandoned.[93] Archaeology bears this out. At some forts in Scotland, bronze *asses*, issued in 86 for the soldiers' pay, have been found in mint condition, indicating lack of use. Large numbers of *asses* were minted in 86 and 87, but while *asses* of 87 reached forts in England, they did not reach forts in Scotland.[94] This coin evidence shows that Scotland was occupied for only a short time. The fortress of Inchtuthil was rapidly abandoned very soon after Agricola's conquests. It must have been a bitter blow. Agricola was awarded triumphal honours by Domitian, the highest award that he could have received, but no further appointments were offered to him.

In the last years of Domitian, the province of Britain extended into Lowland Scotland, the most northerly forts being at Newstead in the east and Drumlanrig in the west.[95]

## Campaigns in Germany

Contemporary with the campaigns in Britain, Domitian waged war against the Chatti, but the dates are disputed. Domitian embarked on it '*sponte*', meaning of his own accord, without provocation.[96] Frontinus claims that 'for the good of the provinces' Domitian wished to crush the Germans who were in arms, mentioning the Chatti by name only when describing their flight into a forest.[97]

The Chatti were formidable enemies. According to Tacitus, they differed from other tribes in that they were united and well-organised. They chose their own commanders, they kept their place in the ranks, recognised and seized opportunities, made camps at night, and most remarkable of all they were disciplined enough, like the Romans, to obey the initiative of their commanders instead of acting individually. Tacitus adds that 'other Germans go to battle, the Chatti make war.'[98] Having described the military talents of this tribe, Tacitus could not bring himself to credit Domitian with a genuine achievement.

Domitian assembled detachments from all four legions of Germania Superior. XXI Rapax was probably replaced at Bonn by the newly raised I Minervia, named in honour of Domitian's favourite goddess Minerva. According to Frontinus, Domitian advanced the *limites*, usually translated as frontiers, along a stretch of 120 Roman miles in Germany.[99] This was thought to refer to the attested frontier line of watchtowers and small forts enclosing the Taunus-Wetterau region of Germany, of Flavian date, and roughly the correct length of 120 miles, but the term *limes*, plural *limites*, was originally used for the road into enemy territory, and did not indicate a frontier until later. Frontinus adds that the advance not only changed the war but subdued Rome's enemies by discovering all their hiding places, suggesting that Domitian penetrated Chattan territory. Dio denies that Domitian saw hostilities at all in Germany, dismissing the campaign as a waste of time because there was no extension of the Empire, meaning that Germany remained unconquered and was not annexed.[100]

Domitian took the title *Germanicus* and celebrated a triumph in 83, which Tacitus dismisses as a sham, claiming that people were paid to dress up as German prisoners.[101] If Domitian had intended to conquer all Germany, he never followed up the campaign against the Chatti. There were other pressing needs on the Danube.

8. The Gallic provinces, the Germanies and the Alpine provinces. To accommodate German settlement in the territory of the left bank of the Rhine in Gallia Belgica, the Romans created two militarily occupied zones under two commanders, with civil administration carried out from the remaining part of Belgica. These zones were made provinces under the Emperor Domitian. The Alps were not under Roman control during the Republic. Augustus annexed the Alpes Maritimae, the Emperor Nero annexed the Alpes Cottiae, and the Alpes Graiae et Poeninae is Diocletian's name for a province annexed in the second century under a slightly different name. Redrawn by Isla Jones after various sources.

## Campaigns in Dacia

The homelands of the Dacians correspond roughly to modern Romania, where several different tribes were first united under the leader Burebista, who *c.59* BC extended control over part of modern Hungary and even attacked the Greek Pontic cities. As Dictator, Julius Caesar planned a Dacian campaign. The project lapsed after Caesar's assassination, but trouble from the tribes beyond the Danube continued. When the troops were withdrawn from Moesia during the civil war of 69, the Dacians intended to destroy the forts but were repelled by Mucianus, marching from Syria to Italy. Vitellius ordered Fonteius Agrippa, proconsul of Asia, to take charge of Moesia.[102] Josephus is the only source for the invasion of Moesia by the Dacians (which he calls Sarmatians) and the death of Fonteius in trying to repel them. Vespasian sent out a new governor, Rubrius Gallus, who restored order and placed more numerous and stronger garrisons on the frontier.[103]

The beginning of the Dacian war is dated somewhere between late 84 and early 86. The Dacians under their new leader Decebalus crossed the Danube, defeated the Roman army in Moesia, and killed the governor Oppius Sabinus. Eutropius adds that a legion was lost.[104] He does not name it, but it is conjectured that it was V Alaudae, originally one of Caesar's legions. The Dacians may have been worried by Domitian's war against the Chatti and decided to pre-empt a Roman attack on Dacia. Dio portrays Decebalus as a shrewd, talented war leader and Domitian as cowardly, lurking in the background in Moesia, living the good life while his commanders did all the work.[105]

Domitian responded to the Moesian situation as rapidly as possible, and his abandonment of Agricola's conquests in Scotland may be connected with the troop movements from Britain and other provinces. II Adiutrix, brought to Britain by Cerialis, was moved to Moesia in 85 or 86, along with IIII Flavia from Dalmatia and I Adiutrix from Pannonia. Later it became normal practice to deal with trouble on the Danube by shunting troops there from the Rhine and then bringing forces from other areas to man the Rhine forts, making use of the good communications established by Vespasian's road from Strasbourg to Raetia, with Domitian's improvements.

Domitian accompanied the troops to the Danube, giving the command of the campaign to the Praetorian Prefect Cornelius Fuscus. Victories are indicated by Domitian's three salutations as

Imperator between February and September 86, bringing the total of his acclamations to fourteen. Probably in the following year, after Domitian returned to Rome, Cornelius Fuscus mounted what should have been a punitive expedition across the Danube but he was defeated and killed. Nothing is known of the immediate aftermath of this disaster, until Domitian had collected another army. He may also have divided Moesia into two zones, Moesia Superior and Moesia Inferior, as part of his preparations for the next round of the war. The governors of these two provinces, respectively Funisulanus Vettonianus and Curiatius Maternus, were both consulars, and Domitian rewarded them, perhaps for work in stabilising the frontier. Mocsy suggests that Funisulanus, previously governor of Pannonia, may have moved to Moesia Superior soon after the defeat of Oppius Sabinus.[106] The final victory was won at Tapae, under Tettius Julianus, probably in 88.

Decebalus had been defeated but not subdued. According to Dio, Decebalus had offered to make peace before the campaign began under Fuscus, and again when the Dacians knew that war was in the offing, but on this second occasion Decebalus' terms were that every Roman should pay him two obols every year, or else he would inflict great damage on them.[107] This is probably Roman propaganda, portraying Decebalus as the enemy who must be destroyed. Decebalus frequently asked for a truce, which Domitian always refused until he suffered a defeat at the hands of the Marcomanni, and then he made terms with Decebalus.[108] The chronology is debatable, but the peace terms belong much more reasonably to the period after the Roman victory at Tapae, so as not to leave the Dacian situation in limbo. The chronological problems surface again below.

Decebalus sent his brother Diegis to negotiate terms, and Domitian gave the latter a gold crown for Decebalus, by which it is assumed that Domitian recognised him as ruler of the Dacians, and a client of the Romans. Domitian also paid Decebalus vast amounts of money, promising more. Various artisans of all trades 'connected with peace and war' were sent to work for the Dacians.[109] In connection with Trajan's Dacian campaigns, Dio explains that money was paid annually, and the skilled artisans were military engineers and builders, who most probably assisted Decebalus to fortify his kingdom.[110]

When Domitian made peace after the battle at Tapae, he may have been planning and even preparing for a resumption of hostilities, perhaps intending to annex Dacia and create a new province, for several reasons: one being that protection of the provinces of the middle Danube could be effected by absorbing territory to the north of the river, and another that there was gold and silver in the country. If he entertained such plans, the restless Marcomanni, the Quadi, the Iazyges of the Hungarian plains, took priority. From this time onwards the Roman military emphasis was on the Danube, where the number of troops increased at the expense of the Rhine frontier.

## The revolt of Antonius Saturninus

A new problem developed closer to Rome in 89, personally threatening to Domitian. Lucius Antonius Saturninus, commanding in Germania Superior, raised rebellion, probably planned in 88. Potentially, Saturninus could call on four legions. XIV Gemina and XXI Rapax were based in the double legionary fortress at Mogontiacum (Mainz), VIII Augusta was at Argentorate (Strasbourg). XI Claudiaat Vindonissa (Windisch)refused to join Saturninus. While marching to Mainz, Domitian summoned VII Gemina from Spain, commanded by Marcus Ulpius Trajanus, the future Emperor Trajan. Before Domitian reached Mainz, the commander in Germania Inferior, Aulus Buccius Lappius Maximus defeated Saturninus, who was killed. The victorious legions received the honorary title *pia fidelis Domitiana*, reduced to *pia fidelis* after Domitian was assassinated. Saturninus' partisans were hunted down and killed, but probably only the officers at Mainz were punished, since the rank-and-file soldiers may have been coerced. Wholesale executions would simply alienate them, and they were needed.

It was said that Domitian took revenge on the senators for this rebellion, but there is no proof that any senators had been connected with it.[111] Sallustius Lucullus, the governor of Britain who probably succeeded Agricola, was killed for naming a spear after himself, which may mean he was part of Saturninus' circle.[112] Domitian became more suspicious and cruel after the revolt.[113] Having learned how easy it had been to raise rebellion, he took steps to prevent a reoccurrence. Two legions would never again occupy a legionary fortress. Saturninus had seized the soldiers' savings from the strong-room in the legionary headquarters to finance his rebellion, so Domitian decreed that no more than 1,000 sesterces should remain in the savings accounts of each soldier. Anyone emulating Saturninus would not have access to so much ready cash.[114]

Drinkwater is certain that it was *c*.90, after the revolt of Saturninus that the two military occupied zones of Gallia Belgica were converted into the two provinces of Germania Superior and Inferior, with Mogontiacum (Mainz) as the capital of Superior, and Colonia Agrippina (Cologne) the capital of Inferior. At the same time the Taunus-Wetterau received more fortifications, linking the Rhine and Danube, and defending the territory of the former re-entrant angle, which was settled by Gauls and called the *Agri Decumates*, meaning ten cantons.[115] Levick prefers to date this settlement to Vespasian's arrangements.[116] Whatever the precise dates, there was now an almost complete frontier line guarded by forts from the Rhine to the Danube, but the western end of the Raetian frontier was not joined to the eastern end of the German frontier for some years.

## The Danube

As soon as the rebellion ended news arrived of trouble in Pannonia, where Domitian arrived probably in the spring of 89. The Marcomanni and Quadi constituted the main threat to Roman security, but the official excuse for Domitian's war against these tribes was that they had not sent help for the campaign against the Dacians.[117] This presupposes that the Marcomanni were bound by terms of friendship to contribute soldiers. These people had been known since Caesar's time, and after they were attacked by Drusus in 9 BC they had migrated to Bohemia. Under Tiberius, Maroboduus, leader of the Marcomanni, was expelled and sought sanctuary in Rome. Subsequent leaders had good relations with Rome. There may have been some inconclusive fighting in 89, but it is just possible that negotiations solved the problems temporarily.

At the end of 89 Domitian triumphed over the Dacians and the Chatti. This suggests that there had been a second war with the Chatti, linked to Suetonius' statement that Saturninus had barbarian allies poised to enter the province, but they were prevented from doing so because the frozen Rhine suddenly thawed.[118] It is more likely that there was never any such threat from the Chatti, and the triumph was really over Saturninus. There was no triumph over the Marcomanni because the wars were not finished and broke out again in 92.

Dio suggests that it was because of a defeat by the Marcomanni that Domitian was induced to make a truce with Decebalus, but it is more likely that peace had already been made, especially since one of the terms allowed the Romans to march through Dacian territory to attack the Marcomanni and Quadi. An inscription recording the career of Gaius Velius Rufus attests that in a war against the Marcomanni, Quadi and Sarmatians, Roman forces did march through the kingdom of Decebalus, specifically named on the inscription.[119] It can be safely assumed that the agreement with Decebalus was in force when the Romans marched through Dacia, but it still cannot be proved whether this expedition occurred in 89 or in 92, and arguments have been made for both dates.

Further complications arise because Suetonius says that Domitian went to war with the Sarmatians because a legion and its commander had been lost, but he provides no dates, no locations, and no name for the legion.[120] The episode has been linked with the undated disappearance of XXI Rapax, perhaps not long after it was moved from Mainz to Pannonia in 89, though some scholars suggest its demise should be dated to the fresh outbreak of war with the Marcomanni in 92. As with the expedition of Velius Rufus there is no absolute proof for 89 or 92.

All that is known of the war of 92 is that it happened, and afterwards the Empire was predominantly peaceful. Domitian attended to the defence of the provinces, continuing the work of Vespasian and Titus. He did not annexe Dacia after the Danube campaigns and made no attempt to regain Scotland after the troops were withdrawn to the Lowlands. The eastern provinces were quiet for the time being, since the Parthians were not aggressive, perhaps because there were now six legions to defend the frontier, one in Judaea, two in Cappadocia and three in Syria. The escalating threat on the Danube was not properly averted until Trajan's two major wars in Dacia.

## The terror

In Rome the reign of terror had begun. Domitian used to say that no-one would believe there were plots against him until he was dead, and he lined his palace corridors and rooms with reflective marble slabs so that he could see if anyone was behind him.[121] Suetonius lists the names of men who were executed, many for seemingly tenuous reasons.[122] Some of the victims may well have been plotting against Domitian, but executions made people afraid and may have engendered the idea of assassination in men who had never contemplated such a thing.

In the end, Domitian's own household staff killed him, probably with the consent of his wife Domitia. No senators were ever proven to have conspired against Domitian, but certain individuals were primed, ready and waiting to act once Domitian was dead. Dio prefaces his account of the conspiracy by saying that he reproduced what he had heard, rather than examining any evidence. He says that a plot already hatched was set in motion more quickly than intended, after a slave discovered a two-leaved wooden tablet under Domitian's pillow containing a list of names. It was assumed that this must be men he wanted to eliminate. Domitian's wife Domitia came across the list and gave 'information to those concerned', so Dio neatly avoids naming the plotters, if he ever knew them. Domitian's successor was Marcus Cocceius Nerva, already very old, and in danger from Domitian because astrologers had predicted that he would become Emperor.[123]

Domitian was forty-five years old when he was killed on 18 September 96. Only the Praetorians mourned his loss. The people of Rome had not been so adversely affected by Domitian's reign as the upper classes, so they were probably indifferent to the demise of one emperor and the advent of a new one. Domitian was not deified, and his memory was damned.

## Nerva

Nerva was chosen as Emperor by the senators and not by the army, so Nerva's pressing need was to ensure that the Praetorians and the armies accepted him. His relationship with the Praetorians was not secure, and a year after his accession they forced him to execute Domitian's killers.

Nerva left most of Domitian's administration intact, but repealed certain harmless acts with exaggerated fuss, as though the new broom was sweeping clean. Exiles were brought home, men imprisoned for treason (*maiestas*) were released, and further treason charges were forbidden.[124] For the Roman populace and the troops, there were cash gifts and some tax exemptions. Landless men in Rome were given allotments, at a total cost of sixty million sesterces, funded by a sale of Nerva's own property and the furnishings of Domitian's palace.[125]

Poor families in Italy were assisted by a new scheme, called *alimenta*, from *alimentum*, meaning food or maintenance of life. It was a three-way arrangement where the state lent money to several small farmers, who then paid the five per cent interest on their loans, lower than normal rates, to their local municipality instead of to Rome, so that the income could be used to support and feed young children until they reached puberty. Two inscriptions from Trajan's reign reveal how it worked. Records were made of small farmers in need of assistance in feeding their children, who provided labour on the farm. State funds loaned to each farmer were based on the value of his property, which provided security. Payments, assumed to be monthly, are listed as sixteen sesterces for legitimate boys and twelve for legitimate girls. Payments for one illegitimate boy and one illegitimate girl were respectively 1,144 and 1,120 sesterces per annum.[126]

Nerva inherited Domitian's war with the Marcomanni in Bohemia. He was not a military man and did not travel to the war zone, but his generals won a victory in 97, and Nerva took the title *Germanicus*. An inscription records a soldier, Quintus Attius Priscus, who earned decorations from the Emperor Nerva.[127] The Marcomanni remained quiet from 97 until the later 160s when the long-term wars broke out under Marcus Aurelius.

Since he had no immediate heirs and was already past middle age, Nerva chose as his successor Marcus Ulpius Trajanus, a military officer who had served under Domitian and supported him at the time of Saturninus' revolt in 89. He was currently governor of Germania Superior. According to Dio, in 97 Nerva went up to the Capitol to announce the formal adoption of Trajan as his son, and in the Senate he appointed him Caesar, by now the usual designation for the successor of the Augustus.[128] Trajan was a wise choice, with a good reputation in the army and as far as possible with the senators and people. He had trodden the fine line between closely involving himself with Domitian and overtly opposing him. Trajan was to be *consul ordinarius* for the second time in 98, and at the beginning of that year Nerva died. Trajan became Emperor.

## Trajan

Trajan's reign lacks documentation, because Suetonius' biographies end with Domitian, and the *Historia Augusta* containing lives of emperors up to the third century begins with Hadrian. Whereas Suetonius sometimes veers towards fantastical stories, the *Historia Augusta* sometimes veers towards the truth. The biographies are supposed to have been written by different authors, but it is now thought that there was only one.

Marcus Ulpius Traianus was the first provincial to become Emperor. The Ulpii, an Italian family, had settled in Spain at Italica, founded by Cornelius Scipio in 206 BC. Trajan was born there in AD 53, and his father had been made a senator by Vespasian. Another Italian family, the Aelii, had also settled at Italica, and in Trajan's day they had been senators for at least four generations. Publius Aelius Hadrianus (Hadrian) was born in Rome in 76. Hadrian's grandfather had married Trajan's aunt. When Hadrian was ten years old, his father Aelius Hadrianus Afer died, and Hadrian became the ward of his cousin Trajan, of praetorian rank at the time.[129]

The new Emperor Trajan went immediately from Germany to the Danube without visiting Rome. He wrote to the Senate to explain that Decebalus was rebuilding his power in Dacia, and Pannonia was threatened. Trajan fought no battles, but probably gathered intelligence and inspected and strengthened frontier defences. Arriving in Rome in 99, Trajan distributed 300 sesterces to each of the people, and added more names to the lists for the corn dole. The armies supported him, so Trajan could afford to root out the Praetorians who had executed Domitian's assassins, and he gave the guardsmen a lower cash gift than other emperors.

## The Dacian wars

Trajan became immensely popular in 101 when he embarked on the first of his two Dacian wars. Decebalus had kept to the terms of the treaty with Rome and had not invaded Roman territory, but Dio says that Trajan was concerned about the amounts of money paid to the Dacians. This was probably not the sole reason for going to war, but it would please the people. A monumental part of the preparations for the war was to cut a road into the rock face of the south bank of the Danube downstream from the Iron Gates gorge. The road platform was too narrow in some places and projecting stone supports had to be inserted to extend a walkway suspended over the river, as recorded on inscriptions.[130]

Trajan took with him the young Hadrian as his quaestor. A huge army was assembled, comprising at least nine legions or large detachments from them, and a number of auxiliary units. Dio's account survives in an epitome and merely summarises Trajan's bravery and justice, and Decebalus' fear of the Romans.[131] There was a battle at Tapae, where Tettius Julianus first defeated Decebalus, but this time there was no satisfactory conclusion. Trajan decided to spend the winter on the Roman side of the Danube. The second season was more successful. The Romans struck at the heart of Dacian territory, forcing Decebalus to submit. According to the terms imposed on him, Decebalus surrendered his war equipment and promised troops for the Romans.

Trajan installed garrisons throughout Dacia.[132] The armies of Moesia and Pannonia would monitor events. It took two years for Decebalus to rearm. He defeated and expelled Trajan's garrisons and attacked the Iazyges, allies of Rome. In 105, the Dacians and other tribes erupted into Moesia. Trajan arrived as quickly as possible and had to deal with the invading tribes so that he could advance without fear of being cut off. He withdrew some troops from Britain, bringing the units out of southern Scotland and sending some of them, such as the Ninth Cohort of Batavians, to the Danube.[133] Some units may have been reshuffled and relocated in Britain. South of the route chosen later for Hadrian's Wall, new forts were built on the road now called the Stanegate, marking the northern limit of Roman occupation in Britain.

In 106 Trajan built a bridge across the Ister, the Danube. Stone piers supported a wooden superstructure.[134] Entering Dacia via the bridge, the Romans captured the Dacian capital at Sarmizegethusa. Decebalus committed suicide moments before the Roman cavalryman Claudius Maximus nearly captured him, as recorded on an inscription.[135]

No territory had been annexed for more than fifty years, but now Dacia became a province under a consular governor with two legions and some auxiliary units. Forts were built to accommodate them, and near the Dacian capital Trajan established *colonia Ulpia Sarmizegethusa*, where an inscription was discovered bearing the name of the first provincial governor, Decimus Terentius Scaurianus, *legatus Augusti pro praetore*.[136] The new province shielded the stretch of the Danube on Dacia's southern border. The Roman victories were marked by three monuments at Adamklissi in southern Romania, a circular *tropaeum* or mausoleum, an altar recording Trajan's first Dacian war, and another circular mausoleum for the second war. Both campaigns were recorded in pictorial detail on the carved reliefs spiralling up Trajan's column in Rome. Trajan took the victory title Dacicus, possibly after the first war.[137]

## Trajan's Empire

During Pompey's eastern campaigns the Nabataean kingdom, centred on Petra, had been made a client kingdom, and had remained so until 106. The territory had become more important given that its neighbours were Syria and Parthia. Trajan took it over, ordering the governor of Syria, Aulus Cornelius Palma, to garrison it.[138] There was no fighting, and the annexation was not necessarily aggressive. Sartre suggests the Nabataean client king Rabbel II had died, and annexation usually followed the death of a client.[139] Trajan reorganised the territory as the new, very large, province of Arabia, comprising the Negev desert, Transjordan and the northern part of modern Arabia, much larger than the Roman province. A legion, probably Trajan's newly created II Traiana, was based at Bostra, perhaps until the Parthian war of 114. The first governor of Arabia, Gaius Claudius Severus, remained in post from 106 through the Parthian wars. The new province gave the Romans better access to the Red Sea and trade routes between Egypt and India, though the Roman navy already assured such contact by patrolling the coasts.

Trajan now spent some years in Rome, where he embarked on a building programme funded by the spoils from Dacia. He had to cut away the southern part of the Quirinal hill to build his Forum and the rows of shops called Trajan's Markets.[140] The complex included a law court and two libraries, one for Latin works and one for Greek. The column recording the Dacian wars stood inside the new Forum. The remains of Trajan's baths are still visible, built over part of Nero's Golden House close to the Viale del Monte Oppio, within sight of the Colosseum. Roads and bridges were built to facilitate communications in Italy, the harbour at Ostia was improved, and building work was carried out at other ports. The *alimenta* scheme that Nerva had established was developed, and in Rome children became eligible for the corn dole to ease the burdens of the poor.

The depopulation and the declining finances of provincial towns required attention. As more of the elite ruling classes became senators, they left their cities and towns to take part in government of the Empire. Finances had declined partly because the elected town and city magistrates squandered corporate resources on ambitious projects which failed, or individual magistrates tried to do better than their predecessors in embellishing their towns and providing entertainments. The affairs of self-governing autonomous communities were not usually directed by provincial governors, and senatorial provinces were usually free of interference by the emperors. Trajan ignored precedent and appointed *curatores* or *correctors* to take over the finances of some towns, Caere in Italy being the first in 113.[141] The correspondence of the Younger Pliny with Trajan makes municipal affairs of Pliny's province of Bithynia the best illustrated of all. He reorganised town and city finances, starting with Prusa (Bursa, Turkey) where money had been spent for not quite legal purposes, and at Nicomedia millions of sesterces had been wasted on two failed attempts to build an aqueduct. Pliny thought that the abandoned stone arches could be finished in brick, and asked Trajan to send an engineer or a specialist in aqueducts.[142] Pliny also reported that the councillors of Apamea would not show their records to him, insisting that their alliance with Rome guaranteed their independence. Trajan replied that Pliny must examine the records 'as my personal wish without prejudice to their privileges'. The autonomy of provincial cities and towns was gradually eroded by instructions issuing directly from Rome.

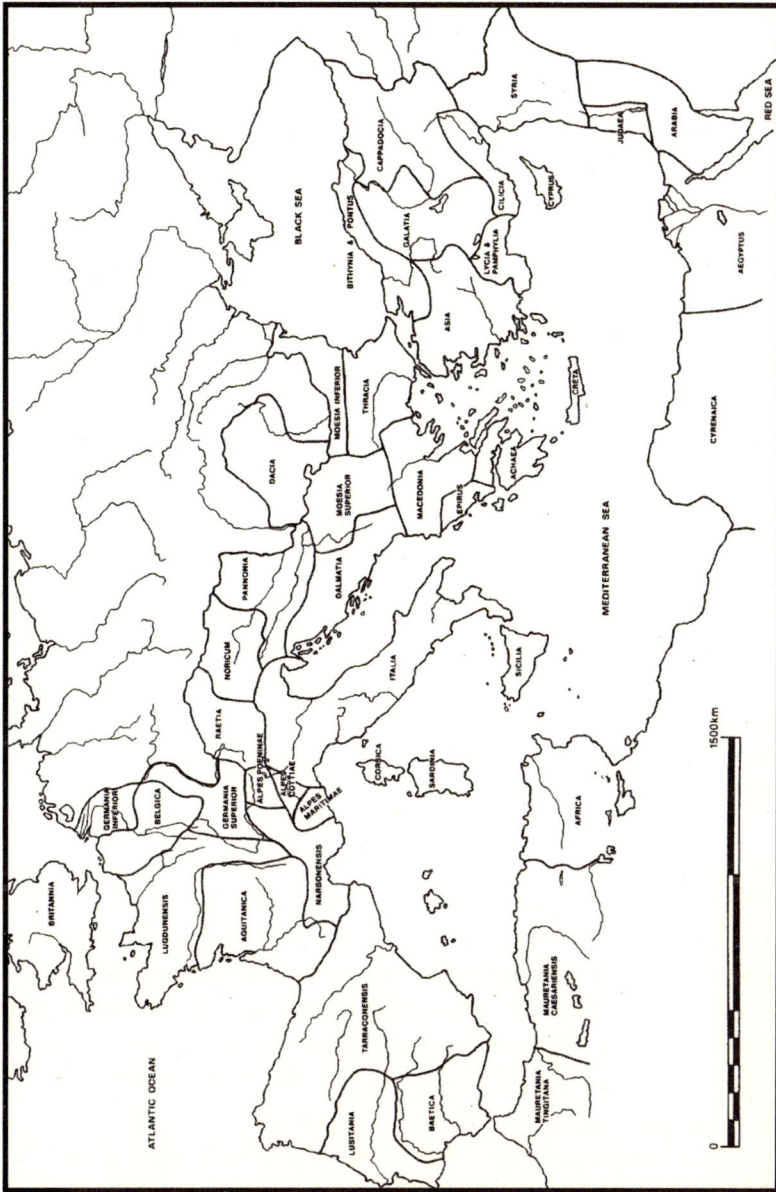

9. The Roman Empire in the second century AD. It reached its greatest extent under the Emperor Trajan (reigned AD 98 to 117) who annexed Dacia on the north side of the Danube, part of Mesopotamia, and the Nabataean kingdom, forming the province of Arabia. Mesopotamia and parts of Dacia were relinquished by Trajan's successor Hadrian. Drawn by Graeme Stobbs.

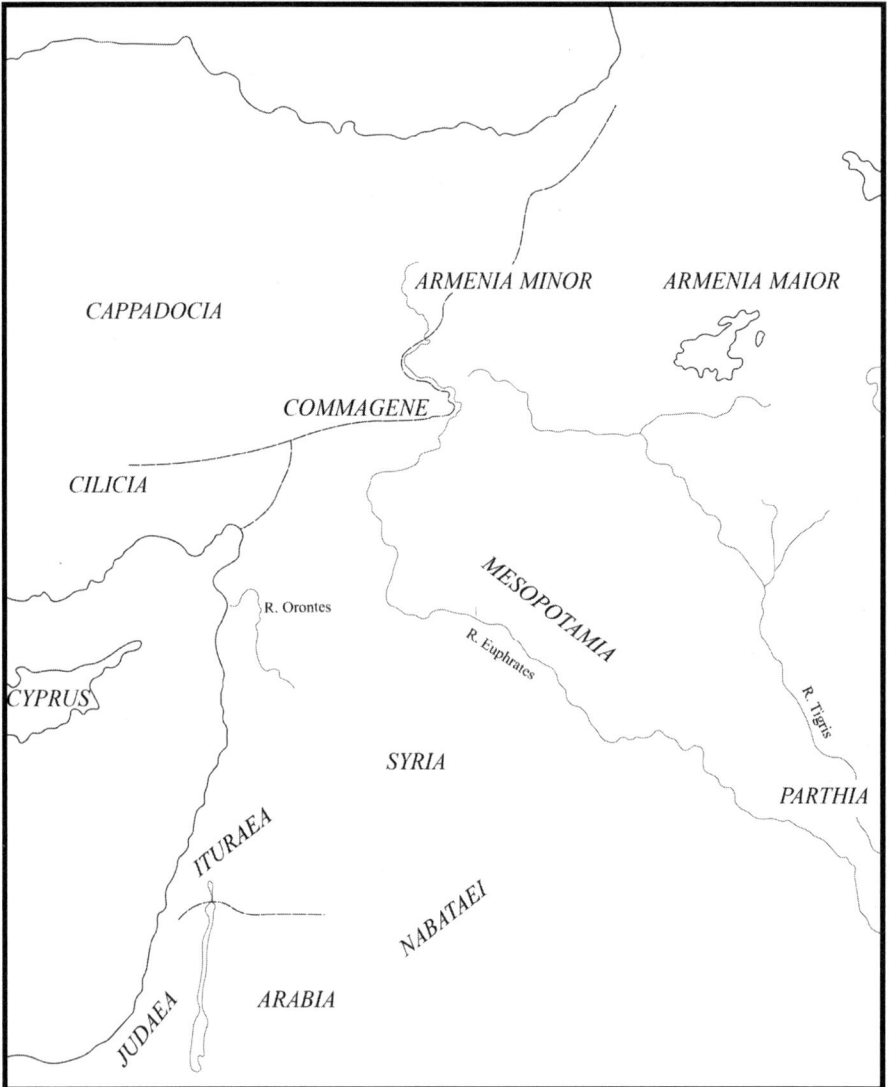

10. Northern regions of the eastern provinces. Commagene belonged to the Syrian kings, but was annexed by Tiberius in AD 17, restored to King Antiochus IV by Caligula who immediately deposed him again, and the country was finally annexed by Vespasian in AD 72 as part of the province of Syria, as was part of Ituraea from 24 BC. Judaea was subdued by Pompey in 63 BC, and organised by his general Gabinius, governor of Syria. Roman procurators were in charge of Judaea until Vespasian made it a province in AD 70. The kingdom of the Nabataei was made into the new province of Arabia under Trajan in AD 106. The Roman made attempts to annex and retain Mesopotamia, under Trajan in AD 114, Lucius Verus in 162 and Severus in 197. None of these conquests survived very long. Redrawn by Isla Jones after Goodman 1997.

## Parthia

The Parthian war was already brewing in 113, when the Parthian King Chosroes removed the Roman nominee from the Armenian throne and installed one of his nephews. It was interpreted as an act of war. Chosroes tried to negotiate. Trajan refused and prepared for war, taking advantage of the internal discord of the Parthians. Though there were several military units already in the east, extra troops were assembled for the campaign, many of them from the Danube provinces. Trajan placed the key province of Syria under Quadratus Bassus, a trusted man who had governed Cappadocia-Galatia for some time. Bithynia-Pontus, formerly governed by senatorial proconsuls, was elevated to an Imperial province with a consular in command, to protect the route from the Danube to the east.[143]

At the end of 113, Trajan set off for the east with the young Hadrian in his entourage, establishing his headquarters at Antioch. In 114 Trajan captured Armenia, and in 115 he overran Mesopotamia, but although it was called a province it was an occupied zone, and that for a very short time. He attacked Parthia in 116, eventually capturing Ctesiphon. The Senate began to plan a triumphal arch to celebrate Trajan's victories, which seemed comparable to those of Alexander because in his despatches Trajan mentioned peoples and places hitherto unknown to the senators, who did not know how to pronounce some of the names.[144]

Trajan's conquests were not secure. Rebellion broke out almost immediately, and Dio says that almost all the soldiers placed in garrisons in the newly annexed provinces were ejected or killed.[145] At Babylon Trajan heard of the uprising in Mesopotamia and sent the Moorish general Lusius Quietus with another commander named Maximus to quell the rebellion. Maximus was killed, but Lusius took the city of Nisibis and burned Edessa, while two other Roman commanders burned Seleucia. Trajan pre-empted any reaction by installing a pro-Roman king, Parthamaspates, on the Parthian throne.[146]

Around this time, there was a great rising of the Jewish population in Cyrenaica, Cyprus, and Egypt. Dio documents the alleged atrocities and the numbers of people killed.[147] Lusius Quietus features once again. He had rendered sterling service in putting down the rebellion in Mesopotamia, commanding his own units of excellent Moorish cavalry. As a reward, in 117 he was made a senator, promoted to suffect consul, and sent to govern Judaea.[148]

Trajan failed to capture the rebellious Hatra, now a ruined site in Iraq. He tried to besiege the city, but the remote site yielded little water or food, and the heat, the sandstorms, and the flies forced the Romans to abandon the siege.[149] By now Trajan was ill. Travelling back to Rome he reached Selinus in Cilicia, where he died, probably from a stroke. His wife Plotina and the Praetorian Prefect Acilius Attianus were with him, but did not immediately announce the death, first informing Hadrian, who was now governor of Syria after Quadratus Bassus was sent to quell trouble in Dacia.

Hadrian was the logical choice as the next emperor, but Trajan had been dilatory in marking him out for the succession and had not formally adopted him. If he had done so, he would have made it much easier for Plotina and Attianus to announce that Trajan was dead and Hadrian was now the emperor, but they had to resort to subterfuge, swearing that Trajan had officially adopted Hadrian on his death bed. Fortunately, the troops in Syria readily accepted Hadrian, who counted his *dies imperii* as 8 August, but it was not an auspicious beginning.

# 10

# From Hadrian to the Antonines and the Development of the Frontiers

Trajan had not indicated that he intended Hadrian to succeed him, and it was Trajan's wife Plotina who signed the letter informing the Senate of Hadrian's adoption. Hadrian wrote to the Senate asking for confirmation of his powers, explaining that the soldiers had already acclaimed him. He asked for divine honours for Trajan, and he prudently doubled the customary donatives to the troops all over the Empire.[1]

Acilius Attianus, Trajan's Praetorian Prefect, had escorted Plotina to Rome bearing Trajan's ashes. He wrote to Hadrian, warning him of opposition, naming names. Baebius Macer, prefect of the city, and the exiled Laberius Maximus were spared, but another exile, Crassus Frugi, was killed. Hadrian denied having anything to do with the demise of Frugi, and he disassociated himself from the execution of four senators. One of them was Lusius Quietus, governor of Judaea, sent home to Mauretania for his brutal put-down of a Jewish rebellion. The other three were Avidius Nigrinus, Palma and Celsus.[2]

The new Emperor was faced with rebellions; the Moors in Mauretania, the Sarmatians on the Danube, the Britons were out of control, and riots broke out in Egypt, Cyrenaica and Judaea.[3] The eastern provinces were dealt with first. Hadrian gave up Trajan's conquests east of the Euphrates and Tigris rivers.[4] Mesopotamia and Armenia, which Trajan had designated as new Roman provinces, were too vast for effective communications, and controlling them called for resources which the Romans did not have, if the northern frontiers were to be protected. Trajan's enterprise has been called fundamentally foolish, and Hadrian's abandonment of them a wise move.[5] Hadrian relieved the Mesopotamians of the tribute levied by Trajan and re-allocated most of the soldiers to other provinces. The Armenians 'were allowed to have their own king', meaning that Hadrian appointed a pro-Roman client king.[6] The Parthian ruler installed by Trajan was moved to Osroene, and Hadrian reverted to the pre-Trajanic borders of the eastern Roman provinces. There would be no trouble for Rome while rivals Chosroes and Vologaeses fought for the Parthian throne. Beyond the frontiers, Hadrian maintained relations with other states, sending gifts to the kings of the Albanians and the Hiberi, whose king Pharasmanes sent gifts in return.[7]

At Antioch Hadrian met Catilius Severus, the new governor of Syria, and then marched for the Danube. Marcius Turbo, who had ended the revolt in Judaea and then extinguished the rebellion in Mauretania, now commanded both banks of the middle Danube, controlling Dacia and Pannonia Inferior, created probably in 106 when Trajan split Pannonia into two provinces.[8] As an equestrian, Turbo would not normally have commanded provincial armies but Hadrian recognised and rewarded ability and loyalty, installing other friends as governors of important provinces. Pompeius Falco, governor of Lower Moesia, also commanded the northern bank of the lower Danube, though the river remained the frontier here, since Hadrian abandoned Trajan's conquests to the east of Dacia. Adjoining the southern borders of Lower Moesia, Aulus Platorius Nepos commanded Thrace.[9] The chronology of these appointments is not established.

Hadrian also gave up control of the Hungarian plain between the southward-flowing Danube and the western side of Dacia, which now formed a bulge north of the middle Danube. Hadrian also removed the superstructure of Trajan's Danube bridge, leaving intact the twenty stone piers built by the architect Apollodorus.[10] If necessary, Roman engineers could build another road using the piers. Dacia was divided into three provinces, all governed by equestrian procurators. Dacia Inferior was designated an unarmed province with no legions. In the north, Dacia Porolissensis was named after its chief town Porolissum, and Trajan's colony at Sarmizegethusa became the capital of Dacia Superior.

Back in Rome, Hadrian cancelled tax debts of nine hundred million sesterces to the treasury (*fiscus*), going back fifteen years.[11] Two marble

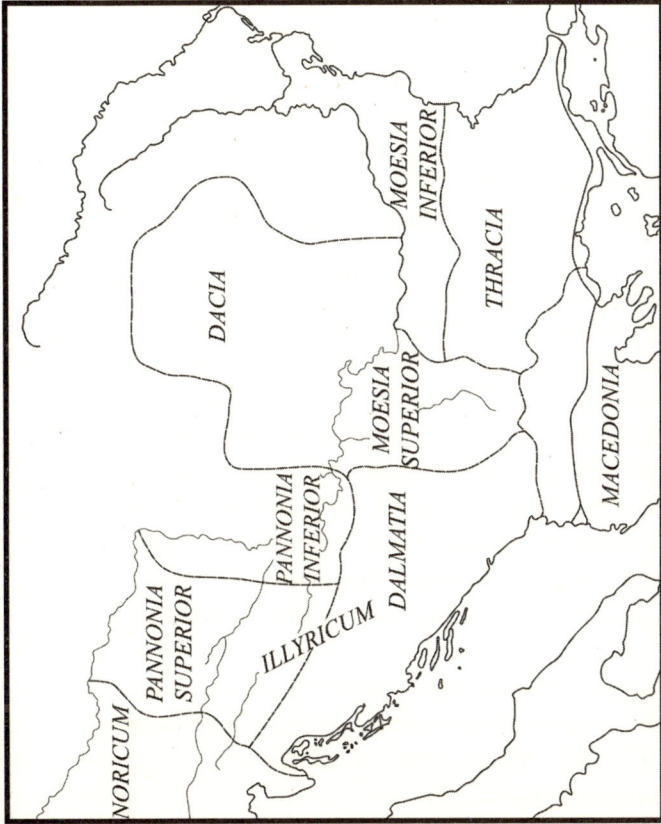

11. The Danube provinces. Illyria became the province of Illyricum under Augustus, but by c.AD 9 it had been divided into Pannonia in the north and Dalmatia in the south, though the name Illyria never went out of use. After AD 106 Trajan annexed Dacia as a new province, which originally extended further west and east, but Hadrian gave up the eastern and western areas, leaving Dacia as a northward facing bulge. Trajan split Pannonia into two, Pannonia Superior and Inferior, and later Caracalla adjusted the boundary between them so that of the four legions each province had two. Moesia with its northern boundary on the Danube was split into two under the Emperor Domitian sometime before 96. Thrace had been a province since AD 46 and Macedonia since 146, shown here with the Via Egnatia running through the northern part, built in stages from two branch roads on the Adriatic coast, eventually reaching Byzantium. Redrawn by Isla Jones after Goodman 1997.

reliefs, now inside the Senate House in Rome, depict men carrying documents, most probably tax records, to be burnt. Another relief is now at Chatsworth House in Derbyshire.

Hadrian rebuilt Agrippa's temple in Rome as a circular domed building added to the façade. It survived as the Pantheon because it was converted to the church of Santa Maria ad Martyres in AD 609.[12] Hadrian's own temple of Venus and Rome was built on a large podium near the Colosseum, but the back-to-back apses visible today were not part of his plan.[13] Another of Hadrian's many buildings is his mausoleum, now the Castel Sant' Angelo and the refuge of the Popes. Hadrian assisted communities across the Empire to build temples and monuments, or built them himself.

## Hadrian's travels and the succession

In 121 Hadrian began his journeys around the Empire, travelling further and faster than any other Emperor.[14] He is portrayed as willing to listen to people, assisting cities, whether or not they were in difficulties, and he provided help after disasters.[15] Gaul was first on Hadrian's list. He built a large aqueduct at Lugdunum (Lyon) and may have built a temple at Condate (Rennes) to supplement the Altar of the Gauls dedicated to the Imperial cult. Hadrian extended its scope to include past emperors. At Alesia, where Julius Caesar defeated Vercingetorix, Hadrian finished the Forum complex begun under Trajan. Hadrian never visited Gaul again, his prime interest being military affairs and defence.[16] Hadrian next visited the German provinces, where he inspected the armies. He travelled on foot or on horseback, not bothering with headgear whatever the climate, and eating the same food as the soldiers, earning the respect of the troops. He made the soldiers feel valued, talking about their lives, attending to their welfare, examining discipline, hygiene, the state of the fort defences and buildings, the cost of the army, the stores, inventories and receipts.[17]

Hadrian visited Raetia, Noricum, and the Lower Rhine, not mentioned by the *Historia Augusta*, which implies that Hadrian went straight from Germany to Britain in 122, where he 'built a wall eighty miles long to separate the barbarians from the Romans'.[18] In 122-123 Hadrian journeyed to Spain, wintering at Tarraco (Tarragona).[19] He improved the facilities at Italica, the ancestral home of the Aelii, and of Trajan's family, the Ulpii. He expanded the town considerably and established roads, installed drainage, and built baths and an amphitheatre. He pondered and finally agreed to the request of the inhabitants to upgrade the *municipium* to a *colonia*, named Colonia Aelia Augusta Italica. Unfortunately, the settlement was liable to landslip, and the inhabited area shrank.[20] Romanization had begun to spread in Spain, and leading men, especially from Baetica, became senators, sharing in the government of the Empire.[21]

From 123 to 125, Hadrian travelled through the province of Asia and the Greek islands, assisting communities financially, and examining the conduct of the governors and procurators.[22] He conferred benefits and new buildings on Athens, some of them listed by Dio.[23] He gave money and an annual corn dole to Athens, which may have been combined with an alimentary system. The same may have applied to Corinth, where a *curator annonae* is attested, and Hadrian also built aqueducts for both cities.[24]

Hadrian was in Rome from 125 to 128, then went to Africa via Sicily, where he climbed Mount Etna to watch the sunrise.[25] The *Historia Augusta* states laconically that Hadrian showed many acts of kindness to the African provinces, without specifying where or how. One of the benefits was purely coincidental, because it rained for the first time in five years.[26] Some African towns and cities were elevated in status. In Africa Proconsularis the *municipium* of Utica was upgraded to a *colonia*, and four other towns now in modern Tunisia were also made *coloniae*, Bulla Regia, Zama Regia, Lares and Thaenae. Bulla Regia was already a *municipium*, but Birley suggests that the other three were probably native settlements.[27] From Hadrian's reign onwards Romans from the African provinces, mostly Africa Proconsularis and Numidia, served in administrative posts in Rome, and became army commanders and provincial governors.

At the end of his African tour Hadrian went to Lambaesis (Lambèse) reviewing the troops in July 128. His speeches were preserved on a long inscription, now fragmented. He praised the soldiers performing in exercises and displays, criticising mildly on occasion, showing that he had watched carefully. One group of men built a stone wall and dug a ditch, and Hadrian pointed out that building in turf blocks of regulation size is much easier than the task the soldiers had set themselves, using heavy stone of unequal shapes and sizes, and yet they accomplished the work in nearly the same time as a turf wall could have been built.[28]

In 130 Hadrian was in Egypt, accompanied by the young Bithynian, Antinous, the love of his life, who drowned in the Nile. An accident, or was he pushed? Antinous became a god. Egyptians believed that drowning in the Nile conferred divinity, but Hadrian would have deified him anyway. A city named Antinoopolis was built near the site of the drowning.[29]

In 131-132 the first signs of unrest broke out in Judaea and in Cappadocia. The revolt in Judaea was the most serious of Hadrian's reign. He had deeply offended the Jews by founding a new city, Aelia Capitolina, on the ruins of Jerusalem, and a temple to Jupiter on the site of the great Jewish temple, destroyed in 70 by Titus.[30] The Romans usually respected religions of other people, but they never even tried to understand Jewish religious beliefs. They underestimated the hatred and the determination of the Jews, under their leader Bar Kochba, who waged a successful guerrilla war, hiding people and supplies in tunnels provided with shafts at intervals to let in air and light. Julius Severus, governor of Britain, was transferred to Judaea. He rounded up small groups whenever possible and hemmed in the rebels, cutting off their food supplies. Judaea was devastated, Dio's estimate of the death toll being 580,000 men killed and an unknown number of casualties from disease and famine.[31] The Jews even now refer to Hadrian in pejorative terms.

On the Danube, the Alani, a tribe from the lands beyond the Caucasus, had attempted to cross into the Roman Empire on more than one occasion. In the 130s they moved towards Cappadocia, where the governor Flavius Arrianus (Arrian) successfully dealt with the threat.[32] Arrian wrote an account of his order of battle against the Alani, called *Acies Contra Alanos*, essential for study of the Roman army.

By 134 Hadrian had returned to Rome. His health was already deteriorating. He designated his successor by adopting Lucius Ceionius Commodus as his son, naming him Lucius Aelius Caesar, but he, too, was ill, his reported symptoms indicating tuberculosis. Early in 138 he died.[33] Now seriously ill himself, Hadrian adopted Titus Aurelius Fulvius Boionius Arrius Antoninus (Antoninus Pius), who in turn adopted two boys, Lucius Aelius Aurelius Commodus, son of Lucius Aelius Caesar, and Antoninus' nephew Marcus Annius Verus (Marcus Aurelius).[34]

Hadrian's aged brother-in-law Lucius Julius Servianus, and this man's grandson Pedanius Fuscus, were eliminated, probably because it was thought that they aimed for the Empire.[35] Shortly before he died, Hadrian wrote the short, brilliant poem, wondering where his soul would go, perhaps to a cold, dark place ('Pallidula, rigida, nudula'). He died probably from heart disease on 10 July 138 at the seaside resort of Baiae.[36] His remains were placed in his mausoleum across the Tiber.

## Frontiers of the Empire

Hadrian clearly had no intention of conquering any more territory. He decided to consolidate and protect what he considered feasible and useful, and so frontiers came into being. It was a momentous U-turn away from continuous conquest. Apart from fighting, it was possible to control peoples outside the Empire by influence, gifts and subsidies, backed up by the immediate presence of the army, and potential reinforcement via the combined military resources of the Empire. The Quadi and Marcomanni, Germanic tribes originally settled around the middle sections of the river Main, moved to Bohemia and Moravia, and the power of their kings, says Tacitus, depended on Roman *auctoritas*, and occasional assistance by Roman armed intervention, and/or money.[37] It was possible to keep the balance among tribes beyond Roman territory of Pannonia and Moesia, because there was no doubt that the emperors could interfere by diplomacy or by armed force.[38] Dio says that Hadrian kept peace with foreign nations because the people beyond the frontiers were aware of the Roman state of preparedness, and received money, so there were no uprisings.[39]

These methods of control and influence were effective, but the addition of physical fortifications and fortified river banks obviated the need for vast manpower resources pinned down near the boundary line. Frontiers were adapted to their local contexts, existing political organisation and social conditions, the geography and geology of the area, and the feasibility of supply lines. It was not possible to devise a uniform frontier strategy to fit all areas. Light defences would serve the purpose in some areas, while others required more robust defences.

The effects of the frontiers have been studied by C. R. Whittaker.[40] The army had been gradually concentrated on the periphery, and this changed the dynamic of the Empire, ending the constant troop movements of previous centuries. As the army became more static, lodged in more permanent bases, the forts and fortresses which were usually built in timber and earth were now built or rebuilt in stone, probably beginning under Trajan. With troops permanently on the edges of the Empire, wealth from the centre also migrated to the periphery with the soldiers, who were unique in receiving regular pay. Everyone else had to earn money from landed estates or by private enterprise, and the remainder of the work force were slaves, earning nothing. The armies formed ready-made corporate and personal markets, not only for food, but pottery, leather, wool, metals, timber, horses, mules, and much more. Production was geared to the needs of

Rome, both at the centre and at the frontiers. In Africa Proconsularis more and more wheat was grown to supply markets in Rome.[41] Egypt was usually considered the prime producer of grain, but from the third century BC the African provinces supplied as much wheat as Sicily and Spain combined.[42] In Nero's reign Egypt provided grain for one third of the year, while Africa provided the other two-thirds.[43] It is not certain how the resources of the Empire were gathered and supplied to the armies, but long-distance trade was a feature of normal provincial and military life, especially when bringing foodstuffs and other items that could not be grown or produced in certain provinces. Linked to army supply in northern Britain, archaeological evidence shows that grain production increased in Northumberland and East Lothian, and supply of pottery from Gaul tailed off as Britain became more self-sufficient in pottery production.[44]

Civilian settlements grew up around long-term military installations, usually called *vici* at forts and *canabae* at legionary fortresses. Camp followers, always swept away by good Republican generals, also became static. Soldiers were forbidden to marry until the reign of Severus, but unofficial families no doubt lived in the civil settlements round the forts. Collection and transport of the *annona* for army rations was probably undertaken by men furnished with army contracts, but there were private business opportunities for merchants (*negotiatores*) who could afford the taxes on imports in supplying the immediate wants of soldiers, and the people of the civilian *vici* and *canabae*.

Hadrian established running barriers in Germany, Raetia, Britain and Africa. These were part of Hadrian's policy, not forced on him because of military disasters, and they did not signify a change from offensive to purely defensive strategy. The frontiers could never be totally impenetrable and were not intended to close off trans-frontier military expeditions, trading activities or relations with the nations and tribes outside the barriers. The frontiers could be moved further out if necessary, as in Antoninus Pius' advance into Scotland and his readjustment in Germany. Some modern scholars think that after Hadrian the Romans fell into a paralysing inertia, unable to think of any other methods of protecting the Empire. This assumes that it is known precisely what the frontiers were intended to do at different times and does not wholly explain why successive emperors retained and repaired the running barriers. Were all emperors from Hadrian to Honorius incapable of thinking outside the box?

## Germany and Raetia

In the *Historia Augusta*, a passage not related to Germany states that Hadrian shut out the tribesmen by high stakes driven into the ground and fastened together in the manner of a palisade.[45] This description fits well with the palisade which Hadrian established on the land frontier of Germania Superior, starting from the Rhine and following the Flavian line enclosing the fertile land of the Taunus-Wetterau region, and then running towards the Danube. Archaeological excavations have revealed evidence of the palisade in several locations in Germany, and dendrochronological studies, a method of dating from tree-ring growth, show that repairs were carried out using new timber. More important, these studies have also shown that the earliest timbers were felled during the winter of 119 to the summer of 120.[46] The timber would need to mature, so perhaps from 119-120 stocks were built up in preparation for building work, which may have already begun by the time Hadrian arrived in 121.

In the neighbouring province of Raetia the frontier was continuous, but parts of it consisted of a flimsy timber fence, labelled the Flechtwerkzaun by archaeologists. Confusingly, the fence sometimes pre-dates the palisade and sometimes replaces it. The western end of the Raetian frontier was not joined with the eastern end of the German palisade until the reign of Antoninus Pius.

The palisade in Germany was protected by a ditch in front of it. Felling timber to build the palisade enabled the Romans to clear the area in front of the ditch, allowing for surveillance. A short distance behind the palisade there were freestanding timber watchtowers, rebuilt more than once, first in timber and later in stone. Gaps have been discovered in the palisade, usually with two large timber posts at each side of the gap and a watchtower set back from it. This probably allowed for patrols to survey the areas beyond the frontier.

There were also small forts (Kleinkastelle in German), close to the frontier but not attached to it. These Kleinkastelle were probably manned by soldiers from the auxiliary forts which were established roughly two kilometres behind the frontier line, and the legions were even more distant. In Raetia there were small forts near the palisade, but auxiliary bases were situated much further back.

Besides the legions and auxiliaries in Germany, but not attested in Raetia, there were also units called *numeri*, which simply means 'units', so the term national *numeri* has been coined to indicate units recruited from tribesmen. *Numeri* were stationed in small forts in the area of the Odenwald, running from Worth on the river Main to the river Neckar at Wimpfen, facing broken hill country that the *numeri* probably patrolled. Inscriptions show that several Odenwald forts were occupied by units of Brittones, but the date when tribesmen were first taken from Britain is not definitely known.[47] The 0.6 ha. Odenwald fort at Hesselbach, established by 100 or earlier, has become the type-site for the *numerus* forts, but *numeri* and their forts were not always the same size. Hesselbach possessed a headquarters building and all the other appurtenances of auxiliary forts, with a commander's house, barracks, storerooms and so on.[48]

## Britain and Hadrian's Wall

According to the *Historia Augusta*, on Hadrian's accession the Britons could not be kept under control.[49] There may have been war in Britain in 118, and another indication derives from Cornelius Fronto's letter consoling Marcus Aurelius for the losses in the Parthian war by reminding him of worse losses under Hadrian in Britain and Judaea.[50] Epigraphic evidence from other provinces attests that Titus Pontius Sabinus led an expedition to Britain bringing vexillations from three legions, 3,000 men in total, and during a war in Britain, Gaius Julius Karus received military decorations.[51]

Pompeius Falco governed Britain until July 122, and he may have been sent direct from Moesia as early as 118 to quell the postulated British revolt. Though various inscriptions record Falco's career, none mention Britain, and the relevant sections of Dio's narrative are lost.[52] Hadrian probably decided to build his wall in Britain even before the war of 118 ended. In 1966, C. E. Stevens suggested that Falco may have started to quarry stone for the new frontier before Hadrian visited Britain.[53] When Stevens wrote, it was not known that trees had been felled in Germany in 119-120, which reinforces his suggestion.[54]

There had been lines of demarcation in Britain before Hadrian's visit in 122, but the concept of a permanent halt behind a pre-Hadrianic fortified line is questionable.[55] During Trajan's Danube wars the Roman forts in southern Scotland were abandoned and the road now called the Stanegate, meaning 'stone street', marked the most northerly occupied zone. Originally thought to connect Carlisle with Corbridge, new evidence suggests that the Stanegate ran from the Solway to the Tyne. The road was provided with forts and fortlets but this does not mean that it was a permanent or even temporary frontier.[56]

The building of the stone frontier indicates that Hadrian never considered any further advance in Britain. Stone may have been used because northern Britain was not densely forested, and a wooden palisade would have been difficult to establish in the stony central sector, where the north-facing Whin Sill runs north of the Stanegate across the Pennines, then turns north, ultimately providing foundations for Bamburgh castle. A north-facing cliff is the ideal place to draw the line.

Nineteenth-century scholars thought that Septimius Severus built the stone wall. Waging war in Scotland from 208 to 211, Severus repaired Hadrian's Wall so thoroughly that there was some justification for attributing it to him. It was thought that Hadrian was responsible for the Vallum, the label invented by the historian Bede for the massive ditch south of the stone wall. To the Romans the term *vallum* referred to the entire frontier system. When inscriptions were discovered recording building work under Platorius Nepos, attested as Hadrian's governor of Britain, the term Severus' Wall was discarded.[57]

The new frontier comprised a ditch north of the stone wall, except where the cliffs made it unnecessary, and an even deeper and wider ditch (the Vallum) to the south, with raised banks of earth on either side of it. The stone wall was to be ten Roman feet wide, later reduced to eight feet, with integral watchtowers and small forts spaced roughly every Roman mile, respectively labelled turrets and milecastles. The auxiliary forts of the Stanegate were probably intended to support these installations, but quite soon after building began, the so-called 'fort decision' was made, to build forts on Hadrian's Wall itself. This involved demolition of work already done to make way for the forts. On the Stanegate some forts were retained, so not all the existing garrisons were moved further north.[58] Hadrian's Wall was further protected by outpost forts along the two main northward routes.

The frontier line would run where geology and geography dictated, and it is possible that it cut across tribal lands of the Brigantes. At Birrens, one of the outpost forts, a legionary called Amandus set up a dedication to the goddess Brigantia, which suggests, but does not prove, that some Brigantes lived outside the frontier.[59] This raises another question: was free passage allowed across the frontier, or was there no unauthorized access into and out of the province? On a river frontier, movement of people was restricted to the bridges, where people crossing from either side could be searched for weapons and their goods could be inspected and taxed. Across the Empire customs dues (*portoria*) were levied on goods inwards and outwards, and there were tolls for using roads, and sometimes fees for permits as well. It is possible that on Hadrian's Wall there were similar restricted access routes serving as inspection and taxation points. Remains of a gate, straddling the wall and projecting north of it, were found at Portgate, near the modern roundabout north of Corbridge, where the A68 crosses the B6318.[60] Not much is known about this gate, but at the Knag Burn, in the valley east of Housesteads fort, there was another gate, inserted in the stone wall in the fourth century. It had a single passageway flanked by guardhouses, and the passage had two gates, one on the north side and one on the south, so it is envisaged that travellers could be let in, both gates or just the exit closed, so that they could be searched and questioned, while the animals, vehicles and goods could be examined and the relevant fees charged.[61] On Hadrian's Wall it was probably the soldiers who performed these tasks and kept the records, but it was an obvious opportunity for extortion even if tax officials were present.

To enable people to cross the Vallum, causeways with gates were provided opposite the forts but not at all the milecastles. It is still not clear whether civilian traffic was allowed to use existing routes through the Wall.[62]

## Africa

The provinces of North Africa stretched from the Atlantic to Egypt, the most westerly being Mauretania Tingitana, where settlement was concentrated near the Atlantic coast, then Mauretania Caesariensis with settlements in a wide belt along the Mediterranean coast. Numidia, bordering on Caesariensis and straddling the borders of modern Algeria and Tunisia, was more densely populated, and housed the single African legion, III Augusta, at Ammaedara (Haidra in Tunisia). It moved to Theveste (Tebessa in Algeria) in 75, then under Hadrian to Lambaesis (Lambèse, Algeria). Africa Proconsularis was situated further east between Numidia and Egypt.

Tingitana and Caesariensis were bounded on the south by the Atlas Mountains and the desert. In Numidia, covering a much smaller area than the two Mauretanias, the Aurès mountains were incorporated in the province. All the provinces were open to the south. This vast stretch of North African territory was very lightly manned, with only one legion based in Numidia and auxiliary units elsewhere, minuscule compared to the large numbers of auxiliary units and three legions in the much smaller area of Britain.

Until the reigns of Vespasian and Trajan there was little advance in the African provinces. Sextius Sentius Caecilianus redefined boundaries under Vespasian and brought order to the two Mauretanian provinces.[63] Trajan pushed the frontiers of the provinces southwards, building new forts, which Hadrian augmented.[64] He created a series of running barriers in eastern Mauretania Caesariensis and Numidia, but the sections were not joined up. The classic work on this is *Fossatum Africae* published in 1949 by J. Baradez (*fossa* means ditch), subsequently augmented by other archaeologists. Cumulative evidence showed that the barriers were built usually of mud bricks, occasionally in stone, and they generally followed the same pattern, with a ditch in front of the wall and a causeway opposite the gateways built at roughly one-mile intervals. The gates had a single passage, gated front and rear, with guard posts on each side. There was usually a tower between pairs of gates, sometimes freestanding in front of or behind the wall, and sometimes attached to it. The towers were presumably used to watch for movement in front of and behind the barrier. On some sectors there were small forts, irregularly spaced. The longest stretch of wall, equipped with a ditch, small forts and towers, was in Caesariensis, running for ninety miles in a roughly oval shape, not quite enclosing the Hodna mountains to the north-west of Lambaesis in Numidia (Lambèse, Algeria).[65] The barriers were placed where seasonal transhumance routes led through cultivated lands, which could potentially disrupt relations between pastoralists and agriculturalists. The running barriers of the African provinces were therefore adapted to the special circumstances of the people and their lifestyles, aimed at internal peacekeeping rather than external defence.

Where the provinces were open to the south, patrols would keep order to a certain extent, and for this the units of *numeri* would serve the purpose, sparing the auxiliary troops for other purposes, just as the *numeri* of Germany supplemented the auxiliaries. In the western sector of Mauretania Caesariensis there was a place called Numerus Syrorum, implying the presence of Syrians, probably archers (*sagittarii*). A *numerus Palmyrenorum* is known from Numidia, possibly raised by Hadrian.[66] External defence in some provinces did not always require large numbers of auxiliaries in closely spaced forts, so once again, defence of the African provinces was adapted to circumstances.

### Beyond the frontiers

There had always been interaction between Romans and the people outside the boundaries. Relations with the tribes, especially beyond the northern frontiers, were not always on a war footing or even inimical, and Hadrian was not in favour of war, which swallowed reserves of manpower and money whether successful or not. His new frontiers made the Roman world more secure, but they were not designed to withstand large-scale invasion of any part of the Empire. From Rome's earliest years most of the trouble with tribesmen on the move was caused by their need for land, and a determination to take it if it was not freely offered.

Subsidies became an effective method of pre-empting incursions into the Empire. If the Romans supplied food as part of the regular subsidies, the primary motives for invading the Empire in a search for food and lands could be removed. The arrangements also helped to keep the peace among the tribes outside the Empire. A tribal leader was only as strong as own right arm, but with Roman backing he could survive longer. If a strong chief was amenable to Roman influence, he could be subsidised in various ways, so that he could then distribute gifts among his people in return for keeping them and his neighbours in order. Gifts and subsidies were already in place when Hadrian became Emperor, and he continued the practice.[67] At the outset of his reign, he investigated the case of the Roxolani of the Danube zone, who complained that the subsidy, *stipendium*, the same word used for the soldiers' pay, had been reduced. It is not stated that Hadrian increased the payment, but he made peace, which suggests that the amounts had been properly negotiated and promises made for the future, presumably on both sides.[68]

The subsidy arrangements benefited the Romans as well. In return for Roman support, a tribal ruler might be asked to contribute warriors if campaigns were to be fought near his area, or better still, part of the agreement would be to send regular batches of recruits for the Roman army, which absorbed the energies of tribesmen who just wanted to fight. When the Brittones were sent to serve in the *numeri* of Germany, their absence may have reduced the potential for skirmishes in northern England and southern Scotland.

## Antoninus Pius

The most frequently quoted reason why Antoninus was given the name Pius derives from his opposition to senators who were determined to prevent the deification of Hadrian. Antoninus argued that it would be a short step from refusing deification to declaring Hadrian an enemy of the state, followed by annulment of all his acts. That would mean that Antoninus' adoption would be annulled, and he would not be Emperor.[69]

There was a dearth of information on the reign of Pius even in antiquity. The epitome of Dio's seventieth book begins with the avowal that 'the account of Antoninus Pius is not found in the copies of Dio probably because the books have met with some accident,' revealing that some of Dio's work was already lost in the later Roman era.[70] Pius' reign is perceived as a golden age, but he inherited peace and security from Hadrian. The golden glow of Pius' reign shines even more brightly in the darkness of later history, when Rome was involved in serious long-term wars on the frontiers caused by the upheavals among the people beyond them.

Total peace over the whole Empire was never possible, and there was some fighting in Pius' reign, but few details in the sources. Pius' few wars were fought via legates, and he retained Hadrian's army commanders and administrative officials.[71] Trouble with the Mauri in Mauretania began probably in 145 and rumbled on for some time, and since the only troops in Tingitana and Caesariensis were auxiliaries, reinforcements had to be brought in from other provinces. Pius' legates forced the Mauritanians to make peace. Other wars included the suppression of the Germans. In Dacia Inferior, trouble erupted for unknown reasons. Legionaries were sent in, anomalously commanded by the equestrian Marcius Turbo, who was upgraded for the purpose to *pro legato*, acting on behalf of what should have been a senatorial legate.[72] Pius' commanders also suppressed rebellions in Achaea and Egypt, and stopped the advance of the Alani, already known in Hadrian's reign.[73]

## Germany and Raetia

Pius moved Hadrian's Odenwald frontier a short distance eastwards, building a new fortified line on the Hadrianic pattern, with the palisade running in a more or less straight line from Miltenberg on the Main to Welzheim and Lorch. The frontier crossed into Raetia, heading north-east to join the Danube south-west of modern Regensburg. The Antonine arrangements finally rationalised the German-Raetian frontier and survived until the invasions of the mid-third century. Probably in the late second century the Raetian palisade was replaced by a stone wall.

The eastward advance was not a territorial conquest, nor a response to trouble. The newly enclosed lands were probably already influenced by the Romans, possibly patrolled from the units on the Hadrianic frontier. The land was fertile, so there would be economic advantages in taking it in.[74] The new forts of the Antonine frontier, called the Outer *Limes* to distinguish it from the Odenwald, were more widely spaced and most if not all of them were occupied by the units from the old frontier. Where routes required supervision, there were smaller forts and towers, stone-built from the beginning, since timber towers have short lives. An element not found on the first frontier is the so-called Pfahlgraben, a rampart of turf and earth accompanied by a ditch, running along the inside of the palisade. It may belong to the insecure era of the Danube wars under Marcus Aurelius.

## Britain

Pius' reasons for a northward advance in Britain, so soon after Hadrian's Wall had been established, may have been a war. The Greek author Pausanias says that although Antoninus never willingly made war, he did so when necessary. Pausanias adds that the Brigantes in Britain were deprived of territory because they had invaded the Genounian district, where the people were subject to Rome.[75] The Genounian district is unknown, but it is assumed that the fighting was in the territory beyond Hadrian's Wall.

Lollius Urbicus was sent to Britain probably in 139. Several inscriptions document his building activities in northern Britain and the *Historia Augusta* informs us that Pius' legate Urbicus defeated the Britons and built another wall of turf (*murus caespiticus*), without saying where it was.[76] By 142, an inscription and several coins show that Pius, in his third consulship and with tribunician power for the fifth time, had been saluted as Imperator for the second time.[77] This reinforces the suggestion that there had been serious trouble in Britain, and a victory was won by Lollius Urbicus. In 143 a coin was issued from the Roman mint portraying the god Mars and the legend MARTI ULTORI, to Mars the Avenger. There is no proof that this concerns Britons, since Pius is credited with crushing the Germans, Dacians and other tribes, but the date is significant, exactly one hundred years after the invasion of Britain under Claudius.[78] The *Historia Augusta* notes that some Britons were removed to distant parts (*summotis barbaris ducto*).[79] For previous generations of scholars, the earliest known inscriptions attesting the *numeri Brittonum* on the German frontier dated to the reign of Pius, so it was thought that Britons must have been sent to man the new Antonine Outer *limes*. Later excavations showed that Brittones had been stationed on the Odenwald, but it is possible that in the 140s Pius sent some Britons to Germany to fill gaps in the British units.

Since Pius would be the first to admit to a lack of military experience, he probably took advice from military men who knew Britain before deciding to build a new frontier across the forty-mile gap between the rivers Forth and Clyde, half the length of the Hadrianic frontier. It was not feasible to keep both frontiers in full operation, so the northward advance involved partial abandonment of Hadrian's Wall. Birley argues that it would not have been abandoned if it had proved entirely satisfactory, but governors of Britain could not make it work. John Gillam concluded that Hadrian's Wall was a tactical success but a strategic failure, because it was in the wrong place to facilitate control of the northern tribes.[80] Hadrian's frontier was not left entirely without troops. There is some evidence that the forts at Chesters, Benwell and Birdoswald were still occupied.[81] The forts were not slighted, but the mounds flanking the Vallum were cut at intervals, and gates were removed from the causeways and milecastles. Auxiliary units in the Pennines were probably redistributed, but it is not possible to chart their movements, or to pinpoint all the units which went north to the new frontier

Lollius Urbicus was probably responsible for the planning and the first building work on the Antonine Wall, but he probably left Britain in 142 or at latest 143, and after his departure little is known of successive governors. Gnaeus Julius Verus is attested as governor in February 158, named on a diploma found at Ravenglass, recording discharge of troops.[82]

The Antonine Wall ran from Old Kilpatrick on the north bank of the Clyde, giving the Romans control of the estuary, to Carriden on the south side of the Firth of Forth. This fort was not attached to the frontier, and there is no evidence that the frontier extended to the east coast. A ditch was dug to the north, wider than the northern ditch of Hadrian's Wall and further away from the frontier line, with a mound of earth on the northern lip of the ditch. There was no ditch to the south, comparable to the Vallum of the Hadrianic frontier, but around the annexes attached to the sides of the forts there was a rampart of turf and an outer ditch. Some annexes contained timber buildings, and probably housed animals, vehicles and equipment. There were also smaller forts on the Antonine Wall, also surrounded by one or two ditches. Other components of the Antonine Wall were the so-called enclosures, defended by a rampart and ditch, and expansions, the latter usually in pairs, founded on square stone bases with the turf superstructure integrated with the turf-built frontier. They were most likely watchtowers, possibly also used for signalling.[83] The Antonine frontier system was supported by forts in the hinterland. Forts at Cramond and Inveresk protected harbours, and in the Lowlands occupation was similar to the Agricolan pattern, except that Agricola or his successor preferred to rely on a series of large forts whereas the Antonine occupation relied on a denser distribution of smaller forts.

The forts of the Antonine frontier were built in turf, except for Castlecary and Balmuildy, built in stone. Balmuildy, built under Urbicus, was equipped with projecting stone wing-walls, suggesting that it may have been planned to build the whole frontier in stone. It was quicker to build with turf, which was readily available, unlike stone which had to be quarried and transported. The soldiers would be assigned to build a particular sector of the turf frontier, and at both ends of the sector elaborate stone inscriptions, known as distance slabs, were set up recording which troops had built the particular stretch. The lack of weathering of the texts and relief sculptures shows that they were deliberately buried when the Romans withdrew from the Antonine frontier. The inscriptions name the units which built the Antonine Wall, all of II Augusta, detachments of VI Victrix and XX Valeria Victrix, and some auxiliary units.[84] Several construction camps, presumably housing the builders, have been discovered. A novel feature of the Antonine Wall was a road south of the frontier line, entering and leaving the forts via their west and east gates, with a supplementary by-pass route skirting the forts.[85]

The date of the withdrawal from the Antonine frontier in Scotland, and the reasons for it, have exercised generations of scholars. At one time it was thought that it had been abandoned and reoccupied twice after it was first built. The first phase was thought to have ended between155 and 158, tying in with a postulated war in Britain in the 150s, for which there is hardly any evidence. Pausanias' reference to troublesome Brigantes, already mentioned in connection with Lollius Urbicus, is not firmly dated, so it was converted into a war in the 150s.[86] Tenuous in the extreme, on the reverse of a bronze coin of 154/155 the personification of Britannia is shown, seated on a rock, with her bowed head supported on her right hand.[87] It was interpreted as Britannia subdued and defeated, despite the fact that the Romans usually made it quite clear in words as well as pictures that they had defeated a tribe or nation.[88] Inscriptions from Birrens, an outpost fort of Hadrian's Wall in south-west Scotland, and from Brough-on-Noe in Derbyshire, attest rebuilding under Julius Verus.[89] In association with signs of burning, this evidence was taken as destruction by Britons. This need not be so, since rebuilding work often involved burning to clear and level the site.

The postulated war of the 150s in Britain now seems like smoke without fire, which is ironic, considering that if it could be shown that there *was* such a war, somewhere between the two walls, it would support the more recent proposition that the Romans began to withdraw from the Antonine Wall, forever, in 158. An inscription found in 1751, dated to 158, reveals that repairs had started on Hadrian's Wall.[90] Nick Hodgson has shown that it was the curtain wall that was undergoing rebuilding, implying that Hadrian's frontier was being recommissioned.[91] This supports Hodgson's earlier conclusion that there was only a single, uninterrupted, occupation of the Antonine Wall.[92] The Roman evacuation of the Antonine frontier and Lowland Scotland was a gradual affair, ending in the mid-160s, but it was Pius who ordered the abandonment of his conquest.[93]

The reoccupation of Hadrian's Wall included some refinements which had been learned in building the turf wall of the Antonine frontier. The problem of accumulation of rainwater that had probably affected the stone wall was solved on the Antonine Wall by the incorporation of drainage channels on a cobble foundation to let water flow through the turf rampart. When Hadrian's Wall was reoccupied, the eastern sector, originally built of turf, was rebuilt in stone, incorporating drainage channels.[94] Communications along the Antonine Wall were facilitated by a road accompanying the frontier, the Military Way, a modern term. A similar road, also called the Military Way, was built when Hadrian's Wall was put back into commission. It is to be distinguished from the modern Military Road, alias the B6318, originally built by General Wade to facilitate troop movements. The lack of such a route was realised in 1745, when English troops were moving from Newcastle against the Pretender at Carlisle. Parts of Hadrian's Wall were used as foundations, and the modern B6318 now seals these sections of the wall.

### The provinces and diplomatic relations under Pius

According to the *Historia Augusta* Pius never made any decisions about the provinces or any matter without first consulting his friends, presumably meaning his *consilium*.[95] Unfortunately, the *Historia Augusta* contains scarcely any other information about the provinces. Pius limited the activities of his procurators in exacting tribute, so as to keep their demands within reason, and he was never pleased if tribute became onerous for provincials. Pius took note of complaints about his procurators, who were made to provide accounts of their activities if they exceeded the limits.[96] If anyone was convicted for extortion, Pius allowed the children of the guilty men to keep their estates, provided that they returned to the provincials what had been purloined.[97] Like all good emperors, Pius assisted cities and settlements where disasters of one kind or another had occurred. He helped to rebuild Narbonne, Antioch and Carthage after fire damage, restored cities in Asia and on Rhodes after earthquakes, and assisted the people of Arabia after a plague.

The *Historia Augusta* briefly describes Pius' extensive arrangements with a variety of nations and tribes, mostly outside the north-eastern and eastern parts of the Empire.[98] Hadrian had exchanged gifts with Pharasmanes, king of the Hiberi of the Transcaucasus, but the king had snubbed his invitation to visit Rome.[99] Under Pius, Pharasmanes did come to Rome, a diplomatic success, but it is not known if any agreements were made. Other kings were assisted by Pius, especially around the Black Sea area, where Rome obtained wheat from what is now south Russia.[100] On the eastern shore of the Black Sea Pius installed Pacorus as king of the Lazi, and he sent troops to the aid of the city of Olbia on the modern river Bug in south-west Russia, against the Tauroscythians, who were subdued and made to give hostages to the city. He settled a dispute between a Roman *curator* and Tiberius Julius Rhoemetalces, a Roman citizen and ruler of the Bosporan kingdom on the eastern side of the Crimea. It is not explained what the dispute was about. Pius restored Abgarus to his kingdom of Osroene bordering the eastern side of the Euphrates. By the reign of Marcus Aurelius the ruler was Mannus, still pro-Roman and therefore ejected by the Parthians. It was important to the Romans to control Osroene via pro-Roman kings, just as it was important to place pro-Roman kings over Armenia, which also involved protecting them from Parthia, and monitoring Parthian intentions. Allegedly by means of a letter, Pius persuaded the Parthian King Vologaeses not to attack Armenia.[101] It was not quite as simple as this, since Pius also sent troops to the east. An inscription records that in Pius' reign, Lucius Neratius Proculus was made commander of several troop detachments in Syria for a Parthian war.[102] Coins issued in 143 in Rome with the legend REX ARMENIIS DATUS show that Pius chose a king for Armenia, but the *Historia Augusta* merely says that Antoninus 'settled the pleas of various kings', which may have included the king of Armenia.[103] Similar coins were issued recording Pius' choice of a king for the Quadi of the middle Danube, who remained quiet for two decades, then joined the Marcomanni in Marcus Aurelius' reign.

While Pius won victories via his legates, and authorized and directed the above diplomacy, he never left Rome, except to visit parts of Italy.

He died in 161, and his reign was the last predominantly peaceful era for Rome and the provinces, before everything started to go wrong.

## Marcus Aurelius and Lucius Verus

Marcus Aurelius was trained for the succession since early youth. He and Lucius Aurelius Verus Commodus (Lucius Verus) had been adopted by Pius when Marcus was sixteen and Lucius about eight. Marcus was betrothed to Pius' daughter Faustina and married her in 145. They were to have many children, but ultimately only one boy survived, Commodus, born in 161. Aged seventeen, Marcus was made Caesar in 139, junior emperor and next in line to the Augustus, and entered his first consulship in 140 with Pius as colleague, and held his second consulship in 145, when he was granted tribunician power, and proconsular power outside the city of Rome and Italy, which completed his powers as heir to Pius.[104] As soon as he became Emperor, Marcus took the name Antoninus and insisted on sharing power with his adoptive brother Lucius Verus.[105] The formalities were observed in the Senate, and Marcus and Verus visited the Praetorian camp, promising 20,000 sesterces to each of the soldiers, and more to the officers.[106]

Marcus was studious and devoted to philosophy.[107] Lucius Verus acquired a reputation, probably not wholly deserved, as a time-waster, devoted to gambling and debauchery. Hadrian had been the last emperor to serve in the army, to govern a province, and to seek knowledge of the Roman world outside Italy, but neither Marcus nor Verus had experience of any of these things. Their joint reign began with a flood of the river Tiber. Houses were destroyed and the situation was compounded by food shortages, which the two Emperors did their best to relieve.[108] More seriously, wars were threatening in different parts of the Empire, the Parthians under Vologaeses threatened Syria, the Chatti invaded Germany and Raetia, and Aufidius Victorinus was sent against them.

Sextus Calpurnius Agricola was sent against the Britons to relieve Statius Priscus, who was called to fight in Armenia.[109] Calpurnius Agricola is well known in Britain from building inscriptions from forts near Hadrian's Wall and further south. There was some fighting, probably in south-west Scotland. In Galloway, home of the Novantae, and in Annandale and Nithsdale, there is not the slightest archaeological evidence from any period for Romanization. The distribution of the Roman outpost forts north of Hadrian's Wall, and the extension of the frontier via watchtowers down the Cumbrian coast, suggest that there was always a perceived threat from this area.

### The wars in the east

When Pius was dying he spoke deliriously of kings with whom he was angry, most likely rulers of states on Rome's eastern borders.[110] The *Historia Augusta* makes it clear that while Pius had successfully deterred Vologaeses from his designs on Armenia, the Parthian king had not relinquished war on the Romans, and he began it under Marcus Aurelius.[111] Vologaeses probably saw his chance to gain ground in Armenia while the inexperienced Emperors Marcus and Verus established themselves. In 161 he installed Pacorus, a member of the Parthian royal house, as king of Armenia. The governor of Cappadocia, Marcus Sedatius Severianus, reacted swiftly, marched out of his province and was immediately surrounded by the Parthians at Elegeia, where he and his entire legion were wiped out.[112] The legion is not named, but it was possibly IX Hispana, last heard of in Britain 108 building a gate at York, and then possibly transferred to the Rhine and after that to the east.[113] After Severianus' disaster, there was no hope of settling affairs in the east by diplomatic means. Rome went to war.

Wars between Rome and Parthia nearly always involved the kingdom of Armenia, and this war of Marcus and Verus was labelled *bellum Armeniacum et Parthicum*. It was fought in two main theatres. Marcus remained in Rome, placing his colleague Lucius Verus in overall command, but the *Historia Augusta* credits Marcus with the strategy and planning of the war while Lucius did everything via legates.[114] Statius Priscus, mentioned above, was sent from Britain to command in Armenia, so it would take some time for him to get there.[115] Troops were placed in Cappadocia, the key to control of Armenia, and Statius captured the Armenian capital Artaxata in 163. He destroyed it and built and garrisoned another city, called in Greek New City, closer to the borders of Roman territory. The title Armeniacus was bestowed on both emperors, which Marcus initially refused, having done nothing to earn it.[116] The victory enabled Lucius Verus to install the pro-Roman Soaemus or Sohaemus, a Roman citizen and a senator, on the Armenian throne in 164. Soaemus' portrait appears on coins with the legend REX ARMENIIS DATUS.[117] The *Historia Augusta* acknowledges the Armenian war in one short paragraph and documents the Parthian war hardly at all. Dio is more informative, but fragmentary. When Vologaeses took control of Armenia via Pacorus, he then aimed for Syria and defeated the governor Attidius Cornelianus, possibly in 162.[118]

The fighting in Armenia and against the Parthians involved taking one legion from Germania Inferior, Pannonia Inferior and Moesia Inferior, plus legionary detachments and presumably auxiliary troops. Shunting troops along from one frontier to another was a predominant feature of wars from this time onwards. The consequent weakening of a more peaceful frontier was noticed by the tribes beyond, who were by no means ignorant and were sufficiently observant to grasp the chances of coming into the Empire to raid, or to seek lands. The wars from the 160s onwards resulted in Roman manpower shortages and difficulties in recruiting replacements. Later, when Marcus was sole Emperor, he had to recruit slaves, gladiators, and even bandits to continue to fill gaps in the armies caused by wars, and the plague which raged for some years.[119] Fortunately for the Romans, Germans would join the armies to fight other Germans, and without the various peoples who made up the Germans, the Roman Empire would probably have collapsed sooner than it did.

Lucius Verus' officers in the Parthian war were chosen for their experience of campaigns. Lucius was accompanied by the Praetorian Prefect Furius Victorinus, and Avidius Cassius, a friend of Marcus from Cyrrhus in Syria, commanded the campaign army. Cassius ended the Parthian war, and in 166 he was rewarded with the consulship and made governor of Syria. When Vologaeses lost the support of his allies, Cassius chased the Parthians down the Euphrates, bridged it, and reached the city of Seleucia on the river Tigris. Apparently, the citizens did not oppose him, and probably some agreement was reached, which Cassius allegedly broke by storming and destroying the city. Later apologists insisted that it was the people of Seleucia who broke faith. Roman wars had to be justified.[120] Cassius also destroyed the Parthian palace at Ctesiphon and led his surviving troops back to Syria.

Lucius Verus and Marcus celebrated a joint triumph in 166, and both received the title *pater patriae*.[121] The triumph and the honours were overshadowed by the threat of war on the northern frontiers, and the aforementioned plague which contemporaries thought originated in the east, possibly Babylon.[122] The nature of the illness is not known, but many civilians and soldiers died, the state finances suffered in consequence, and manpower declined just as extra soldiers were needed. The two Emperors organised religious ceremonies, purified the city, and passed laws forbidding owners of estates to bury their dead within their grounds. State funds were provided for funerals of the poor.

## The Marcomanni, Quadi and Sarmatian Iazyges

Marcus and Verus set out together for the northern war.[123] The chronology is not established, and the scenes on the column of Marcus Aurelius in Rome documenting these wars begin only in the later phases, variously dated from 172, or 174-5. The war had been threatening for some time, but according to the *Historia Augusta* the Roman commanders in the north, using diplomacy rather than fighting, managed to hold off hostilities until the Parthian campaigns ended.[124] Commanders probably dragged out negotiations, giving subsidies and food, with the unspoken reminder that the Roman army was still powerful.

On inscriptions the war is called *bellum Germanicum*. The Romans were not simply fighting the Marcomanni, but several tribes. The *Historia Augusta* says it was a war of many nations, listing the tribes which conspired together from the borders of Illyricum (Pannonia) to Gaul.[125]

The tribes were not always hell-bent on destroying the Empire. In the first stage of the war the *Historia Augusta* reports that some tribes were involuntary migrants retreating from more distant tribes, and wanted to come into Italy, desperate enough to invade.[126] According to Dio some tribesmen penetrated as far as Italy but were defeated by Marcus' generals Pompeianus and Pertinax. Among the dead tribesmen, there were women in armour.[127] This means that whole families were involved, and it was not simply warriors on the warpath, but a migration.[128]

The warriors who fought against the Romans may not have represented their entire tribe, just as in the early Republic the Romans defeated sections of a tribe, only to find more of them on the warpath soon afterwards. When the Iazyges had been defeated, probably in 174, their king Banadaspus tried to make peace, but tribal dissidents opposed to peace imprisoned him. Then in 175 another leader of the Iazyges, Zanticus, asked for peace, and this time there was no dissent.[129] The sometimes precarious standing of tribal chiefs made it more difficult for the Romans to deal with the tribes, like grasping the soap in the bath, where an agreement was no sooner made than it slipped out of control.

Tribes frequently asked for incorporation in the Empire. One method was to be offered lands in an existing province, without damaging the provincials, and another method was the conversion of tribal lands into a Roman province.[130] For the first option, within the provinces there always seemed to be enough lands available. Some provincial lands had never been intensively cultivated, and others had been depopulated by disasters or disease. Some tribesmen would surrender to the reigning emperor in return for lands on which to settle and thereby gain protection from other tribes. Their young men were usually recruited into the Roman army. Dio describes how Marcus settled some of the tribesmen in the northern frontier provinces, Dacia, Pannonia, Moesia, Germany and also Italy, but those settled at Ravenna seized the city. This ended tribal settlement in Italy, and for good measure Marcus expelled earlier settlers as well.[131]

By Marcus' reign, being incorporated in the Empire as a province became more acceptable to the tribes, because pressure from further north was increasing and life inside the Empire was more attractive. During the northern wars Marcus was said to have planned the creation of two provinces, Marcomannia, and Sarmatia for the Iazyges. The *Historia Augusta* affirms that Marcus would have achieved this goal, had it not been for the rebellion of Avidius Cassius in the east.[132] A later passage, possibly scrambling the chronology, declares that in 179 in the wars against the Hermunduri, Sarmatians and Quadi, Marcus would have created provinces, but he died before he could do so.[133] Dio explains how Marcus had stationed 20,000 soldiers in the lands of the Quadi and Marcomanni, and would have subdued the whole region, but his death ended the scheme.[134] Tiberius had thought of annexing Bohemia and Moravia, and by Marcus' day the Danube frontier and the occupation of Dacia made the project more feasible, bringing the Roman Empire up to a mountain frontier, which would have been more secure than the river line.[135]

Probably in spring 168, Marcus and Lucius arrived at Aquileia and, apparently without fighting the tribes retreated, sending envoys asking for pardon. The Quadi sought Roman acceptance of the king they had chosen. Lucius was ready to turn back, but Marcus thought the tribes were feigning a retreat so as to attack later. He and Verus crossed the Alps and took measures to ensure the safety of Italy and Illyricum, Pannonia under its old name. In the winter of 168-169, during the plague, the Emperors returned to Rome, but quite soon after setting off Lucius died, probably from a stroke, at Altinum (Altino).[136]

Marcus returned to Rome with the body and arranged the funeral and Lucius'defication.[137] Rumours that Verus had been poisoned by Marcus or his physician can be ignored.[138]

### Marcus rules alone

Marcus did not choose another colleague until 175, when he elevated his only surviving son Commodus, aged fourteen, to the rank of Caesar. Two years later Commodus became Augustus.

Despite being involved in wars for much of his reign, Marcus assiduously attended to the Senate, the people, the provincials, and the laws. The role of the Senate had declined because senators had no executive role in government, and apathy was setting in. Marcus at all times displayed respect for the Senate, regularly attending meetings.[139] He deferred to senators whenever possible, kept them informed of his plans, and tried to provide meaningful tasks for them, appointing them judges in many inquiries, even those under his own jurisdiction. He employed many men of praetorian and consular rank who had held no magistracies to settle disputes, so they would gain prestige through administration of law. He gave the rank of tribune or aedile to poor but honest senators. He appointed senatorial *curatores* for many communities, usually to regulate the finances.[140] He revived Hadrian's scheme, revoked by Pius, of placing *juridici* in parts of Italy, employing ex-praetors rather than the consulars of Hadrian's reign.[141]

Social mobility was now considerably increased, but paradoxically at the same time distinctions of rank were crystallizing. A special category was that of the retinue of the emperor, the *comites*, singular *comes*, personal friends of the ruler, and eventually official companions. During the later second century new titles came into being to indicate rank among senators and equites, senators meriting the description *clarissimus*, meaning most illustrious or distinguished. Administrative posts in Rome, once entrusted to freedmen, were given to equestrians, including the chief offices, and more procuratorial posts were created for equestrians, whose ranks ultimately depended on their pay grades. Titles denoting equestrian status started with *egregius*, meaning literally outside the common masses, rising through *perfectissimus*, most perfect, to *eminentissimus*, most eminent. Equestrians were also entrusted with an increasing number of military posts, and not only equestrians, but provincials and even sons of freedmen could rise through service in the army. Lowly origins did not hinder a man's career, and Marcus chose the men who were best suited to the tasks he wanted them to perform, but he took the precaution of promoting them to the relevant rank.

Increased social mobility based on merit and ability is illustrated by the careers of two army officers, Helvius Pertinax and Valerius Maximianus. Pertinax was the son of a freedman, and he rose via the army, and also through helpful patrons, since no-one got anywhere without influential assistance. Edited highlights of his career include his service in the Parthian war under Lucius Verus, and as military tribune in Britain. In 175 he reached the suffect consulship.[142] The ubiquitous Valerius Maximianus served in several parts of the empire, as did many military men. His career is documented on several inscriptions from Africa and Dacia. Under Marcus, Maximianus was fleet commander on the Danube, bringing supplies to the troops in Pannonia, and later he commanded detachments of legions stationed north of the Danube in the lands of the Marcomanni and Quadi, at Leugaricio (Trencin, on the river Vah, Slovakia), where the relevant inscription is on a rock face, visible from the rear of a hotel.[143]

Despite the examples of men rising from lowly origins, wealth still ruled and society was more rigidly divided into the haves and the have nots, labelled *honestiores* and *humiliores*. These two broad social classes were treated differently at law, with harsher punishments for *humiliores*, so things had not really changed since the plebeians fought for recognition and status in the fifth century BC.[144] Debt problems had not gone away either. Like Hadrian, Marcus cancelled debts to his private treasury and the public treasury, burning all the documentation in the Forum.[145]

For provincials, Marcus refused to raise extra taxes when he badly needed money to finance the frontier wars.[146] Responding to legal problems, he made it compulsory for provincials to name free-born children within three days of birth, and to record their names as was done in Rome under the prefects of the treasury (*praefecti aerarii*). The records could then be used if a provincial's free status was disputed.[147] This probably indicates that such disputes were fairly common.

Many of the laws that Marcus passed were concerned the freedom and safety of individuals including slaves, rights of inheritance, laws on inheritance taxes, protection of wards and their property. He appointed a praetor to deal with wards to afford closer supervision of the trustees, which was previously the responsibility of consuls. Hadrian had invited lawyers to attend his *consilium* and Marcus employed the lawyer Cervidius Scaevola in his *consilium*.[148] Some of Scaevola's laws, and some of Marcus' rulings, are incorporated in the sixth century compilation of laws under the Emperor Justinian.

## The northern wars resumed

Before Marcus could return to the northern frontiers, he had to solve the manpower shortages and the financial problems. Many soldiers had been lost in the fighting or had died from the plague, leaving gaps to be filled, and the potential territorial and temporal extent of the wars also demanded an enlargement of the army, which in turn increased the wage bill at a time when finances were depleted. As mentioned earlier, over a period of time Marcus recruited any able-bodied men that he could find, even slaves and gladiators.[149] He made the gesture of raising cash by selling off the palace treasures and furnishings. The sales lasted for two months, bringing in gold to pay two new legions, II and III Italica.[150] While raising cash without imposing higher taxes, Marcus also refused to pay the expected donatives to his victorious troops, explaining that the money would have to come from their families.[151]

There were changes in provincial government according to the new circumstances. The *Historia Augusta* notes that some provinces governed by senatorial proconsuls were made imperial provinces, and vice versa some imperial provinces became senatorial provinces.[152] The three Dacian provinces were united under a single governor, Claudius Fronto. The shortage of suitable manpower affected not only the armies but also the choice of suitable governors, a situation compounded when Fronto had to add Moesia Superior to his three Dacian provinces. When Fronto himself was killed fighting Germans and Iazyges, new governors had to be found, Cornelius Clemens for the three Dacias, and the governor of Thrace, Caerellius, took over Moesia Superior.[153]

In autumn 169 Marcus returned to the war against the Marcomanni, beginning the campaign probably in 170, taking the Romans across the Danube. Birley doubts the success of the campaign. Italy was invaded around this time. Ammianus Marcellinus, writing in the second half of the fourth century, describes a siege of Aquileia and the destruction of Opitergium (Oderzo, north of Venice).[154] The Marcomanni, the Quadi, and their allies now had a foothold in northern Italy, and ousting them was the priority, even though Macedonia, Thrace, and Achaea had also been invaded. Marcus was fighting a world war, and he had to rely on his generals to combat these menaces while he concentrated on the Danube area. In the early 170s, the Mauri crossed the Straits of Gibraltar and devastated parts of Spain, principally Baetica. Marcus sent Aufidius Victorinus, a personal friend and probably a member of his *consilium*, to govern the combined provinces of Tarraconensis and Baetica. With only one legion at Legio (Leon) Victorinus needed reinforcements. Some troops were sent from Greece under Gratus Julianus.[155] When the northern wars were almost concluded the Mauri appeared in Spain again in 177, besieging a town called Singilia Barba, near Malaga, something for which raiders did not usually devote time and manpower. Italica suffered as well, and both towns set up inscriptions thanking the procurator of Mauretania Tingitana, Vallius Maximianus, who may have chased the tribesmen leaving Africa into Spain.[156]

By late 171 Marcus was able to negotiate with the tribes, remaining in Pannonia, probably at the legionary fortress on the Danube at Carnuntum (Bad Deutsch-Altenburg, near Petronell, Austria). He dealt with the tribes separately. Dio's enumeration of the arrangements may not belong to this single context of 171, but he perhaps grouped together Marcus' methods of dealing with tribes over a period of time. Some tribes surrendered and their young men were recruited and sent on distant campaign, while other tribes were given lands. One tribe was led by a boy of twelve, Battarius. Marcus promised an alliance and gave money, with which the tribe was able to foil the designs of a neighbouring chief called Tarbus who had entered Dacia demanding cash with menaces. The Roman alliances with tribal leaders usually ensured that the chief and his warriors, supported by subsidies if necessary, could police their own people and protect their borders. The Quadi asked for and obtained peace. The Romans hoped to detach them from union with the Marcomanni and received horses and cattle from the Quadi, together with the promise of return of some of the captives and deserters. They were refused permission to attend markets, in case the Marcomanni and Iazyges infiltrated and gained knowledge of Roman dispositions.[157]

The first scene on the column of Marcus Aurelius depicts the Romans crossing the Danube, probably in 172. The Marcomanni won a battle in which they killed the Praetorian Prefect Marcus Vindex. He may not have been replaced, leaving the other Prefect, Bassaeus Rufus, without a colleague.[158]

Marcus had to rely on his generals to deal with problems in Armenia and Egypt. Martius Verus, governor of Cappadocia, reinstated Soaemus, who had been ejected from Armenia. A rebellion began in

Egypt, triggered by the Bucoli or Bucolici, meaning herdsmen. The revolt became serious enough for Avidius Cassius, governor of Syria and commander of most of the east, to be sent to quell it, with special dispensation from the Senate to circumvent the law forbidding senators to enter Egypt.[159]

The Marcomanni were defeated by the end of 172. Inscriptions show that Marcus took the title *Germanicus*, since he had won the victory himself.[160] Commodus, aged eleven, also received the title.[161] The Quadi and their allies remained unconquered. A famous episode, probably belonging to this war, is depicted on the Marcus column, the so-called rain miracle, when the Quadi had trapped the Romans without access to water and by divine intervention there was a storm and the soldiers drank through their open mouths or from their helmets, and continued fighting.[162] The miracle is variously attributed to Marcus himself, an Egyptian wizard, or the Christians.[163] After this the Quadi avoided pitched battles, and the Romans could not get to grips with them in the old way by pitting entire legions and auxiliaries against them. The war was won by smaller groups of solders, consisting of vexillations from the legions, probably supported by auxiliary units, under different commanders working independently. The Quadi were defeated probably in 173 and made terms but reneged by evicting their pro-Roman king Furtius. They elected another one, Arigaesus, which implies the work of dissident tribal factions. Marcus refused to recognise or treat with the new king. Some of the Quadi joined their neighbours the Iazyges in war against the Romans. Dio describes a battle in winter against this tribe, fought on the frozen Danube. The Iazyges though that they had an advantage, since the tribesmen and their horses were used to moving on the ice. The Romans, now threatened on at least three sides, faced all their foes at once, positioning the bottoms of their shields on the ice and holding them firm with one foot, which sounds very awkward, but they took hold of the bridles of horses, dragging them down, or if they slipped they brought the tribesmen down with them and used their feet to hurl them away.[164] The Iagyges were defeated, sending envoys to make peace, but Marcus was angry with them, and the Quadi too, so angry that he wished to exterminate them.[165]

In 175, Marcus was informed by Martius Verus, governor of Cappadocia, that Avidius Cassius had been declared Emperor in Syria.[166] Cassius commanded most of the Roman east with access to all the similarly vast resources of wealth, food and manpower, and with the armies behind him he would be a formidable enemy. At this point Marcus probably did not know why his close friend seemed to have turned against him. He set off for the east, ensuring that the northern frontiers could be controlled by his commanders. He made arrangements with the Iazyges without informing the Senate, contrary to his usual courteous procedure. Previously he had resettled the Marcomanni and Quadi beyond the Danube, forbidding them to live within five miles of it, and Dio says that the same arrangements were made with Iazyges, who were to remain ten miles away from the river. The Iazyges returned a large number of Roman captives and provided 8,000 cavalry, of which 5,500 were sent to Britain, called Sarmatians. Mounted units with the title Sarmatae are attested later at the fort at Ribchester in Lancashire, England.[167] Marcus also raised troops from the Marcomanni and Quadi, and took them to the east under the command of his trusted officer Valerius Maximianus.[168]

Cassius' reign lasted three months and six days, ending when a centurion and a decurion killed him and cut off his head to send to Marcus.[169] The tragic truth was that Cassius thought Marcus had died, leaving the young Commodus at the mercy of any scheming would-be emperor. Cassius held more power than any other governor, and so he was almost duty bound to take care of the Empire. Sordid rumours inflated the episode into palace intrigue and scandal, not really worth attention.[170]

Before Marcus arrived in the east, Cassius' rebellion was over, but Marcus continued as planned, with his wife Faustina and their son Commodus accompanying him, thus demonstrating that there was a legitimate successor. Cassius' family and friends were not punished, nor were his followers in the east. Marcus wrote to the senators, asking them to spare anyone who sided with Cassius, but he did execute some men for crimes not associated with the revolt, and he exiled the governor of Egypt to an island, burning all his potentially incriminating documents.[171] Dio believed that if Cassius had been captured alive, Marcus would have forgiven him.[172]

Marcus journeyed through some of the provinces. The rebellion had been potentially widespread, so it was important to see what was happening, and to be seen. Sadly, in Cappadocia, his wife Faustina died, at a small town called Halala, which he renamed Faustinopolis in her honour, building a temple to her, and elevating the town to a colony.[173] He seems to have been devoted to Faustina, despite tales of her sexual promiscuity, and was devastated by her death.[174] Before setting off for Rome, Marcus visited Athens, probably a lifelong ambition given his devotion to philosophy.

Towards the end of 176 Marcus and Commodus returned to Rome and celebrated a triumph. The northern wars had not been decisively concluded in 175. Fighting had continued, and a Roman victory earned Marcus his ninth acclamation as Imperator and the second for Commodus. In the late summer of 178, both Marcus and Commodus were back on the northern frontier. Commodus was made Augustus and co-emperor in 177. He was also consul in that year, and in 178 he took a wife called Bruttia Crispina, daughter of Bruttius Praesens.[175] Marcus was already ill when he set off for the north. Galen, Marcus' physician since 168, diagnosed a stomach problem, probably an ulcer.[176]

Not much is known about the campaign in 179. The commander of the Roman forces was Tarrutienus Paternus, who earned a victory after fighting for an entire day. Marcus was acclaimed Imperator for the tenth time.[177] Negotiation and resettlement followed. Envoys came from various tribes, and Marcus judged them on their perceived merits, some receiving Roman citizenship, some exempted from tax or tribute, either for a specified period, or permanently. Three thousand men of the Naristi, usually associated with the Quadi and Marcomanni, were settled in Roman territory. Other tribes were promised subsidies and protection. The main concern of the Iazyges was for protection from their enemies the Quadi, who would be free to attack them unless Marcus defeated them. Marcus placed Quadi under Roman military surveillance, along with the Marcomanni, controlling them by stationing 20,000 soldiers in forts in their territory, including legionary detachments commanded by Valerius Maximianus.[178] The soldiers prevented the tribesmen from farming the land or letting their flocks graze, and when they attempted to migrate the Romans blocked the routes.[179] The result of this harassment seems to have produced a peace of sorts, but Marcus was denied the chance to carry out his alleged plan to subdue al the tribes. He died, traditionally at Vindobona (Vienna), but more likely at Sirmium, in March 180, and Commodus, already co-emperor, took over the Empire, made peace with the tribes, and returned to Rome.

Thereafter, says Dio, the kingdom of gold descended into iron and rust.[180] He was entitled to his opinion. He survived eleven years nine months and fourteen days of the sole rule of Commodus.

# 11

# From Commodus to
# the Severans

From the reigns of Nerva to Marcus Aurelius, the succession was arranged by adoption, but Commodus came to rule the Empire as the legitimate son of Marcus. After his father's death, Commodus brought the Danubian wars to a close by diplomatic means, arranging a treaty with the Marcomanni and Quadi, who were by this time thoroughly oppressed, hemmed in by Roman troops and forbidden to cultivate the fields or to move away. They no longer possessed their former manpower, they lacked food, and Dio says that Commodus could have destroyed them completely.[1] The terms that Marcus had made were revived, and Commodus imposed some conditions of his own. There was to be an annual contribution of grain, later revoked. Instead of recruiting tribesmen for the army each year, Commodus demanded an immediate levy of arms and 13,000 men from the Quadi and a smaller number from the Marcomanni. The tribes were forbidden to make war on the Iazyges, Buri and Vandili, and they were prevented from congregating wherever they chose. From now on they were to assemble once a month in a designated location, supervised by a Roman centurion and some soldiers. Once the terms were agreed, Commodus retained control of a neutral zone just beyond the frontier and withdrew troops from the areas beyond it.[2]

Little is known about the Buri. Although they sent embassies on earlier occasions, they did not want lasting peace, but simply an opportunity to rest and regroup. By Commodus' day their strength had declined, so peace was granted and 15,000 prisoners were returned. Even if the numbers are exaggerated, it seems that much of the Roman army's manpower had been drained by the tribes. All the tribesmen were to take an oath that they would not settle or pasture their herds and flocks within five miles of the Dacian border.

Commodus' actions secured the frontiers and the provinces for several years, without full-scale wars, except for a victory in Sarmatia allegedly won by one of the sons of the Praetorian Prefect Tigidius Perennis, but in reality by the generals under his command.[3] Archaeological evidence suggests that there were raids and minor incidents, and to combat these problems, watchtowers were constructed along the banks of the Danube, attested on a series of inscriptions in which the new towers are labelled *burgi*, described as built *a solo*, from the ground up. The inscriptions usefully explain that they were intended to control the movements of *latrones*, or the diminutive and dismissive form *latrunculi*, or little robbers.[4]

In Rome there were naturally rumours that Marcus' acknowledged illness had been given a boost by doctors, possibly with Commodus' agreement, but not with his participation.[5] Marcus was deified, and a gold statue of him was placed in the Senate House.[6] Thus far, Commodus was doing all the right things. He was only nineteen, but then Augustus had been only the same age when he embarked on his illustrious career, without the wise counsel and grooming for power that Commodus had received from his father. The ancient authors assumed that Marcus could see quite clearly that Commodus was unsuitable, but that he was prevented by his death from doing something about it.[7]

Commodus had been given the best guardians and tutors, and he inherited good advisers from Marcus, but when he became Emperor, he is said to have dismissed or ignored them all.[8] Herodian says that Commodus listened to advisers at first, and he pinpoints the moment when the rot set in to the appointment of Perennis (Perennius in Greek) as Praetorian Prefect. Perennis had a good military record and was ostensibly a good choice for Prefect. He was an able administrator and may have been responsible for organising the neutral zone beyond the Danube frontier, particularly in Pannonia Inferior.[9]

He came as close to supreme power as anyone could, because Commodus more or less abdicated from government and was happy to let Perennis do the work.[10] When things went wrong Perennis was blamed, and gradually came to be hated. It was said that he had brought accusations against most of the men appointed by Marcus to guide the young Emperor, and seized the property of his condemned victims in his insatiable greed.[11] He persuaded Commodus to give the command of the Illyrian armies, meaning the Pannonian troops, to both of his sons, meanwhile getting the soldiers on his side by giving them large donatives, his main reason for wanting lots of money. Perennis was doing what Commodus should have been doing himself, probably to keep the Empire together in the absence of meaningful instruction from its current Emperor, but he stands accused of aiming for personal rule of the Empire by promoting one of his sons. This is Dio's tale, in his account of 1,500 soldiers from Britain coming to Rome to warn Commodus about Perennis.[12] The downfall of Perennis soon followed, and he and his entire family were executed. Perennis' son was summoned to Rome from the Sarmatian war by letter. Not suspecting his fate, he was reluctant to abandon his campaign.[13]

One man among Commodus' favourites had been keen to have Perennis removed. This was Cleander, who rapidly became more notorious than his predecessor. Even when Perennis was still alive, Cleander already possessed almost as much influence.[14] He came to Rome from Phrygia as a slave, but someone brought him into the imperial household of Marcus Aurelius, where he was freed, and as an imperial freedman he became Commodus' chamberlain (*a cubiculo*). After Perennis' death, there was a ridiculous succession of Praetorian Prefects, appointed and removed according to the whim of Commodus. Niger held the post for six hours, and Marcius Quartus for five days.[15] These men had no chance to gain power and influence. Without military experience Cleander could not realistically command the Praetorian Guard, but he could make sure that he was powerful enough to control the two Prefects when things had settled down. He also managed to control virtually everything else, including appointments and promotions, mostly by selling them. Commodus was happy to have Cleander relieve him of tedious duties, to filter approaches to him, and make him secure. He gave Cleander the title *a pugione*, the dagger. Cleander could not only promote individuals but also eliminate them, so the choice for most men was between retiring into private life or being a friend of Cleander, who ruined many men's careers.[16]

Just as Perennis had been blamed for the problems that beset Rome, Cleander was suspected of organising a food shortage, buying up supplies so that he could then appear magnanimous in distributing it to the people. If this is correct, he was hoisted with his own petard, because there were riots, which frightened Commodus into executing his former favourite.[17] Not even the members of Commodus' family were safe. Not surprisingly, there were plots against him, one of them instigated by his sister Lucilla, who persuaded her second husband Pompeianus – imposed on her by Marcus – to kill her brother. She failed, and was banished to Capri, along with Commodus' wife Crispina, accused of adultery. Dio saw for himself how many ordinary men and women were eliminated.[18]

### The provinces

The ancient historians neglect the provinces in favour of concentrating on Commodus' depravities, his appearances in the area as a gladiator, his homosexuality, his growing megalomania in renaming buildings, towns and cities, even Rome, after himself.

In Gaul, Spain, and possibly in the German provinces, a Roman deserter called Maternus gathered an army. Herodian says that all the lands of the Celts and Spain were overrun.[19] It has been questioned whether the uprising was as serious or as widespread as the sources suggest, but it earned the name *bellum desertorum*. The numbers of deserters were too large for police work, and troops had to be sent to combat them.[20] The damage was not limited to the countryside but affected towns and large cities.[21] Even Strasbourg, headquarters of VIII Augusta, was affected, possibly even besieged, in 185. The legion was given the title *pia fidelis constans Commoda*, implying that it remained loyal to Commodus and fought off the gangs. The *Historia Augusta* names Pescennius Niger and Septimius Severus, governor of Gallia Lugdunensis, as commanders against the deserters.[22] Clodius Albinus also marched from Gallia Belgica.[23]

When Maternus realised that he faced a war, he and his followers split up to infiltrate Italy in small groups, probably in 187. There he decided that it was all or nothing. He planned to join the festival in honour of the mother of the gods, held in March, hoping to get near to Commodus during the celebrations and assassinate him, but some of his men betrayed him. Maternus was arrested and beheaded, along with his betrayers.[24]

Dio notes that there were wars beyond Dacia, in which Clodius Albinus and Pescennius Niger gained distinction, but provides no further information or dates. Dio also remarks cryptically that the greatest struggle of Commodus' reign occurred in Britain, when an uprising began and the Britons crossed the wall that divided them from the Roman legions, killing a Roman commander, and

Ulpius Marcellus was sent against the tribesmen.[25] No details of the subsequent campaign have been preserved. There is debate about which frontier was crossed, and the dates when Marcellus governed Britain. It was once thought that the commander who was killed must have been the previous governor, and therefore Commodus must have sent Marcellus out to Britain to take over. In order to accommodate the epigraphic evidence that Marcellus was in Britain *c.*178, and in 182-184, the theory developed that there were two governors with the same name, or Marcellus served two separate terms as governor. More recently it has been pointed out that Dio does not say that Marcellus was sent from some unnamed place to Britain, but that he was sent against the tribesmen, meaning that he was already in Britain, probably since 178 during the joint reigns of Marcus and Commodus.[26]

Marcellus is attested on inscriptions from Benwell and Chesters on Hadrian's Wall.[27] Some forts on this frontier were damaged, indicating that this is most probably the wall which was crossed, given that the Antonine frontier had been abandoned at least two decades earlier. The fighting may have begun in 182 and ended in 184, when Commodus was acclaimed Imperator for the seventh time, and took the title *Britannicus Maximus*.[28]

The war was over, but the soldiers were not happy, and not for the first time in Britain the legionary legates caused trouble, deciding they need their own emperor and choosing one of their number, Priscus. He refused the honour, telling them he was no more an emperor than any of them.[29] In the *Historia Augusta* the Britons are said to have wanted their own emperor, but the natives probably had no say in the matter. According to an earlier passage, the Praetorian Prefect Perennis is blamed for the attempted usurpation because he had appointed equestrians to command the soldiers in Britain, dismissing senators, which means that he had removed the legionary legates.[30] This is when 1,500 soldiers allegedly came to Rome to warn Commodus that Perennis was plotting against him.[31] In Britain, Marcus Antius Crescens Calpurnius is attested as *iuridicus*, and was made governor temporarily until Publius Helvius Pertinax was appointed in 185. Pertinax not only thoroughly suppressed the mutinous soldiers, almost getting killed in the process, but according to the *Historia Augusta* he had to dissuade them from declaring him emperor. He asked to be relieved, and an unknown replacement was despatched.[32]

## The last years of Commodus

After the execution of Cleander, Commodus became very much like Domitian, insecure, unpredictable, and murderous. He removed the Praetorian Prefects, first Regillus and then Julius Julianus, after the latter had enjoyed a brief period as sole Prefect.[33] Towards the end of his reign, Commodus devoted himself to gladiatorial activities and killing animals. Senators were compelled to watch, and it was obligatory to hail Commodus as lord (*dominus*), first among men, and so on.[34] Herodian recounts how Commodus decapitated Mauretanian ostriches using crescent-shaped arrows, and Dio says that Commodus waved an ostrich head in front of the senators, who understood the message that he could do the same to any of them. Dio explains that he and other senators had to cover up their laughter by chewing laurel leaves.[35] One did not laugh at Commodus, unless specifically instructed of course, and then one would have guffawed wholeheartedly until told to stop.

The end was not far off. Commodus chose Quintus (or Marcus) Aemilius Laetus as one of the Praetorian Prefects. It is not known how or when Laetus began his association with Marcia, Commodus' mistress, and Eclectus, the palace chamberlain, but these three decided that the Emperor had to be removed. The assassination took place on the last day of December 192. Eclectus joined the conspiracy because chamberlains were frequently executed, but Marcia's motives are not explained, and she was blamed along with Laetus for encouraging Commodus' crimes.[36] The sources agree that Commodus was poisoned but did not die, and had to be finished off by strangulation.[37] Herodian explains that Commodus had written on a wooden tablet the names of men he intended to execute, but one of his young favourite boys found it, then Marcia took it from him, read what was on it, and sent it to Laetus because his name and that of Eclectus were on the list.[38] This recalls the assassination of Domitian, who also made a list of intended victims, discovered by his wife, who condoned his murder.

Publius Helvius Pertinax was proclaimed Emperor. Having refused the honour while he was in Britain, he now accepted it. According to Dio and Herodian, Pertinax knew nothing about the plot, but the *Historia Augusta* says he did.[39] It would have been prudent for Laetus to find an emperor before killing Commodus, to avoid total anarchy in the scramble for rule of the Empire.[40]

## Pertinax

The new Emperor was the supreme example of social mobility in the Roman world. Starting out as the son of a freedman, he rose to prominence via the army, obtained equestrian then senatorial rank, and afterwards governed provinces. He was voted the title of *pater patriae*, 'father of his country', and accepted it immediately, but he refused the titles Augusta and Caesar for his wife and son, saying that his son should earn the right to be Caesar.[41]

While the people of Rome clamoured to have the dead Commodus thrown into the Tiber, Pertinax arranged for him to be installed in Hadrian's mausoleum, but Commodus' memory was damned. Pertinax had to rescue the Praetorian Prefect Laetus, who faced condemnation by the Senate because he had been party to Commodus' actions. Pertinax persuaded the senators that Laetus did not condone everything that Commodus had done. With one of the Praetorian Prefects on his side, Pertinax had to win over the Praetorian Guardsmen, who worried that they might lose their many privileges, since Pertinax was a known martinet.[42] The Praetorians were not entirely mollified by their donative of 12,000 *sesterces* per man. There was a slight glitch when the oath of loyalty to the new Emperor was taken because the soldiers preferred a senator called Triarius Maternus. Fortunately, he did not want to be an emperor and ran off, having somehow lost his clothes. He left Rome soon afterwards.[43] It was wise to pay the soldiers of the Empire as well, so Pertinax paid more than the donatives promised by Commodus.[44]

Like a Republican general taking over a campaign, Pertinax flushed out the superfluous slaves, concubines and hangers-on in the Imperial household. He arranged for exiles to be reinstated and assisted the families of men killed by Commodus. He organised a new census, reduced customs dues to revive commerce, and granted titles of ownership to waste lands with ten years' tax exemption in order to promote agriculture. To provide funds for the depleted treasury he sold Commodus' goods, and he reduced the expenditure of the imperial household.[45] He seemed destined to reorganise government and administration on a solid basis, but this did not prevent plots from being formed against him. One plot was detected, involving the senator Falco, who was allegedly in cahoots with the Praetorians, but Pertinax persuaded the Senate to pardon him.[46] Inevitably perhaps, he was killed by the Praetorians, probably on the orders of Laetus. Pertinax had stopped the Praetorians from exercising their by now customary licence to damage or seize property, which sounds like a lucrative protection racket.[47] After a reign of eighty-seven days, Pertinax was eliminated and the leaderless Empire was up for sale. Flavius Sulpicianus, the city prefect, and father-in-law of Pertinax, offered vast sums, but the Praetorians thought that if he became emperor he would avenge Pertinax.[48] Sulpicianus was gazumped by Didius Julianus, who promised 25,000 *sesterces* for each Praetorian Guardsman.[49]

## Septimius Severus

Severus came from Africa, the origin of an increasing number of administrative and military personnel. His father was Septimius Geta of the colony of Leptis Magna. The Septimii were probably of Punic origin, while Severus' mother Fulvia Pia was Italian.[50] Aged twenty-eight, Severus became a senator under Marcus. He served in the normal succession of posts, the first meaningful one being that of quaestor in 170. He commanded IV Scythica in Syria, where Helvius Pertinax was governor. From 186 to 189 Severus governed Gallia Lugdunensis, where he helped to suppress the rebel deserter Maternus. He was forty-five years old before reached the consulship in 190, possibly thanks to Cleander, who was noted for creating multiple suffect consulships. In a single year there were twenty-five consuls.[51]

For some time before Commodus was killed, it was obvious that something was rotten in the state of Rome, and there was no designated heir to take over when Commodus died, or was assisted to die, which his unpredictable and dangerous behaviour made increasingly likely. Late in Commodus' reign, Severus was helped by his fellow African, the Praetorian Prefect Aemilius Laetus, who recommended him to Commodus for the post of governor of Pannonia Superior in 191, even though Severus had no experience of commanding armies, or governing a frontier province. Around the same time, Severus' brother Septimius Geta was appointed governor of Moesia Inferior. Thus the two brothers were in command of five legions on the Danube, three under Severus and two under Geta, not forgetting the auxiliary troops.[52]

Severus would not be the only provincial governor keeping a close eye on developments in Rome. The elevation of Pertinax left little time to act upon any plans that keen observers may have made, and Severus had to wait and see what happened next, meanwhile administering to his troops the oath of loyalty to Pertinax. As soon as he arrived in

Pannonia, possibly earlier, Severus had probably begun to sound out colleagues who might support him if he made a bid for Empire. It was not the sort of thing that could be sparked off on a whim. As well as supporters, any would-be emperor required vast quantities of money, clients acting for him in Rome and the provinces, information supplied by agents from all walks of life, and as for any campaign he would need food supplies, access to arms and armour, transport vehicles, horses, mules and oxen, footwear, tents – and above all a proper plan, taking note of potential snags.

Pertinax was killed on 28 March 193, and on 9 April Severus was proclaimed Emperor by his troops at Carnuntum. When he made his move Severus left garrisons to protect Pannonia, and according to the *Historia Augusta* the armies of the Danube and those of the Rhine declared for him, under compulsion from their generals, which indicates that Severus had thoroughly prepared the ground.[53]

Pescennius Niger was also proclaimed Emperor in Syria, before the end of May.[54] Clodius Albinus, governor of Britain, was perhaps proclaimed slightly later than the other two. Severus had the advantage of being closer to Italy, while his rivals were stationed at opposite ends of the Empire. He was in Rome well before the other two could mobilise. He had another advantage in that the horoscope of his second wife, Julia Domna, predicted that she would be the wife of an emperor, and her eastern family circles and her connections would bring influential, wealthy people to Severus' side. The short reign of Pertinax had held great promise of stable government and prosperity, so Severus approached Rome as *ultor Pertinacis*, avenger of Pertinax, a worthy cause which he otherwise lacked.[55] He adopted the name Pertinax, displaying it on his coins.

Didius Julianus, who had just bought the Empire, persuaded the Senate to declare Severus *hostis*.[56] He fortified the city and the imperial palace and despatched troops to stop Severus' march through Italy, but they all possessed a strong sense of self-preservation and joined the new Emperor.[57] Julianus executed Laetus and Marcia, but the Praetorians were not impressed because, according to Herodian, Julianus was incapable of delivering the promised cash, though the *Historia Augusta* claims that he paid 5,000 sesterces above the 25,000 that he had offered.[58] Whatever their grievances, the Praetorians sent messages to Severus. Julianus was killed by a soldier, having been condemned to death by the senators, who declared Severus Emperor. All this was witnessed by Dio.[59]

The Praetorians expected praise, honours and riches for their support of Severus, but were disappointed. The new Emperor called them to a meeting outside the city. He surrounded them with his soldiers, to pre-empt trouble when he dismissed the lot of them. The arrogance and power of the Praetorians had long gone unpunished, and the men had not realised that with armies behind him Severus could manage without them for a while. Some were executed, the rest banished from Rome.[60] Eventually, Severus created a new, larger, Praetorian Guard, numbering 1,500 men, drawn from the legions. Inscriptions confirm that some of the new Praetorians were Illyrians, from the Danube armies, not surprising in view of the fact that Severus governed Pannonia.[61] Usually the Praetorians had been recruited from Italy, Spain, Macedonia and Noricum, and Dio accuses Severus of ruining Italian youth by depriving them of employment as Praetorians.[62] Italian youth was not so keen on being away from Italy with less pay and fewer privileges, which in part accounts for the decrease in numbers of Italians in the armies.

Severus entered Rome in civilian dress. He paid the usual cash gifts to the soldiers and to the people of Rome, a prudent move, as was his promise to the senators that none of them would be condemned to death without trial by his peers. He promised to rule like the exemplary Marcus Aurelius and made every effort to associate himself and his family with this Emperor.

## Pescennius Niger and Clodius Albinus

With two rival claimants to the rule of the Empire, Severus would have to make bargains or fight. Niger had won distinction in Dacia in the 180s, but not much is known about him, despite the attempt to flesh out his biography in the *Historia Augusta*. He was potentially more dangerous than Albinus because he held the eastern provinces, with access to resources greater than anything that Clodius Albinus could gain in the west. Severus decided to go to the east first, but before he could march he needed to neutralise Albinus to prevent him from marching on Rome while the struggle with Niger was in progress. Severus sent a letter by one of his trusted friends, offering Albinus the title Caesar and making him consul *in absentia*. Albinus seemed to be content with this, calling himself Decimus Clodius Septimius Albinus Caesar.[63] It is debatable whether Albinus believed that he would succeed Severus, who had two young sons, or whether he was quite prepared to be Severus' dupe while he gained support in the western provinces, sufficient to leave Britain protected while he fought Severus when the time came. Albinus needed to be ready on the European mainland, not to be forced to fight in Britain with only three legions.

With Albinus content, or playing a waiting game, Severus was ready to face Niger. He recruited Italians, ordered troops from Pannonia to march to Thrace and requisitioned triremes from the Italian coastal cities to supplement the Ravenna and Misenum fleets.[64] He sent orders for the troops in Moesia to set off ahead of him, while he marched through Pannonia. The proconsul of Asia, Asellius Aemilianus, had declared for Niger, who had occupied Byzantium. Severus' general Marius Maximus was ordered to besiege city, but Niger escaped to Nicaea.[65] The first success for Severus was won by his general Claudius Candidus, who defeated Asellius Aemilianus, chased him to Cyzicus and executed him. Candidus went on to confront Niger at Nicaea, where he had to rally the Severan soldiers beginning to give ground amid the narrow passes.[66] Candidus' victory forced Niger to retreat, and shortly afterwards Egypt came over to Severus.[67]

Byzantium had still not surrendered. Dio devotes several paragraphs to a description of its position and it defences, declaring that Severus' siege lasted for three years, which ought to mean that it ended in 196, but it is more likely that it was over by the end of the previous year.[68]

Niger, not decisively defeated, withdrew into Syria, setting up headquarters at Antioch. He needed men and money.[69] He was beginning to lose support. If Severus was to be the winner, communities which had assisted Niger would suffer. Arabia followed the example of Egypt and went over to Severus. A little later, other Syrian cities began to support Severus. Tyre and Laodicea (Latakia, Syria) were punished for deserting Niger.[70] His days were numbered, though. The final battle was fought in spring 194 at Issus, the plain where Alexander the Great defeated Darius. The Roman victory was largely owed to Cornelius Anullinus, a friend of Severus, now commanding the army, while Severus himself remained behind at Perinthus. Niger escaped yet again, but he was captured and killed.[71] The *Historia Augusta* says that initially Severus exiled Niger's family but then executed them all when he heard that Albinus had raised revolt in Gaul.[72] Severus sent Niger's head to Byzantium, to prove that the city was leaderless, but the inhabitants had held out for too long to expect leniency and did not surrender. Severus' fleet cut off the food supplies, forcing Byzantium to submit. The city and its people were destroyed. Dio comments that Severus had thus demolished a Roman base against the barbarians from Pontus and Asia.[73] Byzantium was too strategically important to be left in ruins and was eventually rebuilt.

There was much to do in repairing damage in the east. Cities friendly to Niger were fined, especially Antioch. Cities which had declared for Severus were well paid, receiving lands and revenues once belonging to the cities undergoing punishment. Niger's adherents were driven into the arms of the Persians, until Severus realised that Roman technical and military expertise was vanishing across the Euphrates. Rebellion had begun in Osroene and Mesopotamia, and Roman garrisons had been ejected. Severus made Osroene a province, in the charge of an equestrian procurator, as attested by an inscription which lacks a date.[74] The capital city of Edessa and its surrounding territory was retained by King Abgar. In Adiabene, Nisibis (Nusaybin, Turkey) had been in Roman hands since the expedition of Lucius Verus and had remained loyal to Rome, besieged by Niger's adherents. Severus rescued it and raised it to the status of a *colonia*, with an equestrian in charge.[75]

In the context of Severus' annexation of Osroene, but also concerned with Mesopotamia which Severus invaded in 195, Dio's sour judgement is that the new provinces were a constant source of wars and expense, costing more than they yielded, and putting the Romans in charge of neighbours of the Medes and Persians meant having to protect them.[76] Undaunted, Severus took the titles *Parthicus Arabicus* and *Parthicus Adiabenicus*, and received from the troops six further acclamations as Imperator. As he well knew, he had not secured control of the east.

It may have been at this time that Severus divided the province of Syria into two. The larger, in the north, was renamed Syria Coele with two legions. Syria Phoenice, the smaller southern province, contained only one legion. Theoretically, no governor of the Syrian provinces had access to all three legions. The division was probably made after the defeat of Niger in order to prevent the rise of another would-be emperor, but the date is not established.[77] The two provinces would require two sets of governmental headquarters and extra administrative and financial personnel.

An inscription dated to 195 includes Severus' *Parthicus* titles, and another dated to 196 include only *Arabicus* and *Adiabenicus*, corroborating the statement in the *Historia Augusta* that Severus dropped *Parthicus* from his victory titles in case it provoked the Parthians.[78] This was all that Severus could achieve in the east, because the matter of Clodius Albinus required attention.

After the defeat of Niger, Severus sent Albinus a reassuring letter, calling him brother, indicating that they still shared the Empire.[79] Probably at the end of 195 Albinus promoted himself from Caesar to Augustus, possibly with encouragement from the soldiers in Britain, and perhaps he had secured support of communities and officials in the western provinces. It was tantamount to a declaration of war with Severus, who at some unknown date, possibly even before Albinus made his move, promoted his elder son Septimius Bassianus, about ten years old, to Caesar, and gave him a new name, Marcus Aurelius Antoninus. Later he was called Caracalla, after the Gallic hooded cloak that he wore.[80] Bassianus' new name probably dates from spring 195, but it is not included on coins until 196.[81] The exact dating is less important than Severus' appointment of Bassianus as his successor. Albinus was out in the cold, most unlikely to survive even if he renounced all claims to rule the Empire, and retired to private life. Albinus by himself was negligible. The danger came from his supporting networks of senators, friends, clients, and soldiers.[82]

Severus had Albinus declared *hostis*, an enemy of the people. The Severans referred to the Gallic conspiracy, casting Albinus in the role of usurper to justify war against him. By autumn 197 Albinus had gathered troops from Britain and moved into Gaul. It is not known what steps, if any, he took to protect Britain during his absence. Hadrian's Wall seems to have been largely evacuated, which may have allowed the Britons to overrun the north, but Severus did not launch his expedition to restore order in Britain until 208. Archaeological evidence shows that the auxiliary units attested on Hadrian's Wall in the second century had been replaced in the third century, leading to the supposition that Albinus removed nearly all the troops from Britain.[83]

Besides the British soldiers, Albinus recruited in Gaul, but he did not manage to win over the Rhine legions, and VII Gemina in Spain refused to assist him, for which Severus awarded it the title *pia* or faithful. According to Dio, Albinus' army was equal in size to that of Severus, but Albinus could not have had time to train his troops to act in concert.[84]

In case Albinus marched for Italy, Severus sent a general and soldiers to guard the Alpine passes.[85] No march into Italy took place. Not all of the cities in Gaul were enthusiastic supporters of Albinus, though they could not prevent men from joining him. The governor of Gallia Lugdunensis would not back Albinus and left the province. Trier may have held out against Albinus, which may be the reason why the city was honoured by Severus.[86] Virius Lupus, governor of Germania Inferior tried to stop Albinus, but was defeated. Dio names him only as Lupus, but he must be the same Virius Lupus whom Severus made governor of Britain.[87]

The war was won by Severus' army at Lugdunum (Lyon). Dio describes the battle but not the sack of the city, whereas Herodian says that the soldiers sacked and burned it. There was great loss of life on both sides, and Severus lost his horse and was nearly killed. Albinus committed suicide.[88] When the war ended, the hunt for Albinus' supporters began, first in Gaul, and then in Rome.[89] Dio enumerates thirty-five supporters of Albinus released and twenty-nine executed, while the *Historia Augusta* lists forty-one killed.[90]

According to Herodian, immediately after the defeat of Albinus, Severus divided Britain into two separate commands.[91] He does not specifically mention two provinces, but his phrase will bear that interpretation, except for the lack of contemporary evidence for the division at this date. The earliest attested inscriptions referring to Britannia Superior and Britannia Inferior belong to the era after Severus' death.[92] It may have been Caracalla who divided Britain *c.*213, when he also divided Pannonia into two.

## The Severan dynasty

On his return to Rome after the defeat of Albinus, Severus gave his son Antoninus (Caracalla) the title *Imperator destinatus*, which made it clear that he intended to establish dynastic rule with Caracalla as his immediate successor.[93] Geta, Severus' younger son, was not promoted as rapidly, and Septimius Geta, brother of Severus, was not given any special attention. Severus now secured his connection to the dynasty of Antoninus Pius and Marcus Aurelius, but he had not yet solved the problem of Marcus' son Commodus, whose memory had been damned. This had to be overturned if Severus was to become part of the Antonine dynasty, so he asked the Senate to deify Commodus, which considerably upset Dio, who reports much of the speech that Severus made eulogising Commodus, calling him his brother.[94] It was a preposterous fiction – but after the elimination of Niger, Albinus and their supporters, no-one was going to argue. All pretended to be on the side of Severus, says Dio, and both he and the *Historia Augusta* indicate the beginning of fear and distrust of Severus.[95]

It was important for Severus to appoint provincial governors and army commanders who would not try to follow his own example of making himself Emperor. He had not finished what he had started in the east, and in his enforced absence from Rome he needed loyal men who would look after his interests and obey his commands in return for his patronage and steady promotions in the social, political and military spheres.[96] He kept a close eye on administration of the Empire while he was away from Rome. The seat of government was wherever he happened to be, and inscriptions show that envoys came to him personally rather than to Rome.[97] Envoys came to Severus in Germany after the defeat of Albinus.[98] During Severus' British campaign, an ambassador from Ephesus reached Rome but moved on to Britain to find him.[99]

Since it was the army that had brought Severus to power and ensured his hold on it, he looked after his soldiers. Military pay was last increased under Domitian, almost a century earlier, and military law forbade soldiers to marry and raise families legitimately, so they did so illegitimately. Service in the army had to be made more attractive to replace the enormous number of vacancies when veterans were discharged or men died, not all of them on battlefields, but from accidents and disease. Severus increased pay accordingly and allowed soldiers to marry. Herodian dates this after the defeat of Albinus, but the *Historia Augusta* dates the pay rise to just before the second Parthian campaign.[100] The people of Rome resented it, and Herodian accuses Severus of undermining the discipline of the soldiers and making them greedy for rewards.[101] Pay may have combined cash and rations, since Herodian uses the Greek word meaning corn allowance.[102] Soldiers were afforded even greater social mobility, continuing and enhancing a trend already set in motion by previous Emperors. The power and influence of the senatorial class were being eroded as equestrians rose in power and importance. Like Augustus, Severus was the fount of all patronage and advancement, and it is estimated that more than half of the new procurators that Severus created were of African or eastern descent, reflecting the origins of Severus himself and the eastern connections of Julia Domna.[103] Severus also held the purse strings of the whole Empire, he commanded all the armed forces and was the source of law, but Augustus managed all this tactfully and did not stifle senatorial distinction. While Severus did not deliberately damage senatorial prestige, he did not care a jot for the Senate's sense of its own importance. On the other hand he did not pander to the mob, either.

For the security of Rome, Italy, and his regime, Severus doubled the numbers of the *equites singulares Augusti* from 1,000 to 2,000 and erected an additional set of barracks for them known as *Castra nova equitum singularium*, their original camp relabelled *Castra Priora*. These barracks were situated on the Caelian Hill in the area of the Lateran, possibly after Severus' general Titus Sextus Lateranus was rewarded with a town house on this site. The barracks of the *singulares* were demolished in the early fourth century by the Emperor Constantine. Perhaps not content with an expanded horse guard, Severus also installed a legion, II Parthica, at Alba (Albano), not far from Rome. It was one of three new legions, I, II, and III Parthicae, raised in Italy probably for the second Parthian campaign. After the Parthian war, I and III Parthica were stationed in Mesopotamia where, as in Egypt, the governor was an equestrian, so the legions were also commanded by equestrians, as senatorial legionary legates could not be expected to serve under equestrian governors. With his enlarged Praetorian Guard and the legion at Alba, Severus had at his disposal an estimated 30,000 men, so it would require a very brave or reckless individual to try to take over the Empire while Severus campaigned in the east. Severus also ensured that his adherents held key posts in government and military spheres. From about 199 the commander of the Praetorian Guard was Caius Fulvius Plautianus, from Africa. He was related to Severus' mother and was a longstanding friend of Severus, far too close while they were young, it was said. Plautianus soon rid himself of his colleague Aemilianus Saturninus, and from then on he remained as sole Praetorian Prefect.[104]

### The second Parthian campaign

Vologaeses of Parthia provided justification for the war against him by occupying Mesopotamia, and once again Nisibis (Nusaybin), this time containing a Roman garrison, was besieged. Julius Laetus defended the city, and before Severus arrived Vologaeses withdrew, facing factional strife among his family. Even his own brother was with Severus.[105] Herodian accuses Severus of fighting this war for his own personal glory, but Dio says more realistically the war was waged to win back control of Mesopotamia.[106]

Severus followed Vologaeses along the Euphrates valley, sending troops down it by boat.[107] There was little resistance until he arrived at the Parthian capital at Ctesiphon, and even there it was an easy victory. The city was plundered and sacked, and Dio sneers that this campaign was concerned with loot.[108] Severus halted the pursuit and led the army out of Parthia. The troops acclaimed him as Imperator for the tenth and eleventh occasions. Caracalla was made Augustus, and Geta was made Caesar. This can hardly have been a spontaneous decision, but it was an excellent time to do it, riding on the crest of a wave in 198. Since Severus had now earned the title of *Parthicus* by dint of his own efforts he added *Maximus* to it.

Severus remained in the east probably until the beginning of 202. On 28 January 198 Severus had made sacrifices for the success of his Parthian expedition. The date was deliberately chosen, the centenary of Trajan's *dies imperii*. It connected Severus with the *Optimus Princeps* and, emulating Trajan, he annexed Mesopotamia after the campaigns ended in 198. The new province embraced only the north-western part of Mesopotamia, the capital at Nisibis. The governor was at first an equestrian procurator, later an equestrian prefect, with I Parthica at Singara (Sinjar, Iraq) and III Parthica at Resaina/Rhesaena (Ra's al-'Ayn), each with equestrian commanders. Roman provinces now surrounded the upper Euphrates, stabilising the eastern frontier. Territory in the southern part of Syria Phoenice was added to Arabia, with the desert protecting access to both provinces.[109] For about twenty years there was peace between Rome and Parthia, mostly because the Parthian kings were not powerful enough to disturb it. When the much stronger Persian Sassanids took over from the Parthians in the third century, everything changed.

The only blot on Severus' success was his failure to take Hatra. Dio is the only author to describe two sieges, both abandoned.[110] Birley suggests that Severus received the surrender of King Barsemius and installed a garrison in Hatra, so it may not have been such a dismal failure.[111] After the war, Severus went to Egypt.[112] On the way he visited cities in Syria and Palestine, raising some of them to the status of colonies. In Egypt, he created councils in the chief cities of the *nomes*, the ancient Egyptian administrative districts. The wealthier members of the communities were now responsible for carrying out and financing local public duties. The expense involved resulted in widespread reluctance to serve on the councils. The city of Alexandria had never possessed a council since Augustus had placed it under the control of an equestrian *juridicus*; now Severus endowed it with a council, of the same type as those of the *municipia*.[113]

## Return to Rome

Probably in spring 201 Severus went to Antioch, then set off for Rome via the frontier provinces of Moesia and Pannonia, where he took especial interest in the *canabae*, the civilian settlements around the legionary fortresses, reconstructing the settlement at Viminacium (Kostolac), and raising those of Carnuntum (Petronell/Bad Deutsch-Altenburg) and Aquincum (Budapest) to colonies. He was in Rome by April 202, having become consul with Caracalla as colleague in January.[114]

Severus publicised his conquests on his coinage with the legends VICTORIA PARTHICA MAXIMA, reflecting his new title *Parthicus Maximus*. The abbreviated title *Impp Invicti Pii Augg*, in the plural, refers to Caracalla as co-Emperor.[115] From this time onwards the legend INVICTUS, unconquered, was to feature widely on Severus' coins and titulature. His sons Caracalla and Geta played a prominent part in his triumph, and he celebrated his *Decennalia* or ten years of his reign with appropriate pomp and ceremony, and public festivals and distributions of cash to the people of Rome.[116] The most durable celebration of his ten-year reign and his military achievements is the arch named after him in the Forum in Rome, erected near the Senate house on the spot where, in a dream before he became Emperor, Severus saw Pertinax fall from his horse, which he claimed by mounting it.[117] The arch faced that of Augustus on the other side of the Forum, celebrating the return of the standards by the Parthians in 20 BC. The parallels would not be lost on the Roman people and senators. The sculptures of the arch depict Severus' military victories in Parthia, and the inscription duplicated on the uppermost panels on both sides of the arch records that it was dedicated to Severus and his son Marcus Aurelius Antoninus (Caracalla) by the Senate and people of Rome, in recognition of the restoration of the Republic and the extension of the Empire.

What did restoration of the Republic mean to Romans of the early third century? Senators played no part in decision making, consular elections had died, magistrates and military officers had to be acceptable to the reigning emperor. At least extension of the Empire was correct, and Severus was about to extend parts of the African provinces. *Imperium sine fine* was not quite dead.

## Africa

In 203 Severus and his whole family sailed to Africa, his homeland. He was accompanied by the Praetorian Prefect Plautianus, who had furthered his connection to the Imperial family by betrothing his daughter, Fulvia Plautilla, to Caracalla, who was only fourteen years old when the marriage took place in Rome in 202. Caracalla was hostile to Plautilla from the start, refusing to take meals with her or to sleep with her.[118] Dio, more discerning, attributes Caracalla's behaviour to resentment of Plautianus' power.[119]

During the Parthian war, Severus' generals had been busy in the African provinces, extending the frontiers, taking in more territory, rationalising boundaries, protecting routes and building new forts, though the number of forts and military units in North Africa was still negligible compared to the densely packed frontier installations in Britain, Germany and the Danube provinces. One of the most successful officers was Quintus Anicius Faustus, another African, legate of *III Augusta* from 197 to 201. He was responsible for building new forts protecting Roman territories from raids, policing the transhumance routes, and extending Roman territory across the southern borders.[120] This had been completed before Severus arrived. He continued the extension of Roman control southwards over a much larger area, earning the title of *propagator imperii*, known from several inscriptions in Africa. In Mauretania Caesariensis he advanced beyond the Antonine boundary, establishing a new frontier zone commemorated on inscriptions as the *nova praetentura*. The first moves were made in 198 by Octavius Pudens, another African.[121] Severus moved garrisons into the large gap between Caesariensis and Tingitana, very sparsely settled, as attested by the lack of authentic place-names for the forts, which were named unimaginatively by the titles of the units stationed there, such as Ala Milliaria and Numerus Syrorum.

Severus made Numidia a province in its own right, smaller than the old kingdom but detached from Africa Proconsularis, but there is no confirmation of the new province until 208.[122] Severus concentrated on the eastern African provinces, paying less attention to the western parts of Africa, except to make Auzia in Mauretania Caesariensis a colony.[123]

## Rome and Italy

By 203 Severus was back in Rome, and in 204 he organised the Secular Games, rooted in the Roman past, combining religious ceremonial with games and festivals, occurring once every 110 years, so that no-one ever witnessed more than one celebration in a lifetime, or *saeculum*. Severus and his whole family attended all the celebrations.

The divine and sacrosanct Imperial household, *domus divina*, is attested on inscriptions, the first signs of the widening distance between the emperors and the people that marked the reigns of late third-century emperors.

Like Marcus Aurelius, Severus devoted attention to the law. Some of his pronouncements concerning a wide range of legal matters are preserved in the law codes, especially the *Digest*. Dio praises Severus for his keen interest in the law, his patient attention to the speakers in court, and his willingness to listen to legal experts.[124] Many of Severus' legal pronouncements derive from replies to complaints and appeals for help, and they show that Severus had a genuine concern for individuals, attending to the problems that beset the helpless and destitute people of the Empire.[125]

However much he listened to legal advisers, Severus seemed both deaf and blind to the vast accretion of powers of Plautianus, who was now more to be feared than Sejanus, Perennis and Cleander put together. Plautianus' name infiltrated inscriptions alongside those of the two Augusti. The ancient authors emphasize Plautianus' cruelty, and his influence over Severus, who made him consul in 203 and showered honours on him.[126] Plautianus almost eclipsed Severus, acting as though he was Caesar and receiving petitions addressed to him personally.[127] As Plautianus successively eliminated rivals, Severus could not fail to notice but did nothing to stop the proceedings, until his own brother Septimius Geta, close to death, denounced Plautianus.[128] Caracalla managed to persuade his father that Plautianus was scheming to eliminate the whole family, and on 22 January 205 Caracalla lured Plautianus to the palace and killed him.[129]

After the removal of Plautianus, Severus made a short speech in the Senate without denouncing him. Some men were executed on account of their association with Plautianus, but if any Praetorians were involved with Plautianus, there is no record of punishment. Two new Praetorian Prefects were appointed, first attested in May 205.[130] These were Quintus Maecius Laetus, formerly prefect of Egypt, and Aemilius Papinianus, an Imperial secretary and jurist, who may have served as *praefectus annonae*. In this dual capacity of administrator and jurist he foreshadowed the later role of the Praetorian Prefects who were put in charge of the military food supply and administration.

Severus' troubles were not over after Plautianus' death. Caracalla and Geta had never been the best of friends and their behaviour was atrocious.[131] It was said that the British campaign was launched to distract them from their dissensions, but this was surely not its main purpose. Severus was aging, suffering among other things from gout or possibly arthritis, which forced him to travel in a litter, but he still left Rome and made the arduous journey to the edge of the Roman world. Herodian says that the governor of Britain sent a despatch asking for more troops or the Emperor's personal intervention, because the Britons were causing such destruction.[132]

## *Expeditio felicissima Britannica*

After Clodius Albinus withdrew troops from Britain, the situation from 197 to 208 is variously assessed. Inscriptions record repairs to several forts in the Pennines and on Hadrian's Wall under the governors Virius Lupus, Valerius Pudens and Alfenus Senecio, but despite the assertion of Herodian that damage was done, it cannot be proved that the work was necessary because of destruction by British tribesmen. Virius Lupus was appointed governor of Britain in 197, and in two separate passages Dio records that there was trouble from the tribe called the Maeatae, who lived near the wall that cuts the island in half, and that the Caledonians had broken their promises by preparing to aid them. Since the Caledonians are traditionally assigned to lands north of the old Antonine Wall, it is assumed that this is the frontier to which Dio referred. Lupus was forced to buy peace from the Maeatae at great cost. Dio does not mention fighting before or after this event, but Lupus received some prisoners in return for the payment, which, assuming that they were soldiers, may indicate a skirmish or a battle.[133]

Modern authors argue for and against an invasion by the northern tribes in or after 197. Birley accepted that there was an invasion, while Salway suggested that repairs to forts were necessary because of deterioration over the years.[134] Frere pointed out that the long time span in repairing forts in the north does not indicate urgency.[135] More recently, Mattingly dismisses the evidence for a military crisis after 197 as dubious.[136] There is very little firm evidence that there was serious trouble, but it is even more difficult to prove that something did *not* happen, so the verdict has to be that we don't know. If the army in Britain was fighting a war in 197, why did nine years elapse before Severus arrived? It could be the case that, as Dio affirms, Severus intended to conquer the whole island.[137] It would be a fitting achievement for his reputation as *propagator imperii*.

Severus arrived in Britain in 208, accompanied by his *comites*, his circle of friends, and his campaign army of troops from the Rhine and Danube, possibly II Parthica from Italy and detachments from the Praetorian Guard. He established his headquarters at York, which was the seat of government of the whole Empire, complete with the Imperial secretaries and officials, some of whom are known. The *Codex Justinianus* preserves many of Severus' rescripts, or replies to legal queries from all over the Empire, some of them issued from York during Severus' campaigns.[138] Herodian says that while his father and brother went on campaign, Geta was left behind in York to exercise jurisdiction over the provincial population and the civil administration of the Empire, with a council of the Emperor's friends to guide him. In 210 Geta was finally elevated to Augustus.[139]

The archaeological traces of Severus' two campaigns are slightly more useful than the written evidence. A Severan supply base has been identified on the river Tyne at Arbeia (South Shields), and another at Coria (Corbridge), where an inscription records an officer in charge of the granaries at the time of the British expedition (*tempore expeditione felicissimae Britannicae*).[140] Further north there was a supply base at Cramond on the Forth. At Carpow on the Tay tiles of VI Victrix attest to a legionary base. Two lines of marching camps into Scotland, not securely dated, are assumed to belong to Severus' two campaigns, the first in 208-9, which he led, and the second led by Caracalla alone in 210. The events of these campaigns are not well documented.

Dissension in the Imperial household was always apparent. Dio relates that Caracalla and Severus rode together to meet the Caledonians to arrange terms, and Caracalla drew his sword, as though he intended to stab his father in the back. He did not do so, but Herodian says that Caracalla tried to persuade his father's doctors to hasten his death.[141] There was no need to hurry things along, because Severus was already ill. In 210 he relinquished command of the next campaign to Caracalla. In February 211, preparing a third campaign, Severus died at York, telling his two squabbling sons not to disagree with each other, to pay the soldiers, and to despise everyone else.[142]

Caracalla may have fought this third campaign in 211, but with no recorded result. If Severus really had intended to subdue all Britain, then clearly he failed, but it is possible that all he wanted to achieve was to secure Hadrian's Wall, which he repaired thoroughly, and to demonstrate Roman strength to tribes beyond the frontier. Possibly his plan included building more outposts forts in Lowland Scotland, but this did not happen. Caracalla brought the campaigns to an end and concluded peace with the tribes. He may not have withdrawn the troops all at once, since an inscription from Carpow reveals a Roman presence there after Caracalla's departure.[143] The northern British frontier remained stable for the next eight and a half decades. There may have been a treaty with the Caledonians and Maeatae, quite possibly involving subsidies for the tribes in return for contributions of troops, but this goes beyond the evidence.

Caracalla did not forget about Britain. At some time after 213 the province was divided into two. Herodian attributes the division to Severus, just after the defeat of Albinus in 197.[144] The idea may have been his, but it is considered that Caracalla executed it. The two new provinces were named Britannia Inferior in the north and Superior in the south. Dio says that VI Victrix was in Britannia Inferior, and the other two legions were in Superior.[145] On analogy with other provinces containing only one legion, Britannia Inferior should have been a praetorian province. Birley discusses the various solutions that have been suggested to explain the apparent anomalies, which have not been satisfactorily resolved. The boundary line between the two provinces is not precisely defined, but Lincoln was in Inferior and Chester was in Superior, so a tentative line can be drawn.[146] The division of Britain is analogous with Caracalla's readjustments of the boundaries of the two Pannonian provinces, sometime between 212 and 217. There were three legions in Superior and one in Inferior. Caracalla reassigned Brigetio (Szöny, Hungary) and its legionary garrison from Pannonia Superior to Pannonia Inferior, so that with two legions in each province, a governor's chances of raising rebellion were reduced.

## The Emperor Caracalla

Very soon after the arrival of the Imperial party in Rome, at the end of 211 or at the beginning of 212, Caracalla personally murdered Geta.[147] Caracalla's next move was to secure the support of the Praetorians, telling them that he had been forced to kill Geta in self-defence. The soldiers had sworn allegiance to Geta, but Caracalla's cash erased their memories.[148] In addition to donatives, Herodian says that Caracalla promised to increase army pay by one half, and Dio gives the total cost as 280,000,000 sesterces.[149]

After spending the night in the Praetorian camp, Caracalla eradicated all his brother's supporters, among them the Praetorian Prefect, Papinianus. Dio says 20,000 people were killed, and Herodian names many of them.[150] The Roman world was ordered to forget Geta.

His name was chiselled off inscriptions, his portraits and statues were destroyed, references to him were edited out of all documents including papyri. A massive undertaking; but Geta is still remembered.

Caracalla bestowed influential posts on his supporters, such as Quintus Marcius Dioga, the new *a rationibus* in charge of revenues and expenditure, and Sextus Varius Marcellus, *ratio privata* in charge of Caracalla's personal funds.[151]

## Constitutio Antoniniana

Traditionally in 212, a date not without dispute, Caracalla granted Roman citizenship to all free-born inhabitants of the Empire by an edict recorded in the *Digest*.[152] It was customary to take the family name of whoever enfranchised new citizens, so the name Aurelius, as in Caracalla's official name Marcus Aurelius Antoninus, became very common after the *Constitutio*. All free peoples in all the provinces were now subject to Roman law, and to the inheritance tax, paid by all citizens. Dio says that this tax was Caracalla's main purpose, because he had to recoup the money squandered on the soldiers.[153] The *Constitutio* will have involved the Roman, Italian and provincial administrative staff in unimaginable clerical work to record all the new citizens, but Marcus' legislation making the recording of free births compulsory in the provinces presumably made it easier to establish free status. The equalizing tendencies of the enfranchisement no doubt upset the old nobility.

## The Rhine and Danube frontiers

For some years there had been no serious trouble on the northern frontiers, but in 212-3 Germania Superior was threatened by tribesmen whom Dio, or more likely his later epitomator, calls the Alamanni.[154] The name Alamanni means 'all men', denoting a federation of different tribes who consciously chose to amalgamate at some unknown date, possibly later than 213. These people would become depressingly familiar in the later third century. In Caracalla's time the tribes threatening the Rhine were still labelled Germans, as attested by his victory title *Germanicus Maximus*, adopted after he fought the war against them.[155] He had prepared for this war thoroughly, building or repairing a network of roads in Raetia, setting up large numbers of new milestones commemorating the work. Between the Rhine and Danube he assembled detachments from other parts of the Empire including II Adiutrix from Pannonia Superior, and II Traiana from

Egypt. Unfortunately, the details of the campaign are obscure, but whatever Caracalla and his army achieved it ensured peace for twenty years, and the Emperor was hailed as Imperator for the third time. He rebuilt the gateway through the frontier at Dalkingen, which may have been a customs post as well as a guard house, on the route from Roman territory into Free Germany. It was probably now that he altered the boundaries between the two Pannonian provinces, each with two legions, and Pannonia Inferior would now require a consular governor.

According to Herodian, Caracalla recruited soldiers from among the tribes north of the frontier.[156] This would have been a normal arrangement in any peace treaty, and subsidies for the tribes may have been instituted after the campaign, possibly, as Dio says, favouring one tribe but not another, turning them against each other to take their minds off Roman territory.[157]

## The East

The Parthian Royal House was still as disunited as it had been under Severus. Vologaeses V was preoccupied in fighting for the throne against his brother Artabanus, who eventually emerged as Artabanus V. Caracalla seized the opportunity to start an eastern campaign.[158] Although Herodian says that Caracalla merely wanted the title *Parthicus*, the campaign was well planned.[159] Caracalla summoned King Abgar of Osroene to Rome as a friend, but imprisoned him and took over his kingdom as a base for the campaign, elevating Edessa to a colony in the process. When he summoned the King of Armenia, he met with resistance from the Armenian people.[160]

The Romans marched to the east by way of the Danube provinces, spending the winter of 214 in Macedonia, but then trouble broke out in Alexandria. Caracalla put his general Theocritus in command with orders to attack Armenia, and went to Alexandria, where he massacred many people.[161] The situation in the east had changed when Caracalla returned. Artabanus V was now ruler of the Parthians, not much stronger than Vologaeses, but for some reason Caracalla did not fight.[162] The troops knew that an African soothsayer had prophesied that Macrinus, currently the Praetorian Prefect, would succeed Caracalla.[163] Macrinus was a lawyer, not a soldier, and resentful that Caracalla mocked him for his lack of military experience.[164] Knowing of the prophecy, Caracalla sent orders to Rome to have it investigated by a man he trusted. The reply was that Macrinus was indeed plotting to remove the Emperor, but when the correspondence from Rome was delivered, Caracalla was watching a chariot race and ordered Macrinus to deal with it.[165] Macrinus was in danger even if he destroyed the letter, because there might be a follow-up from Rome. This is how he explained why he had persuaded a centurion among Caracalla's bodyguard to murder the Emperor early in April 217.

## The reign of Macrinus

Marcus Opellius Macrinus had not been the soldiers' first choice as Emperor. They preferred Oclatinius Adventus, Macrinus' colleague, as Praetorian Prefect and as consul in 218. Adventus refused the honour on account of his age, and also because of his low origins as a former mercenary.[166] He had been a member of the *frumentarii*, dubbed not quite accurately in modern terms as secret police. They originated possibly from Domitian's reign, but are more commonly associated with Hadrian, their primary task being to procure grain (*frumentum*), which gave them experience of all the provinces, the governors, the people and the armies. This suited them for special tasks, and they became an instrument of imperial power.[167] Adventus was made city prefect, but Macrinus soon replaced him with Marius Maximus.

Although the army declared Macrinus Emperor, he did not take up the title immediately because he wanted to make it clear that he had not arranged Caracalla's murder for the sole purpose of becoming Emperor himself.[168] Macrinus was a native of Mauretania and had been treasury official (*procurator aerarii maioris*) in 208. In 212 he became Praetorian Prefect.[169] He had survived the fall of his patron Plautianus.[170] As an equestrian he was not of the correct social class, and since he did not immediately travel to Rome he lost the chance to make himself acceptable to the senators and the people. In truth, there was such great relief that Caracalla was dead that anyone, even a non-senator, would be better.[171]

Macrinus finished off the Parthian war, attending to Imperial government by remote control. He wrote to the Senate, explaining that he had adopted the name of Severus, and also the titles Pius Felix Augustus, without waiting for the senators to bestow titles on him of their own accord.[172] Macrinus' son, Diadumenianus, not yet ten years old, was given the additional name of Antoninus, connecting him and his father with the reigns of Antoninus Pius, Marcus Aurelius, and Caracalla. The senators voted Diadumenianus the status of patrician and the title Caesar.[173] There was a division between the soldiers, who had adored Caracalla, and the senators and people, who reviled him, so Macrinus made no move either to deify him or to damn him. Fear of the soldiers prevented anyone else from damning Caracalla's memory.[174]

By appointing men he trusted to important posts, regardless of social standing or rank, Macrinus upset most people. He appointed Marcius Agrippa governor of Dacia and Deccius Triccianus governor of Pannonia. Triccianus demonstrates the new social mobility, having been a soldier in Pannonia, rising to commander of II Parthica and now to provincial governor. The next Emperor, Elagabalus, had him killed.[175]

Meanwhile, King Artabanus of Parthia had launched an offensive against Mesopotamia, but while Macrinus prepared to retaliate, negotiations ended the war. Macrinus was a realist, aware that neither he nor his army was capable of defeating Parthia. He installed the pro-Roman Tiridates as King of Armenia, and paid indemnities to Artabanus. He awarded himself the title *Parthicus Maximus* in his report to the Senate.

Since Macrinus relied more than most on the support of the army, he mollified the soldiers by eventually deifying Caracalla, but he lost whatever support he gained by penny pinching. He wrote to the Senate to explain that it was impossible to pay the wages and the promised donatives to the army, but on the other hand it was impossible to refuse to pay it.[176] He managed to curb the expenses of the army without unduly offending the troops, but he reverted to the Severan rates of pay for the Praetorians, snatching away Caracalla's promise of a pay rise.[177] When Macrinus proclaimed a victory over the Parthians, he seems to have forgotten that this usually involved cash rewards to the soldiers, even though the war had ended by diplomacy. If Macrinus had split up the army into smaller units, distributing them over a wide area, he may have soothed the discontented troops.[178] It was already too late. The family of Julia Domna, Severus' widow, began to take an interest in Imperial rule. Domna had accompanied Caracalla to the east, but she died soon after his murder.[179] She hailed from Emesa (Homs) where her family still lived. Her ambitious sister, Julia Maesa, had two daughters, Julia Soaemias and Julia Mammaea, each of whom had a son. Soaemias communicated with the armies, claiming that her son Varius Avitus Bassianus was the son of Caracalla. On 16 May 218 this boy was declared Emperor by the army, and renamed Marcus Aurelius

Antoninus, better known later as Elagabalus after his ardent worship of the god of the same name.

## Elagabalus

At Macrinus' request, the Senate declared the usurper an enemy of the state. Diadumenianus was made Augustus, to no avail, since the army went over to the new Emperor. Macrinus and Diadumenianus were killed.[180] From Antioch, Elagabalus wrote to the Senate, styling himself Imperator Caesar Antoninus Pius Felix Augustus. An inscription shows that for added security he declared himself a descendant of Nerva.[181] The soldiers wanted to sack Antioch, but were bought off at a cost of 2000 *sesterces* per man.[182] If it was not known already, the episode showed that connection to previous Imperial families did not count for as much as cash with the promise of more, and that Roman armies would casually sack a Roman city to get rich quick.

Elagabalus and his family entered Rome in late September 219. He had ordered a painting of himself in his robes as priest of his divine namesake to be placed in the Senate House.[183] The Romans would probably not have objected to the arrival of the eastern god if Elagabalus had limited observation of the cult to himself and his followers, but he put his god before Jupiter.[184] What his portrait did not reveal was his decidedly odd, even unhinged character, and how much he was under the thumbs of his mother Julia Soaemias and his aunt Julia Maesa.

Dio describes how Elagabalus disposed of Macrinus' followers without making any official statement about their disappearance, or rather murder.[185] To replace these officials, Elagabalus installed his own favourites, allegedly putting actors and circus performers in official posts.[186] Dio laments that Publius Valerius Comazon was made Praetorian Prefect, despite his lack of experience, but the Prefects had been drawn more and more frequently from non-military men. What really annoyed Dio was that Comazon became consul and was city prefect three times, and yet he was only an equestrian, once condemned to the galleys. The senator responsible for condemning him to the galleys, Claudius Attalus, did not survive Comazon's appointment as Praetorian Prefect.[187] Dio then lists some other men killed by Comazon, sometimes with the reasons for their demise. The Senate acquiesced, dutifully condemning the victims posthumously.

In the ancient sources the scandals of Elagabalus' reign take priority over history. Elagabalus' outrageous sexual behaviour with both men and women became legendary, described at length by Dio, who also mentions the preponderant influence of the Emperor's 'husband' Hierocles.[188] The blatant sexual romps were not the prime cause of affront to the Romans, who were more upset by the preponderant influence of the Emperor's unsavoury associates. Julia Maesa tried to control the excesses of her grandson Elagabalus without success, and turned her attention to her daughter Julia Mammaea, mother of Gessius Alexianus Bassianus. Elagabalus was persuaded to adopt this boy, only a few years younger than himself, and the Senate ratified the adoption.[189] Gessius Alexianus was made consul with Elagabalus in 221, and probably through his mother he cultivated the Praetorians, always a shrewd move.[190] Elagabalus was killed on 6 March 222, along with his mother Soaemias and many of his adherents, including Fulvius the city prefect.[191] Comazon was probably the only associate of Elagabalus to survive, and took Fulvius' place for his third term as city prefect. The new Emperor, Gessius Alexianus Bassianus, became Marcus Aurelius Severus Alexander.

## Severus Alexander

The two Praetorian Prefects, Flavianus and Chrestus, were replaced in December 222 by a single Prefect, Domitius Ulpianus, or Ulpian. Dio accuses Ulpian of killing them in order to obtain the post.[192] Ulpian may have been connected to the Severan dynasty, and he was favoured by Julia Maesa. He was a jurist, and in the first decades of the third century administrators and legal experts were more in demand in government than soldiers. The need for military men would soon revive when wars broke out on the eastern and northern frontiers. Dio says that as Praetorian Prefect Ulpian was put in charge of most business of the Empire, and that he corrected many wrongs.[193] The Praetorians killed Ulpian probably in summer 223, not in 228 as previously thought, and afterwards they rioted for three days, burning parts of Rome.[194]

The sources for the reign of Severus Alexander are notoriously unreliable, and it boils down to opinion as to what is authentic and what is not. Dio's account is fragmentary from 229, Herodian's work lacks analysis, concentrating on the drama, and the *Historia Augusta* is mostly but not always fiction. The guiding forces in Severus Alexander's government were his grandmother Julia Maesa, who died in 224, and his mother Julia Mammaea. Though they had influence rather than political power, they were well-connected and could dispense favours, which worked effectively enough. Mammaea received honorary titles, such as *mater castrorum*, or mother of the camp, which Septimius Severus had bestowed on Julia Domna, but Mammaea went several steps further as *mater Augusti et castrorum et senatus atque patriae*, indicating that her influence if not her authority extended over the army, the Senate, and the fatherland. Maesa and Mammaea chose the Emperor's advisers, including sixteen senators.[195] The council comprised seventy members, according to a disputed passage of the *Historia Augusta*, but the personal names which are listed cannot be verified, and it seems that there was no rotation of membership according to the business to be discussed, as was customary under other emperors.[196]

Until the 230s there were no serious external wars, giving Severus Alexander time to repair the damage and restore the government. Some of the old Severan notables filled the magistracies and gravitated to the Imperial court. There is little information about provincial development or decline.

In Parthia, while the Romans restored their government, Ardashir, or Artaxerxes, an Iranian vassal subject to Artabanus V, steadily gained power. In 224 he overthrew the Parthian Arsacid dynasty on the battlefield of Hormizdagan, replacing it with his own Sasanid or Sassanid Persian dynasty, named after Ardashir's Iranian ancestor Sasan.[197] Ardashir quickly absorbed the states around the old Parthian kingdom, and as a result he made contact with Roman territories. He attacked Hatra in 229, and after news reached Rome, Severus Alexander prepared for an eastern campaign.[198] Soldiers were recruited in Italy and the provinces, especially in Pannonia and Dalmatia, the Illyrian provinces which supplied many of Rome's soldiers and generals.[199]

The Romans arrived at Antioch, but before the campaign began the Emperor had to deal with restlessness among his Egyptian troops, and the death of Flavius Heracleo, governor of Mesopotamia, killed by legionaries. There was also a potential usurper called Uranius, who was suppressed.[200] When all was quietened down, coins were issued with the legend FIDES MILITUM and FIDES EXERCITUS, proclaiming the loyalty of the army. Alexander made Antioch his base and marched in three columns, leading the central one himself. Of the other columns to his north and south, one inevitably headed for Armenia, where control was necessary for any eastern campaign. This column was to continue into Media, and the other was aimed at the city of Ctesiphon. The campaign is described by Herodian and related in hagiographic terms in the *Historia Augusta*.[201] There were great losses of soldiers, but the Persians caused no further trouble until the 240s under Ardashir's successor Shapur. Alexander took the titles *Parthicus Maximus* and *Persicus Maximus*, illustrating the change from the Parthian to the Persian regime.

For the eastern campaign Alexander had removed troops from the northern frontiers, and when trouble broke out on the Rhine the remaining soldiers became concerned for the safety of their homes and families.[202] Without concluding an official peace with Ardashir, Alexander wound up the war, returning to Rome at the end of 232 to celebrate a triumph. He then prepared for the war on the northern frontiers. He took with him troops which had fought in Mesopotamia, such as the archers from Osroene and the units of Moors, as well as the detachments of legionaries and auxiliaries.[203] He placed an experienced officer, Julius Verus Maximinus, in command of the recruits, and he was responsible for training them.[204]

Herodian insists that the Illyrians on the borders of Italy were in danger.[205] This is not borne out by archaeology, which shows that attacks on the frontiers were in Raetia in the region of the Altmühl valley, and the German tribes probably concentrated their attacks on the Taunus-Wetterau frontier where *c.*233 forts were destroyed.[206] Severus Alexander chose Mainz as his base, launching an offensive in 234 against an amalgamation of German tribes who were probably now calling themselves Alamanni. So far, the offensive had gone well, but instead of pursuing the enemy, Alexander began to negotiate, allegedly offering money. The Germans were always ready for gold.[207]

The troops were frustrated, having expected a brief and bloody campaign in revenge for the death and damage caused by the tribes.[208] In spring 235 it boiled over. Severus Alexander and his mother were murdered, and the Pannonian soldiers declared for Julius Verus Maximinus, better known as Maximinus Thrax, the Thracian. He may have been involved in the plot, but probably not the actual murder.[209] Herodian puts the elevation of Maximinus before the murder of Alexander.[210]

The Severan dynasty was finished. It was the fourth century author Aurelius Victor who designated this date of 235 as a turning point, when a soldier became an emperor and the so-called third-century crisis began.[211]

# 12

# The Soldier Emperors and the Crisis of the Third Century

The second half of the third century was a stressful time for the whole Empire. Leaving aside the debate about whether the period merits the description crisis, there were common themes all through the period. The army could and did make or break emperors, usually elevating soldiers, and there were twenty emperors in fifty years, some lasting only weeks. Sometimes there was more than one emperor at the same time. Unsuccessful emperors were labelled usurpers, but not all of these aimed at being emperor. Some of them took it upon themselves to protect their provinces because no-one else was able to help. Of the emperors and usurpers, hardly any died peacefully in bed. There was almost constant warfare. The western provinces suffered until the Rhine frontier faded away, while the focus shifted to the Danube and the east. The desperate state of the Empire is illustrated by the plethora of Imperial titles containing the word *restitutor*, restorer, on the Danube, or in the east, or eventually of the whole world.

## Maximinus Thrax

Maximinus was the first soldier to become Emperor, having risen through the ranks. He was perhaps not a Roman citizen but was descended from soldiers of the garrison of Dacia Ripensis.[1] Whatever his origins, the senators confirmed Maximinus as Emperor.Maximinus and made his young son Caesar. Severus Alexander's entourage and his *consilium* were eliminated, though the total of 4,000 killed according to the *Historia Augusta* is surely too high.[2] Resuming the German war, by the end of 235 Maximinus had won a victory.[3] In the following year he defeated the Sarmatians and Dacians. Inscriptions from Pannonia refer to soldiers killed in Dacia (*bello Dacico* or *in expeditione Dacica*), but with no dating evidence.[4]

Maximinus could not leave the frontier to go to Rome to establish himself as Emperor, but he could have sent representatives to explain his actions and policies to the Senate, most especially his need for money. Herodian describes Maximinus seizing money intended for the food supply, stripping temples and reducing good families to penury, possibly by confiscating properties.[5] Maximinus' financial dilemma had important consequences. Some of the wealthy nobles in North Africa protested against the harsh taxation, extracted to the letter by the procurator, who was killed. The best way of avoiding Roman retribution was to make a rival emperor, so the governor of Africa Proconsularis, Marcus Antonius Gordianus Sempronianus, over eighty years old, and his son, became the joint Emperors Gordian I and II.[6]

The Senate confirmed the Gordians in power and declared Maximinus and his son public enemies, probably in April 238. Agents of the Gordians in Rome killed the Praetorian Prefect Vitalianus, loyal to Maximinus, and the city prefect Sabinus was killed in a riot.[7] The governor of Numidia, Capellianus, also loyal to Maximinus, killed the two Gordians but did not seize power, which left the Empire technically leaderless, except that the soldiers of Maximinus had not deserted him. At a meeting of the Senate the government of the Empire was placed in the hands of twenty senators (*vigintiviri ex Senatus Consulto rei publicae curandae*).[8] The title indicates neither a revival of the Republic, nor a senatorial revolution, as has been claimed. The *Historia Augusta* insists that the twenty men were to defend Italy against the Emperor Maximinus, and in another passage that each of them was assigned a particular area of Italy to defend, which is highly unlikely.[9]

Learning that the two Gordians were dead, the senators elected Clodius Pupienus Maximus and Decimus Caelius Calvinus Balbinus as joint Augusti.[10] The people had other ideas, and together with the Praetorians they chose the thirteen-year-old Marcus Antonius Gordianus, nephew of Gordian II and present in Rome. The Senate recognised the boy as Caesar and designated successor of the two current Emperors.[11]

As Maximinus approached Italy from the Danube, Pupienus Maximus marched to meet him, and won a battle. The morale of Maximinus' troops was sinking, especially the men of II Parthica whose families lived close to Rome at their base at Alba, vulnerable to retribution. The legionaries killed Maximinus and his son at Aquileia.[12] The troops went over to Pupienus Maximus, who sent them back to their bases and kept the German soldiers as his bodyguard. This worried the Praetorians, who foresaw redundancy looming while the Germans replaced them. Pupienus Maximus and Balbinus were both murdered, and Gordian III became Emperor. This is where Herodian's narrative ends.

## Gordian III

The new Emperor's government tried to remedy the finances of the Empire. Justinian's sixth-century law code preserves a ruling that procurators at this date were ordered to be more lenient in collecting taxes and revenues.[13] In 241, Timesitheus, a friend of Severus Alexander, was appointed Praetorian Prefect and took on administration and military matters. His career is documented on an inscription from Lyons.[14] Gordian III married Timesitheus' daughter. It was probably on Gordian's orders that III Augusta in Africa was disbanded for its part in the deaths of the first two Gordians. The absence of the legion allowed a certain Sabinianus to bid for power, but the governor of Mauretania Caesariensis restored order.

Civilians in many parts of the Empire found themselves oppressed by the soldiers, as demonstrated by the famous inscription dating to the reign of Gordian III from the Thracian village of Skaptopara, in modern Bulgaria.[15] The village was not on any direct military route, but it possessed hot springs, and soldiers often arrived demanding *hospitium* (in Greek *xenia* or *xeinie*), literally 'hospitality' deriving from Republican and early Imperial practice when soldiers were quartered in official lodging houses rather than in barracks. Both Livy and Suetonius use the term *hospitium* in the context of military quarters.[16] *Hospitium* was theoretically limited to shelter and food, but the soldiers visiting Skaptopara interpreted it as licence to appropriate anything without paying for it. The inhabitants of Skaptopara were ready to set up a stele and display it in public if the Emperor relieved them of the burden. They petitioned Gordian III in 238, and he replied, but referred them to the provincial governor. The result is not known.

In addition to internal problems there were ominous signs of disturbances from outside the Empire. In the west, tribal incursions across the frontiers were probably responsible for the burial of coin hoards, for example in Germany at Kösching and Gunzenhausen, where hoards date between 241-244, roughly contemporary with the destruction of the fort at Künzing and damage to some settlements in Gaul.[17] There were also problems with bandits and unruly Roman soldiers.

From beyond the Danube, the Goths and Carpi invaded Moesia and Dacia, the first time that the Romans encountered the Goths. By the middle of the first century AD the geographer Ptolemy knew of a people called Gutones, probably Goths. It was thought that the tribes came from Scandinavia, migrating in stages into modern Prussia, Poland, and Russia. Their history was not written until the sixth century, so their Scandinavian origin is debatable. The Gothic kings held power for long periods, and they fought skilfully in a more organised fashion than many other tribes. They assimilated other people, while some of them left to join different tribes, or joined the Roman army.

The Emperors Pupienus and Balbinus had sent Tullius Menophilus against the Goths.[18] He defeated the tribes, repaired roads, fortified Marcianopolis in modern Bulgaria, and established a mint at Viminacium (Kostolac). He brought the tribes to terms, but in 241, for unknown reasons, he was removed from command by Timesitheus.

Rome's difficulties gave the Persian king Ardashir an advantage. He raided Mesopotamia in 236, and in 239 he attacked Dura Europos, possibly capturing Hatra, allied to Rome. He occupied Carrhae, Nisibis and possibly Singara.[19] He was ready to cross the Euphrates, threatening Syria, and may have attacked or even taken Antioch, where coin issues ceased from 240-241. While Timesitheus prepared for war in the east, Goths and Germans threatened the frontiers again, possibly because of the removal of Menophilus, who had arranged their treaties, which they anticipated would be swept aside. Timesitheus conducted a short war in 242, and arranged a new peace, probably recruiting tribesmen for the eastern campaign.

Timesitheus and Gordian III reached the east at the end of 242, beginning the campaign the following spring. Ardashir now shared power with his son Shapur, who may have captured Edessa. Timesitheus recaptured Osroene and restored it to Abgar X. At a battle at Rhesaena, the Persians were driven off and the Romans regained Nisibis and Singara. Timesitheus then died. Gordian III decided to continue the march to Ctesiphon with the Praetorian Prefect Marcus Julius Verus Philippus commanding the army, but the young Emperor also died, and fingers were pointed at Philippus. Ancient historians clearly did not know what had happened, relaying different versions of when, where and how Gordian died.[20] The Persian King Shapur carved his own version into the rock-face at Naqs-i Rustem, the text inscribed in Persian, Parthian and Greek. The record is termed *Res Gestae Divi Saporis*, denoted by the initials *RGDS*.[21] In March 244 Philippus was declared Emperor by the troops.[22] The Senate recognised him as Imperator Caesar Marcus Julius Philippus Augustus.[23] He is better known as Philip the Arab.

## Philip the Arab

Philip was born in Arabia to an equestrian family.[24] Philip sent Gordian's ashes to Rome and ensured his deification. Without fighting, he brought the army out of Persian territory, and negotiated peace in 244, losing control of Armenia but retaining Osroene and probably part of Mesopotamia, reconquered by Timesithius.[25] He paid an indemnity to the Persians of 500,000 denarii, and Persian sources say that he also agreed to pay regular tribute.[26] Philip took the titles *Parthicus Maximus* and *Persicus Maximus*.[27] Peace had been bought, but there had been no proper settlement, though Aurelius Victor maintains that Philip organised the east before he left.[28] He placed his brother Priscus in command, as prefect of Mesopotamia.[29] As an equestrian, his command of Mesopotamia was usual but Priscus also governed Syria, a consular command. His title was *rector Orientis*.[30] *Rector* was not a regular or permanent office, but signifies wide-ranging powers, and the expedient of putting equestrians in command of more than one province became more common in the later third century. Zosimus says that Priscus caused offence among the provincials by his harsh rule. [31]

In Rome in July 244, Philip elevated his son Marcus Julius Philippus to Caesar.[32] He would want to secure the succession as soon as possible, so the suggestion that he waited until 246 to make his son Caesar is unlikely.[33] In 247 Philip's wife Otacilia Severa received the title Augusta, and his son became Augustus. Instead of fictitiously connecting himself with a previous Imperial family, Philip deified his father Marinus, who had not been Emperor.

From 246-7 Philip fought the Carpi and Quadi on the Danube. Zosimus describes how the Carpi were forced back and besieged in their fortress, which may be linked to an inscription recording the death of a Praetorian soldier at a fortress of the Carpi in a Dacian war.[34] An honorary inscription from Romula in Dacia Malvensis declares both Philip and his son *restitutores orbis totius*, restorers of the whole world, which despite the hyperbole may have seemed a very real concept to beleaguered provincials.[35]

Philip celebrated the Secular Games sixty years too early in 248, but he was also celebrating a special date, the foundation of Rome 1,000 years before. Legends on the coinage proclaimed ROMA AETERNA. Perhaps convinced by his own propaganda, in the same year Philip terminated subsidies to the Goths. Within a year the tribes united to invade Moesia and Thrace, besieging Marcianopolis in modern Bulgaria. The sixth-century author Jordanes describes the siege from the Gothic point of view.[36]

It was realised that in order to combat tribes who were highly mobile and ranged over large areas it was necessary to combine provinces and their armies under a single command, since a provincial governor, restricted to his territory, could not deal with such invaders. The other side of the coin is that a single leader with increased power could bid for control of the Empire. Tiberius Claudius Marinus Pacatianus had been given an extended command over much of Pannonia and Moesia, and with access to large numbers of soldiers, he rebelled.[37] It came to nothing. Pacatianus was put down by his own troops. In Syria, Jotapianus led a revolt allegedly because of Priscus' over-zealous tax collection.[38]

Philip lost his nerve and offered to resign, dissuaded by the senator Gaius Messius Quintus Decius, who was appointed to the Danube command. He rounded up remaining supporters of Pacatianus, whereupon the soldiers recognised Decius as a better general than Philip and proclaimed him Emperor.[39] Civil war broke out. Two Roman armies, one from Rome and the other from the Danube, converged on the north of Italy, fighting near Verona. Alternative theories place the battle in Thrace, or in Macedonia. Wherever it occurred, Philip was killed, and late in 249 the victor Decius was confirmed as Emperor. The Praetorians helpfully murdered Philip's eleven-year-old son.

## Decius

The Senate granted to the new Emperor the additional name of Trajan, associating him with the Optimus Princeps. The usurper Jotapianus was caught and beheaded, but another maverick arose, Mariades, a noble from Antioch who raided Syria and Cappadocia, going over to the Persians in 251.[40]

Wars on several fronts threatened to fragment the Roman Empire. As one means of reunifying it, Decius reaffirmed the old Roman religion, restoring temples and reinvigorating the cult practices and rituals, earning the title *restitutor sacrorum*, attested on an inscription from Cosa. He marginalised or outlawed cults that he thought antipathetic to Rome, chiefly Christianity, issuing orders throughout the Empire on16 October 249 that everyone should sacrifice to the Roman gods, in return for a certificate testifying that they had done so.[41] The production and distribution of certificates, on whatever medium they were written, called for a supreme clerical effort. The persecution surprised the Christian community. Philip had been tolerant towards them, to the point where the myth grew up that he was the first Christian Emperor, now discredited. St Cyprian, whose letters illustrate events in Africa, complained that many Christians did not have the courage to disobey the authorities. Some Christians perhaps rendered unto Caesar what was his due, and quietly carried on rendering what was due to their own deity, while those who refused to conform were tried and executed. Decius is the arch-tyrant in the works of contemporary and later Christian authors.[42]

In 250, the Carpi attacked Dacia and the Goths invaded Moesia. Surviving Christians construed this as divine retribution. Attempting to make his regime more secure, Decius elevated his son Herennius Etruscus to the rank of Caesar. Living up to his name Trajan, he drove the Carpi out of Dacia, and was granted the title *restitutor Daciarum*.[43] So far, he was successful, but Cniva, the leader of the Goths in Moesia and Thrace, was a match for Decius and his army.

Herennius Etruscus became Augustus in May 251, and Decius' other son Hostilianus attended to civil administration, assisted by the senator Publius Licinius Valerianus.[44] The Roman mob were not impressed, and tried unsuccessfully to create a new Emperor, Julius Valens Licinianus.[45] Meanwhile Decius marched north after the Goths, skirmishing but not bringing them to battle, until they arrived at Abrittus (Razgrad, Bulgaria), where the Romans were defeated and Decius killed. The ancient authors provide several versions of Decius' demise.[46] Herennius Etruscus may have been killed in one of the earlier skirmishes. An Emperor was required, and the legions declared for the governor of Moesia, Trebonianus Gallus, from Perusia. He became Imperator Caesar Caius Vibius Trebonianus Gallus Augustus.[47]

### Trebonianus Gallus

Aware that continuing the war in the Danube zone would prevent him from going to Rome to consolidate his rule, the new Emperor made peace with the Goths, resuming payment of subsidies, possibly on condition that the Goths guarded the Danube area.[48]

Established in Rome, Gallus spared supporters of Decius, and adopted Decius' son Hostilianus.[49] Hostilianus and Gallus' son Volusianus were made Caesars and then Augusti, in echelon with Hostilianus in the lead, but during the plague of 252-3 Hostilianus died.[50] The most important item on Rome's agenda was how to stop the Persian ruler Shapur from taking over the east. Gallus' impending Persian campaign started with the issue of a large quantity of *antoniniani*, the coins used to pay the soldiers, from the Antioch mint.[51] Shapur pre-empted Gallus by taking Nisibis and destroying much of Antioch, according to Zosimus and Shapur's own testimony at Naqs-i Rustem, where he lists thirty-seven towns and fortresses taken from the Romans.[52] The provincials of the east needed help immediately, and Uranius Antoninus of Emesa seized power, defeated a Persian force and began to issue his own coins in 253 and 254, naming him as Lucius Julius Sulpicius Antoninus.[53] He held power for roughly a year and then disappears from the record.

The actions of Uranius Antoninus were construed as usurpation, but his case illustrates a dilemma that became more common during the third century, when the central government could not deal simultaneously with all the problems of the Empire, especially the attacks on the frontier provinces. In the absence of legitimate emperors, the pressurized provincials required someone strong enough to fight back. For this to be effective, the chosen or self-proclaimed leader required the titles and trappings of authority of the emperors, because no other titles would suffice. So-called usurpers were not all rebels, but Romans, whatever their original nationality, firmly adhering to Roman ideals and standards and doing what Rome could not do for them.[54] The problem for legitimate emperors was that this procedure of self-protection could build up a power base that might eventually threaten their hold on the Empire.[55]

## The revolt of Aemilius Aemilianus and the rise of Valerian

Contemporary with the rise of Uranius Antoninus in the east, Gallus was also challenged on the Danube frontier, where the governor of Moesia Inferior, Aemilius Aemilianus, stopped the subsidies to the Goths on his own initiative. He may have crossed the Danube and defeated the tribesmen, rescuing some of the Roman prisoners that Gallus had allowed the Goths to keep. His troops declared him Emperor, but instead of attempting to oust Gallus, he compromised, sending a letter to Rome suggesting a division of responsibilities with the Senate, which he said should be the supreme power, with himself as commander in chief on the Danube and in the east.[56]

Gallus summoned Publius Licinius Valerianus commanding in Gaul to bring the Rhine legions to assist him against Aemilianus, who was on his way to Italy. Before Valerian reached them, Gallus and his son were assassinated by their own troops at Interamna north of Rome. Valerian continued the march, meeting Aemilius at Spoletium (Spoleto), and defeating him. Having been an emperor for less than three months, Aemilius was murdered by his troops. In September 253 Valerian was declared Emperor by the army.[57] The ancient sources claim that the Senate immediately elevated Valerian's adult son Publius Licinius Gallienus to Augustus, but milestones in Numidia show that he was first made Caesar.[58] It is more likely that Gallienus was raised to Augustus when Valerian arrived in Rome.[59] It all looked very promising, since two adult Augusti ought to be able to deal with the problems in two halves of the Empire, Gallienus taking the west and Valerian going to the east to combat the Persian menace.

## Valerian and Gallienus

Shapur had been meddling in Armenian affairs for some time, and in 253 he gave them his full attention, claiming that 'the Caesar lied again and did wrong with respect to Armenia.'[60] The meaning is unclear. Armenia was left open to Shapur as King Chosroes was killed and his son Tiridates fled. It is suspected that Shapur had captured Antioch in 253, but if so, in January 255 Valerian regained it.[61] Damage to the city and its surrounding territory was repaired, and Valerian earned the title *restitutor Orientis*, restorer of the east. By summer 256 Valerian was at Cologne, and Gallienus travelled from the Danube to join him, probably having defeated the tribes.[62] In August 257, Valerian, Gallienus, and Gallienus' son Valerian the Younger were all together, responding to the Frankish threat to Gaul and Germany.[63] Gallienus made Cologne his headquarters and established a mint there, issuing coins naming him *restitutor Galliarum*.

When the Franks had been expelled, Valerian resumed Decius' measures against the Christians. St Cyprian was exiled from Carthage, but he returned and was executed in September 258, thus depriving modern scholars of the best source for events and their chronology. By the spring of 258 Valerian had returned to the east. He left Valerian the younger in Illyricum, where shortly afterwards the army rebelled, led by Ingenuus, and in the turmoil the younger Valerian was killed.[64]

While Valerian was fully occupied in the east fighting against Shapur, Gallienus was re-establishing his authority over the Danube provinces, but probably between 255 and 259 the Goths appeared, threatening the Black Sea coastal cities.[65] At the same time the Alamanni were restless on the frontiers of Germany and Raetia, threatening the *Agri Decumates*, uncomfortably close to Italy.[66] Gallienus left his younger son Saloninus at Cologne as the new Caesar with a guardian known only as Silvanus, and set up headquarters at Milan, where he established a mint. Coins were issued with the legends FIDES MILITUM and FIDES EQUITUM, proclaiming the loyalty of the army and the cavalry.[67]

The year 260 saw the nadir of the Empire. The frontiers were breached, and in the summer Shapur captured the Emperor Valerian. This unprecedented event is recorded by an impressive array of ancient authors.[68] The Persians also recorded it, via relief sculptures supplementing the trilingual written account at Naqs-i Rustem.[69] The date 260 is not without dispute, but Christol points out that in papyrus records from Egypt, up to August 260 Valerian and Gallienus were Augusti and Saloninus was Caesar, but by October 260 officials in Egypt dated events by the regnal years of the two sons of Macrianus, who took command in the east.[70]

## The provinces in the third century crisis

From the 230s onwards there were simultaneous or consecutive problems outside and inside the Empire. The year 235 has been identified as a turning point, when Maximinus succeeded Severus Alexander, and the Roman world entered a period of escalating anarchy. This was not an age of expansion, adding new provinces or extending old ones, but a struggle to keep hold of territory. While this was playing out there were attacks on nearly all the frontiers, and by 260 most of them had been breached.

There were several other factors apart from raiding tribesmen that made up the third century crisis not engendered by the incursions of the tribesmen, but certainly exacerbated by them.[71] An economic decline had already begun before the tribal invasions, and the coinage had been successively debased, to the point where in the mid-third century, the silver content of the *antoninianus*, introduced by Caracalla and worth two *denarii*, was less than five per cent, and Fergus Millar links the debasement of the coinage to the later development whereby the soldiers would be paid half in cash and half in food, or entirely in rations and clothing.[72] Markets declined, towns shrank or were abandoned, and in some provinces the countryside was depopulated. Not all of the provinces had all of the problems all of the time, and probably no-one but the emperors and the high command would have a collective sense of the unfolding drama now labelled a crisis. Most people in Italy and the provinces would see it all as a series of successive disasters of different kinds, not necessarily linked. The concerns of a small farmer in central Gaul would probably be limited to the fact that tribesmen had crossed the Rhine, and he would probably not know or care that the Persians were rampaging through Syria.

There were also internal problems in the provinces. Bandits proliferated, so it became necessary to protect all kinds of settlements not only from invading tribesmen but from the lawlessness that prevailed. The most famous group of bandits was the Bagaudae, farmers and agricultural workers who had nothing to lose, but this group developed later and were more co-ordinated than other bandits.

There were some common features in the responses to the new situation in the western provinces. One was the increasingly burdensome obligations of the decurions and the elected officials of the towns. During troublesome times in all periods, those who can afford to leave usually do so. The third century migration of the wealthy from the cities and towns to large villa estates, possibly fortified, has been detected archaeologically in Gaul and Britain. Lack of funds may have been caused in part by a new expenditure, as those cities and towns that had not already built defensive walls did so in the third century, while existing walls were strengthened or rebuilt. Imperial sanction had to be sought first, but it seems that this was not refused. Possibly for prestige and not defence, cities and towns in Britain had been provided with walls in the second century, considerably earlier than most of the cities in the Gallic provinces.

In the early third century there were only a few walled towns in the Gallic and German provinces. One of the earliest was Autun, established as the *civitas* capital of the Aedui, with imposing gates and a fortified circuit probably of first century date. As in Britain, the colonies received walls quite early, so Aventicum (Avenches), Cologne and Xanten were walled, but Lugdunum (Lyon) was not. Atuatuca (Tongeren) and Bononia (Boulogne) had walls before other cities. The defences of Augusta Treverorum (Trier) incorporated part of the amphitheatre in the walls. Many of the third century town and city walls in Gaul, especially Belgica, were constructed in haste, using tombstones, inscriptions and parts of monuments in the foundations, but usually the walls above the foundations were built with care, from quarried stone, not rubble.[73] Nearly all the third-century city and town defences enclosed a smaller area than the settlements had previously occupied. New walls replaced the earlier ones at Atuatuca (Tongeren) enclosing the city in a much smaller area, and the same shrinkage of town and city size has been observed in Spain, Raetia, and the Upper Danube zone. Some people may have lived outside, and certainly farmlands would be beyond the walls. Depopulation is probable, but there is also evidence of overcrowding, with dwellings being established in earlier gardens and open spaces, and encroaching on streets, or of rooms being divided up into smaller units.

Aurelius Victor reports that the tribes who crossed the Rhine, labelled Germani or Franci, reached Spain.[74] They failed to capture Tarraco, but interested primarily in loot, they moved on to Africa in stolen ships. There are few archaeological traces of destruction of this period at Tarraco.[75] Orosius writing in the fifth century says that signs of damage were still visible in his time, but the damage could have been caused after these first invasions. Some of the cities of the Spanish provinces had been equipped with walls under Augustus, and in the later third century these were either strengthened, or new walls replaced them, as at Barcino (Barcelona), where new fortifications were constructed in front of the Augustan defences. As in Gaul, the new defensive circuits did not enclose entire towns. In the later third century, Rome itself would receive a wall, which excluded some parts of the city.

Africa and Egypt escaped large-scale invasions, but there was still some fighting, mostly on the provincial borders. In Macedonia, Greece and Asia Minor most of the cities were already walled, but the walls had not been kept in good condition, so rapid repairs took place when tribes crossed the Danube and arrived in ships to raid the coast of Asia Minor during the reigns of Valerian and Gallienus. Thessalonica was besieged, but the inhabitants defended their city and drove off the tribes. The Athenians had to rebuild their walls, but the city still suffered much damage until the people resisted, probably in 267, led by Herennius Dexippus, who wrote an account of the defence of the city and the defeat of the barbarians. Civilians in other parts of the Empire were also involved in defence of their own areas, in Gaul and Germany, working with the armies fighting against the Alamanni, and in Pannonia Inferior the usurper Ingenuus fought and defeated the Sarmatians with an army of town dwellers and country people.[76]

In the tumultuous times it is not surprising that local Roman or native commanders took charge of some areas to try to establish order. There were determined efforts in the east and the west to do exactly this. Some Roman commanders assumed power and were labelled usurpers, their biographies provided in the *Tyranni Triginta*, Thirty Tyrants, or Pretenders of the *Historia Augusta*. Not all of these leaders wanted to rule the world, and without them parts of the Empire may have crumbled.

### Gallienus and the secessionist states

Gallienus had to fight to maintain his position. After the defeat of Valerian, Macrianus, *praepositus annonae expeditionalis*, in charge of supplies and logistics, assembled the remnants of the Roman army with the help of Callistus, or Ballista. Neither of them claimed to be emperors, but Macrianus declared his two sons, Titus Fulvius Junius Macrianus and Titus Fulvius Junius Quietus, as Augusti.[77] Macrianus was not content with restoring order in the east. He placed Callistus/ Ballista and his son Quietus in command of the provinces while he took his younger son with him to march for Rome to claim the Empire. He had reached Pannonia before he met Gallienus' general and cavalry commander Aureolus, and both father and son were killed.

The Palmyrene leader Odenathus had initially assisted Macrianus, but perhaps because he could see that the usurpers were doomed, he accepted Gallienus' instructions to eliminate Callistus and Quietus, perhaps being offered the title of *corrector totius orientis*, making him in effect governor of the entire east.[78] The *Historia Augusta* expands on this claiming that Odenathus was made emperor of the east, *orientis factus est Odenathus imperator*.[79] Callistus and Quietus were killed by their Roman troops, who had also seen the writing on the wall. They went over to Odenathus.

Odenathus was a member of the nobility of Palmyra, which was a highly cultured, wealthy city, in the desert roughly midway between Emesa (Homs) in western Syria and Dura Europos on the Euphrates. Possessing a reliable source of water, Palmyra was situated astride the eastern trade routes, where taxes could be levied on the caravans passing through, and fees could be charged for the accommodation of the traders. Odenathus was a Roman citizen and had taken the name Septimius, after the Emperor Severus had granted Roman citizenship to Odenathus' father Hairan. Odenathus held senatorial rank, and by 258 he was *vir consularis*, of consular status, perhaps having been granted *ornamenta consularia* by the joint Emperors Valerian and Gallienus.[80]

Gallienus could not mount a campaign to win back the east and try to rescue his imprisoned father, who died in captivity, and for this apparent neglect Gallienus was accused of lack of filial piety, but in trying to rescue Valerian, Gallienus would probably have lost another army in the east, and in his absence the other parts of the Empire may also have been lost. Since Odenathus seemed capable of bringing everything under control it would be better to use him rather than oust him, so Gallienus negotiated, perhaps arranging a formal treaty *c*.262-3.[81] He recognised the Palmyrene leader as commander in the east, possibly granting him the title of *dux Romanorum*.[82] The titles granted to Odenathus, nominally Gallienus' chosen deputy, were not unusual. It is not certain if Odenathus was given power over Roman administrative officials, but as *dux* he would be entitled to command Roman troops as well as his Palmyrene militia, and Zosimus describes how Odenathus combined his own troops with the legions to pursue and attack Shapur as the Persian army headed back across the Euphrates laden with booty.[83] The territorial extent of Odenathus' power is not clearly established, but he probably controlled Syria, Palestine, Mesopotamia, Arabia, and the eastern areas of Asia Minor.[84] For the time being, the eastern provinces were secure, and still part of the Roman Empire.

Ancient authors say that Odenathus led only one campaign, but Zosimus says that there were two. Conceivably there was an expedition in 262-3 and another four years later.[85] Odenathus liberated Nisibis from Persian domination, and reached Ctesiphon, awarding himself the customary eastern title king of kings. Gallienus granted him the title Imperator, and *corrector totius Orientis*, taking the title *Parthicus Maximus* for himself.[86] It is not certain how much executive power this gave Odenathus, but he was willing to defer to Gallienus, and he certainly kept the peace in his territories, losing no time in marching to meet the Goths when they invaded Asia Minor. Probably in Emesa *c*.267 or 268, Odenathus was murdered, along with his eldest son Hairan/Herodes. It has been suggested that he may have been ready to turn against Gallienus and to seize power in the east, and therefore Gallienus ordered his removal.[87] This is unlikely. Gallienus sent the Praetorian Prefect Heraclianus to take charge in Palmyra, but when the northern tribes crossed the Danube, Zenobia, later Septimia Zenobia, the energetic and ambitious wife of Odenathus, took power with her two younger sons, Herodianus and Vaballathus, and expelled Heraclianus.[88] From then onwards until his death in 268 Gallienus was too hard-pressed to retrieve the situation, which remained unresolved until the reign of Aurelian.

In the west, Marcus Cassianus Latinius Postumus was *praeses* or equestrian governor of Germania Inferior in 259.[89] The frontiers of the Rhine, the Taunus-Wetterau and Raetia had probably lost some of their forts in the 230s, and although some of the damage had been repaired, after 260 the whole line was in tatters. Postumus, the man most capable of defending the German and Gallic provinces, was declared Emperor by the army.[90] It is not certain whether news of Valerian's capture reached Gaul before or after this event, but it was clear that the legitimate Emperors were in no position to help. As proof of his abilities Postumus won a victory over the tribe of Senones or Juthungi, attested as such on an inscription from Augsburg.[91] The tribesmen were returning home after a raid carrying their booty, which Postumus seized and gave to his soldiers, but Silvanus, guardian of the young Saloninus, tried to force the men to return possessions to the original owners. This noble idea failed miserably, resulting in Postumus' siege of Cologne and the deaths of Silvanus and Saloninus.

Postumus' territory was labelled the Empire of the Gauls by the late author Eutropius, and now goes by the modern title *Imperium Galliarum*, or the Gallic Empire.[92] The Augsburg inscription shows that Postumus ruled over the Gallic and German provinces, the Rhine frontier and Raetia, verifying the statement in some ancient sources that Gallienus lost Raetia. An inscription found in Wales attests that Britain was also with Postumus, and a milestone from Lincoln mentions the third Gallic Emperor, Victorinus.[93] Postumus is attested as Emperor on a milestone from Spain dating to 260-262.[94]

The Gallic Empire was a secessionist state but it was governed on Roman lines, with Roman magistrates, Roman laws, and Roman gods. The Augsburg inscription names Postumus and Honoratianus as consuls, and the Gallic Emperors held tribunician power renewed each year, and were protected by a Praetorian Guard. Civil and military government went on as before and provincial boundaries were retained. Senators were not removed from their posts by Postumus, and the coinage was of a better quality than that of Gallienus.[95] In the *Historia Augusta* Postumus is portrayed as courageous and wise,

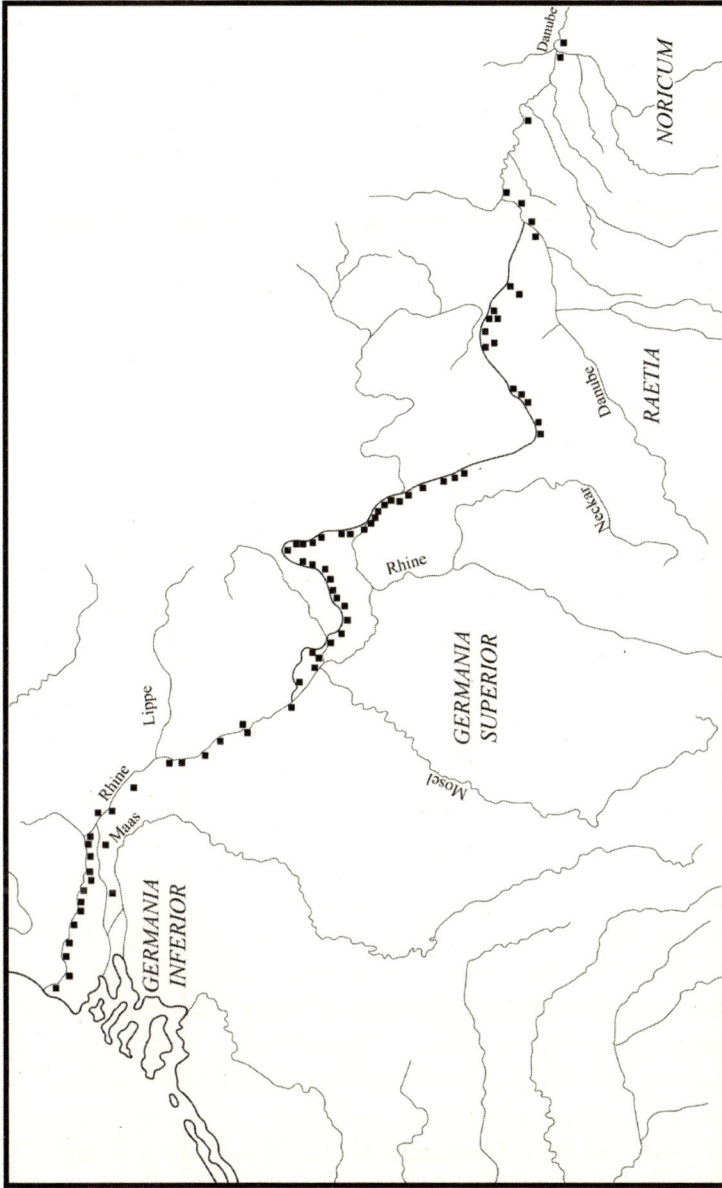

12. Map of the frontier of the Rhine and Upper Danube in the AD 230s. Since the reigns of Vespasian Titus and Domitian efforts were made to close the gap between the German and Raetian frontiers, also enclosing the north facing salient of the Taunus-Wetterau region. Under Hadrian a running barrier was built consisting of a line of timber posts guarded by watchtowers and forts, rationalised under Antoninus Pius. This is what the frontier looked like after raids from Free Germany in the 230s when some forts had been destroyed. Redrawn by Isla Jones after Graeme Stobbs for Southern 2015.

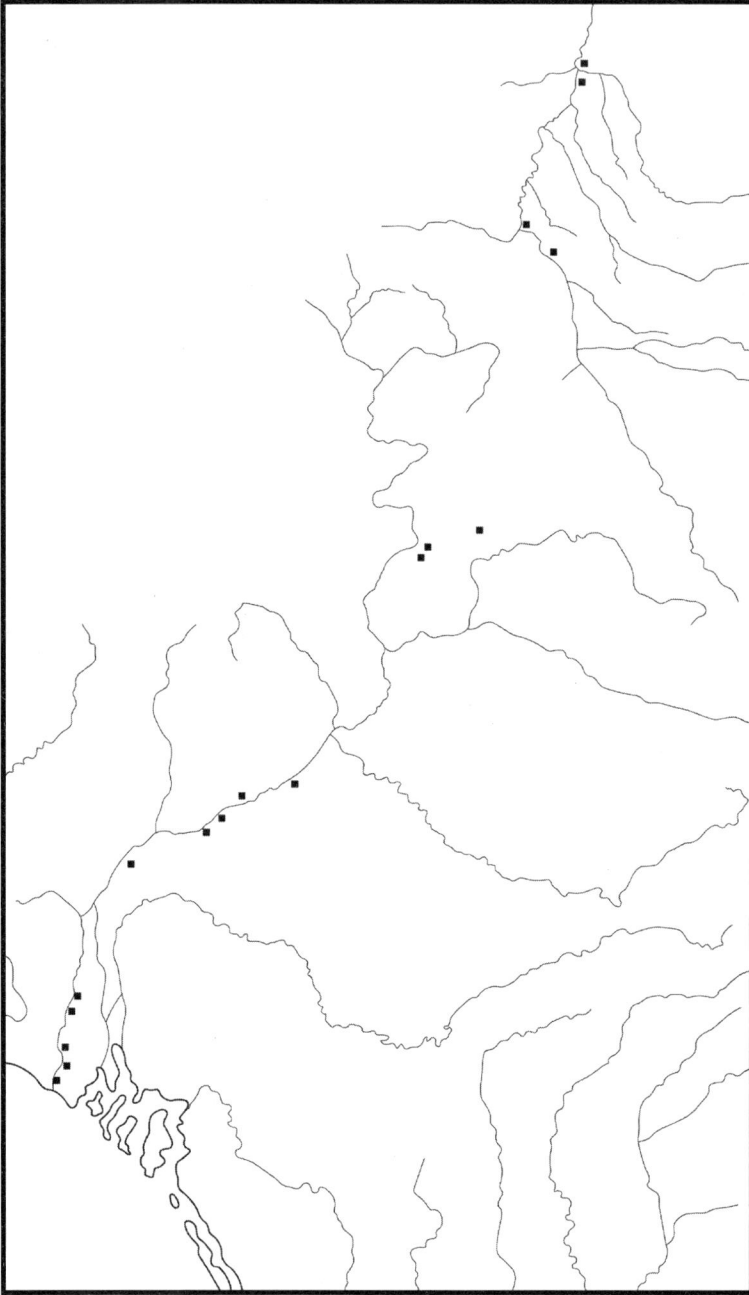

13. Map of the frontier of the Rhine and Upper Danube in the AD 260s. Hardly any forts were still occupied and Gaul, the German provinces, Raetia were endangered. The governor of Germania Inferior, Latinius Postumus, was declared Emperor by his troops and set about protecting what he could, forming what became known as the Gallic Empire in the west. Redrawn by Isla Jones after Graeme Stobbs for Southern 2015.

restoring the security of old, but then the author of this work was strongly opposed to Gallienus.[96]

Did Postumus hope to rule the Empire, as de Blois suggests, or was he content to repair and defend the Rhine frontier and the hinterland, as Drinkwater and König claim?[97] He promoted himself as restorer of the Gallic provinces (*restitutor Galliarum*) and the bringer of security to the provinces (*salus provinciarum*). That was ambitious enough, because many of the frontier forts were abandoned after 260, and there is evidence of widespread destruction.[98] Engaged in the task of pulling everything back together, neither Postumus nor his successors marched on Rome, but a separate state within the Empire could not be allowed to last forever. Though Gallienus recognised Odenathus as ruler of the east, he never recognised Postumus, and possibly in 261and in 265 he made attempts to recover the Gallic provinces.[99] In one of these attempts he was wounded at Trier.[100] Gallienus controlled the routes into Italy through the Alpine passes, and may have regained control of Raetia, but it was the Emperor Aurelian who reunited the *Imperium Galliarum* with Rome.

## Gallienus' reforms

Gallienus was heir to an Empire that was threatening to break up, and the efforts he made to reunite it form the hinge between the Empire of the third century and the early fourth century Empire of Diocletian and Constantine. Aurelius Victor devoted more words to Gallienus' reign than to most others. Modern authors justifiably identify the reign of Gallienus as central to the survival of the Empire in the third century, and the Emperor himself as the originator of several of the institutions of the late Empire, but there was no straightforward linear development leading directly from Gallienus to Constantine.

At Milan, sandwiched between the Gallic Empire in the west and the realm of Odenathus in the east, Gallienus controlled most of Italy, the Balkans, northern Turkey, North Africa and Egypt, the latter countries assuring his food supplies.[101] His financial resources were limited, compounded by a decline in agriculture and trade and tax evasion by the wealthy classes.[102] He could summon only a fraction of the armies. The Persians were held in check by Odenathus, but there were usurpers with sizeable armies in different parts of the Empire, the Goths were raiding Moesia and Thrace and were now using boats to raid rich coastal cities, and the Franks, Alamanni and other tribes were poised to attack the Rhine and the upper Danube.

Probably in 260, Gallienus ended the persecution of the Christians begun by Valerian. He reopened Christian churches, religious buildings and cemeteries.[103] The military and administrative policies of Gallienus were formulated out of necessity. He had to make the best use of what was immediately to hand and try to stay one step ahead of events. Political and military needs dictated what must be done, and circumstances, resources, flexible thinking and ingenuity dictated what could be achieved. By finding ways to solve problems, Gallienus changed the administration of the Empire and the army. The constant wars from the 250s onwards had already engendered extraordinary measures in military and civil administration, resulting in an increase of the powers and importance of the men of military background, and their intrusion into provincial government.[104] Facing more usurpers than any other emperor, Gallienus had increased need for an efficient and loyal army.[105] His fiscal, social, and political policies were subordinated to military needs.[106]

At Milan, Gallienus' army consisted of vexillations from the Rhine and Danube legions, and some auxiliary units, probably the troops which he had assembled for the Rhine campaign in the 250s, including the Praetorians and II Parthica from Italy, accompanied by vexillations from the legions of Britain, Germania Superior and Inferior, Raetia, Noricum, the two Pannonias and the two Moesias, and the three Dacias. The Praetorians and seventeen legions feature on Gallienus' coinage, and it is significant that these coins are found only where Gallienus campaigned, and not at the legionary home bases.

Needing to foster goodwill among the soldiers Gallienus attended to their welfare, their monetary rewards and their advancement, continuing and extending the tradition begun by Hadrian and Severus of broadening the career prospects of ordinary soldiers via distinguished service, so that each man could look forward to becoming a junior officer, then achieving equestrian status, and from there progressing to high rank.

Campaign armies made up of vexillations did not immediately answer Gallienus' purpose. He required mobility and rapid response, to reach the Danube and Rhine provinces and to guard the Alpine passes against invasion by tribesmen from the north, whilst also defending the western passes against troops of Postumus, who may one day invade Italy. The plain of the river Po was good country for horses, and Milan was well placed to enable Gallienus to move quickly into and through the Alps.[107] This was vital, because the Alamanni were actually in the Alpine passes, within immediate reach of Italy.

Gallienus' cavalry was a new departure. The troops that he was able to muster after the loss of the Gallic and Rhine provinces would have included regular *alae* and *cohortes equitatae*, and perhaps the *equites Dalmatae*, from Dalmatia, expert horsemen who may have brought their own mounts. Gallienus may have amalgamated the legionary cavalry from the vexillations with the new cavalry, calling them *promoti*, denoting their transfer from legionary cavalry to a cavalry army, probably regarded as an upgrade.

The horsemen of the mobile cavalry were not brigaded in auxiliary units based in the frontier posts, or attached to any other army, but were able to fight wherever the Emperor wished. The cavalry had its own commander, answerable directly to the Emperor, making it quite distinct from other elements of the army. The first commander, Aureolus, is attested in more than one source, but it is Zosimus who specifically links him with Milan.[108] It is disputed whether this army is the true forerunner of the mobile armies of the later Empire. The Byzantine chronicler George Cedrenus says that Gallienus was the first to employ a mobile cavalry army, implying that he founded the later mobile armies, but continuity from the 260s to Byzantine times cannot be traced. The cavalry probably survived Gallienus in its original form, possibly attested on an inscription dating to the reign of Claudius Gothicus, mentioning *vexillationes adque equites*, the distinction between detachments and cavalry suggesting that the horsemen were still a separate unit, but in Diocletian's reign (284-305) it was no longer at Milan and is not attested as a separate entity.

A new body of military men was established called the *protectores*. The title of *protector* first appeared from about 253 in the joint reigns of Valerian and Gallienus, possibly reserved for Praetorians at first, then under Gallienus as sole Emperor it was awarded to centurions or higher-ranking men, but senators were excluded.[109] *Protector* did not denote a rank, but it was a mark of distinction, denoting loyalty to the Emperor. The *protectores* were not a bodyguard, but probably formed a staff college, a new aristocracy of military men with proven ability.[110] In the fourth century the term became synonymous with centurion.

An important change under Gallienus was the removal of many senators from military commands, which became the preserve of equestrians, all of which is fraught with debate. The senatorial military career had already begun to wane. As early as the Marcommanic wars, Marcus Aurelius employed equestrians in place of senators, first elevating them to the proper rank. Septimius Severus did not bother about rank, and gave equestrians posts usually reserved for senators, and Gallienus continued and extended this policy, fostering military men who had risen from the ranks, professional soldiers of long military experience who had concentrated almost exclusively on the army and had not served their time simply in order to advance their political careers, as senators usually did.[111] Aurelius Victor says that Gallienus issued an edict divorcing senators from army commands, and that under the Emperor Tacitus the senators could have regained military power but they thought only of their personal fortunes and privileges.[112] The edict is doubted, but epigraphic evidence documenting the careers of senators suggests that they held fewer military commands.[113]

After 250 there is a decline in documented senatorial careers, partly because the epigraphic habit was beginning to die out, but also because the first steps on the ladder for promotion had already been removed when the senatorial *tribuni laticlavii* of the legions disappeared. Another factor affecting senators is that from Hadrian onwards military and civil careers had been steadily separated, contributing to the development of specialisation and professionalism in either one or the other, producing senators with no military experience, or senatorial army commanders with little administrative experience.[114] Since military experience was of paramount importance in the mid-third century, Gallienus found it among his equestrian officers, and he placed them in charge of legions as *praefecti*. It was not unprecedented. Augustus appointed equestrian governors of Egypt with the title *Praefectus Aegypti*, and commanders of the Egyptian legions were equestrians. Under Severus, the governor of Mesopotamia was an equestrian, and legions were commanded by equestrians. The full terminology for a prefect of a legion was *praefectus agens vices legati*, indicating that the prefect was acting as substitute for the legate, and without this complete title, according to the law codes, the *praefectus legionis* lacked certain legal prerogatives.[115] The last known senatorial legionary legate was the commander at Caerleon in Wales, and in the Gallic Empire, Postumus retained the senatorial legionary commanders.[116]

Once Gallienus began to employ equestrians, senators lost the potential for military or administrative experience, especially after equestrians more frequently became provincial governors. This, too, had precedents. In the past, if the original governor died or was killed, equestrians had sometimes filled the post, not as governor, but with full authority to act on behalf of the governor, reflected in the title, *agens vice praesidis*. From about 260 onwards, equestrian *praesides* (singular *praeses*) were appointed as governors in their own right, usually in provinces where the legionary legate was also responsible for both military and civil affairs. Senators cannot have been removed in one fell swoop, but it is not certain whether the senatorial legionary legates or provincial governors served their full terms, allowing natural wastage to effect the change, or whether some of them were prematurely recalled to put equestrians in charge. The procedure was probably complete by 262.[117] Gallienus occasionally installed equestrians in place of consular governors of Imperial provinces if there was a military crisis, but senatorial governors of large provinces with two legions were not affected, principally because the legions were in the hands of the equestrian prefects. In provinces governed by senatorial proconsuls, and in those with no troops, Gallienus made no changes.

Though the Senate undoubtedly lost political power and influence in the third century, Gallienus did not annihilate it, and relations between him and the senators were not always hostile. Senators retained their prestigious status, filled many of the customary governmental posts in Rome and they were not deprived of their wealth or otherwise persecuted. If there was a whiff of revolt, it was quickly dealt with, especially since senators could bankroll rebellions.[118] The removal of senators from military commands would probably not have arisen if there had been peace over most of the Empire, but the old methods were no longer appropriate.

The main effect on senatorial careers after Gallienus' reforms was the disruption of the normal *cursus honorum*, the path to the consulship. Senatorial participation in the government of the Empire diminished. In the military sphere, Christol enumerates the losses of twenty-five posts as legate of a legion, and twelve as provincial governors of praetorian rank.[119] Senators had to find alternative routes to the consulship, and further appointments depended on the assistance of the Emperor. Some lucrative posts in provincial government were still open to senators, but roughly fifteen years elapsed between holding the consulship and an important appointment like the proconsulship of Asia, and probably up to twenty-five years elapsed between the first and second consulship, because the emperors often monopolised the post.

Gallienus had the army exclusively in mind in his monetary and financial policies. He did not control the whole Empire, and even before the formation of secessionist states, revenues had already begun to decline while expenditure increased. The coinage had been successively debased and Valerian and Gallienus debased it further while issuing more of it, and there was an alarming lack of uniformity in weights or values of coins.[120] Prices rose, purchasing power declined, so army pay and some taxes were partly transmuted into payments in kind, which laid increasing burdens on the population. Egyptian papyri show that the system was already in operation before 260, frequently recording payment of taxes in kind, not cash.[121]

Direct taxation, the source of much of the state revenue, fell most heavily on the wealthy landowners in Italy and the provinces. In dealing with government of the praetorian provinces, Gallienus placed civil, military and financial matters, including tax collection, in the hands of the new equestrian *praesides*. Income from the mines also decreased, and the state-run mines in north-west Spain closed down, though they had not been exhausted. The problem may have been lack of manpower, since the mines in southern Spain, run by contractors, still functioned, but with reduced output.[122] One source of revenue that Gallienus exploited was the *aurum coronarium*, the traditional contribution of gold crowns from the provinces whenever the Emperor proclaimed a victory.[123]

Without adequate pay, Gallienus' soldiers could not be expected to remain loyal, so he established mints near the various military headquarters, at Milan, Sirmium (Sremska Mitrovica, Serbia), Siscia (Sisak, Croatia), and Smyrna (Izmir, Turkey). As mentioned above, values were not standard, so people began to ignore what the Imperial power said the coins were worth, and they judged by weight instead.[124] While Gallienus' monetary policies ensured that his army functioned, in the end they were disastrous. The army was the sole means of saving the Empire, but it was seen as a drain on finances, while the populace faced rising prices due to inflation. A rift between the army and the civilian population of Rome, Italy, and the provinces was nothing new, but during the reign of Gallienus it widened, despite his coinage announcing *concordia* between the soldiers and the people.[125]

Gallienus had no choice except to concentrate on the immediate dangers, ignoring the Gallic Empire under Postumus, who was kept busy enough defending his territory. Similarly, Gallienus did nothing to regain the east, because for the moment Odenathus' loyalty and ability to defend Syria and the other provinces was not in question. Gallienus' first priority was to prevent the Alamanni from damaging Italy and they were soundly defeated near Milan in 260, remaining quiet until after Gallienus' death.[126] By 262 Gallienus had re-established control of his diminished Empire, but it was clear that there was a long way to go before unification could even be attempted.

After 262, Gallienus launched a propaganda campaign to promote peace and prosperity, adopting Trajan's epithet *optimus princeps*.[127] He celebrated his *Decennalia* in high style in Rome.[128] He associated himself with the powerful Graeco-Roman gods such as Jupiter and Hercules, claiming special protection of Apollo and Diana, and of Sol, the sun god. All these gods were honoured on his coinage, and his own portraits became more idealised, putting him on a higher plane than mere mortals, adopting titles such as Magnus, the Great, and *Invictus*, unconquered, which was also applied to the sun god as Sol Invictus.[129] Gallienus portrayed himself as saviour of the state. Modest emperors got nowhere in these dangerous times.

True to Gallienus' propaganda, there was peace, relatively speaking, between 262 and 265. Gallienus found time for philosophy, promoting Platonism via his favourite Plotinus, whose school flourished as its membership grew. Gallienus encouraged literature and the arts, visiting Athens where he was made exarch of the city and may have been initiated into the Eleusinian mysteries.[130] His mistake was that he did not devote every hour of the day and night to winning back the lost territories, and faith in him waned.

In 265 the Emperor embarked on an unsuccessful campaign to reconquer the Gallic Empire, but in 266 he was called to the Danube to combat the Goths, mostly labelled Scythians by the ancient authors. Gallienus based himself at Siscia (Sisak, Croatia), where the mint was opened in preparation for impending military activity, and archaeological evidence confirms wide-ranging movements of the army in Pannonia.[131] There was no decisive victory, and by 267 the Goths were threatening the Empire from Moesia to the Mediterranean. A group of Goths invaded Thrace through Moesia, the Heruli invaded Greece, attacking Athens, Sparta and Corinth; another group laid siege to Thessalonika. Neither the troops with Gallienus nor those in the provinces could hope to stem the tide, so self-help was the only answer. Some cities already possessed walls. The councillors at Aquileia in northern Italy had fortified their city in 238 and Verona had been walled in 265.[132] The Greeks built a wall across the isthmus of Corinth to stop the incursions of the tribes.[133]

According to the *Historia Augusta*, the walls of other cities needed attention, and Gallienus despatched two men from Byzantium, Cleodamus and Athenaeus, to repair and fortify the cities.[134] Athens was captured, despite its spirited defence by civilians under Dexippus, but the capture is hard to spot in Dexippus' account. In Pannonia, Gallienus defeated the Heruli twice, the first time under their leader Naulobatus, when he received the surrender of the rest and incorporated them into the Roman army, and again at Nestus. Zosimus notes the campaign without citing a victory for Gallienus, attributing it to Claudius Gothicus, who won a battle against the Goths at Naissus.[135] At this point, the cavalry commander Aureolus, one of the most loyal and successful of Gallienus' generals, raised revolt in Milan.

Gallienus left his general Marcianus in command of the campaign against the Heruli and the Goths. Back in Italy Gallienus besieged Aureolus at Milan, unaware that his general Heraclianus was plotting his death. There are conflicting versions of the assassination, and its date.[136] Papyrus evidence suggests Gallienus was murdered in July or August 268.[137] The next Emperor, Claudius II Gothicus, may have been aware of the plot. The soldiers, loyal to Gallienus, were pacified by cash. Aureolus was defeated in battle by Claudius II and killed near a bridge over the river Adda, not far from Milan.[138] Gallienus' cavalry force now required a leader. Eventually, Claudius appointed the future Emperor Aurelian to that role.[139]

## Claudius II Gothicus

The new Emperor Marcus Aurelius Claudius was an Illyrian army officer, allegedly commander of all the troops in the Balkans under Gallienus. The later Emperor Constantine the Great claimed him as an ancestor, so Claudius' alleged glory and success may be invented.[140] At the time of Gallienus' death, Claudius was in command of reserve forces at Ticinum (Pavia).[141] He travelled to Rome to establish his rule and cultivate the senators, who conferred the name of Augustus on him.[142] He persuaded the Senate to deify Gallienus, but refused to punish the plotters. Gallienus' policies were not reversed, equestrians retained command of provinces, and Claudius prudently took care of the armies.[143]

The prefect of the *Vigiles*, Julius Placidianus, was sent against the Gallic Empire and it seems that he regained the eastern part of

Narbonensis and the Rhône valley.[144] Claudius was unable to fight this campaign himself, and the fact that he sent the prefect of the *Vigiles* to begin the task implies a shortage of other commanders, the majority of whom were committed to the struggles against the Goths and the Alamanni. With their acquired naval skills the Goths could disrupt Roman shipping and attack the Mediterranean coastal cities.[145] The Prefect of Egypt, Tenagino Probus, was put in command of a fleet based in Greece to sweep the seas clear of the Goths.[146]

In the meantime, between 266 and 268, Odenathus of Palmyra had been assassinated, and his widow Queen Zenobia had taken command. She took advantage of the situation and ordered an advance into Egypt, rapidly gaining a foothold. Tenagino Probus won a victory but was then defeated and committed suicide.[147] The Palmyrene Royal House was therefore in command of most of the east, and more important, controlled much of Rome's corn supply. At that moment Claudius could do nothing about it.

Claudius' campaigns against the Goths and Alamanni are almost impossible to chronicle, with the result that it cannot be said which tribes he fought and in what order.[148] Claudius probably marched first to the Danube, to conclude Gallienus' wars. Marcianus, left in command, had achieved some success, but Thessalonika and Marcianopolis were still under siege. Claudius claimed a victory at Naissus, earning his victory title Gothicus, and temporarily halting the incursions of the Goths.[149] Some of the Goths were settled on the land in the Balkans, or were sold as slaves.[150] The Goths had not been defeated in their entirety, and dispersed to fight another day.

The Alamanni had been quiet since their defeat in 260, possibly agreeing to a treaty with Gallienus, which would be invalidated when he was killed. The problems of the Empire presented a good opportunity to attack, but the Alamanni were defeated near Lake Garda, and Claudius took the title *Germanicus Maximus*. By summer 270 he was campaigning against the Juthungi in Raetia and Vandals in Panonnia, but he died of the plague that broke out in that year.[151] For a short time, possibly only a few months, his brother Quintillus was Emperor. It did not take Aurelian very long to be proclaimed by his soldiers. Perhaps he had been working on such a development.

### Aurelian: the Empire restored

Lucius Domitius Aurelianus, of obscure origins, was a prominent officer in Claudius' entourage. Aurelius Victor felt it necessary to point out that Aurelian was of low birth, but ancient authors cannot agree on where he was born.[152] His nickname was *manu ad ferrum*, hand on hilt, a good recommendation for an Emperor in these troubled times. The army proclaimed him probably in November 270, while he was leading the campaign against the Juthungi and Vandals. Eminently practical, he seized the mint at Siscia, issuing gold coins to pay donatives to the soldiers. The problem of Claudius' brother Quintillus was solved in April 270, when he committed suicide.

Aurelian finished the war, catching the Juthungi in Raetia when they were on their way home from plundering Italy. He refused to make a treaty when the tribesmen asked for one, but after extracting 40,000 horsemen and 80,000 soldiers, he let the Juthungi go home. The statistics are surely exaggerated, but nonetheless he gained soldiers. Next it was the turn of the Vandals, a confederation of Germanic peoples, already known to the Romans in the first century AD as Vandili, originally settled in modern Poland, moving southwards at the beginning of the third century. Aurelian brought them to terms by a scorched earth policy, starving them into submission. He took 2000 cavalry and gave the remaining tribesmen sufficient food to return home.[153]

The new Emperor marched to Rome as soon as the tribes had moved away. Events of Aurelian's reign are recorded in the ancient sources but without a clear chronological framework, which makes it difficult to discern cause and effect. Aurelian's first problem was not war, but trouble with the workers of the mint, who were apparently creaming off resources for their own benefit. They staged their own revolt, traditionally at the outset of Aurelian's reign, but the episode may have occurred as late as 274 when Aurelian began to overhaul the finances and the coinage.[154] The ringleader at the treasury was Felicissimus, the *a rationalis*, who may have been the tool of more influential men. To quell the revolt, Aurelian simply closed the mint. There was a riot in which Felicissimus was killed.[155]

Aurelian cultivated the goodwill of the Senate and people of Rome, giving 500 denarii to each citizen in the city.[156] He cancelled debts to the Treasury and burnt all the records, making the senators fear him as a populist, but they dutifully bestowed the usual powers on him. They still had the power to do this, but their legislative authority was being absorbed and finally disappeared as the Emperor evolved into a totalitarian ruler and lawgiver. The Senate was not in a position to argue, but there was some opposition to Aurelian from military men.

There were three attempted usurpations, not described in detail in the sources, and quickly put down.[157]

By 271 the Juthungi, the Alamanni, and the Marcomanni had joined forces, launching a serious attack on Roman territory. The ancient sources are not reliable when it comes to tribal names, recording battles with the Suebi and Sarmatians, an invasion of Pannonia by the Scythians, followed by an invasion of Italy by the Alamanni.[158] The Juthungi reached Milan in 271. Aurelian may have fought more than one battle against them.[159] The Juthungi refused terms of peace and made a surprise night attack on the Romans at Placentia.[160] Defeated, Aurelian fought back while constantly on the move, chasing the mobile tribesmen and guessing their next moves. After bringing about a temporary halt by exhausting the tribes, Aurelian proclaimed a victory over the Germans, celebrating it on his coins. It was not decisive. It was now known that the frontiers could be breached, and after 260 the Rhine frontier was hardly protected at all, so Rome itself was in danger. Aurelian called a meeting of the Senate to discuss the project of building a wall round the city.[161]

Rome had not needed walls for the last four centuries, but the tribes were now more mobile with a longer reach, and besides their defensive value, walls and defended gates would have psychological value. Building began probably in 271 and may have been almost complete by the time of Aurelian's death in 274. The soldiers would normally have undertaken most of the work, but they were defending the routes into Italy and fighting wars, so civilian workers built the walls.[162] The circuit was not quite nineteen kilometres, but it excluded some parts of the fourteen regions of Augustan Rome. The work was hastily done, as attested by the incorporation of existing buildings into the circuit. The walls were originally 6 metres high, with square towers roughly thirty metres apart. Most of them are still standing. Repairs were made in the early fourth century by Maxentius, and about a century later Honorius repaired and heightened the walls, and altered some of the gates, reducing the two arched entrances to a single arch. In the sixth century the walls were repaired again by Count Belisarius, sent by the Byzantine Emperor Justinian to try to regain control of Italy.[163]

### The Empire reunited

As the walls of Rome were being constructed, Aurelian set off to win back control of the eastern provinces from Queen Zenobia and her son Vaballathus, the elder of her two boys. Probably by 270 she had taken control of Egypt.[164] She called herself Augusta and Vaballathus Augustus, and she issued coins from the Alexandrian mint bearing a portrait of Aurelian on one side and on the other Vaballathus in the fourth year of his reign. She may have hoped that Aurelian would condone her rule of the east, with himself as senior Emperor and her son as his subordinate. Vaballathus adopted the legitimate titles awarded by Gallienus to Odenathus, *vir clarissimus, Rex, Imperator, dux Romanorum* and *corrector totius orientis*, sometimes written in Palmyrene script.[165]

When armed conflict with the Romans was inevitable, Zenobia elevated Vaballathus to Imperator Caesar Augustus.[166] A milestone from the road from Bostra to Philadelphia bears an inscription showing that Vaballathus adopted Aurelian's name and Roman victory titles.[167]

On the march to the east, Aurelian had to fight a battle with a group of Goths, whose leader Cannabas or Cannabaudes may have been the famous Cniva. The Romans won, and Aurelian took the title *Gothicus Maximus*.[168] By August 271, Egypt had been reconquered and the Alexandrian mint was issuing coins for Aurelian alone. Controversially, the *Historia Augusta* states that it was Marcus Aurelius Probus, the future Emperor, who recovered Egypt.[169] Aurelian spent the winter of 271-272 at Byzantium, marching to Asia Minor in the following spring. Tyana (in modern Turkey) closed the gates against him, so he besieged it, giving orders that when the city was captured, no-one, not even a dog, was to survive, but Tyana was betrayed to him and only the traitor was executed.[170] Other cities, quick on the uptake, opened their gates.

Zenobia's army was commanded by her general Septimius Zabdas. She met the Romans at Immae, east of Antioch. Aurelian ordered his horsemen from Dalmatia and Mauretania to run away when they encountered the Palmyrene heavy armoured cavalry, descriptively called *clibanarii* or ovens, indicating what it was like to wear the armour in a hot climate. The ruse drew the *clibanarii* into an ambush, and the battle was won by the Romans. Zenobia left a garrison at Daphne near Antioch, and escaped.[171] The final battle, a victory for Aurelian, was at Emesa (Homs).[172] Aurelian then besieged Zenobia at Palmyra, where his main problems concerned food, but he persuaded the desert tribes to supply him.[173] Zenobia escaped, riding a female camel, which according to Zosimus are very fast.[174] The Romans caught her as she aimed for the Persians. She had left behind a city where pro- and anti-Roman factions fought each other. Aurelian simply waited, and in summer 272 he captured Palmyra.[175]

The army clamoured for Zenobia's death, but Aurelian wanted her to walk in his triumph, which she did, though Zosimus claims that she died on the journey to Rome.[176] Alternatively, she married a Roman senator, keeping her children with her while her house became a tourist attraction, and her descendants continued to live in Rome.[177]

The capture of Palmyra did not end the problems. Aurelian set out for Rome, leaving his general Marcellinus in command of the much-reduced province of Mesopotamia as *rector Orientis*.[178] He defeated the Carpi on the Danube, taking the title *Carpicus Maximus*, but this victory was not followed through because he had to return to the east. An anti-Roman faction at Palmyra led by Septimius Apsaeus proclaimed Antiochus/Achillus, a distant relative of Odenathus, as king.[179] Antiochus and Apsaeus tried to persuade the Roman governor Marcellinus to join them in rebellion against Aurelian, and they may have been behind the revolt of Firmus in Egypt. Marcellinus did not give a definite answer, prevaricating while he warned Aurelian, who reappeared so suddenly in the east that the Palmyrenes were bewildered. This time Aurelian obliterated Palmyra and it never fully recovered.[180]

In Egypt, Firmus is assumed to have acted in concert with Apsaeus and Antiochus, appropriating exports intended for Rome.[181] The rebellion was quickly put down and Firmus committed suicide. The historian Ammianus Marcellinus comments on Aurelian's severe treatment of Alexandria, destroying the walls, and raising taxes on Egyptian products such as glass, papyrus and linen, bringing extra revenue for Rome.[182] He recruited two new legions which he placed in Syria and Arabia to control the territories he had won from Palmyra.[183] Aurelian adopted the victory title *Palmyrenicus Maximus*, and the *Historia Augusta* says that he was possessor of the whole of the east: *totiusque iam orientis possessor*.[184] His coinage proclaimed him *Restitutor Orientis*, echoed on an inscription referring to him as *Imperator Orientis*.[185] It was important to remind people that after nearly four years Rome now controlled the east again. It remained to regain control of the west.

The Gallic Empire had experienced a rapid turnover of emperors after the death of Postumus. His regime had lasted for over a decade, established on Roman lines. He had kept the provincials safe from incursions and destruction, though he had to acknowledge that he could not defend the whole of the Rhine frontier.[186] His coinage was superior to the coins of the central government, but there is a detectable decline in standards after his death.[187] Internal dissension began probably in 268 with the revolt of Ulpius Cornelius Laelianus, or Lollianus, who lasted for about four months.[188] His name Ulpius may indicate a Spanish origin, and though traditionally he governed Germania Inferior, he may have been governor of Germania Superior, since his rebellion began at Mainz.[189] Shortly after Postumus took up his fifth consulship on 1 January 259, he defeated Laelianus, only to face another usurper, Marius, who survived for only two months. While engaged in the struggle against Marius, Postumus refused to allow his soldiers to sack Mogontiacum (Mainz). He could not control them. They killed him, and once again Roman soldiers sacked a Roman city.

Piavonius Victorinus, consul with Postumus in 268, was proclaimed Emperor in December 269. The Emperor Claudius II Gothicus was about to embark on the Danube campaign against the Goths. In order to guard the Alpine passes while he was absent from Rome, he sent Placidianus, who had been successively prefect of the *Vigiles*, Praetorian Prefect, and consul in 273 with the short-lived Emperor Tacitus. Placidianus gained control of part of Narbonensis, and this may be the context of the revolt of the city of Autun against Victorinus, who besieged and captured the city and punished the inhabitants.[190] The Gallic Empire was beginning to unravel. Victorinus was murdered and unexpectedly, his mother Victoria took over. She promoted the senatorial governor of Aquitania, Esuvius Tetricus, making him an acceptable Gallic Emperor by distributing cash to the soldiers.[191] Tetricus made Trier his base, while Victoria chose Cologne. Britain and Gaul, with the exception of Narbonensis, accepted Tetricus, but enthusiasm was lacking in Spain, and in the city of Argentorate (Strasbourg) in Germania Superior.[192] Tetricus celebrated a *Victoria Germanica*, but little is known of any fighting. Invasions across the Rhine and along the coasts continued. Tetricus could only abandon yet more forts and withdraw the troops. A serious incursion of Germans reached the Loire. Of the coin hoards found in Gaul, some of them must relate to this period of endemic insecurity.

Aurelian mobilised late in 273. It is disputed whether or not there was a battle when the rival armies met at Châlons-sur-Marne. There had probably been some diplomatic contact, and the story goes that Tetricus sent a message to Aurelian, quoting Virgil: 'rescue me undefeated from these troubles' (*eripe me his invicte malis*).[193] In March 274, the mint at Lyons began to issue coins for Aurelian. Coins and inscriptions declared him *Restitutor Orbis,* restorer of the world.[194] Aurelian had, after all, reintegrated three separate empires into one.

In Gaul the army was split up and put into different garrisons, and the reliable Probus was put in charge of repairing the frontier zones.[195] Aurelian held a splendid triumph in Rome, in which Tetricus and Zenobia featured as part of the display.[196] Zenobia remained in Rome, as described above, and Tetricus was not punished but made *corrector Lucaniae* in Italy.[197] An inscription refers to Aurelian as *Britannicus Maximus*, implying that there had been some fighting before Britain was brought back into the Empire.[198]

The reintegration of the Empire was offset by the loss of Dacia, which was evacuated and a new province of the same name was established south of the Danube in parts of Moesia Superior and Inferior.[199] The date is not known, allowing some ancient sources to attribute this to Gallienus. In modern sources the evacuation can be dated to virtually every year of Aurelian's reign, without certainty. There may be a link with Aurelian's victory over the Carpi at the end of 272. Up to this date archaeological evidence reveals normal Roman occupation of Dacia, and a coin hoard discovered in Romania, the modern version of Dacia, contained over 200 coins from the mints at Milan, Cyzicus and Siscia, not one of them later than 272. At this time Palmyra was in revolt, so Aurelian probably evacuated Dacia rather than have it wrested from his grasp by the invading tribesmen. Without giving a precise date, Eutropius says that Aurelian could not defend Dacia so he brought the Romans out, and Christol thinks that the evacuation was begun before Aurelian returned to Palmyra.[200] Aurelian probably organised the move and put officers in charge, then set off for the east. The capital of the new province was at Serdica (Sofia), on the road connecting Viminacium with Byzantium. The old fortresses of Ratiaria and Oescus were strengthened and the forts guarding the Danube crossings were retained, at Drobeta, Sucidava and Barbosi.[201] Some inhabitants of Dacia probably opted to stay in their homes. Epigraphic evidence attests a continued Romanized population after the evacuation, but these people may have been assimilated with the Goths and Carpi who took over. The tribesmen would be kept busy while they occupied the vacated areas, and would probably fight each other for lands, keeping them out of Roman territory. Sometime before 285 the new Dacia was split into Dacia Ripensis in the north, and Dacia Mediterranea in the south.

## Aurelian's last years

After 274, Aurelian, the restorer of the world, became divine, greater than any mortal. He was proclaimed in superlatives, most victorious, most glorious (*victoriosissimus, gloriosissimus*) eternal, invincible, the personification of Hercules, *Imperator deus et dominus* or Emperor, god and lord. Finally, he was *deus et dominus natus*, born as a divine being, which no-one had discerned until now. He began to act the part in all seriousness, wearing a diadem and cloth of gold.[202] Having put the Empire back together, Aurelian had to project an image of an all-powerful ruler, capable of protecting his people, and he needed enemies to fear him. The way in which he went about it was a little over the top. Aurelian had learned a lot from eastern monarchs and he set a trend, utilised to good effect by Diocletian and Constantine.

Aurelian could not rest on his laurels. There were problems that no-one had had time to address for many years. Aurelian had never completed his partial reform of the monetary system in 271, and finances were still in a mess. The treasury had been drained by wars, corrupt officials, and the financial policies of Gallienus who had only a third of the Empire to draw on. Aurelian could begin all over again in 274, especially as revenues had increased now that the Empire was whole.[203] Aurelian thought that everyone ought to contribute to the well-being and defence of the Empire, and focussed on taxing the wealthy, earning him a reputation for rapaciousness, but this was because he took money from people with the loudest voices.

Aurelian was able to reform the coinage because the production of gold and silver, much reduced compared to the early Empire, was now aimed at Rome instead of being diverted to the breakaway states. The currency continued to be produced in gold, silver and bronze, but the Senate was deprived of its customary right to issue bronze coins. Aurelian tried to withdraw all the *antoniniani* with virtually no silver and succeeded in eradicating the bad coinage in Rome and Italy. In other provinces, especially Gaul and Britain, he was less successful, but the percentage of silver and gold was increased in the new coins, and a standard weight and value was established for the silver coinage all over the Empire. The *antoninianus* was replaced by billon coins marked XX, XX.I, XXI, or KA in Greek, which may relate to the five per cent silver content of the coins.[204] It is a sad reflection on the late third-century monetary system that coins with five per cent silver could be regarded as improved.

Postumius Varus, prefect of the city in 271, is the last known *curator alimentorum* or official in charge of the *alimenta*, established by Trajan.[205] Later *curatores* may have gone undetected but it is suggested that Aurelian may have abolished the scheme. Perhaps as an alternative he reorganised the corn dole for the city, distributing bread instead of grain.[206] Aurelian reintroduced Severus' free distribution of oil, which had lapsed, and he added salt and pork to the rations, and wine at reduced cost. His initial plan was to distribute it free of charge, to encourage vine growing and put abandoned lands back into use, but had to compromise and make a charge for the wine.[207] His successors did not alter his arrangements. The distribution of wine revitalised the struggling vine growers of Italy, and the change from the corn dole to the bread ration meant that processors and bakers became part of the system. The taxes of Egypt included grain, which was delivered to the bakers free of charge. The loaves were distributed free to those who could not afford to pay for them, while others bought them at fixed prices. The shippers (*navicularii*) were responsible for the transport of the various goods, and new administrative officials were created, especially on the Nile and the Tiber to oversee transport. The entire operation, collection, transport, warehousing and storage, processing and distribution, was supervised by the *Praefectus Annonae*, who was subject to the city prefect.[208]

In the east Aurelian had seen how the sun god could be a force for unification, and since unification had been a constant theme in his reign and still an ambition, he introduced the worship of this god to Rome. Claudius II Gothicus had put Sol, the sun god, on his coinage, so the idea was not entirely novel when Aurelian produced coins honouring *Sol Invictus*, the unconquered sun, *Sol Conservator*, protector of the state, and *Sol Dominus Imperii Romani*, lord and master of the Roman Empire.[209] Sol was a real visible entity, and worship of him was natural. Probably in 271 Aurelian had started to build a temple to him in the seventh region of the city.[210] It was consecrated in 274, and according to the *Historia Augusta*, corroborated on inscriptions, aristocratic Romans served as priests.[211] There was no suppression of other gods, and no persecution of Christians or Jews.

There was still one nagging source of discontent. The defeat and capture of Valerian had not been avenged, and the Persians were in a disadvantageous position at the moment. After the death of Shapur at the end of 272, the succeeding ruler Hormizd lasted for only a year or so before dying, and the next king Vahram was too preoccupied with his own troubles to attack Roman territory.[212] For Aurelian it was too good an opportunity to miss, and as an admirer of Trajan, the definitive conqueror of the Parthians, Aurelian set out for the east in summer 275. He assembled his army in Illyricum and declared war on the Persians.[213] It was his last decision. At Caenophrurium in Thrace, he was assassinated.[214] The story is garbled and more than one culprit is named, an official of the court called Eros, or a minor clerk called Mucapor. A list of victims intended for execution also features, and pre-emptive action by those named. This time, though, there does not seem to have been a candidate lurking in the background, primed for rule of the Empire. There was no heir and no favoured general marked for the succession, despite the insistence in the *Historia Augusta* that Probus had been designated by Aurelian.[215]

The soldiers were angry about Aurelian's murder and were not inclined to proclaim any of their generals as the new emperor, but nor did any other army opt for one of their own generals, and in contrast to previous occasions when emperors were assassinated, the situation did not descend into civil war.[216] The sources agree that the soldiers asked the Senate to choose an Emperor.[217] The senators chose Marcus Claudius Tacitus, one of their most venerable and aged colleagues, though Zonaras cannot bring himself to believe that there was no military influence, possibly hinting at the Praetorians.[218]

The new Emperor Tacitus requested the Senate to deify Aurelian, whose funeral had been held in Thrace. Since he was already a living god, it is debatable how deification improved Aurelian's afterlife. His legacy is two-edged. He could be regarded as the saviour of Rome because in reunifying the Empire he strengthened it, enabling it to survive for another two centuries, but his authoritarian rule paved the way for the stultifying rigidity that set in with Diocletian and Constantine, and the growing despotism of the fourth century emperors.

# 13

# Diocletian and Constantine:
# A New World

Aurelius Victor seemed to think that under Tacitus the senators allowed a great opportunity for revival to pass them by, but the election of Tacitus hardly constitutes a resurgence of senatorial influence.[1] Tacitus' executed the assassins of Aurelian, and he spent most of his short reign fighting the Goths.[2] His commander was his half-brother Marcus Annius Florianus, Praetorian Prefect, and a victory is indicated by the Emperor's title *Gothicus Maximus*. Tacitus reigned for about six months, dying in suspicious circumstances, at Tyana or Tarsus.[3] The soldiers proclaimed Florianus Emperor, but the troops of the east preferred their own commander, Probus. Florianus faced his rival as soon as possible at Tarsus, but his soldiers killed him, probably recognising Probus as the better commander.

## Marcus Aurelius Probus

Probus' achievements are not well documented. Zosimus considered Probus a good and just Emperor, but his work covers only half the reign, the end of Book I and the beginning of Book II being lost.[4] A coherent chronological narrative of Probus' reign is beyond reach, and the coinage is of no help.[5]

Probus attended to the frontiers, clearing Gaul and the Rhine of the invading tribesmen, re-furbishing the damaged cities, and re-establishing some of the forts. He defeated the Longiones, but one of the chiefs, Igillus, did not return booty and prisoners. After his capture he was punished, along with other captives, by being sent to Britain.[6]

After defeating the Franks on the Rhine, Probus carried the war beyond the frontiers, establishing forts on barbarian soil (*in solo barbarico*), and nine tribal kings submitted to him.[7] In Gaul Probus restored sixty Gallic towns and cities, inflated to seventy by other authors.[8] In winter 278-9 Probus turned to the Danube zones, settling 100,000 Bastarnae on lands in Thrace, which provided recruits for the army and created a partly Romanized zone between the Empire and the tribes beyond.[9] Revolts against Probus were quickly quashed. His generals subdued the people of Ptolemais in Egypt who joined with the notorious Blemmyes, nomads who caused occasional trouble.[10] A usurper, Saturninus, was suppressed.[11] At Cologne there were two potential Emperors, Bonosus and Proculus, both eliminated without much trouble.[12]

Probus celebrated a triumph probably in 281, over Germans and Blemmyes.[13] He had achieved peace over the Empire and had soldiers to spare. He set some of them to planting vines on the hillsides of Moesia.[14] Soldiers were also assigned to draining the marshes near Sirmium.[15] Probus remarked that very soon the Empire would have no need of its armies, needlessly offending the soldiers, some of whom assassinated him at Sirmium as he was preparing for the Persian campaign.[16] The Praetorian Prefect Marcus Aurelius Carus, commanding troops in Raetia and Noricum, became Emperor in 282.

### Carus, Carinus and Numerianus

Aurelius Victor perceived a turning point in 282, because Carus took power with no reference to the Senate.[17] This is not quite true, since Carus sent his elder son Carinus to Rome to deputise for him.[18] Taking over the Persian campaign, Carus made Carinus Augustus to take charge of the western provinces, and his younger son Numerianus became Augustus probably after the first victories over the Persians.[19] The Persian King Vahram II, beset by internal problems, was not strong enough to oppose the Romans, who marched into Seleucia and Ctesiphon. Carus earned the victory title *Parthicus Maximus*, recalling the Parthian regime.[20] The victory facilitated a later diplomatic understanding with the Persians in 288.[21]

At the peak of his success, Carus died. Suspicion attached to the ambitious Praetorian Prefect Lucius Aper, father-in-law of Numerianus. As the army marched out of Persia, Numerianus also died, and Diocles, commanding Numerianus' *protectores domestici*, accused Aper of murdering Numerianus. The story goes that a wise woman in Gaul had told Diocles that he would become Emperor after killing a boar, *aper* in Latin.[22] This tale was probably invented retrospectively.

Diocles killed his 'boar' personally, and on 20 November 284 the soldiers proclaimed him Emperor.[23]

## Diocletian

The new Emperor became Gaius Aurelius Valerius Diocletianus, though in March 285 he was still known in Egypt as Diocles.[24] His early life and career are not known.[25] Carinus, Emperor in the west, was challenged by Marcus Aurelius Julianus, *corrector Venetiae* in northern Italy.[26] Diocletian bided his time until either Carinus or Julianus prevailed, then fought the victor Carinus, either at Marcus in Moesia, or Margus near Belgrade. Carinus lost the battle and his life after his Praetorian Prefect Aristobulus joined Diocletian. Aristobulus remained as Praetorian Prefect and went on to become proconsul of Africa from 290 to 294, and then *praefectus urbi* in Rome. [27] Carinus' soldiers swore allegiance to Diocletian, who probably visited Rome to have the Senate confer power on him.[28]

Diocletian selected Marcus Aurelius Maximianus (Maximian) as his Caesar, but it is argued that Maximian was made Augustus immediately.[29] He was certainly Augustus by 286, a full partner of Diocletian, who took the name Jovius, from Jove or Jupiter, and Maximian became Herculius, Hercules being Jove's assistant. From 285 to 288 Diocletian was occupied on the Danube, and then in the east, while Maximian took charge of the west, but the Empire was not divided, with a firm boundary between east and west.[30]

## Gaul, Britain and Carausius

Raids by the tribesmen crossing the Rhine into Gaul caused great misery. Desperate people who lost everything formed into groups, combining with army deserters. One group was the Bagaudae, led by Amandus and Aelianus, classified as usurpers, because Amandus issued coins naming himself Imperator Caesar Gaius Amandus Pius Felix Augustus.[31] Maximian defeated the Bagaudae, which may have earned him his elevation to Augustus.[32] In 289 a panegyric was addressed to him, not mentioning the Bagaudae, but recognising that the discontent of the people stemmed from the incursions of the tribes.[33]

In 286/7 Marcus Aurelius Mausaeus Carausius was declared Emperor in Britain.[34] Seston though that this rebellion prompted Diocletian to elevate Maximian to Augustus, a step he would not otherwise have taken.[35] Frankish and Saxon pirates had become troublesome around the mouth of the Rhine and the coasts of Britain and Gaul, and

Carausius may have been appointed as fleet commander by Carus or Carinus, or possibly by Maximian.[36] Carausius may have been ordered to build a fleet to use against the pirates.[37] He may have been the last prefect of the *Classis Britannica*, the Channel fleet, but if he had to build a fleet, this could mean that the *Classis Britannica* was defunct.[38] Carausius' base was at Boulogne. He had a good reputation among the troops on both sides of the Channel, and knowledge of the Channel waters. He was successful against the pirates, but soon came under suspicion. He seemed to know when the Franks were about to raid – but intervened only when they were returning to their ships with their booty, which he recaptured, and nothing was restored to the original owners. Even if the rumour was false, Maximian had to be seen to act. He decided to arrest Carausius, but his quarry, probably tipped off, escaped to Britain, where the army declared him Emperor. Salway suggests that the army officers went along with Carausius because they were already compromised.[39] Carausius held onto Boulogne and he commanded some troops in Gaul who were loyal to him. His ships were intact, his crews experienced, and he was said to have allied with the Franks, hiring them as mercenaries.

In saving his own skin Carausius created a new breakaway state, the *Imperium Britanniarum*. He probably had no desire to rule the whole Empire, but he wanted recognition, issuing coins in 290 with Diocletian's head depicted in the centre, flanked by the heads of Maximian and Carausius, bearing the legend CARAUSIUS ET FRATRES SUI, Carausius and his brothers.[40] His coinage was of higher standard than that of the western half of the Empire. There were mints at London and Colchester, and at Rouen and probably Boulogne.[41] Carausius or his advisers quoted Virgil on the coinage, especially *expectate veni* from the Aeneid, declaring that Carausius was the expected one.[42] He styled himself the restorer of Britain (*resitutor Britanniae*). The coins list the legions under Carausius' command, some of which may be only vexillations. Strangely, there is no mention of VI Victrix from York.[43]

Maximian could not attend to Britain until Gaul and the Rhine were safe. By 288 he had dispersed the Frankish raiders, and Diocletian returned from the east to join him, having first been embroiled in war against the tribes of the Danube, chiefly Sarmatians. He won battles but had to fight the Sarmatians all over again four years later, earning the title *Sarmaticus Maximus*. In 286/287 Diocletian avoided a confrontation with the Persians by diplomatic arrangements, perhaps not making a formal treaty, but the Persians sent gifts.[44] Diocletian re-absorbed Mesopotamia and reorganised the Syrian frontier, fortifying Circesium on the Euphrates.[45] The Roman candidate for the throne of Armenia, Tiridates, was installed without opposition.

In 288 Diocletian and Maximian concentrated on the Alamanni, attacking respectively from Raetia and Mainz. By a scorched earth policy and keeping the tribes on the move, the two Emperors finally swept the enemy out of the *Agri Decumates*, which the tribes had occupied since the reign of Gallienus.[46] Franks, Chamavi and Friesians were settled on the lands between the Rhine and the Waal from Nijmegen to Utrecht, and on vacant lands in Gaul.[47]

Maximian could finally turn to Carausius. A panegyric delivered in 289 expected much of his campaign, but it did not happen. In another panegyric of 297, it was said that bad weather prevented the campaign.[48] An invasion of Britain was difficult because Carausius' navy guarded the Channel, and his forts guarded the south coast. It is not yet appropriate to call these the forts of the Saxon Shore, though it could be said that Carausius paved the way for them. It is not possible to pinpoint a date when the Saxon Shore was established, welding into an overall scheme the coastal forts all built at different times and to different designs. In their later forms the forts were oriented to naval operations.[49]

In 293 Carausius lost control of Boulogne to Constantius Caesar, one of the emperors of the Tetrarchy, described below.[50] Carausius lost credibility and was assassinated by Allectus, described with little certainty as finance minister.[51] Allectus controlled Britain for another three years, while Constantius fought the Alamanni in Gaul until 296. He then embarked for Britain, sharing command of the fleet with his Praetorian Prefect Asclepiodotus, who defeated and killed Allectus.[52] Constantius claimed that Carausius' Frankish mercenaries were about to sack London, so he had them killed. Constantius issued the famous medallion from the Trier mint, proclaiming that he had brought back the eternal light to Britain (*redditor lucis aeternae*).[53] This is a fine rhetorical flourish, but had it really been so dark under Carausius and Allectus? By 297 the British provinces were secure enough for Constantius to return to Gaul.

## The Tetrarchy

Diocletian concluded his campaign against the Saracens at the end of 290, but next to nothing is known about it. The Empire was more or less stabilised and secure, with the glaring exception of the regime of Carausius in Britain and part of Gaul. Celebrations were held in 291, not in Rome but in Milan, nearer to the troublesome zones.[54]

Multiple threats to the Empire, often simultaneous, made it imperative for the emperors to appoint permanent deputies. Diocletian created the Tetrarchy, which is not his label but a modern one derived from ancient Greek, indicating territory divided into four areas, each with a tetrarch in charge. Diocletian and Maximian as Augusti were the senior Emperors, and two Caesars were created in ceremonies held on the same date, 1 March 293, in Milan where Constantius was made Caesar to Maximian, and probably in Sirmium, where Galerius was made Caesar to Diocletian.[55] Constantius was the senior Caesar, being cited in first place on official documents.[56] Constantius, whose name Chlorus was applied long after his death, married Theodora, Maximian's stepdaughter, having divorced his first wife Helena, who had given him a son, the future emperor Constantine. Like Maximian, Constantius took the name Herculius, while Galerius adopted Diocletian's title Jovius. Victory titles were held by all four, whether or not they had participated in the relevant wars.[57]

Lactantius and Aurelius Victor both assert that each ruler had his own territory.[58] The Empire was not divided into four permanent zones, but each of the four rulers chose cities in different parts of the Empire as their headquarters, Constantius at Trier, Maximian at Milan, Galerius at Thessalonika, and Diocletian at Nicomedia, but there were several other Imperial residences. The Tetrarchs perhaps had limited licence to make decisions or legislate in the areas where the others were operating, but Diocletian alone had the power to issue edicts pertaining to the whole Empire.[59]

### Wars of the Tetrarchs

From 293 to 296 Diocletian and Maximian took a back seat while Constantius and Galerius fought the wars. A revolt in Egypt *c.* 293 to 295 was suppressed by Galerius.[60] Battles with the Sarmatians were fought on the Danube in 294. Forts were built *in Sarmatia contra Acinco et Bononia*, in barbarian territory opposite Aquincum (Budapest) and Bononia (Vidin, Bulgaria).[61] These forts have been labelled bridgeheads guarding the approaches to the Roman side of the Danube, but it is possible that Diocletian kept the tribes under surveillance from new forts in occupied zones beyond the frontier. No forts have been detected archaeologically.

During the war with the Sarmatians, the bellicose Narses seized power in Persia, but he sent ambassadors to Rome and war was postponed until the Persians invaded Armenia and ousted Tiridates in 295. Galerius finalised operations in Egypt and set off to fight Narses in 296, but at Carrhae he was defeated.[62] A new Persian campaign had to wait for two or three years.

Later Maximian campaigned in Mauretania, taking troops from Germany and the Rhine.[63] Another revolt broke out in Egypt led by Lucius Domitius Domitianus, who declared himself Augustus. He soon died, and Aurelius Achilleus took over, styling himself *corrector* of Egypt.[64] The revolt may have been deliberately timed to coincide with Narses' war against Rome.[65] The excuse for it may have been the announcement of a census and land survey for a new taxation scheme. Tax was usually derived from units of land, *tributum soli* or later *iugatio*, and from a personal tax, *tributum capitis* or *capitatio*. The Egyptian version of these taxes was also based on land and individuals.[66]

The Romans besieged Achilleus in Alexandria. The city fell, and the killing began. Diocletian was said to have vowed that the slaughter would not stop until the blood reached his horse's knees, which it did unexpectedly when his horse fell, bloodying its knees. The carnage was halted and later the Alexandrians erected a statue of the horse, their saviour.[67] Alexandria lost its special status and the right to issue coinage, and Egypt was divided into two provinces, one retaining the name Egypt, governed by the Prefect of Egypt and the other called Thebais, carved out of the original province and divided into two parts, each governed by a procurator under the overall command of an equestrian *praeses*. The census was held, the new tax laws were instituted, and the administration was overhauled, an ongoing process over several years.

A new Persian campaign was launched in 298-9. Diocletian remained in Syria, as Galerius marched through Armenia into Media and Adiabene, winning a victory near modern Erzerum.[68] At Thessalonika, Galerius' headquarters, a triumphal arch was erected, recording his achievements against the Persians. At Nisibis Diocletian and Galerius arranged a treaty with the Persians in 299. Another Tiridates was made King of Armenia, and Mesopotamia was recovered. It was agreed that all trade was to pass through Nisibis, benefitting the Roman economy. Diocletian also strengthened the eastern frontier.[69]

Constantius also won victories on the Rhine.[70] By 303, peace had been established as far as possible over the whole Empire. Working together, Diocletian and Maximian had managed to convert what had been a purely defensive policy into an offensive one. In Rome they celebrated their *vicennalia*, their joint reigns of twenty years, juggling the figures for Maximian's shorter reign. Coins were issued bearing the legend GAUDETE ROMANI, instructing the Romans to rejoice.[71]

After the *vicennalia* Diocletian went to Nicomedia, where he fell seriously ill in 304, which probably convinced Diocletian to abdicate in 305.[72] While in Rome he may have suggested to Maximian that they should both retire at the same time, and in a ceremony in the temple of Jupiter, Maximian allegedly promised that he would comply with Diocletian's wishes.[73] When the time came in 305, Maximian reluctantly obeyed.[74] Diocletian retired to the famous palace at Split, which he had started to build some years earlier.[75] Constantius and Galerius became Augusti, with two new Caesars proclaimed on 1 May 305, Flavius Valerius Severus in the west under Constantius, and in the east Galerius' Caesar was Maximinus Daia, renamed Gaius Galerius Valerius Maximinus. Severus had married Galerius' daughter, and Maximinus was Galerius' nephew.[76] The balance seemed therefore to be in Galerius' favour.

As Augustus, Constantius returned to Britain, asking his son Constantine to join him. Constantine was given permission to leave Galerius' court at Nicomedia. Zosimus says that he expected to be killed, so whenever he changed horses at posting stations, he killed or maimed all the remaining animals to prevent pursuit.[77] Constantine joined his father at Boulogne, though the sources imply that he travelled to Britain later.[78]

All that is known of Constantius' British campaign is that it happened. There is little elucidation in a panegyric delivered after his death.[79] The enemies are named as Caledonians, and for the first time the Picts are mentioned, and Constantius is said to have reached the far north of the island. Archaeology has little to show for this campaign. Constantius took the victory title *Britannicus Maximus* for the second time. Any further plans were cut short by his death at York in July 306. The soldiers proclaimed Constantine as Augustus. The instigator may have been the Alamannic king Crocus, commanding his tribesmen in the expeditionary army.[80] Constantine had to be patient in making his proclamation a reality.

## Diocletian's Empire

The literary, epigraphic and papyrus records for Diocletian's work date to the period after his reign, making it difficult to distinguish between Diocletian's and Constantine's measures. A common denominator was that the emperors became more remote from the people. Even before Diocletian's reign, emperors were not content with the simple victory title such as *Germanicus* or *Britannicus*, but added *maximus*, 'greatest' to their titles, and so became *Sarmaticus maximus*, *Arabicus maximus*, and so on. Under Diocletian and Maximian titles became superlatives. They were *invictissimi*, not just invincible but most invincible, and on an inscription from Augsburg, they were *providentissimi*, most provident, from *providere* meaning to foresee, or to take precautions.[81]

In the Imperial service of the late third century, ranks were also indicated by superlatives, starting with the *vir perfectissimus*, literally 'the most perfect man', rising to *vir eminentissimus*, *vir clarissimus*, and *vir spectabilis*. Anyone serving as *vir clarissimus* became a senator, but the status was not as grand as it once was. Only a few posts as provincial governors remained in the hands of senators.[82] The equestrian class had been progressively promoted, and the tendency to follow almost exclusively a military or a civilian career, already apparent by Hadrian's reign, facilitated the growth of professionalism.

Professionalism also developed in the law, which was recorded mostly in the form of rescripts of the emperors, or replies to queries from provincial governors. Although Diocletian distanced himself from the people, he took an interest in their welfare and many of his rescripts survive, a high proportion of them dealing with minor cases. Probably in 292, the *magister libellorum* Gregorius published his collection of rescripts which he considered useful for the practice of law.[83] His *Codex Gregorianus* was supplemented in 295 by a further collection of rescripts and legal decisions, complied by Hermogenianus, *magister libellorum* under Diocletian and Maximian.

## Field armies, frontier armies and the Praetorian Prefects

Diocletian inherited the military system of the earlier Empire, with legions and auxiliary units defending the now battered frontiers and provinces. Campaign armies were formed from detachments, or vexillations, taken from the armies of the frontiers to supplement the troops stationed in the war zones. There was no standing campaign army to march immediately to threatened provinces or frontiers. In the third century the need for mobility and rapid response increased, which could only be supplied by cavalry. Adapting to the new circumstances, Diocletian and Constantine reorganised their military forces, eventually creating the frontier armies and the mobile field armies, but it cannot be discerned which developmental stages were due to which emperor.

The legions still provided the backbone of the army before the division into field armies and frontier armies. Most of the thirty-four pre-Diocletianic legions survived, and Diocletian added over thirty new legions, which may have been only 1,000 strong.[84] On the other hand the fourth-century author Vegetius says that Diocletian's legions were 6000 strong, and it was difficult to keep them up to strength.[85] Vegetius may have referred to the old-style legions, which Diocletian may have split up into smaller groups to man more than one fort.[86] The *Notitia Dignitatum*, a late Roman list of civil and military offices, records that II Italica, raised by Marcus Aurelius, was distributed over five different forts, and also contributed a unit to the campaign army.[87] In Egypt, II Traiana was also split up among different locations, and Elton explains that by this time the eastern legions had been divided into specialist groups, infantry armed with missiles called *lanciarii* and light cavalry called *promoti*. These specialist units of II Traiana were based respectively at Ptolemais and Tentyra.[88] The legions had always possessed a cavalry contingent, which Gallienus enlarged, and the legionary cavalry could be detached from the parent legion to operate independently. The *promoti* may have been derived from the legionary cavalry.[89]

In 260 the Emperor Gallienus welded together the cavalry units drawn from several different sources, placing them under a single commander. The independent cavalry may have survived into the reigns of Carinus and Diocletian, either of whom, according to Seston, deprived it of its single commander.[90] The Byzantine chronicler George Cedrenus considered that Gallienus' cavalry army was the forerunner of the mobile *comitatenses* of the later Empire.[91] It cannot be demonstrated that the cavalry survived as a distinct body into the late Empire, so the origin of the *comitatenses* is still to be sought.

Diocletian's role in the formation of the *comitatenses* is debated. The argument revolves around the *comitatus*, composed of the friends (*comites*) of the emperors, and picked soldiers accompanying an emperor on campaign. The cavalry, the vexillations and the *comites* of Diocletian are attested in 295 in Egypt.[92] An inscription records a *lanciarius* of *Legio XI Claudia* serving in the *comitatus*.[93] Another inscription honours the three Augusti Maximinus, Constantine and Licinius, dating it somewhere between 307 and 313. It concerns the *praepositus* or commander of a Dalmatian cavalry unit, *praepositus equitibus Dalmatis Aquesianis comit*, but the abbreviated *comit* could indicate *comitatus*, or *comitatenses*.[94] If the correct restoration is *comitatenses*, then it shows that field armies existed probably by 307, only two years after Diocletian abdicated, and Potter argues the *comitatenses* should be attributed to Diocletian, with some reorganisation by Constantine.[95] New commanders of the field armies, the *magister peditum* and *magister equitum*, were probably installed by Constantine.[96] These titles suggest that the *magistri* commanded the infantry and the cavalry, but their roles were not so strictly prescribed.[97]

The division into field armies and frontier armies could not have occurred overnight, but by Constantine's reign it had been achieved. The Theodosian Code of laws, compiled in the early fifth century, contains a letter from Constantine written in 325 concerning exemption from the *capitatio*, or tax on persons, for the soldiers and their families of three different types of armed forces, the *comitatenses* or field armies, the *ripenses/riparienses milites* or frontier armies, and the *protectores*.[98] Other troops, the *alares* and *cohortales*, are distinguished from the first three groups. These belong to the *auxilia*, recruited from tribesmen outside the Empire to guard the frontiers. The tax exemptions for the troops of Licinius, Constantine's rival, were more generous, as shown by the bronze tablet dating to 311 from the Danube fort of Brigetio (Szöny, Hungary).[99]

The *ripenses* later became the *limitanei*, linking them with the *limes*, meaning frontier. The *limitanei* of later times were probably settled on the land in return for military service, and authors of the fourth and fifth centuries projected the term retrospectively into previous reigns, so caution is necessary when the *Historia Augusta* mentions *limitanei* in the army of Severus Alexander, and the Byzantine chronicler John Malalas attributes the *limitanei* to Diocletian.[100] Van Berchem compromised, suggesting that when Diocletian put troops on the frontiers, as Zosimus says, he tied them to the land, but they were not yet called *limitanei*.[101]

The Praetorians receded in importance under Diocletian and were dissolved by Constantine in 312. The new Imperial guards were mounted troops called *scholae*, possibly established by Diocletian but not attested until Constantine's reign as *scholae palatinae*, replacing the *equites singulares Augusti*, which were also disbanded, and their barracks built by Septimius Severus were demolished to make way for the church of St John Lateran.[102]

The Praetorian Prefects survived, with primarily administrative duties, though they were still sometimes put in command of troops. They were second in command to the emperors with wide authority in every sphere of government, responsible for judicial matters and financial affairs. They were chiefs of staff, and quartermasters responsible for supplies to the army and the administrative officials. A few of the Tetrarchic Prefects are known by name.[103] There is debate about whether each of the four Tetrarchs had his own Praetorian Prefect, but it seems that there were only two under Diocletian.[104] It is conjectured that one Prefect was allocated to Diocletian and one to Maximian.[105] After Diocletian's abdication each of the five hopeful successors – Constantine, Maxentius, Severus, Galerius and Licinius – appointed his own Praetorian Prefect.[106] Zosimus insists, incorrectly, that there were permanent regional prefectures, with each Prefect being responsible for his own area, but at this stage they did not control defined territories.[107]

Diocletian repaired the frontiers and may have completed the Rhine-Iller-Danube *limes* connecting the Rhine and the Danube, begun by the Emperor Probus.[108] In the east, Diocletian established roads fortified with towers and forts, the principal route being the Strata Diocletiana, said to connect Egypt with Palmyra, but only about 100 miles of it have been discovered. Diocletian's army reforms and frontier repairs have been interpreted as the establishment of defence in depth, with troops stationed on the frontiers supported by fortified road posts and depots in the hinterland, so instead of stopping invading tribesmen on the frontiers, the Romans would converge on them inside Roman territory.[109]

Zosimus praises Diocletian for securing the frontiers and protecting the Empire, while Constantine took troops away from the frontiers, placing them in cities which did not need protection.[110] This makes it sound as if Constantine stripped the frontiers of all troops, which is nonsense. All emperors were concerned with the protection of the frontiers, and the existence of *ripenses*, *alares*, and so on shows that Constantine did not neglect frontiers.

In the late third century the need for defences became more acute, and the shape of forts changed to meet these needs. Gateways were blocked up, or sometimes the gateway was enclosed by a tower projecting beyond the walls. Projecting U-shaped towers were built along fort walls, and the Danube forts were equipped with fan-shaped projecting corner towers, providing a clearer view of the two walls leading from the corners. Harbours and landing places were defended, and more watchtowers were built.[111] Generally, there was no Imperial policy for the fortification of cities, but in some cases Imperial assistance is recorded, at Grenoble for instance, and there are instances of the army helping to build walls.[112]

As well as making changes in frontier defences, Diocletian reorganised the military command structure. He is said to have finally removed senators from army commands, but Arnheim's examination of the political and social careers of senators between the accession of Diocletian and 395 showed that senators were never totally removed from command.[113] During the Tetrarchy, senatorial proconsuls governed Achaea, Asia and Africa, though the latter two provinces were reduced in size.[114] Equestrian *praesides* governing the provinces took on judicial duties, as shown by the alternative title *iudex* (plural *iudices*) meaning judge, and they were responsible for finances and tax collection.[115] In the later Empire there were still some small provinces such as Mauretania Caesariensis and Isaurica where the governor was also the military commander, in one case listed as *dux et praeses*, military commander and governor.[116] The *dux* (plural *duces*) was a new equestrian officer probably introduced in Gallienus' reign. *Dux* simply means leader, and the first *duces* may have led collections of different troops.[117] A *dux* holding a temporary command would not need a title explaining where he held authority, but when *duces* were appointed as regular military officers their titles showed the area, or areas, where they had authority. The *duces* provided a unified command on one or more frontier zones, regardless of who the provincial governors were. By 289, contemporary sources speak of two separate posts, *duces* as military commanders and *iudices* as governors and administrators.[118] With separate military commanders and civilian governors, the workload of both demanded less broad-based diversity and more specialist knowledge.

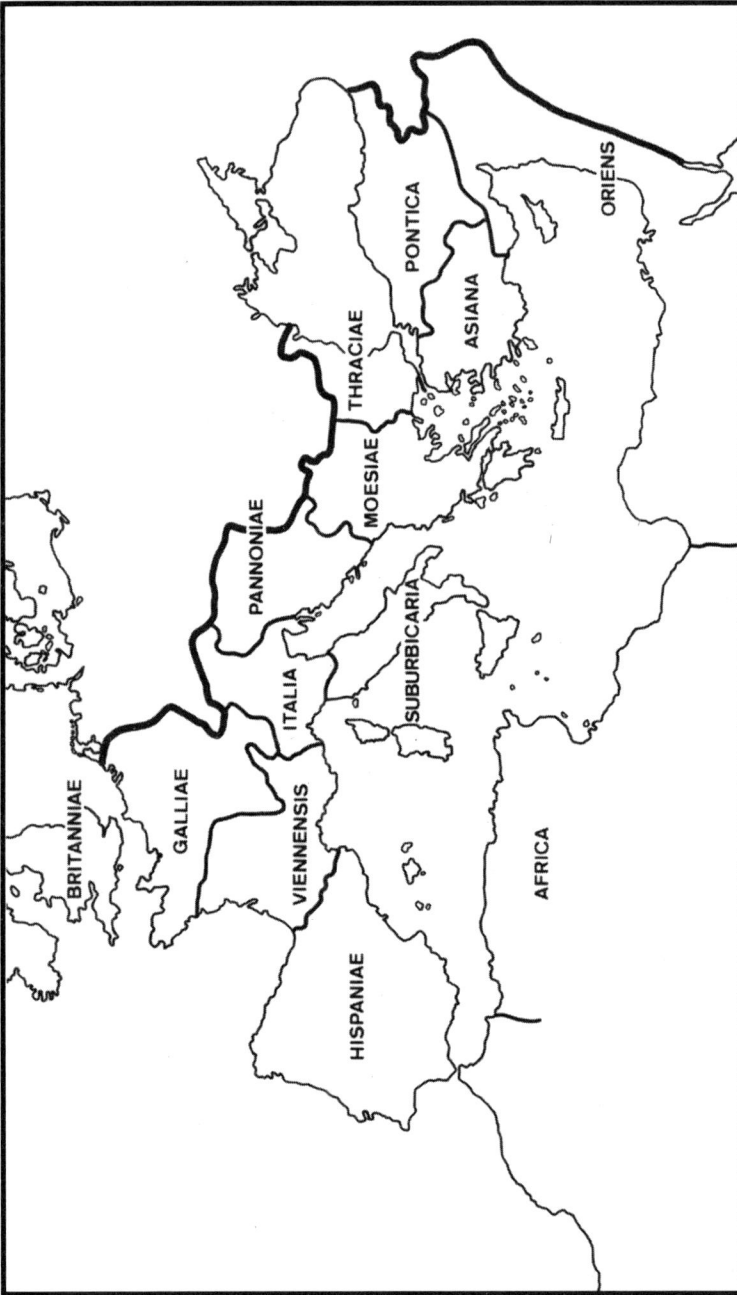

14. Map of the dioceses created by the Emperor Diocletian as part of his reorganisation of the provinces, splitting them all into smaller units and grouping them into dioceses, which were governed by new officials called *vicarii*. These provided an extra rank between the Praetorian Prefects to whom they were directly answerable and the provincial governors, for whose activities they were responsible. Drawn by Graeme Stobbs.

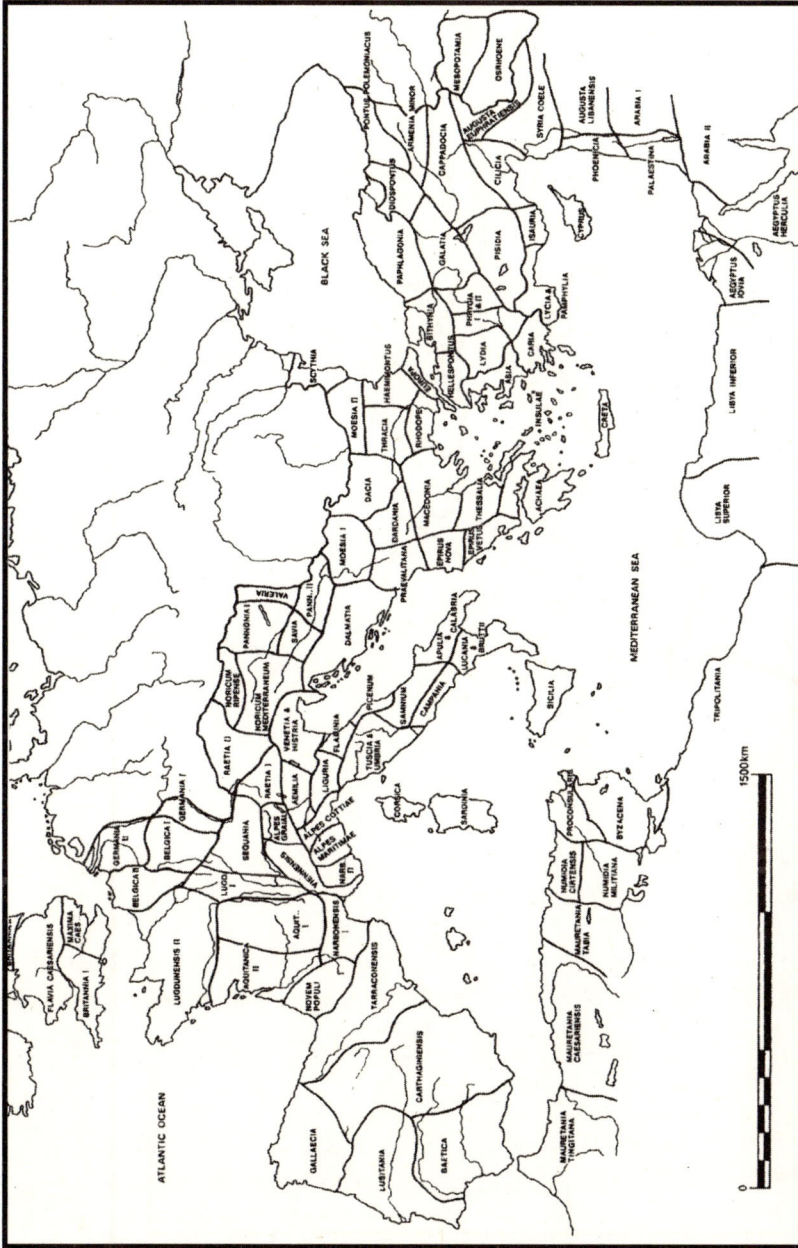

15. Map of the reorganised provinces under Diocletian, with their new names, redrawn boundaries and smaller areas. Drawn by Graeme Stobbs.

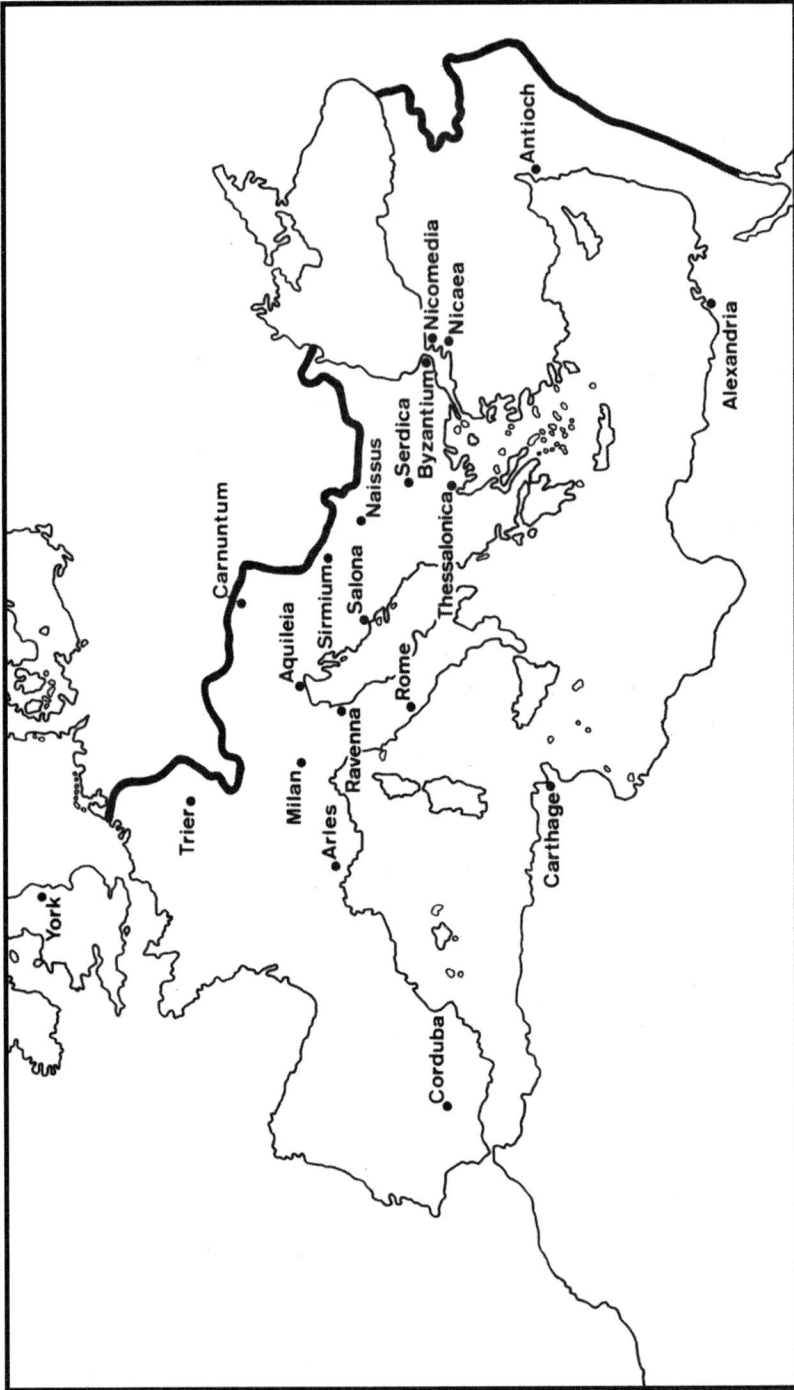

16. Map of the provincial capitals established by the four emperors of the Tetrarchy, who required headquarters within their regions. These were existing cities which benefitted from the presence of the Imperial courts. Drawn by Graeme Stobbs.

*Finance and taxation*

The closest that the Romans came to formulating an annual budget was when the Praetorian Prefects took on administrative, financial and legal duties. When the annual requirements for the Empire were calculated, the Prefects were responsible for apportioning the amounts to be collected from each province. Taxes were collected by the town or city councils, with the shortfall made up by the decurions or council members. The crippling expense of serving on the councils resulted in a decline in numbers of decurions.[119] Avoidance tactics to escape the office became common; to counteract these and to spread the net wider over more candidates for the decurionate, Diocletian lowered the land-holding qualification for service on the councils. Once decurions had been nominated, these unfortunates had no means of escape, and small landholders, or even under-age minors, could be found on municipal councils by the mid-third century.[120]

By far the largest expense was in feeding, clothing and equipping the soldiers. During the third century, the state was unable to pay the troops, and payment in kind was substituted for part or all of the soldiers' wages. The *annona militaris* originally involved compulsory requisitions by order of the emperor when the army was on campaign; items were theoretically paid for as the army passed through each designated area, but more frequently the system was abused, and the collection of the *annona* degenerated into arbitrary requisitioning.[121]

It became a matter of urgency to find some method of taxation that spread the burden fairly and ensured that all provinces contributed to the defence of the Empire. Italy, long exempt from tax, now had to play its part. Under Severus, Italy was subject to requisitioning of food for the *annona militaris*. Probably under Aurelian, Italy had been put on the same footing as the rest of the provinces by its division into different administrative areas tactfully called regions rather than provinces. During the tax reforms of Diocletian, Italy's long-lasting tax exemption ended, except for Rome and its territory up to 100 miles around the city.

Taxation was predominantly based on agricultural production, which naturally varied from region to region, depending on the quality of the soil and the type of crops produced on it. Diocletian introduced a system of assessment based on an agricultural unit called the *iugum*, originally meaning a yoke or a collar for oxen or horses. It was not a uniform measurement but varied according to the type of land and crop. The standard measure for acreage was the *iugerum* (plural *iugera*). A passage from *The Syro-Roman Law Book* explains that five *iugera* of vineyards pay the tax of one *iugum*, whereas twenty *iugera* of grain land pay the tax of one *iugum*. In mountainous terrain, the inhabitants were asked to calculate how much land was required to produce one *modius* or standard measure of wheat of barley.[122]

There was also a tax on manpower, assessed by a head count, *capitatio* from *caput*, head. It was calculated by the amount of labour required by one man to plough and plant the land. A woman's labour was usually, but not always, assessed as half a *caput*. Both the *iugatio* and *capitatio* were needed to make the fair assessment of taxes due from an area. Livestock was also included in the assessments, as the *capitatio animalium*.[123]

Vast amounts of clerical work were required to assess the lands and classify it under various headings, woodland, vineyards, pasture, grain land and so on. This would be part of the census, ideally renewed every five years to keep track of changes. There is some census information for Syria and Egypt, but none for the western provinces.[124] Possibly all the censuses were undertaken quite early in Diocletian's reign, in Egypt perhaps as early as 287, with the edict of the Prefect of Egypt in 297 representing a secondary stage of a system that was already well established.[125] This does not prove that the census began in other provinces in 287.

In order to tackle the problem of inflation and rising prices, Diocletian attempted to reform the currency and to set the maximum amounts that could be charged for a comprehensive variety of goods. Aurelian's attempt to stabilise the value of coins had not been successful. As the amount of precious metal in successive coin issues kept on declining, good coins were hoarded and disappeared from circulation, causing prices to rise. Diocletian's coinage edict was issued before September 301.[126] The preface usually attached to the price edict is now thought to belong to the coinage edict.[127] The three metal coinage was restored, and better quality coins were issued. The mints all issued coins of uniform types, but since there is no information as to how the Diocletianic coins related to each other, it is not known how many of a smaller denomination made one of a higher denomination, and values may have varied in different parts of the Empire.[128] The coinage reform did not have the desired effect.

A few months after this edict, the price edict was issued. It is known from several versions, some of them fragmentary, on wood, papyrus and stone.[129] It contains fascinating information about relative prices of all kinds of goods, listed in minute detail with their recommended retail prices, which, if exceeded, incurred penalties. Potter labels the edict an act of economic lunacy.[130] The edict failed to take into account regional differences, and although it laid down how much could be charged for transport, it failed to add these charges to production costs. If traders could not buy and transport their goods for less than the maximum amount they could charge, they would cease to trade. Lactantius says that goods disappeared from the market, and fights and even deaths occurred over the smallest items.[131] Lactantius is the only source for the effects of the edict, and he gloats about its failure. The price edict was allowed to sink into oblivion.[132]

## The growth of centralization

Nearly all of the evidence for administrative changes comes from Constantine's reign or later, so Diocletian's contributions are sometimes difficult to discern. What follows is what Diocletian achieved. Probably.

Administration of the Empire became more centralized, and more militarised and regimented, earning the label *militia*, while *militia armata* referred to army service. Diocletian organised the administrative personnel in ranks, and divided up business into departments, called *scrinia* (singular *scrinium*) after the boxes containing documents. The earliest reference to the *scrinia* dates to 313, but Diocletian was probably the originator.[133] Officials acquired new titles, *magistri*, from *magister*, meaning master or director. The *ab epistulis* became the *magister epistulorum* and *magister libellorum* took over from the *a libellis*, both of them probably being responsible for correspondence and petitions to the emperors. There was also the *magister memoriae* who may have dealt with foreign relations.[134] The *magister officiorum* in charge of the *scrinia*, and of the military *magistri*, belong to Constantine's reign. Diocletian's *magistri* were members of the Imperial council, the *consilium*, which in the later Empire became the *consistorium*.[135] The equestrians and freedmen who ran the offices behind the scenes were not members of this council.

Beginning under Diocletian and crystallized under Constantine, personal freedom and social mobility were obliterated by state-imposed obligations, extended to all walks of life. Manufacture of goods by private individuals was increasingly controlled by the state, especially for anything concerning the army. Food and raw materials taken as tax in kind had to be processed, so factories for all kinds of production were established, managed by military personnel.

Craftsmen were compelled to join a guild or corporation. Under Constantine, craftsmen had to train their sons in their specific skills, so employment became hereditary, and these workers and their descendants were forbidden to change to a different trade or to move to another area.[136]

The restrictions on personal freedom extended to the rural population. The *coloni*, or tenant farmers, originally possessed a degree of freedom, but in the uncertain times of the third century they needed the support of influential people. Some had abandoned their lands because of failed harvests, or general insecurity. Lactantius says oppressive taxes added to the burdens of the peasant farmers, inducing them to flee.[137] Of necessity, efforts were made to put them back on the land.[138] Not all *coloni* were poor and defenceless, since there is evidence that some of them owned estates in the early fourth century.[139] For those who owned no land, joining with the landowners was an option. Egyptian peasant farmers were already closely associated with their landlords, through whom they paid their taxes. As the fourth century progressed more landowners abandoned the cities where their obligations were becoming too onerous, and the *coloni* gradually came under their control, in what amounted to captivity, but some modern authors dismiss the colonate system as a myth.[140] A law of 332 states that anyone who shelters a *colonus* belonging to someone else must return him and pay the taxes he had avoided.[141] The only alternative for a *colonus* was to join the army, and on occasion landowners, who needed cultivators, competed with the armies in recruiting manpower. Constantine tied the *coloni* to the land, just as tradespeople and craftsmen were tied to their professions.

## Provincial reorganisation

Diocletian reorganised provincial administration across the entire Empire, but once again the evidence is Constantinian or later. At an unknown date towards the end of Diocletian's reign, twelve new administrative units were created, called dioceses, each comprising a group of provinces, and the provinces were split into much smaller areas with new provincial names. There is debate about whether the dioceses were established before the division of the provinces, or vice versa, and about whether the reorganisation was instantaneous, or a prolonged process.[142] The inception of the changes possibly belongs to 293 or 297, but Britain is unlikely to have become a diocese before 296, when Constantius regained control.[143]

Each diocese was controlled by a new equestrian official, or *vicarius*, which denotes a substitute standing in for another official, in this case the Praetorian Prefects, to whom the *vicarii* were directly answerable. No *vicarius* is attested until 298. Diocletian's *vicarii* were permanent officials, slotted into the administrative hierarchy as an extra rank. They were responsible for the conduct of the provincial governors, except the few remaining senatorial proconsuls. The hierarchy was not strictly observed, since the Emperor and the Praetorian Prefects could communicate directly with provincial governors. Boundaries would be re-drawn for each of Diocletian's new provinces, and each smaller province would require a headquarters for the governor. Some new provinces would contain troops, and the forts would probably remain in situ, but the headquarters might be relocated. In a few of the smaller provinces the governor took charge of civilian affairs and also commanded troops, otherwise civil administration and military commands remained separate.

The evidence for the dioceses and the new provinces derives from the fourth century Verona List, the *Laterculus Veronensis*, copies of which were made at later dates, the seventh century version being the one available to historians. The document lists the dioceses, the *vicarii* in charge of them, and the provinces and their governors, all requiring revision and updating. Some of the entries are from the reign of Constantine, thus obscuring the Diocletianic arrangements.[144] The benefits of the subdivision of provinces were that the duties of each governor concerned a smaller population, so he could devote more time to supervising the cities, transport and communications, food supply, judicial cases and tax collection. Lactantius says that splitting the provinces into smaller units made supervision of the populace easier, but he interprets the methods as terrorisation.[145]

## The problem of the Christians

The beginning of Diocletian's reign was peaceful as far as the Christians were concerned.[146] Diocletian at first concentrated on reviving and strengthening the old Roman religion, but he did not enforce worship of Roman gods by all the peoples of the Empire. There was no time during the wars of his early reign to combat religious subversives. The first religious sect to occupy Diocletian's attention was that of the Manichaeans of the eastern provinces, with other groups in Egypt and North Africa. They followed the teachings of Mani, who was considered a heretic by the priests of

Mazda in Persia. Shapur had forbidden the persecution of religious groups, including the Manichaeans, so it seemed to the Romans that the followers of Mani must be favourable towards the Persians, and they were seen as a fifth column in the Roman eastern provinces. Nothing specific was done to eradicate them until 302 when Diocletian visited Egypt, issuing an edict against the Manichaeans that same year. The text is known; how it was put into effect is not elucidated.[147]

In 303 the Christians came under scrutiny. In 295 the proconsul of Africa had to judge a certain Maximilian because he refused to enlist. If this attitude became widespread, recruitment for the armies all over the Empire would be compromised, and if the Christians were to be officially excused from military service, men who simply did not want to be soldiers could suddenly develop a zeal for Christianity. An attempt was made to remove Christians already in the army in case they refused duty. In 298 a Christian centurion called Marcellus refused to take part in celebrations honouring Maximian, probably because sacrifices were involved – to the emperors as gods, or to Jupiter and Hercules.[148] Sacrifice to the Roman gods became the litmus test of a Christian's attitude to Imperial rule. Galerius forced officers to sacrifice or to leave the army.[149] Further conflict was inevitable.

At the beginning of the fourth century the Emperors applied themselves to eradicating Christianity. Galerius, violently anti-Christian throughout his career, took most of the blame. Lactantius says that Diocletian's advisers were afraid of Galerius and advocated persecution.[150] The first anti-Christian edict was issued on 23 February 303, at Nicomedia, where the church was destroyed. Panic ensued, and fires broke out twice in the Imperial palace. Galerius left the city rather than be murdered by the Christians, but Lactantius accuses him of starting the fires and blaming the Christians; clear echoes of Nero.[151]

In summer 303 another edict was issued, ordering arrest of the clergy.[152] A third edict ordered compulsory sacrifice to the gods. In the east, Christians were tortured to persuade them to sacrifice, but the west was not as heavily Christianized as the east, and Constantius and Maxentius merely closed churches and confiscated books.[153] Elsewhere, officials simply told the Emperors that everyone had sacrificed. No-one bothered to check, and some pagans sheltered Christians from the worst of the persecution.

## The rise of Constantine

Constantine's rise to power was not inevitable. He managed to gain supremacy by a combination of talent, guile, effort and luck. When the soldiers in Britain declared him Emperor in July 306, Constantine wrote to Galerius, now Augustus after the abdication of Diocletian, to explain that he had no choice but to concur with the wishes of the troops. Galerius compromised and made him Caesar. Constantine waited and watched for the next opportunity, but there was a rival. In October 306, Maximian's son Maxentius was declared Emperor in Rome.[154] Maximian reappeared, voluntarily according to Zosimus but Lactantius says that Maxentius invited him.[155] Galerius sent his Caesar, Severus, to dislodge Maxentius, but he failed. He was besieged in Ravenna and committed suicide, or alternatively Maximian lured him out and hanged him.[156] Galerius arrived to besiege Rome but could not prevail against Aurelian's walls and returned to the east. Maxentius now held southern Italy, Sicily, Sardinia and Africa, but not Spain, which was in Constantine's hands.[157]

After Galerius's departure, Maximian tried to depose his son, but Maxentius was too well supported in Rome, and Maximian had to flee to Constantine's court at Trier. Constantine married Fausta, daughter of Maximian, who is said to have promised to make Constantine Augustus. Maximian was technically a usurper, so Constantine distanced himself as soon as he could, but first he attended to the Rhine frontier, campaigning against the Bructeri and building a bridge at Cologne.[158] He perhaps began to build the fort at Deutz opposite the city, though the archaeological evidence suggests that it belongs to a later period.

While Constantine and Maximian were in Gaul, Galerius arranged the famous meeting at Carnuntum on 11 November 308. An inscription set up in the Mithraeum at Carnuntum records the fact that the Emperors were reunited.[159] It was not as harmonious as it sounds. Constantine, fully engaged on the Rhine, did not attend. Maxentius was ignored as an outsider, and Maximian had to step down again. Diocletian would not be persuaded to resume rule of the Empire. Whatever influence he possessed ended altogether when he died, probably in 312. Since Diocletian refused to direct affairs in 308, Galerius' colleague Licinius was made Augustus. Constantine and Maximinus became Caesars.[160] Constantine determinedly held onto the title Augustus, bestowed by the army of Britain. Later, Maximinus also adopted it, and Galerius finally confirmed both of them as Augusti.[161]

## The elimination of Constantine's rivals

Constantine claimed that his wife Fausta had informed him of her father's intrigues against him.[162] He marched to southern Gaul and besieged Maximian at Marseilles. It was said that Maximian committed suicide, but his death was suspicious. Constantine obliterated all connection with Maximian. He deified his father Constantius, also contriving to make the Emperor Claudius Gothicus one of his ancestors.[163] In response Licinius attached himself to the house of Philip the Arab. Constantine rejected the Jovian-Herculian cult of Diocletian and turned to Apollo and Sol Invictus, like Aurelian. His new attachment derived from a vision he saw in 310 in Gaul.

Galerius fell ill and died in 311. Lactantius rejoices that he suffered.[164] He had issued the edict of toleration, ignored by Maximinus, that reversed the persecution of the Christians, restored Christian places of worship and reinstated the clergy.[165] In 312 Constantine secured the Rhine and mobilised against Maxentius, who controlled Italy and the African provinces with their agricultural resources. Constantine represented himself as the saviour of Rome and Italy and marched from Gaul to the Alps with a conglomerate army, which defeated Pompeianus, Maxentius' Praetorian Prefect guarding the Alpine passes. Constantine stormed Segusio (Susa) that Maxentius had garrisoned, but he prevented looting and murder, which would have spoiled his image as saviour of Italy. He did the same at Turin, defeating Maxentius' soldiers but sparing the town. Constantine had scored a psychological and political success. Milan opened its gates to him. The road to Rome was open.

Maxentius had strengthened the Aurelian walls, but he chose to meet Constantine outside the city. The battle was fought at the Milvian Bridge, where the Via Flaminia coming northwards from Rome met the Tiber.[166] Maxentius was defeated, probably drowning in the river along with many of his soldiers. A significant event occurred some days before the battle, and the story lost nothing in the telling, how Constantine saw a cross in the sky and was informed that he would conquer in this sign.[167] Lactantius was confident that Constantine witnessed the Chi Rho.[168] In truth, even contemporaries could not agree what Constantine saw, either in Gaul in 310 or near Rome in 312. The evolved story was moved forwards to the night before the battle at the Milvian Bridge, when the soldiers also saw the cross in the sky and were ordered to paint it on their shields.

Maximinus was receding in importance. He was still zealously persecuting Christians, and Constantine failed to stop him. Constantine and Licinius were now the two most important Augusti, further united in 313 at Milan, where Constantine's half-sister Constantia was married to Licinius, isolating Maximinus even further. At Milan, Constantine and Licinius issued an edict of toleration for all religions all over the Empire.[169]

Licinius went to war against Maximinus because the latter had invaded Thrace. As victor in autumn 313, Licinius took over Maximinus' provinces, and conveniently Maximinus fled to Tarsus and committed suicide.[170] Licinius eliminated the families of Maximinus, Diocletian and Galerius, including the women.

Constantine's control of the western provinces was secure, and the Senate confirmed Constantine's chosen title Maximus Augustus, rejecting Licinius' technical seniority. In 315 Constantine celebrated his *decennalia* in Rome, and his triumphal arch next to the Colosseum was dedicated. It had been finished quickly by filching sculptures from monuments of Trajan, Hadrian and Marcus Aurelius, though the relief sculptures on the frieze running round the arch are contemporary, documenting the run-up to the battle of the Milvian Bridge and its conclusion. The panel over the main arch bears the text outlining Constantine's achievements, saving the Empire from the tyrant and his faction, meaning Maxentius.

Rather than going to war precipitately against Licinius, Constantine arranged an intrigue, accusing Licinius of plotting against him so that, in the old Roman style, war against him would be justified. Valens, *dux limitis* commanding the frontier of Dacia, was made Augustus by Licinius.[171] When Constantine won the first round of the war in 316, Valens was eliminated, and Constantine appropriated some of Licinius' territories, the frontier province of Pannonia, part of Moesia, and part of the Balkans.[172] There was a sort of truce with the appointment of three Caesars in 317, one the infant son of Licinius and the other two were Constantine's teenage son Crispus by his first wife Minervina and the infant Constantine by his marriage to Fausta.[173] Each Emperor meticulously shared the consulships.[174]

Crispus campaigned against the Franks on the Rhine, and Constantine campaigned against Goths or Sarmatians, who invaded the Danube provinces in 323. In rounding up the Goths, he crossed into Thrace. Licinius had made war on Maximinus for doing the same thing, but Constantine declared that pushing back the Goths outweighed his entry into Thrace. War was temporarily avoided, though Licinius had provided Constantine with a cause for war by resuming persecution of the Christians, contravening the edict of toleration issued in Milan. In July 324 Licinius and Constantine fought it out at Adrianople (Edirne, Turkey). Licinius was defeated and made for Byzantium. Crispus, commanding the fleet, forced his way through the Hellespont, obliging Licinius to move on, to meet with defeat at Chrysopolis opposite Byzantium. He surrendered, giving up the eastern provinces to Constantine. Under house arrest for a short time, Licinius was killed along with his son Martianus.[175] Constantine was sole Emperor and intended to remain so.

The Constantinian dynasty was established rapidly when Constantine's six-year-old son Constantine was made Caesar, firmly indicating that this post was filled and no-one else need apply. Later he made his other two sons Caesars, but never elevated them to Augusti. While still very young, Constantine's three Caesars were eventually sent to govern dioceses as titular heads.[176] The dioceses of Britain, Galliae, Viennensis and Hispaniae were governed by the twelve-year-old Constantine, based at Trier in 328. The dioceses of Asiana, Pontica and Oriens were governed from Antioch in 335 by Constantius, now aged eighteen, and Constans was fifteen when he was based in Milan to govern Africa, Italia and Pannonia. Constantine retained firm overall control of the Empire.

Constantine could now construct his life history to his own satisfaction. Details of his reign depended on what he wanted his audience to know. His reputation was enhanced and spread by the Christian writers, even though he still honoured Sol Invictus and the pagan religion for some time, but he was becoming less tolerant of religious schism, and in 326 he struck at the Donatists, a schismatic Christian sect in North Africa, led by Donatus. Constantine ordered the *vicarius* of Africa to confiscate Donatist churches.

The main trouble spots in the Empire were the eastern provinces and the Danube, requiring a base of operations close to these areas. Byzantium fitted the bill perfectly. It lay on a triangular promontory, surrounded by the sea, and the land routes from the north and north-west could be blocked by a fortified wall across the peninsula from coast to coast.[177] Constantine re-founded Byzantium as the new capital of the Empire in 324, renaming it Constantinople. He said God had authorized it. By 328 he had built the defensive wall across the peninsula, extending the city limits to the west, enclosing a much larger area than Severus' wall. At the end of 324 a palace was constructed, where the Blue Mosque was built in the seventeenth century. The hippodrome next to the palace followed later, emulating the relative positions of the Imperial Palace and the Circus Maximus in Rome. There were also seven hills and the city was divided into fourteen regions, like Augustus' division of Rome. The Senate of Constantinople ranked lower than the Roman Senate, and its members were not *clarissimi*, most distinguished, but *clari*, merely distinguished.[178]

Constantine called a council of the Christian bishops at Nicaea in June 325 to try to settle the acute differences that had grown up between Christian factions in Egypt, one of them being the Arians, led by Arius, whose version of Christianity differed from that of Rome. Constantine wanted peace and unity, and in his opening address he stressed that internal division in the Church of God was graver than any war.[179] The result of the council was the production of the Nicene Creed, still the basis for Christian belief. Such standardisation was never applied to any of the pagan religions.[180]

Constantine's *vicennalia* in 326 was held in Nicomedia and Rome. For unknown reasons, in that year he executed his son Crispus and his wife Fausta. Both suffered *damnatio memoriae*.[181] In 328, Constantine's mother Helena died. She had journeyed to the Holy Land in 327, discovering a fragment of the True Cross and also the cave in Bethlehem where Jesus was born. She was responsible for the foundation of churches near the site in Bethlehem and on the Mount of Olives where Jesus ascended to heaven. She was buried in the family mausoleum in Rome.[182]

From 328 until 332 Constantine fought in the Danube zone on behalf of the Sarmatians, who asked for help against the Goths. He built a bridge over the Danube, the longest that the Romans ever constructed, and he built roads and camps on the north side of the river.[183] In 329 he campaigned against the Goths in what had been the province of Dacia. After three campaigning seasons the Goths, probably starving, asked for peace. Constantine took the title *Gothicus Maximus*.[184] The treaty arrangements with the Goths included contribution of soldiers for the Roman army, and it allowed them trading privileges on the frontier.[185] In 334 the Sarmatians asked the Emperor for somewhere to settle and were given vacant lands in Macedonia, Thrace, and Gaul. There was no displacement of peasant farmers or Roman landowners, and new settlers would bring lands back into cultivation and pay tax.[186] He made war on the Goths in 336, perhaps a different group of tribesmen in the old province of Dacia. He took the title *Dacicus Maximus*, perhaps establishing forts on the north bank of the Danube.

In 335, Constantine chose Flavius Dalmatius, the son of his half-brother the elder Dalmatius, as a fourth Caesar. Constantine and his Caesars each had a Praetorian Prefect, attested on inscriptions, from Tunisia, Carthage and Antioch.[187] The Prefects would be attached to their emperors, not to a specific territory. That came about in the later fourth century, when the Prefects and their territories are named on inscriptions.[188]

Another son of the elder Dalmatius, Hannibalianus, was made King of Kings of the Pontic peoples, but he was also designated King of Armenia, ready for the ejection of the ruler installed by Shapur II. Having failed to negotiate peace with the Persians, Constantine planned a future campaign taking him to Persia by a route to the river Jordan, where he hoped to be baptized as a Christian.[189] Constantine celebrated his *tricennalia* at Constantinople. He was said to have been assisted in all things by the one true God.[190] Early in 337 Constantine set off for the Parthian campaign, later than he had planned because of illness. At Nicomedia in late May he despaired of recovery, and asked bishop Eusebius of Nicomedia (not the biographer) to baptize him. Death-bed confession of sins and baptism was not unusual. His funeral, conducted by Constantius, combined pagan rituals with Christian ceremonial. He was laid to rest in Constantinople, though the Romans argued he should be buried in Rome.

### Constantine's achievements

Constantine made Christianity the state-approved religion, thus creating the Christian Empire. He did not try to eradicate paganism, but he paved the way for the conversion of the tribes outside the Empire when he chose Ulfilas as bishop of the Goths, whose work was continued by Christian priests.

Having no intention of returning to collegial government, Constantine completed what Diocletian had begun in administration.[191] Bureaucratic centralization continued, with some newly created officials and honorary ranks. Senators of the highest rank were awarded the new title of *vir illustris*, but they were dependent on service to the emperors for their distinction. The equestrians provided nearly all the provincial governors and army commanders, some provincial governors being awarded the rank of *consularis*. Constantine's *comites* were upgraded to high rank. They held administrative posts derived from earlier ones, but with new titles, such as *comes sacrarum largitionum*, responsible for finances. The highest rank of all was *patricius*, the first known holder being Flavius Optatus, consul in 334, but no other is known before Constantine's death.[192]

## The sons of Constantine

Constantine died without having designated any of his Caesars as Augustus. His three sons, Constantine, Constantius, and Constans, are first attested as Augusti in September 337. They said that the soldiers demanded it. The new Augusti arranged the speedy removal of Dalmatius, Hannibalianus, and all members of Constantine's extended family. Two children, Gallus aged twelve and Julian aged six, nephews of Constantine, were spared but were kept in confinement. Constantine II proclaimed himself the senior Emperor, choosing the western provinces, while Constantius II took over Thrace and the east. Constans, still very young, controlled Italy with Illyricum and Africa. Constantine II soon quarrelled with Constans.[193] It is suggested that Constans was manipulated by his officers because they objected to being told what to do by Constantine.[194] In the end Constantine II marched against Constans, only to be defeated and killed at Aquileia. Constans took over his territories, now ruling about a third of the Empire. Constantius II acquiesced because he was tied down in the east. The Persian king Shapur II attacked Rome's eastern possessions in 337, and besieged Nisibis (Nusaybin). Constantius rescued Nisibis by 338, but the Persian war dragged on.

Constans attended to the defence of the Rhine frontier, fighting the Franks in 341-342, and he visited the provinces of Britain in 343. He was in Pannonia in 344, then briefly in Gaul, and then the Balkans from 346.[195] In January 350, when Constans had returned to Gaul, Flavius Magnentius, an officer in the *comitatenses* of Gaul, was declared Augustus by the troops. Constans almost managed to escape to Spain but was killed. Constantius could not immediately respond until he had driven off the Persians from a renewed siege of Nisibis. On his way to Italy, he reached Serdica (Sofia, Bulgaria) in December 350, and met Vetranio, Constans' *magister peditum*, who had seized power in order to prevent Magnentius from taking over the army in the Balkans. Vetranio was not a usurper. Constantius rewarded him with a diadem and sent him off to peaceful retirement. Vetranio's soldiers joined Constantius, who defeated Magnentius in 351 in a bloody battle on the Danube at Mursa (Osijek, Croatia). Eutropius says that there were huge losses at this battle, which according to Zosimus weakened the Roman army for some time.[196] Magnentius escaped. It took a battle at Aquileia in 352 and another in Gaul in 353 to defeat him, but he did not lie down until he knew that Constantius had regained Spain and Africa, and then he committed suicide.[197]

Constantius chose a new Caesar, Gallus, the boy who had been spared when Constantine's descendants were killed. Gallus' half-brother Julian was released from virtual imprisonment since he was six years old, first at Nicomedia and later in Cappadocia. He now went to study at Athens, having developed a passion for philosophy and an aversion to Christianity in favour of the old gods. Gallus, aged twenty-eight, was married to Constantius' sister Constantia, and sent to guard the eastern frontier, but it was soon apparent that he was the wrong choice. Ammianus reports that he ordered the execution of an Alexandrian called Clematius without hearing the case, instructing Honoratus, *comes orientis*, to carry out the sentence. Honoratus informed his superior, the Praetorian Prefect, who protested to Gallus and to Constantius.[198] In 354 Gallus was summoned back to Rome and executed. Zosimus credits Gallus with some success in the east, asserting that the Persians had remained quiet for fear of him.[199]

In Gaul a Frankish officer called Silvanus was made Constantius' *magister peditum* as a reward for deserting Magnentius and helping to defeat him. Silvanus was probably *magister militum per Gallias*.[200] He was accused of treason, framed by means of forged letters allegedly written by him. If he had never planned rebellion, he did so when he was accused. Constantius sent his officer Ursicinus, a man whom Silvanus trusted, to remove the so-called rebel in 355. Ammianus the historian accompanied Ursicinusus.[201]

The Franks and Alamanni crossed the Rhine in 355, and the Franks destroyed and occupied Cologne, according to Ammianus.[202] Constantius summoned Julian from his studies at Athens and made him Caesar in 355 at Milan. Family ties were strengthened by Julian's marriage to Constantius' sister Helena. Julian had not been given any opportunity to gain military experience, but he was assisted by Ursicinus, and the *magister equitum* Marcellus. In 356 Julian campaigned against the Alamanni, concentrating on the lower Rhine while Constantius fought the tribe on the upper Rhine. There was no decisive victory, but Cologne was recovered from the Franks and peace was made with some of their kings.[203] Near Argentorate

(Strasbourg) in the following year, Julian and his officers, including Florentius, Praetorian Prefect of Gaul, brought the Alamanni to battle. In Julian's account he was outnumbered but he won an important victory. Ammianus also gave a detailed description of the battle.[204] The soldiers hailed Julian as Augustus, but he refused the honour.[205] Three years later it was a different story.

After the battle of Strasbourg, Julian chased tribesmen across the Rhine, making expeditions beyond the frontier in 358, receiving the surrender of the Salian Franks and making peace. In the following year, leaders of the Alamanni also surrendered.[206] During the winter of 359-360 the Picts and Scotti/Attacotti attacked Britain, where the Roman troops could not repel the tribesmen without help. Julian was at Lutetia (Paris), but although the Alamanni had ceased to fight, he was not willing to leave Gaul, so he sent his *magister equitum* Flavius Lupicinus to deal with the incursions.[207]

While Lupicinus was in Britain Constantius asked for him to be sent to the east with troops, because he was preparing another campaign against Shapur II, who had demanded that Rome should cede territory to him in 358. Negotiations in 359 had failed to bring peace, and Shapur invaded Mesopotamia and besieged and destroyed the city of Amida (Diyarbakır, Turkey).[208] Constantius was not aware that early in 360 the troops in Gaul had declared Julian Emperor. The official story was that by demanding soldiers from Gaul, Constantius had contravened the promise made to the German soldiers that they would not be sent to serve beyond the Alps, so they protested and made Julian Emperor. This time Julian accepted. He could have refused, as he had done in 357, and modern authors suggest that he had been waiting for the best opportunity.[209] Constantius refused to recognise Julian, who marched for Constantinople. Did he take the German troops across the Alps after all? Before the war started, Constantius died in Cilicia in 361, allegedly naming Julian as his successor.

## Julian and Jovian

As sole Emperor, Julian took on the Persian war, marching to Antioch in May 362, and in the following spring he won a battle at Ctesiphon. Shapur II arrived with the main Persian force and Julian did not risk another battle but marched away. Shapur kept on attacking and skirmishing, and during one of these skirmishes, Julian dashed out without his armour and was wounded by a spear. He died that night, aged thirty-one, having reigned for just over three years.[210] The commander of Julian's bodyguard, Jovian, was chosen Emperor by the army. He made peace with Shapur, and gave up territory, never a popular move for the Romans, but Jovian's alternative was to fight and probably lose the army. Armenia and the eastern parts of Mesopotamia were relinquished, and Jovian agreed to pay subsidies to the Persians.

In accordance with Julian's wishes, Jovian buried him at Tarsus. By February 364 Jovian was dead, probably from natural causes. Zosimus said it was suicide, while Ammianus wondered why there was no investigation of the circumstances.[211] The military high command asked Secundus Salutius to take on the Empire.[212] He had been the army's first choice after Julian's death, but he had refused, and his answer was still the same. Military and civilian administrative officials agreed on Flavius Valentinianus, an army officer from Pannonia.[213] At Nicaea (Iznik, Turkey) Valentinian agreed to become Emperor, but according to Ammianus 'all the centuries and maniples of the cohorts' agreed that there should be two emperors, one for the west and one for the east.[214] In March, Valentinian chose his brother Valens, and both became Augusti.[215]

## Valentinian

Valens took control of the prefecture of Oriens, while Valentinian took control of the western parts of the Empire, including the prefectures of the Gauls, Italy, Illyricum, and Africa.[216]

Britain was still suffering from incursions by northern raiders and the raids escalated in 367, now including Saxons and Franks who were also harassing Gaul.[217] The simultaneous timing of the attacks suggested that this was a conspiracy of the barbarians (*barbarica conspiratione*). Valentinian sent two generals to Britain, first Severus, *comes domesticorum* commanding the household troops, soon replaced by the *magister equitum* Jovinus, but nothing is known of what was achieved. [218] Finally, Flavius Theodosius, *comes rei militaris*, Count Theodosius in English, was sent to Britain. Apart from the panegyric in honour of Theodosius' son, who became the Emperor Theodosius I, Ammianus is the only author to describe the campaign in Britain, often calling Theodosius *dux*. Dividing his army into detachments, Theodosius chased the bands of raiders, recovering the booty and restoring most of it to the original owners, except for what was reserved for the soldiers. The British garrison was probably depleted because of desertions, so Theodosius announced that deserters who returned would not be punished, resuming the campaign in 368.[219] He had more success this year and began to restore and fortify damaged cities, also repairing forts and garrisoning them, and guarding the frontiers with watch-towers.[220] Ammianus mentions only 'Augusta, which men of old called Lundinium'. [221] Theodosius asked for Civilis to be sent as deputy prefect (*pro praefectis*), and Dulcitius as *dux*, but nothing is known about them.[222]

Theodosius went on to remove the *areani/arcani*. Ammianus had described these men in his account of Constans' brief visit to Britain in 343, but that part of his history is lost. In Theodosius' day the *areani* were supposed to gather information about the tribes and pass it on to Roman generals, but they had become corrupted and now passed information in the opposite direction.[223] They may have been Britons recruited for their knowledge of the land and the languages, and their activities are best suited to the frontier, most likely Hadrian's Wall. It is not known how or if intelligence was gathered after the *areani* were removed.

Ammianus says that a province called Valentia was created in Britain.[224] It was neither a new province nor an extra one, so possibly it was a new name for an old one, or part of an old one, and no-one knows where it was.[225] In 368 Theodosius replaced Jovinus as *magister equitum* in Gaul, and later he accompanied Valentinian in campaigns against the Alamanni and the Sarmatians.

Valentinian elevated his son Gratian, aged nine, to Augustus in 367, and in 369 he began to fortify the Rhine from the mouth of the river to Raetia, building earthworks, forts and towers. He also built a fortification on the river Neckar and diverted the river to stop it from eroding the banks near the fort.[226] It sounds as though the Roman Empire was back in business, but trouble began when Valentinian built a fort in tribal territory where he had defeated the Alamanni in 368. Ammianus calls it Mount Piri, which was probably the Heilige Berg at Heidelberg. The Alamanni pleaded with the Roman commander to stop building, but were rebuffed, so they attacked and killed the entire building party.[227] Valentinian also built a fort in the lands of the Quadi in 373, which made the tribesmen fear that they were to be taken over. Even Ammianus admits that it was a fort too far.[228]

While Valentinian fortified the Rhine and the Danube, a rebellion began in North Africa in 373 in protest against corrupt officials, principally Romanus, *comes Africae* and a thoroughly unpleasant, self-seeking and unprincipled individual. He adroitly shifted the blame for his misdeeds to others and got away with it because he was protected by his relative Remigius, Valentinian's *magister officiorum* until 371 and then *magister memoriae*. Eventually, Palladius, described as a tribune and secretary, was sent to Africa to investigate. He was also carrying the wages for the soldiers. Romanus neatly cornered him, getting his officers to swear that they did not require the money. He told Palladius to keep the cash, then promptly threatened to prosecute him for extortion. Consequently, on returning to report to Valentinian, Palladius lied through his teeth, explaining that there was no real trouble in Africa, and Valentinian started to execute people who said otherwise.[229] Ammianus condemns Valentinian for giving his officers far too much unchecked power, while punishing the ordinary soldiers for minor faults.[230] Palladius, who lacked the courage to tell the truth about what Romanus had been doing, hung himself.

It is not surprising that Firmus, a chieftain of the Mauri, rebelled against Romanus. Theodosius was despatched to Africa in 373, and Firmus put up a good fight for two years.[231] When Theodosius discovered evidence of the corruption of Romanus and Remigius, the latter killed himself.[232] Romanus was dismissed from his post and prosecuted, but he produced witnesses to say whatever he told them to say and was acquitted.[233] Theodosius' activities did not benefit him. He was executed in 375.

News reached Valentinian in 374 of devastation in Pannonia by Sarmatians and Quadi, and at the same time Gaul was under threat from the Alamanni under their king Macrianus. Valentinian made peace with Macrianus, who was made an ally of Rome and probably received subsidies, remaining loyal until his death.[234] Valentinian was now free to march to the Danube, choosing Carnuntum as his base, even though it was in ruins. He attacked the Sarmatians and Quadi in spring 375, sending part of his army to burn the settlements, while he crossed the Danube on a bridge of boats. He conducted a destructive campaign until autumn and then retired to winter quarters.[235] At Brigetio (Szö*ny*, Hungary), an embassy from the Quadi arrived, explaining that it was not the tribesmen who had caused all the trouble, but foreigners and brigands. Then they complained about the unjustified building of fortifications in their land. Valentinian, famed for explosive anger, vented it once too often. He died, from apoplexy or a stroke.[236] His son Gratian, only sixteen, succeeded him, remaining in Gaul, while the military commanders persuaded Valentinian's widow to make her four-year-old son Augustus, as Valentinian II, who was to govern Illyricum with the help of the military commander Merobaudes, probably of Frankish origin. Many officers of German extraction had become high ranking military commanders by this time, and they did Rome good service.

## Valens and Gratian

The Goths continued to threaten the frontiers, especially Thrace. Valens defeated a group of them in 369 and made a treaty with the leaders, recruiting tribesmen as part of the agreement. In 371 Valens prepared to regain Armenia, controlled by Shapur II. He drove the Persians out of Mesopotamia and temporarily stopped them from gaining more Rome territory. In that year the Goths invaded the Danube provinces, not raiding but looking for somewhere to settle inside the Roman Empire. They were fleeing from the Huns, previously unknown to the Goths.[237] Valens ordered that the group of Goths called the Tervingi, under their leaders Alavivus and Fritigern, should be given food and lands, and in return they promised to remain peaceful and to provide auxiliary soldiers. They were transported into Thrace. Thus the ruin of the Roman world was brought in, says Ammianus dramatically, but it was not the Goths who precipitated trouble. The Roman officials kept them confined in a small area, extracting high prices for food, even offering them dogs to eat in exchange for one slave. Ammianus blames Lupicinus, now *comes* of Thrace, and the *dux* Maximus for inflicting these atrocities. The hungry Goths had no choice except to find food somehow, and Goths who had been drafted into the Roman army sympathised with them.[238] Soon afterwards another Gothic group, the Greuthungi, crossed the Danube without official permission, and joined up with Fritigern's people. Lupicinus was facing a potential revolt, so he assembled his army and marched against them, losing the greater part of his soldiers, and only just escaping himself.[239]

The final battle was fought at Adrianople (Edirne, Turkey). Valens reached the place in August 378, where he received Gratian's *comes domesticorum* Richomeres bearing a message that Gratian was on his way, and Valens was to wait for him. [240] Gratian was at Sirmium (Sremska Mitrovica, Serbia), so it would take several days before he reached Adrianople, and Valens attacked without waiting for him. Ammianus says that he wanted to deny Gratian a share in the victory.[241] It was a motive not unknown to Republican consuls, sometimes leading to disaster, as happened at Adrianople. Valens was killed, and his body was never found. Ammianus comments that only Hannibal's victory at

Cannae compares with the Gothic victory.[242] The strange thing about Adrianople is that it was the eastern army that was destroyed, but it was the western Empire that started to crumble less than three decades later.

The Goths, failing to capture Adrianople by siege, began to spread out, unopposed. Gratian took over the war, summoning the younger Theodosius, disgraced since his father Count Theodosius was executed, but it is suggested he had been reinstated earlier and given a command on the Danube. Late in 378 Gratian appointed him *magister militum*. In January 379 Theodosius became Augustus.[243]

## Theodosius I

Gratian continued to rule the west, while his half-brother Valentinian II, still a child, ruled Italy and most of Illyricum. Theodosius commanded the eastern Empire and the Danube zone. Thrace and Moesia Inferior had been lost to the Goths, who also moved into Macedonia and Thessaly, but before moving against them Theodosius issued an edict to the inhabitants of Constantinople in February 380 declaring his wish that all people should follow the religion handed down by the apostle Peter, and thereby be known as Catholic Christians, labelling everyone else insane and heretical.[244] Powerful stuff, similar to forcing everyone into a single political party.

It was now time to stem the Gothic advance. As in most tribes, there were rival factions, which Theodosius played against each other to take their minds off moving into any more Roman territory. In 381 he called in troops from the west under the Frankish generals Arbogast and Bauto, who drove the Goths out of Macedonia, Thessaly and Illyricum and back into Thrace. The war ended, and Theodosius made a treaty with the Goths in 382, an arrangement for which he was censured by contemporaries and later historians. Unfortunately, there is no surviving detailed description of the terms.[245] It is assumed that the Goths surrendered and were therefore *dediticii*, but Theodosius' treaty allowed the Goths to live under their own laws, ruled by their own chiefs, remaining on the lands they had overrun in Thrace. They were obliged to furnish recruits, apparently not for the regular armies but for specific campaigns, just as the Romans of earlier centuries had recruited native contingents to fight under their own leaders until the war ended. The Gothic soldiers of the 382 treaty served alongside the army, but did not belong to it as named units, and therefore do not appear in official documents, such as the late Roman list of civil and military offices, the *Notitia Dignitatum*.[246] Theodosius promised subsidies of food, which would presumably cease if the Goths fought against Rome on their own or with other tribes. The treaty seems to be a sensible way of averting war, but it polarised the Roman world. Some Romans advocated Romanizing and Christianizing the Goths. Taking a favourable stance toward Theodosius' arrangements, Themistius asked in one of his orations whether it was better to fill Thrace with corpses or with farmers.[247]

Theodosius encountered the old problem of finding enough recruits for the army, and hanging onto the soldiers already serving. In 365 Valentinian and Valens had rounded up deserters, punishing anyone who sheltered them. They also rounded up camp followers and turned them into soldiers. Valentinian reduced the height qualification for soldiers, and in 367 he passed laws to recruit men who had deliberately chopped off their fingers or thumbs. By the following year he had lost patience, and from then on self-mutilated men were burnt to death. Theodosius punished provincial governors who hindered recruiting officers.[248] In view of the difficulties of finding soldiers it is not surprising that Theodosius recruited thousands of Goths. Nationalism was not deeply rooted among the tribes, so serving under the Romans did not contravene notions of loyalty, as demonstrated by the inscription on a tombstone of a Frankish warrior – *Francus ego cives, Romanus miles in armis* – meaning I am a Frankish citizen and a Roman soldier.[249]

Gratian was losing favour in the west. In 383, Magnus Maximus commanding in Britain was hailed as Emperor by his troops. The sources, gathered together and translated by Birley, do not make it clear whether Maximus was *dux Britanniarum* or *comes litoris Saxonicum*.[250] Originally a Spaniard serving in Britain, Maximus found his way into Welsh legend as Macsen Wledig, immortalised in the *Mabinogion*, and associated with the fort of Segontium near Caernarvon. Gaul and Spain, and later Africa, supported Maximus. He took troops to Gaul, possibly leaving Hadrian's Wall largely undefended, but since he was said to have waged war against invading Picts and Scots, he may have ensured peace for a while.[251] Gratian broke off a campaign against the Alamanni, but when he met Maximus, his troops deserted him and killed him in August 383 at Lyon. Maximus remained in command of most of the west for a few years. He was acknowledged as Emperor by Theodosius, at least until he had settled affairs on the Danube and in the east. Theodosius prevented the Ostrogoths, or the eastern Goths, from crossing the

Danube, then he arranged a peace treaty with Shapur III, whereby he agreed to partition Armenia, with a pro-Roman ruler in one half and a pro-Persian ruler in the other.[252]

In the meantime, Maximus had elevated his son Victor to Caesar in 387 and invaded Italy, the territory of Valentinian II, who fled to Thessalonika with his mother and his half-sister, Galla. Theodosius marched against Maximus, leaving his elder son Arcadius, Augustus from 383, at Constantinople. Maximus moved from Italy, and Theodosius won the first battle at Siscia (Sisak, Croatia), and the second at Pola (Pula, Croatia). Maximus lost the adherence of his troops, and at Aquileia they surrendered him to Theodosius, who executed him in 388. Victor, Maximus's son, was killed a month later in Gaul.

Valentinian II, not yet out of his teens, was restored to power and sent to Gaul, accompanied by the *magister militum* Arbogast. Theodosius married Galla, Valentinian's half-sister, and remained in Italy at Milan, where he encountered Ambrosius, the Nicene bishop of Milan since 374, who developed some influence over him. The Christians were in the ascendancy and had started to turn against non-Christians, and when some Christians burnt down a Jewish synagogue in Mesopotamia, Ambrose persuaded Theodosius not to force the perpetrators to rebuild it. Two years later, in Thessalonika, a Roman general was killed in a riot, and Theodosius ordered the deaths of the rioters. Allegedly 3,000 were killed, and Ambrose demanded that the Emperor should perform a public penance, or face exclusion from the Church. After a delay of eight months Theodosius complied. This prefigured many a struggle between the church and the state into medieval times.

Theodosius returned to Constantinople in 391. His son Arcadius had quarrelled with Theodosius' new wife Galla, and the Goths had taken to raiding again, but Theodosius's trusted assistants, Rufinus, *magister officiorum* since 388, and the general Stilicho, stopped the raiding. Stilicho was the son of a Vandal tribesman, whose ancestors had occupied central Europe at the beginning of the fourth century but had not come into conflict with the Romans. Loyal to the house of Theodosius, Stilicho married the Emperor's niece Serena, and was made *magister utriusque militiae* in 392, a command which did not limit him to a specific area.[253]

In the west, Arbogast had gained so much power as guardian of Valentinian II that he was able to ignore the young Emperor's orders.

Valentinian was found dead in May 392, possibly having committed suicide, but Arbogast came under suspicion. He created a new Augustus, Eugenius, an official at Valentinian's court. Predictably, Theodosius refused to recognise Eugenius, despite the mediation of Ambrose, and proclaimed his younger son Honorius as Augustus in the west in 393. In September 394 the two sides clashed in northern Italy at the battle of the river Frigidus. Arbogast and Eugenius, with an army composed mostly of Franks, were defeated by Theodosius and Stilicho with their army of Goths. Eugenius was captured and killed, and Arbogast committed suicide. Theodosius journeyed to Rome to celebrate the victory. In January 395 he died in Milan, allegedly appointing Stilicho as the guardian of Arcadius and Honorius. At least that is what Stilicho persistently claimed.

## Arcadius and Honorius

After Theodosius' death, his two sons ruled the Empire, Arcadius, aged about eighteen in the eastern half, based in Constantinople, and Honorius aged ten, in the western half, based at Milan and latterly at Ravenna. Viewed retrospectively, the year 395 seems to mark the beginning of the split into two Empires, but contemporaries would not see it in the same light, because Emperors had shared power and ruled different parts of the Empire on several occasions in the past. Both parts of the Empire were sometimes afflicted by the same enemies, one being a Goth who had fought for Theodosius I at the battle of the Frigidus. His name was Alaric, and what he wanted was not a life of raiding but an official appointment for himself as commander of troops, and the pay and food for his men that went with it. In 395-6 he moved into Greece and allegedly sacked Athens, but archaeologically there is no trace of such an event. Stilicho arrived, defeated the Goths, and was declared a public enemy for causing damage in Greece, while Alaric was made *magister militum per Illyricum*, a post which he held until 399.[254]

Alaric commanded a group of tribesmen from different ethnic backgrounds who could be persuaded to follow him. Desertions were frequent, so Alaric had to work hard at uniting his army. When the eastern Empire dispensed with his services, Alaric marched into Italy in 401-2. Stilicho defeated him in 402 at Pollentia and again at Verona, but Alaric was able to withdraw into Pannonia and Dalmatia, collectively known as Illyricum, where he claimed that the inhabitants made him their leader.[255] Illyricum was currently divided between

Arcadius and Honorius, but Stilicho wanted all of it as a recruiting ground. Realising that Alaric could help him, he recognised him as *comes rei militaris*. Stilicho's project was put on hold when Goths and other tribes under Radagaisus invaded the west, crossing the frozen Rhine in winter 405-406. Stilicho defeated Radagaisus, who surrendered at Ticinum (Pavia). 12,000 Goths were taken for Stilicho's army.

Around this time the troops in Britain proclaimed three Emperors in quick succession. The first, Marcus, was deposed by Gratianus, who was killed. The third was probably chosen for his name, Constantine, made the Emperor Constantine III. Honorius heard the news in March 407. Constantine crossed into Gaul, but the response to his arrival was delayed by events of 408. Arcadius died, and it was decided that Stilicho should go to Constantinople, while Honorius dealt with Constantine, who sent envoys apologizing for his usurpation, forced on him by the soldiers. The *magister officiorum* Olympius persuaded Honorius that Stilicho planned to make his son Augustus, so Stilicho was recalled to Ravenna and executed in 408. Honorius had just eliminated the most able commander of the western Empire, allowing Constantine III unopposed entry into Italy in 409, but Constantine's *magister militum* Gerontius besieged him at Arles. Honorius sent troops, Gerontius fled, and Constantine was executed in 411.

By this time the Romans were losing control of the western provinces.

# 14

# The Fate of the Provinces

It is not the intention in this book to document the successive western emperors until the traditional date of the fall of Rome in 476, or of the eastern Roman emperors, but it is appropriate to outline some of the reasons why the east did not share the fate of the west. One of the most important factors was wealth. The east was always wealthier than the west, and could afford large armies to defend the provinces, or buy off opponents such as Alaric and his Goths, more than once. The east had its fair share of palace intrigue, assassinations and usurpations, but from the point of view of defence from external attack, Constantinople, alias Byzantium, was easier to defend than Rome and better placed near trouble spots to the north and east, which is why Constantine chose it as the new capital.

In the eastern Empire there was greater stability than in the west, where the turnover of emperors was more rapid and consequently reigns of these emperors were much shorter, destroying any continuity of policies. Another factor was that the western Empire relied on tribal commanders, principally the Franks, Goths, Vandals and latterly Huns, and the troops were also largely of tribal origin, often raised by treaty at the end of wars, or derived from tribesmen settled on Roman lands with the obligation to provide soldiers. Some of the high-ranking tribal commanders were beginning to realise their power and had started to expect greater rewards. The eastern emperors purged the army of Goths. This had already happened on a smaller scale. For instance, after the Roman defeat at Adrianople, sealed orders had been issued to commanders of the eastern troops to summon the Gothic soldiers to a pay parade, and kill them all. In 386 more Goths were killed at

Tomi (Constanta, Romania). In 400 the Gothic general Gainas was given the command against other Goths under their leader Tribilgild, but instead of fighting each other the Goths joined together and marched on Constantinople. It took another Goth, Fravitta to defeat them. Gainas escaped but was killed by Huns. In 401 Fravitta was consul.[1] He survived until 404 but died as a victim of palace intrigue.[2] Encouraged by the Empress Eudoxia, the civilians of Constantinople rose up against the Goths and killed thousands of them in the city and surrounding area. It was not just racial hatred, but also religious prejudice, since the Goths were Arian Christians, and the orthodox church of Constantinople did not approve. The eastern emperors eventually turned away from settling all manner of tribesmen on the land and employing them in the armies, instead recruiting from more local peoples, such as the hardy Isaurians, Persians and Armenians, who would have a vested interest in protecting their own territory.

In the interests of simplicity, the provinces in this section are referred to by their old names, not by the names of the smaller units into which they were divided by Diocletian, with amendments by Constantine and later emperors.

## *Italy*

Italy cannot be classified as a province, but its history as a country epitomises the fate of the western Empire. Alaric entered Italy and laid siege to Rome in 408, but what he really wanted was money, so he negotiated, extracting five thousand pounds of gold and thirty thousand pounds of silver, which was paid by the senators.[3] In 409 more Goths marched into Italy under Alaric's brother-in-law Athaulf, and the Praetorian Prefect Jovius arranged a truce and further negotiation. The Goths asked for food, and permission to settle in Noricum, near the Danube frontier, which would have moved them out of Italy, but Alaric also wanted a military command as *magister utriusque militiae*.[4] Honorius refused him, so Alaric seized Ostia and cut Rome's food supply. He was in the ascendancy and nominated his own Emperor, Priscus Attalus, who gave him his command, and agreed to win back control of Africa and the food supply. Alaric then besieged Honorius in Ravenna, but when it was clear that Attalus was not going to do as he promised, in 410 Alaric marched back to Rome and took it.[5] It was a psychological shock, magnified in later histories and labelled the sack of Rome, but although the Goths looted and carried off portable wealth, they held the city for only three days without engaging in wholesale destruction, and as Christians, they spared the people who took refuge in churches. One important prize was carried off by the Goths. Alaric captured Galla Placidia, the daughter of Theodosius, and stepsister of Honorius, and took her with him when he marched down the west coast, intending to cross over to Sicily. A storm wrecked his ships, and on returning to the mainland, Alaric died in 411.

In 476, after a rapid succession of emperors of the west, the last Roman, Romulus Augustulus, was deposed but not killed by Odoacer, a prince of the Sciri living east of the Rhine. Their kingdom had been destroyed by the Amal Goths, and Odoacer and many Scirian refugees joined the Roman army.[6] He rose to the post of *comes domesticorum* under the short-lived western Emperor Julius Nepos, but he needed a way of rewarding his Scirians because army pay had ceased. He settled some of his tribesmen on the land in Italy, possibly without disturbing Roman landowners.[7] Before deposing Romulus, he captured the boy's father Orestes and killed him. Romulus was sent to his Campanian estates and made no trouble.

Odoacer acknowledged the eastern Emperor Zeno as supreme, with himself as ruler of Italy, and after considering the situation Zeno recognized Odoacer as such. This is considered the end of the western Roman Empire. Zeno asked Odoacer to reinstate Julius Nepos, driven out by Orestes in 475, but Nepos never returned and was killed in Dalmatia in 480. Odoacer took over Nepos' territory of Noricum in 481, but in 486 Zeno encouraged the Germanic Rugii to invade Noricum, to keep Odoacer away from the Balkans, and prevent him from assisting Leontius, a rival Augustus to Zeno. Odoacer realised that he did not have the military capacity to hold the Danube frontier and abandoned Noricum, bringing the population to Italy to resettle them.

With Odoacer as ruler of Italy based at Ravenna, Rome and the Italian cities and towns hardly changed. Odoacer preserved Roman laws, administrative systems and the Latin language. He was not secure in his rule, since Zeno persuaded Theoderic the Amal to invade Italy. The war was still going on when Zeno died in 491. Odoacer was killed in 493, after losing battles against Theoderic, who called himself king without waiting for approval from Constantinople. He received recognition of a sort from Zeno's successor Anastasius. It was really just an acceptance of the status quo.

Theoderic's reign was one of peace. He promoted Arian Christianity, but not at the expense of the Catholic Church, and he adopted the existing administrative and financial systems. Romans readily took up offices in these spheres. The population merged, as Gothic and Roman landowners shared the same economic concerns. In the military sphere there was a change. From the third century onwards there had been a steady increase in the numbers of officers of tribal origin, many of them reaching the highest ranks. Theoderic, like the leaders of the Visigoths and the Vandals, planned to keep his soldiers apart from Roman civilians, but the elite, wealthy and educated Goths became more like Romans, and an increasing number of Romans served in the Gothic army and began to reach high ranks. In the past Goths would learn Latin as they served as soldiers and were promoted, and now Romans learned Gothic and married Gothic women. If in the past Romans had been upset by the number of tribal officers, the Goths were now upset by the number of Roman officers in the army. Theoderic would perhaps have been able to contain the situation, but he died, succeeded by his nephew Theodehad. At Constantinople the Emperor Justinian refused to recognise Theodehad, and almost straight away ordered the invasion of Italy under Belisarius. This general regained control of Sicily in 535 and arrived at Naples in 536.[8] In that year Theodehad died, replaced by Vitigis, who abandoned Rome.

Justinian's army had regained control of Africa comparatively rapidly, but in Italy the war was hard fought; it damaged the country more effectively than any tribal horde, with lasting consequences. The eastern Empire clung onto Italy long after the collapse of the west, so the country which had been at the centre of the Roman Empire now became a frontier province of the Empire of Constantinople. In the sixth century the north of Italy was lost to the Lombards.

## Britain

Romanization of Britain was not enforced, being left largely to local initiative with encouragement and perhaps assistance from Roman officials, but it was uneven, taking root predominantly in the south. In the north and west the native-style round houses persisted, generally consisting of two to three dwellings around a courtyard and protected by a circuit of one to three earthen banks. Grain would play its part, but the economy was based on cattle and sheep. Finds of Roman artefacts show that some of these native sites were occupied from the first to the fourth centuries, rebuilt as necessary on the same plots.[9] Round houses have also been discovered inside some towns, where the farmers worked the fields outside the urban area.[10] Roman-style villas were not entirely excluded from northern Britain, as was once thought. Villas have been found in Yorkshire and Durham, but they are much more common in the south.

Romanization is judged by the presence in a town or city of Roman buildings such as a forum, a basilica, baths and temples, which fulfilled the needs of the Roman administration, and do not necessarily indicate that the entire native population was wholly Romanized, only that they were governed as if they were. When there is evidence of local councillors erecting or embellishing public buildings, then it can be assumed that these men were content with being Romano-Britons, receiving Roman citizenship after serving as magistrates, and using their wealth as a form of self-advertisement as much as altruistic benefactions.

Until the middle of the fourth century, the keyword concerning Britain seems to be wealth and prosperity, at least in the south, as many more villas were built and they become larger and more elaborate. This growth has been linked to the migration of wealthy people retreating to the countryside to escape from the burdensome expenses of being town councillors, and to an influx of wealthy Gauls coming to Britain as life in Gaul became progressively more dangerous.[11] This is a feature of turbulent times at all periods of history, whereby those who are able to get away do so, leaving the peasantry to join them as servants, or to fend for themselves.

As the fourth century progressed, there was a change in the larger towns. Decline is an emotive word, and in need of qualification and explanation, though there seems to have been such a decline in Britain, probably beginning before 350. Public buildings had been going out of use probably from the beginning of the third century or earlier. Baths fell out of use probably because of changing fashions, lack of money or personnel to keep them functioning, or more practically because the water supply was no longer working properly.[12] The spread of Christianity was probably one reason for the neglect of temples. It is less easy to explain why the forum and basilica in some towns were destroyed or changed their uses. Mattingly enumerates the known examples. London's forum and basilica were destroyed around the beginning of the fourth century, while the site of the forum at Gloucester was paved over with cobbles. At Wroxeter at the beginning of the fourth century and at Leicester a little later, these public buildings were destroyed by fire and not rebuilt. Also during the fourth century, first Caerwent, then Silchester, then Exeter turned their basilicas or the spaces they occupied to metal working, seemingly on an organised basis rather than being colonised by opportunists.[13]

The use of the forum and basilica may have been replaced by large town houses which began to be built in the fourth century, equipped with large rooms interpreted as reception rooms, indicating growth of personal rather than corporate power.[14] The occupancy of the town houses dropped dramatically after 350, but some were still in use in the early fifth century. Were the occupants of these town houses also the owners of the large villas, like the aristocracy of later times with their country estates and their town houses? Wealth in later Roman Britain still derived from ownership of land, so an important magnate would need land and farms. Whoever the owners of villas and town houses were, they had subscribed to *Romanitas*, as shown by the Roman religious and mythological themes depicted probably in their wall paintings which have not survived, and definitely in their surviving mosaics and on their silver ware. The wealthy perhaps became more like lords, their power spilling over into control of local government, or even domination as tyrants.[15]

Troubled times in the late fourth and early fifth century are indicated by the fact that many coins and much fabulous silver ware was buried, as shown by the several hoards which were never recovered by their owners. These finds predominate in the eastern parts of Britain, and so far there is nothing to match them in the west. Theodosius had to bring forces with him to supplement the troops in Britain, which was usual practice, but the army of the later fourth century in Britain was probably reduced in numbers. Only two legions are mentioned in the *Notitia Dignitatum*, II Augusta at Richborough under the *comes litoris Saxonici*, commanding the Saxon Shore, and VI Victrix at York under the *dux Brittaniarum*. Both were probably reduced in size. The last surviving evidence for XX Valeria Victrix is on coins of Carausius, the latest being from 293. It may have been disbanded in the fourth century.[16] The auxiliary units listed in the *Notitia* suggest that the Pennine forts and those of Hadrian's Wall were occupied. An exact date for the British entries in this document remains unclarified, but archaeological evidence also shows that several of the northern and Pennine forts were occupied in the fourth century, and a line of towers was built on the east coast from Huntcliff to Filey, remains of one of them being visible inside Scarborough castle. These fortifications, the late fort at Caer Gybi in North Wales and the forts of the Saxon

Shore along the south coast indicate that it was the coasts that were threatened, by Irish raiders as well as Saxons.

In 406, Britain was still connected to the Empire, otherwise the mutiny and creation of three successive emperors in that year would surely have focused on regional defence and carving out what would become a separate realm in Britain. Four years later, the British provinces were no longer Roman. Zosimus says that as Alaric approached Rome in 410, Honorius wrote to the Britons to tell them to look to their own defence.[17] Some authors suggest that Honorius was acknowledging that Britain was already lost in 409. It is also suggested that Honorius was not writing to the Britons at all, but the Bruttians of Italy, since the context into which Zosimus slots Honorius' letter has nothing to do with Britain.[18] Zosimus also says that attacks from beyond the Rhine prompted the Britons and some Celts to throw off Roman control and live their own lives.[19] Did the Britons eject the Romans, or did the Romans renounce the British provinces because they yielded little profit, not worth the expense of defending them?

There was no recorded serious effort on the part of the Roman government to regain Britain. When bishop Germanus of Auxerre allegedly visited Britain in 429, and again in the 430s, his mission was not to bring Britain back into the Empire; he had a religious task, to counter the influence of Pelagius, declared a heretic in 418, though Germanus is credited with urging the Britons to fight and win a battle against the Picts and Saxons. Were the inhabitants of Britain capable of defending themselves? Tradition states that Honorius withdrew the troops from Britain, but it is not known how many were left after Constantine III took units of the army to Gaul. If such an order was issued from Ravenna, probably some of the soldiers ignored it and remained behind with their families, so there may have been some armed forces, but perhaps not enough. Gildas wrote his *De Excidio Britanniae* (*On the Destruction of Britain*) somewhere between 490 and 550, and in this work he says that the Britons asked for help from the general Aetius, in his third consulship, which dates to 446.[20] Aetius was the last great general of Rome, reaching high rank, and from the 430s, though he never tried to be emperor, he was effectively the real ruler of the west. In 446 he was on the Danube preparing for an onslaught of the Huns, and he could not spare time or energy in regaining Britain.

Up to 409/410 coins from the Empire were still reaching Britain, as far north as Hadrian's Wall, but after 410 Roman coins are rare.[21] If economic life survived it was probably via barter, with goods or services exchanged for other goods. It would probably shrink to regional or highly localised zones. Roads may have been maintained for a while, but travel for long distances probably became unsafe. The times were ripe for the emergence of powerful local lords, who controlled their own private armies, dispensed justice and governed the regions that they could defend. From the later fourth century there may have been a need for unofficial locally organised defence against low-grade threats from robbers, perhaps locals as well as invaders, such as those Count Theodosius rounded up in 367-8. Spain was afflicted by the same problems, and some of the landowners armed their workers. When Gildas describes the British appeals for help from Aetius, it may not have been lawless bands causing the trouble, but the depredations of the self-proclaimed lords of their own regions, who in the absence of a central government could become like princes, subject to no laws except their own.

Life in Britain did not cease after 410, but it was not Roman life.[22] Excavations have shown that some sites were occupied into the fifth century. At Wroxeter, parts of what had been the baths and basilica complex were still used, even without the roof, and the floor was levelled and paved with stone roof tiles, perhaps for a market area. Later a timber hall was built on the site.[23] In the mid-sixth century timber buildings were erected over the levelled basilica. Timber buildings were built on the site of the granaries at Birdoswald fort on Hadrian's Wall, and the basilica discovered underneath York Minster may have stood until the seventh century.[24]

Evidence of continued use of a building does not always reveal who was using it, just as discovery of artefacts of Germanic origin does not automatically signify an aggressive invasion of Saxons, as reported by Gildas, who portrays the Saxons as the villains. Germanic troops were already serving in the Roman army in Britain in the fourth century. Similarly, the continued arrival of quantities of goods from the Mediterranean and beyond arriving at Tintagel for some centuries after 410 does not prove that Ygraine and Uther Pendragon, assisted by Merlin, gave birth to Arthur at this site. What it does show is that contact between Britain and the remnants of the Roman Empire had not ceased.

Britain was divided into several kingdoms, whose names and territorial extent changed over time, but three main kingdoms eventually emerged, now known by the names applied to them by the Anglo-Saxons. Scotland preserves the name of the Scotti, originally from Ireland, but its name is Alba. Wales is named after the Anglo-Saxon Wealas, meaning Britons, but its own name is Cymru. England is named after the Angli. Collectively, they are all part of Britain, or Britannia.

## Gaul

The provinces of Gaul had a head start of a century or so on Britain in terms of Romanization, but after the turmoil of Julius Caesar' ten-year conquest, it took some time to convert a tribal society into a Roman province. The process of Romanization of Gaul is analysed and discussed in Gregg Woolf's *Becoming Roman*. Once the process of integration into the Empire had begun, the Romans, as usual, cultivated the elite groups, and Gallic aristocrats played a greater part in the public life of the Empire than the Britons.

The later third century saw the beginning of a decline as the frontiers were neglected and infiltration of the Germanic tribes beyond the Rhine gradually became an influx that never really ceased, but in some cases there was a blend of cultures rather than an abrupt change from Roman to Germanic ways of life. Roman administrative control of the German provinces and Gallia Belgica diminished after 31 December 406 when Alans, Suevi and Vandals crossed the frozen Rhine in search of lands for settlement. Thereafter, the frontier zones had to look after themselves, becoming almost autonomous.[25]

In 412, Athaulf, brother of Alaric, took the Visigoths into Gaul. He and his tribesmen joined the usurper Jovinus, who was supported by the Burgundians, first known to the Romans in the region of the river Main in the later third century. Athaulf soon joined Flavius Constantius, a native of the Balkans, whose early career was with the army of the eastern Empire, and together they defeated Jovinus. Athaulf married Gallia Placidia in 414. She was the stepsister of Honorius and had been kidnapped from Rome by Alaric. Athaulf was forced out of Gaul and into Spain by Flavius Constantius, who denied the Goths access to supplies. Athaulf was killed, then a leader called Wallia or Vallia took over.

Constantius settled some of the Goths in southern Gaul in 417, and in 418 the Visigoths under Wallia received food when he returned

Placidia, the widow of Athaulf, to the care of Constantius, who married her. Wallia was sent to fight Vandals and Alans in Spain, and after he defeated them he and his Goths were settled in Aquitania Secunda and part of Narbonensis Prima, with Toulouse, but not Narbonne.[26] There is no surviving record of local disruption, so the Goths were possibly given Imperial lands, or abandoned farms.[27] Wallia's domain in Aquitania evolved into the Visigothic kingdom, which survived until 507 when the Franks took over.

When the Romans relocated the administrative centres to Arles and Milan, the previous centre at Trier was not so well defended and the Franks besieged it several times. Flavius Constantius organised a council of the Gallic provinces in 418, but no representatives of the northern provinces attended.[28] Coinage and pottery disappeared, several buildings, especially villas, were deserted and not reoccupied, and some public buildings changed their usage, as in Britain. In general, power was transferred from the cities and towns to the rural landowners, who had probably played an important part on the local councils, so taking up the reins to govern a local area would not be such a radical change. Some of the bishops who ran things in the cities and towns and surrounding territories became estate owners. They were generally better educated, their power deriving from wealth. It is suggested that the cities and towns were worse affected than the rural areas, largely because of the cessation of trade.[29]

Probably in the 440s Aetius settled some of the Alans in Armorica, not without protest from bishop Germanus, who addressed his concerns to the court at Ravenna. About the same time, Armorica was also infiltrated by people from the south-west of Britain.[30] The fact that the area became Brittany, not Alania or something similar, indicates that the Britons were more Romanized and perhaps wealthier and more influential. A decade later, Attila and the Huns moved into Gaul. The Visigothic King Theoderic fought for the Romans to protect their territory and the general Aetius drove Attila away from Orleans, fighting a battle variously called the Catalaunian Plains or the Mauriac Fields, near Troyes, in 451. Aetius won a splendid victory. Attila then attacked Italy, but died in 453. The empire of the Huns disintegrated.

In the south of France life continued more or less undisturbed through most of the fifth century, at least for the wealthy landowners who managed to maintain their living standards, as described in the letters of Sidonius Apollinaris, bishop of Clermont-Ferrand, but he emphasises the positive, not inquiring too closely into the sometimes not so friendly relations between Goths and Romans.[31]

From the late third century the Roman government was not strong enough to make war on all the tribes who came into Gaul, so on the basis that if you can't beat them, join them, or rather join them to yourselves by alliances and allocating lands, and if possible employ them as allies to fight other tribes. Some parts of the provinces were ceded to tribal rulers in the early fifth century. When the Goth Wallia died, he was succeeded by Theoderic, who controlled his kingdom of southern Gaul until 451.[32]

The tribes were probably settled as *foederati*, a term which in the past denoted recruitment of tribesmen from outside the empire, but was now extended to those settled within it, and later still in the sixth century it referred to regular troops, with pay and a rank structure. The arrangements with the tribes, which sometimes had to be renewed after occasional lapses of loyalty, probably included some form of support, money or food, in return for the obligation of providing soldiers, which at least in part enabled Aetius to gather an army of German troops with which to oppose Attila, who also used German tribesmen in his army, at the battle of the Catalaunian Fields. Gradually, more tribes were settled in parts of Gaul, with their leaders recognised by the Roman government, but such leaders could also arise from among the Gallic commanders in the Roman army, the prime example being the Gaul Aegidius, appointed *magister militum per Gallias* by the western Emperor Avitus when he was newly proclaimed in Gaul in 455. Avitus' reign lasted less than a year, but Aegidius retained his appointment when Majorian became Emperor in 456. After this Emperor's death in 461, the *comes* Ricimer attempted to replace Aegidius, who objected and formed a domain of his own based at Soissons. Acting under his own authority he worked on Rome's behalf by fighting against the tribes infiltrating Roman territory, rescuing Lyon from Burgundian control and defending Arles from the Visigoths under Theoderic II, with help from Childeric, King of the Salian Franks, who controlled much of northern Gaul. On his death in 469, Aegidius' son Syagrius succeeded him, and according to Gregory of Tours, both Aegidius and Syagrius were regarded as kings, not Roman officials.[33]

The two most successful tribes invading late Roman Gaul were first the Visigoths and then the Franks. King Euric of the Visigoths was an ambitious ruler who came to power after murdering his elder brother Theoderic in 465/466. Realising that the western Romans were in no position to stop him as emperors were made and destroyed in rapid succession, he expanded his territory, attacking the Bretons in 469, driving out King Riothamus, and gaining Tours and Bourges. Then he turned south to begin a siege of Arles in 471, prompting the western Emperor Anthemius to send an army under his son Anthemiolus to relieve the city, formerly the administrative centre after the move from Trier. Anthemiolus was killed. Elton points out that this was the last time the Imperial government tried to intervene in Gaul.[34] From this time cities and towns had to fend for themselves. By 475 Euric controlled everything west of the Rhone, but it took him until 476 to capture Arles and Marseilles, which gave him control of the Mediterranean coast. While he fought for supremacy in Gaul, Euric sent some of his soldiers into Spain in 473, and three years later he had established his Visigothic kingdom controlling the whole of Spain except for the Suevic kingdom in the north-west.[35]

By 476 Italy was ruled by Odoacer, so it was up to the eastern Emperor Zeno to recognise Euric as king of what he held.[36] Euric did not turn against the Roman population and wipe them out, but worked with the landowners, most of whom who were willing to co-operate with him, not necessarily because they were disloyal to Rome, or abject cowards. There was no sense in putting up a futile resistance and losing everything – farms, houses, status, and livelihood – as seems to have happened in Britain, where landowners disappeared. From Euric's point of view, it was not sensible to destroy the landowners and have to start from scratch to build up the economy when there were people there who knew how to do it, or rather they knew how to direct their tenants and peasant farmers to do it for them. The landowners could extract rents, and out of the rents they could afford to live and also pay taxes, and like the Romans used to do when acquiring new territories, the Visigoths took over a system that worked, appointing their own tax collectors. Perhaps the peasants were not badly affected. If they were oppressed, they exchanged one set of oppressors for another, working on the farms and paying rents as before.

In governing the country Euric required Roman officials who knew the systems, the customs, the regulations and the law.[37] He produced a law code, the *Codex Euricianus*, drawn up with the help of Roman legal experts. It embraced Romans and Visigoths indiscriminately, and concerned everyday matters, including landholding.[38] Latin was kept alive as the official legal language, as well as in the Christian

Church, as German Arians gradually adopted Catholicism. Euric died in 484, succeeded by his son Alaric II, who also issued a law code, the *Breviarum*, a cut-down version of the *Codex Theodosianus*, but continuing the practice of catering for Romans and Visigoths. His kingdom ended in 507, as he lost a battle against the Franks south of Poitiers.

The Franks had been known to the Romans since the end of the third century, when the Emperor Maximian arranged a treaty with them in 286, on the basis of which they became *foederati* and contributed large numbers of soldiers to the Roman army in the fourth century, while many of their commanders served as officers, readily combining Roman and Frankish identity.[39] Like the soldier who was a Frankish citizen and a Roman soldier, the Frankish Mallobaudes was at one and the same time *comes domesticorum et rex Francorum* commanding the household troops and recognised as King of the Franks.[40] He was not ruler of the entire tribe. There were other groups of Franks at different times, under different leaders, such as the Salian Franks, who had occupied part of Gallia Belgica around Tongres in the mid-fourth century, and Merovingian Franks allegedly descended from Merovech, born of a sea-creature like a bull and the wife of a Frankish nobleman, and the line continued through Childeric and his son Clovis.

Childeric had supported Aegidius against the Visigoths in 468, and by the 470s he controlled Belgica Secunda and Tournai.[41] His son Clovis amalgamated several groups of Franks to extend Frankish control over most of Gaul, defeating Syagrius, son of Aegidius, in 481 at Soissons, and the Visigoth Alaric II in 507. Clovis was baptised as a Catholic Christian at Reims, not so much a conversion but a political move in the interests of unity. He died in 511. His descendant Clothar, through his second wife Clotild, became king of all the Franks in 558. Clothar's four sons inherited his kingdom in 561, and made their separate headquarters at Paris, Reims, Soissons and Orleans, without dividing up their joint territory into four separate zones.[42] The country we know as France had been born, and had survived its infancy. The Franci obviously decided the name of the country and its people. Six centuries after the end of the Roman period, the artist who designed the Bayeux Tapestry knew perfectly well that the invaders of Britain in 1066 were Normanni, but the combatants at Hastings are labelled Angli et Franci. The Germans go one better and still call the country the Kingdom of the Franks, Frankreich.

*Spain*

The diocese of the Spains eventually included Ibiza, Mallorca and Minorca, and the *vicarius* of the diocese was also responsible for the administration of Mauretania Tingitana, closer to Spain than it was to the command of the *comes Africae*. Tingitana was the source of several invasions of Spain by the Mauri, and it had its own military commander, the *comes Tingitanae*, whose units of the field army and garrison troops confronted raiders and bandits.[43]

Spain had been within the Roman domain since the third century BC, long before Gaul. An aristocracy had grown up calling themselves senators, whose members had taken part in the central government, in provincial government, and as commanders in the Roman army. The Emperor Theodosius I was originally from Spain and had probably retired to his estates at Cauca (Coca) when his father Count Theodosius was executed. In January 379 he was made Augustus, reigning as the Emperor Theodosius I until 395. Spain was peaceful at this time, and many men of Spanish origin were brought to Theodosius' court. But these were Spain's halcyon days.

There had been signs of trouble from the mid-third century onwards as tribes crossed the Rhine, eventually threatening northern Spain. In the fourth century the threats increased, so the history of the Spains reflects what was happening in Britain and Gaul, in that towns and cities which did not have walls rapidly acquired them, but the fabric of buildings deteriorated and was not repaired. Mining and production declined, centres of manufacture and distribution tended to become more localized, and the wealthy moved out from towns to villas.[44] When the central government was unable to help, the development of local self-defence was inevitable, and the landowners armed their workers.

The beginning of the end of Roman Spain can be tied in with the usurper Constantine III from Britain, who crossed the sea into Gaul in 407 and sent his elder son Constans, elevated to Caesar, to take charge of Spain, with the help of the British general Gerontius, and the praetorian prefect Apollinaris, whose grandson was the author Sidonius Apollinaris. The Spanish family of Theodosius were defeated trying to oppose Constans.[45] In the account of these events, as Richardson points out, VII Gemina is not mentioned, though it appears in the *Notitia* at its headquarters in Leon, while the Theodosian forces are described as private armies. Were there no regular troops left in Spain?[46]

When the Suevi, Alans and Vandals entered Spain in 409, it was said that Gerontius had invited them in so that he could use them against Constantine III, implying that he had planned this for some time. He did not make himself emperor but raised one of his soldiers called Maximus instead. Gerontius killed Constans in battle, and then moved against Constantine III at Arles, but Gerontius' soldiers would not face Flavius Constantius, sent from Honorius' court. Gerontius killed himself. Constantine was executed in 411. Later Gerontius' chosen Emperor Maximus made another bid for power, but in 422 he was executed.[47]

Only Tarraconensis was under the control of the Emperor Honorius. The rest had been divided up between 409 and 411 by the invading tribes. In the north-west the Suevi occupied the part of Gallaecia nearest the ocean. Their neighbours were the Hasding or Asding Vandals, a new name for one of two groups, the other being the Siling Vandals who occupied Baetica. The Alans occupied Lusitania and Carthaginensis.[48] These tribes could draw on the tax revenues that were presumably diverted from Rome.[49] The situation changed when Flavius Constantius made an arrangement with the Goth Wallia, who came to power after the death of Athaulf. Wallia wiped out the Siling Vandals in Baetica, and so depleted the Alans who until now had dominated the Suebi and other Vandals, that they were forced to join the Hasding Vandals settled in Gallaecia. In 418 Wallia and the Goths were then settled in Aquitania by Constantius, as described above.

The Hasding Vandals and the Alans were ruled by Gunderic, but since the focus in the 420s was on Italy and Gaul, little is known of what they were doing until Gunderic died in 428, succeeded by his half-brother Geiseric, who in 429 took his people out of Spain to Africa.[50] When the Vandals left, parts of Spain were up for grabs by other tribes, but while the Roman general Aetius was repairing the damage in Spain, the Suevi were left to their own devices. They did not move, though their lands were among the poorest of the country. Their chance came when Aetius planned a campaign to regain control of Africa, and then the Suevi did act, in 439. They took Emerita (Merida), Hispalis (Seville) and finally gained Baetica and Carthaginensis.[51] Three military commanders in succession were sent to Spain, Asturius in 442 and Merobaudes in 443, to clear the Bagaudae from Tarraconensis; and in 446 Vitus, *magister utriusque militiae*, was sent against the Suevi, but the tribesmen won a resounding victory and ended up with control of nearly all Spain, and its revenues.[52] Carthaginensis was regained by the Emperor Majorian in 460, the last time an imperial expedition entered Spain. The *magister militum* Nepotianus was left in command when Majorian returned to Italy in 461 to meet death at the hands of Ricimer. Spain was not strategically important any longer, compared to the loss of Africa.[53]

By 476, Euric had established his Visigothic kingdom in Spain, controlling all of it except for the Suevi kingdom in the north-west, as described above. The passages concerning the co-operation between landowners and the invaders of Gaul apply equally well to Spain. The traditional date for the fall of the Roman Empire is 476, by which time the Visigoths ruled Spain. Is the same date also the end of Roman Spain? Or had it ceased to be Roman when the Suevi controlled most of it in the 440s? Or did the end come as far back as 409 when the tribesmen crossed the Pyrenees? It is perhaps better to enquire what survived. Roman provincial life generally continued in Spain and southern Gaul.[54] Pagan religions had been gradually eradicated over the Empire by edicts dating from the 380s, leaving the Catholic Church supreme, especially after 587 when King Reccared of the Arian Visigoths was converted.[55] The Church kept alive the use of Latin, preserving literacy and education at least among the clerics.

Justinian managed to regain control of a small part of south-west Spain in 552, while the war to regain Italy was still going on. He had a brilliant excuse in that a Visigothic noble called Athanagild rebelled against Agila, the legitimate Visigothic King, and asked for Justinian's help. An expedition set off commanded by Liberius, who was getting on in years. He had been praetorian prefect of Italy under Odoacer and Theoderic. Athanagild presumably knew that he would have to pay for the favour, in this case with land. The new Roman province of Hispania, a shadow of its former self, included control of the Balearic Islands, commanded by a *magister militum* appointed from Constantinople. The area was part of the Byzantine Empire until 624.[56]

The Visigothic kingdom of Spain lasted until the arrival of the Muslim forces in the eighth century, but modern Spanish derives from Latin, not the language of the Visigoths, and the name of the country in several languages preserves its Roman label, Hispania.

## Africa

The history of the late Roman provinces of the west is intertwined, and the same significant people and tribes turn up repeatedly, in this case the Vandals and some Alans under Geiseric, who crossed from Spain to Africa in 429. The invasion forces were not large and were possibly ferried in batches across the Straits of Gibraltar into Mauretania Tingitana, the shortest sea-route.[57] They perhaps employed ship-owners whom the Visigoths had befriended, until they learned seafaring for themselves.

The African provinces, principally Numidia, Byzacena (or Byzacium), and Proconsularis were coveted prizes. Attila had tried to cross from Sicily, and Wallia attempted the longer crossing from Barcelona, but storms wrecked his fleet. For Geiseric, Africa was not only rich but safe, and not easy to invade with an army, as demonstrated by the failure of Attila's and Wallia's plans. The government of Mauretania Tingitana was in the hands of the *vicarius* of the diocese of the Spains, with an army commanded by the *comes Tingitanae*, but this army was not strong enough to withstand the onslaught of Geiseric's experienced soldiers. They had no trouble in progressing eastwards, marching towards Numidia, many miles away. Near the border of Numidia in 430 Geiseric defeated the army commanded by Bonfacius, *comes Africae*, who took refuge in Hippo Regius (Annaba, Algeria), the home town of St Augustine. Geiseric besieged the place. Augustine died there during the siege, which lasted for more than a year, while Geiseric's followers looted and destroyed the countryside, and as Arian Christians they aimed for the Catholic churches.[58]

By 433 Aetius was the dominant power in the western Empire, but he could not fight on the two main fronts in Gaul and Africa without help, so he asked for troops from the eastern Empire, and the commander Aspar was sent against Geiseric. He based himself in Carthage in 431. When he risked battle Geiseric defeated him, but Aspar did not leave Carthage until 434. By then the Emperor Valentinian III had realised that he could not hold Africa and also attend to other problems, and he arranged a treaty with Geiseric on 11 February 435, giving him control of part of Numidia, Mauretania Sitifensis and Caesariensis, while the Romans held on to the rest of Numidia, Proconsularis and Byzacena.[59]

In October 439, Geiseric ignored the treaty and marched on Carthage, forcing his way into the city. He may have known that there were not many soldiers left in Carthage while wars were fought elsewhere. Once in possession of Carthage, he could strangle Rome's food supply. He also attacked Sicily, another source of food for Rome, and besieged Panormus (Palermo), the base of the Roman navy, but bad weather forced him to return to Carthage in 440. He must have known that retribution would come, and forces from the western and eastern Empires were assembled to attack Carthage from Sicily. Geiseric, an Arian Christian, must have thought he was under divine protection when the Huns took advantage of the withdrawal of troops from the Danube and crossed the river, forcing the contingents of the eastern army to return from Sicily. Unable now to wage war on Geiseric, the Romans made another treaty with him in 442. He would have to be offered something rather better than the control of the provinces of the western parts of North Africa, so the Romans swapped their wealthy provinces for Geiseric's, leaving him in control of part of Numidia, with Proconsularis and Byzacena, and of course Carthage. Geiseric was recognised as friend and ally of the Roman people, and he sent grain to Rome, as well as his son Huneric as a hostage.[60] The treaty merely recognised the hard fact that the Romans were in no position to remove him.

The landowners of Proconsularis were sacrificed to expediency, since Geiseric confiscated their holdings to pay his soldiers. He did not take lands in Numidia or Byzacena. It is suggested that the Vandals were given only the tax revenues, but Heather argues from legal documents mentioning allotments that the Vandals were given lands. Farms may have been taken over complete with the labour force.[61] The peasants of Proconsularis would perhaps not notice the change except that their rents would be collected by Vandal landowners. Displaced Romans were compensated as far as possible by Valentinian's laws to protect them from prosecution by money lenders, who were also forbidden to charge interest on loans made after the landowners had been expelled.[62]

The landowners as well as the Roman high command expected to be able to recover Africa. The Emperor Majorian attempted to bring this about, gathering his army off the coast of Spain, but Geiseric had learned of the assembly of the fleet and destroyed it.[63] Shortly afterwards, Majorian was killed by the general Ricimer, who had served two previous western emperors. The next attempt to regain Africa occurred in 468, when the eastern Emperor Leo I assembled a massive fleet and military forces from west and east, under the overall command of Leo's brother-in-law Basiliscus. One of the generals under Basiliscus, called Marcellinus, regained Sardinia and then occupied Sicily, but was killed there, and another general, Heraclius, commanded Egyptian troops in Tripolitania, where locals were keen to help them eject the Vandals.[64] The fleet under Basiliscus landed on the African coast at Cape Bon, and prepared to disembark the army. Before there was a battle, Geiseric sent in fire ships, the most terrifying weapon in the days of wooden ships. Oared ships stood a chance of escaping once they had got under way, but it seems that the wind was against the fleet so sails were useless. Basiliscus and the surviving ships returned to Constantinople.[65]

The eastern Empire had thrown great resources into this naval expedition and took a long time to recover financially. Peace was made with the Vandals, mostly because there was no chance within the foreseeable future that either the west or the east could dislodge them. Geiseric died in 477, three years after the eastern Emperor Leo. He had been a resourceful, talented leader, who had managed to persuade his people to follow him for all those miles from Spain to Numidia, and then into Carthage. Less than thirty years after his death the Byzantine Emperor Justinian sent a force under the general Belisarius to reconquer Africa. There had been rebellions against the Vandals in Sardinia, and in Libya, so it was a propitious time to invade, and the excuse was provided by the Vandal usurper Gelimar when he ousted King Hilderic. In 533 the invasion began, supported by local people, and a Vandal force was defeated not far from Carthage. Then the support of the locals was lost by the imposition of taxes as the Moors and Berbers became the main enemy, and the generals squabbled among themselves.[66] This belongs to the history of the Byzantine Empire, so fast-forwarding a little, the end came with the Arab conquest. By the end of the seventh century the Arabs had conquered all of North Africa from the Atlantic to Egypt.

## Raetia and Noricum

Although the northern border of Raetia was the Danube, thus placing it within the Danube provinces, Raetia belonged to the diocese of Italy. It was split into two provinces, one to the west and one to the east, while Noricum was split into northern and southern provinces. Noricum Ripense in the north was bordered by the Danube, taking its name from *ripa* meaning riverbank. The southern province was called Noricum Mediterraneum, not that it came anywhere near the Mediterranean Sea, but it was literally in the 'middle territory' between the Alps and Noricum Ripense.

There were gaps in the defences of the Upper Rhine and the Upper Danube even before the end of the fourth century, and Gratian tried to pre-empt penetration of tribesmen through the frontiers and thereby guard his rear before he set off to join Valens at Adrianople. [67] Before the Rhine frontier collapsed in 406, the Vandals were able to raid Raetia, opening the way through the Alpine passes and into Italy. In the first half of the fifth century there were frontier troops or *limitanei* in Raetia and Noricum, but no field armies, which were usually needed elsewhere because the interiors of the provinces now needed defence as well as the frontiers, and resources were restricted, leaving too little to support the frontier soldiers.[68] Eventually they were not paid at all, as demonstrated by the famous tale relayed by Eugippius, the biographer of St Severinus and historian of the last decades of Noricum and Raetia. The soldiers of the fort at Batavis (Passau) on the eastern border of Raetia, at the confluence of the Inn and the Danube, decided to send a few of their number into Italy to ask for their pay. Some days later their bodies floated past the fort.[69] It does not matter whether or not this is true, for the end of Roman rule was probably something like that. The soldiers probably stayed at home with their families, sharpened their swords, and did their best to defend their communities.

By the early fifth century, troop numbers in the Danube garrisons had declined or disappeared, and the central government could not adequately defend the frontiers. The Gothic leaders Radagaisus and Alaric passed through Noricum in 405 and 407, causing enough damage to ruin two towns. Eventually Virunum (Zollfeld, Austria) was abandoned, though it had been the old capital of the undivided province, and then of Noricum Mediterraneum. In its place Tiburnia (Teurnia), further west, became the new capital. Villas, too, were deserted. New types of settlement grew up from the beginning of the fifth century, called *castella*, interpreted as refuges, not simply for temporary crises but for permanent occupancy.[70] The *castella* were usually built on slopes of hills where access was difficult, with a wall surrounding the settlement. It is considered that since so many of them were built, most of them in southern Noricum, that they probably were not all constructed in a single building programme after 400, so it is possible that older hill forts may have been refurbished. Hilltop refuges were not confined to Noricum and Raetia, though Johnson suggests that the hilltop sites in the Alps may have been official military sites for the defence of Italy.[71] Protection of the passes through the Alps would have concerned the emperors of the west and their successors, the Goths Odoacer and Theoderic, especially after the abandonment of the Raetian frontier and northern part of Noricum.

According to Zosimus, for a short time until about 428, a general called Generidus united the commands of Raetia, Noricum Ripense, Pannonia Prima, and Dalmatia.[72] After 460 the situation in Noricum is documented in Eugippius' life of St Severinus. Eugippius lived in Noricum Ripense, and wrote his biography in 511, nearly three decades after Severinus' death. Severinus was a man of energy and ability, and in the absence of any Roman governor in Noricum Ripense when he arrived there in 460, 'directed by God' he rallied the population and helped them to organise their own defence. Farms were still occupied for a while and produced food, but soon there were shortages, and Severinus tried to provide food from wherever he could, even bringing supplies from Italy.[73] He negotiated with the tribesmen, the Germanic Rugii and the Alamanni, who raided the farms, and perhaps succeeded in putting a temporary stop to their depredations, but it was a losing rearguard action. The people had to move into Lauriacum (Lorch), and then into settlements further east, up to Faviana (Mautern), but this land had been taken over by the Rugii, who had made Faviana tributary to them. Severinus died in January 482 and was buried at Faviana. Without him, the cause was lost. The last time that anything like a Roman force appeared in Noricum was in 487, when Odoacer had to fight the Rugii, who had been encouraged to invade Italy by the eastern Emperor Zeno.[74] Odoacer and his brother defeated the Rugii but could no longer defend Noricum Ripense, so the southern province and the Alps became the northernmost frontier of Italy. The Roman population and Severinus' remains were taken to Italy, accompanied by Eugippius. The Roman towns and forts of Ripense were still occupied, but not by Romans, and immediately after the defeat of the Rugii, in 489 the Lombards moved in.[75] In the first century the Lombards were settled in the region of the lower Elbe.[76] By the mid-sixth century they had moved into Pannonia and Noricum, and from there they invaded Italy in 568.

### Pannonia, Moesia and Dacia

Pannonia had been divided into four provinces by Diocletian. Bordering Noricum in the western sector, Pannonia Prima's northern frontier was the Danube, and south of it was the new smaller province of Savia. The eastern sector, surrounded to the north and the east by the Danube, was Valeria, with Pannonia Secunda to the south. Moesia had been split into two parts when Aurelian inserted the new Dacia between them. Aurelian's new province may have occupied only the area of Diocletian's Dacia Ripensis, with what became Dacia Mediterranea added later.[77] Diocletian divided western Moesia into Moesia Prima in the north and Dardania to the south, while Moesia Secunda lay east of Dacia on the lower Danube, reaching the Black Sea. This area was important for the defence of the Byzantine Empire, and consequently the frontier here lasted longer than that of the middle Danube.

As mentioned above, the commands of Raetia, Noricum Ripense, Pannonia Prima, and Dalmatia were united by Generidus, but little else is known about him.[78] By about 420, even if Generidus was still in command, Pannonia was occupied by the Huns, who had been neighbours of Pannonia for some time. Though an attempt was made in 427 to oust them, probably by the eastern Empire rather the battered west, the reality of the situation was recognised in 433 when large areas of Pannonia were granted to the Huns.[79] Then Attila arrived in 441. As he captured cities which belonged to the eastern Empire, Ratiaria, Viminacium, Singidunum, Sirmium and Naissus, evacuation of territory began, as in Noricum Ripense when the Roman population were moved out. The middle Danube was left to non-Romans. The Huns settled until their own empire collapsed, and then the Goths, followed by a succession of other tribes, moved in.

Moesia Prima did not suffer as much damage as Pannonia, and avoided the settlement of tribesmen, who were placed in Dacia Ripensis and Moesia Secunda. The frontier of Moesia Prima was not threatened to the same extent as other parts and was not so heavily defended, with the result that when Attila appeared it was not garrisoned. The northern sectors were evacuated. Moesia Secunda was garrisoned and defended as part of the eastern Empire, and at the end of the sixth century the border troops were well-organised and efficient, impressing the *magister militum per Thracias*.[80]

The mid-fifth century saw the end of Roman rule in the northern parts of Pannonia, in Moesia Prima and Dacia Ripensis. In Moesia Secunda, the Roman population was not eradicated, nor was Christian worship. Bishops bringing the relics of saints to Italy may not represent all the Christian communities of the Danube provinces. Some Roman Christians may have stayed, some of the more dedicated harbouring a mission to convert the Huns and the Arian Goths. Just as early tribes of Italy and the Romans readily absorbed other peoples, so did the northern tribesmen, and just as the term Roman did not denote people from Rome, the terms Huns, Goths and so on did not denote groups of people with pure ethnic backgrounds. If some Romans remained in the evacuated parts of the Danube provinces, there may have been some integration and assimilation, and the Romans probably behaved in the variety of ways in which people behaved in more recent occupied countries.

## Dalmatia

Before the Flavian era Illyricum was divided into two separate provinces, Dalmatia in the south and Pannonia in the north, though the use of the name Illyricum persisted. Under Diocletian the name was used for the two dioceses, the Moesias and the Pannonias, and later Illyricum was used for military commands, for instance the military post of *magister militum per Illyricum* was given to Alaric, and one of the four prefectures was that of Illyricum.

In the early fifth century in the beleaguered Danube area some of the inhabitants left their towns and cities to live on defensible hillsides, but others fled into Dalmatia from Pannonia and from northern parts of Dalmatia itself, their numbers causing problems about how to accommodate them. This situation is familiar to many modern countries in the twenty-first century. Instructions were issued in 415 about the movements of the refugees and how to deal with them.[81]

As the Vandals increased their power and learned how to use sea-going vessels, the Dalmatian coasts were threatened. Aetius was unable to attend to this threat and sent the commander Marcellinus, who on the death of Aetius turned against the western government, but he did help the Emperor Majorian to take back control of Sicily from the Vandals. After this, Marcellinus returned to Dalmatia. The eastern Emperor Leo I made him *magister utriusque militiae*. It was probably Ricimer who ordered the death of Marcellinus, and without him there was seemingly no-one to stop the Suevi from entering Dalmatia. Marcellinus' nephew Julius Nepos took over the government and his colleague Nepotianus commanded the troops as *magister militum Dalmatiae*. Nepos was instrumental in removing the western Emperor Glycerius, who was forcibly retired to a monastery at Salona (Split). Nepos became Augustus, confirmed by Leo I, but then Nepos was quickly deposed by Orestes, who sent him back to Dalmatia, where he was still legally Emperor of the west, but powerless. He was assassinated in 480. By this time Odoacer ruled Italy. He executed Nepos' assassins, but he may have used the death of Nepos to add Dalmatia to his kingdom. His successor Theoderic was confirmed in possession of the province, ruling Dalmatia and Italy well, providing peace and security, which lasted under his successor. In 535 the *magister militum per Illyricum*, Mundus, fought two battles against the Goths and won both, but he was killed in the second one, which resulted in the evacuation of Dalmatia for a while.[82] The Romans returned when Justinian's general Belisarius attacked Italy, and the assault on Dalmatia was led by Constantianus. The Goths left Salona and in 536 retreated to Ravenna, and another victory over them in 537 ensured that they did not try to regain Salona. In the second half of the sixth century, a Roman *praeses* governed Dalmatia, and military affairs were under a Gothic *comes Dalmatiae et Saviae*, the latter referring to the small province of Savia in southern Pannonia, bordering Dalmatia. Unlike the western provinces, which were irretrievably lost, Dalmatia remained as part of the Empire of Constantinople and the Byzantine Empire until 1204.[83]

## Macedonia and Greece

The term Greece does not signify a province, but embraces Achaea, Crete, Thessaly, Epirus and Macedonia, all of which underwent various boundary changes from Augustus onwards, sometimes attached to another province and sometimes becoming an independent province. Under Diocletian, all were in the diocese of Moesia. When the four praetorian prefectures were established, the diocese was under the prefect of Illyricum. On its eastern border Macedonia was divided from Thrace by the river Nestus, but its other borders are not so explicitly defined. In Diocletian's scheme, Macedonia was one of ten provinces in the diocese of Moesia, but Constantine split this diocese into two separate dioceses of Dacia and Macedonia, still part of the prefecture of Illyricum. After the battle of Adrianople, the western Emperor Gratian retained the prefecture of Illyricum but gave to the eastern Emperor Theodosius control of the dioceses of Macedonia and Dacia. These were returned to Valentinian II.[84] Greece had been subject to raids by various tribes from the late second century, first the Costoboci, then the Heruli, Germanic tribesmen who invaded via the Black Sea in the 260s, Franks in 280, Goths just before the battle of Adrianople and Vandals in the second half of the fifth century. From the mid-third century fortifications were the order of the day, as in many other provinces, and some of the walls incorporated older monuments, as Aurelian had done in Rome.[85]

Macedonia in particular came under increasing threat from the Ostrogoths. Running through northern Greece and Macedonia was the Via Egnatia, first laid down around 130 BC and named for the proconsul of Macedonia, Gnaeus Egnatius, and later extended to Byzantium connecting the west with the east, but in the late Empire it also became a route for tribal invasions, notably Alaric in 395, who caused much damage.

The local authorities in cities and towns began to build or refurbish fortifications, which were particularly splendid at Thessalonica. At an unknown date after the late fourth century Macedonia was split into two parts, Macedonia Prima and Secunda, and Thessalonica was the capital of Prima, while Stobi became the capital of Secunda. The harbour at Thessalonica had been enlarged by Constantine the Great, and from the late fourth century until the late fifth it became an international trading hub, growing prosperous as a result, enabling the wealthy to build luxurious fortified villas, the Christians to build large churches, and small manufacturing industries to flourish.

This all came to an end in the early seventh century. Several earthquakes wrecked some of the cities, and disaster was followed by invasions of Slavs, who originated in what is now Poland. They arrived on the Danube *c*.500, combined with the Bulgars, a confederation of Turkic tribes whose name is not strictly an ethnic term, being derived from Turkish *bulgha* meaning 'disruptive'. They were allied with Constantinople against the Ostrogoths but then began to attack territories of the eastern Empire, until the Avars subdued them.[86] From about 580 the Slavs and Avars joined forces, the Slavs having overrun much of Greece. The origins of the Avars are disputed. They were nomads from central Asia who came to control the lands north of the Black Sea, and from the last three decades of the sixth century they established themselves as a separate state in Pannonia, having dislodged the Gepids who occupied it, and the Lombards, with whom they at first had an alliance. The Avars took Sirmium, and in the years between 620 and 680 the praetorian prefect of Illyricum disappears, possibly resurfacing as the urban prefect of Thessalonica. In Macedonia, when the Avars and Slavs invaded it was a familiar story. The countryside became deserted as people fled, and locally organised defence was the only option, since the government at Constantinople was fully engaged with the conflict with Iran. The recovery of Greece began in the late seventh century, but Macedonia had to wait until the early ninth century for its reincorporation into the Byzantine Empire.[87]

*Thrace*

When Thrace was annexed by Claudius there were no cities to provide the substructure for government, so centres had to be created. The province was divided into *strategiai*, governed by a *strategos* appointed by the governor, originally an equestrian procurator until Trajan appointed a consular legate. Trajan also built new cities, which promoted Romanization, though Thracian language and customs were not submerged. Thrace was a source of soldiers for the Roman army, but at first had few troops since the defence of the province in its earlier years lay with the legate of Moesia. Thrace was never urbanised compared to other provinces, but it supported many Imperial estates, and in the late Roman period these agricultural lands supplied food to Constantinople, gaining more importance in the seventh century when Egypt was overrun by the Arabs. Major routes from the north and west passed through Thrace, but as with the Via Egnatia connecting the Adriatic with Constantinople, roads which facilitated movements of messengers and troops also facilitated invasions by tribesmen. Diocletian created the diocese of Thrace, which was divided into four smaller provinces, and also included the Danube frontier, incorporating Moesia Inferior in its new guise as Moesia II and Scythia, north of Moesia II and bordering the western coast of the Black Sea. The *magister militum per Thraciam* commanded part of the eastern field army in the diocese. Since Thrace lay to the west of Constantinople it was important for the defence of the city, but when the pressures of the tribes increased in the late fifth century, the eastern Emperor Anastasius built defences with the accurate title of the Long Walls, sixty-five kilometres west of Constantinople, and stretching for forty-five kilometres from the Black Sea the Sea of Marmara across the peninsula, which would at least delay invaders from getting too close to the city. It has been suggested that the Long Walls originated with Theodosius, who built a wall across the peninsula closer to Constantinople, so Anastasius only had to repair the Long Walls.[88]

The cities which grew up in Thrace were too few and far between to contribute to the defence of the province, and in the sixth century Justinian built forts in Thrace, numbered and located by Procopius in his work, *On Buildings*, a panegyric on Justinian's public works.[89] In the seventh century the Slavs controlled western Thrace, while the eastern Empire controlled the only the eastern sector, but by the eighth century the Slavs had been subdued. The security of Thrace was vital for the security of Constantinople, so it would not be relinquished lightly.

## Asia Minor

The territory of Asia Minor approximates to modern Turkey. Diocletian divided the country into two dioceses of Asiana and Pontica. Asiana comprised Lycia and Pamphylia, and the old province of Asia, from which seven new provinces were made, one called Asia, obviously much reduced compared to the old province, but it was anomalous in that it was governed from Pergamum by a senatorial proconsul who reported to the Emperor, not the Praetorian Prefect.[90] In the north and east of Asia Minor, the diocese of Pontica comprised the old provinces of Bithynia-Pontus, Galatia and Cappadocia, but Cilicia on the south-eastern coast of Turkey belonged to the diocese of Oriens. The *vicarii* of the dioceses would be answerable to the Praetorian Prefect of the east, which along with the three other prefectures developed probably after Constantine's reign.

The cities of the old province of Asia were among the wealthiest of the Empire, until the invasions of the Goths in the mid-third century, when they suffered badly, leading to the decline of some of the smaller cities. As in many cities of the Empire, fortifications were rapidly built, often using public monuments as part of the defences. From the end of the fourth century the spread of Christianity in Asia Minor ensured the disappearance of pagan temples, some of which provided the building materials for new buildings, both religious and secular. In the later period Lycia and its coast, in the south of modern Turkey, became prosperous because the communities had access to the trade of Egypt, Syria and Constantinople, the profits accounting for the number of new churches and stone-built houses in the settlements by the sea. Similarly, the coastal areas of Cilicia prospered. From the fourth to the sixth centuries, the hitherto unimportant harbour at Corycus, north-east of modern Silifke, flourished, with extensive trading connections, exporting olive oil, wine and timber. Strong fortifications enclosed the town, which contained stone houses and many churches.[91]

The eastern zones of Asia Minor, Cappadocia and Galatia, in the Diocletianic diocese of Pontica, were less urbanised, but in Galatia the small villages prospered even into the mid-sixth century. Cappadocia was important because routes passed though the country connecting Constantinople with Antioch, and trade routes running north and west from the Cilician Gates used a pass through the Taurus mountains north of Tarsus, which was one of only two routes which could accommodate wheeled traffic. In 371-2 the Emperor

Valens divided Cappadocia into two parts, Prima in the eastern sector and Secunda in the more urbanised west. Cappadocia Prima had only one city, Caesarea, while the countryside was filled with many Imperial lands. The province was governed by a *praeses* but the Imperial lands were administered by the *comes domorum*, with equal powers to the governor. He was answerable to the *comes rei privatae*, whose department was responsible for Imperial estates. With the division came conflict in the eastern zone between the *praeses* and the *comes*, and religious conflict in both provinces between two metropolitan bishops, Basil, whose jurisdiction was limited to the only city, Caesarea, while his counterpart Anthimus, bishop of Tyana, the capital of Secunda in the south-west of the province, could claim jurisdiction over several cities, which Basil attempted to usurp.[92]

### The provinces of the eastern Empire

When the western provinces were lost in the fifth century the eastern Empire had to take charge of the provinces that were left. Constantinople controlled all the Mediterranean, with the exception of the Spanish and Gallic coasts, from the Mauretanias to Egypt, the Middle East, the coasts of modern Turkey and Greece and all the islands including Cyprus, Rhodes and Crete, Dalmatia, Italy and the Adriatic. The upper and middle Danube zones were lost, but the lower Danube remained important for the defence of Constantinople. There were multiple enemies for what can perhaps now be called the Byzantine Empire.

A struggle began with the Persians in the early years of the sixth century. After a period of peace between Persians and Romans, the Persian attacks resumed in 502 and lasted until a truce was arranged in 506/507, then rumbled on until fresh hostilities began in 530-532, when Justinian arranged the so-called Endless Peace, which did not live up to its name. Probably in the period 507 to 530, fortified posts were established beginning at Circesium (Buseire) on the Euphrates in Syria, running northwards to the south-eastern shore of the Black Sea. The building work was not necessarily carried out by the central government, but by local authorities.[93] In 561, peace was arranged for fifty years.

In the middle of the sixth century Justinian managed to regain control of Italy, Africa and a small part of south-west Spain, which he took over in 552 while the war to regain Italy was still going on. As mentioned earlier, Athanagild rebelled against Agila, the Visigothic

King, and asked for Justinian's help. The new Roman province of Hispania was part of the Byzantine Empire until 624 when the Arabs conquered it.[94]

Apart from fighting, the eastern Romans dealt with the tribes in the same ways that had worked since the early years of the Empire. They made alliances with some tribal groups, either because a particular tribe asked for an alliance or because an alliance would perhaps stabilize relations with troublesome peoples. Tribal manpower was utilised to help to fight other tribes, or in some cases, the government set one tribe against another and let them do all the fighting. The Emperor Maurice (reigned 582-602) paid the Frankish King Childebert to attack the Lombards.[95] From the allied tribes Constantinople recruited soldiers, and sometimes opted to preserve the loyalty of allied or non-allied tribes by settling them on the land, and by subsidies, gifts, money and food. The whole had to be constantly monitored, since tribes changed their allegiance and they were highly mobile, leaving their settlements for something better, as when Geiseric left Spain for Africa.

Relying on their resources, always greater than the western Empire, the eastern emperors sometimes bought peace. In 574 Tiberius was made Caesar by Justin II, who was ill, and in 575 he negotiated peace with the Persians for 45,000 *solidi*. Likewise in 597/598 the Emperor Maurice paid off the Avars.[96] As in the earlier Empire, these payments did not usually secure a lasting peace but provided a breather, allowing for attention to be paid to other enemies or other problems, some of which were internal rather than external. Other tribes demanded and received annual tribute in return for giving back territories they had overrun, with the danger that they could increase their demands when they were in a strong position while Constantinople was stretched by wars on different fronts.

The eastern Empire could still mount expeditions inside or outside its territory. In 591, the Persian ruler Hormizd IV was toppled by the usurper Bahram. Hormizd's son Khusro II succeeded him for a short time and was then ousted. He sent appeals for help to Constantinople. After some delay, the Emperor Maurice agreed to send troops to restore Khusro in 591. The Romans were successful and received in return control of Armenia and eastern Mesopotamia, where garrisons were installed. There were also military expeditions across the Danube, against the Slavs and the Avars, from 593 to 602.

Attempts at usurpation did not cease. The Emperor Maurice had become unpopular with the soldiers because he had been forced to reduce pay, but what tipped the balance was when Maurice ordered the army under his brother Peter to go into winter quarters north of the Danube where they had been campaigning.[97] The army could still make emperors and chose the centurion Phocas towards the end of 602, and marched on Constantinople. Phocas ordered the deaths of Maurice and all his family, and reigned until 610, but in 608 Heraclius, exarch of Africa based at Carthage, one of the main ports from which food supplies were sent to Constantinople, also seized Alexandria, the other main port, and he strangled the supplies to the capital. Territory had been lost under Phocas, and this was the last straw. He lost support and was killed in November 610. Heraclius became Emperor.[98]

By the beginning of the seventh century Constantinople was beginning to lose parts of this still extensive Empire. The old enemies, the Persians, resumed their attacks on the eastern frontiers, and overlapping with their attacks a new enemy appeared that neither the Romans nor the Persians were strong enough to defeat, the Arabs. The Persians managed to capture much of the diocese of Oriens, comprising in Diocletianic times the old provinces of Cilicia, Syria, Arabia Palaestina, Cyprus, Egypt, and Cyrenaica, which became Libya Inferior and Superior, later Prima and Secunda.

The Persian advance was rapid. The eastern part of Cappadocia was invaded in 609-610, and the capital Caesarea was taken, but in 612 the Romans won it back.[99] Antioch was taken in 610/611, probably at the same time as Apamea and Emesa. Damascus fell in 613, and Jerusalem was lost when it was besieged in 614, amid great slaughter of Christians. In 613 the Emperor Heraclius led the army in person, breaking the tradition from 395 that fighting was usually conducted by generals. He was defeated near Antioch and had to withdraw, unable to defend Syria. In Egypt, Pelusium was taken in 616/617, and after a siege Alexandria fell in 619, when the Persians occupied Egypt. In 623 they captured Rhodes.[100] Heraclius decided to take the war into Persia. He collected troops in Armenia, devoting time to training them, and he made an alliance with the Avars in 623. He set off in 624, achieving some success, but then the Persians talked to the Avars and in 626 they combined and marched to besiege Constantinople. The Avars arrived first, while the Persians were delayed by the Roman fleet which stopped them from crossing from Asia. The Avars lifted the siege. Late in 627 Heraclius entered Persia and won a battle at Nineveh, and in 628, Khusro having been deposed by his son Kavadh, peace was made.

In summer 629, the Persian commander Shahrbaraz who had commanded the forces destined to attack Constantinople, learned that he was to be executed, so he planned to usurp the throne. He was assisted by Heraclius, in return for the evacuation of Syria and Egypt.[101] Everything must have seemed almost perfect. The two wealthiest provinces were back under the control of Constantinople, and the ruler of Persia owed a favour to Heraclius; but not for long, since he ruled for barely two months. The civil wars that followed nevertheless kept the Persians occupied and away from the eastern Empire.

Only seven years later a new force emerged from the Palestinian and Syrian desert, rapidly and unexpectedly turning the tables. The Arabs under their name Saracens had provided troops, especially cavalry, to assist the Roman army, while the various tribes had been regarded as bandits. Now they were united, and efficient in war. What had happened? The answer is Mohammed and the rise of Islam, which had welded the Arabs together. After Mohammed's death in 632, the Arabs besieged Damascus in 635, and in 636 at the battle of the Yarmuk they defeated the Roman field army, the first to be required in the Arab lands because until now the tribes had limited themselves to raiding. In the following year the Arabs defeated the Persians at Qadisyya, and Ctesiphon was abandoned. The eastern Roman Empire had fought constant wars against tribes and the Persians, and the Persians themselves had fought civil wars after their defeat by the Romans in 628, and both had been weakened.[102] The Arabs soon took over Roman territory. Syria was abandoned by the Romans after the battle of the Yarmuk and the Arabs moved in. Jerusalem fell to them in 638, Egypt fell in 641 and by the late seventh century the Arabs controlled all of North Africa, where the Berber tribes joined them, providing the manpower to enable them to extend into Spain.[103] The Byzantines made efforts to regain Alexandria in 645 and Carthage in 697, probably to re-establish the grain supply if they could hang onto the two cities and their ports. They lost both within a year of gaining them. Carthage was abandoned and a new Arab settlement was built.[104]

This was the end of the Empire that had begun as a cluster of huts on the Capitol and the Palatine in Rome in the eighth century BC.

# Notes

## Abbreviations

And see Bibliography.

*AA Archaeologia Aeliana*
*ANWR Aufstieg und Niederganag
    der Römischen Welt. Berlin: de
    Gruyter*
*BRGK Bericht der Römisch-Germanisch
    Kommission*
*CIL Corpus Inscriptionum Latinarum*
*CJ Codex Justinianus*
*C.Th. Codex Theodosianus*
CWAAS Cumberland and Westmorland
    Antiquarian and Archaeological
    Society
*HA Historia Augusta*
*ILS Inscription Latinae Selectae*
*JHS Journal of Hellenic Studies*
*JRS Journal of Roman Studies*
*LL de Lingus Latina (see under Varro)*
*PBSR Papers of the British School at
    Rome*
*P.Oxy. The Oxyrhynchus Papyri,* eds. P.
    Grenfell *et al.* 1898 to date.
*RG Res Gestae Divi Augusti.*
SANT Society of Antiquaries of
    Newcastle upon Tyne
*ZPE Zeitschrift fur Papyrologie and
    Epigrafik*

## 1 Seven Kings and One Republic

1. Cic. *Rep.* 2.3.5; 5.10; 6.11; Livy 5.54.4; Dudley 1967, 5.
2. Strabo *Geog.*5.3.7.
3. Braund 1987, 56 (in Wacher 1987).
4. Carandini 2017, 149-150.
5. Carandini 2017, 149.
6. Carandini 2017, 218.
7. Carandini 2017, 152; 283-6C; Smith 2000, in Coulston and Dodge 2000, 23-24.
8. Livy 1.3.1- 1.4.2.
9. Tac. *Ann.*12.24.
10. Carandini 2017, 79; 220.
11. Varro *LL* 5.41; Platner and Ashby 1926, 471-473; Claridge 2010, 6.
12. Carandini 2017, 150; 325-326.
13. Livy 1.21.5; Carandini 2017, 150; 425.
14. Carandini 2017, 150-1; 165, 220; Coarelli 2014, 84-86; Carandini 2017, 165.
15. Carandini 2017, 151.
16. Carandini 2017, 151; 152-3; Coarelli 2014, 51-4; Cic. *Rep.* 2.31.
17. Cornell1995, 121; 125.
18. Coarelli 2014, 54-57; Cornell 1995, 95 fig. 9.
19. Cornell 1995, 60-63.

20. Carruba 2006.
21. Livy 1.8.5-7; Dion. Hal. 2.15.1-4.
22. Cornell 1995, 60, 412 n.34; Sherwin-White 1973, 8.
23. Livy 1.9.6-15.
24. Livy 1.9.5 to 1.13.6.
25. Livy 1.13.6-7; Dion. Hal. 2.7.1-3.
26. Livy 1.13.8.
27. Livy 1.8.7; Dion.Hal. 2.12.4; 13.1-3.
28. Livy 1.15.8; Dion. Hal. 2.13.1-4.
29. Livy 1.14.4-11; 1.27.3; Cornell1995, 301-3.
30. Dion. Hal. 2.54.1-55.6; Livy 1.15.1-5.
31. Plut. *Rom.* 27.6; Livy 1.16.1; Dion. Hal. 2.56.4-6.
32. Livy 1.15.8.
33. Livy 1.17.8 -18.5; Dion. Hal. 2.57.1-4; 4.40.2.
34. Plut. *Numa* 1.1-2.
35. Carandini 2017, 150; Livy 1.18.6-10.
36. Dion. Hal. 2.76.6; Livy 1.22.1.
37. Livy 1.24.3-9.
38. Livy 1.27.7-11; 1.28.5; Dion. Hal. 3.24.3-6; 3.28.9-10.
39. Dion. Hal. 3.31.2-4; Livy 1.30.2.
40. Dion. Hal. 3.34.1-5.
41. Livy 1.32.1; Dion. Hal. 3.36.1.
42. Cic. *Rep.* 2.5; 2.33; Livy 1.33.9; Dion Hal. 3.41.4; 3.44.1-2; Pliny *NH* 3.56; 31.89; Meiggs 1973,16-17.
43. Livy 1.33.2-9; Dion. Hal. 3.38.3; Meiggs 17.
44. Dion. Hal. 3.37.3; Livy 1.32.3.
45. Salmon 1982, 4; 184, n.34; Livy 1.24.3-9; 1.32.5-14. Plut. *Numa* 12; Dion. Hal. 2.72.2.
46. Dion. Hal. 2.72.6-9.
47. Dion. Hal. 2.72.6-9; Billows 2007, 314-316.
48. Livy 1.32.6-14;1.33.1; Dion. Hal. 3.37.4.
49. Livy 1.33.5.
50. Dion. Hal. 3.45.1-2.
51. Livy 1.33.7.
52. Strabo *Geog.* 5.3.7; Carandini 2017, 326.
53. Livy 1.33.8.
54. Carandini 2017, 153.
55. Scullard 1967, 221; Cornell 1995, 139.
56. Dion. Hal. 3.39.2; 40.4; 48.3.
57. Livy 1.34.12; Dion. Hal. 3.41.4.
58. Dion. Hal. 3.46.1; Livy 1.35.1-6.
59. Dion. Hal. 3.49.3; Livy 1.35.7.
60. Livy 1.38.4.
61. Dion. Hal. 3.50.4-6.
62. Dion. Hal. 3.51.1-54.3.
63. Livy 1.36.1-2; Dion. Hal. 3.55.1-4.
64. Livy 1.36.2.
65. Livy 37.1-2; Dion. Hal. 3 56.1-2.
66. Livy 1.37.3-5; Dion. Hal. 3.56.3-3.57.1.
67. Livy 1.38.1-2.
68. Dion. Hal. 3.50.2-3.
69. Dion. Hal. 3.66.1.
70. Cornell 1995, 128, quoting Pliny *NH* 36.107.
71. Livy 1.35.10; 1.36.6; Dion. Hal. 3.67.4-5; Carandini 2017, 154.
72. Dion. Hal. 3.69.1; Livy 1.38.7.
73. Livy 1.41.6.
74. Cornell 1995,127, 424 n.25; Cic. *Rep.* 2.37.
75. Varro *LL* 5.45-54.
76. Livy 1.44.12; Cornell 1995,173-9, esp. 175, for discussion of the number of tribes.
77. Livy 1.44.1; Dion. Hal. 4.15.6.
78. Livy 1.44.2; D.H. 4.22.2; Beard 2105, 98.
79. Keppie 1984, 17; Forsythe 2007, 31; Cornell 1995, 184; Rich 2007, 18.
80. Keppie 1984, 17.
81. Livy 1.43.1-9; Dion. Hal. 4.16-21.
82. Rich 2007, 17-18.
83. Cornell 1995, 184-5.
84. Livy 1.43.11; Dion. Hal. 7.59.2-8.
85. Cic. *Rep.* 2.39.
86. Carandini 2017, 154.
87. Coarelli 2014, 11; 538.
88. Dion. Hal. 4.22.4-24.6; Lewis and Rheinhold 1990, vol. I 67-68.
89. Dion. Hal. 4.9.7 to 4.10.6; Livy 1.57.10-12.
90. Dion. Hal. 4.12.1-3; Livy 1.46.1.

91. Livy 1.46.4; Dion. Hal.4.6.1-4.7.5; see also Cornell 1995, 123 fig.14 for a family tree.
92. Livy 1.47.8-48.7; Dion. Hal. 4.38.2-6.
93. Livy 1.48.8; Cic. *Rep.* 2.37.
94. Dion. Hal. 4.41.1-4.
95. Livy 1.49.9; 1.50-52; Dion. Hal. 4.47.1-48.3.
96. Livy 1.52.1-6.
97. Livy 1.53.5 to 54.10; Dion. Hal.4.58.1-3.
98. Livy 1.55.1; 56.3; D.H. 4.63.1.
99. Livy 1.55.1; Dion. Hal. 4.59.1; Cic. *Rep.* 2.35-6; 44; Cornell 1995, 129-30.
100. Carandini 2017, 154.
101. Livy 1.56.1.
102. Coarelli 1995, 32-33.
103. Carandini 2017, 155.
104. Platner and Ashby 1926,126-7; Livy 1.56.2; Dion Hal. 3.67.5; 4.44.1; Pliny *NH* 36.24; 36.104.
105. Livy 1.57.1-3; Dion. Hal. 4.64.1.
106. Livy 1.57.6-11; Dion. Hal. 4.64-67.
107. Livy 1.59.12; 1.60.1; Dion. Hal. 4.85.2-4.
108. Dion. Hal. 5.1.1; Polyb. 3.22.1-2.
109. Cornell 1995, 231.
110. Lintott 1999, 31; Cornell 1995 237.
111. Coarelli 2014, 45; 313; Claridge 2010, 281-2.
112. Lintott 1999, 29.
113. Livy 1.26.2-12.
114. Dion. Hal. 2.9.2.
115. Livy 5.32.8.
116. Livy 1.24.3-9; 1.32.6-14.
117. Livy 1.38.1-2; Polyb. 36.4.1-3.
118. Livy 1.24.3-9.
119. Cornell 1995, 174-5; 257; Livy 2.16.5; Dion. Hal. 5.40.5; Livy 2.16.4-5.
120. Livy 1.60.1-3; 2.6.5-2.7.1.
121. Livy 2.9.1-2.13.5.
122. Livy 2.10.1- 13.
123. Tac. *Hist.* 3.72.
124. Livy 2.6.2-3.
125. Livy 2.15.1-7; 2.19.4.
126. Livy 2.21.5.
127. Dion Hal. 4.72-75.
128. Livy 2.56.2; Cornell 1995, 116; 265; 379; Lintott 1999, 53-55.
129. Cornell 1995, 25.
130. Lintott 1999, 109; Livy 2.18.4-9; 2.29.11; Dion. Hal. 5.70-77.
131. Salmon 1982, 183 n. 19.
132. Lintott 1999,110.
133. Livy 22.8; Plut. *Fab.* 4.1.
134. Cic. *Rep.* 1.63; 2.56.
135. Dion. Hal. 4.75.1-2; 4.76.1; 4.84.5.
136. Dion. Hal. 3.61.
137. Cornell 1995, 229.
138. Livy 3.55.12.
139. Salmon 1982, 183 n.19; Cornell 1995, 230.
140. Varro *LL* 5.80; 87.
141. Livy 7.3.5-7.
142. Cornell 1995, 228-9; 442 n.47.
143. Beard 2015, 132-3; Cornell 1995, 359-360.
144. Livy 6.42.10; Cornell 1995, 337.
145. Livy 8.23.11-12; 8.26.7; Cornell 1995, 360.
146. Lintott 1999, 115.
147. Cornell 1998, 248; 369-70.
148. Cic. *Leg.* 3.7.
149. Lintott 1999, 50-51; 117-8.
150. Cic. *Leg* 3.7; Livy 4.24.5.
151. Livy 4.24.4-9.
152. Livy 2.33.1.
153. Dion. Hal. 11.68.8; Livy 3.30.7.
154. Cornell 1995, 259.
155. Livy 4.49.6; Lintott 1999, 122; Cornell 1995, 277; 341.
156. Livy 3.55.13; Cornell 1995, 254.
157. Livy 3.55.16-11; Lintott 1999, 129.n. 29.
158. Dio 49.43.1.
159. Cic. *Leg* 3.7; *de Offic.* 2.16.55-57.
160. Tac. *Ann.* 11.22.
161. Livy 3.57.10.
162. Livy 3.50.1-58.6.
163. Cornell 1995, 462 n.17 notes the more important modern discussions.
164. Livy 4.6.8.
165. Cornell 336, table 8.

166. Livy 4.54.2-6.
167. Livy 4.56.1-3; 5.12.9-10; Cornell 1995, 336, table 8.
168. App. *BC* 1.1.8.
169. Cornell 1995, 270; 329.
170. Livy 6.42.9-11.
171. Livy 7.42.2.
172. Cornell 1995, 337.
173. Livy 8.16.1.
174. Livy 7.1.7; 7.6.8-7.7.1.
175. Rutulus' career: Livy 7.16.1; 7.17.6-9; 7.21.4; 7.22.7; 7.28.6; 7.38.8.
176. Livy 7.23.1-7.25.1.
177. Cornell 1995, 225-6; 266.
178. Livy 2.34.5-6.
179. Livy 3.6.1-9.
180. Cornell 1995, 268; 459 n.98 referring to Garnsey 1988, 168-72.
181. Livy 2.52.1.
182. Livy 2.34.3
183. Rickman 1980, 32-4.
184. Cornell 1995, 268.
185. Livy 2.23.1.
186. Livy 2.24.6-7.
187. Livy 2.31.8-10.
188. Livy 2.31.7.
189. Livy 2.32.1-2.
190. Livy 7.28.9.
191. Livy 7.42.1; Cornell 1995, 322.
192. Livy 2.41.1-3. Dionysius says it was only the Roman land that was to be divided. Dion. Hal. 8.77.2.
193. Cornell 1995, 270; 329.
194. Livy 2.32.7-8.
195. Dion. Hal. 6.63.3; Cornell 1995, 257-8; 448 n.61.
196. Livy 2.43.2-11.
197. Livy 2.44.1-6.
198. Livy 2.48.1-4.
199. Boatwright (et al.) 2004, 82.
200. Gellius *Attic Nights* 16.13.9.
201. Alba Fucens: Salmon 1969, 61, fig. 6; plates 30-33. Cosa: Salmon 1969, 30-31, fig. 3; 36-37 fig. 4.
202. Salmon 1969, 71-72; 177 n.107; Livy 27.38.3; 36.3.4.
203. Salmon 1969, 49.
204. Cic. *Pro Plancio*. 19; see also Cic. *Pro Balbo* 31; *de Offic.* 1.35.

205. Livy 38.36.7.
206. Cornell 1995, 365.
207. Rich 2008, 69; Burton 2011, 82.

## 2 The Assimilation of Italy and the First Provinces

1. Polyb. 3.22.1-3.23.6; Cornell 1995, 211; 440 n.13.
2. Cornell 1995, 212-3.
3. Rickman 1980, 32.
4. Polyb. 3.24; Diod. Sic. 16.69.1; Livy 7.27.2.
5. Cornell 1995, 294.
6. Livy 2.22.5.
7. Livy 2.30.8-10.
8. Livy 8.4.8.
9. Livy 2.33.3-9; Dion. Hal. 6.95.1-3.
10. Livy 2.41.1.
11. Dion. Hal. 8.69.2; Cornell 1995, 300.
12. Livy 2.41.10.
13. Livy 2.64.10-11; 3.4.10-11; 3.5.9.
14. Livy 2.53.4-5.
15. Livy 2.39.2-7; 2.40.1-12.
16. Livy 3.15.5-9; 3.16.6.
17. Livy 3.18.1-10.
18. Livy 3.26.1-3.
19. Livy 3.26.7-29.9.
20. Livy 3.57.8.
21. Livy 3.59.8-3.63.4.
22. Livy 3.65.3-70.11.
23. Livy 4.26.1-4.29.6.
24. Livy 4.35.2; 4.37.4; 4.45.3- 4.47.7.
25. Livy 6.12.2-4.
26. Livy 2.38.6; 3.8.6-10.
27. Livy 3.15.4; 3.2. 2; 3.22.5.
28. Livy 3.1.8.
29. Dion. Hal. 9.58.3-5.
30. Livy 3.1.8; 3.24.10; 3.25.5-9.
31. Livy 4.30.1.
32. Scullard 1967,107-8.
33. Livy 2.44.7-2.47.12.
34. Livy 2.50.1-11.
35. Livy 2.51.2-9; 2.54.1.
36. Livy 4.17.1-20.7.
37. Livy 4.21.6-22.6; 4.23.5-4; 4.25.7-8.
38. Livy 4.30.5-14; 4.31.1-4.35.2.

39. Livy 4.58.6-4.59. 10.
40. Diod. Sic.14.16.5; Livy 4.59.11-4.60.8.
41. Rich 2007, 18.
42. Livy 4.41.3; 5.1.3-9.
43. Livy 5.8.4-13; 5.12.5-13.
44. Livy 5.19.1-11.
45. Livy 5.21.1-5.22.8.
46. Livy 5.21.9.
47. Livy 5.26.3-5.27.15.
48. Livy 6.4.3-6.
49. Livy 5.35.2-5.36.10.
50. Livy 5.37.3.
51. Livy 5.38.1-5.41.4.
52. Livy 5.39.9- 5.43.6.
53. Livy 5.46.6-5.47.10.
54. Livy 5.49.1- 5.50.7; 6.4.2.
55. Livy 5.54.2-5.55.5; 6.4.6.
56. Livy 6.4.7-11.
57. Cic. *Planc.* 19; *Balb.* 31; *de Offic.* 1.35.
58. Livy 6.25.1-6.26.8; 6.36.2.
59. Cornell 1995, 323; Livy 6.26.8.
60. Livy 6.26.8.
61. Livy 9.42.8-9.43.24.
62. Livy 9.55.5-17.
63. Livy 23.19.16-23.20.2; Salmon 1982, 162, 205 n.470.
64. Livy 6.9.4.
65. Livy 6.3.1-6.4.3.
66. Livy 7.11.5-6; 7.15.2; 7.15.2-10.
67. Livy 7.17.6-9.
68. Livy 7.19.1-4
69. Livy 7.19.4; 8.6.8.
70. Livy 7.29.3-7.
71. Livy 7.31.1-4.
72. Cornell 1995, 347.
73. Livy 7.31.8-12; 7.33.6.
74. Livy 7.32.2.
75. Livy 7.33.5-18.
76. Livy 7.34.1-7.36.13.
77. Livy 7.38.1-3.
78. Livy 7.38.5-7.39.2.
79. Livy 7.39.7-7.42.7.
80. Livy 7.41.3; Cornell 1995, 262.
81. Livy 2.24.6-7.
82. Livy 7.42.1.
83. Livy 8.28.1-9; Dion. Hal.14.9.
84. Livy 7.25.5-9.
85. Livy 8.2.5-13.
86. Livy 8.3.9-8.6.7.
87. Livy 8.11.3-4.
88. Livy 8.8.19-8.10.10.
89. Livy 8.11.5-15. 8.12.4-8.13.18.
90. Livy 8.14.1.
91. Livy 8.14.2-4.
92. Livy 8.14.5-8.
93. Carandini 2017, 400; tables 208; 211.
94. Livy 8.14.8; 8.14.12.
95. Livy 8.17.11.
96. Livy 8.14.
97. Livy 8.11.16.
98. Cornell 1995, 351.
99. Pliny *NH* 3. 56-59.
100. Livy 8.14.10-11; 8.17.12.
101. Livy 8.17.12; 8.21.10.
102. Livy 9.20.5.
103. Livy 9.20.10.
104. Livy 8.8.3-5.
105. Cornell 1995, 354; 465 n.29.
106. Livy 8.8.3-14.
107. Polyb. 6.19.1- 6.24.3-4
108. Livy 9.30.3.
109. Cornell 1995, 354; 465 n.29 lists the sources.
110. Burton 2011, 82.
111. Rich 2008, 67; 69; Burton 2011, 82 n.19; 135 n.130.
112. Polyb. *Hist.* 2.23-24.
113. de Ligt 2011, 116-117.
114. Livy 8.22.5-10.
115. Livy 8.23.9.
116. Livy 8.23.17.
117. Livy 8.25.5- 8.26.7.
118. Livy 8.36.9-8.37.2.
119. Livy 9.2.1-9.12.9.
120. Livy 9.15.1-2; 9.18.7-8.
121. Livy 9.27.1-14.
122. Livy 9.29.1-5; 9.31.1; 9.32.1-9.33.2.
123. Livy 9.36.1-9.40.21.
124. Livy 9.38.1-9.43.24.
125. Livy 9.44.5-9.45.4.
126. Livy 10.6.3-10.9.1-2.
127. Livy 10.9.8-9; 10.10.1-5.
128. Livy 10.11.6-10.12.3.
129. Livy 10.12.3-4.
130. Livy 10.13.1 -10.14.4.
131. Livy 10.14.5-10.15.6.

132. Livy 10.15.12-10.17.12.
133. Livy 10.18.1-10. 21.6.
134. Livy 10.21.7.10.
135. Livy 10.21.11-10.24.18.
136. Livy 10.12.1-10.26.13.
137. Livy 10.26.13-10.29.20.
138. Livy 10.31.1- 10.37.5.
139. Livy 10.38.1-10.39.6.
140. Livy 10.39.8-10.42.7
141. Livy *Per.*11.
142. Scullard 1967, 119.
143. Polyb. 2.18.6-9.
144. App. *Samn.* 6.1-2; *Gall.* 11.
145. Salmon 1969, 62; Polyb. 2.19.7-2.21.1.
146. Livy 10.25.11;10.26.8;10.26.14;10.29.3.
147. Cornell 1995, 360.
148. Livy 9.42.2.
149. Livy 8.17.11.
150. Livy 9.41.7; 9.43.7; 9.43.21; 10.5.12; 10.41.12.
151. Livy 8.13.6-9.
152. Livy 8.20.7; 9.24.14; 9.28.6.
153. Livy 8.16.2-14.
154. Livy 8.3.6; 8.24.1.
155. Dion. Hal. 19.5.1-5; Dio frag. 39.6-9; App. *Samn.* 7.2; Cornell 467 n.43.
156. App. *Samn.* 7.3.
157. Plut. *Pyrr.* 14.3-5.
158. App. *Samn.* 10.1-3.
159. Plut. *Pyrr.* 21.9.
160. Keppie 1984, 235 n.8.
161. App. *Samn.* 12.1; Plut *Pyrr.* 24.
162. Polyb. 1.6.
163. Polyb.1.20.13-16.
164. Polyb. 1.9.1-1.10.2.
165. Polyb. 1.10.1-1.11.3.
166. Gargola 2007, 148; Hoyos 1998, 53-57.
167. Polyb. 1.11.4-8.
168. Burton 2011, 129; 237 n.134.
169. Diod. Sic. 23.1.4; 23.2.1; Polyb. 1.9-12.
170. Front. *Strat.* 1.4.11; Polyb. 1.11.9; 1.20.13-16.
171. Polyb. 1.12.1-4.
172. Polyb. 1.16.4-11.
173. Diod. Sic. 23.4.1; Polyb. 1.16.3; Burton 2011, 134-136.
174. Polyb. 1.18.1-7.
175. Polyb. 1.19.1-15.
176. Polyb. 1.20.1-3.
177. Polyb. 1.20.9-16.
178. de Souza 2007, 359-363.
179. Polyb. 1.21.1-3.
180. Polyb. 1.21.4-1.23.10; *ILS* 65.
181. Polyb. 1.24.3-4.
182. Polyb. 1.25.7-1.28.14.
183. Polyb. 1.29.1-10.
184. Polyb. 1.30.1-1.34.12.
185. Livy *Per.*18; App. *Sic.*1.
186. Polyb. 1.36.10.1-37.10; 1.38.6-1.39.6.
187. Polyb. 1.38.1-1.39.15; 1.40.1-1.43.8.
188. Polyb. 1.46.4; 1.59.8.
189. Polyb.1.44.1-1.48.11.
190. Polyb. 1.49.1-1.52.3.
191. Polyb.1.56.1-58.1-6.
192. Polyb.1.59.5-1.63.3.
193. Polyb 1.66.1- 1.81.1.
194. Polyb 3.28.1-3.
195. Polyb. 3.27.1-6; App. *Sic.* 2.3.
196. Polyb. 1.84.1-1.85.7. 1.86.1-1.88.7
197. Hoyos 2019, 20.
198. Lintott 1993, 28.
199. Livy 45.17.7.
200. Pliny *Letters* 10.79.1.
201. App. *Sp.* 99.
202. Rutilius: Serrati 2000a, 113.
203. Cic.*Verres* II.2.32ff.
204. Wilson 1990, 18; Serrati 2000b, 126-130.
205. Cic. *Verres* II.3.13.
206. Serrati 2000b, 131; Livy 21.49.7-8.
207. Wilson 1990, 18; Rickman 1980, 37.
208. Jones 1974, 119-20; Rickman 1980, 37-45.
209. Polyb. 1.24.7.
210. Polyb. 1.71.1-7; 1.79.1-3; 1.82.7.
211. Polyb. 1.83.1-11; Burton 2011, 301-2.
212. Polyb. 1.88.8.
213. App. *Sic.* 2.3.

214. Polyb. 3.10.3; 3.15.10; 3.27.7-8. 3.30.4.
215. Lazenby 1978, 21.
216. Harris 1978, 192-193; Rosenstein 2012, 68-69.
217. Gargola 2007, 149.
218. Strabo *Geog.* 5.2.7.
219. Tac. *Ann.* 2.85.
220. Livy 23.21.6.
221. Polyb. 1.79.7; Strabo *Geog.* 5.2.7.
222. Rosenstein 2012, 263.

## 3 Hannibal, and the Provinces of Spain and Macedonia

1. App. *Ill.*7.
2. Polyb. 2.2.4; 2.4.7-9.
3. Polyb. 2.8.3-13.
4. Polyb. 2.10.8-2.12.2.
5. Sampson 2016, 82-84; Dio frag. 49.7; Polyb. 2.12.3-4.
6. App. *Ill.*7-8.
7. Polyb. 2.16.1.
8. Diod. Sic. 5.3.
9. Sampson 2106,54-56; Zonaras 8.18; Polyb. 2.20.1-2.21.8.
10. Polyb. 2.23.1-2.24.17; Eutropius 3.5; Livy *Per.* 20.
11. Rosenstein 2012,73, table 3; Brunt 1971, 44-60.
12. Polyb. 2.22.1-2.31.10.
13. Polyb. 3.9.6-9; 3.11.5-7.
14. Richardson 1986, 21; Dio frag. 48.
15. Polyb. 2.13.1-4.
16. Richardson 1986, 26-27.
17. Livy 21.2.7; App. *Sp.*7; Polyb.2.13.6-7; 2.22.9-11.
18. App. *Hann.* 2-3; *Sp.* 7; Polyb. 3.30.1-2; Richardson 1986, 21-22.
19. Polyb. 3.15.8-11.
20. Livy 21.17. 4.
21. Polyb. 3.20.1-3.21.8; 3.29.1-10; Livy 21.18.1-14.
22. Livy 21.17.1-9.
23. Livy 21.32.1-2; Polyb 3.41.8.
24. Polyb. 3.60.9; 3.61.7-9; 3.69.14; Livy 21.51.5-7.
25. Livy 22.16.10-15.
26. Polyb. 3.66.9; Livy 21.46.7-10.
27. Polyb. 3.67.1-68.4; 3.69.5-75.7.
28. Polyb. 3.77.3-6; 3.84.6-3.85.4; Livy 21.63.5-22.7.1.
29. Livy 22.31.1.
30. Polyb. 3.87.6-9; Livy 22.8.6-7; 22.11.1-6; Rosenstein 2012, 138.
31. Polyb. 103.4-8. 3.104.1-105.11; Livy 22.25.11-22.30.6.
32. Rosenstein 2012, 141; 147; Polyb. 3.107.7; 3.108.1; Livy 22.61.14; 25.6.7.
33. Polyb. 3.107.9-12; 3.110.8-111.1; Livy 22.36.1-5;22.43.1-44.35.
34. Rosenstein 2012,141; Polyb. 3.113.3-4; Livy 22.45.6-8.
35. Polyb. 3.113.8-9; Livy 22.43.10; 22.46.8-9; 22.47.5.
36. Polyb. 3. 114.1-116.13; Livy 22.45.5- 22.50.12.
37. Livy 22.51.1-4.
38. Livy 23.24.6-23.25.5.
39. Polyb. 6.58.2-13; Livy 22.58.1-22.61.10; 23.25.7-8; Rosenstein 2012, 148.
40. Livy 23.14.1-4; 23.35.5-9.
41. Livy 22.14.3-10; 24.16.18; 24.18.12; 25.20.4; 25.22.3.
42. Livy 25.8.1-10.10; 25.15.5-17; Polyb. 8.27.1-9; 8.30.68; 8.31.2. 8.
43. Livy 23.14.5-23.15.6; 23.17.1-7.
44. Livy 22.49.14; 22.54.1; 23.1.6-7; 23.7.1-2.
45. Livy 22.14-16.
46. Lazenby 1978, 87.
47. Livy 26.11.6.
48. Livy 26.12.1- 26.16.5.
49. Livy 26.26.6-16.
50. Livy 23.32.16-17.
51. Livy 23.34.1-9; Polyb. 7.9.1-17 provides the text.
52. Livy 24.10.4; 24.20.12; Waterfield 2014, 47.
53. Livy 24.40.2-17; 24.44.4.
54. Waterfield 2014, 419.
55. Livy 26.26.1-4.
56. Polyb. 9.42.5-8; 23.8.10; Waterfield 2014, 52.
57. Livy 27.30.16; 28.7.17-18.
58. Livy 28.5.15-28.7.14; 29.12.16.

59. Polyb. 7.2.1-7.3.9; Livy 24.4.1-24.7-9.
60. Livy 24.35.1-24.36.6.
61. Livy 25.23.4- 25.24.7; Polyb. 8.37.1-12. Polybius' account is lost after this point.
62. Livy 25.31.9.
63. Livy 25.24.8- 25.28.9.
64. Livy 26.23.1; 26.28.3. 26.28.10-11; 26.32.6.
65. Livy 27.12.4-6.
66. Livy 26.40.1-18; 27.8.19; Rickman 1980, 37.
67. Livy 27.5.1-19; 27.7.12; 27.8.16-18.
68. Livy reports this episode twice, with different statistics. 27.29.7-8; 28.4.5-7; 28.20.16.
69. Livy 26.28.7-13.
70. Livy 27.15.4- 16.9.
71. Livy 27.12.1-27.15.1.
72. Livy 27.21.5; 27.15.6- 27.17.14.
73. Livy 27.36.10; 27.38.1-51.13.
74. Livy 28.10.4-5; 28.11.8-11.
75. Livy 30.20.1-4; Lazenby 1978, 51.
76. Polyb. 3.76.1-13; Richardson 1986, 36-37; Lazenby 1978, 126.
77. Polyb. 3.76.1-13; 3.95.1-3.97.8; Livy 21.40.1-21.41.11; Lazenby 1978, 126-128; Richardson 1986, 36-37.
78. Livy 23.26.1-23.29.17; 23.32.5-7; 23.48.4-23.49.14.
79. Livy 24.41.1-24.42.11; Richardson 1986, 41.
80. Livy 24.49.7-8; 25.32.1-25.39.18.
81. Livy 26.17.1-16.
82. Livy 26.18.1-26.20.6.
83. Polyb. 6.7; 9.6; 10.10; Livy 26.41.1-47.10.
84. Livy 27.17.4-5; Polyb. 10.38.3-10.40.3.
85. Polyb 10.39.7-8; Livy 27.18.1-19.2.
86. Livy 27.19.2-12.
87. Livy 28.13.6; 28.15.11; 28.35.1-13; Polyb. 11.21.1-124.9; Richardson 1986, 50-51.
88. Richardson 1986, 54; Livy 28.24.3-4; 28.31.5-34.12.
89. Livy 28.17.3.
90. App. *Sp.* 38.
91. Livy 29.14.1.
92. Livy 29.13.3; 29.24.9.
93. Livy 29.35.4-15.
94. Livy 30.1.10.
95. Livy 30.4.1-4.
96. Livy 30.4.9 -30.7.3.
97. Livy 30.7.13- 30.8.9.
98. Lazenby 1978, 218.
99. Livy 30.27.1-30.31.10; 30.32.1-30.35.11
100. Polyb. 18.35.9; Livy 30.37.1-6.
101. Livy28.12.3-8.
102. Livy 21.17.1; 22.22.1; 25.3.6; 27.22.7.
103. Livy 28.38.1; 29.1.19- 29.3.6.
104. Livy 29.13.7; 30.2.7. Richardson 1986, 64-65.
105. Livy 31.20.1-7; 32.7.4; 33.27.1-5.
106. Richardson 1986, 76.
107. App. *Sp.* 99.
108. Livy 31.10.1-4.
109. Livy 21.21.1-22.3; 21.47.4-49.3.
110. Livy 32.28.1; 32.29.5-31.6.
111. Livy 31.1.10.
112. Livy 31.3.3-6.
113. Livy 31.14.5.
114. Livy 31.5.2-4; 31.6.3-6; 31.7.1-15.
115. Livy 31.6.1; 31.8.5.
116. Polyb.16.29.1-16.34.12; Livy 31.17.1-31.18.9.
117. Livy 31.14.3.
118. Livy 31.23.1-12.
119. Livy 21 27.1-21.28.4.
120. Livy 31.33.1-31.40.10; 32.28.3-4.
121. Livy 32.1.1-32.7.10.
122. Livy 32.10.1-32.23.9
123. Polyb. 18.9.3-18.10.3; Livy 32.28.8-9; 32.32.5-32.35.13.
124. Livy 32.25.1-12; 32.38.1-32.39.4.
125. Polyb. 18.22.1.
126. Hoyos 2017, intro to Livy *History of Rome* books 31-34, p.xxxiii.
127. Polyb. 18.22.1-27.7; Livy 33.7.1-33.10.10. Livy admits to using Polybius' account of the battle.

128. Polyb. 18.34.1-18.39.6; Livy 33.11.1- 33.13.15.
129. Polyb. 18.42.1-5; Livy 33.13.1-5; 33.25.4-7.
130. Polyb. 18.39.3-7; 18.44.1-18.45.12; Livy 33.30.1-31.6-11.
131. Polyb. 18.46.1-15; Livy 33.32.1- 33.33.8.
132. Livy 34.26.1-34.29.14.
133. Livy 34.30.1-34.40.7.
134. Livy 34.52.1-12.
135. Livy 33.19.6-33.20.13.
136. Polyb. 18.47.1-2; 18.50.1-9; Livy 33.39.1-7.
137. Livy 33.45.1-33.49.8.
138. Polyb. 18.39.2-4.
139. Livy 35.31.1-35.40.1.
140. Livy 35.20.12-35.21.1.
141. Livy 35.42.1-35.47.8.
142. Livy 35.48.1-36.3.12.
143. Livy 36.4.1-9.
144. Polyb. 20.3; 20.7.3-5; Livy 36.5.1- 36.6.5.
145. Livy 36.7.1-36.8.6.
146. Livy 36.9.1-36.13.9.
147. Livy 36.14.1-36.28.9; 36.30.1-6.
148. Livy 36.33.1-36.34.10.
149. Livy 37.1.1-37.7.16.
150. Livy 36.41.1-7.
151. Polyb. 21.10; Livy 37.18.10-12.
152. Polyb 21.11; Livy 37.25.4.
153. Polyb. 21.13.1-21.15.13; Livy 37.34.1-37.36.9.
154. Polyb. 21.16.1-21.17.12; 21.43.1-27; Livy 37.38.1-37.45.21; 38.38.2-18.
155. Livy 37.47.6-37.51.10; 38.1.1-38.9.13; 38.44.1-6.
156. Livy 37.52.3 Polyb. 22.2-4.
157. Livy 37.55.5-56.6; Rosenstein 2012, 197-8.
158. Polyb. 22.18.1-10; Livy 39.23.5-12; 40.16.3.
159. Polyb. 25.3.1-8; Livy 40.58.
160. Livy 41.22.3; 41.25.5-6.
161. Livy 42.2.1-2; 42.5.8-10; 42.6.3-4; 42.11.4-5.
162. Livy 42.25.1-13.
163. Livy 42.27.1-8; 42.31.8.
164. Livy 42.30.8-11.
165. Livy 42.37.1-42.38.7; 42.45.1-8; Polyb. 27.3.1-5; 27.4.1-10.
166. Livy 42.49.10; 42.55.1.
167. Livy 42.57.1-42.61.11.
168. Polyb. 27.8.1-13; Livy 42.62.12.
169. Livy 43.9.4-43.10.8.
170. App. *Ill.* 2.9.
171. Livy 44.30.1-44.32.5.
172. Polyb. 28.3; Livy 43.14.1-10; 43.17.2-10.
173. Livy 44.1.1- 44.7.7.
174. Livy 44.17.1- 44.18.5; 44.20.1-44.21.11.
175. Livy 44.30.1.
176. Livy 44.32.5-11.
177. Livy 44.34.10; 44.35.10-24.
178. Livy 44.36.1-44.39.9; Plut. *Aem.* 14.
179. Plut. *Aem.* 19.1, following Polybius 29.17.1.
180. Livy 44.40.1-44.46.11; 45.5.1-45.8.8; App. *Ill* 2.9.
181. Livy 45.16.1-2; 45.17.1-3; 45.18.1-8.
182. Livy 45.29.1-45.30.8.
183. Livy 43.4.5-6.
184. Livy 42.56.1-5; 42.63.1- 12.
185. Livy 43.8.7.5-43.8.10.
186. Waterfield 2014, 184-5.
187. Livy 43.4.5-13.
188. Polyb. 29.7-8; Livy 45.24.7.
189. Livy 45.25.1-12.
190. Livy *Per.* 46.
191. Livy 44.29.6-8.
192. Livy 45.10.1-15.
193. Livy 45.21-45.25.4.
194. Polyb. 30.31; Livy *Per.* 46.
195. Cic. *Balb* 35-36.
196. Livy 45.28.6-8; 45.31.1-2.
197. Polyb. 30.13.
198. Livy 45.31.9-11.
199. Livy 45.27.1-4; 45.31.1-15.
200. Livy 45.34.1-6; Plut. *Aem.* 29; Waterfield 2014, 201-204.
201. Livy 45.37.11-12.
202. Livy 45.40.1-5; Diod. Sic. 31.8.10-12; Plut. *Aem.* 32-34.
203. Livy 45.40.7; Plut. *Aem.* 35.
204. Livy *Per.* 48-52; Zonaras 9.28; Vell. 1.11.1-2.

205. Waterfield 2014, 220-222.

## 4 The Two Spains and the Provinces of Africa, Asia and Transalpine Gaul

1. Richardson 1986, 77; Livy 32.28.11.
2. Richardson 1986, 96 n.1; Livy 35.1.1-3.
3. App. *Sp.*51; 55; 59.
4. Richardson 1986, 149-152.
5. Livy 39.56.1-2.
6. Livy 33.21.6-9.
7. Livy 34.7.4-34.21-8.
8. Livy 34.21.7.
9. Richardson 1986, 95.
10. Livy 39.30.1-39.31.18; 39.42-1-3.
11. Livy 40. 35.1-14; 40. 39.1-40.40.15; *Per* 41.
12. Strabo *Geog.* 3.4.13.
13. App. *Sp.* 43-44.
14. Richardson 1986. 107-8; 112.
15. Lintott 1993, 29.
16. Livy 43.2.1-12.
17. Livy 43.3.1-4.
18. App. *Sp.* 57-58.
19. App. *Sp.* 45-47.
20. Polyb. 35.2.1-3; App. *Sp.* 48-50; Richardson 1986, 143.
21. App. *Sp.* 49-51.
22. App. *Sp.* 59-60.
23. Livy *Per.* 49.
24. App. *Pun.* 68-69; Livy *Per* 47.
25. Livy *Per* 48; Polyb. 36.2.1-4.
26. Harris 1979, 234-240.
27. Polyb. 36.3.1; Livy *Per.* 49; App. *Pun.* 74-80.
28. App. *Pun.* 80-85.
29. Livy *Per* 49; App. *Pun.* 98-104.
30. Polyb. 36.16.5.
31. App. *Pun.*105-109; Livy *Per* 50.
32. Livy *Per.* 50; App. *Pun.* 110-112.
33. App. *Pun.* 113-125.
34. App. *Pun.* 113-132; Livy *Per.* 51.
35. *CIL* 1.585; Lewis and Rheinhold 1990, vol. I, 276-283.
36. Broughton 1929, 21-29.
37. App. *Pun.* 135; Broughton, 1929; Raven 1993, 50-51.
38. Livy *Per* 51.
39. Pausanias 7.15.4; Livy *Per.*52.
40. Livy *Per.* 52; Polyb. 39.4.6.
41. Pausanias 7.16.9-10.
42. Polyb. 39.5.2; Waterfield 2014, 225.
43. Polyb. 39.4-6; Pausanias 7.15.9.
44. Strabo *Geog.* 8.6.23.
45. Waterfield 2014, 226.
46. Waterfield 2014, 228.
47. App. *Sp.* 61-64.
48. Livy 33.43.2; Richardson 1986,132.
49. App. *Sp.* 67-69.
50. App. *Sp.* 70-79.
51. Richardson 1986. 189-190.
52. App. *Sp.* 76-79.
53. App. *Sp.* 79-80; 87.
54. App. *Sp.* 81-83; Richardson 1986, 149-150.
55. App. *Sp.* 84.
56. App. *Sp.* 85-86.
57. App. *Sp.* 87- 98.
58. App. *Sp.* 99.
59. Richardson 1986, 120.
60. Richardson 1996, 14.
61. Livy 28.37.10; Richardson 1986, 74; 1996, 103.
62. App. *Sp.* 38.
63. Strabo *Geog.* 3.2.1; Richardson 1986, 119.
64. Livy *Per* 55; Richardson 1986, 132; 147; 153.
65. Richardson 1986, 156-157.
66. App. *BC* 1.7-8.
67. Plut. *Tib.* 9.
68. Lintott 1993, 62.
69. App. *BC* 1.9.
70. Plut. *Tib.* 11-12.
71. Plut. *Tib.* 13-15; App. *BC* 12-13.
72. Plut. *Tib.*13.
73. App. *BC* 1.10.
74. App. *BC* 1.18-19.
75. Plut. *Tib.* 14.
76. App. *BC.* 1.14-15.
77. Plut. *Tib.* 19.
78. App. *BC.* 1.17.
79. App. *BC* 1.18.

80. Livy *Per* 59; Vell. 2.4.4.
81. Plut. *Gaius* 1; App. *BC* 1. 21.
82. Plut. *Gaius* 2.
83. Livy *Per.* 60.
84. Plut. *Gaius* 4; Lintott 1992b, 78.
85. Plut. *Gaius* 5; App. *BC* 1.22; Livy *Per.* 60.
86. Plut. *Gaius* 5.
87. Lintott 1992b, 78.
88. Plut. *Gaius* 7.
89. Plut. *Gaius* 6; App. *BC* 22.
90. Plut. *Gaius* 5; Rickman 1980, 158.
91. Rickman 1980, 159; App. *BC* 21.
92. Livy *Per.* 60.
93. Plut. *Gaius* 9.
94. Plut. *Gaius* 14-17; App. *BC* 25-26; Livy *Per.* 61.
95. Lewis and Rheinhold 1990 vol I. 342-344.
96. Livy *Per.* 59.
97. Jones 1937, 58.
98. Lintott 1992a, 35.
99. Lintott 1992a, 34.
100. Millar 1981, 196-7
101. Jones 1937, 60-61.
102. Jones 1937, 62.
103. Rivet 1988, 3.
104. Strabo *Geog.* 3.4.6; 4.1.5.
105. Strabo *Geog.* 4.1.5; 4.6.3.
106. Ebel 1976, 31.
107. Polyb. 3.95.6-8; Livy 22.19.2-12.
108. Livy *Per* 47; Polyb. 33.9-10.
109. Livy *Per* 60.
110. Strabo *Geog.* 4.1.5; Livy *Per.* 61; Ebel 1976, 68-69; Rivet 1988, 40.
111. Livy *Per.* 61.
112. Ebel 1976,72-73.
113. Rivet 1988, 43.
114. Ebel 1976,35; Rivet 1988, 46.
115. Ebel 1976, 97-99.
116. Drinkwater 1983, 7-8; Rivet 1988, 48.
117. Sall. *Jug.* 5.6-7; 9.3.
118. Sall. *Jug.* 7.1-7; 11.5-12.5; 14.1-15.5.
119. Sall. *Jug.* 20.3-26.3.
120. Sall. *Jug.* 27.1-5.
121. Sall. *Jug.* 29.1-7.
122. Sall. *Jug.* 35.1-36.5.
123. Sall. *Jug.* 36.4-38.4.

124. Sall. *Jug.* 47.1- 55.8.
125. Sall. *Jug.* 46.7.
126. Plut. *Mar.* 6.
127. Sall. *Jug.* 55.1-65.5.
128. Sall. *Jug.* 73.2-7; Plut *Mar.* 8.
129. Sall. *Jug.* 84.1-86.3. Plut *Mar.* 9.
130. Sall. *Jug.* 75.1-82.3.
131. Sall. *Jug.* 87.1-91.7.
132. Sall. *Jug.* 96.1-3.
133. Sall. *Jug.* 92.5-96.1-3.
134. Sall. *Jug.* 97.1-99.3.
135. Sall. *Jug.* 102.1-113.6 ; Plut *Mar.* 10; *Sul.* 3.
136. Sall. *Jug.* 65.1.
137. App. *Ill.* 11; Livy *Per.* 47; 62.
138. App. *Ill.* 10; Livy *Per.* 56.
139. App. *Ill.* 10; Livy *Per.* 59.
140. Livy *Per* 60; Plut. *Gaius* 1.
141. Livy *Per* 62.
142. Livy *Per* 63; App. *Ill.* 5; Eutropius 4.24.
143. Livy *Per* 65.

## 5 From Marius to Pompey and the New Eastern Provinces

1. Livy *Per.* 63; Strabo *Geog.* 5.214; Plut. *Mar.* 16; Tac. *Germ.* 37.
2. Livy *Per.* 65.
3. Livy *Per.* 67.
4. Livy *Per* 67; Plut. *Mar.* 19; 25; Tac *Germ.* 37.
5. Plut. *Mar.* 14.
6. Front. *Strat.* 4.2.2.
7. Livy *Per.* 67. Plut. *Mar.* 15.
8. Livy *Per.* 68; Plut. *Mar.* 21.
9. Plut. *Mar.* 16-24.
10. Plut. *Mar.* 25-26.
11. Plut. *Mar* 29.
12. App. *BC* 1.28; Mackay 2009, 108-109.
13. App. *BC* 1.28; Plut. *Mar.*29; Mackay 2009, 109.
14. Lintott 1992, 97.
15. Mackay 2009, 109-111.
16. Mackay 2009, 159.
17. Lintott 1992, 97-98.
18. Plut. *Mar* 29.
19. App. *BC* 1.30.

20. App. *BC* 1. 31; Livy *Per* 69.
21. App. *BC* 1.32-33; Plut. *Mar.* 30.
22. Plut. *Mar.* 31.
23. App. *BC* 1.35-36.
24. Gabba 1992, 104.
25. App. *BC* 1.35.
26. Gabba 1992, 110 n.30.
27. Livy *Per*.71; App. *BC* 1.36.
28. Dart 2014, 9-2.
29. App. *BC* 1.37-38.
30. App. *BC* 1.42; Gabba 1992, 115; Dart 2014, 18.
31. Livy *Per* 67; App. *BC* 1.39-40.
32. Plut. *Mar.* 33.
33. *ILS* 8888.
34. App. *BC* 1.42; Dart 2014,122.
35. Livy *Per.* 74; App. *BC* 1.49; Dart 2014 122.
36. Plut. *Mar.* 32.
37. App. *BC*.1.40.
38. Livy *Per*.72; App. *BC* 1.38; Dart 2014, 99-100.
39. App. *BC* 1.43.
40. App. *BC* 1. 46.
41. App. *BC*.1.47-48.
42. App. *BC* 1.49; Livy *Per*.80.
43. App. *BC* 1.51-52.
44. App. *BC* 52; Livy *Per*.74.
45. Gabba 1992, 126-127; Sherwin-White 1973, 157-158.
46. Diod. Sic.37.2.13-14; Sherwin-White 1973, 146.
47. Livy *Per.* 98; Gabba 1992,156 n.2; Dart 2014, 211.
48. Dart 2014, 185-187.
49. Sherwin-White 1973, 150.
50. Gabba 1992, 128.
51. Plut. *Sul.* 5.
52. Hind 1992, 140.
53. App. *Mith.* 11-21; Hind 1992, 144-147.
54. App. *Mith.* 22.
55. App. *Mith* 23-27; Hind 1992, 149-150.
56. Plut. *Sul.* 8; *Mar.* 35.
57. Livy *Per.* 67; App. *BC* 1.55-56; Plut. *Mar.* 8.
58. Plut. *Sul.* 8; *Mar.* 32; Dart 2014, 185-187.
59. Plut. *Sul.* 8-9.
60. App. *BC* 1.7-58; Plut. *Sul.* 9; *Mar.* 35.
61. App. *BC* 1.59.
62. Plut. *Mar.* 36-41; App. *BC* 60-62; 67.
63. App. *BC* 1.63; Livy *Per.* 77.
64. App. *BC* 1.64.
65. Plut. *Sul.* 10.
66. App. *Mith* 28-29; Livy *Per.* 78.
67. Plut. *Sul.* 11-13; App. *Mith* 33.
68. Plut. *Sul.* 14.
69. App. *Mith* 42-45; Plut. *Sul.*16-18.
70. Plut. *Sul.* 22.
71. App. *Mith.* 49-51; Plut. *Sull.* 20-21.
72. App. *Mith.* 54-56.
73. App. *Mith.* 51; Livy *Per.* 82.
74. App. *Mith.* 52.
75. Plut. *Sul.* 23-24; Hind 1992,160 n.92.
76. Plut. *Sul.* 25; App. *Mith.* 59-60.
77. Plut. *Sul.*17; Hind 1992, 162.
78. App. *Mith.* 61.
79. Plut. *Sul.* 25.
80. Plut. *Mar.* 41; App. *BC* 1. 64.
81. App. *BC* 1.65.
82. App. *BC* 1.66-68.
83. Seager 1992a, 177; App. *BC* 1.68; Plut. *Pomp.* 3.
84. Plut. *Mar.* 41-42.
85. Seager, 1992a, 165-207, esp. 179.
86. App. *BC* 1.71-75. Plut. *Mar.* 46.
87. Livy *Per.* 80.
88. App. *BC* 1.77-78; Seager 1992a, 184.
89. App. *BC* 1.79; Plut. *Sul.* 27.
90. Plut. *Cras.* 4-6.
91. Plut. *Pomp.* 6; App. *BC* 1.79-80.
92. App. *BC* 1.80; Plut. *Pomp.* 8.
93. App. *BC* 1.85-6; Plut. *Sul.* 28.
94. Richardson 1986. 163.
95. App. *BC* 1.87-88.
96. App. *BC* 1.89.
97. Seager 1992a, 187; 191; App. *BC* 1.91-92; Plut. *Sul.* 28.
98. Plut. *Sul.* 29; App. *BC* 1.92-93.
99. Plut. *Sul.* 30.
100. Seager 1992a, 197; Livy *Per.* 89; Plut. *Sul.* 33.
101. App. *BC* 1.96; Plut. *Pomp.* 10.

102. Val. Max. 6.2.8; Syme 1939, 27.
103. Plut. *Pomp.* 10.
104. Livy *Per.* 86.
105. Plut. *Pomp.* 11.
106. App. *BC* 1.80.
107. Plut. *Pomp.* 2; 12.
108. Plut. *Pomp.* 14.
109. Livy *Per.* 89.
110. Plut. *Pomp.* 14.
111. App. *BC* 1.98.
112. Plut. *Sul.* 33.
113. Livy *Per.* 89.
114. App. *BC* 100.
115. Cloud 1992, 414-515.
116. App. *BC* 1.101.
117. App. *BC* 1.97.103-6; Plut. *Pomp.* 15; *Sul.* 38.
118. Seager 1979, 14.
119. Gruen 1974, 14-16; Seager 1992b, 209.
120. App. *BC* 1.107.
121. Plut. *Pomp.* 16; *Brut.* 4.
122. App. *BC* 1.107; Plut. *Pomp.* 15-17; *Sul.* 34.
123. Livy *Per.* 90.
124. Plutarch's *Sertorius* gives most detail about the war in Spain; App. *BC* 1.108-115.
125. Cic. *de Imp.* 62.
126. Plut. *Pomp.* 19.6; *Sert.* 21.5.
127. App. *BC* 1. 109.
128. App. *BC* 1.110 is alone in saying that Metellus was present at the battle; Plut. *Pomp.* 18; *Sert.* 19; Greenhalgh 1980, 237.
129. Livy *Per.* 92; Plut. *Sert.* 21.
130. Sall. *Hist.* 2.98; Greenhalgh 1980, 51-2.
131. Seager 1979, 19.
132. Sall. *Hist* 2.98.10; Seager 1979, 19-20.
133. App. *BC* 1.112.
134. Greenhalgh 1980, 55-6.
135. App. *BC* 1.113.
136. Plut. *Pomp.* 20; *Sert.* 27.
137. Seager 1992b, 221.
138. Cic. *Balb.* 19; 32; 38.
139. Pliny *NH* 3.18; Sall. *Hist.* 3.89
140. Livy *Per.* 90; 93.
141. Livy *Per.* 91 Eutropius 6.2.2.
142. Livy *Per.* 92; 95.
143. Livy *Per.* 95-97; App. *BC* 1.116-120; Plut. *Cras.* 8-10.
144. Plut. *Cras.*11.
145. Plut. *Pomp.* 21.
146. Seager 1979, 27 n.111; Aulus Gellius *Attic Nights* 14.7.2.
147. Livy *Per.* 97; Plut. *Pomp.* 21.
148. Plut. *Pomp.* 22; App.*BC* 1.121; Sall. *Hist.* 4.45.
149. Gruen 1974, 28-30; Livy *Per.* 97; Vell. 2.
150. Seager 1979, 18; 1992, 211; Greenhalgh 1980, 65.
151. Seager 1979, 24.
152. Livy *Per.* 98.
153. Plut. *Pomp.* 23.
154. Seager 1979, 33 n.44.
155. Gruen 1974, 22; 30; 538-539; de Souza 1999, 145; Rickman 1980, 50-51; Seager 1992b, 213; Vell. 2.31.2-3.
156. Cic. *de Imp.* Dio 36.22.
157. Plut. *Pomp.* 25; Dio 36.37.1.
158. Vell. 2.31.1; Tac. *Ann.* 15.25; Seager 1979, 35.
159. Plut. *Pomp.* 25; Dio 36.24.1.
160. Sall. *Hist.* 5.24; Vell. 2.23.1.
161. Plut. *Pomp.* 25; Vell. 2.31; Rickman 1980, 51.
162. Plut. *Pomp.* 26; Livy *Per.* 99; App. *Mith.* 94.
163. App. *Mith.* 95; Florus 3.6.7-14, translated in Leach 1978, 213-2.
164. Plut. *Pomp.* 28; App. *Mith* 96; Strabo *Geog.* 8.7.5.
165. Sherwin-White 1992, 234-5.
166. Livy *Per.* 94; 95; Plut. *Luc.* 7; 9-11; App. *Mith.* 72-78.
167. App. *Mith.* 82-83.
168. App. *Mith.* 84-87; Plut. *Luc.* 21-23.
169. App. *Mith.* 89.
170. Seager1979, 31-2. App. *Mith.* 88.
171. App. *Mith.* 90; Dio 36.2.2.
172. Plut. *Pomp.* 30; *Luc.* 35; App. *Mith.*97.
173. Seager 1979, 43.
174. Dio 36.45.3; Seager 1979, 45.

175. Plut. *Pomp.* 31; *Luc.* 36; Dio 36.46.1-2.
176. Dio 36.47.1- 36.49.8.
177. App. *Mith* 104; Dio 36.48.2-36.53.4; Plut. *Pomp.* 32-33; Vell. 2.27.3.
178. Seager 1979, 50, n. 54.
179. Dio 36.53.5-36.54.5.
180. App. *Mith.* 103.
181. Dio 37.1-37.5.1.
182. Seager 1979, 49.
183. Dio 37.5.2-5.
184. Plut. *Pomp.* 34; Vell. 2.40.1; Dio 37.6.3
185. Sartre 2005, 38; App. *Syr.* 49-51; *Mith* 106.
186. Dio 37.7a; App. *Syr.* 49.
187. App. *Mith.* 114.
188. Sartre 2005, 40.
189. Jos. *AJ* 14.46.
190. Jos. *BJ* 1.139; *AJ* 14.53; Dio 37.11.1-37.14.2.
191. Jos. *AJ* 14.72-73; Dio 37.15.2.-16.4.
192. App. *Mith.* 113.
193. Dio 37.14.1-2.
194. App. *Mith*.114-115.
195. App. *Mith.* 114.
196. Seager 1979, 53; Dio 37.20.2.
197. Strabo *Geog*.12.3.1.
198. App. *Mith.* 114-5.
199. Sartre 2005, 42-44.
200. App. *Mith.* 118.
201. Sherwin-White 1992, 269-270.

## 6 Caesar, the Conquest of Gaul, and the Civil War

1. Wiseman 1992a, 342-3; Seager 1979, 58.
2. Gruen 1974, 389-396.
3. Seager 1979, 63.
4. Wiseman 1992a, 351.
5. Sall. *Cat*.18.
6. Gruen 1974, 416-417.
7. Dio 37.29.1.
8. Sall. *Cat*. 33.
9. Sall. *Cat*. 39-43.
10. Dio 37.34.1.
11. Sall. *Cat.* 51.1-43; App. *BC* 2.6; Suet. *DJ* 14; Dio 37.36.1-2.
12. Sall. *Cat.* 55.6.
13. Sall. *Cat.* 56-61; Dio 37.39.1-37.40.2.
14. Plut. *Caes.* 12.
15. Plut. *Caes.* 11; App. *BC* 2.8.26; Suet. *DJ* 54.
16. App. *BC* 2.2.9.
17. Suet. *DJ* 20.
18. Cic. *Ad Att.* 2.3.
19. Plut. *Caes*.14; Dio 38.5.1-2; Gruen 1974, 72; 398-9; 403.
20. Dio 38.3.2-3.
21. Dio 38.4.3.
22. App. *BC* 2.10; Plut. *Pomp.* 47.
23. Plut. *Caes.* 14; Gruen 1974, 397.
24. Wiseman 1992b, 371; App. *BC* 2.12; Dio 38.7.1.
25. App. *BC* 2.11; Plut. *Caes* 14; Suet. *DJ* 20.
26. Gruen 1974, 400-403, Suet. *DJ* 20; App. *BC* 2.10; Dio 38.7.3.
27. Suet. *DJ* 20.4; App. *BC* 2.13.
28. Dio 38.7.4-6.
29. Gruen 1974, 239-240.
30. Suet. *DJ* 20; App. *BC* 2.12; Dio 37.41.2-4; 38.9.2-4.
31. Dio 37.47.1.
32. Suet. *DJ* 22.
33. Cic. *Ad Att.* 2.18.
34. Plut. *Caes*.14; Suet. *DJ* 20.
35. Cic. *Ad Att.* 2.18-2.19.
36. Caes. *BG* 1.2-29; Dio 38.31.2-38.33.6.
37. Drinkwater 1983, 12.
38. Strabo *Geog.* 4.3.4; Caes. *BG* 1.31.
39. Plut. *Caes*.19; Dio 34.3; Caes. *BG* 1.33; 1.36.
40. Dio 38.34.2; 38.36-46.
41. Caes. *BG* 1.38-40. Dio 38.50.4.
42. Dio 39.6.1-39.9.3.
43. Plut. *Caes.* 20; Caes. *BG* 2.1.
44. Caes. *BG* 2.3-5; Dio 39.1.3-4.
45. Caes. *BG* 2.5-10; 2.16-28.
46. Caes. *BG* 2.35; Dio 39.5.1.
47. Cic. *Ad Fam.* 1.7.10; Gruen 1974, 100.

48. Suet. *DJ*. 24.1-2; Plut *Pomp.* 51; *Caes.* 21; App. *BC* 1.17.62.
49. Caes. *BG* 3.7-28; Dio 39.44.1-2.
50. Caes. *BG* 4.1-19; Dio 39.48.4-5.
51. Caes. *BG* 4.20-21; Suet *DJ* 58.
52. Caes. *BG* 4.29.
53. Caes. *BG* 4.25.
54. Caes. *BG* 4.24; 4.33.
55. Caes. *BG* 4.37-38.
56. Caes. *BG* 5.6-7.
57. Caes. *BG* 5.10.
58. Caes. *BG* 5.18-23.
59. Plut. *Caes.* 23; *Pomp.* 53; Suet. *DJ* 26. Dio 39.64.1.
60. Gruen 1974, 450-451.
61. Caes. *BG* 5.26-48; Dio 40.7-9.
62. Caes. *BG* 49-52.
63. Caes. *BG* 6.1-4.
64. Caes. *BG* 6.34.
65. Caes. *BG* 6.36-42; Dio 40.32.3-5.
66. Dio 40.45.1.
67. Dio 40.46.-50.
68. Plut. *Pomp.* 55; App. *BC* 2.24.90-93; Dio 40.51.3; 40.53.1.
69. App. *BC* 2.23.87; Dio 40.52.1; 40.55.2.
70. Gruen 1974, 455.
71. Gruen 1974, 456-458; Dio 40.51; Suet. *DJ* 26; 28; App. *BC* 2.25.96.
72. Caes. *BG* 7.9.
73. Caes. *BG* 7.10-34.
74. Caes *BG* 7.35-40; Dio 40.35-37.
75. Caes. *BG* 7.44-52.
76. Caes. *BG* 7.55-65.
77. Caes. *BG* 7.69-74.
78. Caes. *BG* 7.75-88.
79. Caes. *BG* 7.90.
80. Caes. *BG* 8.2.
81. Caes. *BG* 8.3.
82. Caes. *BG* 8.4-24.
83. Caes. *BG* 8. 30-44.
84. Caes. *BG* 8.48-49.
85. Caes. *BG* 8.52.
86. Caes. *BG* 8. 54.
87. Drinkwater 1983, 18-20.
88. Cic. *Ad Att.* 5.11.2.
89. Suet. *DJ* 28-29; Caes. *BG* 8.53. Dio 40.59.1; Livy *Per.* 108; Gruen 1974, 463 n.50.
90. Gruen 1974, 463 n.50; 492-3.
91. Suet. *DJ* 50.
92. Cic. *Ad Fam.* 8.6.5; App. *BC* 2.28; Gruen 1974; 480-485.
93. Suet. *DJ* 29; App. *BC* 2.27; Plut. *Pomp.* 58; *Caes.* 30.
94. Plut. *Pomp.* 57.
95. App. *BC* 2.28.
96. Cic. *Ad Fam* 8.10.12.
97. Caes. *BG* 8.52-55; Plut. *Pomp.* 56.3; 57.4.
98. App. *BC* 2.30.
99. App. *BC* 2.31; Plut. *Pomp.* 59; 40.64.4; 40. 66.1.
100. App. *BC* 2.32.
101. Cic. *Ad Att.* 7.6; 7.7.
102. Cic *Ad Att.* 7.8.5.
103. Caes. *BC* 1.1; Plut *Pomp.* 59; C 30; App. *BC* 2.32; Dio 41.1.
104. Caes. *BC* 1.5.
105. Plut. *Caes.* 31.
106. Caes. *BC* 1.5; App. *BC* 2.33; Dio 41.3.
107. Suet *DJ* 31-33; Dio 41.4; Plut. *Caes.* 32.
108. Rawson CAH 424.
109. Suet *DJ* 32; Plut. *Pomp.* 60; Caes. 32.
110. Caes *BC* 1.6; 1.30; App *BC* 2.34. Dio 41.3.3.
111. Caes *BC* 1.14; Plut. *Pomp.* 60; App *BC* 3.37; Dio 41.6.1.
112. Dio 41.2-4. Plut. *Caes* 34.
113. Caes *BC* 1.9-11.
114. Caes *BC* 1.25.5; 1.26.2.
115. Cic. *Ad Att.* 8.11a; 8.11b-d.
116. Caes *BC* 1.15-23.
117. Dio 41.5.1-6.1; 41.10.3.
118. Caes. *BC* 1.25-28; App. *BC* 2.40; Plut. *Caes.* 35; P.62-64.
119. Dio 41.18.1.
120. Caes *Afr.* 19; 40; Dio 41.41.1-41.42.7
121. Dio 41.117; App. *BC* 2.41; Plut. *Caes.* 35.5.
122. Suet *DJ* 34.
123. Caes. *BC* 1.33-37; 2.1-16.
124. Caes. *BC* 1.37-87; App.2.42-42; Dio 41.18-24; Plut. *Caes.* 36.
125. App. *BC* 2.47; Dio 41.35.
126. Caes. *BC* 3.1.1-3.2.1.

127. Caes. *BC* 3.1.2. Plut. *Caes.*. 37.
128. App. *BC* 2.48; 2.54.
129. Caes. *BC* 3.4-5.
130. Caes. *BC* 3.11-13. App. *BC* 2.52.
131. Caes. *BC* 3.13.
132. Plut. *Caes*. 38; App. *BC* 2.57; Dio 41.46.
133. Dio 41.48; Caes. *BC* 3.15-19.
134. Gelzer 1968, 230-231.
135. Cic. *Ad Fam.* 9.9.
136. Caes. *BC* 3.49.
137. App. *BC* 2.62-63; Plut *Caes*. 39; Dio 41.51.
138. Caes. *BC* 3.76-81; App. *BC* 2.65-66; Dio 41.52; Plut. *Pomp.* 66-67; *Caes*. 40.
139. Caes. *BC* 3.84-86.
140. Caes. *BC* 3. 89.
141. Caes. *BC* 3.88-97; Plut. *Pomp.* 69; *Caes*. 44. 2.75-82; 41. 41.58-63.
142. Caes. *BC* 3.97-97.
143. Suet *DJ* 30; Plut. *Caes*. 46.
144. Dio 42.21.
145. Dio 42.27.3.
146. Plut. *Ant*. 9.2; 10; Dio 42.32-33.
147. Plut. *Pomp.* 73-80; App. *BC* 2.86; Dio 42.3-4.
148. Plut. *Caes*. 48-49; Dio 42.34-35.
149. Caes. *Alex*. 1-2.
150. Dio 42.39; App. *BC* 2.90.
151. Caes. *Alex*. 9-12.
152. App. *BC* 14-26; Plut Caes 49; Suet *DJ* 64; Dio 42-40.
153. Caes. *Alex*. 20-31.
154. Caes. *Alex*. 33.
155. App. *BC* 2.90.
156. Caes. *Alex*. 34.
157. Caes. *Alex*. 35-41; Plut. *Caes*. 50.
158. Caes. *Alex*. 67-76.
159. Plut. *Caes* 50.
160. Dio 42.49.
161. Plut. *Caes*. 51; Dio 42.52-54.
162. App. *BC* 2.93; Plut *Caes.*51; Dio 42.52-54.
163. Caes. *Afr*. 1-2; Dio. 42.57.4.
164. Caes. *Afr* 3; Dio 42.58.
165. Caes. *Afr*. 6-7.
166. Caes. *Afr* 11-18; App. *BC* 2.95.
167. Caes. *Afr*. 20.
168. Caes. *Afr*. 25; Dio 43.3.
169. Caes. *Afr*. 24; 30-34;37.
170. Caes. *Afr*. 41-2; 48.
171. Caes. *Afr*. 38-56.
172. Caes. *Afr*. 53; 62-63.
173. Caes. *Afr* 79-80; Dio 43.
174. Caes. *Afr* 80-88; Dio 43.10-11.
175. Caes. *Afr* 93-94.
176. Dio 43.9.
177. Caes. *Afr* 87-88; Dio 43.10-11.
178. Dio 43.1.4; 43.47.3; Gelzer 1968, 278 n.1; 288.
179. Plut. *Caes*. 55.
180. Dio 43.19.
181. Dio 43.21.3-43.22.4; Suet. DJ 41.3; Plut. *Caes*. 55.
182. Dio 43.24.4; 43.25.2.
183. Suet. *DJ* 41; Dio 43.25.3.
184. Cic. *Ad Fam.* 9.15.4.
185. Suet. *DJ* 40; Dio 43.26.
186. Suet. *DJ* 52
187. Suet. *DJ* 79; Nic. Dam. *Aug*. 28.
188. Dio 43.29.1-43.31.1.
189. Dio 43.29.1-43.30.5.
190. Caes. *Sp*. 3-5; Dio 43.31.4; 43.32.6.
191. Dio 43.33.2; Caes. *Sp*. 6;19.
192. Caes. *Sp.*22-24.
193. Caes. *Sp*. 28.
194. Caes. *Sp*. 29-31.
195. Plut. *Caes*. 56.
196. Caes. *Sp*. 36-39.
197. Caes. *Sp*. 32.
198. Caes. *Sp*. 33-42.
199. Lewis and Rheinhold 1990 vol 1, 453-461.
200. Richardson 1996, 120-121.
201. Cic. *Phil*. 2.34.
202. Cic. *Phil*. 2.34.
203. Plut. *Ant*. 11; Cic. *Phil*. 2.78.
204. Huzar 1978, 74.
205. Plut. *Ant*.11.3; Cic. *Phil*. 2.79-84.
206. Suet. *DJ* 76; App. *BC* 2.106; Dio 43.44.
207. Dio 44.6.5-6; Huzar 1978,76; Weinstock 1971.
208. Dio 44.11; 46.17.
209. Plut. *Caes*. 61.
210. Suet. *DJ* 79; App. *BC* 2.109; Pelling 1988, 144 enumerates the possible motives.

211. App. *BC* 2.117; Dio 44.19.
212. Suet. *DJ* 82; Dio 44.19.5.
213. Cic. *Ad Att*.14.21; 14.14.
214. App. *BC* 2.118.
215. App. *BC* 2.118; Dio 44.22.
216. App. *BC* 2.125; 3.5; Dio 44.53. Plut. *Ant*.15; Pelling 1988, 15.
217. Cic. *Phil*. 2.35-6; 2.93; 5.11-12. Syme 1939, 97-111; Pelling 1988, 156.
218. App. *BC*. 2.127-28; 2.133-5.
219. Cic. Ad Att. 4.10; 14.14.
220. Cic. Ad Att. 14.13; *Phil*. 2.95; 5.11-12.
221. Cic. Ad Att. 14.6; 14.9; 14.14.
222. Dio 44.34.
223. Dio 45.24; Syme 1939, 107.
224. Suet. *DJ* 83.
225. Syme, R. 1988, 159ff; Schmitthenner, W. 1952.
226. Suet. *DJ* 84.
227. Cic. *Ad Att*. 14.10; Dio 44.36-49; App. *BC* 2.144-7; Plut. *Ant* 14.6-8; Pelling 1988 153-4.
228. Cic. *Ad Att*. 14.10.
229. Suet. *DJ* 72.

## 7 Antony Falls, Octavian Rises

1. Suet. *Aug*. 8; 89; Nic. Dam. *Aug*. 16; Vell. 2.59; App. *BC* 3.9; Dio 45.3.
2. Suet. *Aug*. 8; App. *BC* 3.10; Cic. *Ad Att*. 14.12.
3. Cic. *Ad Att*. 14.5; 14.10.
4. Cic. *Ad Att*. 14.11; 14.12.
5. Cic. *Ad Fam*. 6.8.1.
6. Cic. *Ad Att*. 14.11; 14.12.
7. Nic. Dam. *Aug*. 18.
8. Nic. Dam. *Aug*. 28.
9. App. *BC* 3.28; Nic. Dam. *Aug*. 28.
10. App. *BC* 3.14-20.
11. *RG* 2.
12. App. *BC* 3.25.
13. App. *BC* 3.40; 3.43; Dio 45.12; Suet. *Aug*. 10; Nic. Dam. *Aug*. 31.
14. Cic. *Ad Att*. 16.8; 16.9.
15. App. *BC* 3.45-46.
16. Nic. Dam. *Aug*. 28.
17. Cic. *Phil*. 5.16.45-46.
18. *RG* 1.
19. Cic. *Ad Fam*.11.20; 11. 21.
20. Vell. 2.62.5.
21. Dio 46.44.2; App. *BC* 3.89-90.
22. Dio 46.46.2; App. *BC* 3.94.
23. Dio 47.17.
24. Dio 46.46.1.
25. Dio 46.48.2; App. *BC* 3.94.
26. App. *BC* 3.95.
27. App. *BC* 3.80.
28. Cic. *Ad Fam*. 11.9.1; 11.10.3.
29. App. *BC* 3.98.
30. App. *BC* 3.96.
31. App. *BC* 4.2.
32. App. *BC* 4.7; Dio 47.2.2.
33. Millar 1973, 51; Gowing 1992; Bleicken 1990.
34. App. *BC* 5.132.
35. App. *BC* 4.2-3.
36. App. *BC* 4.3; Keppie 1983.
37. Dio 47.15.2-4.
38. App. *BC* 4.6.
39. Dio 47.8; Plut. *Ant*. 21; Vell. 2.66.
40. Vell. 2.66; Dio 47.7; App. *BC* 4.19-20.
41. Livy *Per*. 120.
42. App. *BC* 4.8-11.
43. App. *BC* 4.1.
44. App. *BC*. 4.32; Dio 47.16; Plut *Ant*. 21.
45. Dio 47.18.4; 47.19.3; 51.22.1.
46. *ILS* 73 and 73a.
47. Dio 47.21.
48. Dio 47.29.1-4.
49. Dio 47.21.4-7. Cic. *Ad M. Brut*. 1.2a.2.
50. Cic. *Phil*.10. 25-26.
51. App. *BC* 3.63; 78.
52. App. *BC* 4.106.
53. App. *BC* 4.110-114; Dio 47.42-45.
54. Suet. *Aug*. 13.2.
55. App. *BC* 4.137-139; Dio 47.39.
56. App. *BC* 5.3; 5.22; Dio 48.12.5.
57. App. *BC* 5.12.
58. App *BC* 5.5; Keppie 1983, 60.
59. Osgood 2006, 108-151.
60. Dio 48.4.1.
61. Dio 48.6.1-4.

62. Plut *Ant*. 30; App. *BC* 5.52; Pelling 1988, 198; 1996,15.
63. App. *BC* 5.18-24; 5.27-48; Dio 48.13-14.
64. App. *BC* 5.48; Dio 48. 14.6 Suet. *Aug*. 15.
65. Plut. *Ant*. 23.2-4.
66. App. *BC* 5.7.
67. Plut. *Ant*. 25; App. *BC* 5.8; Dio 44.39.
68. App. *Sy* 51.
69. Dio 48.24.4-26.5.
70. App. *BC* 5.56; Dio 48.7; 48.16.
71. App. *BC* 5.59; 5.64; Dio 48.28.
72. App. *BC* 5.75.32.
73. Plut. *Ant*. 31; App. *BC* 5.65; Dio 48.31.
74. Plut. *Ant*. 32; App. *BC* 5.67-69; Dio 48.38.
75. App. *BC* 133-144.
76. Pelling 1988, 201; Reynolds, 1982, nos. 10; 12; 13.
77. Dio 49.19-20.
78. Plut. *Ant*. 35; App. *BC* 5.93-95; Dio 48.54.
79. Plut. *Ant*. 23; Pelling 1988, 217; Huzar 1978, 148-149.
80. Dio 49.23.
81. Plut. *Ant*. 39; Dio 49.25-26; Vell. 2.82.
82. Plut. *Ant*. 40-51; Dio 49.28-29.
83. App. *BC* 123-126.
84. Dio. 49.42. 2-49.43.1.
85. Huzar 1978, 181.
86. Plut. *Ant*. 54.
87. Dio 49.39.
88. Plut. *Ant*. 54; Dio 49.40.3-49.41.3.
89. Dio 50.2.
90. Plut. *Ant*. 57.4; Dio 50.3.
91. Suet. *Aug*. 17.
92. Plut. Ant. 58.4-59.1.
93. Syme 1939, 282 n.1; Huzar 1978, 208.
94. *RG* 25.2.
95. Plut. *Ant*. 61-62.
96. Dio 50.11-13.
97. Plut. *Ant*. 68.
98. Dio 50.15.
99. Dio 50.33.
100. Plut. *Ant*. 67.
101. Plut. *Ant*. 69.
102. Plut *Ant*. 72; Dio 41.6; 51.7.
103. Plut. *Ant*. 81.
104. Plut *Ant*. 77; 83-86; Dio 51.12.-13; Pelling 1988, 318-320; Huzar 1978, 227.
105. Dio 51.19.3-5.
106. *RG* 27.1.
107. *ILS* 8995.
108. Dio 57.17.1; Tac. *Ann*. 2.59.
109. Millar 1981,184.
110. Millar 1981, 182.
111. Alston 1995, 86-92.
112. Dio 51.20.1.
113. Suet *Aug*. 22.
114. *ILS* 81.
115. Levick 2010, 69.
116. Vell 2.89.
117. Suet. *Aug*. 28.
118. Dio 53.11.1-53.12. 53.17.1.
119. Strabo *Geog*. 17.3.25.
120. Dio 53.12.4.
121. Suet. *Aug*. 47; Dio 53.12.3-4.
122. Dio 53.13.1.
123. Dio 53.32.5.
124. Syme 1939, 314; Kienast 1982,74-75; Raaflaub 2009, 209, 218.
125. Dio 53.32.5.
126. Sherk 1988, p5, no.2B.
127. Dio 53.14.4.
128. Broughton 1929, 56-57; App. *Pun* 136.
129. Tac. *Ann*. 4.23.
130. Strabo *Geog*. 4.1.1.
131. Drinkwater 1983, 20-21; 97.
132. Drinkwater 1983, 22; 95.
133. Dio 53.22.5.
134. *ILS* 212 col. 2, lines 36-40=Sherk 1988 no. 55.
135. Livy *Per*. 139; Dio 53.22.5.
136. *RG* 26; Cooley 2009, 220.
137. Dio 54.4.1.
138. Dio 53.12.6; 54.20.5.
139. Dio 54.32-33.
140. Dio 55.1-2; Vell 2.97.
141. Tac. *Ann*. 4.44.
142. Drinkwater 1983 54-55; Wightman 1985, 55.

143. Dio 54.5.1-3; Richardson 1996, 134-5.
144. Dio 49.23.3; 51.2.1-2.
145. Coolidge 2009, 7.
146. Wilkes 1969, 46-47.
147. App. *Ill.* 29.
148. Livy 40.34.
149. Strabo *Geog.* 5.1.7.
150. Strabo *Geog.* 4.6.8-9; Alfoldy 1974, 53.
151. Vell. 2.29.3.
152. *CIL* 5.1389; 1838=*ILS* 1349.
153. *RG* 30; Cooley 2009, 247; Dio 54.34.3-4.
154. Dio 53.12.5-7; *ILS* 3320.
155. Vell. 1.39.3; Suet *Tib.* 16-17.
156. Vell 2.116.
157. Dio 55.29.3.
158. *ILS* 1349.
159. *RG* 15.
160. *RG* 16.1.
161. *RG* 3.
162. Keppie 1983, 74; 82.
163. *RG* 15.
164. *RG* 28.
165. Tac. *Ann.* 4.5.
166. De la Bedoyere, 2017, 72.
167. Dio 54. 25.6; 55.23.1.
168. Nippel 1995, 96-97; Fuhrmann 2012, 116-117.
169. Vell. 2.92.
170. Lott 2004, 81; 89.
171. Fuhrmann 2012, 116 n.94.
172. Tac. *Ann.* 1.2.
173. *RG* 10; Dio 53.32.2.
174. Tac *Ann.* 3.56.2.
175. *RG* 6.2; Bleicken 1990, 104.
176. Galinsky 1996, 13; Magdelain 1947.
177. Dio 53.1.3; *RG* 7.2.
178. Dio 51.19-20; Fishwick 1987.
179. Dio 51.19.1-51.20.6.
180. *RG* 8.1.
181. Dio 51.21.4.

# 8 Augustus to Nero; the Provinces of Greece, the Danube, Britain and Thrace

1. Dio 53.32.1.
2. *RG* 5.
3. Vell. 2.94; Dio 54.9.4-6; Suet. *Aug.* 21; *Tib.* 9; Tac. *Ann.* 2.3.
4. Dio 54.10.5-6; Crook 1996a, 91-92; Levick 2010, 89-90.
5. Tac. *Ann.* 1.2.1; Lacey 1996, 3-5; 12; 14; 210-32.
6. Talbert 1984, 21.
7. *RG* 6.
8. Dio 54.10.5; 54.30.1; Suet. *Aug.* 27.
9. Dio 56.10.3; Suet *Aug.* 34.
10. Dio 52.19.1-2.
11. Gaius *Institutes* 1.17.2.29; 2.195; 3.56; Tac. *Ann.* 13.27.
12. Tac. *Ann.* 1.5-6; Dio 55.10a.10.
13. Dio 53.30.1-2; 53.53.31.3.
14. Suet. *Tib.* 7.
15. Suet. *Aug.* 64.
16. Dio 54.10a.9.
17. Vell 2.101; Dio 54.10.17- 21; 10a.4-6.
18. Vell 2.99; Suet *Tib.* 10; 12.
19. Dio 55.10a.4-9.
20. Suet *Tib.* 15.
21. Suet. *Aug.* 99.
22. Dio 57.2.1.
23. Raaflaub and Samons, 1990, 417-454.
24. Suet. *Aug.* 19.
25. Suet. *Aug.* 101.
26. Dio 56.33.1-6.
27. Tac. *Ann.* 1.4.
28. Dio 57.2.3.
29. Vell. 2.104.
30. Suet. *Tib.* 25.1.
31. Suet. *Aug.* 100.3-4; Dio 56.34-42.
32. Tac. *Ann.* 4.37-38.
33. Tac. *Ann.* 1.11; Dio 57.1.1.
34. Tac. *Ann.* 1.7.
35. Vell. 2.126; Tac *Ann.* 1.15.
36. Tac. *Ann.* 1.72-73; 4.30.
37. Tac. *Ann.* 1.16-30; Dio 57. 4-5.
38. Tac. *Ann.* 1.8; 1.31-49; Dio 57.5-6.
39. Tac. *Ann.* 1.45-51; 1.56-72.
40. Tac. *Ann.* 2.6-26; 2.41.
41. Tac. *Ann.* 2.5; 2.42.
42. Tac. *Ann.* 2.43.
43. Tac. *Ann.* 3.16-17.

44. Tac. *Ann.* 2.53-58.
45. Tac. *Ann.* 2.59.
46. Tac *Ann.* 2.69-82; 3.7-18; Dio 57.6-10.
47. Dio 57.19.1-8; Tac. *Ann.* 4.2.
48. Vell. 2. 127.
49. Tac. *Ann.* 4.1.
50. Dio 57.21.4.
51. Tac. *Ann.* 4.8; Dio 57.22.1-4.
52. Tac. *Ann.* 4.7.
53. Tac. *Ann.* 4.39.
54. Tac. *Ann.* 4.35.
55. Dio 58.4.5-8.
56. Dio 58.3.8.
57. Tac. *Ann.* 4.57; 4.67; Dio 58.1.
58. Tac. *Ann.* 4.59.
59. Dio 58.4-7.
60. Dio 58.9.1-58.11.6.
61. Dio 58.14.
62. Tac. *Ann.* 6.19; Suet. *Tib.* 61.
63. Dio 58.25.4.
64. Tac *Ann.* 1.80.
65. Suet. *Tib.* 32; Dio 57.10.5.
66. Vell 2.126; Tac. *Ann.* 4.13; Dio 57.17.7.
67. Tac. *Ann.* 2.52.
68. Tac. *Ann.* 3.20-21.
69. Tac. *Ann.* 3.73-74; 4.23-25.
70. Drinkwater 1983, 28; 34 n. 138.
71. Tac. *Ann.* 3.41-42.
72. Dio 57.17.5; Jones 1937 182.
73. Tac. *Ann.* 2.42; Dio 57.17.6.
74. Suet. *Vesp.* 8.
75. Suet. *Cal.*13-14; Dio 59.27.1-3.
76. Dio 59.8-10.
77. Suet. *Cal.* 16; Dio 59.20.
78. Suet. *Cal.* 25; Dio 59. 23.7.
79. Tac. *Ann.* 6.45; 6.48; Suet. *Cal.* 26; Dio 59.10.
80. Suet. *Cal.* 14.2-3; 27; Dio 59.8.
81. Dio 59. 21.1; 59.25.1; Suet. *Cal.* 26; 37.
82. Dio 59.21.2-3; Suet. *Cal.* 39.
83. Suet. *Galba* 6.2-3; Drinkwater 1983, 36; 50 n.7.
84. Dio 59.22.5.
85. Suet. *Cal.* 24.
86. Suet. *Cal.* 46.
87. Suet. *Cal.* 46; Drinkwater 1983, 36.
88. Suet. *Cal.* 44; 48.
89. Suet *Cal.* 49; Dio 59.25.2-5.
90. Dio 59.29.7.
91. Suet. *Cal.* 59.
92. Suet. *Claud.* 10-11.
93. Suet. *Claud.* 10.
94. Suet. *Claud.* 14.
95. Suet. *Claud.* 20.
96. Suet. *Claud.* 21.
97. Suet. *Claud.* 14-15; 23.
98. *ILS* 212; Sherk 1988, no. 55.
99. Tac. *Ann.* 11.23-25.
100. Suet. *Claud.* 25.
101. Suet. *Claud.* 28; Levick 1990, 82-83.
102. Dio 60.15.1-4; Suet. *Claud.* 13; 35.
103. Dio 60.14; 15.5.
104. Tac. *Ann.* 29-39; Suet *Claud.* 26-27; 36-37; Dio 60.5; 61.1.6a. 61.31.1-5.
105. Suet. *Claud.* 27; Tac. *Ann.* 12.9.
106. Tac. *Ann.* 12.25.
107. Suet. *Claud.* 43-44.
108. Dio 60.25.4-6.
109. Dio 60.17.3.
110. Dio 60.9.1-5.
111. Suet. *Galba* 7.
112. Jones 1937, 96.
113. Dio 60.17.3-4.
114. Jones 1937, 106.
115. Suet. *Claud.* 17.
116. *RG* 32; Dio 49.38.2; 53.22.
117. Strabo 2.5.8; 4.5.1-3.
118. Dio 60.19.1-5.
119. Dio 60.21.1-60.22.2.
120. Tac. *Ann.* 4.72-74.
121. Tac. *Ann.* 11.18-19.
122. Dio 61.30.3-4.
123. Tac. *Ann.* 12.27; *Germ.* 28.5; Levick 1990, 154.
124. Levick 1990, 156;165.
125. Tac. *Ann.* 12.29-30; Moscy 1974, 41.
126. Levick 1990, 133; 157.
127. Millar 1981, 224.
128. Jones 1937, 18.
129. Jos. *AJ.* 19.238-9.
130. Jos. *AJ* 19.326-7.
131. Jos. *AJ* 19.341.

132. Jos. *AJ*. 20.137; *BJ*. 2.247; Tac. *Ann*. 12.23; Suet. *Claud*. 28.
133. Tac. *Ann*. 12.54.
134. Jos. *AJ* 20 160-166.
135. Levick 1990,157.
136. Dio 60.28.7.
137.Tac. *Ann*. 11.10; 12.10-14.
138. Tac. *Ann*. 12.44-51; 13.6.
139. Suet. *Nero* 8; Tac. *Ann*. 12. 69.
140. Suet. *Nero* 9; Tac. *Ann*. 13.2-3.
141.Tac. *Ann*. 13.5; 13.28.
142. Tac. *Ann*.13.28-31.
143. Suet. *Nero* 9.
144. Suet. *Nero* 5.
145. Dio 61.3.3-61.4.1; Tac. *Ann*. 13.5.
146. Tac. *Ann*. 13.1; Dio 61.6.4-5.
147. Tac. *Ann*. 13.14.
148. Griffin 1984, 73; Tac. *Ann*. 13.14.
149. Suet. *Nero* 33; Tac. *Ann*. 13.15-16; Dio 61.7.4.
150. Suet. *Nero* 34.
151. Tac. *Ann*. 13.19-20.
152. Suet. *Nero*. 34; Tac. *Ann*. 14.1-8.
153. Tac. *Ann*. 16.6.
154. Suet. *Nero* 35.
155. Dio 61.7.5.
156. Tac. *Ann*. 14.14.
157. Suet. *Nero* 12.3.
158. Suet. *Nero* 28-9; 48-9.
159. Suet. *Nero* 26-29; Dio 61.8-9; 17-18; 62.25-28.
160. Tac. *Ann*. 13.25; Dio 61.9.3-5.
161. Suet. *Nero* 37.
162. Tac. *Ann*. 15.48-66.
163. Griffin 1984, 166-170.
164. Dio 62.25; Suet. *Nero* 35.
165. Suet. *Nero* 36-37.
166. Tac. *Ann*. 15.38-40.
167. Dio 62.16; Suet. *Nero* 38.
168. Tac. *Ann*. 15.
169. Tac. *Ann*. 43.
170. Suet. *Nero* 16.
171. Tac. *Ann*. 15.44.
172. Tac. *Hist*. 1.6; Suet. *Nero* 19; Dio 63.8.
173. Griffin 1984, 228.
174. Griffin 1984 108-9.
175. Suet. *Nero* 18-19.
176. Tac. *Ann*. 15.32.
177. Tac. *Germ*. 37.2.
178. Tac. *Ann*. 13.6.
179. Tac. *Ann*. 13.8-9.
180. Tac. *Ann*. 13. 34-35.
181.Tac. *Ann*. 13.36-46.
182. Dio 62.19-4-20.1.
183. Tac. *Ann*. 14.23-26.
184. Dio 62.20.3.
185. Tac. *Ann*. 15.1-17.
186. Tac. *Ann*. 15.24-31.
187. Suet. *Nero* 13; Tac. *Ann*. 16.14.
188. Tac. *Ann*.12.40; 14.19; *Agric*. 14.
189. Tac. *Ann*. 14.31.
190. Dio 62.2.
191. Tac. *Ann*. 14.31.
192. Tac. *Ann*. 14. 33-37.
193. Dio 62.1; Suet. *Nero* 18. Tac. *Ann*. 14.38.
194. Tac. *Agric*. 16.
195. Tac. *Ann*.14. 38-39.
196. Tac. *Hist*. 1.60; Agr. 16.
197. Tac. *Hist*. 5.9-10.
198. Tac. *Hist* 5.10; Jos. *BJ* 3.1-6.
199. Suet. *Nero* 23.
200. Dio 62.19.2.
201. Dio 63.22- 23; Suet. *Galba* 9.2.
202. Dio 63.24.
203. Dio 63.27.1a.
204. Suet. *Nero* 47-49; Dio 63.27.2-29.3.
205. Tac. *Hist*. 1.10.
206. Suet. *Galba* 11.
207. Tac. *Hist*. 1.7.
208. Suet. *Vit*. 7.
209. Tac. *Hist*. 1.12; Suet. *Galba* 16; Plut. *Galba* 18-22.
210. Tac. *Hist*. 1.14-18.
211. Suet. *Galba* 17; *Otho* 5.
212. Tac *Hist*. 1.52.
213. Suet. *Otho* 8.
214. Suet. *Galba* 20; *Otho* 6.
215. Tac. *Hist*. 1.46.
216. Tac. *Hist*. 2.39.
217. Tac. *Hist*. 2.40-49.
218. Tac. *Hist*. 2.55; 2.89.
219. Jos *BJ* 4.585-604; Tac. *Hist*. 2.6-7.
220. Tac. *Hist*. 1.10.
221. Dio 64.2.
222. Tac. *Hist*. 2.96-97.
223. Tac. *Hist*. 3.2-8.
224. Dio 64. 10.1- 15.2.

225. Tac. *Hist.* 3.12; 3.28-34.
226. Tac. *Hist* 3.74; Suet. *Dom*.1; Dio 64.17.
227. Tac. *Hist* 4.11; Jos *BJ* 4.654.
228. Tac. *Hist*.3.86; Dio 64.22.
229. Dio 65.2.3; Suet. *Dom.* 1.

## 9 From the Flavians to Trajan, and the Provinces of Dacia and Arabia

1. *ILS* 244.
2. Brunt 1977, 95; Levick 1999, 86.
3. Levick 1999, 66-67.
4. Tac. *Hist.* 4.12-14.
5. Tac. *Hist.* 4.15-18.
6. Tac. *Hist.* 4.18; 21; 36.
7. Tac. *Hist.* 4.59-60.
8. Tac *Hist.* 4.61; 4.67-69.
9. Tac. *Hist.* 4.71-78; Levick 1999, 110-112.
10. Tac. *Hist.* 4.79; 5.14-26.
11. Tac. *Hist.* 2.84.
12. Suet. *Vesp.* 16.3.
13. Levick 1999, 95-106 discusses Vespasian's finances.
14. Tac. *Hist.* 2.84.
15. Suet *Vesp.* 23.3; Dio 65.14.5.
16. Tac. *Hist.* 4.53; Dio 65.10.2.
17. Suet. *Vesp*.8.5.
18. Levick 1999, 99; 135.
19. Tac. *Ann.* 4.46.
20. Campbell 2006; Bishop 2012; Pollard and Berry 2012.
21. Suet. *Vesp.* 8.
22. Jos. *BJ* 7.219-243.
23. Tac. *Hist.* 1.63; 1.68; 2.59; Suet. *Vit.* 10.
24. Pliny *NH* 3.30; Richardson 1996, 189.
25. Levick 1999, 138-9.
26. Richardson 1996, 188.
27. *ILS* 254.
28. Suet. *Vesp.* 8.
29. Levick 1999, 146.
30. Tac. *Hist.* 3.45.
31. Tac. *Hist* 3.45.
32. Tac. *Agric.* 17.
33. Tac. *Agric.* 17.
34. Birley 2005, 69.
35. Tac. *Agric.* 7.
36. Tac. *Agric.* 18-20.
37. Tac. *Agric.* 22-23.
38. *RIB* Vol. 2 fascicule 3, nos. 2434.1-3.
39. Tac. *Agric.* 19.4.
40. Tac. *Agric.* 21.1-2.
41. Drinkwater 1983, 58; Levick 1999, 160-1.
42. Tac. *Hist.* 4.4.
43. Suet. *Vesp.* 15.
44. Tac. *Ann.* 16.33; Suet. *Vesp.* 15.
45. Suet. *Vesp.* 23.
46. Suet. *Titus* 6.2.
47. Suet. *Titus* 9.1-2.
48. Dio 66.19.
49. Suet. *Titus* 1.
50. Dio 64.25.1-5.
51. Suet. *Titus* 8.1.
52. Tac. *Agric.* 23.
53. Birley 2005, 84 n.71; Tac *Agric.* 24.
54. Dio 66.24.1.
55. Suet. *Titus* 8.
56. Tac. *Hist.* 4.40.
57. Suet. *Titus* 8.5.
58. Tac. *Hist*.1.1.
59. Suet. *Dom.* 1.3; Tac. *Hist.* 4.39.
60. Dio 66.26.2-3.
61. Suet. *Dom.* 1.3; 3.1.
62. Dio 67.4.3.
63. Talbert 1984, 16.
64. Suet. *Dom.* 13.2; Dio 67.4.7.
65. Jones 1979, 21; 29; 39-42.
66. Suet. *Dom.* 10.2-4.
67. Jones 1979, 28; Levick 1982, 62.
68. Talbert 1984, 402.
69. Suet. *Dom.* 8.1.
70. Suet. *Dom.* 9.
71. Suet. *Dom.* 8.2.
72. Suet. *Dom.* 7.2; 14.2.
73. *ILS* 6088; 6089.
74. Richardson 1996, 208-209.
75. *ILS* 6087; Richardson 1996, 196.
76. Suet. *Dom.* 4.5.
77. Suet. *Dom* 4.
78. Suet. *Dom.* 9.1.
79. Suet. *Dom.* 19.
80. Suet. *Dom.* 20.

*Rome's Empire*

81. Suet. *Dom.* 5.
82. *Chronographus Anni 354.*
83. Speidel 1994, 29-37.
84. Suet. *Dom.* 7.3.
85. Alston 1994, 113-123.
86. Suet. *Dom.* 12; Dio 67.3.5.
87. Tac. *Agric.* 26.
88. Tac. *Agric.* 30; 33.
89. Tac. *Agric.* 29.
90. Tac. *Agric.* 30-32.
91. Tac. *Agric.* 33-38.
92. Tac. *Agric* 10; 28; Dio 39.50.4; 66.20.1-3.
93. Tac. *Hist.* 1.2.
94. Hobley 1989, 69-74.
95. Wooliscroft and Hoffmann 2006.
96. Suet. *Dom.* 6.1.
97. Front. *Strat.* 1.1.8; 2.3.23.
98. Tac *Germ.* 30.
99. Front. *Strat.* 1.3.10.
100. Dio 67.4.1.
101. Tac. *Agric.* 39.
102. Tac. *Hist.* 3.46.
103. Jos. *BJ* 7.91-95.
104. Eutrop. *Breviarium* 7.24.3.
105. Dio 67.6.1-3.
106. Mocsy 1974, 82.
107. Dio 67.6.5.
108. Dio 67.7.2.
109. Dio 67.7.2-4.
110. Dio 68.6.1-2; 68.9.1-4.
111. Jones 1974, 530; 1992, 147.
112. Suet. *Dom.* 10.3.
113. Suet. *Dom.* 10.5.
114. Suet. *Dom.*7.3.
115. Drinkwater 1983, 60.
116. Levick 1999, 160.
117. Dio 67.7.
118. Suet. *Dom.* 6.2.
119. *ILS* 9200.
120. Suet. *Dom.* 6.1.
121. Suet. *Dom.* 14.3-4; Pliny *NH* 36.196.
122. Suet. *Dom.* 10.
123. Dio 67.15.3-6.
124. Dio 68.1.1-2.
125. Dio 68.2.1-2.
126. *ILS* 6675 from Veleia near Parma; *ILS* 6509 from the vicinity of Beneventum; Lewis and Rheinhold 1990, vol. I. 255-259. 3rd ed.
127. *ILS* 2720.
128. Dio 68.3.4.
129. *HA Hadrian* 1.3; 1.4; 2.1.
130. *ILS* 5863; *AE* 1973, 473.
131. Dio 68.6.1-58.9.7.
132. Dio 68.97.
133. Birley 2005, 108-109
134. Dio 68.13.1-5.
135. Sherk 1988, no.117; *AE* 1969-1970, 583; M. Speidel *JRS* 60 1970, 142-153.
136. *CIL* 3.1443.
137. Dio 68.10.2.
138. Dio 68.14.5.
139. Sartre 2005, 87.
140. Dio. 68.16.3.
141. *CIL* 11.3164; *ILS* 5918a.
142. Pliny *Letters*.10.17a; 37; Lewis and Rheinhold 1990 Vol 2, no. 69.
143. Birley 1997, 66-67.
144. Dio 68.29.3.
145. Dio 68.29.4.
146. Dio 68.30.3.
147. Dio 68. 33.1-2.
148. Birley 1997, 74; 324 n.21.
149. Dio 68.31-1-4.

## 10 From Hadrian to the Antonines and the Development of the Frontiers

1. Dio 69.2.2; *HA Hadrian* 5.2; 6.1-4.
2. Dio 69.2.5-6; *HA Hadrian* 5.8; 7.1-3; Birley 1997, 87-89.
3. *HA Hadrian* 5.2.
4. *HA Hadrian* 5.3.
5. Kennedy 1987, 280.
6. *HA Hadrian* 11-12.
7. *HA Hadrian* 17; 21.
8. *HA Hadrian* 6.7.
9. *HA Hadrian* 4.2; Birley 1997, 84.
10. Dio 68.13.
11. *ILS* 309; *HA Hadrian* 7.6; Dio 69.8.1; Birley 1997, 97-8.
12. Coarelli 2014, 286.
13. Coarelli 2014, 98-99.

14. Dio 69.5.2; *HA Hadrian* 13.5.
15. Dio 69.5.2-3; *HA Hadrian* 21.5-7.
16. Drinkwater 1983, 75; 90 n.16.
17. Dio 69.9.1-5; *HA Hadrian* 10-11.
18. *HA Hadrian* 11.2.
19. *HA Hadrian* 12.3.
20. Richardson 1996, 222-224; 255.
21. Richardson 1996, 229-230.
22. *HA Hadrian* 13.10.
23. Dio 69.16.1-2.
24. Alcock 1993, 113; 124-125; 181.
25. *HA Hadrian* 13.1-4.
26. *HA Hadrian* 13.3-4; 22.14.
27. Birley 1997, 206-207.
28. *CIL* 8.2532; 18042; *ILS* 2487; 9133-5; Sherk 1988, no.148.
29. Dio 69. 11.2-4; *HA Hadrian* 13.6; Birley 1997, 247-248.
30. Dio 69.12.1-3.
31. Dio 69.13.1-14.2; Birley 1997, 268-276.
32. Dio 69.15.1.
33. Dio 69.17.1; 69.20.1; *HA Hadrian* 23. 10-11; 23.16.
34. Dio 69.21.1; *HA Hadrian* 24.1-7; Birley 1997, 294-295.
35. Dio 69.2.6; 17.1-2; *HA Hadrian* 25.8.
36. Birley 1997, 302; 357 n.6 regarding the medical evidence.
37. Tac. *Germ.* 42.2.
38. Mocsy 1974, 41.
39. Dio 69.9.5-6.
40. Whittaker 1994.
41. Broughton 1929, 28.
42. Livy 31.50; 36.31.
43. Jos. *BJ* 2.383-385; Rickman 1980, 67-71.
44. Millett 1990, 159-160.
45. *HA Hadrian* 12.6.
46. Birley 2005, 118-119 n. 82.
47. Southern 1989, 118-122.
48. Baatz 1973.
49. *HA Hadrian* 5.2.
50. *HA Hadrian* 5.2; Fronto *De Bello Parthico* 2.
51. *ILS* 2726; *AE* 1951.88.
52. Birley 1997, 90; 2005, 114-119.
53. Stevens 1966, 39, 62.
54. Birley 2005, 118; Hodgson 2009a.
55. Crow 2004, 116-118.
56. Dobson 1986, 2; Hodgson 2009a, 11-14.
57. *RIB* I 1340; 1427; 1634;1637;1638; 1666; 1935.
58. Hodgson 2009a, 15.
59. *RIB* 2091; Breeze and Dobson 2000, 46; Hodgson 2009a, 15.
60. Breeze 2006, 184.
61. Daniels 1978, 137.
62. Welfare 2000; Breeze 2006, 314-315; Breeze 2014, 115.
63. Daniels 1987, 240.
64. Daniels 1987, 242.
65. Daniels 1987, 241, fig.10.8; Birley 1997, 209-210.
66. Southern 1989, 137.
67. Dio 69.9.5-6; *HA Hadrian* 17.10-12; 21.14.
68. *HA Hadrian* 6.8.
69. Dio 70.1.2-3.
70. Dio 70.1.1.
71. *HA Pius* 5.3.
72. Birley 1987, 61.
73. *HA Pius* 5.4-5.
74. Maxfield 1987, 160.
75. Pausanias *Description of Greece* 8. 43.3.
76. *RIB* 1147; 1148; 1276; 2191; 2192; *HA Pius* 5.4.
77. *ILS* 340; Birley 2005, 137.
78. Kent 1978, 297; plate 89 no. 312.
79. *HA Pius* 5.4.
80. Birley 1987, 60; 2005, 139; Gillam 1961, 66-67.
81. Breeze and Dobson 2000, 91-2.
82. *AE* 1997.1001; Birley 2005, 147.
83. Woolliscroft 1996; 2008.
84. Breeze and Dobson 2000, 98.
85. Breeze and Dobson 2000, 96.
86. Pausanias *Description of Greece* 8. 43.3.
87. Ireland 1996, 93 no 143.
88. Breeze and Dobson 2000, 118-119; Birley 2005, 147-148.
89. *RIB* 283; 2110.
90. *RIB* 1388; 1389.
91. Hodgson 2011, 66.
92. Hodgson 1995.
93. Hodgson 2009b, 192.

94. Breeze and Dobson 2000, 94.
95. *HA Pius* 6.11.
96. *HA Pius* 6.1-2; 7.8.
97. *HA Pius* 10.7-8.
98. *HA Hadrian* 9.6-10.
99. *HA Hadrian* 13.9; 17.11-12.
100. Rickman1980, 26; 96.
101. *HA Pius* 9.6.
102. *ILS* 1076.
103. *HA Pius* 9.7; Kent 1978, 296 plate 87 no. 306.
104. *HA Marcus* 6.3-4.
105. Dio 71.1; *HA Marcus* 7.5.
106. *HA Marcus* 7.9.
107. *HA Marcus* 1.1; 2.1; 2.6.
108. *HA Marcus* 8.4.
109. *HA Marcus* 8.6-7.
110. *HA Pius*12.7; Birley 1987, 121.
111. *HA Pius* 10.7; *Marcus* 8.6.
112. Dio 71.2.1; Birley 1987, 121-122.
113. *RIB* 665; Pollard and Berry 2012, 98.
114. *HA Marcus* 8.10-14; 20.2.
115. *HA Marcus* 8.8.
116. *HA Marcus* 9.1.
117. Dio 71.3.1; Birley 1987, 131
118. Dio 72.2.1; *HA Marcus* 8.6; Birley 121.
119. *HA Marcus* 21.6-7.
120. *HA Verus* 8.3-4; Dio 71.2-3.
121. *HA Marcus* 12.7.
122. *HA Verus* 8.1.
123. *HA Marcus* 13.1-14.1.
124. *HA Marcus* 12.13.
125. *HA Marcus* 22.1; 7.
126. *HA Marcus* 14.1.
127.Dio 71.3.2.
128. Birley 1987, 168-169.
129. Dio 72(71).16.
130. Mocsy 1974, 186-7.
131. Dio 72.11.4-5; *HA Marcus* 22.2; 24.3.
132. *HA Marcus* 24.5.
133. *HA Marcus* 27.10.
134. Dio 72 (71). 20.1-2.
135. Birley 1987, 253-4.
136. *HA Marcus* 14.8; *Verus* 9.10-11.
137. *HA Marcus* 20.2.
138. *HA Marcus* 15.3-4; *Verus* 11.2.
139. *HA Marcus* 10.1-9.
140. *HA Marcus* 10.2.
141. *HA Hadrian* 22.13.
142. Birley1987, 207; 2005, 172-4.
143. *CIL* 3.13439=*ILS* 9122.
144. Birley 1987, 139.
145. Dio 72(71).32.2.
146. *HA Marcus* 17. 4-5; 21.8-9.
147. *HA Marcus* 9.7-8.
148. *HA Marcus* 11.10.
149. *HA Marcus* 21.6-7.
150. *HA Marcus* 17. 4-5; 21.8-9.
151. Dio 71.3.3-4.
152. *HA Marcus* 22.9.
153. Birley 1987, 161; 164.
154. Birley 1987, 164; Ammianus 29.6.1.
155. *HA Marcus* 21.1; 22.11; Birley 1987, 168.
156. Richardson 1996, 231-233.
157. Dio 72(71).11.1-5.
158. Dio 72(71).3.5; Birley 1987,171.
159. Dio 72(71).4.1-2.
160. *HA Marcus* 12.9.
161. *HA Comm.* 11.13.
162. *HA Marcus* 24.4.
163. Dio 72(71).8-10.
164. Dio 72(71). 7.1-5.
165. Dio 72(71).16.2.
166. Dio 72(71). 23.3.
167. *RIB* 583; 594; 595; Dio 72(71).16.1-2.
168. *AE* 1956,124.
169. Dio 72(71).27.1a-28.1.
170. *HA Marcus* 24.5; Dio 72(71).22.2-23.3.
171. *HA Marcus* 24.8-9; Dio 72(71).28.2-4.
172. Dio 72(71).30.4.
173. *HA Marcus* 26.9.
174. Dio 72(71).29.1; 30.1.
175. Dio 72(71).33.1; *HA Marcus* 27.8.
176. Birley 1987, 196-197.
177. Dio 72(71).33.3.
178. *CIL* 3.13439=*ILS* 9122.
179. Dio 72(71).18.1-21.1.
180. Dio 72(71).36.4.

## 11 From Commodus to the Severans

1. Dio 73(72).2.1-2.
2. Dio 73(72).2.2-4.
3. *HA Comm.* 6.1-2; Herodian 1.9.10.
4. *CIL* III 3330; 3332; 10312; 10313; *ILS* 395; 8913.
5. Dio 72(71).33.4.
6. Dio 72.34.1; *HA Marcus* 18.3.5.
7. Dio 72 (71).36.4; Herodian 1.4.3-6; *HA Marcus* 28.10.
8. Dio 73.1.2; *HA Comm.* 3.1.
9. Whittaker on Herodian 1.6.8 in the Loeb edition.
10. Dio 73(72). 9.1-10.1.
11. Herodian 1.8.1-2; 1.9.1.
12. Dio 73(72).9.3.
13. Herodian 1.9.4-10.
14. Dio 73(72).12.1.
15. *HA Comm.* 6.6-9.
16. Ammianus 26.6.9.
17. Dio 73(72).13.1-6.
18. Dio 73(72). 4.1-6.
19. Herodian 1.10.1.
20. *HA Comm.* 16.2.
21. Herodian 1.10.2-3.
22. *HA Niger* 3.3; *Severus* 3.8.
23. Whittaker note to Herodian 1.10.3.
24. Herodian 1.10.3-11.
25. Dio 73(72).8.1-6.
26. Birley 2005, 164-167.
27. *RIB* 1329; 1463; 1464.
28. Birley 2005, 164.
29. Dio 73(72).9.2a.
30. *HA Comm.* 6.2; 8.4.
31. Dio 73(72).2$^2$-4.
32. *HA Pertinax* 3.6-8.
33. Dio 73(72).14.1; *CIL* 14.4378.
34. Dio 73(72).20.2.
35. Herodian 1.15.5; Dio 73(72).21.
36. *HA Comm.* 15.2; *Pert.* 5.2.
37. *HA Comm.* 17.1-2; Dio 73(72).22.4-6.
38. Herodian 1.17.1-12.
39. Dio 73.22; 74.1.1-2; Herodian 1.17; *HA Pertinax* 4.4.
40. Birley 1988, 84.
41. *HA Pertinax* 5.6; 6.9.
42. Herodian 2.4.4; Dio 74.1.3.
43. *HA Pertinax* 6.4-5.
44. *HA Pertinax* 6.6; 7.6; 9.1.
45. *HA Pertinax* 6.6-9.9; Herodian 2.4.6.
46. Dio 74.8.5; *HA Pertinax* 10.1-7.
47. Herodian 2.4.4; 2.5.1.
48. Herodian 2.6.9.
49. Dio 74.11.1-6; *HA Pertinax* 13.7; *Didius* 3.2.
50. Birley 1988, 212-221.
51. *HA Comm.* 6.9.
52. Birley 1988, 83.
53. *HA Severus* 5.3-5.
54. Dio 74.14.3-4.
55. *HA Severus* 5.5.
56. Dio 74.16.1.
57. Dio 74.16.4-17.1.
58. Herodian 2.7.1; *HA Julianus* 3.2.
59. Dio 74.17.2-5.; *HA Julianus* 8.6-8.
60. Dio 75.1.1-2; Herodian 2.13.1-9.
61. *CIL* VI 210=*ILS* 2013.
62. Dio 75.2.5-6; Herodian 2.1.4.5.
63. Dio 74.15.2; *HA Albinus* 6.8.
64. Herodian 2.14.6-7.
65. Birley 1988, 110.
66. Dio 75.6.4-5.
67. Birley 1988, 110.
68. Dio 75.10.1-12.1.
69. Herodian 3.2.10.
70. Birley1988, 112.
71. Dio 75.8.3.
72. *HA Niger* 6.1-4.
73. Dio 75.14.4.
74. *ILS* 1353 referring to C. Iulius Pacatianus, *proc. provinc. O[sr] hoenae.*
75. Dio 75.1.2; 3.2. (at the end of book 75 in the Loeb edition).
76. Dio 75.2-3.
77. Birley 1988, 114; Millar 1993, 121; Christol 1997, 24; Sartre 2005, 135-6.
78. *ILS* 417; 418; *HA Severus* 9.11.
79. *HA Albinus* 7.1-6.
80. *HA Severus* 10.6.
81. Birley 1988, 122; Christol 1997, 15; 62 n.9.

82. Dio 73.8.1; 76.6.2; Herodian 2.15.1.
83. Birley 1988, 124; Salway 1991, 221-31; 1993, 165-7.
84. Dio76.6.1; Birley 1988, 124.
85. Herodian 3.6.10.
86. *ILS* 419, dated prior to 198.
87. Dio 76.6.2; Birley 2005, 183-186; Christol 1997, 16.
88. Dio 76.6.1-7.4; Herodian 3.7.1-8.
89. *HA Severus* 12.1-6; Herodian 3.8.1.
90. Dio 76.8.4; *HA Severus* 13.5.
91. Herodian 3.8.2.
92. *CIL* VIII 2080 (Britannia Superior); *CIL* VIII 5180 (Britannia Inferior); Birley 2005, 333.
93. *ILS* 442; 446; 447.
94. Dio 76.7.4-8.4; *HA Severus* 11.4.
95. Dio 76.8.5. *HA Comm.* 17.11; *Severus* 12.8-13.9.
96. Birley,1988 and Christol 1997, 26-8 examine the careers of Severus' adherents.
97. Millar 1993,121.
98. *ILS* 1143.
99. *AE* 1971, 455.
100. Herodian 3.8.4-5; *HA Severus* 17.1.
101. Herodian 3.8.8; Watson 1969, 188 nn.231-3; Campbell 1984, 185-6; Birley 1988, 128; 196.
102. Whittaker on Herodian 3.8.5; Dio 78.34.3; Develin 1971.
103. Birley 1988, 196.
104. Dio 6.14-16; Herodian 3.10.6-7; Birley 1988, 128-9; Christol 1997, 28-9.
105. Dio 76.9.3.
106. Herodian 3.9.1; Dio 76.9.1.
107. Dio 76.9.3.
108. Dio 76.9.4.
109. Bowersock 1983, 110; Birley 1988, 134.
110. Dio76.10.1; 76.11.1-12.
111. Birley 1988, 133.
112. Dio 76.13.1.
113. Dio 51.17.2; *HA Severus* 17.2; Birley 1988, 137.
114. Herodian 3.10.1; Christol 1997, 29.
115. Christol 1997, 30.
116. Dio 76.1.1-5; Herodian 3.10.
117. Herodian 2.9.5-6; Birley 1988, 155.
118. Herodian 3.10.5-8.
119. Dio 77.3.1.
120. Christol 1997, 25-6; Birley 1988, 146-53.
121. Birley 1988, 148; Christol 1997, 25-6.
122. Birley 1988, 147; Christol 1997, 63 n.7.
123. Birley 1988, 148-54; 212-21; Christol 1997, 25-6.
124. Dio 77.17.1; Birley 1988, 164-5.
125. Lewis 1996; Coriat 1997.
126. *HA Severus* 15.4.
127. Dio 76.14.1 - 15.2a.
128. Dio 76.2.4.
129. Herodian 3.11.1 - 12.12, not wholly reliable; Dio 77.3.1-4.5.
130. *CIL* VI 228; Christol 1997, 35.
131. Dio 77.7.1-2; 11.1;14.1; Herodian 3.13.3-6.
132. Herodian 3.14.1.
133. Dio 75.5.4; 77.12.1.
134. Birley 1988, 171; Salway 1991, 221-7.
135. Frere 1987, 157-8.
136. Mattingly 2006,123.
137. Dio 77.13.1.
138. Birley 1988, 174-51.
139. Herodian 3.14.9.
140. *RIB* 1143.
141. Dio 77.14.1-7; Herodian 3.15.2.
142. Dio 77.15.2
143. *JRS* 55, 1965, 223.
144. Herodian 3.8.2.
145. Dio 55.23.3; 23.66.
146. Birley 2005, 333-336.
147. Herodian 4.3.1 - 4.4.2; Dio 78.1.4 - 2.6.
148. Dio 78.3.1; Herodian 4.5.1.
149. Herodian 4.4.7; Dio 78.36.3.

150. Dio 78.4.1; Herodian 4.6.
151. Christol 1997, 37.
152. *Digest* 1.5.17; Sherwin-White 1973, 279-87; 380-93; Wolff 1978.
153. Dio 78.9.5.
154. Dio 78.13.4; 15.2.
155. Christol 1997, 65 n.9.
156. Herodian 4.7.3.
157. Dio 78.14.3; 20.3.
158. Dio 78.12.2-3.
159. Herodian 4.10.1; in note 4 on this passage Whittaker points out the careful planning.
160. Dio 78.12.1a.
161. Dio 78.18.1; 21.1-4; 22.2; Herodian 4.8.6-9.8.
162. Dio 79.1.1. Herodian 4.10.1-5.
163. Dio 79.4.1-2.
164. Herodian 4.12.1-3.
165. Herodian 4.12.5-8.
166. Dio 79.14.1-4.
167. Furhmann 2012, 152-3.
168. Dio 79.11.4-6; Herodian 4.14.1-3.
169. *HA Macrinus* 4.7.
170. Dio 79.11.2.
171. Dio 79.15.2;18.4; 26.2.
172. Dio 79.16.2.
173. Dio 79.17.1; 19.1.
174. Dio 79.17.2-4.
175. Dio 79.13.4; 80.4.3.
176. Dio 79.36.2-3.
177. Dio 79.12.7.
178. Dio 79.29.2.
179. Dio 79.23.1-4.
180. Dio 79.38.1; 39.1-40.5; Herodian 5.4.7.
181. *CIL* VIII 10347.
182. Dio 80.1.1.
183. Herodian 5.5.6.
184. Dio 80.11.1-2.
185. Dio 80.4.3-5.1.
186. Herodian 5.7.6.
187. Dio 80.4.1-2.
188. Dio 80.13.2 -15.4.
189. Dio 80.17.2.
190. *HA Elagabalus* 13-16.1; Dio 80.19.1a.
191. Dio 80.20.2; Herodian 5.8.8.
192. Dio 80.2.2.
193. Dio 80.1.1; 2.2.
194. Dio 80.2.5; Christol 1997, 54; 68 n.13; Herodian 7.11-12 places this riot, or possibly another one, in 238.
195. Herodian 6.1.2.
196. *HA Severus Alexander* 15.6-16.3; Crook 1955, 87-88.
197. Herodian 6.2.1; Dio 80.3-4; Dodgeon and Lieu 1991, 9-16; Christol 1997, 73-4.
198. Whittaker note to Herodian 6.5.1.
199. Herodian 6.3.1; 6.4.3.
200. Zosimus 1.12.
201. Herodian 6.5.1-6.6.6; *HA Severus Alexander* 55.1-3; 57.3.
202. Herodian 6.7.3.
203. Herodian 6.7.8.
204. Herodian 6.8.1.
205. Herodian 6.7.2.
206. Schönberger 1985, 414-8.
207. Herodian 6.7.9-10.
208. Zosimus 1.13.1.
209. *HA Maximinus* 7.
210. Herodian 6.8.3-9.8.
211. Aurelius Victor *de Caes.* 24.7-9; Christol 1997, 69.

## 12 The Soldier Emperors and the Crisis of the Third Century

1. Whittaker note 3 on Herodian 6.8.1.
2. Herodian 6.9.7; 7.1.3; *HA Maximinus* 8.6; Crook 1955, 92.
3. Herodian 7.2.1-9.
4. *CIL* 3.4857; 5218=*ILS* 2309; *AE* 1909, 144; 1965, 223.
5. Herodian 7.3.5.
6. Herodian 7.4.2-3; 5.1-8.
7. Herodian 7.6.6-9; 7.7.4.
8. Herodian 7.10.2-5; Zosimus 1.14.2; *CIL* 14.3902=*ILS* 1186; *ILS* 8979.
9. *HA Maximinus* 32; *Gordiani* 10.2.
10. Herodian 7.7.2.

11. Herodian 7.10.6-9.
12. Herodian 8.1.5-5.7-9; *HA Maximinus* 32.
13. *CJ* 10.3.2.
14. *CIL* 13.1807=*ILS* 1330.
15. *CIL* 3.12336=*IGR* I 674.
16. Livy 33.29.2; Suet. *Tib.* 37.1.
17. Schönberger 1964; 1969, 176-7; 1985, 474-5.
18. *HA Maximinus* 21.6; 22.1; Herodian 8.2.5.
19. Zonaras 12.18.
20. *HA Gordiani* 29-30; Zosimus 1.18-19; Eutropius 12.2.2; *Epit. de Caes.* 27.2; Zonaras 12.17.
21. The relevant passages are translated in Dodgeon and Lieu 1991, 34-5; 45.
22. Zosimus 1.19.1; Zonaras 12.18; Eutropius 9.2.3.
23. *CIL* 3.3203.
24. Zosimus 1.18.3; *HA Gordiani* 29.1; *Epit. de Caes.* 27.2.
25. Dodgeon and Lieu 1991, 45-6.
26. *RGDS* lines 9-10, Greek version; Dodgeon and Lieu 1991, 45; 358 n.25.
27. *CIL* 3.4634; 10619=*ILS* 507; *CIL* 6.1097=*ILS* 506; *AE* 1935, 27.
28. Aurelius Victor *de Caes.* 28; Christol 1997, 99; 116 n.1.
29. Zosimus 1.19.2.
30. *CIL* 3.141595.5=*ILS* 9005.
31. Zosimus 1.20.2.
32. *CIL* 6.793=*ILS* 505; *CIL* 3.14191; *AE* 1960, 356.
33. Christol 1997, 99; 116 n.1.
34. Zosimus 1.20; Loriot and Nony 1997, 40 no. 12; *AE* 1965, 223.
35. *CIL* 3.8031.
36. Jordanes *Getica* 89.
37. Zosimus 1.20.2.
38. Aurelius Victor *de Caes.* 29.2; Zosimus 1.20.2; Potter 2004, 239.
39. Zosimus 1.21.1-3.
40. Potter 2004, 248.
41. *CJ* 10.16.3.
42. Eusebius *History of the Church* 6.41.9; Lactantius *de Mort. Pers.* 4.4.1-3.
43. *CIL* 3.1176=*ILS* 514.
44. Zonaras 12.20.
45. Cyprian *Ep.* 55.9; Aurelius Victor *de Caes.* 29.2-3.
46. Jordanes *Getica* 101-3; Zosimus 1.23.3; Zonaras 12.10; Aurelius Victor *de Caes.* 29.4.
47. *CIL* 11.1927
48. Zosimus 1.23.2; Zonaras 12.20; Christol 1997, 127; 167 n8; Wolfram 1988, 46.
49. Zosimus 1.25.
50. Aurelius Victor *de Caes.* 30.2.
51. Christol 1997, 128.
52. *RGDS* 4-9.
53. Potter 2004, 249-250.
54. MacMullen 1966, 213.
55. Wolfram 1988, 47-8.
56. Eutropius 9.5; Zosimus 1.28.1. Zonaras 12.20.
57. Zosimus 1.29; Aurelius Victor *de Caes.* 32.1; Eutropius 9.7; Zonaras 12.22; Orosius 7.22.1.
58. Christol 1997, 131; 169 n.2.
59. Eutropius 9.8.1; *Epit. de Caes* 32.2.
60. *RGDS* line 4.
61. Potter 2004, 254; 638 n.167.
62. Drinkwater 1987, 21-2; Christol 1997, 132-135.
63. Christol 1997, 136; 170 n8; Zosimus 1.30 dates this earlier, contradicted by Schönberger 1985, 422-3.
64. Christol 1997, 137; 170 n.1.
65. Zosimus 1.31-35; de Blois 1976, 3; Ridley 1982, 141 n.61.
66. Zonaras 12.24.
67. de Blois 1976, 27.
68. Zosimus 1.36.2; Zonaras 12.23; *HA Valerian* 4.2; Aurelius Victor *de Caes.* 32.5; Eutropius 9.7; Orosius 7.22.4; Lactantius *de Mort. Pers.* 5.
69. *RGDS* lines 19-37, translated in Dodgeon and Lieu 1991, 57.
70. Christol 1997, 139; 179 nn. 4; 7; *P. Oxy.* 2186; 1476; Dodgeon and Lieu 1991, 2; 57-65.

71. Millar 1981, 241; Drinkwater 1983, 214.
72. Millar 1981, 241-2.
73. Drinkwater 1983, 212; Wightman 1985, 223.
74. Aurelius Victor *de Caes.* 33.3.
75. Richardson 1996, 250-251.
76. Potter 2004, 250-1.
77. Zonaras 12.24; *HA Thirty Tyrants* 12.10; 18; *Gallienus* 1.3-5.
78. Potter 2004, 159.
79. *HA Gallienus* 3.3.
80. Christol 1997, 148; Potter 1996, 283.
81. *CIL* 8.22765.
82. Zonaras 12.23.
83. Zosimus 1.39.1.
84. de Blois 1976, 33-4.
85. Zosimus 1.39-40; Zonaras 12.24; Eutropius 9.10; Orosius 7.22; *HA Gallienus* 10.12.
86. Loriot and Nony 1997, 91-3 no. 46.
87. *HA Gallienus* 10; Eutropius 9.13.2; Orosius 7.22.
88. Zosimus 1.40.2; *HA Gallienus* 13.4-5; 14.1.
89. de Blois 1976, 7 n.21.
90. de Blois 1976, 33; *HA Thirty Tyrants* 3.9.11; Zosimus 1.38.2; Aurelius Victor *de Caes.* 33.7; Zonaras 12.24.
91. *AE* 1993, 1231, translated in Potter 2004, 256; Loriot and Nony 1997, 76-7 no.36; Christol 1997, 171 n.6.
92. Eutropius 9.9.1.
93. *ILS* 560; 565.
94. *ILS* 562; *CIL* 2.4919; Richardson 1996, 250; Drinkwater 1987, 27-8; 116-8; König 1981, 55-6 lists all the inscriptions.
95. Loriot and Nony 1997, 69-74; 78 n.23.
96. *HA Thirty Tyrants* 3.1-7.
97. de Blois 1976, 7; 259-73; Drinkwater 1987, 34; 85; König 1985, 55.
98. Schönberger 1985, 423.
99. *HA Thirty Tyrants* 3.5; Zonaras 12.24; Christol 1997, 146.
100. *HA Gallienus* 4.4-6.
101. Potter 2004, 257.
102. de Blois 1976, 13-5; Petit 1974, 193-4; 198.
103. de Blois 1976, 175-84, esp. 177; 178-9.
104. Christol 1986, 35-6; 45-6.
105. de Blois 1976, 13; 47; Christol 1997, 143-4.
106. de Blois 1976, 117.
107. de Blois 1976, 26-30; Southern and Dixon 1996, 11-14.
108. Zosimus 1.40.1; Zonaras 12.25.
109. Christol 1997, 394-5.
110. Parker 1935, 180; 220.
111. For an overview from Severus to Gallienus see Devijver 1989, 316-338; de Blois 1976, 37-44; Loriot and Nony 1997, 125.
112. Aurelius Victor *de Caes.* 33.31-4; 37.5-7.
113. de Blois 1976, 57-8; 117.
114. de Blois 1976, 60-1; 68; 72-7; Christol 1986, 39-40.
115. de Blois 1976, 47 n.108.
116. Christol 1986, 43-4 n33.
117. Christol 1986, 45-6.
118. de Blois 1976, 82; 144-5.
119. Christol 1986, 17-8; 66.
120. Crawford 1975, 569; Callu 1969; Petit 1974, 200.
121. Loriot and Nony (1997, 164-5); *P.Oxy.* 2282; 2346; 3109; 3111.
122. Richardson 1996, 253.
123. de Blois 1976, 90-1.
124. de Blois 1976, 90 n.253.
125. Christol 1997, 149.
126. Christol 1997, 145; de Blois 1976, 6.
127. de Blois 1976, 135.
128. *HA Gallienus* 7.2.
129. Christol 1997, 151; de Blois 1976, 148-9; *CIL* 14.5334.
130. de Blois 1976, 185-6.
131. Christol 1997, 150; Loriot and Nony 1997, 87-9 no. 43.
132. *CIL* 5.3329.

133. Potter 2004, 250; Zonaras 12.26; Zosimus 1.29.2-3.
134. *HA Gallienus* 13.6.
135. Zosimus1.39-40; 43.2; *HA Gallienus* 13; *Claudius* 9.
136. Zosimus 1.40.1-2; *HA Gallienus* 14.1.7; 4-9; Zonaras 12.25 gives two versions of the murder of Gallienus.
137. *P. Oxy.* 1119.
138. *HA Thirty Tyrants* 11.4-5; *Claudius* 5.1-3.
139. *HA Aurelian* 18.1.
140. *HA Claudius* 14.18; Aurelius Victor *de Caes.* 33.28; 34.1.2; Ammianus 31.5.17; Zosimus 1.46; Zonaras 12.26.
141. Cizek 1994, 80.
142. *HA Claudius* 4; Eutropius 9.11.3.
143. Cizek 1994, 82-3; Christol 1997, 157.
144. *CIL* 11.2228=*ILS* 569.
145. *HA Claudius* 6.4; Ammianus 31.5.15.
146. Zosimus 1.44.2; Zonaras 12.27.
147. *HA Claudius* 11.2.
148. Cizek 1994, 81; Christol 1997, 157.
149. *HA Claudius* 1.3; 3.6; 6-8; 11.4; Aurelius Victor *de Caes.* 34.3-8; Eutropius 9.11.2; Zosimus 1.43-45; Zonaras 12.26.
150. *HA Claudius* 9.4-6.
151. Aurelius Victor *de Caes.* 34.5; *HA Claudius* 12.1-2; Zosimus 1.46.1; Zonaras 12.26.
152. Cizek 1994, 11-12; Aurelius Victor *de Caes.* 35.1; Eutropius 9.13.1; *HA Aurelian* 3.1.
153. Cizek 1994, 89; 359 n.8; Zosimus 1.48.2; 49.1.
154. Cizek 1994, 169-72; Aurelius Victor *de Caes.* 35.5-6.
155. Eutropius 9.14.
156. *HA Aurelian* 48.5.
157. *HA Thirty Tyrants* 12.14; 13.3; Zosimus 1.49.2; *Epit. de Caes.* 35.3.
158. *HA Aurelian* 18.2; Zosimus 1.48.1-2; 1.49.1.
159. *HA Aurelian* 18.3.6.
160. *HA Aurelian* 21.1-4.
161. *HA Aurelian* 21.9; Zosimus 1.49.2; Eutropius 9.15.1.
162. Cizek 1994, 101.
163. Coarelli 2014, 12-13; Cizek 1994, 98-102; Richmond 1930; Todd 1978; Ivaldi, R. 2005.
164. Dodgeon and Lieu 1991, 87-8.
165. Loriot and Nony 1997, 93 no. 47A.
166. Dodgeon and Lieu 1991, 83-101.
167. *AE* 1904, 60=*ILS* 8924.
168. *HA Aurelian* 22.2; Eutropius 9.13.1; Orosius 7.23.4; Jordanes *Rom.* 290.
169. *HA Probus* 9.3.
170. *HA Aurelian* 22.5-24.6.
171. *HA Aurelian* 25.1; Zosimus 1.50.1-4; Eutropius 9.13.2; Jordanes *Rom.* 290.
172. *HA Aurelian* 26.1; Cizek 1994, 111.
173. *HA Aurelian* 28.2.
174. Zosimus 1.55.2-3; *HA Aurelian* 28.3.
175. Zosimus 1.55.1; Dodgeon and Lieu 1991, 96-9.
176. *HA Thirty Tyrants* 30.27; Aurelian 30.1; 30.2l; 33.2; 34.3; Zosimus 1.59.
177. Eutropius 9.13.2.
178. Cizek 1994, 185; Christol 1986, 113-4.
179. *HA Aurelian* 31.2; Dodgeon and Lieu 1991, 101-3.
180. Zosimus 1.61.1; Cizek 1974, 116.
181. *HA Aurelian* 32.2; Dodgeon and Lieu 1991, 103-5; Cizek 1994, 114-5.
182. Ammianus 22.16.15; *HA Aurelian* 45.1; Cizek 1994, 172.
183. Cizek 1994, 116-7.
184. *CIL* 5.4319; Christol 1997, 162; *HA Aurelian* 28.4.
185. *AE* 1936, 129.
186. Drinkwater 1987, 28-34; 89.
187. Drinkwater 1987, 175; Cizek 1994, 75.
188. *Epit. de Caes.* 32.4; Eutropius

9.9.1; *HA Gallienus* 21.5; *Thirty Tyrants* 3.7; 4.1; 5.1; 5.4; 5.5; 5.8; 6.3; 8.1; 31.2; *Claudius Gothicus* 7.4.
189. Drinkwater 1987, 177.
190. Drinkwater 1987, 37.
191. Drinkwater 1987, 37-44.
192. Cizek 1994, 117; 261 n.10.
193. Virgil *Aeneid* 6.365 Aurelius Victor *de Caes.* 35.4; Eutropius 9.13.2; *HA Thirty Tyrants* 24.3.
194. Cizek 1994, 121; Loriot and Nony 1997, 113 nos. 66-7.; *CIL* 6.1112ff; 12.5561; 8.10217.
195. Aurelius Victor *de Caes.* 35.3; *HA Thirty Tyrants* 24.4; *Probus* 12.3-4.
196. *HA Aurelian* 33.2; Eutropius 9.12; Zosimus 1.61.1 places the triumph before the end of the Gallic Empire.
197. Cizek 1994, 156; Aurelius Victor *de Caes.* 35.5; Eutropius 9.13.2; *HA Thirty Tyrants* 24-5.
198. Cizek 1994, 120.
199. Cizek 1994, 123-52.
200. Eutropius 9.8.2; 9.15.1; Christol 1997, 159.
201. Christol 1997, 150-1.
202. Cizek 1994, 186.
203. Cizek 1994, 172; *HA Aurelian* 39.6; Aurelius Victor *de Caes.* 35.7; Eutropius 9.15.1.
204. Cizek 1994, 172-5; Harl 1996, 143-8; Christol 1997, 177-8.
205. *CIL* 6.1419.
206. *HA Aurelian* 47.1.
207. *HA Septimius Severus* 18.3; Aurelius Victor *de Caes.* 35.7; *HA Aurelian* 35.2; 48.1.
208. Rickman 1980, 198-209 esp. 187 and 197.
209. Cizek 1994, 175-82.
210. Aurelius Victor *de Caes.* 35.7; *HA Aurelian* 1.3; 25.6; 28.5; 35.3; 39.2; Eutropius 9.15.1; Zosimus 1.61.2.
211. *HA Aurelian* 35.3; Cizek 1994, 181-2; *CIL* 6.1397; 1418; 1673; 1739; 1740; 2151.
212. Cizek 1994, 195.
213. *HA Aurelian* 35.4.
214. *HA Aurelian* 35.4; Aurelius Victor 35.8; Eutropius 9.15.2; Zosimus 1.62.1.
215. *HA Probus* 6.2-7.
216. *HA Aurelian* 40.2; *Tacitus* 2.5.
217. Aurelius Victor *de Caes.* 35.10; *HA Aurelian* 40.3; 41.3; *Tacitus* 2.6; Cizek 1994, 204.
218. Zonaras 12.28.

# 13 Diocletian and Constantine: A New World
1. Aurelius Victor *de Caes.* 35.9-12.
2. *HA Aurelian* 37.1; *Tacitus* 13.1; Aurelius Victor *de Caes.* 36.2.
3. *HA Tacitus* 13.2; Zosimus 1.63.2; Zonaras 12.28; Cizek 1994, 214; 216.
4. Crees 1911, 20.
5. Crees 1911, 17-8; Christol 1997, 184-5.
6. Zosimus 1.66.2; 68.3.
7. *HA Probus* 13.5.
8. *HA Probus* 13.5-8; Crees 1911, 104.
9. *HA Probus* 18.1-3; Zosimus 1.7.1.
10. *HA Probus* 17.2; Zosimus 1.7.1.
11. *HA Probus* 18.4-5; *Four Tyrants* 7-11; Aurelius Victor *de Caes.* 37.2-4; Zosimus 1.66.1.
12. Eutropius 9.17; Aurelius Victor *de Caes.* 37.2-4.
13. *HA Probus* 19.2.
14. Eutropius 9.17.
15. Aurelius Victor *de Caes.* 37.2-4.
16. *HA Probus* 18.1; 21.2; Aurelius Victor *de Caes.* 37.4; Eutropius 9.17.
17. Aurelius Victor *de Caes.* 37.5.
18. Christol 1997, 187; 248 n.21.
19. Christol 1997, 187-8.
20. Zonaras 12.30; Aurelius Victor *de Caes.* 38; Eutropius 9.18.
21. Winter 1988, 141.
22. *HA Carus* 14.3.
23. *HA Carus* 13.

24. *P. Oxy.* 47; Williams 1985, 240 n.37.
25. Zonaras 12.31; Aurelius Victor *de Caes.* 39.1.
26. Zosimus 1.73.1; *Epit. de Caes.* 38.6.
27. Aurelius Victor *de Caes.* 39.15; Barnes 1982, 97.
28. Christol 1997, 192; 250 n.3.
29. Nixon and Rodgers 1994, 47.
30. Potter 2004, 282-3.
31. Barnes 1982, 10.
32. Salway 1991, 287; Christol 1997, 195.
33. *Pan. Lat.* 10 (2).4.
34. *RIB* 2291=*ILS* 8928.
35. Seston 1946, 57-81; Williams 1985, 48; 241 n.5.
36. Christol 1997, 193 opts for Carus; Barnes 1982, 10-11, and Bowman 2005b, 70-71 opt for Maximian.
37. Aurelius Victor *de Caes.* 39.19; Eutropius 9.21.
38. Casey 1994, 103.
39. Salway 1991, 289.
40. Casey 1994, 110.
41. Barnes 1982, 11.
42. Virgil *Aeneid* 2.282.3.
43. Casey 1994, 92.
44. Winter 1988, 137-9; Barnes 1982, 51 dates this to 287.
45. Ammianus. 23.5.2.
46. Williams 1985, 45-51.
47. Williams 1985, 51; 73.
48. Nixon and Rodgers 1994, 107; Williams 1985, 55-6; 242 n.21; Christol 1997, 193-5.
49. Johnson 1989, 43. Mann 1989, 2; 10-11.
50. Williams 1985, 71; Barnes 1982, 60.
51. Aurelius Victor *de Caes.* 39.41; Eutropius 9.22; Salway 1991, 305; Williams 1985, 72.
52. Salway 1991, 305-12; Casey 1994; Christol 1997, 197.
53. Kent 1978, p.324 no. 585; Christol 1997, plate p.198.
54. Barnes 1982, 52; Williams 1985, 56-8.
55. Barnes 1982, 52; 62 n.73.
56. Christol 1997, 196; Nixon and Rodgers 1994, 50-1.
57. Barnes 1982, 17-29; 254-7 tables 4-7.
58. Lactantius *de Mort. Pers.* 7.2; Aurelius Victor *de Caes.*
59. Barnes 1982, 42; Williams 1985, 67; 243 n.12; Potter 2004, 343.
60. Barnes 1982, 62 nn.74-5.
61. *Chronica Minora* I, 230.
62. Aurelius Victor *de Caes.* 39.34; Eutropius 9.25; Ammianus 14.11.10.
63. Christol 1997, 200; Speidel 1984, 406.
64. Barnes 1982, 54; Williams 1985, 81; 244-5 n.1.
65. Williams 1985, 81.
66. Bowman 2005b, 82; Wilkes 2005, 320.
67. Eutropius 9.23-24.
68. Dodgeon and Lieu 1991, 125-39; Winter 1988, 152-215; Christol 1997, 251 n.13.
69. Dodgeon and Lieu 1991, 136-8; Williams 1985, 85; Winter 1989.
70. *Pan. Lat.* 6(7).6.2-3.
71. Christol 1997, 211-3; plate 211.
72. Williams 1985, 186-200.
73. *Pan. Lat.* 7(6) 15.16; Lactantius *de Mort. Pers.* 20.4.
74. Eutropius 9.27.1; Aurelius Victor *de Caes.* 39.48.
75. Williams 1985, 65.
76. Aurelius Victor *de Caes.* 40.1; 40.8; Zosimus 2.8.1; Lactantius *de Mort. Pers.* 18.13-14; 19.16; Williams 1985, 191; Barnes 1982, 39.
77. Zosimus 2.8.3; Lactantius *de Mort. Pers.* 24; Eusebius *Life of Constantine* 1.21; Aurelius Victor *de Caes.* 40.2-4.
78. Cameron 1993, 48.
79. Pan Lat. 7(6).4.3.
80. Salway 1991, 322-3.
81. *ILS* 618.
82. Elton 2018, 40.
83. Potter 2004, 295; Elton 2018, 40.

84. Seston 1946, 299; Jones 1964, 56; 68; Southern and Dixon 1996, 30-33.
85. Vegetius *De Re Militari*. 2.2-3; 2.31.7; Duncan-Jones 1978, 553.
86. Duncan-Jones 1978, 549.
87. *Not. Dig. Occ.* XXXV 17-19; 21-22.
88. Elton 2012, 327; 2018, 99-100.
89. Southern and Dixon 1996, 12.
90. Seston 1946, 305-7; van Berchem 1952, 106-8; 1977, 542.
91. George Cedrenus *Compendium Historiarum* 454 in Migné vol. 121, 495.
92. *P.Oxy*. 43 col. 2, 24-8.
93. *CIL* III 6196=*ILS* 2781; Casey 1991, 10-12.
94. *CIL* 3. 5565=*ILS* 664.
95. Potter 2004, 453-4.
96. Zosimus 2.33.3.
97. Potter 2004, 454.
98. *C.Th*. 7.1.18; 7.4.14; 7.20.4.1; Potter 2004, 451.
99. *AE* 1937, 232.
100. *HA Severus Alexander* 58; John Malalas *Chron*. 12.308.
101. Van Berchem 1951, 21.
102. For the demise of the Praetorians see de la Bédoyère 2017, 255-7.
103. Williams 1985, 110; 249 n.20; Rees 2004, 26.
104. Lo Cascio 2005, 171.
105. Kelly 2012, 185
106. Barnes 1982, 124-8; Kelly 2012, 186.
107. Zosimus 2.33.1-2.
108. Drack 1980; Drack and Fellman 1988; Southern and Dixon 1996, 43 fig. 7.
109. Luttwak 1976; Williams 1985, 91-101.
110. Zosimus 2.34.
111. Johnson 1983, 253; Southern and Dixon 1996, 23-33.
112. Johnson 1983, 62-3 n.45; *CIL* XII 2229; Liebeschuetz 1992, 4-6.
113. Arnheim 1972; Campbell 2005, 118
114. Elton 2018, 40.
115. Williams 1985, 52; 94; 108-9.
116. *Notitia Dignitatum Oc*. XXX.
117. Campbell 2005,123.
118. *Pan. Lat*. 10(2) 3.3.
119. Garnsey 1974.
120. Williams 1985, 133-4; 251 n.8; MacMullen 1976, 166-7; 288-9 nn.54-59; *CJ* 4.13.3; 4.26.1; 10.39.3.
121. Williams 1985, 117-9.
122. Lewis and Rheinhold vol 2, 1990, 420.
123. Corbier, 2005, 360-86; Christol 1997, 208-9.
124. Cameron 1993, 36-8.
125. Seston 1946, 279-80; 289; Williams 1985, 118-9; Christol 1997, 209.
126. *AE* 1973, 526a; Barnes 1982, 17-8.
127. Barnes 1982, 18; Corcoran 2000, 205-233.
128. MacMullen1976, 113-5.
129. Erim and Reynolds 1973.
130. Potter 2004, 335.
131. Lactantius *de Mort.Pers*. 7.5-7.
132. Williams 1985, 128-32; 224-7; Potter 2004, 334-6.
133. *C.Th*. 6.35.1; Williams 1985, 110.
134. Potter 2004, 372.
135. *CJ* 9.47.12.
136. MacMullen 1976, 163; Williams 1985, 136ff.
137. Lactantius *de Mort. Pers*. 7.3.
138. MacMullen 1976, 173.
139. *C.Th*. 5.19.1; 11.1.4; 12.1.33; MacMullen 1976, 180.
140. Goffart 1974.
141. *C.Th*. 5.17.1; MacMullen 1976, 179-80.
142. Barnes 1982, 224-5; Christol 1997, 209; Rees 2004, 25.
143. Bowman 2005b, 76; Lo Cascio 2005, 180; Wilkes 2005, 707.
144. Barnes 1982, 147-174 lists the provincial governors under Diocletian and Constantine.
145. Lactantius *de Mort. Pers*. 7.4.
146. Eusebius *History of the Church* 8.1.1-6.

147. Christol 1997, 210-2; 252 n.7.
148. Campbell 1994, 237-8; Christol 1997, 210-11; 252 n.6.
149. Eusebius *History of the Church* 8.4.
150. Lactantius *de Mort. Pers.* 11.
151. Lactantius *de Mort. Pers.* 10-11.
152. Eusebius *History of the Church* 8.6.8-9.
153. Christol 1997, 212
154. Barnes 1982, 12-13.
155. Zosimus 2.10.2; Lactantius *de Mort. Pers.* 26.7.
156. Zosimus 2.10.1-3.
157. Barnes 1982, 13; 197-8.
158. Barnes 1982, 70; *Pan. Lat.* 6(7).12.1ff; 4(10). 18.1.
159. *CIL* III 4413; Christol 1997, 219.
160. Lactantius *de Mort. Pers.* 32.1.
161. Nixon and Rodgers 1994, 216 n.9.
162. Zosimus 2.11.
163. *Pan. Lat.* 6(7).2.1-3.
164. Lactantius *de Mort. Pers.* 35.3.
165. Lactantius *de Mort. Pers.* 24; Eusebius *History of the Church* 8.17.
166. Zosimus 2.15-2.17.
167. Eusebius *Life of Constantine* 1.27.
168. Lactantius *de Mort. Pers.* 44.
169. Lactantius *de Mort. Pers.* 48; Eusebius *History of the Church* 10.5.2-14.
170. Lactantius *de Mort. Pers.* 45-49.
171. Barnes 1982, 15.
172. Barnes 1982, 198; 313-324.
173. Barnes 1982, 83-5.
174. Barnes 1982, 95; Christol 1997, 241-2.
175. Barnes 1982, 76; Zosimus 2.28.1; Eutropius 10.6.1-3; Aurelius Victor *de Caes.* 41.8-9.
176. Eusebius *Life of Constantine* 4.51-2.
177. Odahl 2010, 232; Potter 2013, 239-40.
178. Pohlsander 1996, 62.
179. Eusebius *Life of Const* 3.12.1-2; Potter 2004, 418-420.
180. Drake 2012, 131; Potter 2013, 233.
181. Aurelius Victor *de Caes.* 41.11; Potter 2013, 245.
182. Eusebius *Life of Constantine* 3.46-47.
183. Odahl 2010, 226.
184. Eusebius *Life of Constantine* 4.5; Aurel. Victor *de Caes.* 41.13.
185. Potter 2004, 444; Heather 2005 74-5.
186. Liebeschuetz 1991, 11; Odahl 2010, 255-6.
187. *AE* 1925,72; 1981, 878; 1985, 823.
188. Kelly 2012, 186.
189. Eusebius *Life of Constantine* 4.56-7; 61-2; Zonaras 13.4; Dodgeon and Lieu 1991, 143-179.
190. Barnes 1981, 258-60; Odahl 2010, 267-8.
191. Lo Cascio 2005, 181.
192. Kelly 2012, 198; Elton 2018, 66.
193. Ammianus 20.6.2; Zonaras 13.5.5-15.
194. Potter 2004, 462.
195. Potter 2004, 464-5.
196. Eutropius 19.12; Zosimus 2.51.1.
197. Elton 2018, 74.
198. Ammianus 14.1.3; 1.10; Potter 2004,475.
199. Zosimus 3.1.
200. Ammianus 15.5.2; Elton 2018, 75.
201. Ammianus 15.5.21-31.
202. Ammianus 15.8.19.
203. Ammianus 16.3.1-2.
204. Ammianus 16.12.1-62.
205. Ammianus 16.12.64.
206. Ammianus 17.8.1-5; 18.2.14-19.
207. Ammianus 20.1-2.
208. Ammianus 19.1.1-8.12.
209. Potter 2004, 503; Elton 2018, 78; Mitchell 2007; 75-6.
210. Ammianus 25.3.1-23.
211. Zosimus 3.63.2; Ammianus. 25.10.12-13.
212. Potter 2004, 521.
213. Ammianus 26.1.3.
214. Ammianus 26.2.3.
215. Ammianus 26.4.3; Zozimus 3.63.3.

216. Ammianus 26.5.1; Potter 2004, 522; Elton 2018, 121.
217. Ammianus. 20.1.1-3; 26.4.5; 27.8.3.
218. Ammianus 27.8.1-2.
219. Ammianus 27.8.6-9; Birley 2005,435.
220. Ammianus 28.3.1-2; 28.3.7.
221. Ammianus 28.3.1.
222. Ammianus 27.8.10; 28.3.6.
223. Ammianus 28.3.8.
224. Ammianus 28.3.7.
225. Birley 2005, 399-400.
226. Ammianus 28.2.1-4.
227. Ammianus 28. 5.1-9.
228. Ammianus.6.2.
229. Ammianus 28.6.17-24.
230. Ammianus 27.9.4.
231. Ammianus 29.5.1-55.
232. Ammianus 28.6.7; 30.2.10-11.
233. Ammianus 28.6.25-30.
234. Ammianus 30.3.1-6.
235. Ammianus 30.5. 1-19.
236. Ammianus 30.6.1-6.
237. Ammianus 31.3.8.
238. Ammianus 31.4.1-9.
239. Ammianus 31.5.1-3.
240. Ammianus 31.12.4-5.
241. Ammianus 31.12.4-7.
242. Ammianus 31.12.10-19.
243. Potter 2004, 546.
244. Potter 2004, 556; *CTh* 16.1.2.
245. Heather and Moncur 2001, 259-260.
246. Heather 1991, 162-3.
247. Themistius Orations 16.211 a-b; Heather and Moncur 2001, 280 for translation.
248. Potter 2004, 548-9.
249. James 1988, 42.
250. Birley 2005, 443-447.
251. Birley 2005, 449.
252. Elton 2018, 139.
253. Elton 2018, 147.
254. Burns 1994, 161-2; 166-7; 183.
255. Burns 1994, 180-1; Elton 2018, 176.

## 14 The Fate of the Provinces

1. Cameron 1993, 17; Elton 2018, 155.
2. Burns 1994, 174.
3. Elton 2018, 178.
4. Elton 2018, 179.
5. Zosimus 6.6-13.
6. Mitchell 2007, 203; Heather 2005, 367.
7. Heather 2005 428.
8. Geary, 1999, 122; Elton 2018, 267.
9. Russell and Laycock 2019, 163; 169; 173.
10. Mattingly 2006, 340.
11. Cleary 2004, 416; 425.
12. Mattingly 2006, 341.
13. Mattingly 2006, 336.
14. Cleary 2004, 419.
15. Mattingly 2006, 532.
16. de la Bedoyere 1999, 43; 59.
17. Zosimus 6.10.2.
18. Birley 2005, 461-2.
19. Zosimus 6.5.2-3.
20. Heather 347-8.
21. Wood 2004, 429; Elton 2018, 181.
22. Russell and Laycock 2019, 227.
23. Mattingly 2006, 338.
24. Wood 2004, 429-30.
25. Heather 2005, 394.
26. Rivet 1988, 107.
27. Mitchell 2007, 110; 204; Elton 2018, 182-3.
28. Wightman 1985, 300-302.
29. Wightman 1985, 306; 309; Mitchell 2007, 203.
30. King 1990, 210.
31. Mitchell 2007, 206.
32. Mitchell 2007, 110; 204; Elton 2018, 182-3.
33. Mitchell 2007, 119; 211; Gregory of Tours 2.12.27.
34. Elton 2018, 216.
35. Heather 2005, 415-7.
36. Heather 2005, 429.
37. Heather 2005, 421.
38. Mitchell 2007, 206-7.
39. James,1988.

40. Mitchell 2007, 211; Ammianus 30.3; 41.10.
41. Heather 2005, 418.
42. Mitchell 2007, 214.
43. Richardson 1996, 270-271; Heather 2005, 270.
44. Richardson 1996, 277-280.
45. Zosimus 6.4.3.
46. Richardson 1996, 298-9.
47. Richardson 1996, 300; Heather 2006, 237.
48. Richardson 1996, 300-301; Heather 2006, 208.
49. Heather 2005, 208-9; 241.
50. Heather 2006, 266.
51. Richardson 1996, 302-3; Heather 2006, 344.
52. Heather 2006, 345.
53. Elton 2018, 213-4.
54. Heather 2006, 438.
55. Richardson 1996, 305.
56. Cameron 1993, 121; Elton 2018, 221.
57. Heather 2005, 267-9.
58. Heather 2005, 270-271.
59. Heather 2005, 285-6; Elton 2018, 188.
60. Heather 2005, 291-2.
61. Heather 2005, 292-3.
62. Heather 2005, 295; Elton 2018, 190.
63. Heather 2005, 398-9; Elton 2018, 213.
64. Heather 2005, 400-401; Elton 2018, 214.
65. Heather 2005, 402-6; Elton 2018, 241-2.
66. Mitchell 2007, 142; 348; 381.
67. Heather 2005, 177.
68. Elton 2018, 235.
69. Eugippius *Life of St Severin* 20.1.
70. Alföldy, 1974, 215-7; Johnson 1983, 240.
71. Johnson 1983, 240.
72. Zosimus 5.46.2; Mocsy 1974, 348; Alföldy, 1974, 213.
73. Alföldy, 1974, 223; Eugippius *Life of St Severin*. 12.7; 29.1; 44.1.
74. Alföldy, 1974, 223; Eugippius *Life of St Severin*. 44.1.
75. Christie 1995, 21.
76. Tac. *Germania* 40.
77. Mocsy 1974, 274.
78. Zosimus 5.46.2; Mocsy 1974, 348; Alföldy, 1974, 213.
79. Mocsy 1974, 349-350.
80. Elton 2018, 315.
81. *C.Th.* 6.29.12; Wilkes 1969, 419.
82. Wilkes 1969, 425-6; Elton 267.
83. Wilkes 1969, 419-426.
84. Elton 2018, 133; 139.
85. Heather 1999, 475.
86. Golden, 1999, 354.
87. Golden 1999, 325-6; Fowden 549-550.
88. Mitchell 2007, 106.
89. Jones 1937, 27; Procopius *Buildings* 4.11.
90. Elton 2018, 38; 41.
91. Mitchell 2007, 337-8.
92. Jones1937, 185-6; 190.
93. Mitchell 2007, 339-340.
94. Cameron 1993, 121; Elton 2018, 221.
95. Elton 2018, 294.
96. Elton 2018, 290; 298.
97. Mitchell 2007, 408-410; Elton 2018, 299.
98. Mitchell 2007, 411-2; Elton 2018, 300-302.
99. Mitchell 2007, 412.
100. Mitchell 2007, 412-3; Elton 2018, 334-5.
101. Elton 2018, 334-340.
102. Elton 2018, 342-349.
103. Mitchell 2007, 349.
104. Mitchell 2007, 411-419; Elton 2018, 349.

# Bibliography

**Ancient Sources**
Ammianus Marcellinus
Appian *BC Civil Wars*
Appian *Gall. Gallic History*
Appian *Hann. Hannibalic War*
Appian *Ill. Illyrian Wars*
Appian *Mith. Mithridatic Wars*
Appian *Pun. Punic Wars*
Appian *Samn. Samnite History*
Appian *Sic. Of Sicily*
Appian *Sp. Wars in Spain*
Appian *Syr. Syrian Wars*
Aurelius Victor *de Caesaribus*
Caesar *Alexandrian, African and Spanish Wars*
Caesar *Civil War*
Caesar *Gallic War*
Cicero *Ad Att. Letters to Atticus*
Cicero *Ad Fam. Letters to his Friends*
Cicero *De Imp. De Imperio Gnaei Pompeii* or *Pro Lege Manilia*
Cicero *De Legibus*
Cicero *De Officiis*
Cicero *De Re Publica*
Cicero *Pro Balbo*
Cicero *Pro Plancio*
Cicero *Verrine Orations*
Dio *Roman History*
Diodorus Siculus
*Epitome de Caesaribus*
Eugippius *Life of St Severin*
Eusebius *History of the Church*
Eusebius *Life of Constantine*
Eutropius *Breviarum ab Urbe Condita*. Trans. H. Bird. Liverpool Univ. Press. 1993.

Frontinus *Aqueducts of Rome*
Frontinus *Stratagems*
Gaius *Institutionum Iuris Civilis*. Trans. E. Poste. Oxford Univ. Press.
Gellius *Attic Nights*
Gregory of Tours
Herodian *History of the Empire*
*Historiae Augustae*
Jordanes *Getica=Gothic History of Jordanes* trans. C. Mierow
Jordanes *Romana*
Josephus *Jewish Antiquities*
Josephus *Jewish War*
Julius Solinus
Lactantius *De Mortibus Persecutorum*
Livy *History of Rome*
Livy *Periochae*, summaries of books 37-40; 46-142.
Orosius
Ovid *Fasti*
Plutarch *Parallel Lives*
Pliny *NH Natural History*
Plutarch *Parallel Lives*
Plutarch *Aemilius Paulus*
Plutarch *Antony*
Plutarch *Caesar*
Plutarch *Gaius Gracchus*
Plutarch *Pompey*
Plutarch *Romulus*
Plutarch *Tiberius Gracchus*
Piny *Natural History*
Polybius *The Histories*
Pomponius Mela
Procopius *On Buildings*
Saint Cyprian *Lettres* Paris, 1925, 2 vols.
Sallust *Histories*
Sallust *War with Catiline*
Sallust *War with Jugurtha*
*Scriptores Historiae Augustae*: see *Historiae Augustae*.
Strabo *Geography*
Suetonius *Twelve Caesars*
Tacitus *Agricola*
Tacitus *Annals*
Tacitus *Germania*
Tacitus *Histories*
Valerius Maximus *Memorable Deeds and Sayings*. Trans. D. Wardle 1998. Oxford Univ.
  Press.
Varro *On the Latin Language*
Vegetius, Publius *Ars Mulomedicinae*
Vegetius, Flavius *Epitoma Rei Militaris*. Trans. N. P. Milner 1993. Liverpool Univ. Press.
Velleius Paterculus *Compendium of Roman History*
Virgil *Aeneid*

Vitruvius *The Ten Books on Architecture*. Translated by M.H. Morgan. New York: Dover Publications Inc.

Zonaras

Zosimus *New History*, trans. R. T. Ridley, Australian Assoc. for Byzantine Studies, 1982.

**Modern works**

Alcock, S. 1993, *Graecia Capta: the landscapes of Roman Greece*. Cambridge Univ. Press.

Alföldy, G. 1974, *Noricum*. Routledge.

Alston, R. 1995, *Soldier and Society in Roman Egypt: a Social History*. Routledge.

Arnheim, M. T. W. 1972, *The Senatorial Aristocracy in the Later Roman Empire*. Clarendon Press.

Baatz, D. 1973, *Kastell Hesselbach und andere Forschungen am Odenwaldlimes*. Limesforschungen 12.

Badian, E. 1958, *Foreign Clientelae 264-70 BC*. Oxford: Clarendon Press.

Balsdon, J. P. V. D. 1979, *Romans and Aliens*. Duckworth.

Barnes, T. D. 1982, *The New Empire of Diocletian and Constantine*. Harvard Univ. Press.

Beard, M. 2015, *SPQR: a history of ancient Rome*. Profile Books

Beard, M. and Crawford, M. 1985, *Rome in the Late Republic: problems and interpretations*. Duckworth.

Bidwell, P. (ed.) 2008, *Understanding Hadrian's Wall*. The Arbeia Society.

Billows, R. 2007, 'International relations', in Sabin (et al.), 2007a, 303-324.

Birley, A. R. 1987, *Marcus Aurelius: a Biography*. Routledge. Rev. ed.

Birley, A. R. 1988, *Septimius Severus: The African Emperor*. Routledge. Rev. ed.

Birley, A. R. 1997, *Hadrian: the Restless Emperor*. Routledge.

Birley, A. R. 2005, *The Roman Government of Britain*. Oxford Univ. Press.

Bleiken, J. 1990, *Zwischen Republik und Prinzipat; Zum Charakter des Zweiten Triumvirats*. Vandenhoek und Ruprecht.

Boatwright, M. T. (et al.) 2004, *The Romans: from village to Empire*. Oxford University Press.

Bowersock, G. W. 1983, *Roman Arabia*. Harvard Univ. Press.

Bowersock, G. W. (et al) (eds.) 1999, *Late Antiquity: a guide to the post-classical world*. Belknap Press of Harvard Univ. Press.

Bowman, A. K. et al. (eds.) 2005, *The Crisis of Empire AD 193-337*. Cambridge Ancient History vol. 12. Cambridge Univ. Press. 2nd ed.

Bowman, A. K. 2005b, 'Diocletian and the first Tetrarchy', in Bowman 2005, 67-89.

Braund, D. C. 1984, *Rome and the Friendly King: the character of client kingship*. Croom Helm.

Braund, D. 1987, 'The legacy of the Republic' in Wacher1987 (ed.), 55-68.

Braund, D. (ed.) 1988, *The Administration of the Roman Empire 214 BC to AD 193*. University of Exeter Press.

Breeze, D. 2006, *Handbook to the Roman Wall*. SANT. 14th ed.

Breeze, D. 2014, *Hadrian's Wall: a history of archaeological thought*. CWAAS extra series no. XLII.

Breeze, D. and Dobson, B. 2000, *Hadrian's Wall*. Penguin, 4th ed.

Broughton, T. R. S. 1929, *The Romanization of Africa Proconsularis*. Johns Hopkins. University Press. Reprinted 1972 by Greenwood Press.

Brunt, P. A. 1971, *Italian Manpower 225 BC-AD14*. Oxford.

Burns, T. S. 1994, *Barbarians Within the Gates of Rome: a study of Roman military policy and the barbarians c.373-425 AD*. Indiana Univ. Press.

Burton, P. J. 2011, *Friendship and Empire: Roman diplomacy and imperialism in the middle Republic (353-146 BC).* Cambridge Univ. Press.

Callu, J. P. 1969, *La Politique Monétaire des Empereurs Romains de 238 à 311.* Paris.

Cameron, A. 1993, *The Mediterranean World in Late Antiquity AD 395-600.* Routledge.

Campbell, J. B. 1984, *The Emperor and the Roman Army 31 BC to AD 235.* Clarendon Press.

Campbell, 2005, 'The army', in Bowman 2005, 110-131.

Carandini, A. (et al.) (eds.) 2017, *The Atlas of Ancient Rome.* 2 vols. Princeton Univ. Press, 2017

Carruba, A. M. 2006, *La Lupa Capitolina: un bronzo medievale.* De Luca Editore d'Arte.

Casey, J, 1991, *The Legions in the Later Roman Empire:Fourth Annual Caerleon Lecture.* National Museum of Wales.

Casey, J. 1994, *Carausius and Allectus: The British usurpers.* Batsford.

Christie, N. 1995, *The Lombards: the ancient Langobards.* Blackwell.

Christol, M. 1986, *Essai sur l'Evolution de Carrières Sénatoriales dans le Deuxieme Moitié du IIIe Siecle après J.-C.* Paris.

Christol, M. 1997, *L'Empire Romain du IIIe Siècle: histoire politique 193-325 aprés J.-C.* Editions Errance.

Cizek, E. 1994, *L'Empereur Aurélien et son Temps.* Les Belles Lettres.

Claridge, A. 2010, *Rome: An Oxford archaeological guide.* Oxford Univ. Press.

Cleary, S. E. 2002, 'Britain in the fourth century', in Todd 2004, 409-427.

Cloud, D. 1992, 'The constitution and criminal law', in Crook, J. A. (et al.) 1992, 491-530.

Coarelli, F. 2014, *Rome and Environs: an archaeological guide.* University of California Press.

Cooley, A. E. 2009, *Res Gestae Divi Augusti: text, translation and commentary.* Cambridge Univ. Press.

Corbier, M. 2005, 'Coinage and taxation: the state's point of view AD 193-337', in Bowman 2012, 327-392.

Corcoran, S. 2000, *The Empire of the Tetrarchs: Imperial pronouncements and government AD 284 to 324.* Clarendon Press. 2nd ed.

Coriat, J.-P. 1997, *Le Prince Législature: la technique législative des Sévères et les methods du création du droit imperiale a la fin du Principat.* Ecole Francaise de Rome.

Cornell, T. J. 1995, *The Beginnings of Rome: Italy and Rome from the Bronze Age to the Punic wars (c.1000-264 BC).* Routledge.

Coulston, J. and Dodge, H. (eds.) 2000, *Ancient Rome: the archaeology of the Eternal City.* Oxford School of Archaeology Monograph 54.

Cowan, R. H. 2009, *Roman Conquests: Italy.* Pen and Sword Military.

Crawford, M. 1975, 'Finance, coinage and money from the Severans to Constantine', ANRW II.2, 560-593.

Crees, J. H. E. 1911, *The Reign of the Emperor Probus.* London Univ. Press.

Crook, J. 1955, *Consilium Principis.* Cambridge Univ. Press.

Crook, J. A. (et al.) (eds.) 1992. *The Last Age of the Roman Republic 146-43 BC.* Cambridge Ancient History Vol. 9. 2nd ed.

Crow, J. 2004, 'The northern frontier of Britain from Trajan to Antoninus Pius: Roman builders and native Britons', in Todd 2004, 114-135.

Curchin, L. A. 1991, *Roman Spain: conquest and assimilation.* Routledge.

Daniels, C. M. 1978, *Handbook to the Roman Wall with the Cumbrian coast and outpost forts.* Harold Hill and Son. 13th ed.

Dart, C. J. 2014, *The Social War, 91 to 88 BCE; a history of the Italian insurgency against the Roman Republic*. Ashgate.

de Blois, L. 1976, *The Policy of the Emperor Gallienus*. Nederlands Instituut te Rome.

de la Bédoyère, G. 1999, *Companion to Roman Britain*. Tempus.

de la Bédoyère, G. 2017, *Praetorian: the rise and fall of Rome's Imperial Guard*. Yale Univ. Press.

de Ligt, L. 2007, 'Roman manpower and recruitment during the middle Republic', in Erdkamp 2007, 114-131.

de Souza, P. 1999, *Piracy in the Graeco-Roman World*. Cambridge Univ. Press.

de Souza, P. 2007, 'Military forces: B naval forces' in Sabin (et al) (eds) 2007a, 357-367.

de Souza, P. and France, J. (eds.) 2008, *War and Peace in Ancient and Medieval History*. Cambridge Univ. Press.

Develin, R. 1971, 'The army pay rises under Severus and Caracalla and the question of *annona militaris*', *Latomus* 30, 687-695.

Devijver, H. 1989, *Equestrian Officers in the Roman Imperial Army*. J.-C. Gieben.

Dobson, B. 1986, 'The function of Hadrian's Wall', *AA* fifth series, vol. 14, 1-30.

Dodgeon, M. H. and Lieu, S. N. C. 1991, *The Roman Eastern Frontier and the Persian Wars (AD 226-363): a documentary history*. Routledge.

Drack, W. 1980, *Die Spätrömische Grenzwehr am Hochrhein*. Archäologische Führer der Schweiz 13. Zurich.

Drack, W. and Fellman, R. 1988, *Die Römer in der Schweiz*. Theiss.

Drake, H. A. 2012, 'The impact of Constantine on Christianity', in Lenski 2012a, 111-136.

Drinkwater, J. F. 1983, *Roman Gaul: the three Gauls 58 BC -260 AD*. Croom Helm.

Drinkwater, J. F. 1987, *The Gallic Empire: separatism and continuity in the north-west provinces of the Roman Empire AD 260-274*. Stuttgart.

Dudley, D. R. 1967, *Urbs Roma: a sourcebook of classical texts on the city and its monuments*. Phaidon Press.

Duncan-Jones, R. 1978, 'Pay and numbers in Diocletian's army', *Chiron* 8, 541-560.

Ebel, C. 1976, *Transalpine Gaul: the emergence of a Roman province*. Brill.

Edmondson, J. (ed.) 2009, *Augustus*. Edinburgh Univ. Press.

Elton, H, 2012, 'Warfare and the military' in Lenski 2012a, 325-346.

Elton, H. 2018, *The Roman Empire in Late Antiquity: a political and military history*. Cambridge Univ. Press.

Erdkamp, P. (ed.) 2007, *A Companion to the Roman Army*. Wiley-Blackwell. Reprinted 2011.

Erdkamp, P. (ed.) 2013, *The Cambridge Companion to Ancient Rome*. Cambridge Univ. Press.

Erim, K. T. and Reynolds, J. 1973, 'The Aphrodisias copy of Diocletian's edict on maximum prices', *JRS* 63, 99-110.

Erskine, A. 2010, *Roman Imperialism*. Edinburgh University Press

Fields, N. 2010, *Roman Conquests: North Africa*. Pen and Sword.

Fishwick, D. 1987, *The Imperial Cult in the Latin West*. Leiden: EPROR.

Forsythe, G. 2011, 'The army and centuriate organization in early Rome', in Erdkamp 2011, 24-42.

Fowden, E. 1997, 'Macedonia' in Bowersock 1999, 549-550.

French, D. H. and Lightfoot, C. S. (eds.) 1989, *The Eastern Frontier of the Roman Empire*. British Archaeological Reports S 553, 2 vols. Oxford.

Fuhrmann, C. 2012, *Policing the Roman Empire: soldiers, administration and public order*. Oxford Univ. Press.

Gabba, E. 1992, 'Rome and Italy: The Social War', in Crook, J. A. (et al.) 1992, 104-128.

Galinsky, K. 1996, *Augustan Culture: an interpretive introduction*. Princeton Univ. Press.

Gargola, D. J. 2007, 'Mediterranean empire (264-234)', in Rosenstein and Morstein-Marx 2007, 147-166.

Garnsey, P. 1974, 'Decline of the urban aristocracy in the Empire', *ANRW* 2.1, 229-252

Garnsey, P. 1988, *Famine and Food Supply in Graeco-Roman Antiquity*. Cambridge Univ. Press.

Garnsey, P. and Whittaker, C. R. (ed.) 1983, *Trade and Famine in Classical Antiquity*. Cambridge Univ. Press.

Geary, P.J. 1999, 'Barbarians and ethnicity', in Bowersock 1999, 107-129.

Gelzer, M. 1968, *Caesar: politician and statesman*. Harvard Univ. Press.

Gillam, J. P. 1958, 'Roman and native, AD 122-97', in Richmond 1958, 60-90.

Goffart, W. 1974, *Caput and Colonate: towards a history of late Roman taxation*. *Phoenix* supplementary volume.

Golden, P. B. 1999, 'The Bulgars' in Bowersock 1999, 354.

Gowing, A. M. 1992, *The Triumviral Narratives of Appian and Cassius Dio*. Univ. Michigan Press.

Greenhalgh, P. 1980, *Pompey: The Roman Alexander*. Weidenfeld and Nicolson.

Greenhalgh, P. 1981, *Pompey: The Republican Prince*. Weidenfeld and Nicolson.

Griffin, M. T. 1984, *Nero: the end of a dynasty*. Batsford.

Gruen. E. S. 1974, *The Last Generation of the Roman Republic*. Univ. California Press.

Harris, W. V. 1979, *War and Imperialism in Republican Rome 327-70 BC*. Oxford Univ. Press. Reprinted 1992 with corrections.

Heather, P. 1999, 'Goths', in Bowersock 1999, 475.

Heather, P. 2005, *The Fall of the Roman Empire: a new history*. Macmillan.

Heather, P. and Moncur, D. 2002, *Politics, Philosophy, and the Empire in the Fourth Century: select orations of Themistius*. Liverpool Univ. Press.

Hind, J. G. F. 1992, 'Mithradates' in Crook J.A. (et al) 1992, 129-164.

Hodgson, N. 1995, 'Were there two occupations of the Antonine Wall?', *Britannia* 26, 29-49.

Hodgson, N. 2009a, *Hadrian's Wall 1999-2009: a summary of excavation and research prepared for the Thirteenth Pilgrimage of Hadrian's Wall 8-14 August 2009*. CWAAS and SANT.

Hodgson, N. 2009b, 'The abandonment of Antonine Scotland; its date and cause', in Hanson 2009, 185-93.

Hodgson, N. 2011, 'The provenance of *RIB* 1389 and the rebuilding of Hadrian's Wall in 158', in Hanson 2009, 185-193.

Hoyos, D. 1998, *Unplanned wars: the origins of the First and Second Punic Wars*. Berlin.

Hoyos, D. 2019, *Rome Victorious: the irresistible rise of the Roman Empire*. I. B. Tauris.

Huzar, E. G. 1978, *Mark Antony: a biography*. Univ. Minnesota Press

Ireland, S. 1996, *Roman Britain: a sourcebook*. Routledge.

Ivaldi, R. 2005, *La Mura di Roma*. Newton and Compton Editori.

James, E. 1988, *The Franks*. Blackwell.

Johnson, S. 1976, *Roman Forts of the Saxon Shore*. Elek.

Johnson, S. 1983, *Late Roman Fortifications*. Batsford.

Johnson, S. 1989, 'Architecture of the Saxon Shore forts', in Maxfield 1989, 30-44.

Jones, A. H. M. 1937, *Cities of the Eastern Roman Provinces*. Oxford Univ. Press

Jones, A. H. M. 1964, *The Later Roman Empire 284-602*. Blackwell, 2 vols.

Jones, A. H. M. 1974, *The Roman Economy: studies in ancient economic and administrative history*. Blackwell.

Jones, B. W. 1992, *The Emperor Domitian*. London.

Kelly, C. 2012, 'Bureaucracy and government', in Lenski 2012a, 183-294.

Kennedy, D. 1987, 'The frontiers: the east', in Wacher 1987, 266-308.

Kent, J. P. C. 1978, *Roman Coins*. Thames and Hudson.

Keppie, L. 1983, *Colonisation and Veteran Settlement in Italy 47-14BC*. British School at Rome.

Keppie, L. 1984, *The Making of the Roman Army: from Republic to Empire*. Routledge. Reprinted 1998.

Kienast, D. 1982, *Augustus: Prinzeps und Monarch*. Darmstadt: Wissenschaftliche Buchgesellschaft.

King, A. 1990, *Roman Gaul and Germany*. British Museum Publications

König, I. 1981, *Die Gallischen Usurpatoren von Postumus bis Tetricus*. Beck'sche Verlag.

Lacey, E. K. 1996, *Augustus and the Principate: the evolution of the system*. Francis Cairns.

Lazenby, J. F. 1988, *Hannibal's War; a military history of the Second Punic War*. University of Oklahoma Press. First published 1978.

Leach, J. 1978, *Pompey the Great*. Croom Helm.

Lenski, N. (ed.) 2012a, *Cambridge Companion to the Age of Constantine*. Cambridge Univ. Press.

Lenski, N. 2012b, 'The reign of Constantine', in Lenski 2012a, 59-90.

Levick, B. 1990, *Claudius*. Batsford.

Levick, B. 1999, *Vespasian*. Routledge.

Levick, B. 2000, *The Government of the Roman Empire: a sourcebook*. Routledge, 2nd ed.

Levick, B. 2010, *Augustus: image and substance*. Longman.

Lewis, N. 1996, 'The humane legislation of Septimius Severus', *Historia* 45, 104-113.

Lewis, N. and Rheinhold, M. (eds.). 1990, *Roman Civilization: selected readings. Vol. I. The Republic and the Augustan Age*. Columbia University Press. 3rd ed.

Lewis, N. and Rheinhold, M. (eds.). 1990, *Roman Civilization: selected readings. Vol. II. The Empire*. Columbia University Press. 3rd ed.

Liebeschuetz, W. 1992, 'The end of the ancient city', in Rich 1992,1-49.

Lintott, A. 1992a, 'The Roman Empire and its problems in the late second century', in Crook, J.A. (et al.) 1992, 16-39.

Lintott, A. 1992b, 'Political history 146-95 BC', in Crook, J. A. (et al.) 1992, 40-103.

Lintott, A. 1993, *Imperium Romanum: politics and administration*. Routledge.

Lintott, A. 1999, *The Constitution of the Roman Republic*. Oxford University Press.

Lo Cascio, E. 2005, 'The new state of Diocletian and Constantine: from the Tetrarchy to the reunification of the Empire', in Bowman 2005a, 170-183.

Loriot, X. and Nony, D. 1997, *La Crise de l'Empire Romain 235-285*. Armand Colin.

Lott, J. B. 2004, *The Neighbourhoods of Imperial Rome*. Cambridge Univ. Press.

Mackay, C. S. 2009, *The Breakdown of the Roman Republic: from oligarchy to empire*. Cambridge Univ. Press.

MacMullen, R. 1966, *Enemies of the Roman Order; treason, unrest and alienation in the Empire*. Harvard Univ. Press.

MacMullen, R. 1976, *The Roman Government's Response to Crisis AD 235 to 337*. Yale Univ. Press

Magdelain, A. 1947, *Auctoritas Principis*. Paris: Belles Lettres.

Mann, J. C. 1989, 'Historical development of the Saxon Shore', in Maxfield 1989, 1-11.

Matthews, J. F. 1989, *The Roman Empire of Ammianus*. Duckworth.

Mattingly, D. 2006, *An Imperial Possession: Britain in the Roman Empire*. Allen Lane.

Maxfield, V. A. 1987, 'The frontiers: mainland Europe', in Wacher 1987, 139-197.

Maxfield, V. A. (ed.) 1989, *The Saxon Shore: a handbook*. Univ. Exeter Press.

Meiggs, R. 1973, *Roman Ostia*. Clarendon Press. 2nd ed.

Migné, J. P. (ed.) *Patrologia Graeca*. Belgium. 161 vols.

Millar, F. 1981, *The Roman Empire and its Neighbours*. Duckworth. 2nd ed.

Millar, F. 1993, *The Roman Near East 31 BC to AD 337*. Harvard Univ. Press.

Millett, M. 1990, *The Romanization of Britain: an essay in archaeological interpretation*. Cambridge Univ. Press.

Mitchell, S. 2007, *A History of the Later Roman Empire AD 284-641*. Blackwell.

Mocsy, A. 1974, *Pannonia and Upper Moesia: a history of the middle Danube provinces of the Roman Empire*. Routledge.

Nippel, W. 1995, *Public Order in Ancient Rome*. Cambridge Univ. Press.

Nixon, C. E. V. and Rodgers, B. S. 1994, *In Praise of Later Roman Emperors: The Panegyrici Latini*. Univ. California Press.

Odahl, C. M. 2010, *Constantine and the Christian Empire*. Routledge.

Osgood, J. 2006, *Caesar's Legacy: civil war and the emergence of the Roman Empire*. Cambridge Univ. Press.

Parker, H. M. D. 1935, *History of the Roman World AD 138-337*. Methuen.

Pelling, C. B. R. (ed.) 1988, *Plutarch: life of Antony*. Cambridge Univ. Press

Petit, P. 1974, *La Crise de l'Empire: des derniers Antonins à Diocletién*. Editions de Seuil.

Platner, S. B. and Ashby, T. 1926, *A Topographical Dictionary of Rome*. Oxford University Press.

Pohlsander, H. A. 1996, *The Emperor Constantine*. Routledge.

Potter, D. 2013, *Constantine the Emperor*. Routledge.

Potter, D. S. 1996, 'Palmyra and Rome: Odenathus' titulature and the use of Imperium Maius', *ZPE* 113, 271-185.

Potter, D. S. 2004, *The Roman Empire at Bay AD 180-395*. Routledge.

Potter, T. W. 1987, *Roman Italy*. British Museum Press.

Raaflaub, K. A. 2009, 'Political significance of Augustus' military reforms', in Edmondson (ed.) 2009, 203-228.

Raaflaub, K. A. and Samons, L. J. H. 1990, 'Opposition to Augustus', in Raaflaub and Toher 1990, 417-454.

Raaflaub, K. A. and Toher, M. (eds.) 1990, *Between Republic and Empire: interpretations of Augustus and his Principate*. Univ. of Los Angeles Press.

Raven, S. 1993, *Rome in Africa*. Routledge. 3rd ed.

Rawson, E. 1992, 'Caesar: civil war and dictatorship' in Crook, J. A. (et al) 1992, 424-467.

Rees, R. 2004, *Diocletian and the Tetrarchy*. Edinburgh Univ. Press.

Reynolds, J. 1982, *Aphrodisias and Rome*. Society for the Promotion of Roman Studies.

Rich, J. (ed.) 1992, *The City in Late Antiquity*. Routledge.

Rich, J. 2007, 'Warfare and the army in early Rome,' in Erdkamp 2007, 7-23.

Rich, J. 2008, 'Treaties, allies and the Roman conquest of Italy,' in de Souza and France 2008, 51-75.

Richardson, J. 1976, *Roman Provincial Administration 227 BC to AD117*. Bristol Classical Press.

Richardson, J. 1986, *Hispaniae: Spain and the development of Roman Imperialism, 218-82 BC*. Cambridge Univ. Press.

Richardson, J. 1996, *The Romans in Spain*. Blackwell.

Richmond, I. A. R. 1930, *The City Wall of Imperial Rome*. Oxford.

Richmond, I. A. R. (ed.) 1958, *Roman and Native in North Britain*. Nelson.

Rickman, G. 1980, *The Corn Supply of Ancient Rome*. Clarendon Press.

Rivet, A. L. F. 1988, *Gallia Narbonensis*. Batsford.

Rosenstein, N. 2012, *Rome and the Mediterranean 290 to 146 BC: the Imperial Republic*. Edinburgh University Press.

Rosenstein, N. and Morstein-Marx, R. 2007, *A Companion to the Roman Republic*. Blackwell. Reprinted 2010.

Russell, M. and Laycock, S. 2010, *UnRoman Britain: exposing the great myth of Britannia*. History Press.

Sabin, P. et al (eds.) 2007a, *The Cambridge History of Greek and Roman Warfare vol. I: Greece, the Hellenistic world and the Rise of Rome*. Cambridge Univ. Press.

Sabin, P. et al (eds.) 2007b, *The Cambridge History of Greek and Roman Warfare vol. 2: Rome from the Late Republic to the Late Empire*. Cambridge Univ. Press.

Salmon, E. T. 1967, *Samnium and the Samnites*. Cambridge Univ Press.

Salmon, E. T. 1969, *Roman Colonization under the Republic*. Thames and Hudson.

Salmon, E. T. 1982, *The Making of Roman Italy*. Thames and Hudson.

Salway, P. 1991, *Roman Britain*. Clarendon Press.

Salway, P. 1993, *Oxford Illustrated Roman Britain*. Oxford Univ. Press.

Sampson, G. C. 2016, *Rome Spreads Her Wings: territorial expansion between the Punic Wars*. Pen and Sword.

Sartre, M. 2005, *The Middle East Under Rome*. Belknap Press of Harvard Univ. Press.

Schmitthenner, W. 1952, *Oktavian und das Testament Caesars: eine Untersuchung zu den Politischen Anfangen des Augustus*. Munich: C.H. Beck'sche Verlag.

Schönberger, H von. 1964, 'Die Römerkastell Künzing Grabung 1962', Saalburg Jahrbuch 21 1963-4, 46-48.

Schönberger, H von. 1985, Die römische Truppenlager der frühen and mittleren Kaiserzeit zwischen Nordsee und Inn', *BRGK* 66, 321-497.

Scullard, H. H. 1967, *The Etruscan Cities and Rome*. Thames and Hudson.

Seager, R, 1979, *Pompey: a political biography*. Blackwell.

Seager, R. 1992a, 'Sulla', in Crook J. A. (et al.) 1992, 165-207.

Seager, R. 1992b, 'The rise of Pompey', in Crook J. A. (et al.) 1992, 208-228.

Serrati, J. 2000a, 'The coming of the Romans: Sicily from the first to the fourth century BC', in Smith and Serrati (eds.) 2000, 109-114.

Serrati, J. 2000b, 'Garrisons and grain', in Smith and Serrati (eds.) 2000, 126-31.

Seston, W. 1946, *Dioclétien et la Tétrarchie; guerres et réformes*. Boccard.

Sherk, R. K. (ed.) 1988, *The Roman Empire from Augustus to Hadrian*. Translated Documents of Greece and Rome vol. 6, Cambridge Univ. Press.

Sherwin-White, A. N. 1973, *The Roman Citizenship*. Clarendon Press, 2nd ed.

Sherwin-White, A. N. 1992, 'Lucullus, Pompey and the East', in Crook, J. A. (et al) 1992, 229-273.

Smith, C. 2000, 'Early and archaic Rome', in Coulston and Dodge (eds.) 2000, 16-41.

Smith, C, and Serrati, J. (eds.) 2000. *Sicily from Aeneas to Augustus: new approaches in archaeology and history*. Edinburgh University Press.

Southern, P. 1989, 'The *numeri* of the Roman Imperial army', *Britannia* 20, 81-140.

Southern, P. 1997, *Domitian: tragic tyrant*. Routledge.

Southern, P. 2008, *The Empress Zenobia: Palmyra's rebel queen*. Continuum.

Southern, P. 2014, *Augustus*. Routledge. 2nd ed.

Southern, P. 2015, *The Roman Empire from Severus to Constantine*. Routledge. 2nd ed.

Southern, P. and Dixon, K. R. 1996, *The Late Roman Army*. Routledge.

Speidel, M. P. 1984, *Roman Army Studies vol. I*. Amsterdam.

Speidel, M. P. 1994, *Riding for Caesar: The Roman Emperors' Horse Guards*. Batsford.

Steel, C. 2013, *The End of the Roman Republic 146 to 44 BC*. Edinburgh Univ. Press.

Stevens, C. E. 1966, *The Building of Hadrian's Wall*. Kendal.

Syme, R. 1939, *The Roman Revolution*. Oxford Univ. Press.

Talbert, R. J. A. 1984, *The Senate of Imperial Rome*. Princeton Univ. Press.

Todd, M. 1978, *The Walls of Rome*. Elek.

Todd, M. (ed.) 2004, *A Companion to Roman Britain*. Blackwell.

Van Berchem, D.1952, *L'Armée de Dioclétien et la Réforme Constantinienne*. Paris: Imprimerie Nationale

Wacher, J. (ed.). 1987, *The Roman World*. Routledge and Kegan Paul. 2 vols.

Waterfield, R. 2014, *Taken at the Flood; the Roman conquest of Greece*. Oxford University Press.

Watson, G. R. 1969, *The Roman Soldier*. Thames and Hudson.

Weinstock, S. 1971, *Divus Julius*. Oxford Univ. Press.

Welfare, H. 2000, 'Causeways, at milecastles, across the ditch of Hadrian's Wall', *AA* fifth series, vol.28, 13-25.

Whittaker, C. R. 1994, *Frontiers of the Roman Empire: a social and economic study*. Johns Hopkins Univ. Press.

Wightman, E. M. 1985, *Gallia Belgica*. Batsford.

Wilkes, J. 1969, *Dalmatia*. Routledge.

Wilkes, J. 2005, 'Provinces and frontiers', in Bowman 2005a, 212-268.

Williams, S. 1985, *Diocletian and the Roman Recovery*. Batsford, reprinted by Routledge 1997.

Wilson, R. J. A. 1990, *Sicily under the Roman Empire: the archaeology of a Roman province 36 BC-AD 535*. Aris and Phillips.

Winter, E. 1988, *Die Sasanadischen-römischen Friedensvertrage des 3 Jahrhunderts nach Christi*. Peter Lang.

Winter, E. 1989, 'On the regulation of the eastern frontier of the Roman Empire in 298', in French and Lightfoot 1989, 555-571.

Wiseman, T. P. 1992a, 'The Senate and the populares, 69-60BC', in Crook, J. A. (et al) 1992, 327-367.

Wiseman, T. P. 1992b, 'Caesar, Pompey and Rome, 59-50 BC' in Crook, J. A. (et al) 1992, 368-423.

Wolff, H. 1978, *Die Constitutio Antoniniana und Papyrus Gissensis 40.1*. Cologne.

Wolfram, H. 1988, *History of the Goths*. Univ. California Press.

Wood, I. 2004, 'The final phase', in Todd, M. 2004, 428-442.

Woolf, G. 1998, *Becoming Roman: the origins of provincial civilization in Gaul*. Cambridge Univ. Press.

Woolliscroft, D. J. 1996, 'Signalling and the design of the Antonine Wall', *Britannia* 27, 153-177.

Woolliscroft, D. J. 2008, 'Signalling on Roman frontiers', in Bidwell 2008, 91-98.

Woolliscroft, D. J. and Hoffmann, B. 2006, *Rome's First Frontier: The Flavian occupation of northern Scotland*. History Press.

# Index

**Constantius**; nicknamed Chlorus; made Caesar under Maximian at creation of Tetrachy, and restores the breakaway province of Britain to Rome 413-414; becomes Augustus at Diocletian's retirement, takes Valerius Severus as his Caesar 416; campaigns in Britain with his son Constantine, dies in AD 306 at York, and army proclaims Constantine as Augustus 416

**Constantius II**; war against Shapur II to relieve siege of Nisibis 437; defeats usurper Magnentius at Mursa 438; frees Julian and his half-brother Gallus from captivity, raises Gallus and Julian to rank of Caesar to command respectively in the east and on the Rhine 438; Gallus executed 438; Julian defeats Alamanni and troops proclaim him Emperor, and Constantius dies in Cilicia 439

**Cornelius Scipio, Publius** (consul 218); defeated by Hannibal in Italy 86-7; commands in Spain and killed 94

**Cornelius Scipio, Gnaeus**, brother of above; commands in Spain while Hannibal fights in Italy 86; joined by Publius in Spain, and defeated and killed 94

**Corsica** made a province with Sardinia 81-82

**Cornelius Sulla, Lucius** 145-146; gains and loses command against Mithradates 147; marches on Rome 147; defeats Mithradates 147-148; reorganises province of Asia 148-149; returns to Rome and defeats enemies 150-152; made Dictator and legislates to strengthen Senate 153; weakens tribunes of the plebs 153; death 154

**Crassus** see Licinius Crassus, Marcus

**Dacia**; Dacians invade Moesia in AD 69, repelled by Mucianus 297; after another invasion of Moesia Domitian mounts two campaigns against Decebalus the Dacian leader, and makes peace 297-298; province annexed after Trajan's two campaigns 305; divided into three provinces 312; Decius drives the Carpi out of Dacia 380; evacuated by Aurelian, new Dacia established in Moesian territory, split into Dacia Ripensis and Dacia Mediterranea 405-406

**Dalmatia**; province created from southern half of Illyricum 136; 471; use of the name Illyricum persisted and Alaric was given command of Illyricum 471; in fifth century population of Dalmatia flee into Pannonia 471; Vandals threaten the coasts, Marcellinus put in command, but killed, and Suevi tribesmen enter the province unopposed 471; Marcellinus' nephew Nepos takes command, but is assassinated, and Odoacer ruler of Italy takes over Dalmatia 471-472; province evacuated briefly 472; until 1204 Dalmatia remained part of the eastern empire 472

**Decius**; Senate awards the name Trajan 379; outlaws Christianity and revives old religion 379-380; drives the Carpi out of Dacia and then fights Goths, but defeated and killed 380

**Dictatorship** 32-33; Sulla as Dictator 153; Caesar made Dictator for life 197; post abolished by Mark Antony 201

**Diocletian** defeats Carinus, Augustus in the west, and takes over his soldiers 411; recognises that he needs a colleague, appoints Maximian as Augustus to control the west, against bandits in Gaul, Frankish pirates on the west coast, and Britain, controlled by Carausius, 411-412; Diocletian mounts two campaigns against Danube tribes, chiefly Sarmatians 412; treaty with Persians, takes control of Mesopotamia, installs pro-Roman ruler in Armenia 413; joins Maximian on northern frontier to evict invading tribes, settles some on lands 413; Constantius restores Britain to the Empire 413; Diocletian creates Tetrachy with two Augusti and two Caesars, with Diocletian in overall command 414; puts down Egyptian revolt and creates two provinces 415; celebrates twenty year rule in AD 304 in Rome with Maximian, goes to Nicomedia, falls ill, and in 305 he abdicates 416; Diocletian's reign: social ranks crystallised, signified by specific titles, equestrians were promoted, the

renounces further conquests, creates running barriers guarding edges of the Empire, and uses subsidies to control natives outside the boundaries of the Empire 317-318; 323-324; damage in Ad 230s and 260s on northern frontiers 388; Diocletian repairs and augments frontiers, design of forts changes and military commanders (*duces*) command large stretches of frontiers 421; Constantine attends to Rhine frontier, his son Crispus campaigns against Franks, Constantine fights Goths on the Danube 431; 433; Valentinian fortifies Rhine and Danube 441

**Galba**; governs Hispania Tarraconensis 271; declares loyalty to Senate, decides to remove Nero 272; arrives in Rome with Salvius Otho, governor of Lusitania, but alienates the Praetorians 272; Otho has Galba killed and becomes Emperor 273

**Galerius**; made Caesar under Diocletian when Tetrachy created, suppresses revolt in Egypt, fights Sarmatians on Danube, and builds forts north of river 414-415; campaigns against Persians, defeated, but victorious in second campaign 415; persecutes Christians 430; issues edict of toleration 432; besieges Maxentius in Rome but fails 431; death 432

**Gallienus**; made co-emperor with his father Valerian 382; faces Goths attacking Black Sea coasts and Alamanni threatening Germany and Raetia 383; Shapur captures Valerian 383; Macrianus and two sons claim the Empire 386; Odenathus of Palmyra protects the east after Valerian captured by Shapur 386 -388; Postumus in Gaul declared Emperor by the army, and Gallic Empire begins 388; Gallienus attempts to regain control of Gallic Empire 391; trouble with several usurpers and with Goths, Franks and Alamanni on northern frontiers 391; ends persecution of Christians 392; commands legionary vexillations from several provinces, forms special cavalry army with its own commander based at Milan 392-393;

creates *protectores* from selected military men 393; removes many senators from military commands, employs equestrians as *praefecti* of legions and *praesides* governing provinces 393-395; resources of Gallic Empire and some part of the east denied to Gallienus, causing financial difficulties, debased coinage and price increases, taxes paid in produce not cash and soldiers paid partly in supplies until new mints established 396; campaign against the Goths on the Danube but no victory 397; campaign against Goths interrupted by revolt of Aureolus commanding the new cavalry army; Gallienus assassinated, succeeded by Claudius Gothicus 398

**Gaul and Gauls**; Sack of Rome 53-55; conquered by Julius Caesar in ten year campaign 173-182; remains an occupied zone until Augustus established three provinces of Belgica, Lugdunensis and Aquitania, and The Province renamed Gallia Narbonensis 182; Claudius awards citizenship to Gauls 256; after 406 frontiers fail and Roman control of Gaul south of the Rhine diminishes 457; infiltration of Visigoths, some under Wallia 457-458; Roman administrative centre moved from Trier to Arles 458; Attila and Huns move into Gaul, defeated and driven out by Roman commander Aetius 458; Euric King of the Visigoths enters Gaul and expands his territory 459-460; western Emperor Anthemius fails to eject Euric, who then rules on Roman lines until Franks arrive 460-461

**Germany**; Caesar campaigns beyond the Rhine 175-176; German tribes settle on left bank of Rhine, Romans create an occupied zone called Germania later divided into two regions administered from Gallia Belgica 227-228; Drusus campaigns in Free Germany 227; Domitius Ahenobarbus reaches the Elbe 227; two provinces created from occupied zone called Germania Superior and Inferior under Domitian 228

# Index